Orpheus in Nineteenth-Century Symbolism

Studies in the Fine Arts: The Avant-Garde, No. 61

Stephen C. Foster, Series Editor

Professor of Art History
University of Iowa

Other Titles in This Series

No. 60	*American Realist Painting, 1945–1980*	John L. Ward
No. 62	*American Artists in Paris, 1919–1929*	Elizabeth Hutton Turner
No. 65	*The Early Sculpture of Jean Arp*	Margherita Andreotti
No. 66	*Issues in Abstract Expressionism: The Artist-Run Periodicals*	Ann Gibson
No. 67	*Max Ernst: The Psychoanalytic Sources*	Elizabeth M. Legge

Orpheus in Nineteenth-Century Symbolism

by
Dorothy M. Kosinski

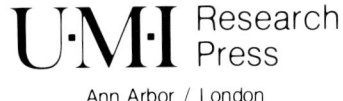

Ann Arbor / London

Copyright © 1989
Dorothy M. Kosinski
All rights reserved

Produced and distributed by
UMI Research Press
an imprint of
University Microfilms Inc.
Ann Arbor, Michigan 48106

Library of Congress Cataloging in Publication Data

Kosinski, Dorothy M.
  Orpheus in nineteenth-century symbolism /
by Dorothy M. Kosinski.
    p. cm.
    Bibliography: p.
    Includes index.
    ISBN 0-8357-1868-9 (alk. paper)
    1. Orpheus (Greek mythology)—Art. 2. Arts, Modern—19th century.
3. Symbolism in art. I. Title.
  NX652.O7K67 1989
  700'.9'034—dc19   89-4732
                                                                    CIP

British Library CIP data is available.

For Eleanor

It is well known and quite understandable that the preoccupation with mythology has something intoxicating about it, and the man who does research in myth must always, become to a certain degree a poet of theogonies.
—F. Dümmler, on W. H. Roscher's
Ausführliches Lexikon der grieschischen und römischen Mythologie

Contents

Preface   xi
  The Scholarly Literature: Symbolist Studies
  Significance and Implications

Acknowledgments   xix

1 The Myth of Orpheus: Metamorphosis in Art and Literature   1
    Orpheus/Orphism
    Orpheus-Priest
    Magical Music: Orpheus Charms the Animals
    The Judeo-Christian Orpheus: Orpheus-David-Christ
    Orpheus and Eurydice—The Romance—Orpheus' Journey to Hades
    The Death of Orpheus
    The Oracular Head

2 Orpheus in the Nineteenth Century: The Intellectual Context   49
    Comparative Studies of Myth and Philology
    Syncretic Histories of World Civilization
    Occultism, Alternative Religions
    Mysticism and the Symbolist Aesthetic: Art as Religion
    Correspondences: The Synaesthetic Ideal
    Gustave Moreau's *La Vie de l'humanité*

3 Orpheus Taming the Animals, Pacifying Mankind   81
    Henry de Groux
    Emile Fabry
    Franz von Stuck
    Melchior Lechter, Artists of the Secession
    Pierre Puvis de Chavannes, Alexandre Séon, Henri Martin
    Alphonse Osbert

x   Contents

4   Orpheus and Eurydice: Orpheus in Hades   115
     Orpheus Pleads before Pluto
     Orpheus Leads Forth Eurydice
     Orpheus' Fateful Glance
     Eurydice Swept Away
     The Role of Eurydice in Occultist Texts
     Orpheus' Glance: Meaning and Interpretations

5   Orpheus Lamenting   151
     Gustave Moreau
     François Louis Français
     Pierre Puvis de Chavannes
     Alexandre Séon
     F. Holland Day
     Auguste Rodin

6   The Death of Orpheus   189
     Emile Lévy
     Paul Baudry
     Auguste Rodin
     Gustave Adolf Mossa
     Gustave Moreau: The Dead Poet and Themes of Religious Syncretism
     The Severed-Head Motif
     Contrasting Interpretations
     The Impact of Moreau's *Orpheus* on Other Artists
     Orpheus versus Saint John the Baptist: Apollonian-Dionysian
        Dichotomy

7   Orphic Imagery in the Twentieth Century   243
     The Symbolist Aesthetic and the Emergence of Abstraction
     Orpheus as Symbol in the Works of Selected Authors and Artists
     Psychoanalytic Interpretation: The Role of Eurydice
     Orpheus and Twentieth-Century Music
     Epilogue

Notes   291

Bibliography   371

Index   423

Preface

Orpheus is poet, musician, initiate, priest, magician, civilizer, heroic intruder in Hades, lamenting lover, victim of Dionysian fury. Already in the sixteenth century B.C., Ibycus invokes "famous Orpheus." The multiplicity of these roles and the richness of this mythic personality are indeed captivating, and have inspired countless interpretations and depictions over centuries. The appeal of Orpheus, however, is due not only to the rich and varied texture of the myth, but perhaps more significantly, to its profound implications, its expression of essential psychological or cultural truths. Orpheus is the archetypal artist—in the company of figures such as Prometheus, Daedalus, Hephaestus or Amphion—whose art is magical, of divine inspiration, and linked to the obscure dawnings of civilization. The myth of Orpheus captivates the imagination because it is about art, about our notions of the sources of inspiration, the nature of creativity.

Within the context of the nineteenth century, this multivalent mythical figure of Orpheus seems implicit in many of the most important intellectual and aesthetic currents of the period—religious syncretism, decadent pessimism, the androgynous concept, the synaesthetic ideal, Rosicrucian mysticism, occultism, and Wagnerism. Orpheus is the prophet or priest, descending and returning from the realm of the dead; the poet-magician, embodying the ideal combination of the arts; the isolated and tormented artist, expressing a conflict between aesthetic idealism and impure earthly imperatives. How Orpheus comes to figure so importantly in Symbolism defies precise definition because the way in which the durable truth of myth becomes cultural currency is itself elusive. This imprecision notwithstanding, the myth of Orpheus offers a focus by which to analyze a nexus of ideas, and simultaneously, a means to synthesize a complex of cultural currents.

An overview of the many descriptions and depictions of Orpheus in literature and the plastic arts from antiquity through the eighteenth century provides an essential introduction to the myth itself. The basic narrative itself is complex, consisting of a sequence of events: Apollo endows Orpheus with the lyre and magically powerful music. With the Argonauts, Orpheus performs a priestly function. He is identified, as well, with Dionysus, and therefore a priest of the orphic cults. He is linked to the beginnings of civilization. Orpheus soothes primitive man, but moreover charms animals and animates rocks and trees; the magical power of his music gains his entry to Hades to retrieve his wife Eurydice. Tragically, however, he transgresses the rule of the gods of the Underworld: looking back too soon, he loses Eurydice forever. Orpheus' song becomes lamentation. Perhaps it is his unfailing devotion to Eurydice which inspires the anger of the Maenads. Alternatively, the women's cruel madness, their murder of Orpheus, tearing him limb from limb, is the result of a Bacchic ritual, or the anger over his institution of a homosexual cult. The final episode of the myth, however, is one of transcendance. The poet's head and lyre continue to emit song. Apollo preserves the oracular head; the lyre is transformed into the constellation.

The myth is not static but is transformed as the moments of the narrative are selected, neglected and variously interpreted. Two fundamentally different interpretations emerge: one emphasizes the romantic tale and gives special importance to the role of Eurydice. This view grew in importance in the Middle Ages, particularly in the context of moralized versions of Ovid's *Metamorphoses* and commentaries on other classical texts. In a fourteenth-century romance, Orpheus becomes the courtier, the Medieval king, Sir Orfeo. Eurydice is his queen. Gluck's 1774 opera, which witnessed many popular revivals in the nineteenth century, is certainly within this tradition. The dramatic core of the myth is entirely stripped away as a happy ending is imposed. Jacques Offenbach's *Orpheus in the Underworld* presents an outright parody of the myth.

In contrast to this tradition which essentially trivializes the myth, another approach plumbs its depth, discovering profound meaning. Orpheus is the harbinger of civilization. He is the archetypal artist and musician, leader of religious cults, a priest or magus. Orpheus plays a significant role in the early Christian period and in the Neo-Platonic milieu of Marsilio Ficino, in which the conflation of pagan and Christian themes was important. The Symbolists partake of this second tradition, rediscovering the religious significance and psychological intensity of the myth. For them, Orpheus is poet, martyr, priest, magician.

Religious, mythological, and cultural syncretism are dominant characteristics of the intellectual fabric of Romanticism and Symbolism as well. The complex investigations of myth, religion, and history which proliferated throughout the nineteenth century are expressions of a broadly significant impulse to create vast, all-encompassing systems which synthsize man's development, past, present, and future. In painting and sculpture, epic works such as Rodin's spiritually encyclopedic *Gates of Hell,* Gauguin's *Who Are We? Where Do We Come From? Where Are We Going?* or Edvard Munch's *The Dance of Life,* may be considered as expressions of this impulse.

The myth of Orpheus is often a central theme in the universal histories and syncretic mythographies, as well as in the various alternative religions and occult groups which proliferated at this time. In the syncretic studies of world religions by G. F. Creuzer and others, Orpheus links the esoteric traditions of east and west, thereby confirming these scholars' underlying theory that there exists a common source for man's development (an evolution which they envisaged as essentially spiritual or religious). Theosophy celebrates Rama, Krishna, Pythagoras, Orpheus, Christ, and Buddha as prophets of a single truth.

As one of the early harbingers of civilization, Orpheus plays a key role, as well, in the palingenetic studies and cyclical histories of man proposed, for example, by Pierre Simon Ballanche. These schemes often present a negative pattern of development, in effect a movement toward disintegration. The apocalyptic destruction of civilization is resolved ultimately in a reintegration, a return to the harmony of Paradise, the perfect unity of the primoridal androgyne. This notion of a cyclical history informs Delacroix's paintings in the Library of the Palais Bourbon, as well as Paul Chenavard's ill-fated decorative scheme for the Pantheon and Gustave Moreau's complex, multipaneled work, *La Vie de l'humanité.* In each of these explorations of man's disintegrative development, conflating pagan and Christian iconography, Orpheus plays a central role. In Moreau's painting, and, for instance, in a theatrical project by Joséphin Péladan, Orpheus is juxtaposed with Cain and Abel, classical mythology united with the Book of Genesis. It is important that the Symbolist concepts of art and symbol evolve in the context of the study of the history of religion, mythology and philology in which Orpheus plays a significant thematic role.

The narrative sequence of the myth itself provides the organizational principle for the discussion that intentionally includes an international variety of artists, and works in different media; a discussion stressing the evolution of themes and motifs from Romanticism through Symbolism, the complex interconnections between art, literature and music which dominate the period.

Mallarmé's concept of the poet's role as summoning forth the orphic voice in the world succinctly articulates the Symbolists' preoccupation with the notions of artist as priest, art as religion, art object as revelation. Their emphasis on Orpheus' magical powers differentiates their interpretations of the traditional motif of Orpheus amidst the animals, taming beasts, animating rocks and trees, from earlier presentations which often explored the variety and beauty of the flora and fauna of the pastoral landscape. Works by Puvis, Osbert, and Lechter manifest, moreover, the Symbolists' interest in an aesthetic expression that communicates directly through the abstract power of visual form, line, and color.

Despite powerfully dramatic interpretations by artsits such as Lord Leighton, Watts, Burne-Jones, Feuerbach and Rodin, the Symbolists demonstrate relatively minimal interest in the role of Eurydice, the romantic tale of Orpheus' undying love, the gothic horror of his quest in Hades. They emphasize instead the poet's grief and lamentation following the second and ultimate loss of Eurydice. In *Orpheus Lamenting at the Tomb of Eurydice*, 1891–97, Gustave Moreau uses the myth to transform his personal grief and anguish, granting these emotions mytho-poetic proportions. In this painting, as well as in works by Puvis de Chavannes and Alexandre Séon, the landscape has special significance. The Theosophist, Edouard Schuré, described these as psychological landscapes, playing a role analagous to that of the Wagnerian orchestra. Through nuances and harmonies it modulates emotions of the interior drama, prolonging those feelings in time and space. The Symbolists develop an antinaturalist concept of the landscape, exploring the popular concepts of synaesthesia and correspondences, to create landscapes which express an interior reality. For Auguste Rodin, Orpheus' lamentation is a powrful expression of the sculptor's perception of the anguish of creativity, a dominant motif in his oeuvre.

It is especially Orpheus' death which most fascinated the Symbolists. In contrast to images from earlier periods, the Symbolists eschew the sexually aggressive image of the onslaught of the crazed Maenads, in favor of the aftermath of the Bacchic destruction. In melancholic, almost serene scenes of the dead poet, Moreau explores a conflation of images of Orpheus and Christ, a manifestation of the religious syncretism which is so important to the Symbolists. Significantly, the Symbolists are the first artists since antiquity to portray Orpheus' severed head. In antiquity, the poet's severed head was celebrated as an oracle; his lyre transformed into the constellation. For the Symbolists, Orpheus' severed head is also magical, symbolic of their antimaterialist, idealist vision of art. The severed head may be considered as an image of the apotheosis of the work of art in death, not unrelated to Nietzsche's concept of the Dionysian aspect of creation. The Symbolists' presentation of the severed head of Orpheus is greatly idealized, ethereal, fine, serene. Delville and Redon both bathe the head in limpid pools of water, emphasizing with this muffled, absorbing body of liquid the introspective, thoughtful quality of the poet's visage. Redon's lush watery or flowered environments express the poet's orphic victory of creative harmony with his world.

The image of Orpheus or the orphic theme continues as a significant motif in twentieth-century art and literature. For example, Orpheus is of dominant importance in the works of Cocteau, Zadkine, and Seuphor; and is significant as well in the works of Marc, Chagall, Dufy, Masson, and Beckmann. Of course

Rilke, as well as Valéry, Apollinaire, and Anouilh, explore the theme in their writings. In twentieth-century music, Stravinsky is the great interpreter of the myth of Orpheus.

In a more general sense, however, the survival of the image of Orpheus in the twentieth century reveals the important impact of Symbolism on the emergence of abstraction in the first decades of the new century. The major themes which revolve around Orpheus in the Symbolist milieu—the significance of the occult, of the spiritual, the prominence of the theory of correspondences and the synaesthetic ideal, the appreciation of music as the artistic paradigm—all endure in a significant manner, serving to inform the evolving idealist, a nonfigurative aesthetic of the twentieth century.

The Scholarly Literature: Symbolist Studies

Nineteenth-century Symbolism seems to have been rediscovered and popularized in the 1970s in a spate of exhibitions in Brussels, London, Madrid, Munich, New York, Paris, Rotterdam, and Turin. These exhibitions, which are manifestations of a maturing revisionism in the art historical appraisal of the nineteenth century, provided an ever-expanding international roster of artists, greater breadth and depth in the array of the visual documents, an increasingly sophisticated selection and analysis of the aesthetic and intellectual issues, and more and more elaborate documentation. The catalogues which accompanied these exhibitions, along with other publications by Robert Delevoy, Edward Lucie-Smith, and Philippe Jullian, remain the basis for any examination of the period. Robert Goldwater's *Symbolism*, published posthumously in 1979, provides one of the most elegant analyses of the complex issues which arose in the 1880s. Sven Loevgren's *The Genesis of Modernism* provides an extraordinarily insightful analysis of the impact of the Symbolist aesthetic on the evolution of abstraction in the twentieth century. The many extraordinarily important monographic studies also grew in sophistication over the years, responding quite clearly to the increasingly complex picture of this period presented in the more general studies mentioned above. In the 1980s exhibitions continue to broaden the scope of Symbolism, exploring its manifestations, for instance, in Hungary and Scandinavia.

Symbolism, as its aesthetic programme emerged from or was informed by poetry, music, or the occult, demands a contextual, interdisciplinary methodology. The phenomenon of tantalizing, yet frustratingly vague and unexplained juxtapositions of images and textual passages from Mallarmé, Verlaine or Wagner, for instance, is perhaps an indication of the scholars' intimidation by the complexities of a foreign discipline or quite simply a reflection of the difficulty of achieving an accurate picture. The Symbolist aesthetic perhaps emerges more coherently in the context of literary criticism, as the gap between theory and practice, that is, between the symbolic or the traditionally allegorical and the Symbolist (Aurier's opposition of "idéiste" and "idéaliste") is less unsettling than in the visual arts.

Indeed, the quantity and quality of literary studies is somewhat staggering. *The Symbolist Movement in the Literature of European Languages*, edited by Anna Balakian, offers not only a compendium of essays representing the essential aspects of literary criticism: a definition of Symbolism and attendant questions of methodology; an investigation of its international and national manifestations; monographic studies of key figures; examination of essential themes; the impact of Symbolism on music and the visual arts but a comprehensive bibliography as well. The works by Balakian, Michaud, Peyre, Raymond are among the most useful presentations of the subject of Symbolism in general; the works by Mercier and Pierrot, the best on the occultist/mystical milieu. Mario Praz' *The Romantic Agony*, first published in 1930, is of course a brilliant example of an interdisciplinary study of essential Decadent themes of Romanticism and Symbolism. Probably the most important recent art historical study of this complex thicket of the relationship between occultism and the Symbolist aesthetic is Filiz Eda Burhan's "Vision and Visionaries: Nineteenth Century Psychological Theory. The Occult Sciences and the Formation of the Symbolist Aesthetic."

Within literary history or criticism, studies of individual themes are relatively numerous. Witness, for instance, studies of the myth of Orpheus or the Orphic theme in the literatures of the nineteenth and twentieth centuries by Bays, Cattaui, Juden, Kushner, Rehm, Riffaterre, and Strauss. The seven essays devoted to "Le mythe d'Orphée au XIXe et au XXe siècle," presented in the May 1970 issue of the *Cahiers de l'Association International des Etudes Françaises* are also particularly helpful. As counterparts within the realm of art historical studies, one can point only to a thorough article by Maria-Louisa Frongia. Three studies focus on the myth and depictions in antiquity: Provoost, Schoeller, and the brief article by Dynes. Of course, mythological compendia and studies of Orpheus and Orphism include analyses of imagery in the visual arts. Friedman and Gros Louis study the evolution of the myth in the literature and arts of the Middle Ages; Buck, Walker, and Ziegler focus on Orpheus in the Renaissance. Theodore Johnson's essay in *The Register of the Spencer Museum of Art* uses the image of Orpheus on a seventeenth-century tapestry in the Museum's collection as the starting point for a brief but inspired overview of the myth and its presentation in the visual arts and literature also, well into the twentieth century.

Significance and Implications

The popularity of the myth of Orpheus or the theme of orphism emerges significantly early in the nineteenth century, in the context of Romanticism. Orpheus figures importantly in synthetic mythographic studies and universal histories, in occultism and alternative religions which all proliferated in that period of intellectual syncretism. From the vantage point of an iconological study or an examination of the history of an idea, one may conclude not only that the Symbolists' Orpheus derives from this very milieu but, moreover, that crucial elements of the Symbolist aesthetic—for instance the very definitions of symbol, sign, and myth or the insistence on the sacerdotal essence of art—evolve (along with or more precisely tied to the theme of orphism) from these same sources. In other words, the delineation between Romanticism and Symbolism appears transparent not only because of the transmission of a theme, but because of a significant conceptual continuum. The increasing importance of the orphic theme, as opposed to the figure of Orpheus himself, is in keeping with the intended suggestivity or hermeticism of Symbolism. In the works of Alphonse Osbert, for instance, the specifically mythological is substituted with an evocative poetry of music-making and contemplation, paradigmatic images, moreover, of the synaesthetic potential of colors and forms. In Rodin's oeuvre, the figure of Orpheus is absorbed into a complex personal symbolism about the nature of art and the vocation of the artist. Ultimately, and wonderfully consonant with the aesthetic programme of Symbolism, the mythic hero, Orpheus, disintegrates (or more aptly is dismembered) into his underlying or primary meanings. The orphic theme, for instance, is embodied in an abstract device such as the five golden strings stretched across Gallen-Kallela's landscape composition, *Waterfall at Mäntykoski*. Orpheus becomes, perhaps, Mallarmé's "the Figure that Nothing is" (from "Richard Wagner, rêverie d'un poète français").

Acknowledgments

This book issues from my professional formation at New York University's Institute of Fine Arts and I hope reflects in a positive way that institution's intellectual diversity and absence of methodological rigidity, characteristics which I valued so highly throughout my training there. Gert Schiff's generous support and advice, in particular his encouragement of my interdisciplinary interests, are enormously appreciated. His very careful reading of the initial manuscript was especially helpful. Colin Eisler is, to no small extent, responsible for my interest in the theme of the archetypal artist. Robert Rosenblum's teaching and scholarship in the field of nineteenth-century art continues to be a source of inspiration.

Angelica Rudenstine has been unstinting in her interest and help since I first worked with her at The Guggenheim Museum in 1977. I am grateful for the challenge of her professional standards, for her colleagueship and friendship.

My preliminary research in Europe during the preparation of the book was made possible through the generous financial support of the Institute of Fine Arts. Among the many people who were exceedingly generous indeed throughout those early stages of research and preparation are: Roseline Bacou, Cabinet des Dessins, Louvre, Paris; Anna Balakian, New York University; Bernard Ceysson, Musée d'Art et d'Industrie, Saint-Etienne; Sarah Faunce, The Brooklyn Museum; Geneviève Lacambre, present Chief Curator, Musée Gustave Moreau and Musée d'Orsay, Paris; Françine-Claire Legrand, Musée d'Art Moderne, Brussels; Edward Lucie-Smith, London; Geneviève Monnier, Paris; Jean Paladilhe, former Director, Musée Gustave Moreau, Paris; Giselle Ollinger-Zinque, Musée d'Art Moderne, Brussels; and Patrick Roger, Galerie Coligny, Paris. I was privileged to be able to discuss my work with the families and descendants of some of the artists discussed in this book. I wish to thank Madame David, Olivier Delville, Monsieur et Madame Edmond Delescluze-Fabry and Yolande Osbert for their extraordinary generosity with their time, memories and archives. Many private collectors very graciously allowed me to visit their homes in order to view their Symbolist works of art.

The following libraries and archives were crucial to my research: Joséphin Péladan archives, Bibliothèque de l'Arsenal, Paris; Papus archives, Bibliothèque Municipale, Lyon; Bibliothèque Nationale, Paris; archives, Musée Gustave Moreau, Paris; archives, Musée Nationale d'Art Moderne, Brussels; archives, Musée d'Orsay, Paris; the New York Public Library; and the Witt Library, The Courtauld Institute, London, as well as the following photographic archives all in Paris: Bulloz, Roger-Viollet and Agraci. Many other colleagues and institutions diligently responded to my requests for photographic material for this book.

Many friends and colleagues contributed in important ways to this project. I am especially grateful to: Ingrid Bowen, Emily Braun, Valdina de Koenigsberg Chirico, Susan Grace Galassi, and Lucy Flint Gohlke.

I am deeply grateful for the untiring support and encouragement of my husband, Thomas Krähenbühl. In fulfilling a variety of essential roles, including those of counselor, editor, translator and all-round assistant, he was instrumental in the realization of this book. I would be remiss if I did not acknowledge, as well, William McCarty-Cooper's contribution in providing the professional environment in which this project could be completed.

1

The Myth of Orpheus: Metamorphosis in Art and Literature

A study of the myth of Orpheus in nineteenth-century Symbolism demands at the outset a substantial investigation of the origins of the myth and its subsequent transformation over the centuries. This effort to clarify or differentiate core significance from accreted references has two-fold importance: first, to establish a sufficiently refined understanding of a particularly complex myth; and secondly, to provide the historical background which acts as foil to the Symbolists' attitude toward the myth. The basic narrative of the myth embraces three successive episodes: the magic of the musician/priest calming man and beast, his descent to Hades, and his death by dismemberment. Other significant elements of the myth include Orpheus' participation in the journey of the Argo; his alliance with Apollo, seemingly contradicting his role as priest of the Orphic cults; and the miraculous survival of the poet's severed head as oracle. Orpheus' roles are varied: he is poet-musician, prophet-priest, psychopomp, grieving husband, and—following the varied explanations of his death—chastened initiate, religious martyr, or homosexual victim.

Orpheus/Orphism

The source for this complexity is found in antiquity—in the evolution of two distinct yet inextricably intermingled personae: the mythical Orpheus, the legendary poet-teacher; and the purportedly historical Orpheus, leader of the Orphic cults that emerged in the sixth century B.C.[1] The former, embracing the first of the three major episodes of the myth, presents the musician whose lyre-playing charmed rocks and trees and calmed primitive man at the dawn of civilization. Orpheus is shaman and teacher, whose musical power and pacific role clearly identify him with the god Apollo. In contrast, the Orpheus of the religious cults is the author of poems expounding a cosmogony which differs significantly from Hesiod's.[2] The birth, passion, and rebirth of Zagreus-Dionysus is the core of the Orphic cosmogony. Moreover, Orpheus' own fate—his descent into Hades and death by dismemberment—parallel the story of the Orphic deity himself. These poems also explain an anthropogony which forms the basis for the Orphics' conception of the dual nature of man, a mixture of good and evil; their belief that the body is a prison of the soul, a notion of guilt similar to the Christian concept of Original Sin; and fear of retribution in another life, a belief in the transmigration of souls.[3] The Orphics adhered to an ascetic regimen and specified rituals aimed at ultimate release from the cycle of rebirth and leading to reunification with the godhead.[4]

Orpheus is identified, then, with both Apollo and Dionysus, and is an accommodation of the philosophical, aesthetic, and spiritual concepts symbolized by these divinities. It will subsequently be made apparent how this rich, if sometimes confusing, complexity of Orpheus' Apolline-Dionysian character became especially appealing to later generations of the nineteenth century, who progressively turned away from earlier, rosier, perceptions of antiquity—one thinks of Winckelmann's "edle Einfalt und stille Grösse"—to embrace an aesthetic that takes into account the irrational, or darker, side of human psychology (the obvious counterpart to the reference to Winckelmann is, of course, Nietzsche).[5]

Orpheus-Priest

Invariably Orpheus is presented as the lyre player, the *citharede*, bound by the power of his music to the god Apollo. Apollonius of Rhodes, in the *Argonautica*,[6] emphasizes Orpheus' alliance with Apollo, his crucial priestly function, leading sacrifices to the god throughout the arduous journey of the ship Argo.[7] Orpheus' music constitutes an intonation to the god Apollo, exhorting his companions to offer proper sacrifices following the amazing apparition of Apollo, accompanying the dances and rituals of the youths in honor of Phoebus. He directs the offerings to Apollo in order to save the Argo from endless wandering on Lake Tritonian. His lyre is dedicated to Apollo.[8] The magical power of his music is his heritage from Apollo:

> Men say that he by the music of his songs charmed the stubborn rocks upon the mountains and the course of rivers. And the wild-oak trees to this day, tokens of that magic strain, that grow at Zone on the Thracian shore, stand in ordered ranks close together, the same which under the charm of his lyre he led down from Pieria.[9]

Despite this evidently special relationship to Apollo, Orpheus' priestly function marks him as an effective intercessor with all of the gods. His plaintive song to the nymphs saves the Argonauts from devastating thirst.[10] Moreover, his magically seductive music becomes an important defensive weapon during the journey, drowning out the voices of the Sirens.[11] Orpheus continually insists upon the importance of proper and timely rituals. It is he who initiates the heroes into the sacred mysteries:

> By the injunctions of Orpheus they touched at the island of Electra (Samothrace), daughter of Atlas, in order that by gentle initiation they might learn the rites that may not be uttered, and so with greater safety sail over the chilling sea.[12]

Often, Orpheus is specifically identified as a native of Thrace, a follower of Dionysus, and initiator of the Orphic mysteries. There are references, for example, in Aristophanes' *The Frogs* and Horace's *Ars Poetica* to Orpheus' teaching of the rites of the Orphic cult and his proscription of the eating of flesh, advocating instead a vegetarian regimen. Orpheus is clearly identified with Orphism by Pindar with a reference to the concept of reincarnation.[13] Aeschylus' identification of Orpheus and Dionysus is unmistakable in his lost play, *The Bassarae*. A red-figured column crater from the fifth century depicts a wreath-crowned Orpheus, seated amidst Thracian youths, playing his lyre (fig. 1.1). It is curious that the first representation of Orpheus as a Thracian, with a costume of Phrygian cap, boots, etc., does not occur until the middle of the fifth century B.C.[14]

There is a profound tradition which names Orpheus as priest and initiate. Already in the sixth century B.C. he is called, "famous Orpheus,"[15] a legendary figure whose renown situates him in the generation before Homer and Hesiod, indeed, at the very dawn of civilization.[16] In *Rhesus*, Euripides refers to Orpheus as he "who first instructed your people in the rites of mystery and secrets revealed."[17] Aristophanes lists Orpheus along with Musaeus, Hesiod and Homer, one of a pantheon of legendary poets who bring civilization to mankind.[18] For Horace, Orpheus is the "holy prophet," who, along with Amphion, promoted the growth of civilization:

> Remember the glorious history of poetry which—as the stories of Orpheus and Amphion show—has from the very infancy of the race promoted the cause of civilization. Then, from Homer on, it has inspired valour, has taught wisdom, has won the favour of princes, and has afforded relief after toil. Never need you be ashamed of the muse.[19]

In the Renaissance, Boccaccio links Orpheus to the origins of Greek religion, the building of temples, the invention of songs.[20]

This tradition of Orpheus' role as theologian and civilizer is sustained in mythographic texts of the seventeenth and eighteenth centuries. Natalis

Comes, in *Mythologie*, citing Horace and Pausanias (*Boeotia*), stresses Orpheus' role as harbinger of civilization, theologian:

> [A]nd by the sweetness of his discourses he made them follow a more courteous and humane way of life, assembling them in cities, teaching them how to construct buildings, instructing them how to conduct themselves and to obey the public laws and to maintain the rules of marriage.[21]

The extensive commentary in book 11 in the 1632 edition of George Sandys' translation of Ovid's *Metamorphoses* views Orpheus' music as "the authority of law ... that concord ... which had reduced wild people to civility"; and Orpheus himself as "the life of philosophy."[22] Similarly, the 1732 edition of the Garth/Dryden translation of the *Metamorphoses*, citing Diodorus Siculus, Horace, and Apollodorus, emphasizes Orpheus' music as an elemental source of culture and religion.

Orpheus is presented, however, not only as poet-priest, instrument of the dawn of civilization, part of a mythical generation before Homer and Hesiod, but, moreover, he is often described as the native of some exotic locale, the source for his knowledge of the mysteries and the magical power of his music. Herodotus and Diodorus Siculus, for instance, point to Egypt as the origin of Orpheus' knowledge of sacred rituals. The commentary to book 10 of the 1732 edition of the Garth/Dryden edition of the *Metamorphoses* includes an extensive discussion of the major theories concerning Orpheus' origins:

> Vossius assures us that the Phenician word *Ariph*, which signifies *learned*, gave rise to the Fable of Orpheus, or else, according to Mr. Furner, the Hebrew word *Rapha*, which is as much as to say *to cure*, is what made that pretended Orpheus pass for a great physician. Monsieur Le Clerc pretends that by confounding two Greek words, it was said that Orpheus was an able Singer instead of saying that he was an Enchanter, or Magician, and the Hymns which are attributed to him resemble rather Conjurations than Divine Odes.[23]

Citing Horace's description of Orpheus as interpreter of the gods, the commentator adds: "He had learned in *Egypt*, where he travelled, the mysteries and Ceremonies of the ancient Religion of the Egyptians, and he ought to be regarded as the Father of the Theology of the ancient Greeks."[24] The commentary includes a discussion of Orpheus' links to Thrace and/or Asia:

> Mr. Loercher brings him from *Asia* to *Thrace*; and he pretends that it was Orpheus who, with Eumolpus and Linus, carried Poetry and Music into Greece, the use of which was 'till then unknown in that country, and that this was the Occasion that so many Fables were published concerning them.[25]

Magical Music: Orpheus Charms the Animals

It is Orpheus' enchantment of people, animals, rocks and trees that is the most popular expression of the extraordinary power of his music. In Aeschylus' *Agamemnon*, Aegisthus speaks of "Orpheus . . . whose voice of rapture dragged all creatures in his train."[26] In Euripides' *Iphigenia in Aulis*, Iphigenia regrets that she does not possess Orpheus' magical powers, so as to be able to convince her father to spare her life: "O my father / If I had the tongue of Orpheus / So that I could charm with song the stones to /Leap and follow me, or if my words could / Quite beguile anyone I wished—I'd use / My magic now."[27] Euripides also makes reference to Orpheus taming wild beasts in *The Bacchae*.[28] A brief epigram by Simonides offers a particularly beautiful evocation of this scene: "Above his head there hovered birds innumerable, and fishes leapt clean from the blue water because of his sweet music."[29]

The image of Orpheus surrounded by the animals becomes increasingly popular among Hellenistic and late antique writers and artists. Diodorus Siculus and Antipater of Sidon mention Orpheus among the beasts, Orpheus the shepherd endowed with music of magical power.[30]

Perhaps the most famous references to Orpheus the musician are by Virgil and Ovid. In the *Metamorphoses* Ovid mentions the trees, rocks and animals charmed by the poet. The most striking passage of his description, however, is the remarkably detailed and extremely beautiful enumeration of all of the various trees that gather around Orpheus, forming his shade, on an otherwise barren hill.[31]

A passage by Philostratus the Younger, describing a painting of Orpheus amidst the animals, further reflects the widespread popularity of this image in the late antique. Philostratus names the specific animals and birds: a lion, a boar, a deer, a hare, "chattering daw," "cawing crow," the eagle of Zeus, wolves and lambs, which gather about the poet. Like Ovid, he also enumerates the trees: pine, cypress, alder, poplar. But here Philostratus introduces an extraordinary image to capture the magic of the scene. The trees are moved or torn up by the power of the music and "stand about Orpheus with their branches joined like hands, and thus, without requiring the craft of man, they enclose for him a theatre, that therein the birds may sit on their branches and he may make music in the shade." Orpheus himself is described in vivid detail: he is young, barely bearded, wearing a tiara; his expression is tender and alert; his garment flows with the motion of his body. The left hand strikes the strings while the right foot marks time; the right hand grasps the plectrum of the lyre which rests on his thigh.[32]

The numerous depictions in the late antique of Orpheus amidst animals and trees are consistent with these descriptions. A fragmentary Italo-Etruscan sculptural group dating from the end of the second century or first decades of the first century B.C. shows the poet seated, nude, with wreathed head. The instrument he once held is now missing. A lion, hare, and another animal are gathered at his feet, while an owl is perched on his thigh (fig. 1.2).[33]

Orpheus amidst the animals was frequently depicted on Roman mosaics, frescos, sculptures and coins.[34] Elaborately detailed descriptions of the animals and trees come to dominate these images, a trend entirely consistent with the generally realistic thrust of Roman art. Furthermore, this deemphasis of the figure of Orpheus in favor of the surrounding flora and fauna undoubtedly reflects the gradual dissolution of his religious significance during the Empire. This shift in emphasis is clear, for instance, in Marcus Terentius Varro's *De Re Rustica*. This work, written in 36 B.C. in the form of conversations, is devoted largely to the subject of farming. In Varro's work, Orpheus is a minstrel, accompanied by a troupe of real animals, who entertains at a banquet. This description is a fine example of the general shift away from cult image to the depiction of Orpheus as an excuse for the portrayal of a variety of animals and a lush landscape.[35]

Orpheus amidst the animals and surrounded by elaborate landscape is an image of durable popularity, appealing especially in those later periods in which the landscape plays an important role. A sampling of the numerous depictions of Orpheus in the Renaissance through the Baroque might include several versions among the prints of Marcantonio Raimondi, a work by Giovanni Bellini (fig. 1.3), the decoration of two Gonzaga palaces in Mantua: by Giulio Romano in the Palazzo del Tè and by Mantegna in the Palazzo Ducale (fig. 1.4), a painting by Il Padovanino (fig. 1.5), the heroic composition by Luca Giordano in the Palazzo Reale, Aranjuez (fig. 1.6), and the sculptural group at Hellbrunn Castle in Salzburg.[36]

A particularly fascinating image of Orpheus amidst the animals is a pavement dating from 1480–90 in the Chapel of St. Catherine in the Church of St. Dominic in Siena (fig. 1.7). Chastel attributes this work to Beccafumi or Francesco di Giorgio.[37] Here Orpheus is surrounded by a variety of animals, most prominently a unicorn, lion, panther, and boar. Other animals and birds lurk in the four stylized trees. The entire composition is encircled by a river indicated by delicate, calligraphic waves, in which swim a number of ducks and geese. The image is quite unusual in that Orpheus does not play a lyre or other instrument but, rather, holds a mirror. The mirror is frequently a symbol of occult powers, activating the celestial bodies (note the sun and moon visible at the top of the composition). If this is Orpheus, he is portrayed as the magician, one of the *prisci-theologi* of the Neo-Platonists. The importance of Orpheus to Ficino and the circle of Lorenzo the Magnificent will be examined briefly below.[38]

An elaborate landscape, teeming with an array of mundane or exotic animals, often dominates the depictions of Orpheus in the works of Northern

Baroque artists such as van Bulert, P. Coecke, van Aalst, C. van de Passe, A. Cuyp, Fr. Pourbus I, Th. van Thulden, or Fr. Snijders. For example, in Roeland Savery's *Landscape with Orpheus and the Thracian Women* (fig. 1.8), the mythological subject seems merely a pretext for an elaborate exploration of a picturesque landscape filled with a great number of animals and birds. Orpheus is barely visible in the midst of the complex scenery.[39]

Sometimes the image is invested with a specific symbolic significance. A "Roemer," or large glass for wine, dated 1611, shows the lyre-playing poet amidst ox, parrot, elephant, elk, ostrich, bear, and squirrel (fig. 1.9). The coat of arms identifies Prince Maurice of Orange (1567–1625) as the owner. This provenance indicates that Orpheus has a symbolic value, intended to augment the image of the ruler as a "prince of peace." Orpheus as peace-maker is similarly the central symbolism of Agnolo Bronzino's portrait of Cosimo I as Orpheus (fig. 1.10).[40]

The Judeo-Christian Orpheus: Orpheus-David-Christ

An especially interesting variation on the image of Orpheus amidst the animals is the Judeo-Christian Orpheus, wherein Orpheus becomes a visual and symbolic analogue for the figures of David, in the Old Testament, and the Christian Good Shepherd. This interpretation, emerging also in the late antique, differs significantly, however, from those presentations in which the central mythic figure is submerged in a panoramic presentation of landscape and animals. The conflation of Orpheus, David, and Christ depends upon the magical quality of Orpheus' song, its calmative and inspiring effect.

The conflation of David and Orpheus is found in works spanning the third through the sixth centuries A.D., in Jewish catacomb and synagogue paintings, and in mosaics and manuscript illuminations.[41] The basis for this identification of David and Orpheus is clear: both are lyre players, renowned for the enchanting power of their music. (David soothes Saul with his playing.) They are both, additionally, the authors of sacred songs—Orpheus of the cosmogonic hymns, and David of the psalms. In addition, David organized the music in the Temple. Moreover, both are part of noble, even godly, lineages. The parallel continues with David's role as ideal king or prince of peace, taming wild animals, the shepherd of the tribes of Israel and Judah.[42] Perhaps the earliest identification of David with Orpheus is in the first century B.C., in Psalm 151 of the Essenian scriptures or Dead Sea Scrolls. Here David is described as the shepherd, tending his flock through the magical effect of his cithara. A later source, the Talmud Hagigah, elaborates upon the magical qualities of David's music, describing its ability to move inanimate objects and relating that the enchanting sounds made the entrails of Abraham's goat vibrate.[43]

This conflation of Orpheus and David evolved, therefore, within the context of Judaism. The focus of this attempt to identify Orpheus with the Jewish tradition was the so-called Testament of Orpheus or Diatheke.[44] This document, in fact written in the third century B.C. by an Alexandrian Jew, was promoted as an extremely ancient text by Orpheus himself. It records Orpheus' final statement to his son/disciple Musaeos, denying the pantheon of pagan divinities, and instructing him to embrace the one, true god. The obvious purpose of this forgery was to establish Orpheus as a monotheist and hence establish the precedence of Judaism. The Alexandrian Jews attempted, therefore, to convince the Greek rulers of Alexandria that they had been worshipping the God of the Jews all along.

Later, the Testament was used by Christian apologists in their efforts to establish the superiority and precedence of their monotheistic religion. The preeminence of Christ, the Good Shepherd, is augmented by the association with both David and Orpheus. This association of Orpheus-David-Christ continues to figure in Christian tracts from the second through the thirteenth centuries, as well as in works of art through the fourteenth and fifteenth centuries.[45]

The image of Orpheus can be found in Christian catacombs or on sarcophagi, dating from the second half of the third century well into the fifth century. In the fresco of the catacomb of Domitilla the hat and boots help to identify the lyre-playing figure as the Thracian Orpheus (fig. 1.11).[46] The basis for this association of Orpheus and Christ is, of course, the similarity between the image of Orpheus surrounded by animals tranquilized by his music and Christ, and the Good Shepherd, as presented in John 10:11–15, and 27–28; Matthew 18:12–13; and Luke 15:5–6. This identification of Orpheus and Christ may depend, moreover, on other important similarities as well. For instance, there is a parallel between Orpheus' Hades journey in search of Eurydice and Christ's harrowing of hell, an episode especially popular in the apocryphal gospels. There are a number of significant parallels between the orphic cults and Christianity: belief in a soul separate from the body; a concept of common guilt or Original Sin; faith in life after death; adherence to rules of conduct, an ascetic regimen in order to attain a better life after death. Moreover, Christ's passion and resurrection echo the central episode of the Orphic theogony—Zagreus-Dionysus' death and rebirth. A third-century cylinder seal adorned with a crucifixion and inscribed, "Orpheus-Bakicos" evidences an appreciation of these similarities.[47]

This conflation of Orpheus and Christ figures in medieval authors' efforts to transform the pagan myth into a Christian allegory. Thirteenth- and fourteenth-century moralized editions of Ovid's *Metamorphoses* distort the basic myth to accommodate abstract concepts of good and evil. Eurydice, for example, is often presented as an instrument of lust and passion to contrast with Orpheus, the embodiment of virtue and reason.[48] An anonymous manuscript from the end of the thirteenth or beginning of the fourteenth century explains: "Thus . . . Orpheus clearly denotes Jesus Christ, Divine Word, the teacher of good doctrine, who by his preaching had converted many nations of men."[49] In Bersuire's influential *Metamorphosis Ovidiana*, the fifteenth book of *Reductorium Morale*, ca. 1325–37, Orpheus is once again identified with Christ: "Let us speak allegorically and say that Orpheus, the child of the [sun], is Christ the son of God the Father . . . Christ-Orpheus wished himself to descend to the lower world and thus he retook his wife, that is, human nature."[50]

The Renaissance Neo-Platonists were interested in the *Testament*. Ficino, Agrippa, Steuco, and Pico quote portions of the *Testament*. Like Dante, Ficino presents Christ as the Orphic shepherd. Consistent with Ficino's general effort to accommodate the pagan religions to Christianity, his translation of the *Testament* does not stress Orpheus' recantation of the pagan gods, but instead attempts to demonstrate how many gods are aspects of a single godhead.[51]

The Florentine Neo-Platonists not only perceived the similarities between Orpheus and Christ but, moreover, named Orpheus as one of a succession of *prisci theologi*. These great thinkers, products of different periods and cultures, reveal the same Divine or mystic truth. Ficino enumerates these spiritual leaders:

> In things pertaining to theology there were in former times six great teachers expounding similar doctrines. The first was Zoroaster, the chief of the Magi; the second Hermes Trismegistus, the head of the Egyptian priesthood; Orpheus succeeded Hermes; Aglaophamus was initiated into the sacred mysteries of Orpheus; Pythagoras was initiated into theology by Aglaophamus; and Plato by Pythagoras. Plato summed up the whole of their wisdom in his letters.[52]

This lineage, often expanded with the addition of such figures as Adam, Abraham, Moses, and the Druid priests, became a central concept in the Neo-Platonists' syncretism.[53] Orpheus therefore played a role not only in the Neo-Platonists' reconciliation of Platonism and Christianity, but also in the even broader context of their association of many ancient theologies and philosophies. Orpheus was a crucial link in this syncretic system—between the mysteries of Egypt and Greece, and then, in his role as author of the *Testament*, between paganism and Christianity.[54]

It is worth noting the religious or philosophical syncretism common to those periods in which Orpheus enjoys a special popularity. The polytheistic environment of the late antique (embodied by the famous lararium of the Emperor Alexander Severus, including busts of his ancestors, statues of Christ, Abraham, Orpheus, and the first century Neo-Pythagorean mystic, Apollonios of Tyana) may be compared to the Florentine Neo-Platonists' vision of mystical wisdom, or (and significantly in this context) to the renewed appreciation of mysticism and the occult, a syncretic understanding of myth and religion which flourished in the nineteenth century.[55]

The Neo-Platonists' claim to their own role in this succession of mystical teachers is made clear by Ficino's personal identification with Orpheus. With a profound knowledge of the Orphic literature, having translated the *Hymns*, the *Argonautica* and the *Testament*, he imagined himself to be the new Orpheus. Poliziano and Lorenzo the Magnificent refer to him as "Orpheus."[56] A poem by Naldo Naldi claims Ficino as one of the *prisci theologi*. A 1521 bust of Ficino by Andrea Ferrucci portrays the poet holding a book in a manner that clearly suggests comparison with the traditional pose of Orpheus holding his lyre.

The Neo-Platonists' Orpheus, *priscus theologus*, is initiate and teacher, civilizing poet and ideal artist. He is a symbol of harmony and excellence; his music is the power of love over the universe, his art an expression of the harmony of the spheres. According to Ficino, Orpheus' art is divinely inspired, the result of Platonic *furor*. Indeed Orpheus is a perfect illustration of Ficino's great poet possessed by four types of *furor*: the poetic, the religious (Bacchic), the prophetic and the amorous.[57]

Furthermore, the power of Orpheus' music, to calm, inspire, even heal, was said to derive from his knowledge of the harmony of the universe.[58] Orpheus embodied the Pythagorean principle of the harmony of the spheres (derived from Pythagoras' concept of mathematical ratios as the determinants of musical intervals) which fascinated the Neo-Platonists and was a central element in the Renaissance humanists' perception of the nature of the cosmos, the body and soul, their understanding of architecture, art, music and medicine.[59]

Based on this tradition of Orpheus' divine inspiration and his initiation into the essential harmony of the universe, he emerges in emblem books, iconologies and mythological commentaries as a symbol of music, harmony, or eloquence. At the end of the fifth century, in his *Mitologiae*, Fulgentius presents Orpheus as a symbol of eloquence, based on an etymological analysis of his name, "oraia phone," or "best voice." In his fourteenth-century *Commentary*, Nicholas Trivet identifies Orpheus with "sapientia" and "eloquentia."[60] Subsequently, Orpheus is identified as "an eloquent and wise man," his noble character strongly contrasted to that of Eurydice, of "Appetitum," all that is coveting and desiring in man. His harmonious and eloquent music produces a profound tranquilizing effect on the soul—exercises, even, medicinal properties.[61]

Orpheus and Eurydice—The Romance—Orpheus' Journey to Hades

In contrast to the tradition that portrays Orpheus as theologian, initiate, civilizer, a symbol of harmony and eloquence, there develops, especially in the Middle Ages, an interpretation of the myth which emphasizes the relationship of Orpheus and Eurydice. The tragic story of Eurydice, which was first elaborated by Ovid and Virgil, becomes increasingly important. The serious, religious, priestly functions of Orpheus are pushed to the background as Orpheus—the husband and lover—and the romantic, melodramatic potential of the myth are brought to the fore.

Undoubtedly, the most influential texts concerning Orpheus are Ovid's *Metamorphoses*, book 10, 1–85 and book 11, 1–66, and Virgil's *Georgics*, book 4, 453–527. Both versions recount Eurydice's death, Orpheus' unsuccessful venture into Hades, his death at the hands of the Ciconian women, and the transformation of his severed head into an oracle. There are, however, some noteworthy differences between the two texts. For instance, though in each case Eurydice dies of a snake bite, Ovid places her in the company of the naiads while Virgil portrays her demise while fleeing the amorous advances of the beekeeper, Aristaeus. Virgil recounts the story of Orpheus and Eurydice in his four books devoted to *Horticulture*. The myth is presented in the context of the seer Proteus' explanation to Aristaeus of the plague which has troubled him—punishment, in fact, for his role in Eurydice's death. In Ovid's account, when Orpheus rashly turns to behold his wife, Eurydice "has no reproach to bring against her husband."[62] Eurydice's elaborate response in Virgil's account is tinged with anger: "What madness, Orpheus, what dreadful madness hath ruined my unhappy self and thee? Lo, again the cruel Fates call me back and sleep veils my swimming eyes. And now farewell! I am swept off, wrapped in uttermost night, and stretching out to thee strengthless hands, thine, alas! no more."[63]

One of the most enduringly popular moments of the myth is Orpheus' quest for Eurydice in Hades, the moment of his fateful glance and her disappearance. One of the most famous depictions of Orpheus and Eurydice is a beautiful fifth-century B.C. relief, known to us through three Roman copies. Orpheus, in the company of Hermes, leads Eurydice from the Underworld (fig. 1.12).[64]

Another tradition emphasizes, instead of Orpheus' dramatic quest, a detailed and picturesque depiction of the Underworld. Both Virgil and Ovid include lengthy and colorful descriptions of the Underworld. Virgil writes:

> Even the jaws of Tartarus, the lofty portals of Dis, he entered, and the grove that is murky with black terror, and came to the dead, and the King of terrors, and the hearts that know not how to soften at human prayers. Startled by the strain, there came from the lowest realms of Erebus the bodiless shadows and the phantoms of those bereft of light, in multitude like the thousands of birds that hide amid the leaves when the evening star or a wintry shower drives them from the hills—mothers and men, and bodies of high-souled heroes, their life now done, boys and unwedded girls, and sons placed on the pyre before their fathers' eyes. But round them are the black ooze and unsightly reeds of Cocytus, the unlovely mere enchain-

ing them with its sluggish water, and Styx holding them fast within his nine fold circles. Nay, the very halls of Hell were spell-bound, and inmost Tartarus, and the Furies with livid snakes entwined in their locks. Cerberus held agape his triple mouths, and Ixion's wheel was stayed by the still wind.[65]

Ovid, too, focuses on the unusual penetration of Orpheus' music into the realm of the dead, the cessation of all activity:

All with his words, the music made the pale phantoms weep: Ixion's wheel was still, Tityos' vulture left the liver, Tantalus tried no more to reach for the water, And Belus' daughters rested from their urns, And Sisyphus climbed on his rock to listen. That was the first time ever in all the world the Furies wept.[66]

A number of vase paintings from southern Italy, dating from the fourth century B.C., are decorated with depictions of Orpheus pleading with Pluto and Persephone, enthroned in a columned architectural structure. The scene typically includes Pluto and his bride, Hercules wrestling with Cerberus, Sisyphus, and the judges Aiakos, Triptolemos, and Rhadamantys. Eurydice is often not even included in these scenes, indicating perhaps that these depictions have less to do with the poignant tale of the poet's ill-fated quest for his wife, and refer more to Orpheus the priest or initiate (he is portrayed in his Phrygian garb), and the Underworld journey, of central importance to the Orphic cult. This interpretation is further reinforced by the fact that Orphism was particularly popular in Southern Italy where these vases originate.[67]

The greatest emphasis on the romantic story of Orpheus and Eurydice emerges in the Middle Ages. The myth, as found in Latin texts and the writings of Christian Apologists, was essentially reread and rewritten, in the context of the medieval courtly ideal, and a severe, all-pervasive moral code. The important aspects of Orpheus' character become his noble origins (as either son of King Oeagrus or of the god Apollo), the extraordinary charm of his musicianship, and the bravery of his journey into Hades. The mythic personality is transformed into medieval terms, becoming Orpheus the nobleman, Orpheus the minstrel, and Orpheus the courtly lover (fig. 1.13). It is in this context that the relationship between Orpheus and Eurydice becomes preeminent. The character of Eurydice herself becomes increasingly important, and subject to extraordinary interpretive symbolism. She is sometimes the sinful side of Orpheus' nature, or she represents the good he cannot attain, and sometimes represents Orpheus' love for the Church.

This tradition can be traced to the sixth century, and Boethius' moralizing *Consolation of Philosophy*, Fulgentius' *Mitologiae*, and then, through the numerous glosses and commentaries which followed, on through the fourteenth century. Another important source are the various moralizations or Christian elaborations of Ovid's *Metamorphoses* which were written from the twelfth through the fourteenth centuries. Salutati's *De laboribus Hercules* and Boccaccio's *Genealogia deorum gentilium*, both dating from the end of the fourteenth century, continue this interpretation. The medieval rewriting becomes increasingly elaborate in the many exercise poems (*ekphrases*) which dealt with this myth and many other stories from classical mythology as well. Probably the most complex and innovative works in this line of development are the fourteenth-century anonymous romance, *Sir Orfeo*, and Robert Henryson's fifteenth-century *Orpheus and Eurydice*, which balance the moral and ethical interpretation with a secularized romance.[68]

The transformation of the classical myth, evolving through centuries of moralizations and ethical allegorizations, and the accommodation of the story to the secular medieval romance and the courtly tradition, is marked. Important aspects of the myth, considered crucial in other periods—Orpheus the Argonaut, Orpheus the priest or initiate, Orpheus the monotheist, even Orpheus the tamer of the beasts—become secondary to the focus on Orpheus' journey into Hades seeking his wife. The poet's fateful backward glance becomes a symbol of corruption.[69]

Orpheus is placed in the middle of a strict moral code, a polarity between good and evil, light and darkness, heaven and hell, the spiritual and the material. In this context of moral choice, Eurydice does not remain for long a neutral figure, but is more and more often identified with evil, becoming an active agent in Orpheus' corruption. In the commentaries on Boethius, her character becomes more clearly defined. For Nicholas Trivet, ca. 1334, Eurydice is named "the affections." "But Eurydice, as she flees through the meadow, that is, the folly of present life, treads on a serpent, not crushing it but casting herself down, that is, joining herself to the sensuality by which she is bitten, and dies."[70] As previously discussed, Orpheus is increasingly identified with wisdom and eloquence. Eurydice is passion and sensuality. She becomes the new Eve, identified with the snake which kills her. Incredibly enough, Aristaeus, her pursuer, comes to symbolize virtue. The commentary by Peter of Paris is remarkable for its deviation from the classical myth. Here, Eurydice is the nagging wife whom Orpheus himself kills.[71] The brief allegorical outline in John of Garland's *Integumenta Ovidii* demonstrates with great clarity the evolution of the moral interpretation into a severe formula, with seemingly no meaningful connection whatever with the original character of the myth: "Field is Pleasure, Wife is Flesh, Viper is Poison, Man is Reason, Styx is Earth, Lyre is Speech."[72]

Perhaps the most striking distortion by the medieval commentators is the imposition of a happy ending. Peter of Paris seems to suggest that Orpheus does comply with the gods' condition and succeeds in retrieving Eurydice.[73] Thierry de Trond's *ekphrasis* provides a happy ending, indeed a resounding victory for Good and Art. "So, trusting with all the power of his spirit in the divinity of his art, bravely he took what he desired from Styx by force. Thus art, aided by firm purpose, vanquished nature, showing that all things yield to Lady Virtue."[74] In *Sir Orfeo*, consistent with medieval romance, his quest to retrieve Heurodis from the Underworld ends in heroic triumph. An illustration to a 1493 *Ovide moralisé* shows Eurydice, led forth from Hades, delivered by fiendish devils to the singing Orpheus. The costumes and settings in these illustrations are strikingly contemporary; visual parallels to the transformation of Orpheus into King Orfeo of Winchester. Orpheus becomes the medieval minstrel and Eurydice the fetching damsel in distress. It is not difficult to understand how the late antique conflation of Orpheus and David, with emphasis on the magic of their song, and their noble origins, was easily transformed into the conventional medieval characters of talented minstrel with entree into royal court, or even king. Another convention of the medieval romance—love by reputation—is incorporated by Robert Henryson into *Orpheus and Eurydice*. Eurydice, Queen of Thrace, falls in love with Orpheus upon hearing of his great beauty and talent. The classical myth becomes more and more remote as Orpheus and Eurydice are portrayed as lovers and their courtship and marriage are treated as the focus of the story.[75]

In *Sir Orfeo*, the quest of the King for his wife takes place in a Celtic otherworld not resembling the classical notion of Hades. As discussed already, Henryson accommodates the myth to the conventions of medieval romance literature. Orpheus' lofty reputation wins Queen Eurydice's love. His quest, through the spheres and in the underworld, is the extraordinary feat or task incumbent upon the hero. Orpheus' lamentation for his dead wife takes the form of the medieval complaint. The familiar terrain of classical mythology is transformed into a Celtic world of fairies (Proserpine is their queen) and dragons.

The evolution of the myth from the thirteenth through the fifteenth centuries, granting new importance to Eurydice's role, inevitably inspires new pictorial treatments of the myth, including depictions of Eurydice's encounter with the serpent; Orpheus pleading for her release in Hades; and the moment of Orpheus' fateful glance back. In the fourteenth and fifteenth centuries, illustrated editions of the moralized Ovid begin to include depictions of Eurydice (fallen to the ground in a swoon), pursued by the shepherd Aristaeus, and the dragon-serpent.[76] Eurydice's story is often incorporated into vast landscapes: Titian's *Orpheus and Eurydice* is typical of his robust mythological landscapes (fig. 1.14). Depictions of Eurydice's death figure in the works of Flemish seventeenth-century artists including, for example, the dramatic scene by Erasmus Quellinus (fig. 1.15).[77]

Orpheus leading Eurydice from Hades or pleading before the Underworld divinities were also very popular images that inspired a variety of pictorial interpretations. *Orpheus in Hades* by Henry Met de Bles (fig. 1.16) presents an unusual Bosch-inspired vision of Hades, including fiery vistas, horrific tortures, fantastic creatures, half-human, half-rocky structures. More typical, perhaps, are depictions of Orpheus pleading before an imposing assemblage of enthroned divinities. Two noteworthy examples of this type are Giulio Romano's *Orpheus before Pluto and Persephone,* in the Sala degli Metamporphosi in the Palazzo del Tè, Mantua, ca. 1530 (fig. 1.17), and Tintoretto's dramatic ceiling painting in the Modena Galleria Estense (fig. 1.18).[78]

Other depictions emphasize the encounter between Orpheus and the ferocious Cerberus. Mantegna's decorations for the Palazzo Ducale, ca. 1473, Mantua, depict this encounter. This motif was apparently particularly favored by sculptors from the sixteenth century through the nineteenth century, for example, Pietro Francavilla's *Orpheus* of 1598 (fig. 1.19).[79]

Orpheus' tragic glance at Eurydice, popular in antiquity and invested with strong moral implications in medieval interpretations, remains one of the most frequently depicted episodes of the myth. The interpretations vary in emphasis: some explore the tension during the couple's ascent from the Underworld; others focus on the brutality of the separation as Eurydice is snatched from Orpheus' grasp; in still others, Eurydice is depicted alone, struggling against invisible forces which threaten to engulf her and return her to Hades. Canova's *Orpheus* and *Eurydice,* 1779 (figs. 1.20a,b), explores the intense and profound emotions which explode as tragedy befalls them. Orpheus and Eurydice are individual sculptural pieces, and the real space between them underlines their tragic separation, and serving as a void which reverberates with the anguish and supplication communicated by their gestures. This episode remains popular throughout the nineteenth and twentieth centuries, as artists and writers attempt to come to terms with the perplexing nature of Orpheus' action, and explore the ambiguous psychological symbolism of his glance.[80]

The Death of Orpheus

Clearly, the dramatic climax of the myth, the moment which invests the entire story with meaning, is Orpheus' violent death. The death simultaneously transforms the poet-priest into a gory victim and a pathetic martyr, as well as setting the stage for the triumphal finale, the magical song of severed head and lyre, by which his art transcends his brutal death.

The dominant tradition attributes Orpheus' death to the madness of the Thracian women. There are less popular explanations for Orpheus' demise: he is blasted by Zeus' lightning bolt as punishment for the revelation of mysteries or sacred secrets.[81] Pausanias offers three explanations for Orpheus' death: the anger of the Thracian women; the punishment of Zeus' lightning; and Orpheus' suicide because of unbearable grief over Eurydice's death.[82]

There is throughout the centuries a wide variety of explanations for the women's madness. Virgil attributes the women's rage to Orpheus' steadfast devotion to his wife. Ovid, too, speaks of Orpheus' grief and his life isolated from other women. Others point to a religious basis for his murder. The Athenian orator Isocrates (436–338 B.C.) in *Busiris*, 391 B.C., lists Orpheus' dismemberment among the deaths of other poets and civilizers, punished for revealing sacred secrets.[83] The mythographer, Conon, suggests that the women are furious because Orpheus has refused to initiate them.[84] One fifth-century red-figured Krater shows the approach of the armed women, as Orpheus sits singing to a peaceful crowd of men. In Aeschylus' *The Bassarids*, it is Dionysus who sends his Maenads to destroy Orpheus, because the poet continues to worship Apollo and refuses to honor him.[85] On the other hand, within the context of the Orphic religion, Orpheus' death serves to emphasize his bond to the god, Zagreus-Dionysus, who is similarly dismembered. Orpheus dies, therefore, as victim of Dionysus, or as primary leader of his cult.

Hyginus offers an explanation for the women's fury that does not at all involve the revelation of mysteries or initiation. He explains that it is Venus who incited the women to lust after the chaste poet. This is the goddess' revenge against Orpheus' mother, Calliope, who as Zeus' judge, gave Persephone possession of Venus' beloved Adonis.[86]

As with the other episodes of the myth, medieval mythographers rely on a strict moral standard in their interpretations of the women's motivation. Arnulf d'Orléans (*Ovid moralisé*, ca. 1125) interprets their murderous attack as a reflection of the nature of women in general, prone to lust and vice. Bersuire equates the women with cruel princes and tyrants.[87]

Perhaps the most popular explanation for the women's fury is anger and jealousy because Orpheus shuns their sexual advances. Orpheus withdraws from society because of an impenetrable grief at the loss of his wife. Also, there is a significant tradition that does not attribute Orpheus' refusal to the women, to asceticism, or fanatical grief, but to his homosexuality. Phanocles, an Alexandrian poet from the second century B.C., is the first to mention Orpheus' homosexuality.[88] Ovid espouses this explanation for the poet's disdain of the women: "His life was given to young boys only, and he told the Thracians that was the better way: enjoy, that springtime, Take those first flowers."[89] Pausanias is very specific, attributing the women's jealousy to Orpheus' seduction of their husbands.[90] Moralizing medieval authors either entirely ignore this aspect of the myth or choose to interpret Orpheus' homosexuality as a righteous avoidance of sensual pleasure and carnal temptation in the form of woman.[91]

The attack of the Thracian women is frequently depicted on fifth-century B.C. vases (fig. 1.21). Orpheus continues to clutch his lyre as he falls to his knees. He is surrounded by a group of women, their bodies covered with tattoos, their hair fiercely bristling, bearing stones, spears, arrows, and farm implements as weapons.

The depiction of Orpheus' death varies little, in fact, over the centuries.[92] An illustration from Lydgate's *Fall of Princes*, ca. 1450 (fig. 1.22) presents Orpheus, helplessly crumpled at the feet of a spear-bearing crowd of women. The only significant difference with portrayals in the antique is the transformation with contemporary garb of the attacking women into bourgeois housewives. Illustrated editions of Ovid's *Metamorphoses* invariably include the image of the poet's death.[93] Mantegna depicts the death of Orpheus in the Camera degli Sposi, in the Palazzo Ducale, in Mantua (fig. 1.23). A print after another lost work by Mantegna was one inspiration for Dürer's *Orpheus*, ca. 1494 (fig. 1.24). Dürer introduces the theme of homosexuality by means of an inscription—"DER ERST PUSERAN"—written on a scroll suspended on a tree behind Orpheus.[94] The putto, fleeing beneath a fig tree whose branch is stripped bare, has also been interpreted as an allusion to the homosexual theme.[95]

The significance of the theme of homosexuality is elucidated by briefly tracing the connections between the works of Mantegna, Dürer, and Poliziano. The Camera degli Sposi in the Gonzaga Palace in Mantua was the site for the performance of Agnolo Poliziano's pastoral drama, *Il Favolo di Orfeo*, in 1471–72. This work was commissioned by Cardinal Francesco Gonzaga upon the visit of Duke Galeazzo Maria Sforza.[96] There is a connection not only between Mantegna's work and Poliziano's play, but also a likely link with Dürer's drawing. *Il Favolo di Orfeo* was printed for the first time in 1494, the date of Dürer's drawing. Moreover, that was the year of Poliziano's death and the year of the northern artist's journey to Italy. Considering Dürer's admiration for the noted humanist, his drawing may well have been intended to commemorate both his death and the newly printed drama.[97]

Poliziano's work begins with Virgil's episode of Aristaeus' pursuit of Eurydice. Also, it briefly recounts Orpheus' failed quest for Eurydice in Hades. The emphasis is on Orpheus' reaction to this tragedy. He is transformed by his guilt and angrily denounces women and militantly espouses homosexual love, or the love of young girls.

> Sorrowing and disconsolate I shall abide in my affection as long as the heavens shall give me life. And since my fate has been so cruel never more shall I wish for woman's love. Henceforth I would cull new flowers, maidens in their spring when all are fair and lithe. This is a love more gentle and sweet. Let the love of woman bind me no longer. Let there be no longer any to prate to me of women. For dead is she who held my heart. Who would converse with me let him not talk to me of woman's love. How wretched the man who changes his purpose for a woman, or even for her is happy or sad! Or who barters for her his liberty, or who puts faith in her pretences or her words. She is ever lighter than a leaf before the wind. A thousand times a day she will or will not. She follows him who flees. From him who wishes her she hides, and like the wave upon the shore she comes and goes.

Of this is Jove assured who scorns the sweet amorous tie that binds him and in heaven enjoys his beautiful Ganymede; and on earth Phoebus enjoyed Hyacinth. To this holy love Hercules surrenders, he who was the world and was won by fair Hylas. The married man I urge to seek divorce, and all to flee the company of woman.[98]

This harsh diatribe leaves no doubt about the reason for the Thracian women's anger. The work ends with the poet's destruction.

Orpheus was, as well, a popular image in the circle of Giorgione.[99] Giorgione's *Concert champêtre,* ca. 1508 (fig. 1.25), has been interpreted as Orpheus singing to a young male companion, while the two women stand some distance away, excluded from their company.[100] Ovid, Poliziano, as well as Phanocles' elegy may have been the sources for this theme of Orpheus' homosexuality. The elegy, which might have been known to Giorgione via the *Florilegium,* compiled by the fifth-century A.D. author Stobaeus, describes Orpheus' song to his beloved Calais. It is this particular passage which has been compared to the Giorgione.

Or else, as the son of Oeagrus, Thracian Orpheus, with his whole heart loved Calais, the son of Boreas. Ofttimes in the shady wood he sat him down to sing his desire and his heart ne'er came to rest. But, ever alert, his amorous longing chafed him, while his eyes looked upon blooming Calais. Gathering about him, the cruel women of Thrace sharpened their keen-edged swords and killed him, for that, first among the Thracians, he had set the example of loving boys and had scorned the love of women.[101]

The Oracular Head

Phanocles' elegy describes the passage of Orpheus' severed head down the Hebrus River to the isle of Lesbos.[102] Lucian explains how Orpheus' head was preserved in a temple of Bacchus and his lyre in a temple dedicated to Apollo.[103] Conon describes the passage of Orpheus' head until its recovery at the mouth of the River Meles near Smyrna.[104] In *The Life of Apollonius of Tyana,* Philostratus describes the oracular power of the severed head and Apollo's eventual silencing of its prophecies.[105]

The nineteenth-century Symbolists' numerous depictions of Orpheus' severed head constitute, in a sense, a revival of an image popular in antiquity, especially the fifth and fourth centuries B.C., but neglected in subsequent centuries. Several red-figured vases from the fifth century depict men and women inclining to hear the word emanating from the head. The severed head, in fact, appears quite animated, with open eyes and mouth. A red-figured kylix (fig. 1.26) apparently portrays Apollo, forbidding someone from recording the oracular statements. The subject also appears frequently in Etruscan art, from the fourth to third centuries B.C. (see, for example, fig. 1.27).[106]

This image did not, however, disappear entirely in the intervening centuries. Boccaccio, in his *Genealogia*, uses Orpheus' severed head as a symbol of genius:

> The serpent, or time, as the list of the legend demonstrates, tried to eat the head, that is, the name and fame of Orpheus or those works performed by this genius, since men of genius thrive by the head. . . . Nothing stands in the way of time, and to be sure the serpent could not have gone hungry save to this extent, that a famous man lives [on] by his lyre, that is, his genius as is reported by an older poet.[107]

In *Lycidas*, 1638, Milton's great elegy on the death of his friend King Edward, there is a reference to Orpheus' head floating on the River Hebrus.

The episode is also maintained in mythographic texts throughout the sixteenth through the eighteenth centuries. Natalis Comes describes the head transported on the river and also the transfiguration of the lyre into the nine-starred constellation.[108] The illustrations by Tempesta for Ovid's *Metamorphoses* include the scene of Apollo turning the dragon to stone, and retrieving the poet's head from its jaws (fig. 1.28). In lines 55–60 of book 11, Ovid describes how Apollo saves the poet's head from the attack of a fierce serpent or dragon, as it washes ashore on the island of Lesbos, near the town of Methysma. The poet's instrument, in this case a violin, floats on the river. (Apollo himself holds the more traditional lyre.) A similar scene is included in the background of the illustration to book 11 in the Sandys 1632 English edition of the *Metamorphoses*. The commentary interprets the preservation of the head as a symbol of the transmission of knowledge. "So the scattered relics of learning, expulsed from one country, are transported to another as here unto Lesbos: Pittacus, Arions, Sappho and Alcaeus, being all of the Island, who succeeded Orpheus in the fame of lyrical poetry."[109] In the tradition of medieval moralizations, the dragon which attempts to devour the head is, "Detraction and Serpentine Envy." The text also relates two stories concerning the fate of the lyre: its transformation into the constellation; and its enshrinement in Apollo's temple at Lesbos whence it was later stolen by Neanthus. In the Garth/Dryden 1732 commentary to book 10, the oracular head is a symbol of Orpheus' victory after Death, "put in the Rank of Demi-Gods and Heros." The Lesbian Dragon symbolizes the ignorant critic who attacks the reputation of the poet to gain fame.[110]

The myth of Orpheus, then, includes the following sequence of events: Orpheus' adventure with the Argonauts; Orpheus charming the animals, trees, and rocks; Orpheus and his wife, Eurydice; Orpheus in Hades; Orpheus' death at the hands of the Maenads or Bacchantes; Orpheus' head and lyre floating on the River Hebrus. Clearly, however, and crucial for an appreciation of the Symbolists' interpretation, the myth is not static but changes in meaning, indeed, is significantly transformed as various moments of the narrative are selected, neglected, and variously interpreted. Two fundamentally different traditions emerge: one emphasizes the romantic tale and gives special importance to the role of Eurydice. In contrast to this tradition which essentially trivializes the myth, another approach plumbs its depth, discovering profound meaning. Orpheus is the harbinger of civilization. He is the archetypal artist and musician, leader of religious cults—a priest or magus. The Symbolists partake of this second tradition, rediscovering the religious significance and psychological intensity of the myth. For them, Orpheus is poet, martyr, priest, and magician.

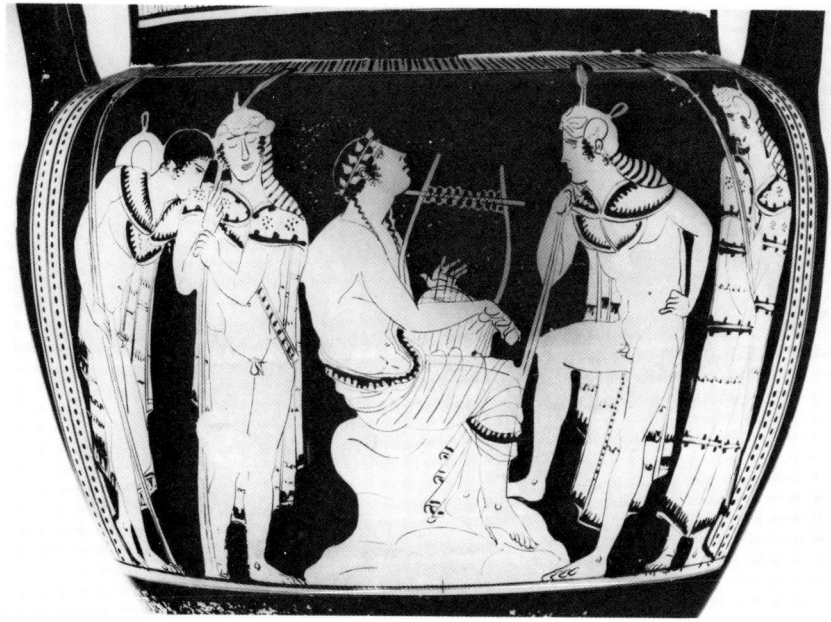

Figure 1.1. *Orpheus Singing to the Thracians*, 5th century B.C.
Red-figured vase painting, column-crater.
(Antikenmuseum Berlin, Staatliche Museen Preussischer Kulturbesitz)

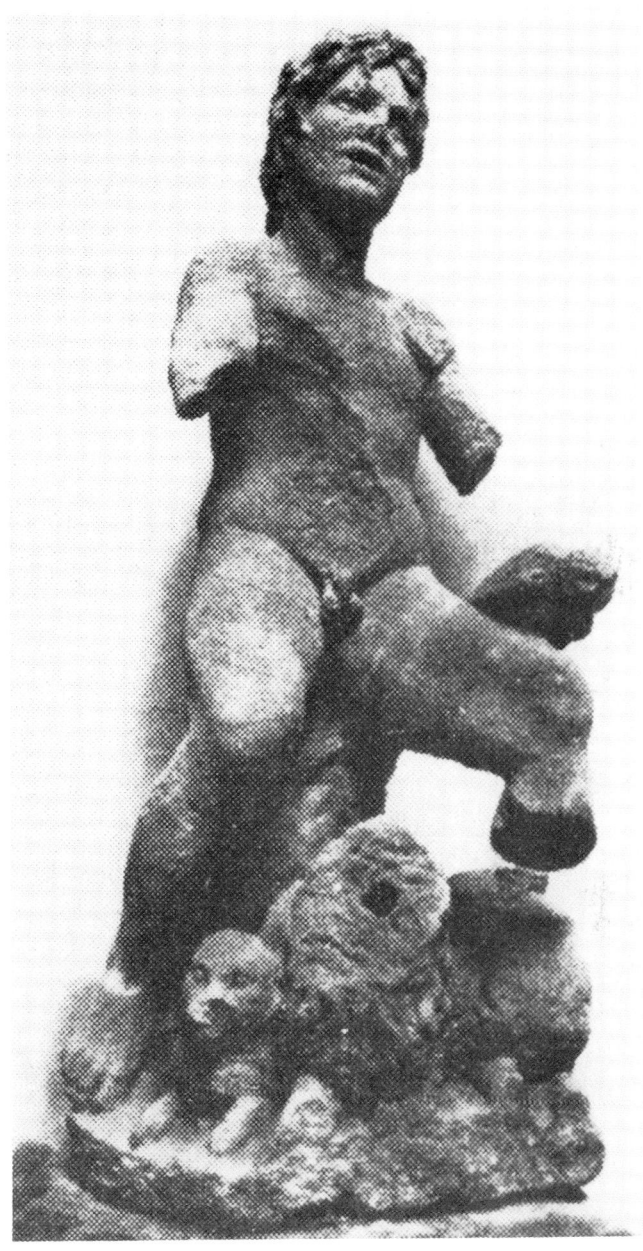

Figure 1.2. *Orpheus amidst the Animals*, 2nd–1st century B.C. Italo-Etruscan sculpture.
(*Museo Capitolino, Rome; Foto Archivio Musei Capitolini*)

Figure 1.3. Giovanni Bellini, *Orpheus*, ca. 1515 Transferred from wood to canvas. (*National Gallery of Art, Washington; Widener Collection*)

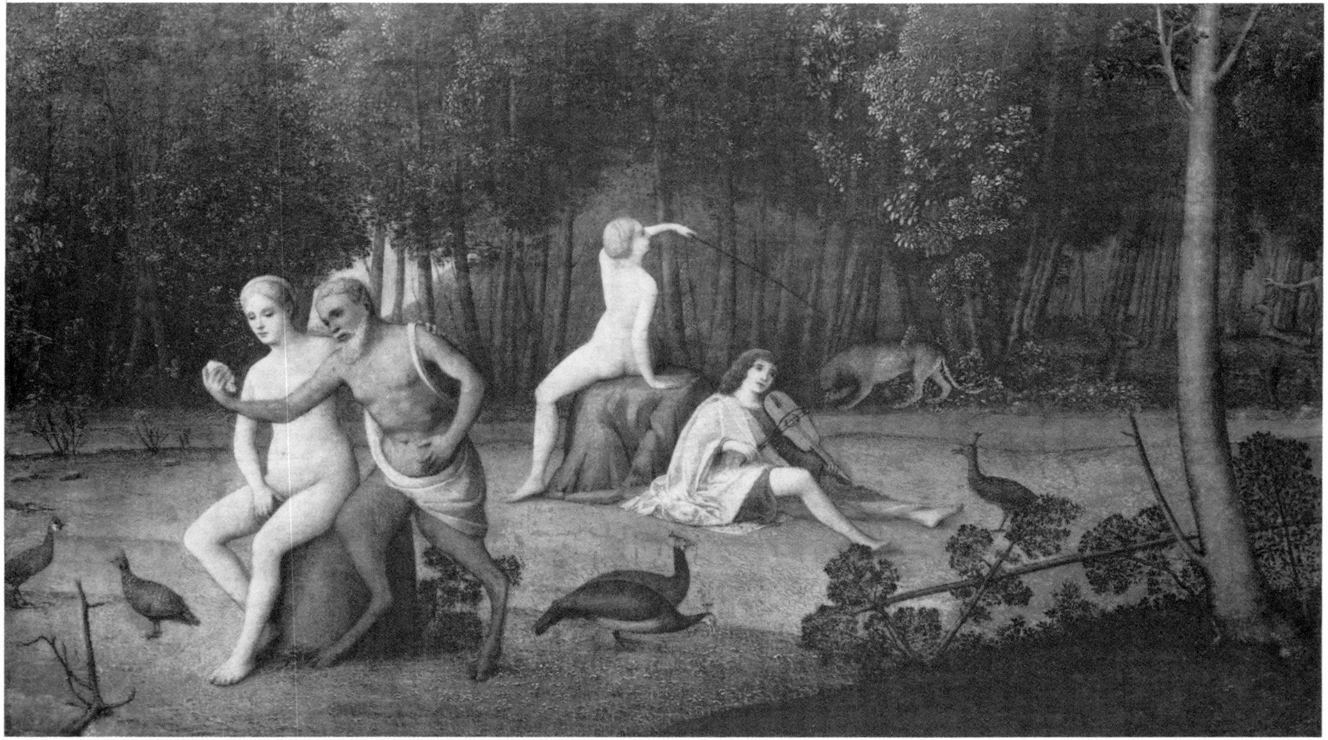

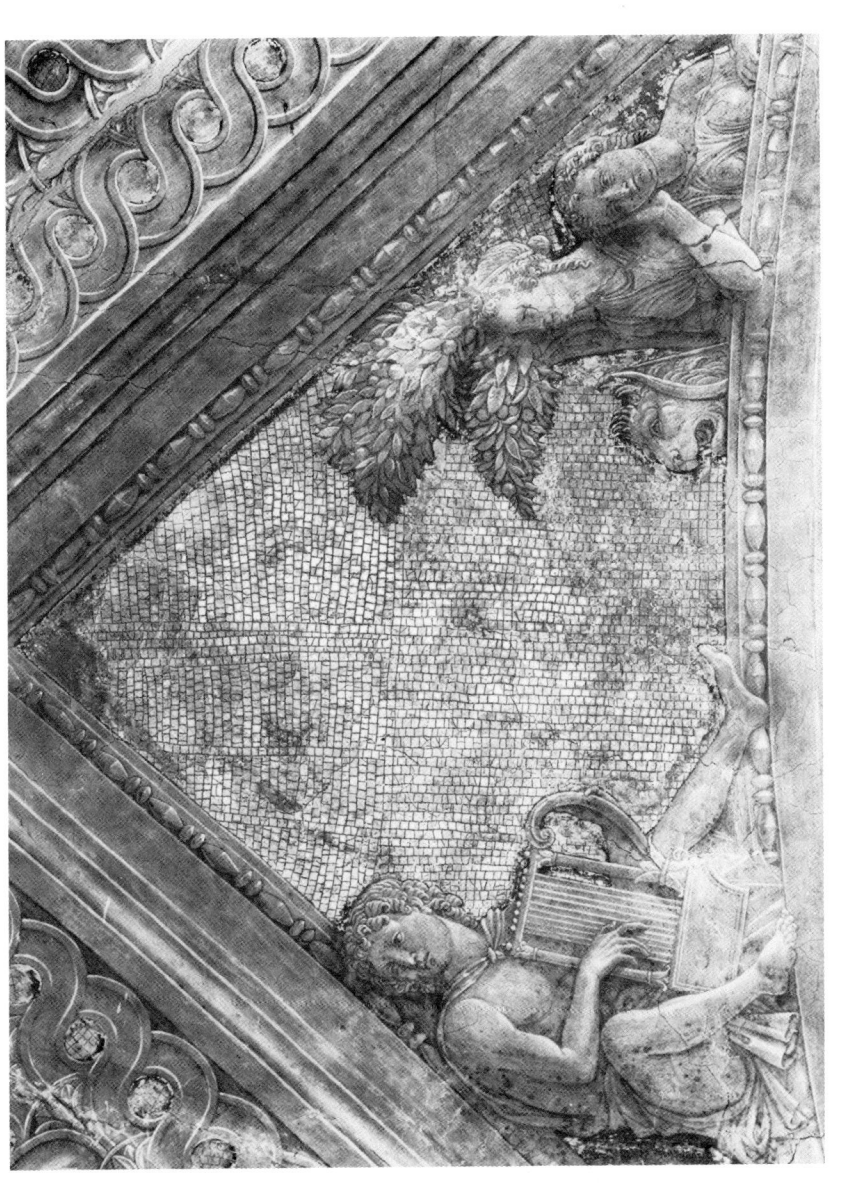

Figure 1.4. Andrea Mantegna, Orpheus Playing the Lyre, 1473 Fresco.
(Camera degli Sposi, Palazzo Ducale, Mantua; Foto Giovetti, Mantua)

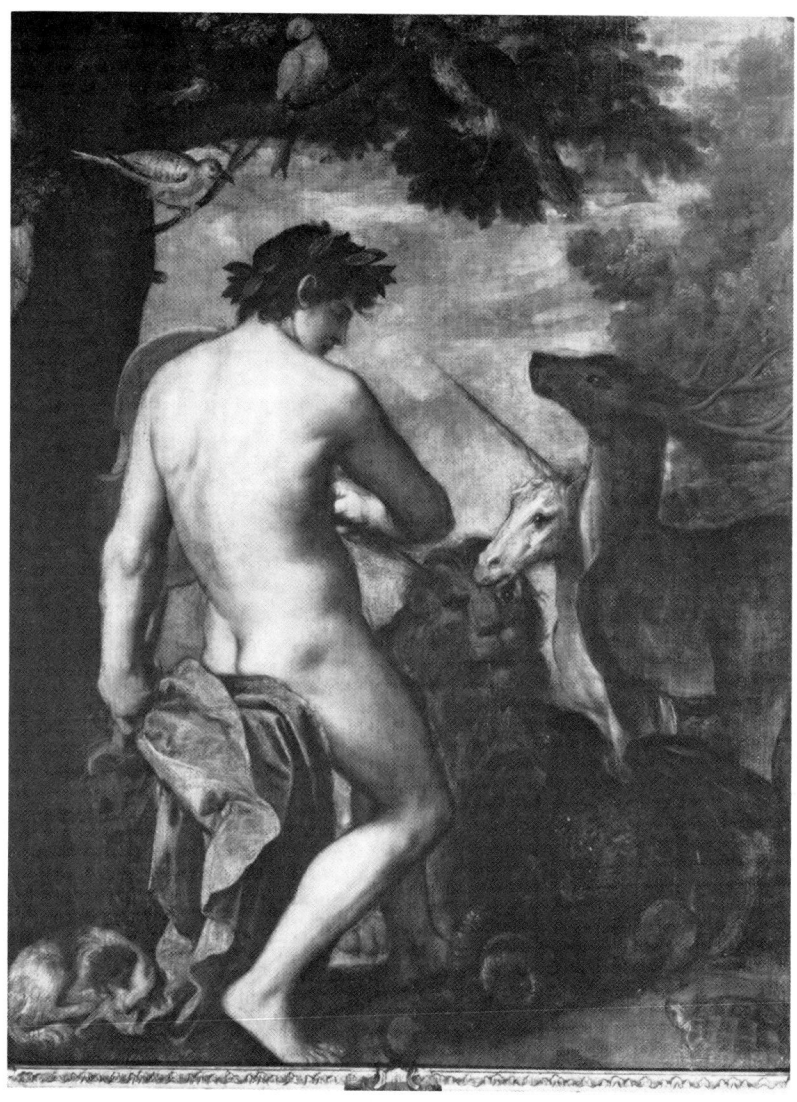

Figure 1.5. Il Padovanino, *Orpheus Enchanting the Animals*, early 17th century
Oil on canvas.
(*The Wellington Museum, Apsley House, from the Spanish Royal Collection; photo courtesy the V & A Picture Library*)

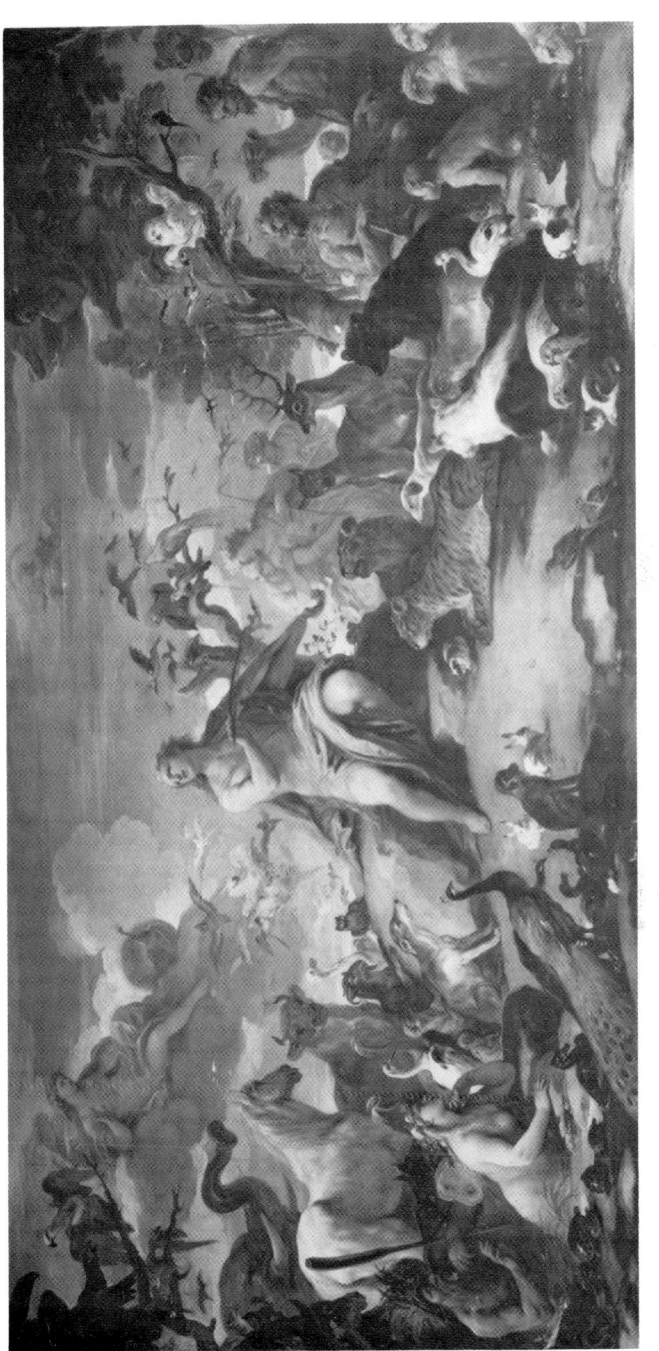

Figure 1.6. Luca Giordano, *Orpheus*, ca. 1696
Oil on canvas.
(*Palacio Real, Aranjuez; fotografía cedida y autorizada por el patrimonio nacional*)

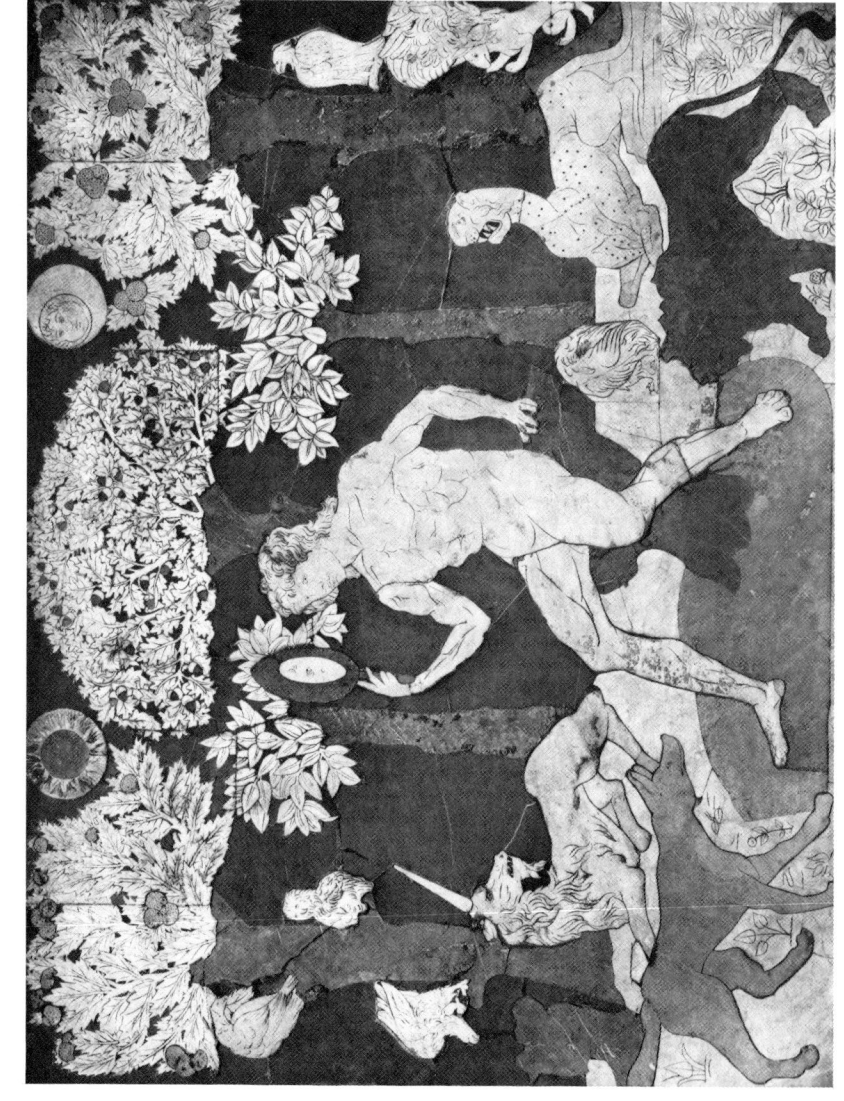

Figure 1.7. Beccafumi or Francesco di Giorgio, *Orpheus*, 1480–90 Mosaic pavement, Chapel of St. Catherine. (*Church of St. Dominic, Siena; photo Alinari*)

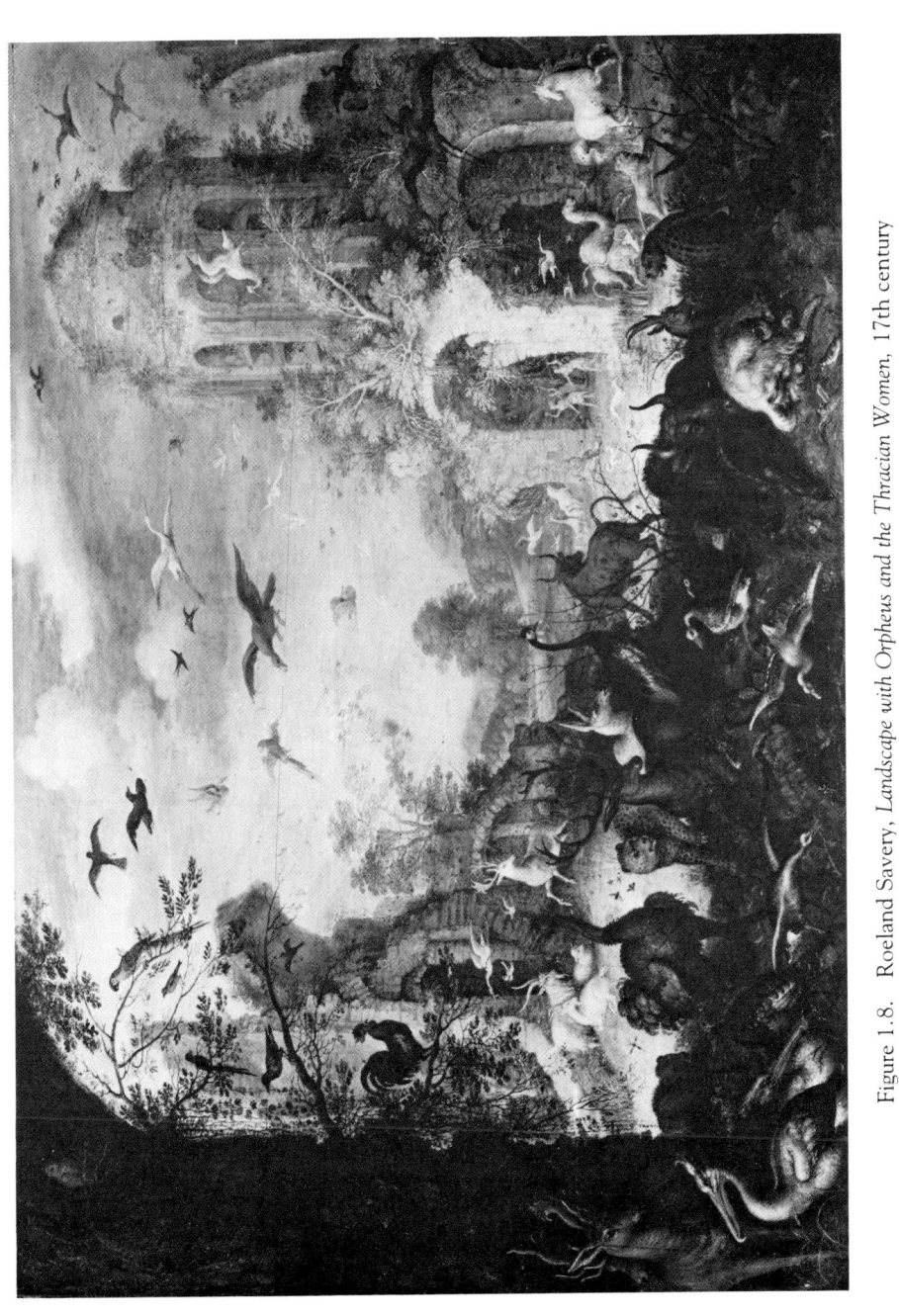

Figure 1.8. Roeland Savery, *Landscape with Orpheus and the Thracian Women*, 17th century (*Kunsthistorisches Museum, Vienna*)

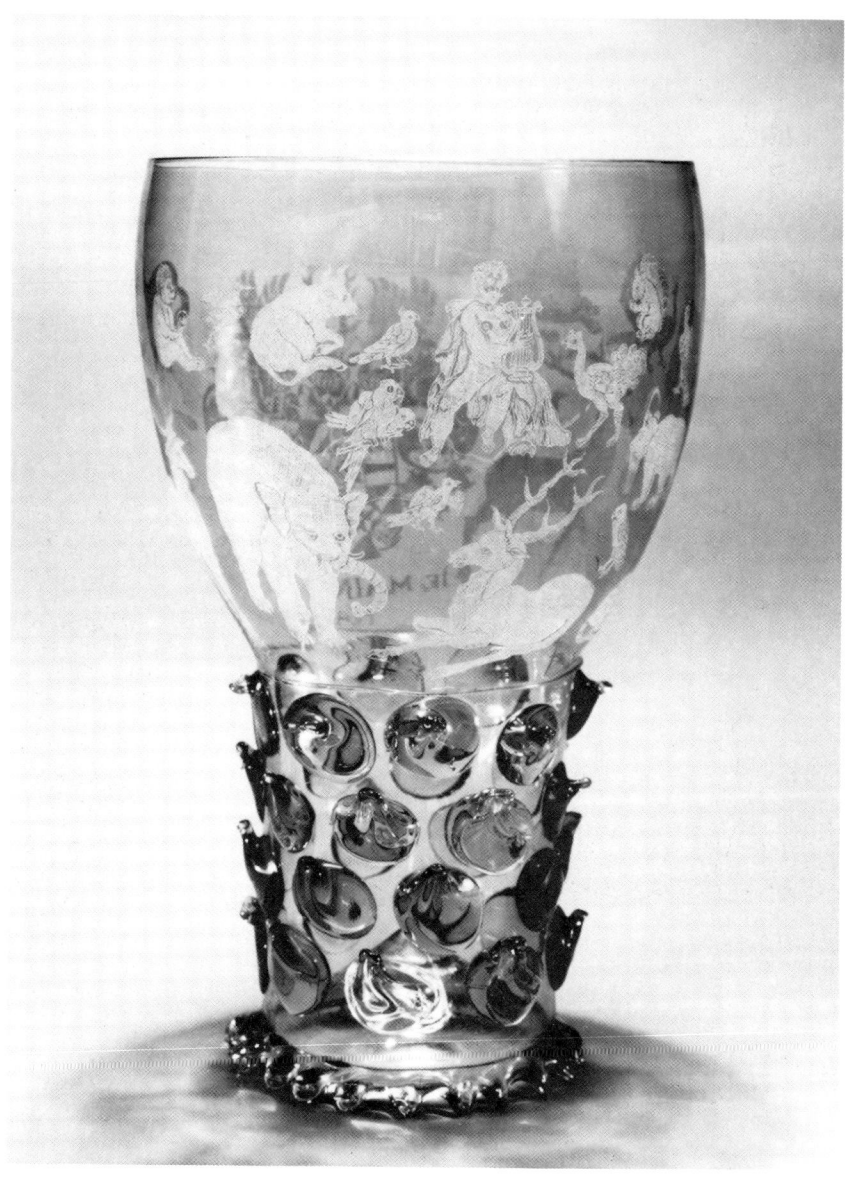

Figure 1.9. *Orpheus*, 1611
Dutch "Roemer."
Oil on panel.
(Museum Boymans-van Beuningen, Rotterdam; photo: Dick Wolters)

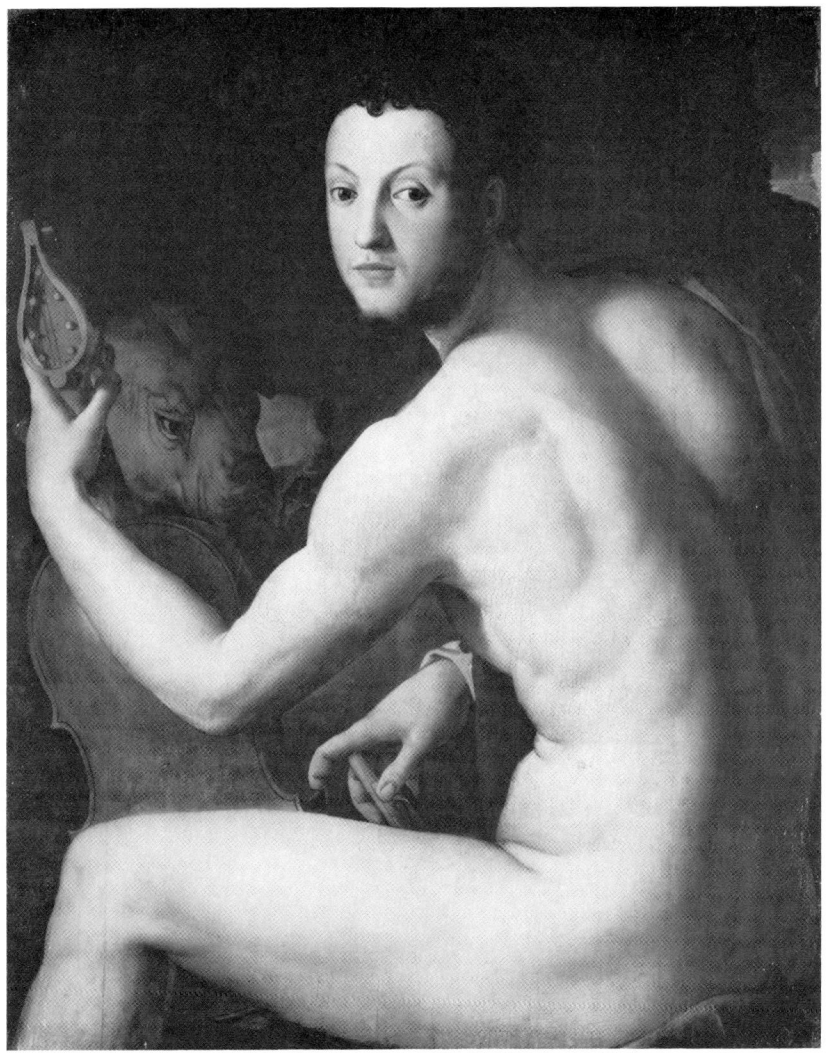

Figure 1.10. Agnolo Bronzino, *Cosimo I as Orpheus*, 1540–42
Oil on wood panel.
(Philadelphia Museum of Art; given by Mrs. John Wintersteen)

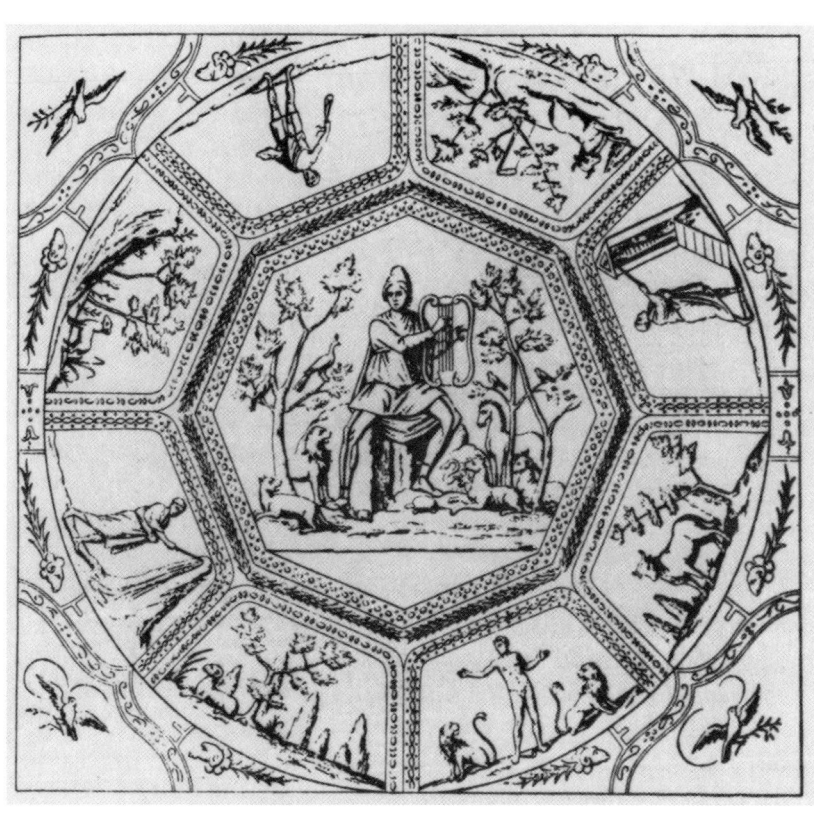

Figure 1.11   *Orpheus*, 3rd century
Ceiling fresco.
(Catacomb of Domitilla, Rome)

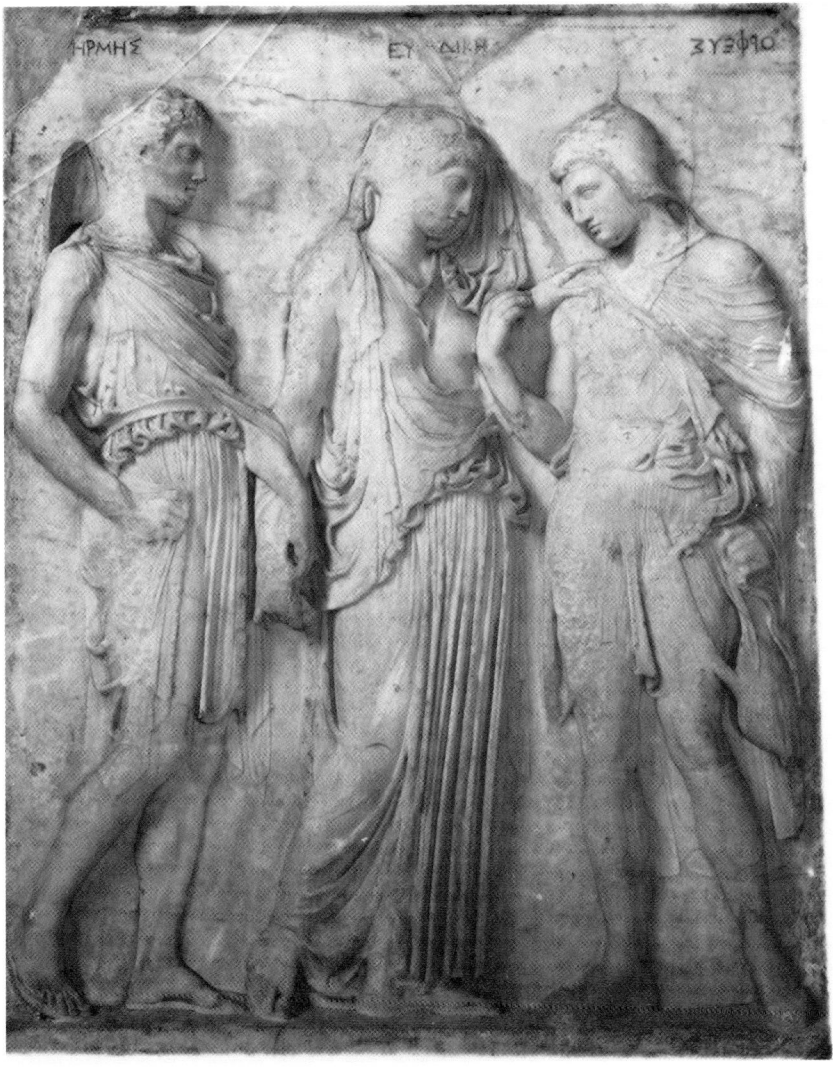

Figure 1.12. Hermes, Eurydice, Orpheus, 5th century Attic relief sculpture.
(National Museum, Naples; photo courtesy Soprintendenza delle Province di Napoli e Caserta)

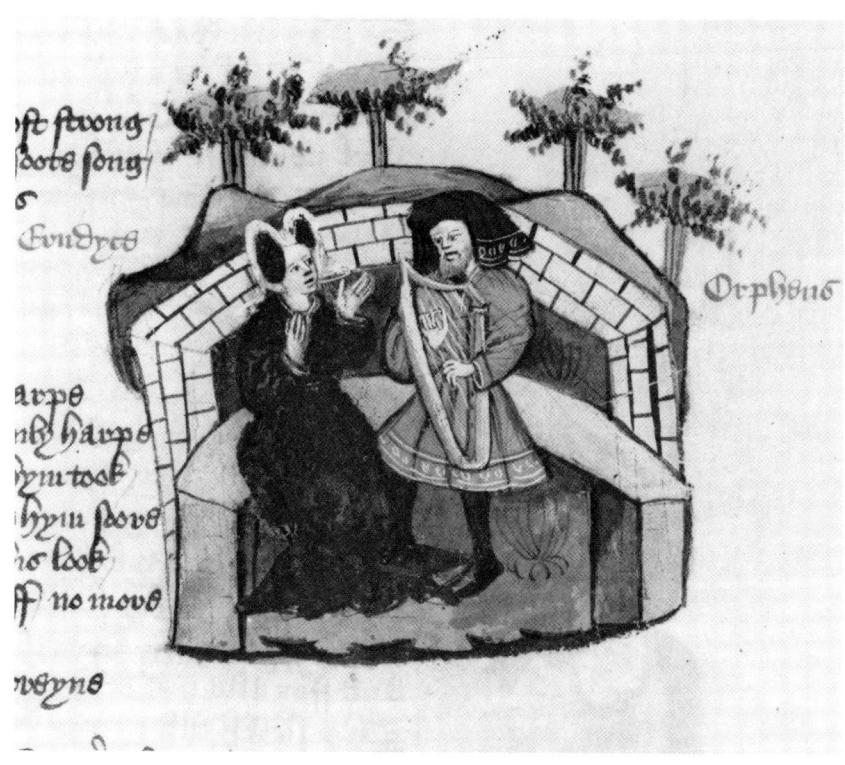

Figure 1.13. *Orpheus and Eurydice Courting*, ca. 1450
Illustration from Lydgate, *Fall of Princes*.
(The British Library. Harley 1766, 76r)

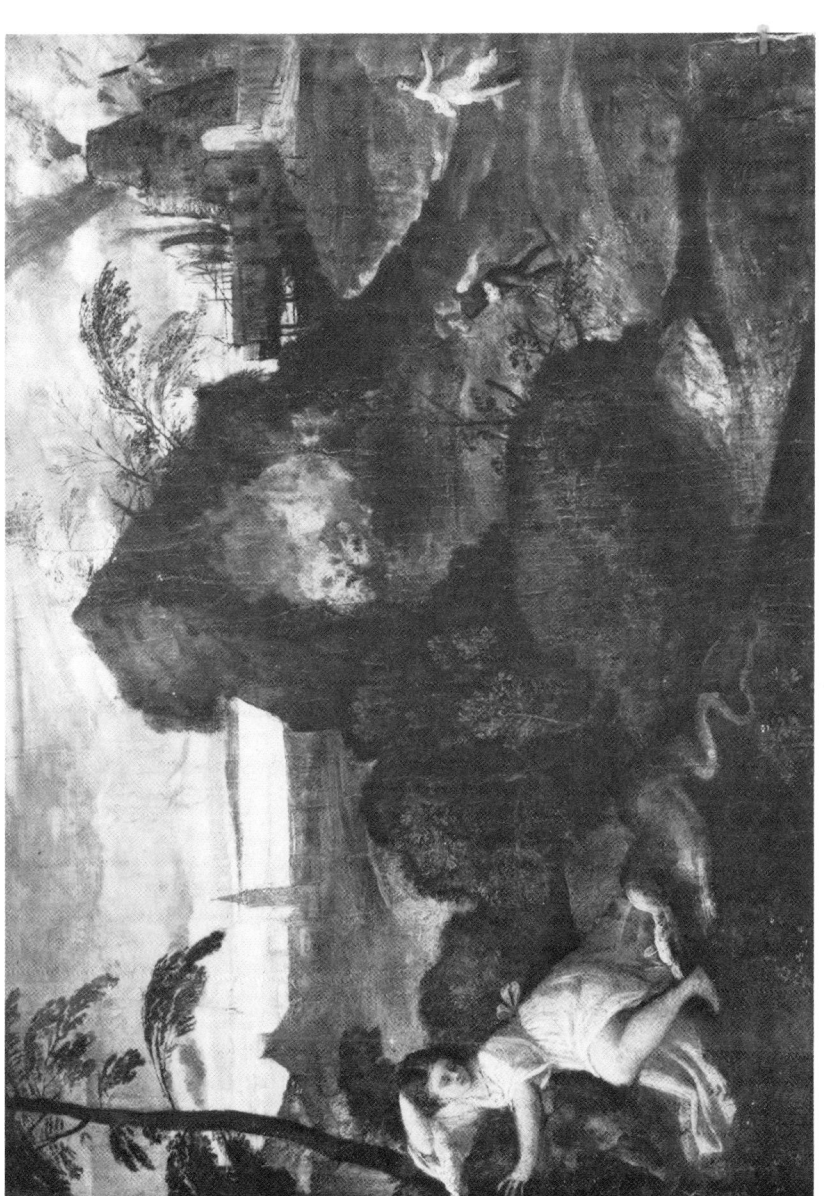

Figure 1.14. Titian, *Orpheus and Eurydice*, ca. 1510. Oil on panel. (*Accademia Carrara, Bergamo*)

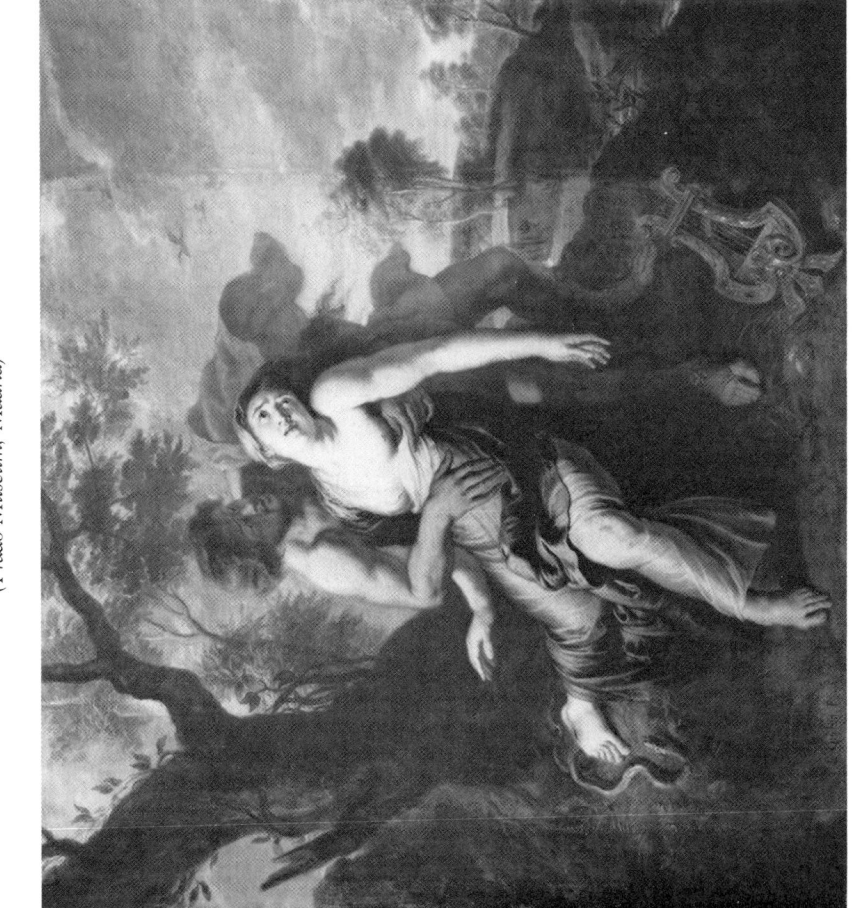

Figure 1.15. Erasmus Quellinus, *Eurydice*, 17th century Oil on canvas. *(Prado Museum, Madrid)*

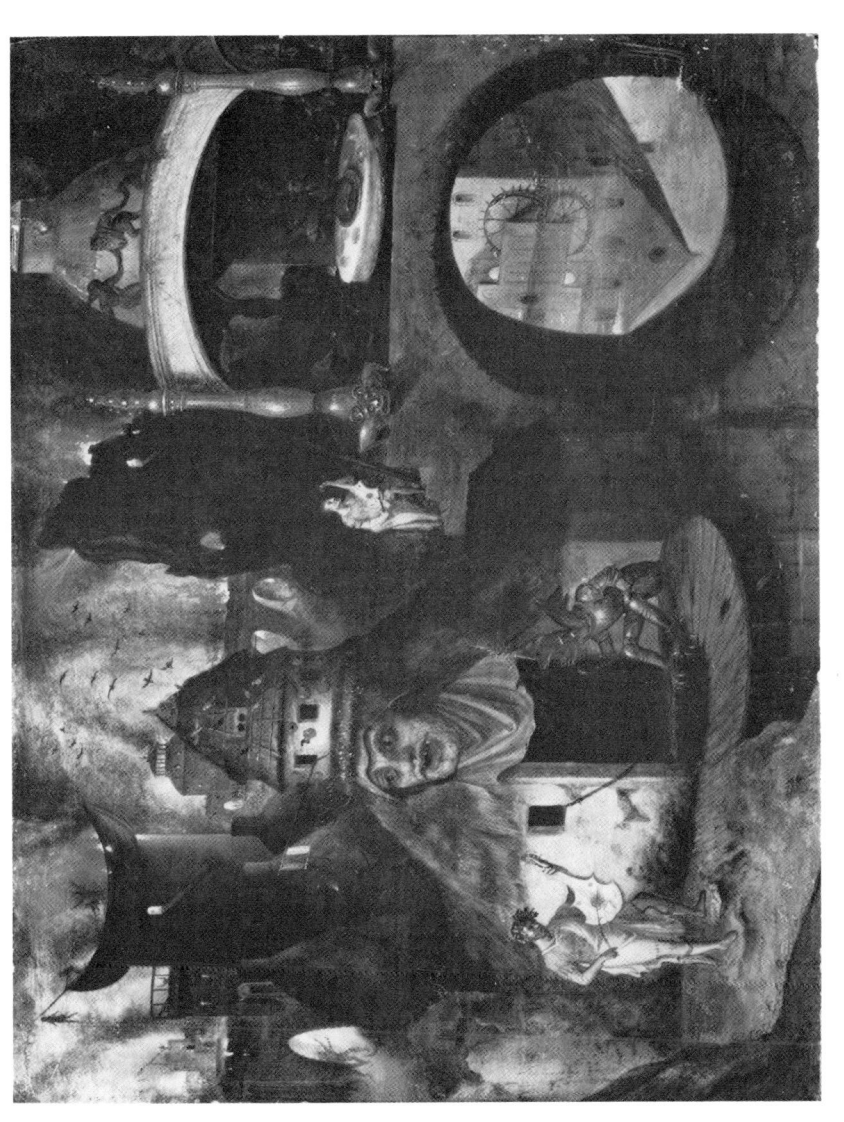

Figure 1.16. Henry Met de Bles, *Orpheus in Hades*, ca. 1515–1550 Oil on panel.
(*The Fine Arts Museums of San Francisco, gift of The de Young Museum Society*)

Figure 1.17. Giulio Romano, *Orpheus before Pluto and Persephone*, ca. 1530
Fresco.
(*Sala di Ovidio, Palazzo del Tè, Mantua; Photocolor, Mantua*)

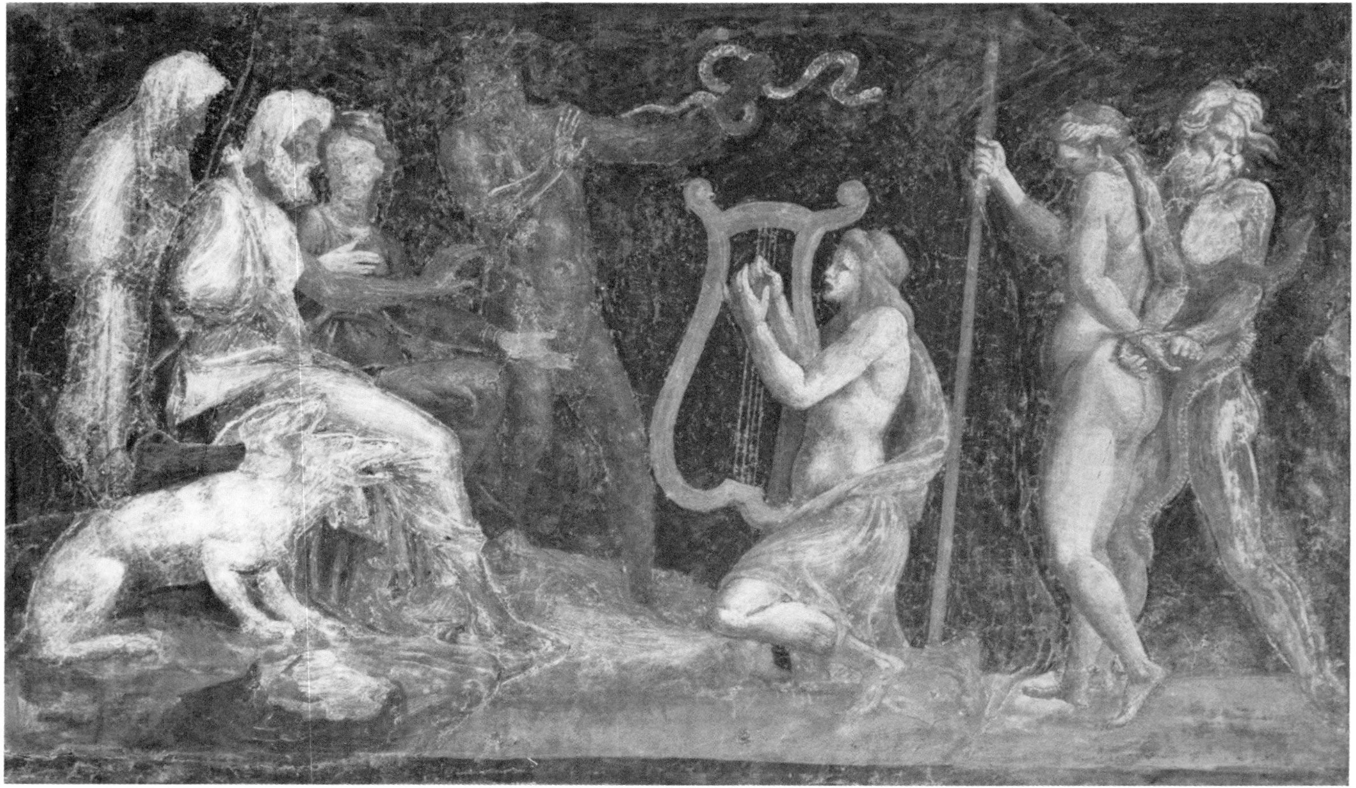

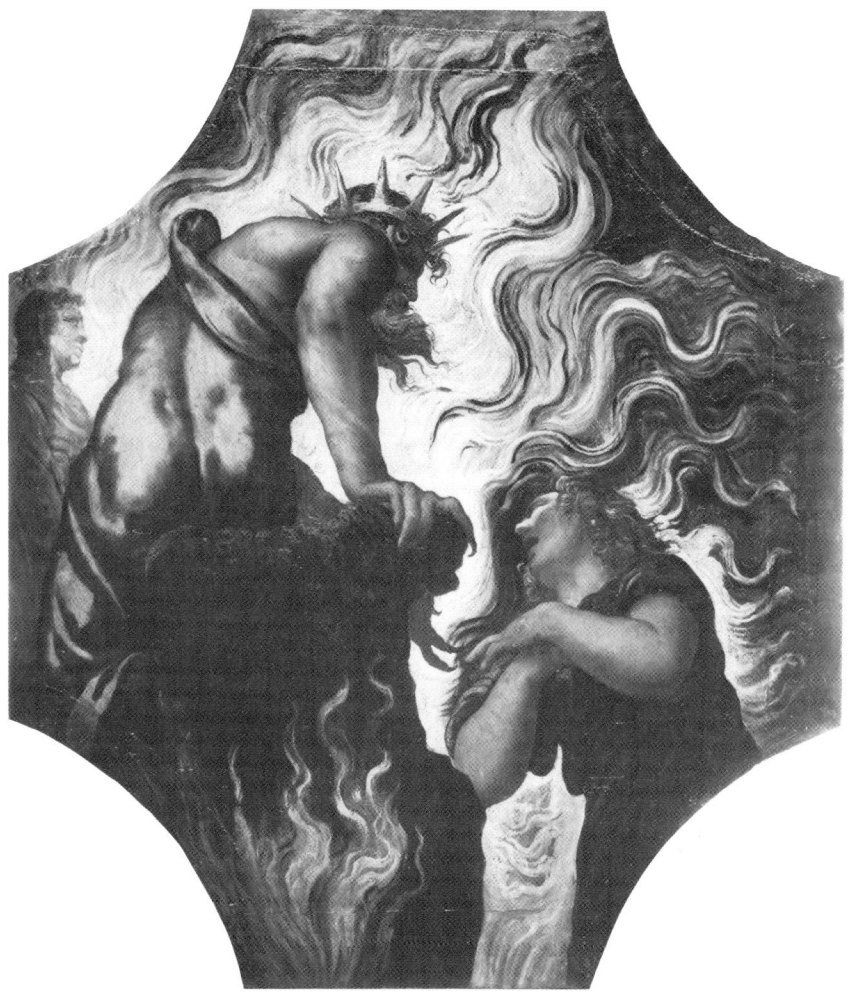

Figure 1.18. Jacopo Tintoretto, *Orpheus Pleading to Pluto*, ca. 1550
Oil on panel.
(Galleria Estense, Modena)

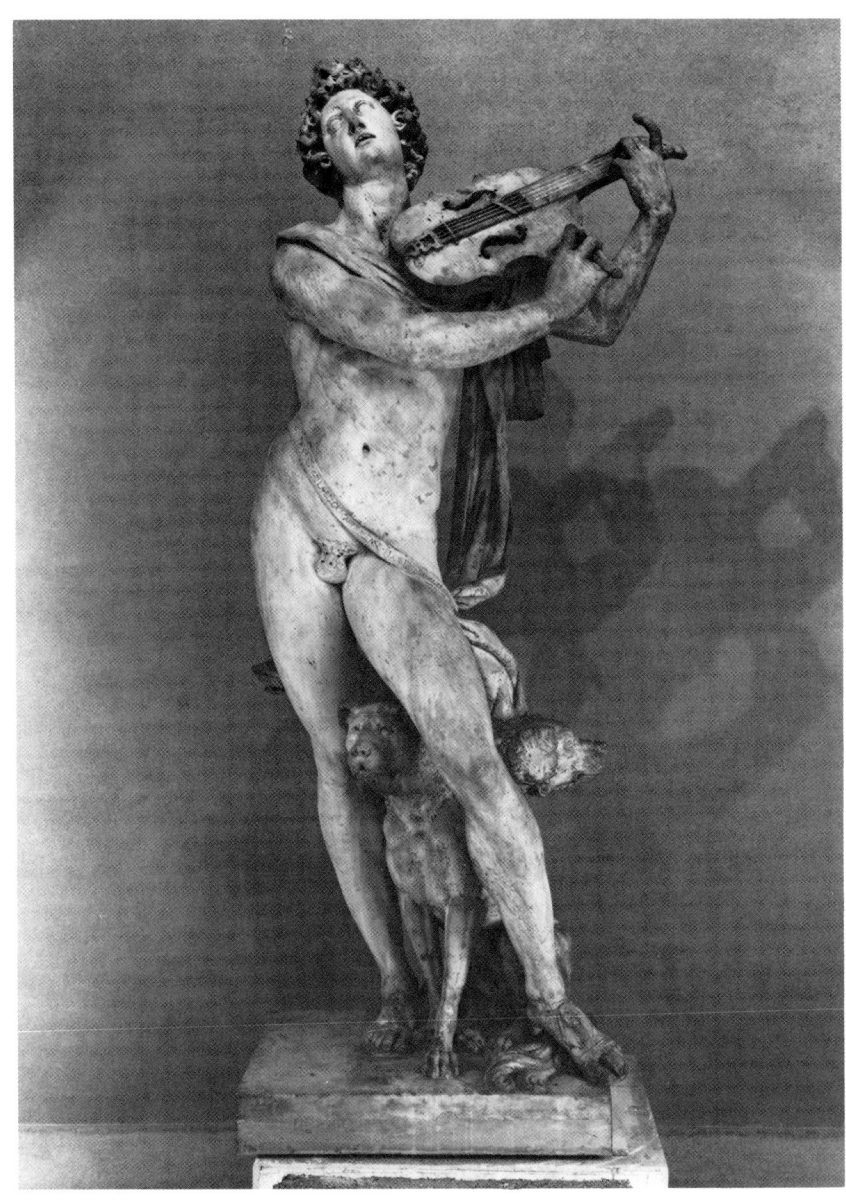

Figure 1.19. Pietro Francavilla, *Orpheus*, 1598
Marble.
(Louvre, Paris; Cliché des Musées Nationaux, Paris)

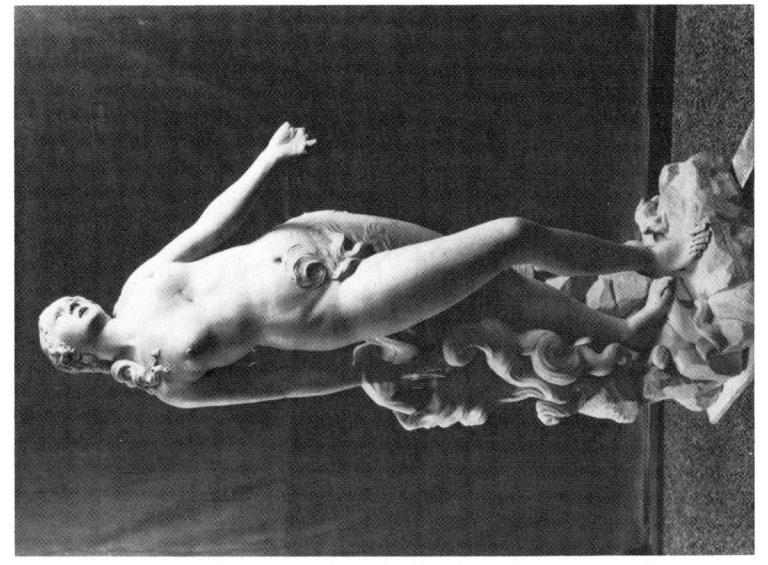
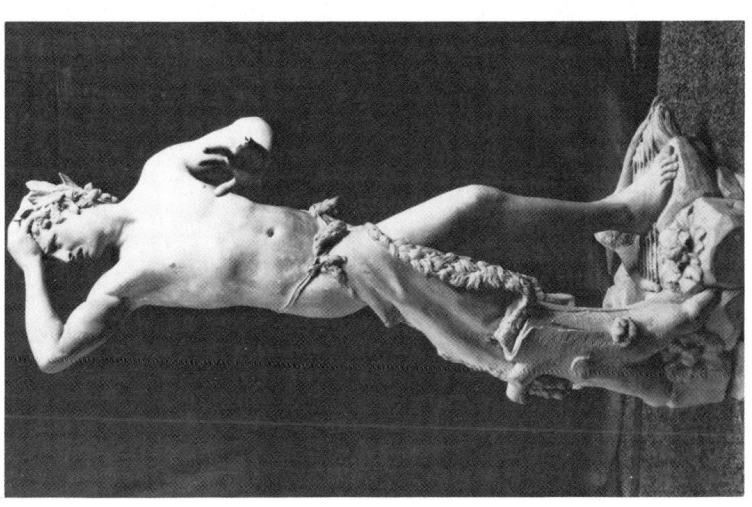

Figure 1.20a and b. Antonio Canova, *Orpheus and Eurydice*, 1779 Marble.
(Museo Correr, Venice; *Reale Fotografia Giacomelli*)

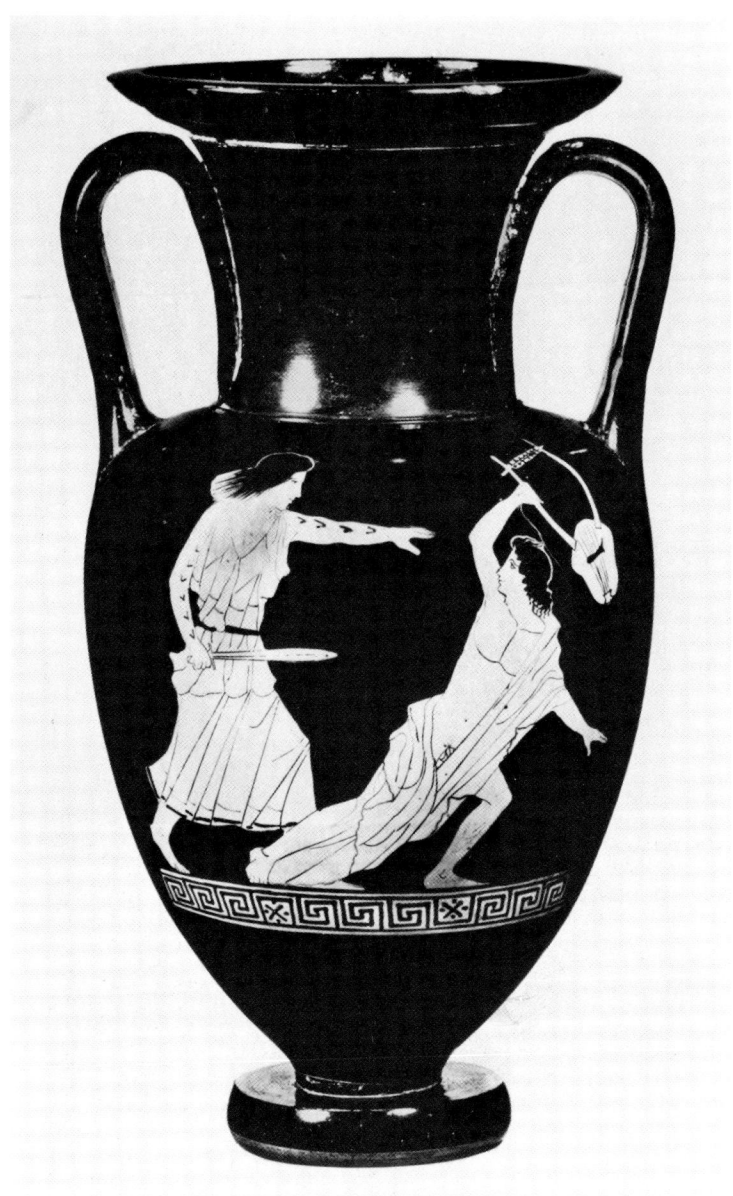

Figure 1.21. *Death of Orpheus*, ca. 430 B.C.
Red-figured attic amphora.
(*Staatliche Antikensammlungen und Glyptothek, Munich*)

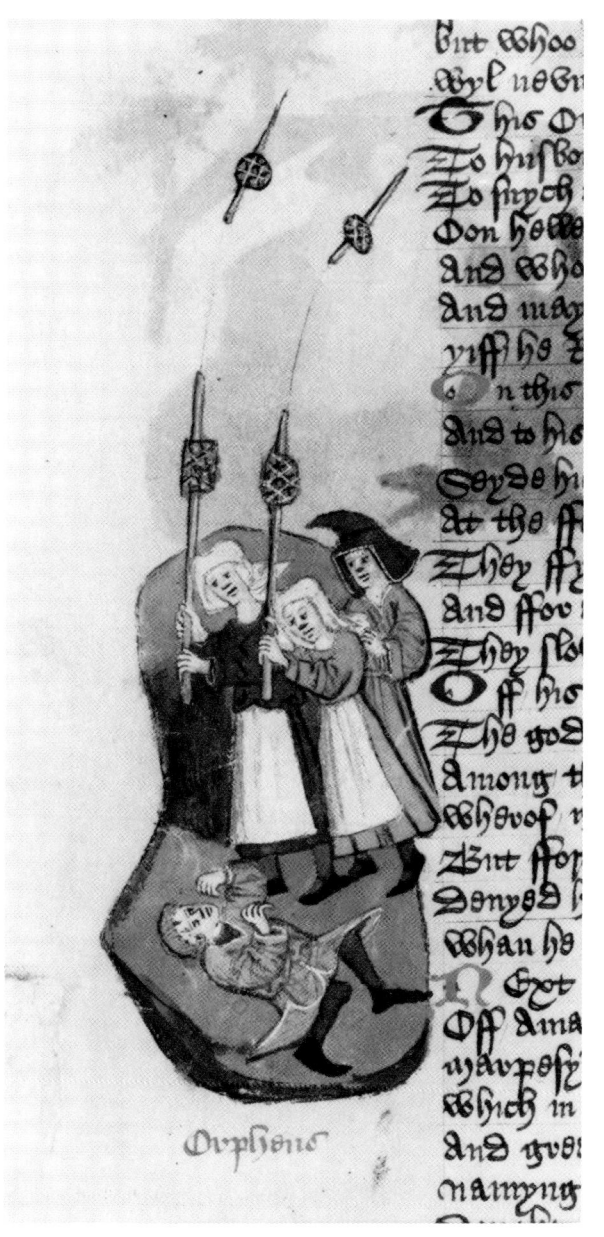

Figure 1.22. *Death of Orpheus*, ca. 1450
Illustration from Lydgate, *Fall of Princes*.
(The British Library. Harley 1766, 76v)

Figure 1.23. Andrea Mantegna, *Death of Orpheus*, 1473
Fresco.
(Camera degli Sposi, Palazzo Ducale, Mantua; Foto Giovetti, Mantua)

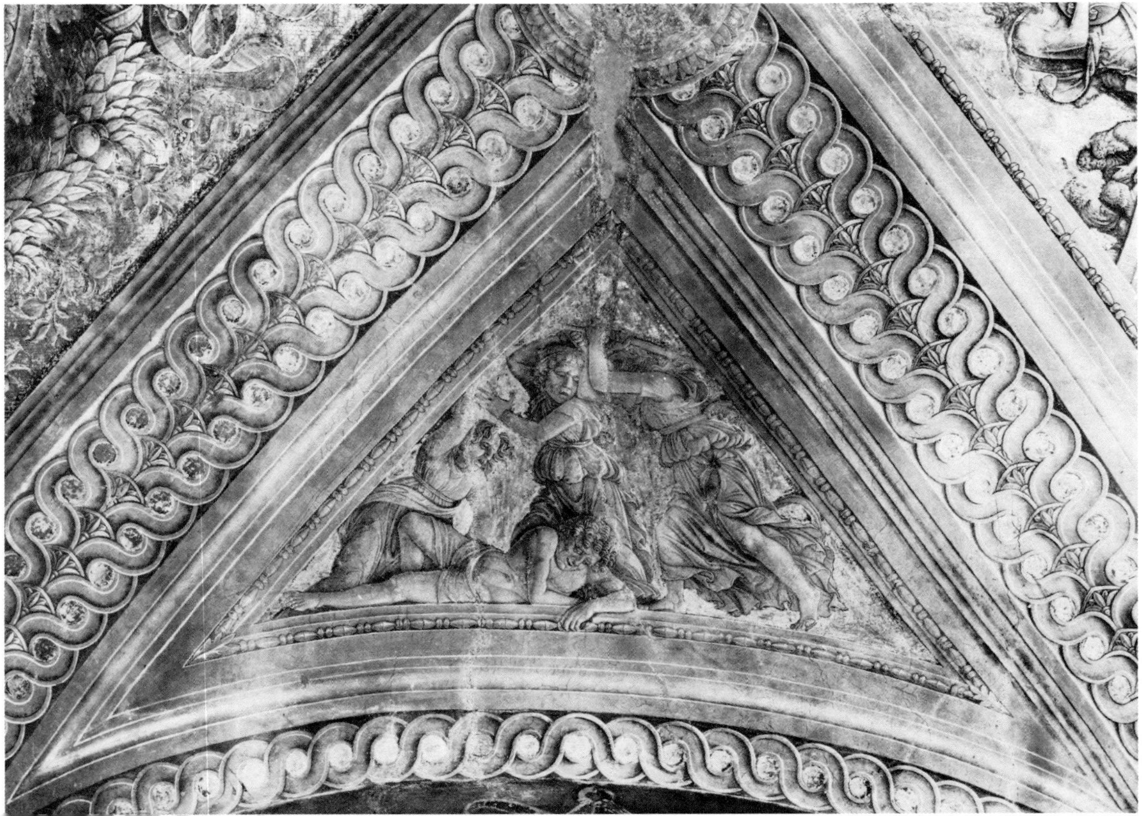

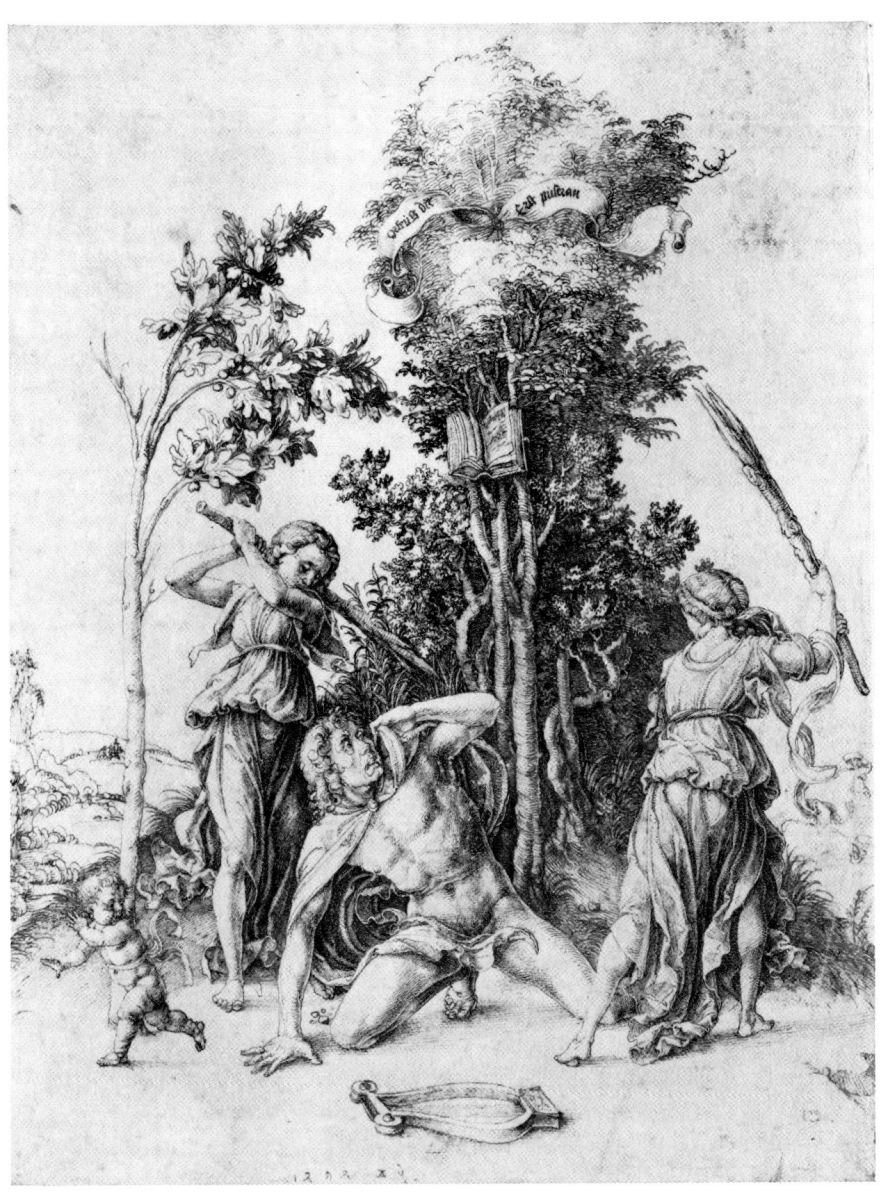

Figure 1.24. Albrecht Dürer, *Death of Orpheus*, ca. 1494
Pen drawing.
(*Hamburger Kunsthalle; Ralph Kleinhempel GMBH & Co., Hamburg*)

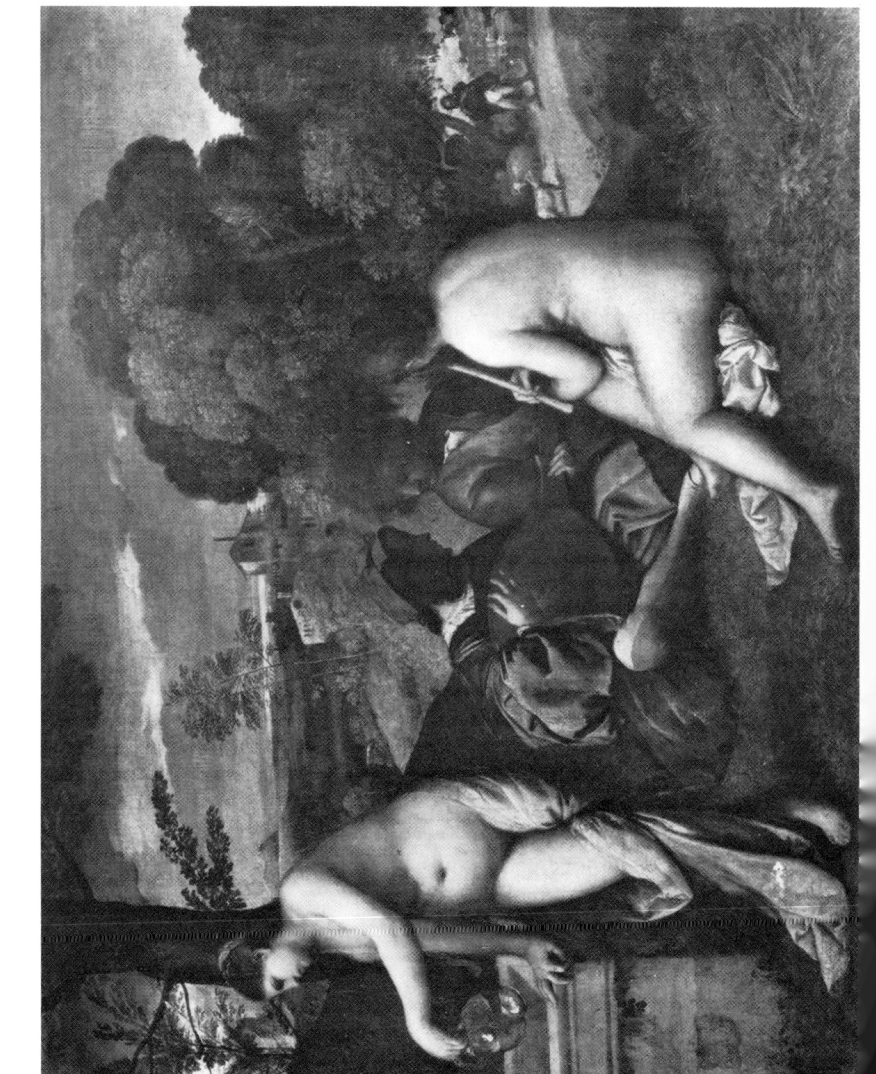

Figure 1.25. Giorgione, *Concert champêtre*, ca. 1508
Oil on canvas.
(*Louvre, Paris; Cliché des Musées Nationaux, Paris*)

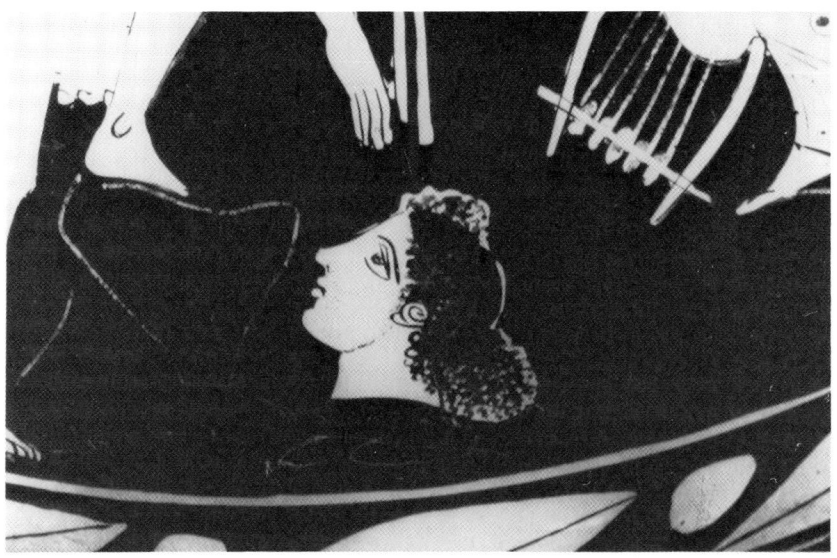

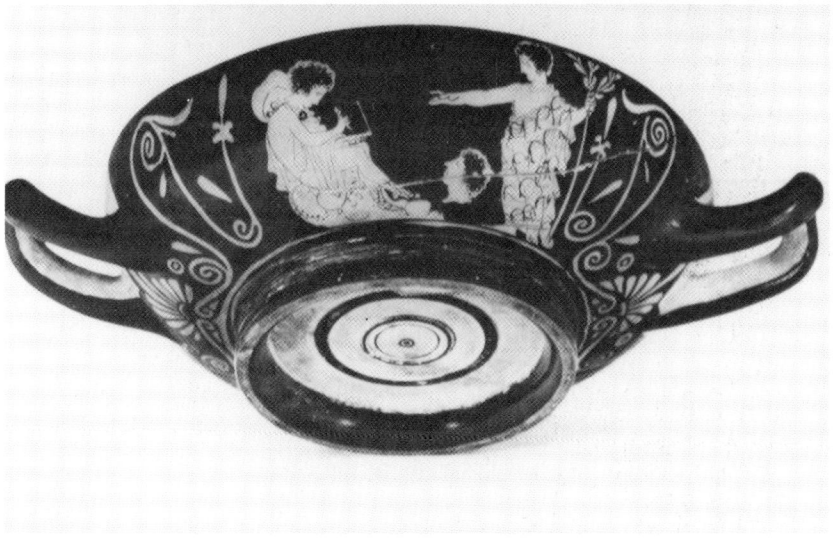

Figure 1.26. *Orpheus' Oracular Head*, 5th century B.C.
Red figured kylix
(Corpus Christi College, Cambridge)

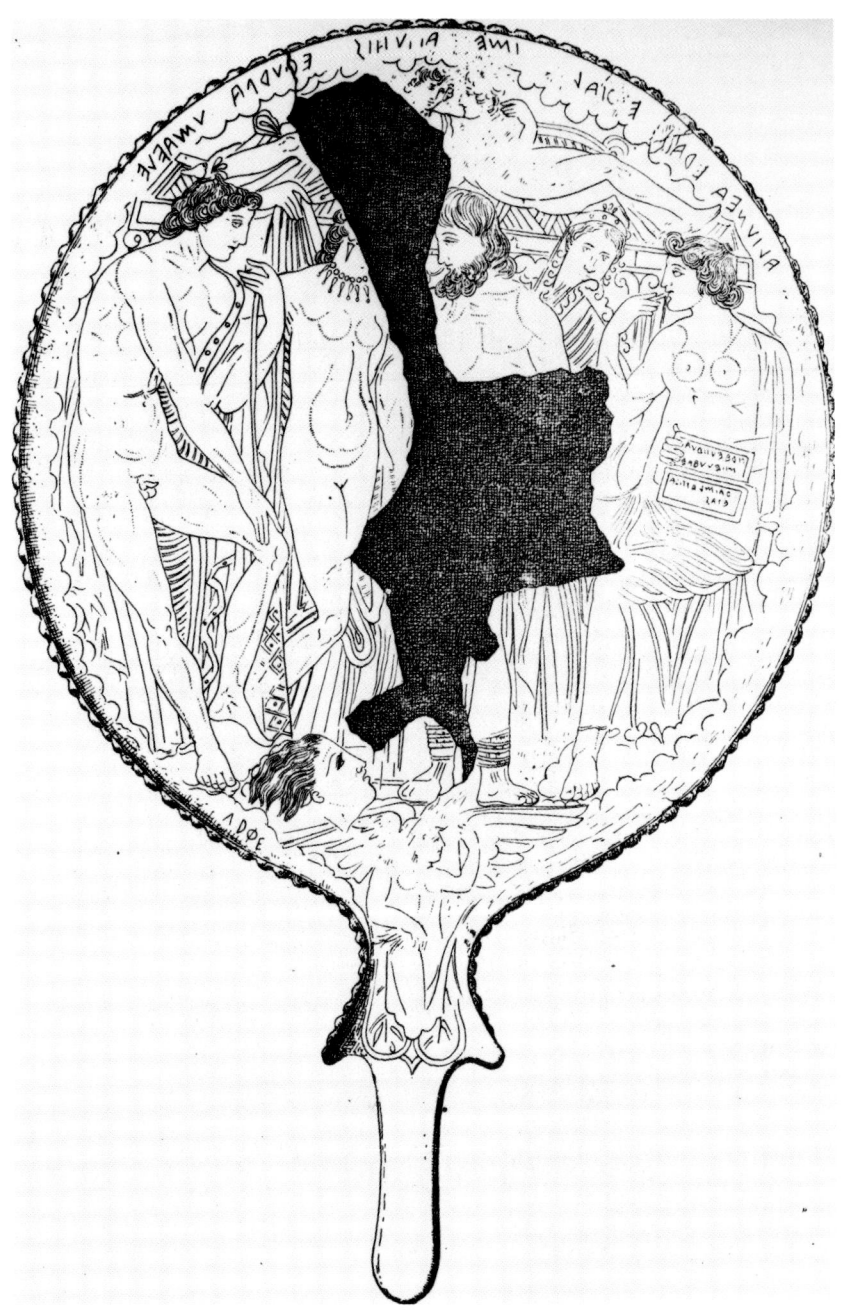

Figure 1.27. *Orpheus' Oracular Head*, 4th–3rd century B.C. Etruscan mirror.
(*Museum, Siena; Soprintendenza Archeologica per la Toscana—Firenze*)

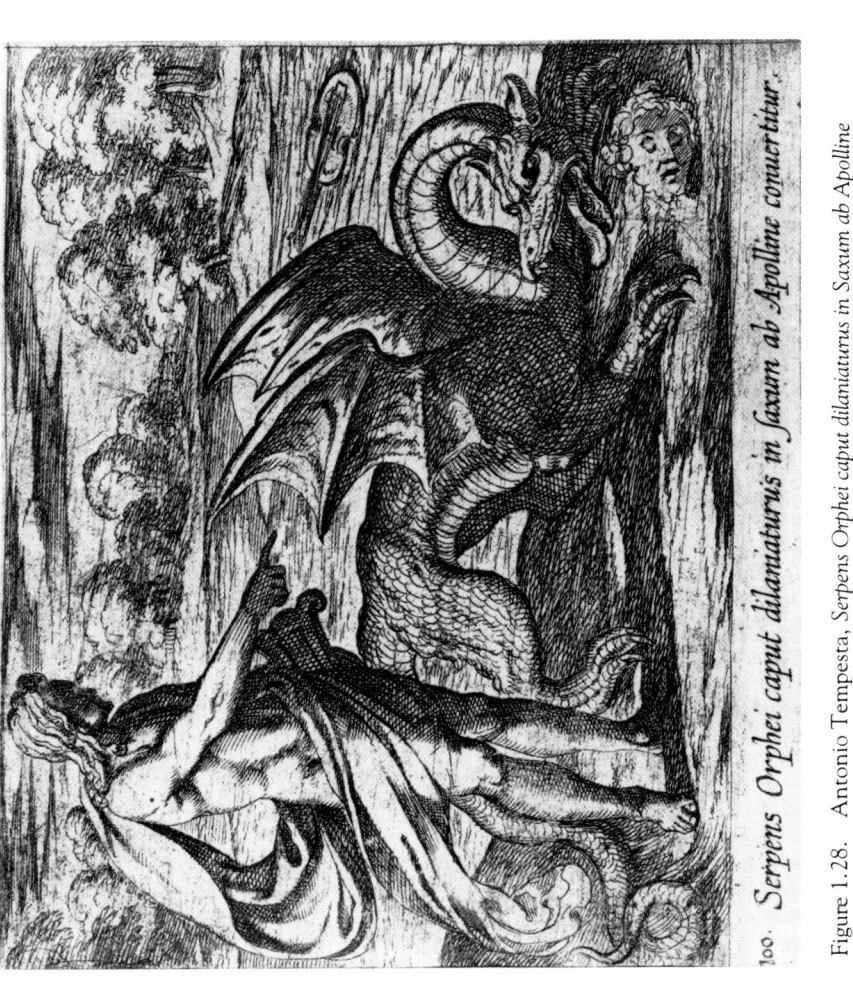

Figure 1.28. Antonio Tempesta, *Serpens Orphei caput dilaniaturus in Saxum ab Apolline conuertitur*, 1606
Illustration from Ovid, *Metamorphoseon . . . Ovidianarum*, Amsterdam, pl. 100. (Bodleian Library, Oxford, Douce O 112)

2

Orpheus in the Nineteenth Century: The Intellectual Context

To understand a catalogue of depictions of Orpheus in the nineteenth century as a reflection of nothing more significant than a superficial coincidence of interest by essentially unrelated artists would be, in fact, to miss the point. For the Symbolists, Orpheus has a very specific meaning: he is priest, initiate, martyr, ideal artist whose work magically summons the Orphic voice in the world; a set of meanings which embody essential aspects of the Symbolist aesthetic—art as religion, the artist as priest, the art object as revelation. The Symbolists' interest in Orpheus, as well as their preoccupation with myth and religion are, moreover, part of a broader intellectual current in the nineteenth century.

This period witnessed a profound interest in and the serious study of ancient religions. Myths and legends were considered the keys to penetrating past cultures, the path to understanding the current direction of society, even the means of predicting the future of mankind—the bases of broad philosophical systems. There was an intoxication with the notion of an initial golden age of civilization. Searching for the matrix of civilization, philologists examined the origins of language, literature, and religions of cultures past and present. Linguists traced the development of language, positing an original era of communication involving the exchange of pure, uncorrupted forms. As historians of religion sought for a universal derivation of all sacred doctrines, the traditional rigid boundaries separating the Judaeo-Christian tradition from the Greco-Roman pantheon and from Eastern religions softened. Mythographers' analyses of disparate bodies of myths and legends emphasize transcendent truths. Symbolism clearly partakes of this generally syncretist appreciation of cultural history, myth, religion, and language.

Significant conflation of pagan and Christian imagery enriches the works of Moreau, Puvis, Redon, and others. Gauguin's interest in the devout peasantry of Brittany, and especially his intermingling of Tahitian myth and Christian subjects, is evidence of this pervasive syncretism. The interest in Hinduism, shared by Redon and Mallarmé among others, reflects a general curiosity about non-Western religions. The eccentric mysticism of the Nabis or Sâr Péladan's Rosicrucians are expressions of a more widespread fascination with alternative religions, the occult, and theosophy. Orpheus' emergence as an important symbol within this intellectual environment is comparable to his importance within the syncretism of late antiquity or to Orpheus' role in the philosophical syncretism that dominated the humanist circles in the Renaissance.

The thrust of this chapter, then, is to discover the meaning of Orpheus in the context of the intellectual syncretism of the nineteenth century as expressed in world mythographies, comparative studies of religion and philology, universal histories and palingenetic theories of world civilization, and the burgeoning of occultism and alternative religions. These realms of study are not mutually exclusive, rather, there is a rich exchange of ideas between the students of myths, the syncretic historians, the occultists, and the artists and writers of this period. Crucial concepts of the Symbolist aesthetic—the importance of myth, the significance of symbol, the meaning of language, the mystical notion of art as religion and the related ideals of the universal work of art, correspondences, and synaesthesia—evolve in or, at the very least, are informed by this broader intellectual context. Orpheus as mythic poet, musician, and priest is the central symbolic crux of these various realms, offering us, therefore, a key to understanding a complex network of ideas.

Comparative Studies of Myth and Philology

Georg Friedrich Creuzer and the Fascination with India.
Myth, Symbol, and Language

Georg Friedrich Creuzer's encyclopedic study of world religions, *Symbolik und Mythologie der alten Völker,* first published in 1810, building upon the vision of myth and religion that emerged in the latter part of the eighteenth century, is a seminal work, influencing subsequent developments in the field, defining the course of heated scholarly debate during the nineteenth and well into the twentieth century.[1] The essential characteristics of Creuzer's work are his syncretic model for the growth and development of world religion; the notion of India as the root of later religious forms, specifically for the emergence of Greek pantheism; the importance of the mystery cults; and a differentiation of myth and symbol. Orpheus, in his roles as initiate in Eastern mysteries, priest of the Dionysian cults, bringer of civilization to Greece, figures importantly in Creuzer's work, linking the esoteric traditions of East and West, and confirming thereby the author's central theory that there exists a common source for all of man's development (an evolution envisaged as essentially spiritual or religious).

Creuzer's conviction that the roots of culture were to be found in Indian language and religion reflects a burgeoning enthusiasm for India which warrants a brief tangential examination in this context. India figures significantly in the realm of syncretic histories and mythographies and comparative philological studies, for instance, in the important works of Friedrich Majer, J. J. Wagner and Joseph Görres.[2] This fascination with India was shared by Goethe, Schopenhauer, Wagner, and Nietzsche.[3] It is significant, moreover, that the interest in Indian religion emerged in the context of linguistics, specifically the study of Sanskrit, the advancements in the one field informing the development of the other.[4]

A clear example of the interplay between linguistics and comparative mythography is found in the career of F. Max Müller. Müller, who studied with the noted linguist Eugène Burnouf, is most respected for his translations of sacred Eastern texts.[5] His writings, however, also include rather popularized mythographic studies (*Comparative Mythology*, 1856; *Introduction to the Science of Religion*, 1873; and *Contributions to the Science of Mythology*, 1897) which reflect his training in linguistics. The essential tenets of his studies of myth are that all myths derive from an effort to explain the power of the sun, and all myth derives from language. Müller sees language as the first myth, positing an original mythopoeic age.

The impact of Müller's all-encompassing solar myth, as well as his linguistic bias, is evident in the works of George W. Cox (*A Manual of Myth in the Form of Questions and Answers* and *The Mythology of Aryan Nations*). The subheadings in the latter work include "The Relation of Mythology and Language." Cox relies upon etymological analyses of words and names to emphasize the essential meaning of myths which transcend cultural limitations, reading individual narrative elements of myths in terms of broader symbolic significance. The *Manual of Myth,* intended as a children's mythology, presenting Greek, Latin, Egyptian, Assyrian, Vedic, Persian, and Norse legends in clear and simple terms, includes an entry on Orpheus and Eurydice which is paradigmatic of his approach:

> What is the name of Orpheus? It is the same as the Indian Ribhu, a name that seems at a very early period to have been applied to the sun. In the Veda it is applied to many deities. In its original sense it seems to have denoted creative power or energy. In the opinion of some, Orpheus represents the winds, who tear up the trees as they course along, chanting their wild music. Does the name Eurydice resemble any others? It comes from the same word from which have been formed such names as Europa, Eurytos, Euryphassa, and many others, all denoting the broadspreading flush of the dawn across the sky.[6]

Cox's differentiation of myth and symbol, his understanding of myth as a finite expression of an abstraction, implies an aesthetic idealism which appealed to the Symbolist poet, Stéphane Mallarmé. Mallarmé's translation of *Mythology of Aryan Nations* in 1880 completes the circuit, then, between mythography, philology, and Symbolist poetry.

Creuzer's monumental work commences with the religions of India, Persia, and Egypt, and proceeds to the primitive and classical religions of Greece and Rome. Clearly, for Creuzer, the Indian religion represents the highest spiritual order, a monotheistic system of pure symbolic form. In contrast, he considers the gods and myths of the Greeks as mere contrivances to explain truths of a pure spiritual order. Myths are crude explanations, feeble representations of symbolic forms. His conviction that the pure symbols of the Indian religion are preserved in mystery cults accounts for the emphasis given to this subject. Two volumes in Guigniaut's translation are devoted to the Orphic cults of Dionysus, the Eleusinian and Samothracian cults of Proserpina and Ceres, Pythagoreanism and the Neo-Platonic mysteries.

Orpheus is crucial, then, to Creuzer's scheme for the westward movement of Indian spiritual enlightenment. Orpheus is initiated into the Eastern mysteries in Egypt. He is priest of the Dionysian cults, author of sacred hymns, bringer of civilization to Greece. More than once, Creuzer cites Herodotus concerning the derivation and importance of the Orphic cults.

> Thus, according to the testimony of the father of history, the orphic doctrines are in essence Egyptian doctrines. In his eyes, the orphic dogmas, also called Bacchic, Egyptian and Pythagorian, are all one and the same.[7]

This theory of the origin and dispersal/evolution of religion invokes a kind of Platonic model, contrasting a spiritual ideal (Indian religion) with a spiritually inferior, (or derivative) religion (the mythology of the Greeks). The heart of this issue is Creuzer's differentiation of symbol and myth.

> In symbol a universal concept takes on earthly garment, and steps meaningfully before the eye of the soul as an image. In myth the pregnant soul expresses its presentiments or knowledge in a living word. It is also an image but of the kind that, in a way different from symbol, goes through the ear to attain inner meaning.[8]

Creuzer laments the loss of the shadowy indefiniteness of the monotheism of Eastern religions ("The oneness called Divinity") to the clearly defined images of Greek polytheism. For this, he indicts Homer ("The tyranny of Homeric poetry").

His light puts the priestliness of the asiatic primal epic in the shadow. What the Near East had taught and practiced, partly openly, partly esoterically, was forgotten by the Greeks amid the full clarity of their Olympus.[9]

Instead, he champions the "masters of the old Ionian philosophy," who "sought to bring the susceptible soul of the Greeks from the excitements of myths back to calmness, to bring the contemplation of the One and All back from the distractions of the Many."

Creuzer's fundamental concepts—the distinction between symbol and myth and the Indian origins of Greek religion—were the focus of a swirl of scholarly debates. Among Creuzer's major opponents were J. H. Voss, G. Hermann, Lobeck, Schelling, K. O. Müller, Welcker, Preller, Buttmann, Voelcker, Schwenck, Gerhard, and Panofka.[10] Voss, an eminent translator of Homer, came to the defense of Homer's importance, accusing Creuzer of imposing a Neo-Platonic or Christian bias on Greek religion. Schelling, for instance, worried that Creuzer's notion of symbol stripped myths of meaning, reducing them to a mere series of allegories. K. O. Müller, probably Germany's foremost classicist of the period, and the center of the Hellenic school, defended the independent development of Greek religion. This controversy inspired numerous publications and contributed significantly to the growing sophistication of the fields of comparative mythology or religion, philology, and archaeology.

Creuzer's impact in France was no less significant. Joseph Daniel Guigniaut's translation appeared in 1825–41, with an introduction to the plates by Alfred Maury and a preface by Ernest Vinet. Guigniaut's work was, in fact, not merely a translation of Creuzer's work, but also included a review of the state of scholarship in Germany, an outline of the general context for Creuzer's ideas, and a description of the controversy which *Die Symbolik* stirred.[11] Creuzer's influence is apparent, furthermore, in the works of Benjamin Constant, Edgar Quinet, and Ernest Renan.[12] The historian Edgar Quinet, who had studied in Heidelberg and was thus especially influenced by Görres and Creuzer, envisaged *De l'origine des dieux*, 1828, and *Le Génie des religions*, 1842, as part of a vast universal history of religion and social evolution.[13]

Ernest Renan was, in fact, one of Creuzer's most vehement critics, attacking his philosophical mysticism which offended Renan's own rationalist approach. Renan objected strongly to Creuzer's insistence on India as the source of the Greek religion and also to his emphasis on symbol: "Mr. Creuzer's principal error is that written in the title of his book. He is too *symbolic*."[14] Despite this criticism there were certain important bases of agreement between Renan and Creuzer. Renan praises Creuzer's enthusiastic appreciation of the spiritual validity of ancient religions and especially his syncretic approach: "It was highly instructive and a great revelation to see them for the first time, united in a scientific *Pantheon*, all the gods of humanity—Indian, Egyptian, Persian, Phoenician, Etruscan, Greek, Roman."[15] He shares with Creuzer, as well, a notion of the importance of the mystery cults in the development of religion.[16] Also, it is clear that a notion of language (the concept of the mythic image as the concretization of innumerable perceptions and the expression of a primary language), derived from the fields of philology and linguistics, informs Renan's works as it did Creuzer's.

> Greek mythology, seen in its first efflorescence, is nothing but a reflection of the sensation of immature and delicate oranges, without dogma, theology or decree.... All of nature is thus reflected in these primitive perceptions as still unnamed divinities. As Creuzer claims, language itself was the fecund source of gods and heros. Mythology is a second language, born like the first from the echo of nature in human consciousness, just as inexplicable as the first, and as impervious to analysis as the first, but whose mystery is revealed to he who understands the forces hidden in spontaneity, the secret accord of nature and the spirit, this perpetual hieroglyphics on which is based all expression of human sentiment. Each god appears to us like a complete cycle, a conceptual field, an intonation of the harmony of things.[17]

Myth, symbol and language are then the key elements in the evolving perception of the development of world religions. The Belgian religious historian, Comte Eugène Félicien Albert Goblet d'Alviella, advocates the Orient, Egypt, Chaldea, and also India as the great original centers of cultural diffusion.[18] The symbol—"One could define symbol . . . as representation that does not aspire to a reproduction"[19]—is the basis of art, speech, all written communication, our very thought, and, of course, of all religions, manifestations of one universal truth, and is the basis of Goblet d'Alviella's syncretic ideal:

> One can conceive of a religious state in which all cults would become purely symbolic. Nothing would inhibit them from maintaining with pious care, the rites and traditions of their heritage; it is only that they would do so above all with the symbols of the truths common to all religions, and, therefore, they would treat one another—as one perceives the relationship between the rites of certain churches—as local manifestations but equally legitimate forms of a universal religion. Such syncretism appears, at first glance far removed from us.[20]

It is significant that this notion of symbol maturing in the context of studies of religion comes to inform the Symbolist aesthetic that emerges in the final decades of the nineteenth century. Crucial elements of Symbolism—the sacerdotal function of art, the priestly role of the artist—derive, in part, from this religious context in which the notion of symbol is refined. This crossover of ideas from the realm of histories of religion and universal mythographies is demonstrated, for instance, in F. Brunetière's article "Le Symbolisme contemporain" which appeared in 1891 in *La Revue des deux mondes*, the same journal that published Goblet d'Alviella's "Migration des symboles" the previous year. Brunetière cautiously applauds the Symbolists' attack on the narrow and superficial focus of naturalism and embraces the Symbolists' attention to mystery and shadow, their desire to pull away the veil and address the essence of things beneath the surface.[21] He contrasts mere allegory and true symbol in his concept of symbol as a revelation of the mysterious ties between man and nature. Brunetière's depends upon Görres' *La Mystique* and explicitly cites Guigniaut's presentation of Creuzer's, *Les Religions de l'antiquité*, "to explain, through more and more general symbols, the enigma of the world, of man, the laws of the universe."[22] Brunetière embraces a Neo-Platonic view that "a religion is nothing but symbolic—similarly, all art is nothing but symbol, and language is nothing but symbol."[23] Drawing upon Creuzer's syncretic idealism, Brunetière proclaims "All symbol is in this sense, a kind of revelation," and thereby catapults the aesthetic into the realm of religion and myth, claiming a sacerdotal function for art and the artist.[24]

Similarly, in his 1889 publication, *L'Art symboliste*, Georges Vanor stresses the role of the symbol in his idealist aesthetic, tracing, furthermore, its derivation in a religious context: "The origin of symbol, the son of religion . . . up until our days, each religion endowed the primordial ideas of its creed with symbols."[25] Vanor's aesthetic is unabashedly Platonic: The material world is an assemblage of reflections of a transcendent spiritual realm. The role of the poet is to discover the symbols, decipher their meaning and reveal this mysterious truth.

In "Les Romantiques allemands et les Symbolistes français," Jean Thorel emphasizes the approach to symbol common to these two schools, indeed stresses the universal significance of symbols as manifestations of a single, universal truth.

> In this sense, Symbolism is eternal, since it is the very basis of all poetry. It is precisely because symbol plays this synthetic role, nourishment for the senses, for the soul, for the spirit, that it is, in its essence superior to comparison and to allegory, which distinguish and separate that which symbol unites and joins together to create one and the same thing.[26]

Not surprisingly, Creuzer's *Symbolik* figures in Thorel's discussion of the approach to the symbolic in the nineteenth century.[27]

Syncretic Histories of World Civilization

The essential thrust of the comparative mythologies and histories of religion is a search for a unifying principle, an all-encompassing explanation of the genesis and the nature of man's spiritual being. Guigniaut explains this basic concept:

> This simple and sublime religion of nature, revealing the divinity to man with its works ... which is in its totality a cult, a philosophy, a poetry, and of which one catches a glimpse in the cradle of all pagan beliefs, of all religious systems and mythologies in antiquity from India to Greece to Italy, from Scandinavia to the Celts, to Egypt, Assyria and Bactria.[28]

A similar quest for a synthetic, transcendent principle inspires a number of syncretic histories of human civilization.[29] By unveiling the shadowy beginnings or origins of civilization, these syncretic historians reach back before historic time, and thereby overlap in subject matter and methodology with the mythographers and philologists. Myth was accepted as a valuable document of man's earliest ages; language was studied as a key for unlocking man's earliest expressions; religion was recognized as the unifying principle of all societal development. These philosophies of history, syncretic visions of mankind, blending in a peculiar mixture of religion, mythology, philology, philosophy, and the occult, proliferated in the early decades of the nineteenth century.[30] In France, among the most important authors of these syncretic histories or philosophies of history are Cousin, Michelet, Ballanche, Eckstein, Hugo, Quinet, Leroux, Ste.-Beuve, Laprade, and Chenavard.[31]

Edgar Quinet, Jules Michelet

It would be difficult, indeed, to discern a clear differentiation between the works of the comparative mythographers and the syncretic historians, as both subscribe to a mystical vision of man's development, a perception of the history of mankind as essentially a spiritual development. In *De l'origine des dieux*, 1828, Quinet defines history as "an eternal cult to which each civilization adds a rite, often bathed in blood."[32] In *Le Génie des religions*, he proposes "deducing political and civil society from religion."[33] Michelet's historical philosophy is clearly presented in his *Bible de l'humanité*, 1864:

> Humanity is incessantly setting down its soul in a common Bible. Each great people writes in its own verse. These verses are very clear, but of diverse forms, of a very free manner of writing—here in a great poem, in historical recitals, there in pyramids, in statues ... successive and superimposed languages. It is not, as one might suppose, a history of religions. This history can no longer isolate itself, set itself apart. We emerge from classifications altogether. The general thread of life which we follow is woven of twenty united threads which cannot be isolated except by tearing them out. With the religious thread are constantly tangled those of love, family, law, art and industry. Moral activity includes religion and is not contained within it. Religion is cause, but much more, effect. It is often a frame within which true life is performed; often it is a vehicle, an instrument of native energies.[34]

Michelet's optimistic vision of an ideal state of understanding—"a great harmony across space and time"[35]—closely parallels the ideal of religious syncretism described by Guigniaut in "Mythologies," and later elaborated by Goblet d'Alviella in "Migration des symboles."

Pierre Simon Ballanche, Paul Chenavard

A related expression of this mystical vision of mankind's development is found in the theory of social palingenesis, a concept of social evolution through cycles or stages of development. This scheme is the inspiration for Pierre Simon Ballanche's vast and rambling epic, "Orpheus." Similarly, Paul Chenavard's proposed series of works for the Pantheon were organized according to this historical principle. He grapples, moreover, with this encyclopedic view of history in the immensely complicated painting, *Social Palingenesis* or *La Philosophie de l'histoire* of 1848 (fig. 2.1). This painting, which is in actuality a study for the central mosaic which was to have been installed beneath the central dome of the Pantheon, summarizes the iconography of the entire program. Orpheus figures prominently as well in two epic poems in which Chenavard planned to give further expression to his notion of history.[36]

Ballanche's "Orpheus," written in 1827 and published in 1830, is the only completed portion of *La Palingénésie sociale ou théodicée de l'histoire*.[37] This rambling epic, characterized by a lofty if confused ambition to ascertain the truth of history, the meaning of religion, and the significance of man in the universe, combines religion, mythology, philology, philosophy, and occultism. Ballanche espoused a theory of palingenesis, a concept of evolution through cycles or stages of development. Although focused on a conventional Christian notion of Fall and Redemption, this cyclical vision of history involves, as well, a belief in reincarnation, or metempsychosis. Mankind evolves in a series of stages that parallel the biological sequence of youth, maturity, and death. Mankind struggles through eternally repeated cycles of fall and expiation, test and redemption, until he reattains a state of pefection—the perfect unity of Adam, the primordial Androgyne.[38] This arduous evolution toward the ideal of perfect unity takes places through the ascension of what Ballanche terms the "plebian principles."[39] In each plebeian age, the initiate reveals a higher wisdom that overwhelms the established, traditional patrician law. Despite his creative syncretism, Ballanche's philosophy of social palingenesis functions within the perimeters of Christian or Catholic doctrine: Christ is the supreme initiate, Christianity is the last step before perfection, and the truths of all earlier religions are contained within Christianity.[40]

Ballanche's "Orpheus" spans fifteen centuries of history but is focused primarily on the history of Rome. The narrative involves stories within stories: the blind bard, Thamyris, and the Egyptian priests explain Aeneas' arrival in

Italy to King Evander of Latium. A major theme here, as with the comparative mythographers, is the transmission of sacred truths from the East via Egypt to Greece. The story of Orpheus is folded into this complex narrative. Ballanche imaginatively, even wildly, combines myth, legend, and historical fact without regard for chronology, original content, or meaning. He is interested less in the traditional figure of Orpheus than in his role as initiate, revealer of truth, instrument of man's evolution from one palingenetic stage to another. In the prologue Ballanche explains that Orpheus is an abstraction, a powerful symbolic expression of the traditions of antiquity.[41] This manipulation of myth is entirely consistent with Ballanche's concern with the "poetry of thought,"[42] his concepts that "religion is an allegorical history of nature," and that "mythology is a condensed history."[43]

The extent of Chenavard's indebtedness to Ballanche is revealed in important characteristics of his series of paintings and sculpture proposed in 1848 for the Pantheon in Paris, as well as the outlines for his two epic poems: the central symbolic role of Orpheus, religious syncretism, a degenerative cyclical history, and a system of analogies between stages of mankind's development and the growth of the individual. Chenavard's ill-fated program for the Pantheon was to have consisted of 111 painted panels, 5 mosaics, 6 statues, and a monument to universal religion. The program, which would have comprised scenes both from the Old and New Testaments and from ancient and modern history (including vignettes from the ancient Near East, Greece, Rome, the Middle Ages, the rise of Islam, the Crusades, the Renaissance, the expansion of America, and episodes from the lives of Luther, Voltaire, and Napoleon), embodies the concept of the encyclopedic epic of modern man. The monument to universal religion was a symbolic amalgam of the Brahminic cow, the Persian gryphon, the Chaldean Sphinx, the Egyptian Bark of the Dead, the Ark of the Covenant, all surmounted by the Chalice of the Last Supper. This sculpture (included at the center of the 1848 painting, *Social Palingenesis*), which was to have been executed in granite and marble, was conceived as an altar for all the peoples of the world.[44]

Chenavard's gloomy theory of history is precise. Time begins with the year 4200 B.C., reaches its halfway point and zenith with the birth of Christ, and deteriorates to a final destruction in A.D. 4200. These 8,400 years are derived from a 1:100 comparative ratio with an individual's ideal lifespan of 84 years. This cycle is divided into four phases: Adam and Eve to the Tower of Babel; the Tower of Babel to the birth of Christ; the birth of Christ to the rise of America; and the rise of America to the end of civilization in 4200. Each of these broad cultural, religious, and societal stages was to be embodied in the decoration of the four great piers of the Pantheon. The focus of each scheme was a single great initiate, a concept like Ballanche's "spontaneous men."[45] The first phase was identified as the Age of Gold (religion, centered on the figure of Moses); the second was the Age of Silver (poetry and Homer); the third the Age of Bronze (philosophy and Aristotle); the fourth the Age of Iron (science and Galileo).

Chenavard also conceived two epic poems with the theme of Orpheus, one proposed in outline to his friend Laprade in 1839 and the second sketched out towards the end of his life. Like Ballanche, Chenavard discovered in Orpheus a profound expression of his historical philosophy. He planned to explore the four phases of history through the story of the relationship of Orpheus and Eurydice. In the first stage, Orpheus is in Egypt, where he begins architecture, building a temple to the goddess Psyche. The second stage unfold in Greece as Orpheus honors Psyche in her human form, Eurydice, with his sculpture. In the third phase, Eurydice is revived as the Virgin Mary through the power of Orpheus' music. This time Orpheus expresses his love through painting. In the final stage, Orpheus (the ideal) is destroyed by his brother Typhon (the embodiment of materialism). Chenavard traces his religious-artistic ages with the context of the myth of Orpheus, manipulating myth and history with a freedom similar, once again, to the creative invention of Ballanche.[46]

Occultism, Alternative Religions

The interest in esoteric religions and occult philosophies may be compared to the efforts of the universal historians and syncretic mythographers to link past and present, to absorb the variety of man's history into a single unifying truth. The exclusive doctrines of conventional religions were rejected in favor of a syncretic vision embracing a succession of multiple revelations through centuries. Typically, Orpheus was the focus, the metaphoric key in these occult schemes. It is not at all surprising that many of the major historians and mythographers, including Edgar Quinet, Jules Michelet, and Alfred Maury, studied and wrote extensively on esoteric religions and magic.[47]

Eliphas Lévi

The Abbé Alphonse Louis Constant, known as Eliphas Lévi, was one of the most colorful and prominent occultists. His extensive writings reveal his youthful training for the priesthood, his interest in Fourierisme and other socialist-mystical movements, as well as his syncretist religious philosophy.[48] He writes: "All the universe is but a sublime temple, having but one king, one sun and one God."[49] Esoteric truth, however, is not readily accessible and Lévi grants therefore an extremely important role to the artist-prophet or artist-priest in deciphering the symbolic correspondences and revealing the higher form of reality. Orpheus plays a seminal role, the primary initiate, as it were, in a long tradition of esoteric learning: the ancestor of Plato, Pythagoras, the Alexandrians, Pascalis Martines, and his disciples.

> The true poets are sent to earth by gods. The great initiator of Greece and its first civilizer was also its first poet.... The fable of Orpheus is entirely a dogma, a revelation of sacerdotal destinies, a new ideal issued forth from the cult of beauty. One has said that beauty is the splendor of truth. It is thus to this great enlightenment of Orpheus that one must attribute the beauty of the form revealed for the first time in Greece.[50]

Lévi combines pagan myth and biblical tale. For example, in "Magie en Grèce," a chapter in *Histoire de la magie* (1860), Lévi conflates Medea's murder of her brother with Cain's fratricide. In *Clef des grands mystères* (1861), Adam and Eve and Cain and Abel are manipulated as symbols of different sides of the human personality or psyche. Lévi synthesizes all religions, using myth and Bible interchangeably to inform his occult philosophy.[51]

Joséphin Péladan

The mystical philosophy of Joséphin Péladan, who adopted the title Sâr Mérodack to emphasize his supposed descent from that Assyrian king, was profoundly influenced by Eliphas Lévi. His manipulation of myth in unusual historical contexts, his emphasis of Orpheus reveals as well the impact of Ballanche and Chenavard. Péladan was in fact, like Chenavard, a native of Lyon and had in 1895 in *L'Artiste,* devoted an article to that artist.[52] Between 1892 and 1896 Péladan organized the Salons Rose + Croix Catholique, which constituted a crucial link between the occultist milieu and Symbolist artists and writers.[53] His *Rose + Croix esthétique,* published in conjunction with the first exhibition, was an especially powerful articulation of the concept of art as religion, artist as priest: "Artist; you are priest: Art is the great mystery . . . a masterpiece . . . a divine ray descends as if to an altar. . . . Artist you are king. . . . Art is the true empire. . . . Artist, you are magician; art is the great miracle and proves our immortality."[54]

Péladan was, moreover, a prolific writer, whose works are permeated with the occultist's typical preoccupation with syncretism.[55] Invariably Péladan links paganism and Christianity, establishing a succession of great philosophers or initiates (including, of course, Orpheus) who reveal a single truth. "God did not talk more or less to Moses than to Orpheus, to Manou than to Zoroaster, to Cakya Mouni than to Meni, to Rama than to Krishnah."[56]

This fluid syncretism characterizes his play *La Terre d'Orphée*. This work, which exists only in manuscript oultines, was intended as the third part of a trilogy entitled *Les Idées et les formes*. The other two sections of this trilogy were entitled *La Terre du Sphinx (Egypte)* (1900) and *La Terre du Christ (Palestine)* (1901).[57] Péladan combines the biblical story of Cain and Abel with the myth of Orpheus and Eurydice. In one version of *La Terre d'Orphée*, Jubal (named in Genesis 4:22 as one of Cain's own descendants and ancestor of all who play the lyre and flute) is Cain's victim. Péladan conflates biblical and pagan martyrdoms by substituting the musician Jubal for the traditional victim, Abel. Péladan's manipulation of the basic story from Genesis is even more extensive in another version of his play. Noah's descendant, Japheth's son Tubal (easily confused with Cain's descendant Tubal-Cain, ancestor of all metalworkers), is pitted against Hebel (Abel). The brothers' conflict is a result of their attentions to the same woman, Eurydice.[58] Eurydice is a follower of Orpheus, the hierophant who returns from his initiation in Crete to bring sacred truth to Thrace. Finally, Eurydice falls victim to a band of priestesses who betray Orpheus' Apolline teachings and reestablish human sacrifice and other forbidden acts. As if in concession to the traditional myth, Péladan's Orpheus attempts to retrieve Eurydice from death but is himself a victim of the Maenads.[59]

Papus (Gérard Encausse)

Papus, or Gérard Encausse, may be considered the most important occultist of the 1880s and 1890s. His writings are permeated with the same themes that dominate the works of Eliphas Lévi, as well as the works of his fellow Lyon natives Ballanche, Chenavard, and Péladan.[60] His "Vie de Christ," conceived as a response to the positivist studies of David Friedrich Strauss and Joseph-Ernest Renan, advocates a syncretic view of religions. Christ is the culmination in a series of cycles of revelation. Orpheus, moreover, is important in a spiritual hierarchy that includes Zoroaster, Abraham, Moses, Lao-Tze, Buddha, Pythagoras, and many other initiates, all revealing a universal, alchemical truth.[61] Papus designates the primary stages of the development of human civilization, when man adopts certain philosophical or theosophical concepts, the "regne hominel." For the Hebrews this "regne hominel" is represented by Adam; for Zoroaster, by Kai Omurdz; for the Brahmas by Pouou; for the Chinese, by Pen-Kou.[62] Like the mythographers and universal historians, Papus emphasizes the role of the East in the process of initiation, attributing the creation and revelation of the great mysteries to the priest of Osiris in Egypt.[63] His successive cycles of revelation and reincarnation are ultimately resolved with the reintegration of the individual with the collective being, the oneness of Adam, the primordial Androgyne.[64] Moreover, Papus bases his historical process on what he calls "la méthode analogique," by which parallels between the cycle of the single day and the seasonal cycle of the year are established.[65] Hence, dawn is the springtime of the day, midday is summer, dusk is autumn, and night is winter. Furthermore, dawn is compared to the first quarter of the moon, day to the second quarter, evening to the third quarter, and night to the full moon.

Edouard Schuré

The popularity of Theosophy during this period is another reflection of the profound appeal of a mystical-syncretic philosophy. Syncretism is the conceptual cornerstone of *The Secret Doctrine,* written by Helena Patrovna Blavatsky, founder of the Theosophical Society:

> It is perhaps desirable to state unequivocally, that the teachings, however fragmentary and incomplete, contained in these volumes, belong neither to the Hindu, the Zoroastrian, the Chaldean, nor the Egyptian religion, neither to Buddhism, Islam, Judaism nor Christianity exclusively. The Secret Doctrine is the essence of all these. Sprung from it in their origins, the various religious schemes are now made to merge back into their original element, out of which every mystery and dogma has grown, developed, and become materialised.[66]

Edouard Schuré's *Les Grands Initiés,* first published in 1889, is a highly influential Theosophical text that celebrates Rama, Krishna, Hermes, Moses, Pythagoras, Orpheus, Plato, Christ, and Buddha as prophets of a single truth.[67] Throughout his writings, Schuré chants his praises to Orpheus like an insistent incantation: "master of the initiates, divine enchanter, marvelous Orpheus."[68] Like Creuzer, Schuré claims Orpheus as the great hierophant, priest of Dionysian mysteries who brings to Greece the truths of sacred Egypt: "the living lyre and the mouth of gold through which the divine torrent flooded all Greece with Dionysian waves, making it one great Temple of Beauty."[69]

The enormous popularity among the Symbolists of Schuré's *Les Grands Initiés* was by no means an isolated phenomenon. Rather there was significant contact and a real flow of ideas between the occultist and the Symbolist circles. Many of the avant-garde reviews (*La Vogue, Le Coeur, L'Etoile, L'Aurore, La Revue Blanche, Mercure de France, Psyche, La Plume*) which proliferated in the 1890s encouraged contributions by the Symbolist artists and writers and the occultist-spiritist writers, as well. Edmond Bailly's bookstore on the Chaussée d'Antin, La Librairie de l'Art Indépendante, specializing in occult literature, was an important meeting place of the Symbolists, bringing together Maurice Denis, Stéphane Mallarmé, Joris-Karl Huysmans, Villiers de l'Isle Adam, Henri de Regnier, Pierre Quillard, and L. H. Herold.[70] Gustave Moreau's extensive library included *Les Grands Initiés* as well as Eliphas Lévi's *Fables et symboles.* The idealist aesthetics of Gauguin and Aurier clearly draw upon their knowledge of Swedenborg. Similarly, the theosophical basis of the aesthetic of the

Nabis, Sérusier, Ranson, and Lacombe is easily discernible. Maurice Denis knew Papus, and was, in particular, familiar with his translations of Eliphas Lévi's works. The spiritist, Ernest Hello, was a familiar figure to many of the Symbolists, including Denis, Emile Bernard, and Huysmans. Villiers de l'Isle Adam recommended Eliphas Lévi's works to Mallarmé. Gauguin was surely familiar with Eliphas Lévi who had been a friend of the artist's grandmother, Flora Tristan. Sérusier was decidedly influenced by St. Yves d'Alveydre. The occultist, Wronski, influenced not only Baudelaire, Balzac and Eliphas Lévi, but also the major theorists of the Post-Impressionist period, including Charles Henry and Gustave Kahn.[71]

Mysticism and the Symbolist Aesthetic: Art as Religion

The occultist milieu was an important source for the Symbolist concept of the religious essence of art. Similar to the manner in which the notions of symbol and myth matured in the context of syncretic mythographies and universal histories and were subsequently transmitted into the realm of Symbolist aesthetics; so the Symbolists' ideas of the transcendent nature of poetry or art, the sacred function of the poet-artist, are reinforced by, if not adopted directly from, occultism and mysticism. A major theme for instance, for Fabre d'Olivet, that master of the esoteric, is the religious function of art. For him, poet is priest. Naming Moses and Orpheus among his syncretic succession of great Initiates, Fabre d'Olivet explains the religious origin of poetry:

> From the early ages of Greece, Poetry—consecrated to the services of the altar—only left the confines of the temples for the instruction of the people: It was like a sacred language through which the priests, charged with presiding over the mysteries of religion, translated the will of the gods. One gave the name "Poetry" to this sacred language.[72]

Saint Yves d'Alveydre's vision of the poet as the living embodiment of the Divine principle in the world, reveals his study of Fabre d'Olivet:

> The Verb is the existence of Being, the Evidence of its identity, the Providence of its Perfection, God even, engendered from himself. The Verb is the Eternal Present in the Presence of the Eternal, its objectivity creator in person, the generic genius of divine genius, the maker of spaces, the archetype, the poet-god, god speaking.[73]

Stéphane Mallarmé

Stéphane Mallarmé's mystical aesthetic, so strongly imprinted with occultist ideas, exercised a profound impact on a generation of younger artists and writers who gathered at his Tuesday salons. Mallarmé captures the fundamentally religious nature of the work of art in his concepts of Le Livre—Instrument spirituel, Le Grimoire, L'Oeuvre, Le Verbe, La Parole. In his famous *Autobiographie,* a letter written in 1885 to Verlaine, Mallarmé's poet is an alchemist who gives himself with self-sacrificial devotion to his art, the "Grand Oeuvre." Not surprisingly, Mallarmé likens the Poet to Orpheus:

> ... a book, that is a book which is architectural and premeditated, not a mere collection of accidental, be they marvelous inspirations.... I'll go further and say: The Book (persuaded that in fact there is but one) undertaken without the knowledge of whomever wrote it, even Geniuses. The orphic explanation of the Earth, that is the only duty of the poet and the literary game *par excellence:* since even the rhythm of the book, thus impersonal and living, right up to its pagination, juxtaposes itself with equations of this dream or Ode.[74]

Mallarmé departs from the Romantic tradition of the poet who expresses personal emotions which he sees reverberate in nature. Instead, the Poet is the mouthpiece or medium for the divine truth which finds expression in the chastened purity of the Work:

> The pure work implies the elocutory disappearance of the poet, who cedes intuition to words, by the shock of their mobilised inequality. They ignite themselves with reciprocal reflections like a virtual trail of brilliance on gems, replacing perceptible respiration with the ancient lyrical breath or the enthusiastic personal direction of the phrase.[75]

The Word, "La Parole," is the source of the magic and power of art, the poet's means to conjure up the pure, spiritual essence of reality:

> What good, therefore, is the marvel of transposing the fact of nature into its vibrating near disappearance according to the game of the word; if it is not so that the pure idea emanates, without the disturbance of a close or concrete reminder, the pure notion.
>
> I say: a flower! And out of the oblivion in which my voice relegates no contour, as much as anything else but the known calyxes, the idea itself musically rises, sweet, the absence of all bouquets.[76]

Charles Morice

Charles Morice, one of the principal apologists for and theorists of Symbolism, explicitly acknowledges occultism as source for the concept of art as sacred, the poet as initiate:

The occult sciences constitute one of the principal corners of art. The true poet is first an initiate. The reading of magical texts awakens in him the secrets of which he always had the virtual knowledge.[77]

In *Demain, questions d'esthétique,* Morice answers Anatole France's attack of the mystical tendencies of Symbolism:

> Prerequisites for Mallarmé's disciples are allegories and all the esoterism of ancient theurgies. No poetry without a hidden meaning. . . . Don't reproach them, Monsieur, for being mystics and for being infatuated with the esoterism of ancient theurgies. Let them search—outside all defined gospels (in this time when all gospels are falling to ruin)—for a religion that would at once satisfy their heart and their reason—in the common basis of all religions and of all metyphysics, the thrill of mystery (about which certain questions have always made humanity tremble), in the hieroglyphs of ancient Egypt, in the magical texts of Paracelsus and the meditations of Spinoza—don't condemn them so quickly—Are you entirely sure that they're wrong?[78]

Morice's aesthetic is essentially mystical. This vocabulary of mysticism—artist-priest, revelation, the infinite and transcendent, higher consciousness—permeates the critical and aesthetic debate that surrounded Symbolism.

Richard Wagner

Undoubtedly, one of the most comprehensive statements of this association of art and religion is Richard Wagner's "Religion and Art," which appeared in the *Bayreuther Blätter* in October of 1880. (The English edition quoted here was published in 1897.) Wagner idealizes art as the substitute for a now degenerate and meaningless orthodox religion.

> One might say that when Religion becomes artificial, it is reserved for art to save the spirit of religion by recognizing the figurative value of the mythic symbols which the former would have us believe in their literal sense and revealing their deep and hidden truth through an ideal presentation.[79]

Wagner's artist also has a religious, revelatory mission. He is the "Tone-Poet/Seer." Also, like the Theosophists or Palingenesists, Wagner advocates a succession of revelations or initiates:

> The artistic teller of the great world tragedy, never lied, was ever sent to humankind at epochs of its direst error, as mediating friend: us, too, will he lead over to that reborn life, to set before us there in ideal truth the "likeness of this passing show."[80]

The Nabis

The Nabis—in the very name adopted for their group, their life-style, the subjects and style of their works of art as well as in a pervasive vocabulary (Sérusier names his painting *The Talisman* and Ranson called his studio "The Temple")—express their conviction of the religious essence of art. Ranson, Lacombe, and Sérusier were fascinated with Theosophy, while Maurice Denis was drawn more toward a rather orthodox Catholicism.[81]

In his writings, Maurice Denis carefully differentiates symbol and allegory, emphasizing the correspondence between this world and a super reality, positing art as revelation or the creation of a mystical state of being. In a 1918 lecture entitled, "Le Symbolisme et l'art religieux," he acknowledges the sources of his aesthetic:

> Our aspirations, our mysticism weren't in truth always very orthodox. We created a peculiar mixture of Plotinus, Edgar Poe, Baudelaire and Schopenhauer. Little theosophical reviews flourished. There were Madame Blavatsky, Péladan, the exhibitions of the Rose + Croix. Finally, we submitted to the influence of German philosophy which one had never been taught in school.[82]

Jean Delville

Jean Delville, a close friend and ardent follower of the Sâr Péladan, exhibited at the Salons Rose + Croix over several years. In Brussels, Delville himself assisted in the formation of two art groups, Pour l'Art and Art Idéaliste, both devoted to his ideal of the sacred role of art. Delville eschews the parochial divisions of modern religions, advocating instead a theosophical vision of cultural and religious syncretism. He openly gives credit to those who influenced his idealist aesthetic, including Péladan, Wagner, Bulwer-Lytton, St. Yves d'Alveydre and Madame Blavatsky. A confirmed Theosophist, Delville contributed to the British theosophical magazine, *Orpheus*, begun by the poet-painter Clifford Bax in 1908.[83] A 1910 translation of his major work, *The New Mission of Art: A Study of Idealism in Art* (including a preface by Bax and an introduction by Edouard Schuré), was dedicated to the members of the Orpheus Art Circle. This book constitutes a thorough presentation of Delville's aesthetic idealism, summed up in the aphorism: "Idealism and Art are the same thing."[84] Delville's idealist artist is a magician, prophet, seer, or alchemist, inspired by a higher power which acts through him. Not surprisingly, the image of Orpheus figures significantly in Delville's paintings.

Correspondences: The Synaesthetic Ideal

The idealism of the Symbolist aesthetic finds expression in the related ideas of the theory of correspondences, synaesthesia, and the musical ideal. The Symbolists' emphasis of the religious essence of art and the sacerdotal function of the artist-priest implies the existence of a reality that transcends the ordinary world. The artist is capable of deciphering the hieroglyphs of this world, of penetrating the mysterious truth of the ideal realm, and of communicating the hidden correspondences between the two realities in a universal language of symbols. Synaesthesia and the total work of art are ideas which represent the Symbolists' attempt to surpass the limited, descriptive vocabulary of the ordinary work of art, and to embrace this universal language of symbols. Music (a kind of abstract equivalent of the mythic Orpheus) is adopted as the ideal art form because of its nonmimetic, immaterial quality.

These key concepts of the Symbolist aesthetic are the heritage of the Neo-Platonism and mysticism of the Romantics. Many of the same themes figure prominently in the works of Wackenröder and Schiller.[85] These concepts are nurtured in the occultist or mystical milieu throughout the nineteenth century. Swedenborg, who was enormously popular with the Romantics and later also with the Symbolists, speaks in *La Nouvelle Jérusalem* of a language of correspondence.[86] Eliphas Lévi's collection of poems, *Les Trois Harmonies*, published in 1845, included "Les Correspondances," a lengthy poem which explores the secret harmonies in nature, revealed by poets and prophets. It begins:

> The perception of exterior harmonies creates poets.
> The clear comprehension of interior harmonies makes prophets.[87]

Later, in 1851, in an article entitled "L'Allégorie," published in *Dictionnaire de la littérature chrétienne* in *La Nouvelle Encyclopédie théologique*, Lévi explores further the notion of universal correspondences and concludes that "Poetry itself is nothing but the awareness of these harmonies and correspondences."[88]

Even a rudimentary overview of the applications of the themes of correspondences and the musical ideal reveals their extraordinary importance to the aesthetic theories of the Romantics and the Symbolists. Eugène Delacroix's symphonic compositions and his theoretical writings, too, reflect his fascination with music. In his Journal, he quotes Madame de Staël's *De l'Allemagne*:

> Man has in his soul, innate perceptions that real objects will never satisfy, and it is to these perceptions which the imaginations of the painter and of the poet know how to give form and life. The first art, music, what does it imitate?[89]

Charles Baudelaire's poem, "Correspondances," is undoubtedly the most noted expression of these concepts of correspondences and synaesthesia. Moreover, these ideas play an important role in the poet's discussion of Delacroix's works and theoretical writings.[90] The theory of correspondences is central in the poet's appreciation of Richard Wagner.[91]

The cult of Wagner became, in itself, one of the dominant themes of the late nineteenth century.[92] The Symbolists' championship of Wagner was based on the important parallels between the composer's idealist aesthetic and their own. The principal elements of Wagner's musical revolution—his eschewal of discrete and thematically or narratively defined songs for an endless stream of melody, and his manipulation of leitmotifs, or musical themes symbolically identified with particular themes or characters—parallel the Symbolists' movement away from the mimetic role of the work of art and toward exploration of the abstract power or direct expressive force of forms or symbols. The ideal synthesis of all the arts, the *Gesamtkunstwerk*, is the central theme of Wagner's 1849 *Art of the Future*. Wagner's aesthetic ideal is an artistic language (clearly related to the concept of correspondences) which would transcend the mundane barriers of the everyday world and give expression to the powerful but invisible forces of the universe. Music is the key to this universal language. In *Oper und Drama*, Wagner discusses music as the primordial art, deriving from primitive man's cry, and, in turn, generating speech.[93]

Mallarmé finds music to be the ideal analogy to express the purity of the Work. In "La Musique et les lettres," 1894, he invokes the unity of all the arts, that is, the principle of correspondences.[94] Synaesthesia and the musical ideal are, similarly, dominant themes in the theoretical program of the Symbolist aestheticians. In *De la vérité et de la beauté*, Morice writes:

> [S]ervants of the gospel of Correspondences and of the Law of Analogy will give, according to the forces of their spirit and the good faith of their heart, vast syntheses, a melodious and luminous explanation of mysteries, glorified in the Reality of Fictions.[95]

Aurier, another major theorist of the Symbolist aesthetic, proponent of "idéisme," similarly emphasizes the spiritual essence of art. He invokes the Neo-Platonic theories of Plotinus to explain his synthetist concepts of the expressive power of color and line.[96] Maurice Denis' arguments about an art which transcends the limits of mere representation depend explicitly on Aurier's theories. Gauguin's synthetism depends significantly on a theory of correspondences derived from Baudelaire and Delacroix. The theory of correspondences, the notions of universal nondescriptive symbols, of music as the immaterial, nonmimetic ideal art form, encourage the evolution of an aesthetic of abstraction, in which the mythic figure of Orpheus becomes disembodied and absorbed into the theory on a purely conceptual level.[97]

Perhaps the most facile manifestation of the Symbolists' fascination with the concepts of synaesthesia and correspondences is their experimentation with the "piano of colors," or colored music. Rene Ghil's *Traité du verbe* and Alfred Binet's, "L'Audition colorée," which appeared in *La Revue des deux mondes*, in 1892, explored analogies between specific vowel sounds and colors. Des Esseintes' "l'orgue à bouche," Mariano Fortuny's experimentation with theater lighting adopted in 1906 at the Théâtre de la Comtesse de Béarn, and Loïe Fuller's inventive incorporation of colored lights in her performances are manifestations of this general fascination.[98] The 1911 painting, entitled *Music*, by Luigi Russolo reveals the Futurists' interest in this Symbolist theme. The Marseillais Symbolist Valère Bernard collaborated in 1913 with his friend, the composer Carol Berard, on a piano of colors.[99]

Religious, mythological, or cultural syncretism must be considered a dominant characteristic of the intellectual fabric of Romanticism and Symbolism. The myth of Orpheus is often a central theme in the cyclical or universal histories and syncretic investigations of myth and religion, and also in the alternative religions and occult groups which proliferated at this period. Orpheus embodies the concept of artist as priest, an idea important to both occultist and Symbolist artist and poet. The concept of correspondences is a crucial element of Symbolist aesthetic idealism: the artist-priest reveals the mysterious relationship between this world and an ideal or transcendent realm via a universal language of symbols. Synaesthesia, the total work of art, the musical ideal, moreover, are elements of the Symbolist concept of the ideal art form. It is significant that the definitions of myth, symbol, and language are refined in the context of religion as well as aesthetics.

Gustave Moreau's *La Vie de l'humanité*

Further clarity may be brought to this discussion of intellectual syncretism through a coda, devoted to one work by Gustave Moreau, *La Vie de l'humanité*. This painting is paradigmatic of Moreau's aesthetic: the significance of Orpheus and the mingling of pagan myth and biblical story are typical both of the artist's fascination with the priestly poet-initiate and of his preoccupation with religious and cultural syncretism. This painting, however, reflects more than an individual artist's obsession with the orphic mysteries; It is, as well, a manifestation of the broad intellectual and philosophical current in the nineteenth century that generated universal histories, palingenetic theories, world mythographies, syncretic studies of religions, and an enthusiasm for the occult and for mysticism.

Indeed, a number of specific parallels exist between Moreau's *La Vie de l'humanité* and literary works or theoretical texts by the syncretist historians and occultist philosophers of the nineteenth century. For instance, several compositional, thematic, and iconographic elements are common to the painting and to works by the mystic philosopher and writer Pierre Simon Ballanche, the philosopher and painter Paul Marc Chenavard, and the mystics and occultists Eliphas Lévi, Joséphin Péladan, and Papus. The most significant points include the central importance of Orpheus, the juxtaposition of pagan myth and biblical story (specifically the myth of Orpheus and passages from Genesis), the prominence of the redemptive Christ, a cyclical pattern for mankind's development—most frequently perceived as a degeneration or negative unfolding—and a system of parallels between these ages of mankind and the stages of the life of the individual.

Moreau's painting (fig. 2.2) has the imposing appearance of an altar, the ten images surrounded and unified by a heavy gilt frame. The sequence of the panels—nine rectangular images arranged in three rows of three panels each, surmounted by the semicircular lunette with the image of Christ—implies a cyclical movement of history, a disintegration redeemed by the victory of the greatest initiate, the Resurrection of Christ. The top row depicts Adam and Eve: The Age of Gold—"Prayer," "Ecstasy," and "Sleep"; the middle row, Orpheus: The Age of Silver—"Inspiration" (fig. 2.3), "Song" (fig. 2.4), and "Tears" (fig. 2.5); the bottom row, Cain and Abel: The Age of Iron—"Work," "Rest," and "Death." The Greek myth of Orpheus is thus sandwiched between two stories from Genesis.

Moreau's own commentary on the work focuses on the complex interrelationships of the individual panels. The painting is intended to present the stages of mankind's development (golden age, silver age, iron age), and the growth of the individual (childhood, youth, maturity). It is arranged, moreover, according to the cycle of the day (morning, noon, evening). Moreau also delineates more subtle progressions: levels of religious or spiritual concentration (prayer, ecstasy, sleep), of artistic effort (inspiration, song, tears), and of productive labor (work, rest, death).

The development and increasing sophistication of mankind, the movement from primitive to civilized state, is viewed as a gradual deterioration, a fall from grace, a corruption of innocence. The sequence within the vertical columns expresses this process of degeneration: from prayer to inspiration to work, from ecstasy to song to rest, from sleep to tears to death. Indeed, a loss of Paradise may be seen as the overriding theme of the nine panels, connecting the biblical and mythical stories: Adam and Eve are compelled to leave Paradise; Orpheus' serene world is shattered by his loss of Eurydice—he loses the transforming power of his music and ultimately his own life as punishment for his untimely revelation of the mysteries or transgression of divine rules; Cain stains the earthly paradise with the murder of his brother Abel. Unifying all is sin itself: Original Sin, Orpheus' glance back at Eurydice, Cain's murder of Abel.[100]

Between the Paradise of first man and the corrupt world of societal man, Orpheus represents the incipient stages of civilization. Indeed, the central panel of the entire work presents the Apolline Orpheus bathed in the brilliant sunlight of midday, singing and playing his lyre, attended by his muse, surrounded by becalmed beasts and flourishing trees, enchanting all by the power of his music. Classical mythology is filled with the embodiments of civilization, the harbingers of knowledge and art: Prometheus, Daedalus, Hephaistos, as well as Orpheus. Moreau specifically acknowledges the appropriateness of pagan mythology to represent the beginnings of civilization: "Intelligence and poetry are much better personified in these whole epochs of art and imagination (pagan antiquity) than in the Bible, steeped as it is in feeling and religiousness."[101] The artist's commentary, however, does not provide a specific explanation for the source of his inclusion of Orpheus in this otherwise Christian context.[102]

An obvious parallel to and likely source for Moreau's inclusion of Orpheus in a biblical context is the frequent depiction of Orpheus in Early Christian art. Artists in the early Christian period exploited the parallel between the magic of Orpheus' music and the calming effect of the Divine Word and perceived in the image of Orpheus among the beasts an analogy to Christ surrounded by his flock.[103] In the generally syncretic atmosphere of the dying days of paganism, and especially in the context of the correspondences between Orphism and Christianity, the lyre-playing Orpheus among the becalmed animals was frequently depicted in catacombs, on sarcophagi, and in other contexts as well.

That the excavations of the catacombs during the latter half of the nineteenth century were widely known and well documented makes it likely that Moreau was aware of this tradition. He was probably familiar with the famous image of Orpheus from the ceiling of the catacomb of Domitilla (see fig. 1.11).[104] This painting is a clear precedent for the depiction of Orpheus taming the animals in the center of a Christian iconographic scheme. In a central octagonal, the lyre-playing Orpheus, clearly recognizeable by his Phrygian attire, sits among various animals, flanked by trees. Eight smaller scenes encircle this central image: four pastoral settings (two with rams, two with bulls) alternate with four biblical subjects (Moses drawing water from a rock, Daniel as orant between two lions, Christ raising Lazarus, David with his slingshot). The commentary that accompanies this image in P. R. Garucci's *Storia della arte cristiana nei primi otto secoli della chiesa* (1873) identifies Christ as the new, the real Orpheus: "Christ, the nonfabulous Orpheus, truly he led man from animal existence to a life of reason and taught him the way of virtue and happiness."[105] This statement is consonant with the syncretism of the universalist historians, who viewed Orpheus as one of a succession of initiates culminating in Christ. Moreau, however, was probably interested less in a specific compositional model than in the correspondence between the intellectual syncretism of the nineteenth century and the religious syncretism of the Early Christian period.

Thus it is important to examine how the painting manifests this broad intellectual current of the period and to analyze specific elements that it shares with the works and theories of universal historians, mythographes of world religions, and occultists.

An earlier manifestation of this syncretism—and a highly influential one—is Eugène Delacroix's cycle of paintings executed between 1838 and 1847 for the Library of the Palais Bourbon in Paris (fig. 2.6). Orpheus is represented there as instituting civilization, a level in man's education or initiation. This movement towards sophistication is, however, intereprered as a gradual loss of purity leading ultimately to man's fall. Delacroix's work may well be a source for Moreau's notion of Orpheus' role in the degenerative movement of history.

One may discern in Delacroix's work—as well as in Moreau's—the influence of Giovanni Battista Vico's cyclical theory of history. In his *Scienza nuova* (1744) Vico posited history as a succession of constantly repeating cycles. His philosophy was humanistic. Humanity, he believed, creates its institutions: language, religion, mythology, and society are products of man's will. And all of man's creations are subject to historical analysis. Vico's *Scienza nuova* had widespread impact on the intellectual circles of the nineteenth century. His influence is reflected in the works of Ballanche and Chenavard, and also in Edgar Quinet, Jules Michelet, and Philippe Benjamin Buchez, especially in their concepts of a universal history—their synthesis of language, myth, and religion—as well as their belief in a spiritual center to man's existence and development.[106]

Indeed, it is within this context that the rationale of Moreau's *La Vie de l'humanité* becomes lucid. His juxtaposition of Orpheus with Adam and Eve and Cain and Abel is no longer baffling when compared with the imaginative syncretism that allowed Ballanche to inject Orpheus into Roman history, or Chenavard to deconstruct and reconstruct the story of the love of Orpheus and Eurydice to express different stages of mankind's development. Eliphas Lévi's creative synthesis of all religions, in particular his juxtaposition of Medea and Cain in *Histoire de la magie* (1860), or Joséphin Péladan's combination of Cain and Abel with Orpheus and Eurydice in his play *La Terre d'Orphée* are, in addition, two specific examples of the syncretist religious philosophy of the occultists which also inform Moreau's painting.

Moreau's choice of Orpheus and pagan antiquity in general to symbolize intelligence and poetry, to represent the dawnings of civilization, parallels Ballanche's use of Orpheus as a symbolic entity: "Orphée ... une puissante expression des traditions antiques les plus générales."[107] The central role played by Orpheus in Moreau's painting, in Ballanche's writings or Chenavard's work, or in the mystical philosophies of Schuré, Péladan or Lévi is fostered by the fluid syncretism which embraces all religions as the manifestations of a single truth.

Specific aspects of Moreau's program reflect, as well, the schemes of the syncretist philosophers. The theme of the parallels between the ages of mankind and the stages in the life of the individual (golden age, silver age; childhood, youth, etc.) is common to Moreau's painting, Ballanche's theory of palingenesis, Chenavard's extrapolation of the progress of history from the average 84-year lifespan of the individual, or Papus' notion of "analogie," or the correspondence between the cycle of a single day and the seasonal cycle of the year as the basis of his model of the historical process.

Moreau's painting, then, is consonant with a significant intellectual phenomenon in the nineteenth century involving a desire to create broad, all-encompassing systems of man's development—past, present, future. This impulse is manifested in the proliferation of universal histories and synthetic world mythographies as well as in the interest in mysticism. It is not surprising that the multivalent figure of Orpheus—poet, musician, initiate, magician, heroic intruder in Hades, lamenting lover, victim of Dionysian fury, but especially harbinger of civilization, archetypal artist, leader of cults, and priest—should play a crucial role in this syncretic intellectual environment.

The syncretic attitude is evident in the mixture of pagan and Christian imagery that enriches not only Moreau's work but that of Puvis de Chavannes, Redon, and many others. Gauguin's interest in the devout peasantry of Brittany and especially his conflation of Tahitian myth and Christian subjects are other expressions of this syncretism. The interest in Hinduism shared by Redon and Mallarmé reflects a profound curiosity about non-Western religions. And a more general fascination with alternative religions, the occult, and Theosophy can be found in the eccentric mysticism of the Nabis or Sâr Péladan's Rosicrucians. This all-encompassing vision of man's history and development may be considered a dominant characteristic of the intellectual fabric of both Romanticism and Symbolism, an important theme in the works of artists from Delacroix to Rodin. Indeed, such epic works as Rodin's *Gates of Hell* (1880–1917), Gauguin's *Who Are We? Where Do We Come From? Where Are We Going?* (1897), or Munch's more psychologically oriented painting, *The Dance of Death* (1899–1900), reflect this utopian search for universal truths.

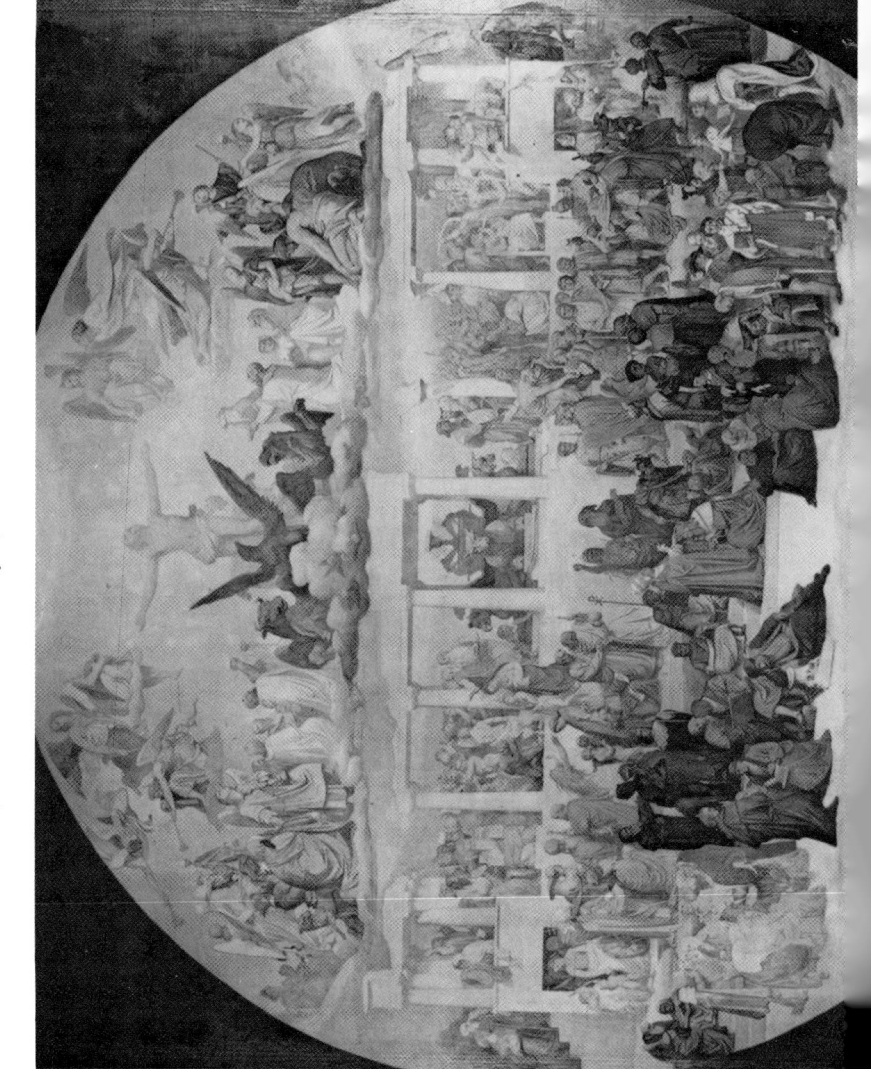

Figure 2.1. Paul Chenavard, *Social Palingenesis* or *La Philosophie de l'histoire*, ca. 1848
Oil on canvas.
(*Musée des Beaux-Arts, Lyon*)

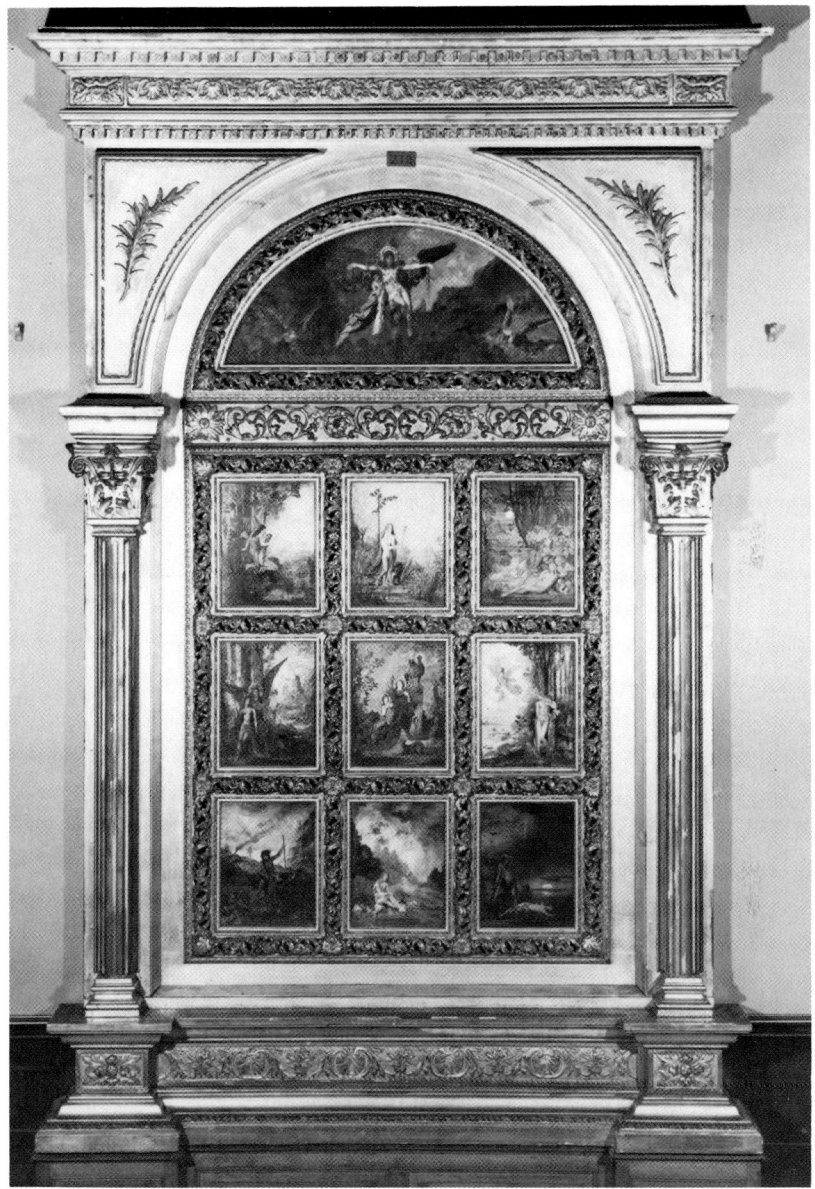

Figure 2.2. Gustave Moreau, *La Vie de l'humanité*, 1886
Oil on panel.
*(Musée Gustave Moreau, Paris; MGM 1974, #216;
Cliché des Musées Nationaux, Paris)*

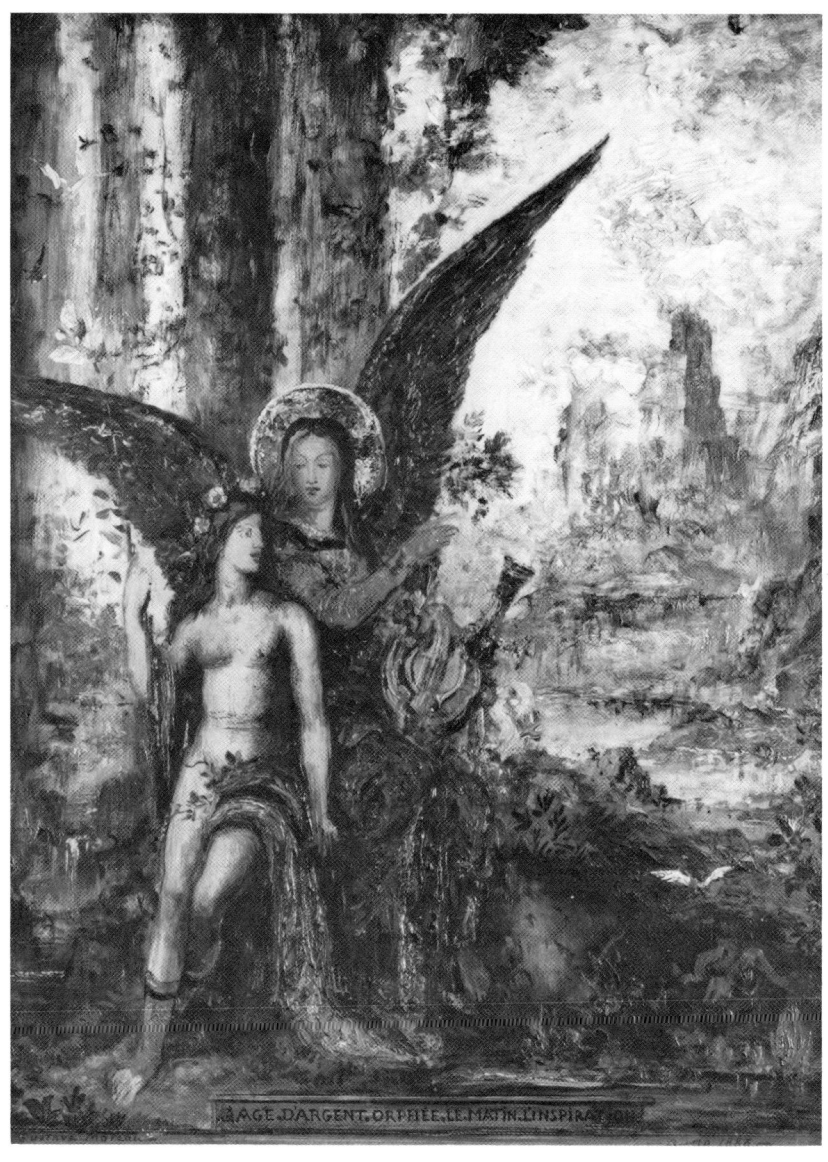

Figure 2.3. Gustave Moreau, *Le Matin, l'inspiration*
Panel from *La Vie de l'humanité*, 1886.
(Musée Gustave Moreau, Paris; Photo Bulloz, Paris)

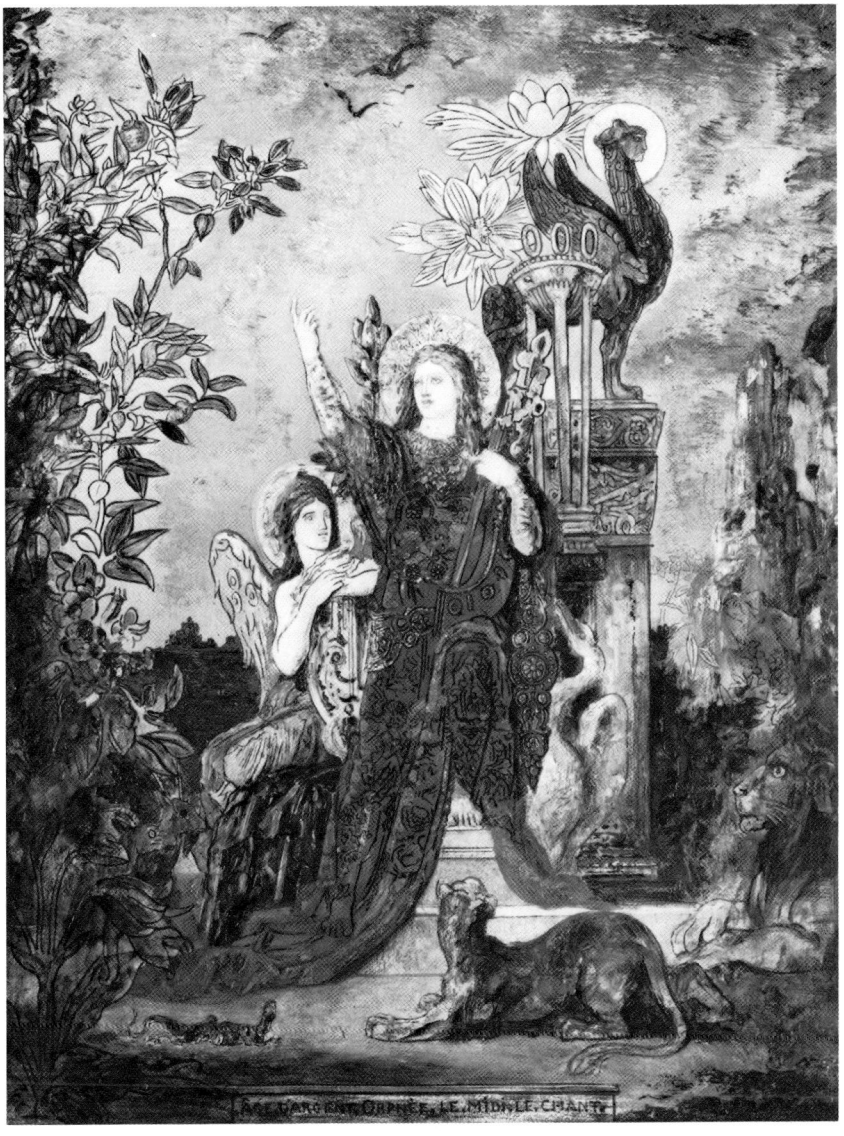

Figure 2.4. Gustave Moreau, *Le Midi, le chant*
Panel from *La Vie de l'humanité*, 1886.
(Musée Gustave Moreau, Paris; Photo Bulloz, Paris)

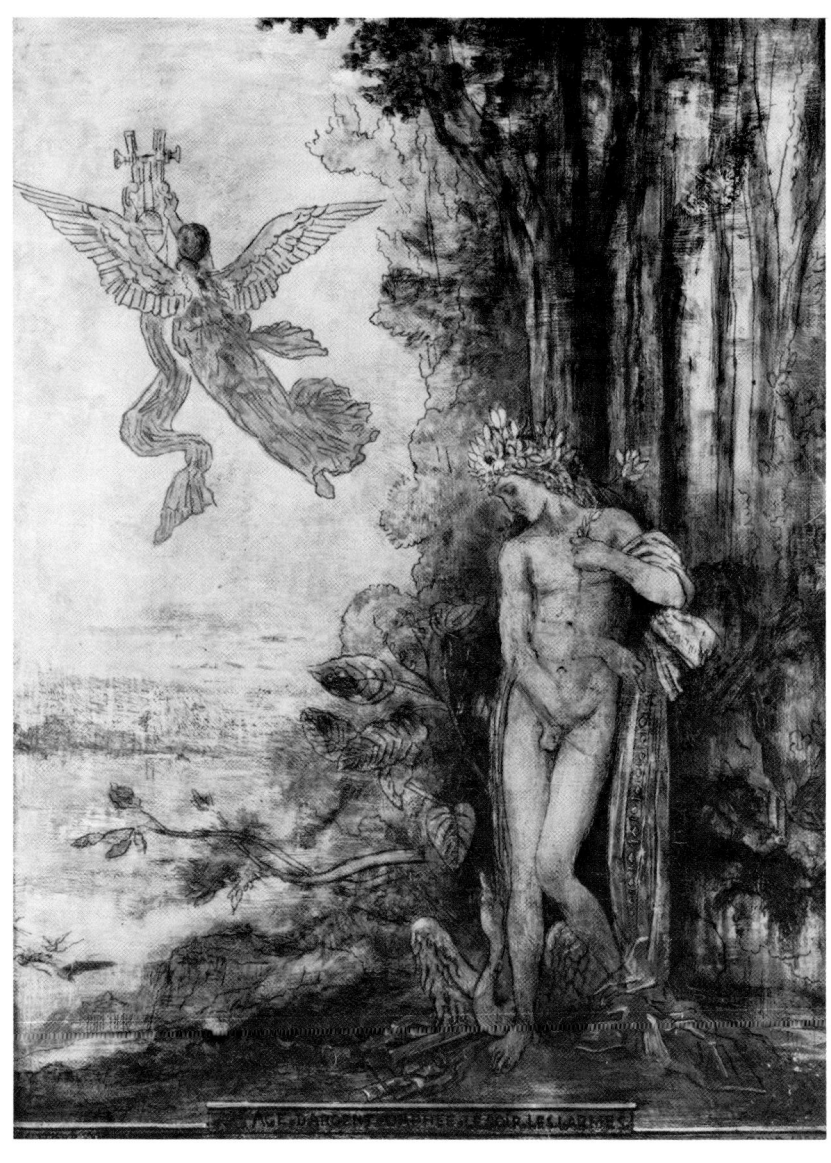

Figure 2.5. Gustave Moreau, *Le Soir, les larmes*
Panel from *La Vie de l'humanité*, 1886.
(Musée Gustave Moreau, Paris; Photo Bulloz, Paris)

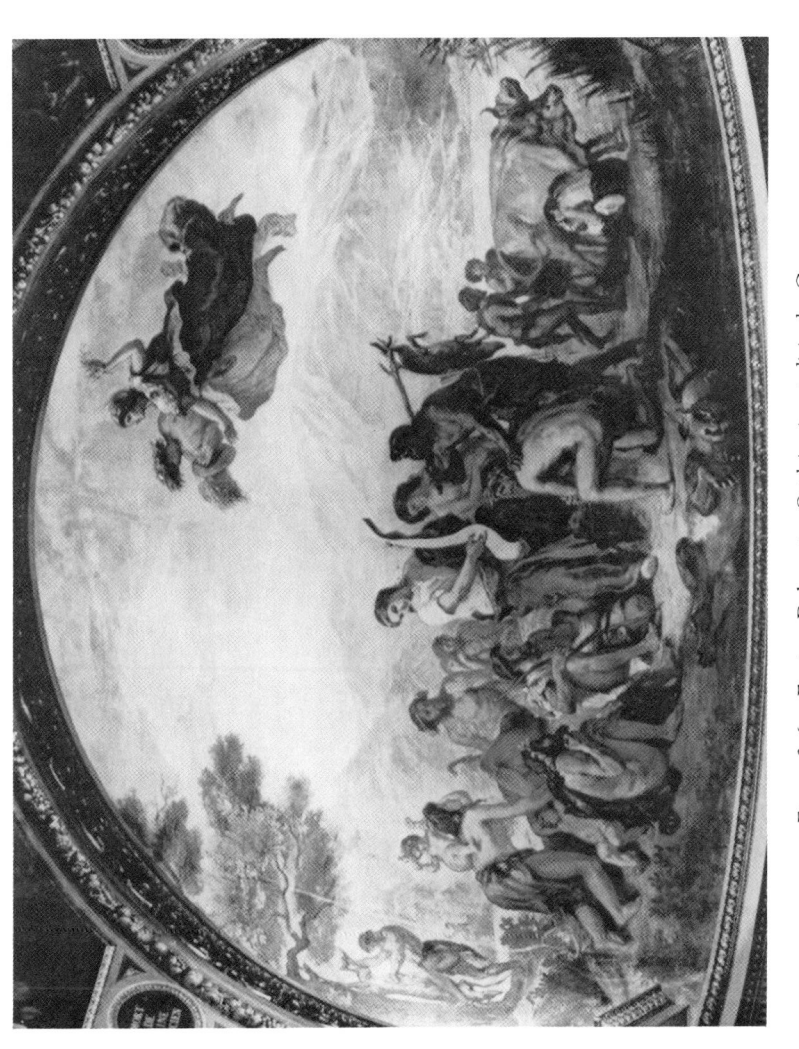

Figure 2.6. Eugène Delacroix, *Orphée vient policier les Grecs encore sauvage et leur enseigner les arts de la paix*, 1838–47
Mural.
(Library, Palais Bourbon, Paris)

3

Orpheus Taming the Animals, Pacifying Mankind

The image of Orpheus amidst a circle of captivated animals or humans symbolizes the inspirational or magically sedative effect of his music. As outlined already in chapter one, the motif is, however, subject to a broad range of interpretation. For the Romans, the scene of Orpheus taming the beasts became the excuse for a rich and varied assemblage of animals. In the context of Jewish and Early Christian art the similarity of the motif to the lyre-bearing David, on the one hand, and Christ-the-Good-Shepherd, on the other, was exploited. In the Medieval Romance, and moralized editions of Ovid's *Metamorphoses*, the animals are suddenly transformed into dragons or corrupting devils. Renaissance presentations of this scene are rife with Neo-Platonic and humanist overtones. In the hands of Dutch artists of the Baroque period, Orpheus is barely noticeable, engulfed by an elaborate panoramic landscape.

Nineteenth-century interpretations vary as well. Some artists are drawn to the motif merely as a vehicle for the depiction of an exotic array of animals. For the Symbolists, however, the power of Orpheus' music is an exceedingly serious theme, a reflection of the priestly role of the artist. As discussed at length in the previous chapter, Moreau's *La Vie de l'humanité* presents Orpheus as harbinger of civilization to primitive mankind, one link in a long chain of initiation. The central panel (see fig. 2.4) presents the poet in song, surrounded by an array of animals including lizard, lion, and birds. Moreau, however, emphasizes the sacerdotal function of the poet: he clutches an elaborate instrument and is draped in hieratic robes; he leans against a fantastic altar and is accompanied by a winged figure who listens with rapt attention; Orpheus' gesture—his hand and eyes raised to the heavens—is one of dramatic declamation.[1] Another work by Moreau, *La Poésie sacrée*, 1908 (fig. 3.1), depicts the androgynous poet, adorned with halo, bearing a jewel-bedecked lyre. He strides amidst a swarm of miniature demons: symbols, it seems, for the torments of this physical existence.

An examination of a few of the more conventional interpretations of the motif will demonstrate by contrast the priestly, hieratic emphasis given by the Symbolists.² Orpheus among the beasts was quite naturally a preferred motif for artists who specialized in animal subjects. John MaCallan Swan, an *animalier* who established an international reputation for his naturalistic treatment of wild cats, painted two versions of Orpheus amidst the animals, the first submitted to the Royal Academy in 1894 (fig. 3.2), the other in 1911. The earlier painting presents a youthful, even androgynous, nude Orpheus, stepping, or more precisely, dancing amidst an array of lions, tigers, and panthers. His music seems to provoke a kind of intoxicated frenzy, as the animals roll at his feet, even follow his every motion with bold intensity.³

In Tadeusz Styka's *Orpheus* (fig. 3.3), the poet is also surrounded by a number of large cats who snarl, rubbing against his legs as if intoxicated by his music. In contrast to Swan's lithe youth who appears to dance amidst the animals, Styka's Orpheus is a more majestic figure, clothed in classicizing drapery, playing an enormous, indeed ponderous, lyre. The poet, his face transfixed, seems to swoon under the effect of his own music. The treatment of the face and hair reveals Styka's study with Jean Jacques Henner. Henner's impact is evident, moreover, in Styka's dashing impasto, infusing not only the figure but the surrounding landscape with a quality of emotional intensity.⁴

In contrast, the Symbolists' interpretations of this motif consistently deemphasize the animals and shift focus rather to the figure of the poet himself. Like Moreau, these artists (including Puvis de Chavannes, Henry de Groux, Franz von Stuck, Henri Martin, Emile Fabry, Nikolaus Gysis, Marie-Alexandre Coudray, Antoine Bourdelle, Melchior Lechter, Martin Brandenburg, Ferenc Helbing, Alexandre Séon, and Alphonse Osbert) emphasize the poet's priestly role, the magical quality of his music. Often, the narrative details of the myth are suppressed in favor of a heroic figure, embodiment of poetic inspiration or the sacerdotal mission. In Alphonse Osbert's works, not only are the animals absent but the figure of Orpheus himself is barely recognizable amidst a delicate landscape which exemplifies the Symbolist notions of correspondences, synaesthesia, the psychological landscape.

Henry de Groux

Very little biographical information is available about the Belgian Symbolist, Henry de Groux. The image of Orpheus, however, which he chose as the cover illustration for the special 1899 issue of *La Plume* dedicated to him, may at least communicate something of his self-concept as artist (fig. 3.4). It includes a dramatically heroicized image of Orpheus (in a stance reminiscent of the traditional pose of Moses with the tablets) clothed in flowing garb and holding a lyre. The animals do not gather calmly at his feet but instead their bodies form a seething mass, a physical embodiment of the intensity of the poet's song.[5]

In another version (fig. 3.5), Orpheus reclines on a hill, a rather elaborate landscape unfolding before him. Here too, the animals surge towards him as though physically compelled by the power of his music (or energized by de Groux's characteristically agitated linear style). Orpheus and the beasts are contained in the upper portion of the composition, and appear, thereby, to float above the landscape. The bending branches of the trees accentuate this impression of the figures held aloft, as though buoyed by a rush of air. De Groux seems to compare the sound of Orpheus' music and the rush of wind through the trees.

Emile Fabry

The image of Orpheus constitutes a significant motif in the easel paintings as well as in the many large-scale murals by the Belgian Symbolist, Emile Fabry.[6] The exhibition catalogues of Pour l'Art, the Symbolist group which Fabry founded along with Jean Delville and Xavier Mellery in 1893, include *Le Poète, La Poésie lyrique,* and *Orphée*.[7] Though his works include fairly conventional images of the poet surrounded by various animals, Fabry stresses the poet's sacerdotal role, with stark, mysteriously hieratic presentations. Fabry's notion of the priestly function of the artist was undoubtedly informed by the Sâr Péladan's Rosicrucian aesthetic (he exhibited at the Rose + Croix Salons from 1893 to 1895) as well as by his friend Jean Delville's theosophical mysticism.[8]

Half of the mural, *War and Peace*, ca. 1919 (fig. 3.6), for the University of Cardiff—that portion devoted to the theme of peace—is dominated by Orpheus, symbol of harmony. The poet holds his lyre aloft, while another male nude offers him a transparent sphere (symbol perhaps of the harmony of the cosmos). In the background another male harvests grain. A female nude is seated, a nude body seems to shoot horizontally from her head. Flowers cover the globe on which she sits and emerge from the right as well. In contrast, that half of the composition devoted to war is fiercely bellicose: a male nude sits in a melancholic pose, a rider gallops on a stallion, a woman desperately attempts to protect her fetus/child from a ferocious armed man. Fabry achieves a certain bizarre intensity through the accentuation of anatomy, with special emphasis of facial features, including the accentuation of an unusually protruding forehead. Orpheus' expression resembles the medallion-face which peers down from between the two sides of the mural. These peculiar facial distortions are actually quite typical of Fabry and may be compared with the gaunt expressions and hallucinatory gazes of the visages in the frontispiece for *Les Heures harmonieuses*, 1897, in *Les Parques*, 1898, or *Les Gestes*, 1895.[9]

It is tempting to discern the impact of the Swiss Symbolist Ferdinand

Hodler (whom Fabry much admired) in the solemn, ritualistic gestures of Fabry's figures. Their mannered stylization probably reflects more the impact of Blake, Fuseli and the Pre-Raphaelites, artists whom Fabry discovered during his sojourn in England during World War I. A shared interest in the myth of Orpheus might have been the basis for a special appreciation of Sir Edward Burne-Jones. In an 1870 gouache (fig. 3.7), Burne-Jones uses Orpheus to represent lyric poetry. (Other works by the British artist with the theme of Orpheus will be discussed in chapter 4.)[10] The intense visages, but also Fabry's taut, sculptural stylization of the human anatomy, may attest to this interest in Burne-Jones. One might compare, for instance, Fabry's *Music*, 1925 (fig. 3.8), with a variety of works by Burne-Jones: *Depths of the Sea*, 1887; *Car of Love*, 1870; or *Wheel of Fortune*, ca.1882.[11] Fabry's interest in Michelangelo may have been transmitted through Burne-Jones, who learned much from the master through his diligent study of such works as Michelangelo's *Deposition*, which hung in the National Gallery. In addition, the floating figures in Fabry's works—emanating from the woman's head in *War and Peace*, and from the lyre-player's head in *Music*, and even the two seemingly suspended women who flank Orpheus in the Théâtre de la Monnaie mural—may, likewise, be inspired by the troublesomely weightless bodies which appear in many of Burne-Jones's works.

Poetic or artistic inspiration is the thematic focus of both *Music*, 1925, and also the mural for the Théâtre de la Monnaie (fig. 3.9).[12] In *Music*, Orpheus' right hand is raised to his temple, suggesting a contemplative pose as well as the rhythmic strumming of his lyre. The poet's taut body and stony stare emphasize this state of intense concentration or inspiration. The female form which emerges, arrow-like, from his forehead, appears like the physical embodiment of his profound thoughts.[13] The entire environment, at once thick with flapping wings of birds and undulating with ripples of water, seems to reverberate palpably with the intensity of Orpheus' concentration. In the Théâtre de la Monnaie mural, Orpheus' anatomy is similarly fierce, even horrifyingly tense, his face a contorted mask of inhuman concentration. Here it is the lyre itself which emerges from his head, an extension of his erect, columnar body, another example of the physical manifestation of the poet's creativity and inspiration. The poet, standing firmly on the globe of the earth, is the intermediary between the natural world and a transcendent plane, symbolized by the lyre which extends into the heavens, surrounded by unearthly light and winged cherubs.

Franz von Stuck

In contrast, Franz von Stuck's interpretations (three versions dating from 1891, 1897–98 and ca. 1924) of the motif of Orpheus amidst the animals are characterized by a serene classicism and calm grandeur.[14]

The depiction of Orpheus and the animals in the Villa Stuck (fig. 3.10), decorating an entire wall of the music room, is highly stylized and nonillusionistic. The poet's brown nude body and giant lyre, supported on one knee, are crisply outlined against a radically simplified landscape consisting of black earth and white sky. Beneath the poet, a white or ochre lion, flat as a cut-out, is similarly contrasted with an undifferentiated background of black. The entire composition of Orpheus and the animals is enclosed by a large gilt frame in the shape of a pedimented temple facade. The triangular pediment is subdivided by three vertical gilt elements into three sections. Orpheus is enclosed in the central section of the pediment. Animals, portrayed as stark silhouettes, either white against black, or black against white (the black and white landscape is continuous), are enclosed in the small angles of the pediment as well as in the rectangular framed areas below.[15]

Surely, Orpheus is thematically appropriate for the music room. However, it is necessary to press beyond this straightforward explanation and penetrate some of the complexities of the iconographic program of the music room, and the villa as a whole. The villa constitutes a highly personal statement of the artist's aesthetic. It is a living environment transformed into a temple devoted to the arts. Painting, sculpture, and architecture, as well as the decorative arts (furniture) are harmonized to form a unified aesthetic environment. Stuck juxtaposes his own work with objects from antiquity. His collection included a cast of the celebrated classical relief of Orpheus, Eurydice, and Hermes (see fig. 1.12). At one point, Stuck used this relief as the focal element in an "altar." Stuck assembled three different altars: the first included a cast of the cult statue of Athena; the second, the Orpheus relief; and the third, his own painting, *Sin*. This theme of the religious nature of art is surely present in the music room, in the golden temple facade superimposed over the images of Orpheus and the animals. Stuck emphasizes Orpheus' priestly function and uses the myth to articulate his own deep feelings about the spiritual nature of artistic creation. Orpheus, representing the ideal synthesis of the arts, may be considered, moreover, the perfect personal symbol for Stuck, who in his own house played the multiple roles of architect, painter, sculptor, and designer.

Music, moreover, is a significant theme in von Stuck's oeuvre more generally. Music, dance, love, play are all means of transcending man's base instincts (symbolized often by the crude physique and rough action of centaurs), of controlling particularly the conflict between man and woman, and generally the means of creating a world of serenity and harmony. In the music room, the central motif of the pacifying power of Orpheus' music is amplified by depictions of dance, the ring dance, eavesdropping, the see-saw, teasing.[16] Three quotations from *The Merchant of Venice*, majestically inscribed on the walls in gold, refer to Orpheus' important role, and the general significance of music as a source of harmony.[17]

The theme of Orpheus' music and harmony is extended, moreover, to the ceiling of the music room. On the ceiling, the same penetrating blue color that was used on the adjacent walls becomes a celestial background for spheres, planets, and encircling rings all delineated in gold. With this astronomical chart, Stuck seems to allude to the Pythagorean-Platonic tradition, which emphasizes Orpheus' knowledge of the perfect harmony, the rhythm of the cosmos, based on his initiation into the harmonic vibrations of the spheres.[18] (The second Shakespearean quote similarly refers to the harmony of the spheres.) The music room is intended as an environment of perfect harmony, the ideal ambiance for the reception of music. Orpheus reigns over an environment of music, dancing, and piping whereby man and beasts are reconciled, the animals sit tamely side-by-side, and man overcomes his own baser instincts. Anyone who enters the room is surrounded by these pacific images, as well as the constant and magical whirling of the celestial bodies overhead. Moreover, photographs reveal that a statue of Diana was once placed directly below Orpheus and also that a statue of Athena was situated in one of the corners on the opposite side of the room. The inclusion of Diana, the chaste goddess, might well be construed as a reference to Orpheus' own enduring devotion to his wife, Eurydice. Athena's presence, undoubtedly in her role as patron goddess of arts and crafts, adds emphasis to the pervasive theme of the synthesis of all the arts, the ideal *Gesamtkunstwerk*.

Melchior Lechter, Artists of the Secession

The poet's divine inspiration is the theme, once again, of *Orpheus*, 1896 (fig. 3.11), by the Berlin artist, Melchior Lechter. Orpheus is pale, transfixed, stiffly erect, as columnar as the trunks of the birch trees that form a curtain behind him. He wears priestly vestments, a robe of gold and green studded with gold stars. The gothicized stylization of hands, face, and hair, his garments, the type of lyre he carries adds to the sacerdotal aura of the image. Orpheus' head, surrounded by a thin golden halo, is turned upward, frozen in concentration on some unseen, otherworldly realm. One imagines that this hallucinatory state is amplified by the field of poppies through which he walks. The flowers' thick, intoxicating perfume finds tangible form in the dense purple haze that filters upward, pervading the entire atmosphere. The colored clouds of the flowers' perfume and the poet's music mingle and reverberate in the forest of birches whose strictly parallel trunks are like pipes of a giant natural organ (one thinks of Baudelaire's "temple ou de vivants piliers," in "Correspondances").[19] This is a synaesthetic image: "Les parfums, les couleurs et les sons se répondent."[20] The painting explores the popular Symbolist ideal of the correspondence between the senses. The image, moreover, implies the correspondence between the natural world and a parallel Platonic plane. The poet, as priest or initiate, deciphers the hieroglyphs of nature to reveal the transcendent reality (Baudelaire's "confuses paroles").[21] Undoubtedly, Lechter was influenced by his association with the literary avant-garde circle of Stefan George in Berlin. Lechter illustrated books by George, Jean Paul, Maeterlinck and Friedrich Wolfers. George (whom Lechter portrayed once as priestly poet or mystical knight) was obsessed with the theme of the poet as chosen being and priest. Lechter's gothicized stylization may be compared with the esoteric mythical allusions and archaic stylizations characteristic of George's works.[22]

One might compare Lechter's painting with another image of Orpheus by a Berlin Secessionist artist, Martin Brandenburg (fig. 3.12). The somber young poet wanders a meadow under a glowering, stormy grey sky. The melancholy or torment of the poet is symbolized by the curling briars which entangle his feet and form a seemingly endless trail behind him. This depressive landscape contrasts sharply to the flowing shapes and brilliant colors which constitute a band across the top of the painting. The contrast between the somber tonality and the bright colors, between the naturalistic landscape and the abstract meandering shapes, may symbolize, once again, the correspondence between the natural world and a transcendent realm.[23]

There are indeed many examples which illustrate the widespread fascination during the *fin-de-siècle* with the poet's priestly role. A lithograph by the Hungarian Secessionist painter and graphic artist, Ferenc Helbing, portrays a muscularly heroic Orpheus, playing a massive lyre (fig. 3.13). The diagonal row of swans which cuts through the sky seems, in fact, to emanate directly from the instrument, a physical manifestation of the poet's music.[24] The 1900 medal by the French sculptor, Marie-Alexandre-Lucien Coudray (fig. 3.14), focuses on Orpheus' face. The poet's delicate, idealized features are infused with demonic fury, an expression of anguish or crazed ecstasy. The poet's hair is an elegant mass of swirling curls, stylistically typical of Art Nouveau.[25] A comparable image of idealized visage, transformed with supernatural inspiration, is found in *Genius with Lyre* (fig. 3.15), an 1888 lithograph by the Greek-born, Munich based artist, Nikolaus Gysis.[26]

Pierre Puvis de Chavannes, Alexandre Séon, Henri Martin

Orpheus is a strikingly prominent theme in the works of Pierre Puvis de Chavannes and his student, Alexandre Séon. This is the subject of a pastel dated 1890 (fig. 3.16), and dedicated to the wife of Philippe Gille (1831–1901), critic, dramatist, and author of opera livrets. Orpheus, crowned with laurel wreath and clothed in loose drapery, strides amidst a tree-studded slope by the seaside. With one hand he clutches his huge lyre while the other reaches to the heavens in dramatic declamatory gesture. Actually this pastel focuses upon and enlarges the figure of Orpheus included in the background of *Les Bûcherons*, 1871–74. This is Orpheus the harbinger of civilization, inspiring or guiding the industrious activity of early mankind. Séon's drawing of Orpheus (fig. 3.17) portrays the poet as an imposing, monumentalized figure. His sacred role is emphasized by the laurel wreath and aureole.

Henry Martin, whom Puvis recognized as his "héritier," painted *Orpheus*, ca. 1894 (fig. 3.18). This painting may well have been directly influenced by Puvis' *Les Bûcherons* or the Gille pastel. The poet's gesture with upraised arm, even the manner in which he grasps his lyre, are almost identical with Puvis' presentation of Orpheus. Similarly, the flying muses which accompany Orpheus in the Martin painting may well derive from the hovering figures which are frequently depicted in Puvis' works, for example, in *The Dream* (see fig. 5.6), 1883, and *The Poet*, ca. 1896 (fig. 3.19).[27] Certainly, however, the dominant themes of Henri Martin's works, artistic inspiration or poetic reverie, are informed by Puvis' idyllic and pastoral scenes.[28]

Alphonse Osbert

Alphonse Osbert's paintings are similarly replete with subjects of poetic reverie. The influence of Puvis as well as Séon is evident not only in this thematic orientation, but also in Osbert's reductive, even abstract style and flat, chalky surfaces. Almost all of Osbert's works present somewhat androgynous figures, playing lyres, draped in garments which suggest classical antiquity. The surrounding landscapes are soft, idyllic scenes evocative of moody reverie or poignant melancholy. The emotional tenor ranges from languor to lamentation, gentle reverie to somber introspection. Osbert was very aptly called "un peintre de l'âme."[29] Indeed, the compositions are largely similar except for subtle differences in mood. Considering the important similarities between Osbert's works, the discovery of a painting inscribed "ORPHÉE" (fig. 3.20) allows one to explore the orphic theme in all of Osbert's works.[30] Indeed, there is nothing to differentiate the painting of Orpheus from the other works, as Osbert suppresses any narrative details of the myth in favor of a subtle evocation of mood.

Corot's arcadian idylls and pastoral scenes, executed during the Second Empire, offer an interesting precedent for Osbert's works. Like Osbert's paintings, works such as *Morning, Dance of the Nymphs*, 1859, *Dance of Nymphs*, 1860–65, or *Souvenir de Mortefontaine*, 1864 (fig. 3.21), depict nonspecific scenes, only vaguely mythological, rather generally evocative explorations of poetic fantasies.[31] Corot's series of *souvenirs* reflect the rococo revival which flourished during the Second Empire. Charles François Jalabert's delicately erotic and elegant *Orpheus* (fig. 3.22), exhibited in the 1853 Salon, is another manifestation of this vogue. Théophile Gautier's 1857 description of Corot's paintings could well apply to Osbert's works of 40 to 50 years later:

> These Elysian woods and meadows, these glimmering skies, this realm of ideal weather in which our painter-poet wanders, lost in dreams, treading lightly on the dewy grass, gazing towards the first faint flush of dawn.[32]

Corot's memory-veiled *souvenirs* have been compared to Nerval's evocation of youthful love in *Sylvie*; similarly, Osbert's subtle association of particular times of day with emotional states of being might well be compared with the Romantic poet's intense identification with nature.

Even more specifically, Corot's own fascination with Orpheus, his many works with this theme, provide the closest antecedents for Osbert's poetry.[33] Corot's notebooks and sketches reveal that the ballet and theatre were major inspirations for his mythological fantasies. For instance, *Dance of the Nymphs* may correspond to his appreciation of *Les Sylphides*. Similarly, the 1861 painting of *Orpheus Leading Eurydice from the Underworld* (fig. 3.23) may have been inspired by Gluck's *Orfeo*. Jean Leymarie has suggested that the ballet served not only as a source for specific scenes or subjects, but also, and perhaps more significantly, the music—the musical concept of variations on a theme—inspired Corot's repeated and subtle reworking of essentially the same subjects.[34] Similarly, subtle variations of a single motif are at the heart of Osbert's work. A perusal of Osbert's titles reveals his intense preoccupation with music: *Etude pour harmonie virginale*, 1894; *Hymne à la mer*, 1895; *Joueuse de flûte*; *Femme à la lyre*; *Les Chants de la nuit*, 1896; *Une Muse*, 1901; *Soir lyrique*; *Harmonie d'automne*; *Les Voiles de la brume et la musique du soir*; *Clair de lune*; *Lyrisme*.[35]

Osbert carefully establishes a correlation between mood or emotion, the landscape motif, music, and the formal properties of his painting. His use of delicate gradations of color clearly reveals his association with Seurat and Denis, and his interest in Neo-Impressionist color theory and Symbolist psychoaesthetics. Synaesthesia, or the ideal of correspondences, is a central aspect of Osbert's work as he attempts (with color, line, and plane) to create the pictorial equivalent for music or sound and emotion. Osbert's paintings, then, can be associated with the dominant theme of correspondences in Symbolist poetry. One thinks of Verlaine's sonorous verses. Osbert's paintings must also be understood in the context of the psychological landscape, another crucial theme of Symbolist painting, explored further in chapter 5.[36]

The image of Orpheus taming the animals or pacifying primitive man is transformed by the Symbolist artists' deemphasis of the narrative details which characterize traditional interpretations of the motif. The landscapes of Puvis,

Osbert, and Lechter demonstrate these artists' interest in a form of visual expression which communicates directly through the abstract power of form, line, and color. In general, Orpheus amidst the beasts becomes a vehicle for exploring the Symbolists' fascination with the poet's priestly function, his role as the chosen one, recipient of divine inspiration. The poet is the initiate, capable of deciphering the symbols or hieroglyphs in nature, and, through the power of his music, of revealing the transcendent truths of the cosmos. Orpheus taming the animals embodies the Symbolist concept of music as the ideal art form. Moreover, he embodies the desired synthesis of all the arts, the correspondences between forms and sensations, both essential concepts of the Symbolist aesthetic.

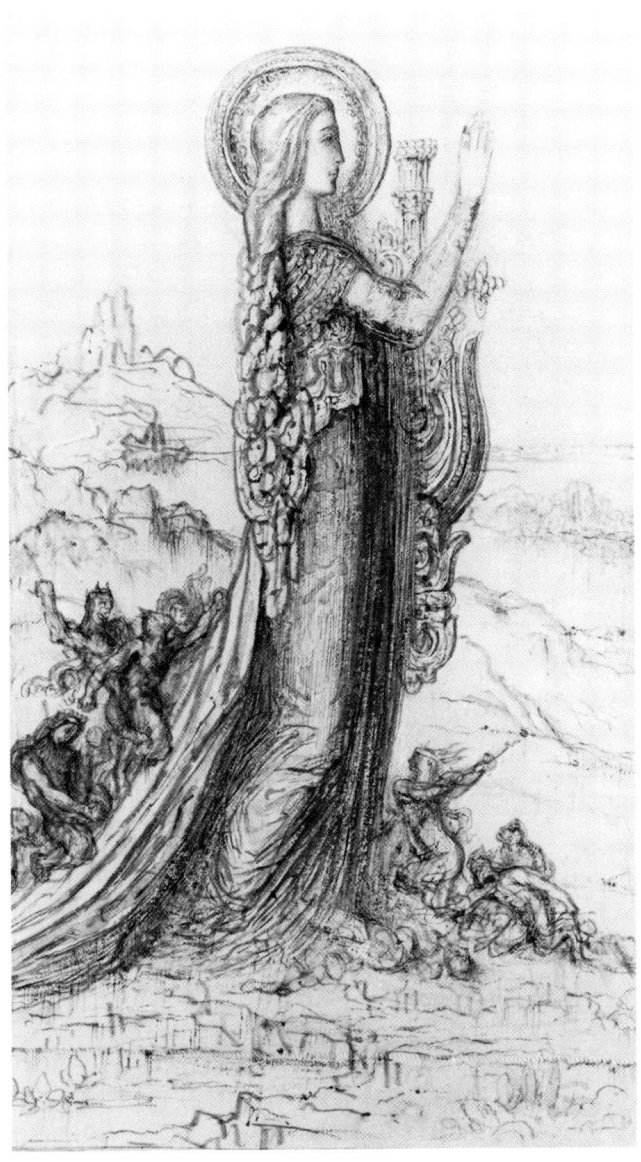

Figure 3.1. Gustave Moreau, *La Poésie sacrée*, 1896
Watercolor and pencil.
(Musée Gustave Moreau, Paris; MGM 1974, #516; Cliché des Musées Nationaux, Paris)

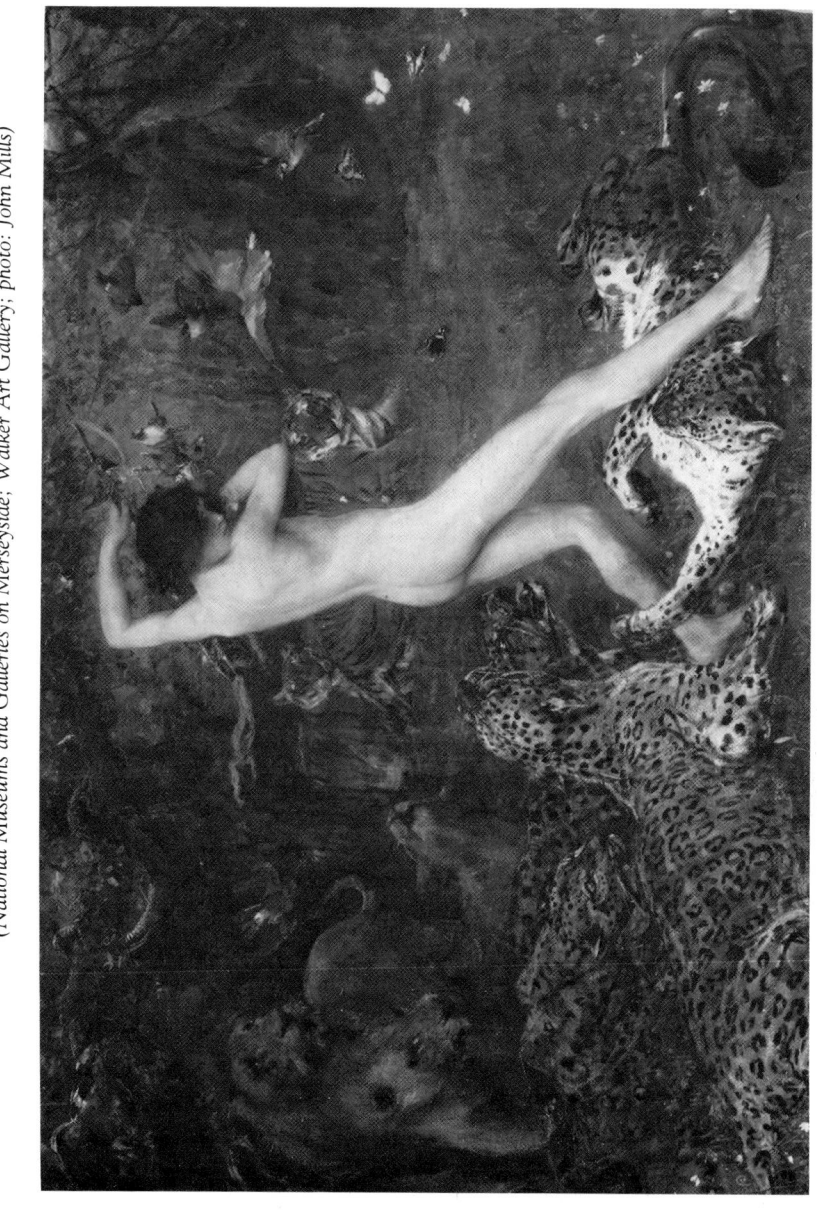

Figure 3.2. John MaCallan Swan, *Orpheus*, 1894 Oil on canvas.
(*National Museums and Galleries on Merseyside; Walker Art Gallery; photo: John Mills*)

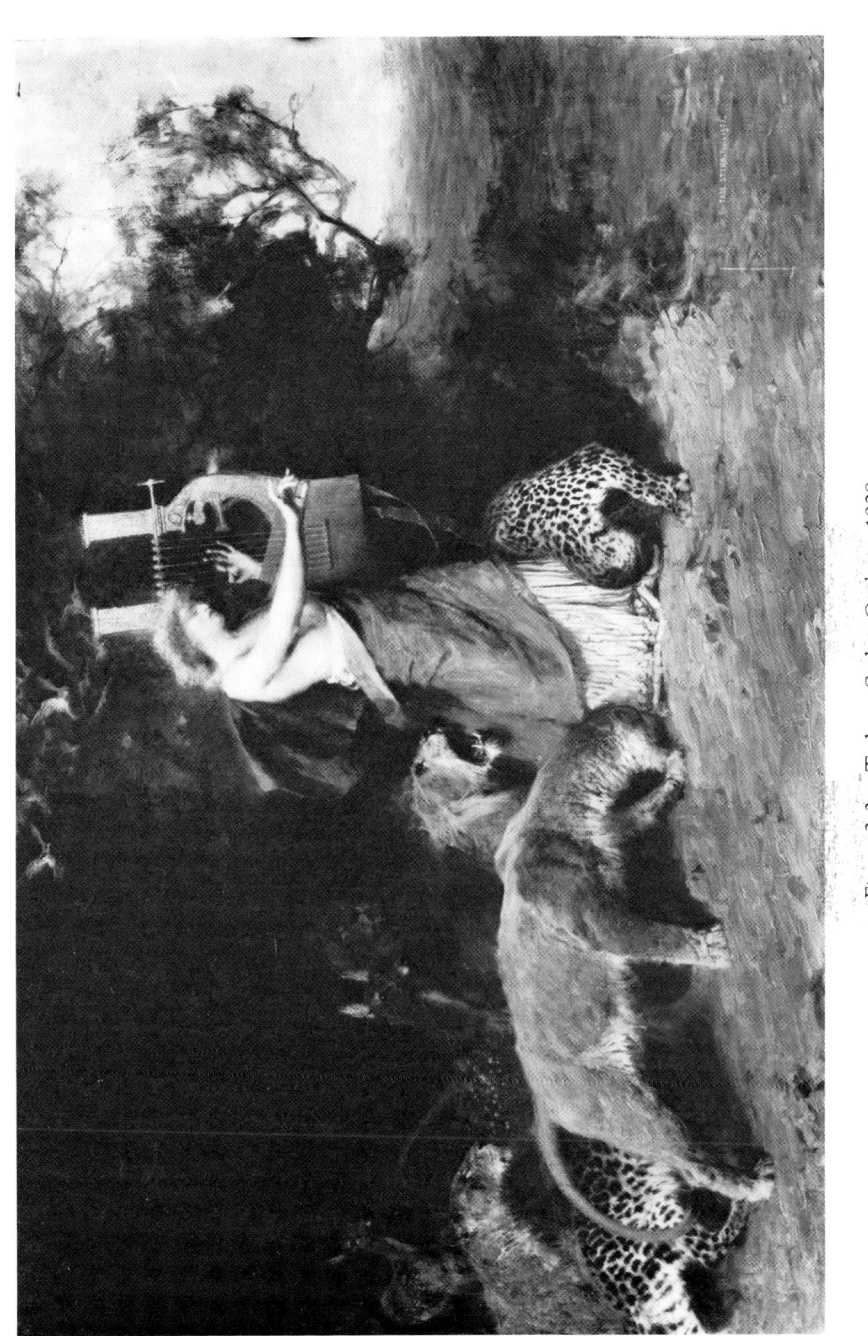

Figure 3.3. Tadeusz Styka, Orpheus, 1908
Oil on canvas.
(Photo: Roger-Viollet, Paris)

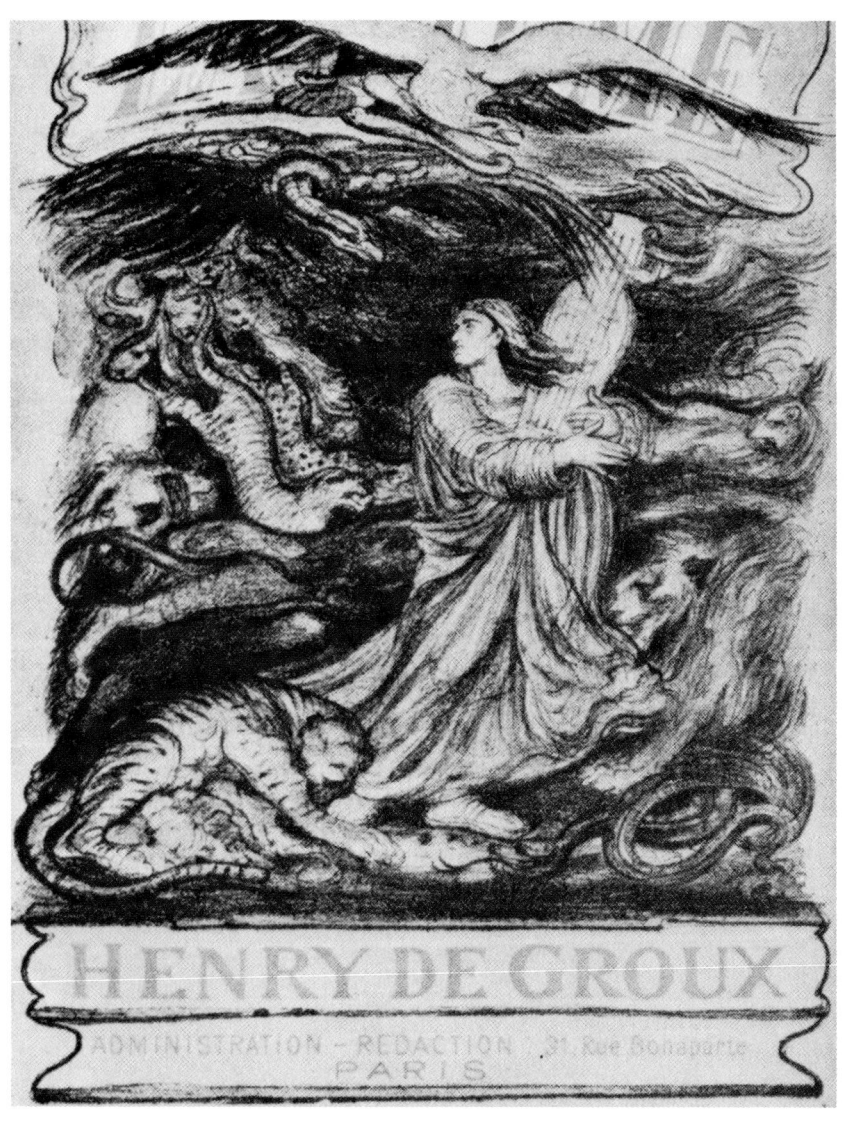

Figure 3.4. Henry de Groux, *Orpheus*
Cover of special issue of *La Plume*, 1899.

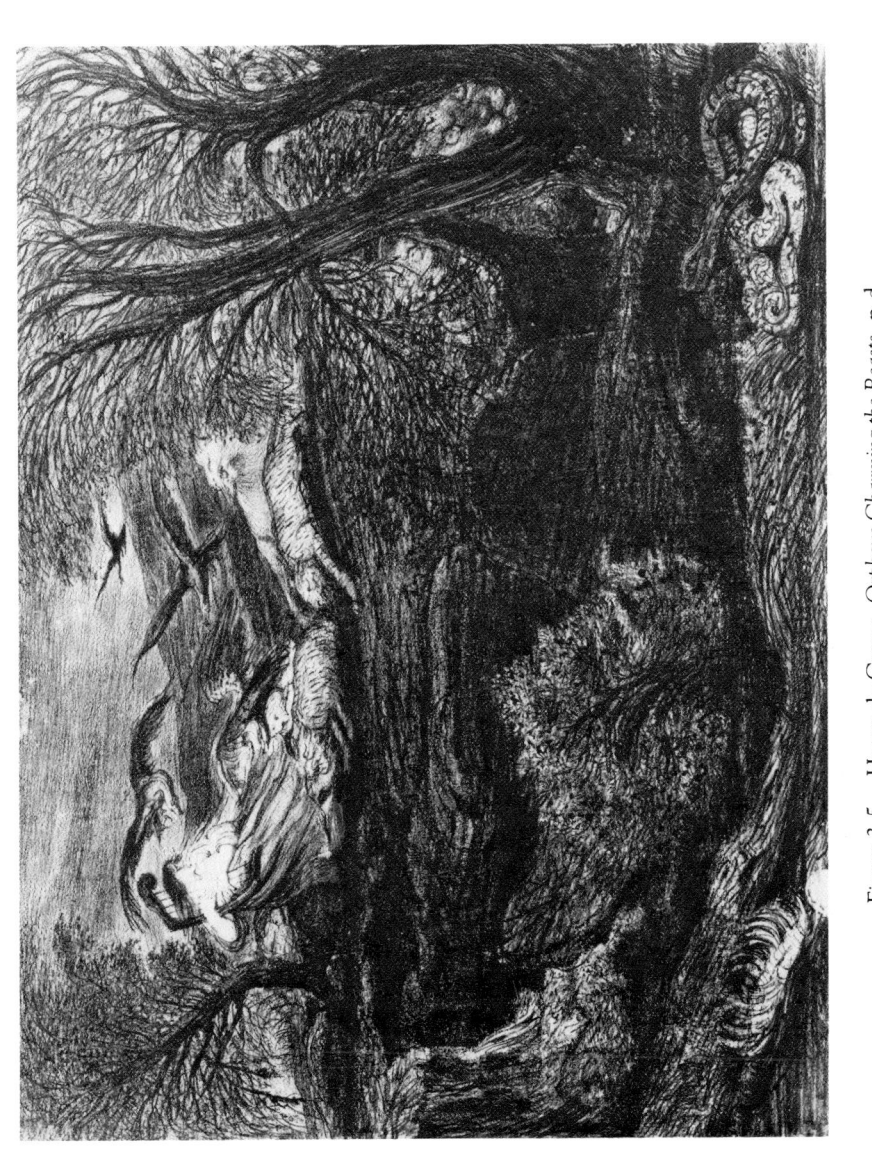

Figure 3.5. Henry de Groux, *Orpheus Charming the Beasts*, n.d. (*Bibliothèque Royale Albert Ier, Brussels, Cabinet des Estampes*)

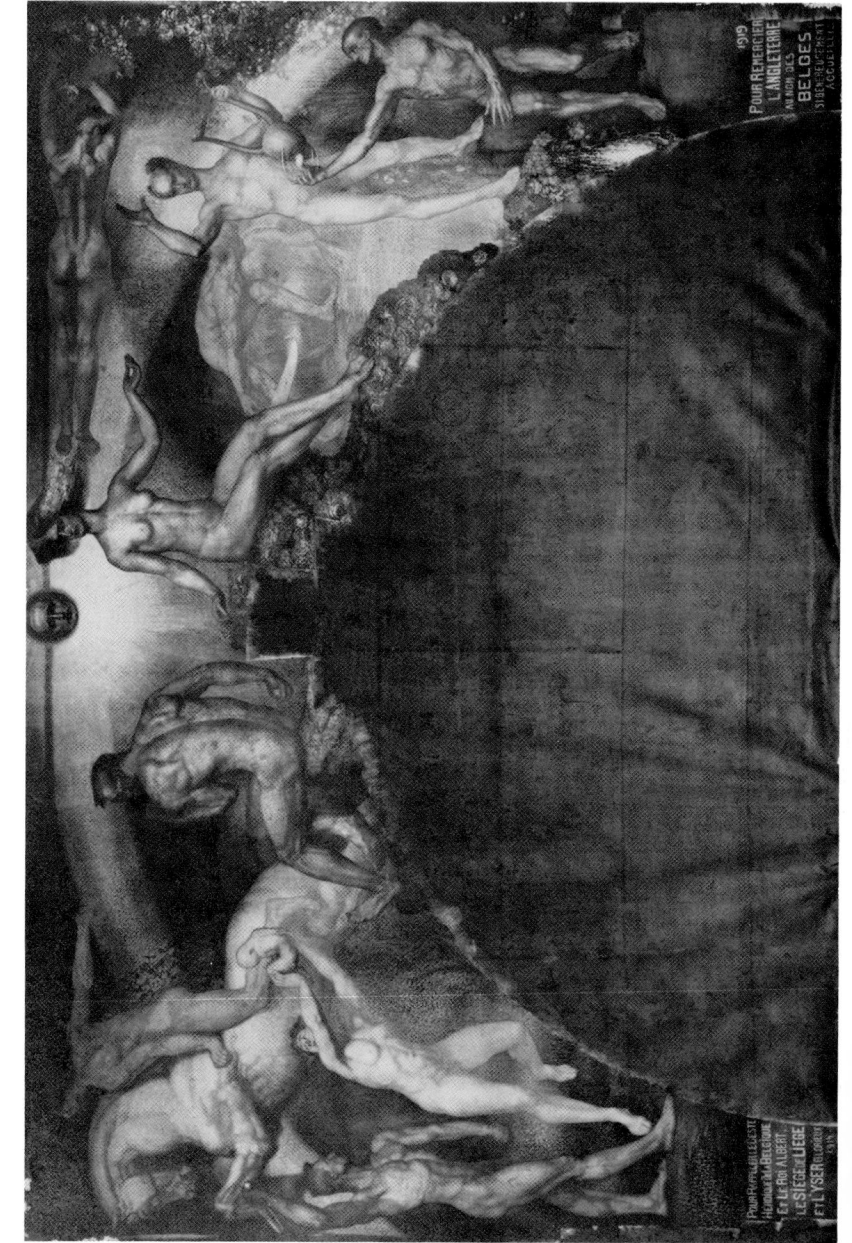

Figure 3.6. Emile Fabry, *War and Peace*, ca. 1919
Mural.
(*University of Cardiff; photo courtesy Mme. Deleclure-Fabry*)

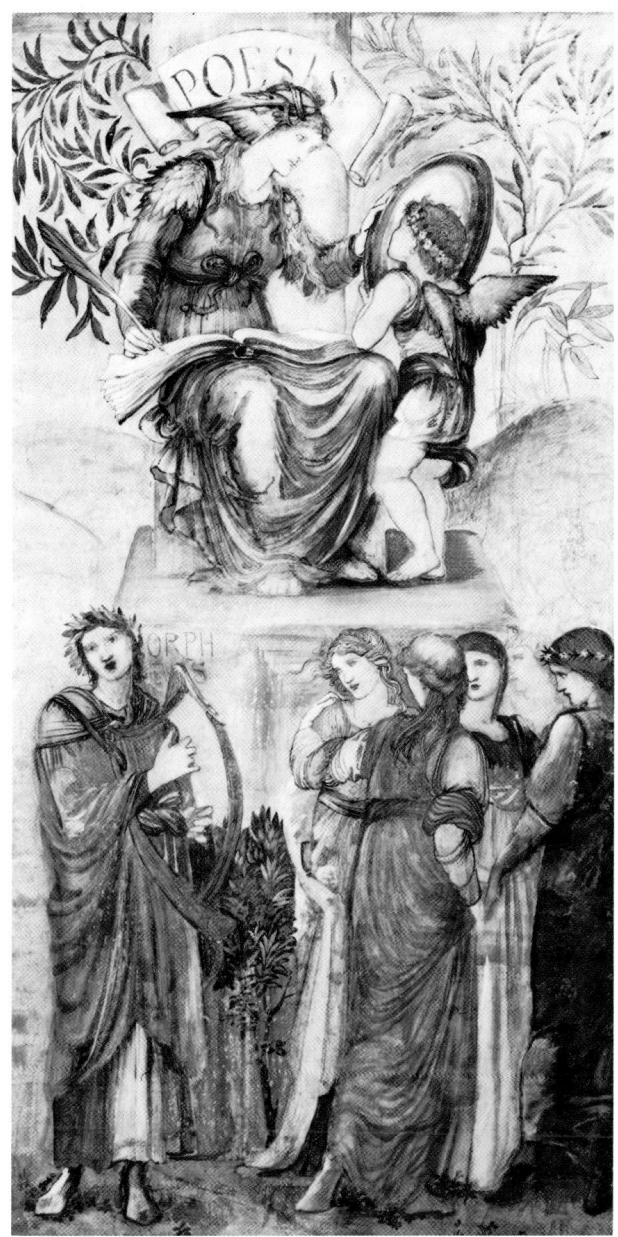

Figure 3.7. Edward Burne-Jones, *Poesis*, 1870
Gouache on paper.
(Photo courtesy Sotheby's, London)

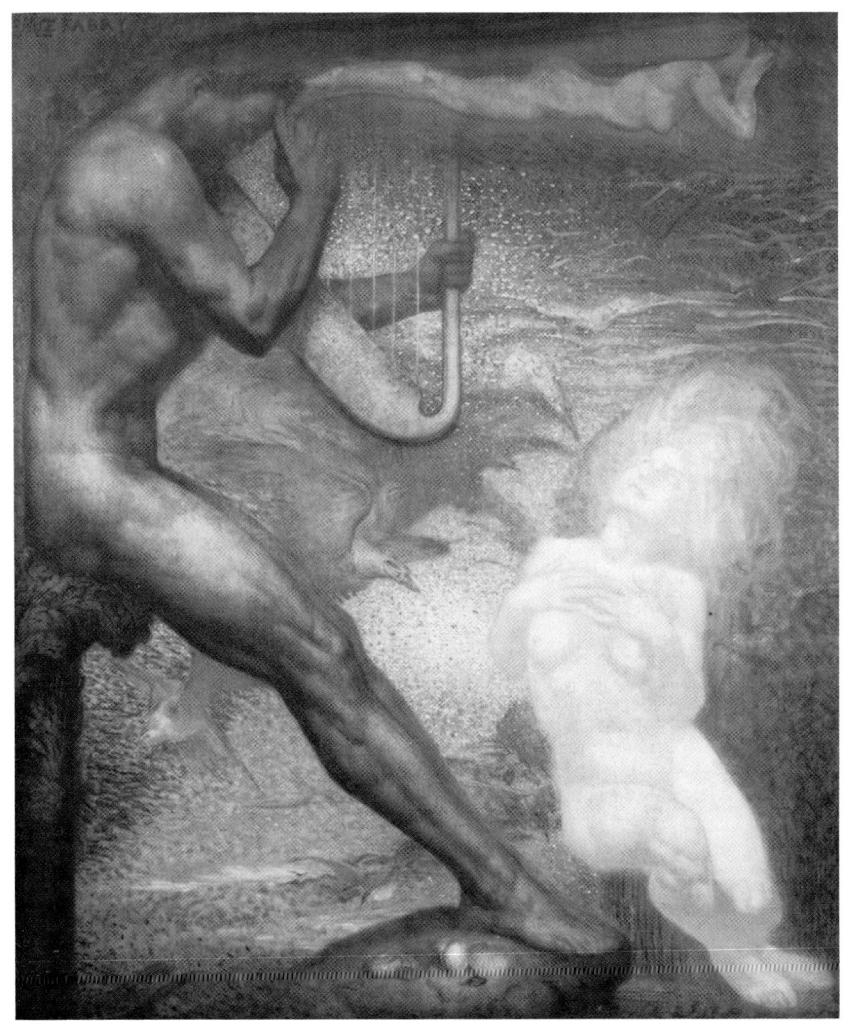

Figure 3.8. Emile Fabry, *Music*, 1925
Oil on canvas.
(Photo courtesy Mme. Delecluze-Fabry; photo E. Dulière, Brussels)

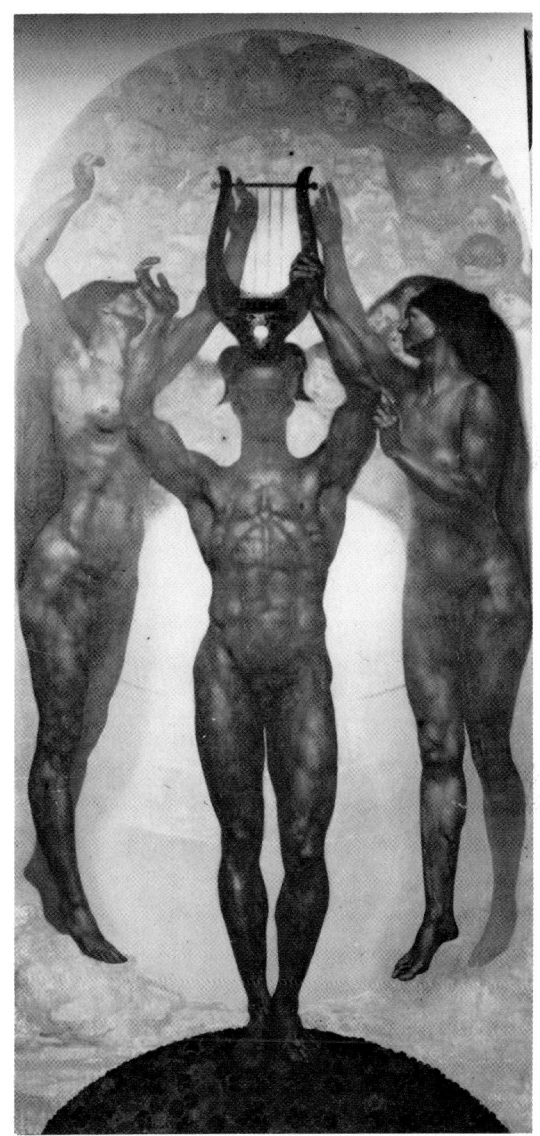

Figure 3.9. Emile Fabry, *Orpheus*, ca. 1890
Mural.
(Théâtre de la Monnaie, Brussels; photo courtesy Mme. Delecluze-Fabry)

Figure 3.10. Franz von Stuck, *Orpheus and the Animals*, 1897–98 Mural.
(Music room, *Villa Stuck*, Munich)

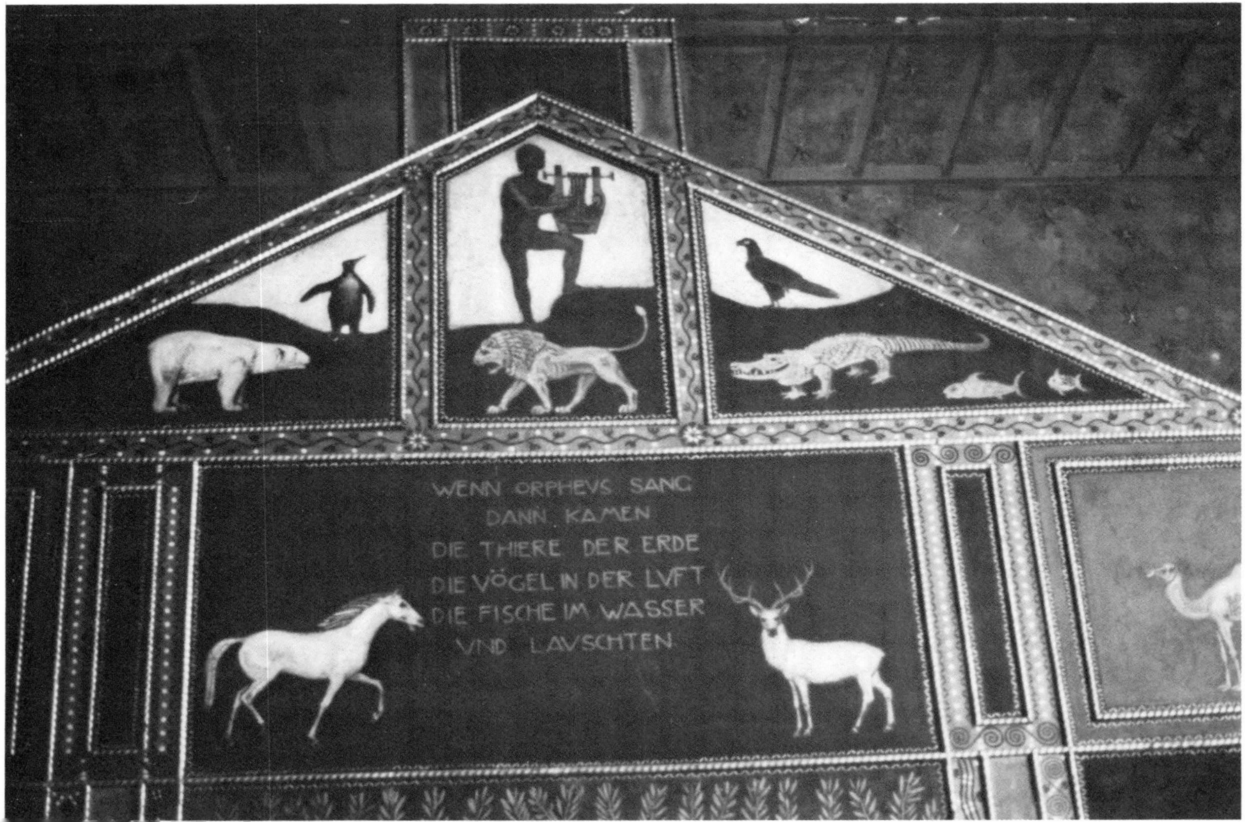

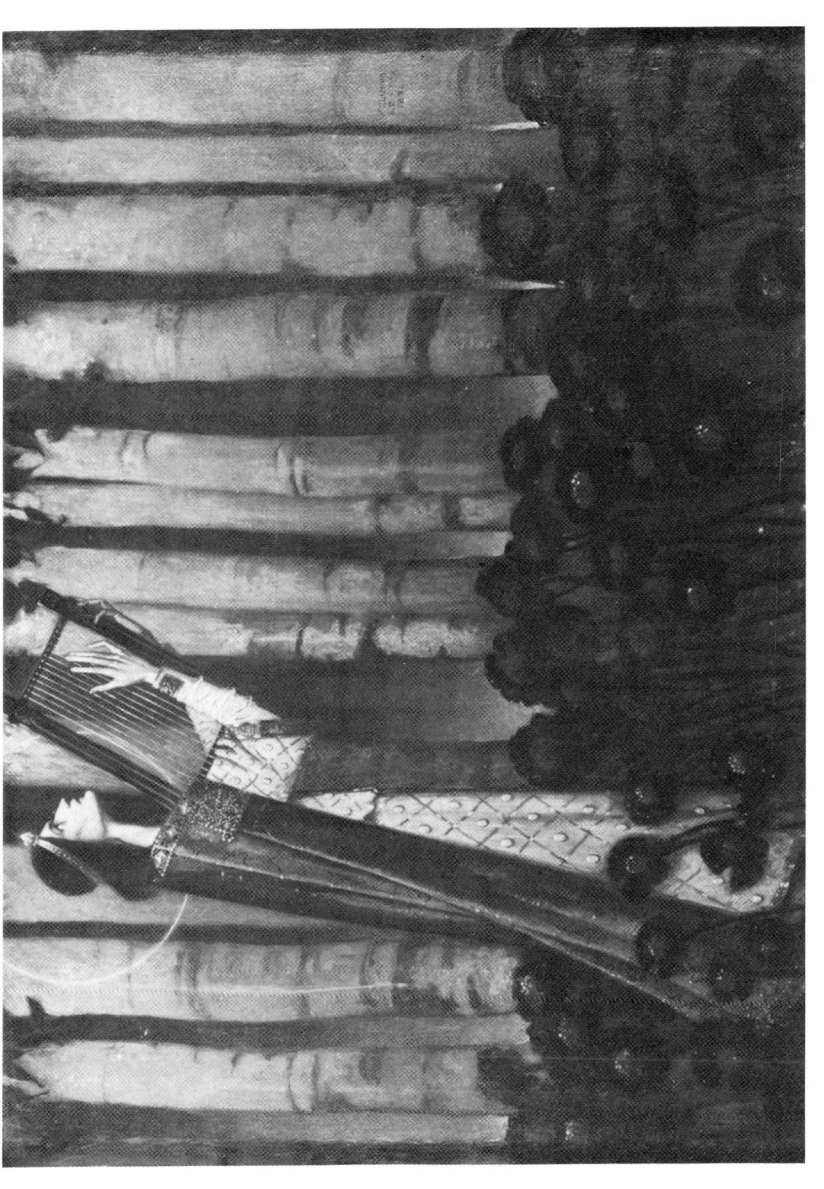

Figure 3.11. Melchior Lechter, *Orpheus*, 1896
Oil on canvas.
(*Westfälisches Landesmuseum für Kunst und Kulturgeschichte, Münster;* photo: *Westfälisches Landesmuseum für Kunst und Kulturgeschichte, Münster*)

Figure 3.12. Martin Brandenburg, *Orpheus*, 1899
Oil on canvas.
(*Hans Gerd Neef, Cologne*)

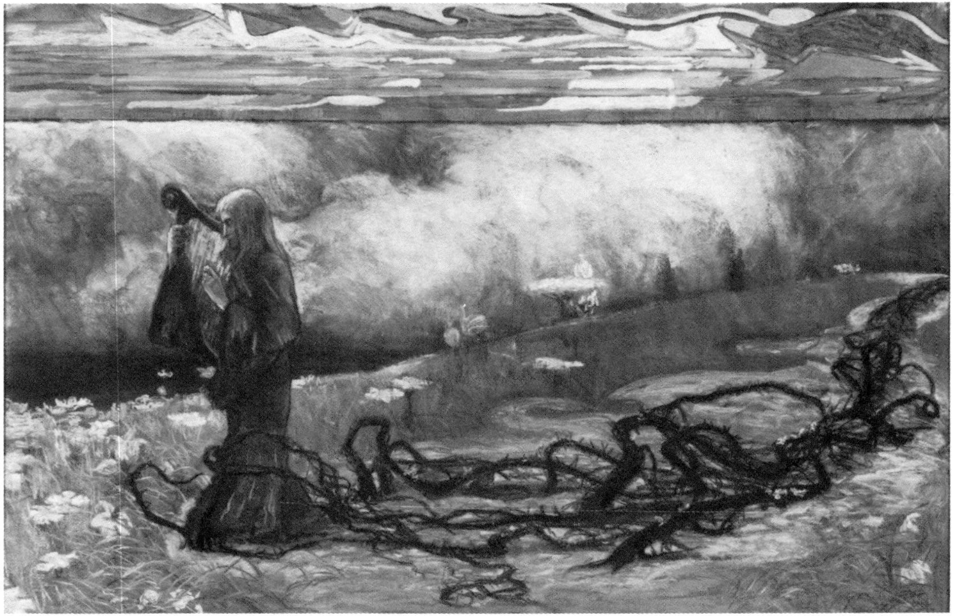

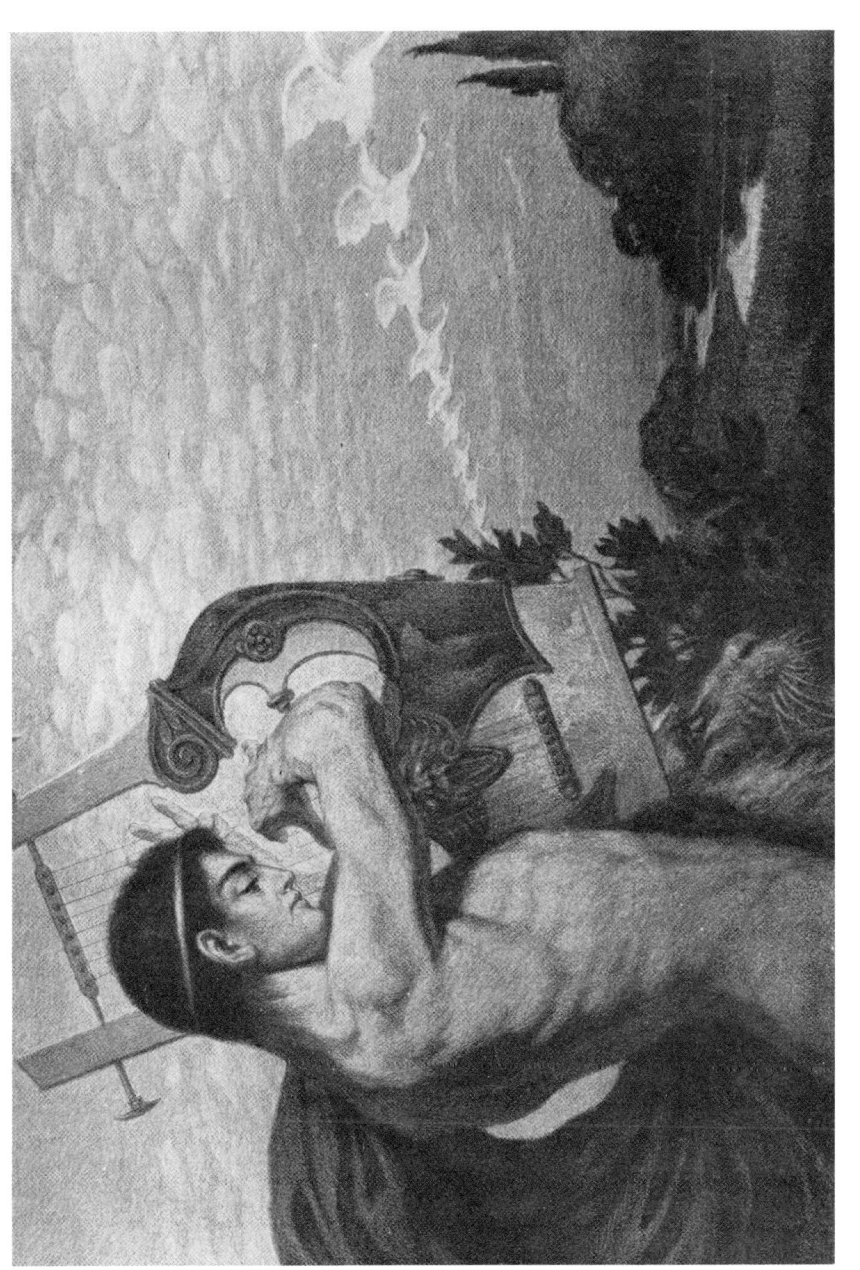

Figure 3.13. Ferenc Helbing, *Orpheus*, n.d. Colored lithograph. (*National Gallery of Hungary, Budapest; photo: Mester Tibor*)

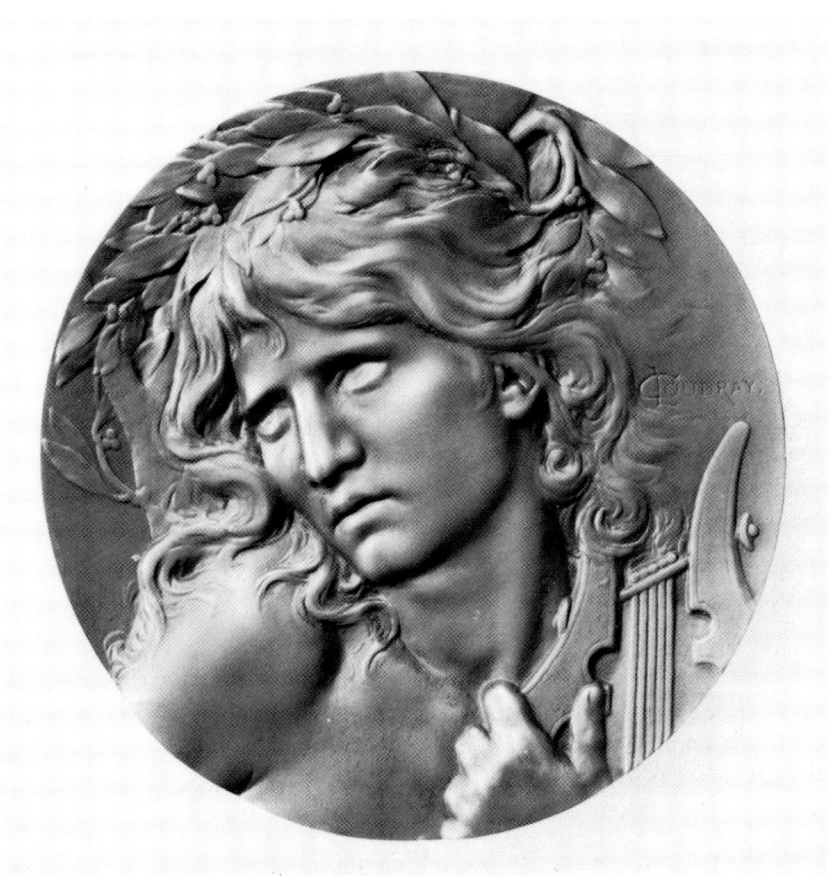

Figure 3.14. Marie-Alexandre Coudray, *Orpheus*, 1900 Bronze medal.
(The British Museum, London)

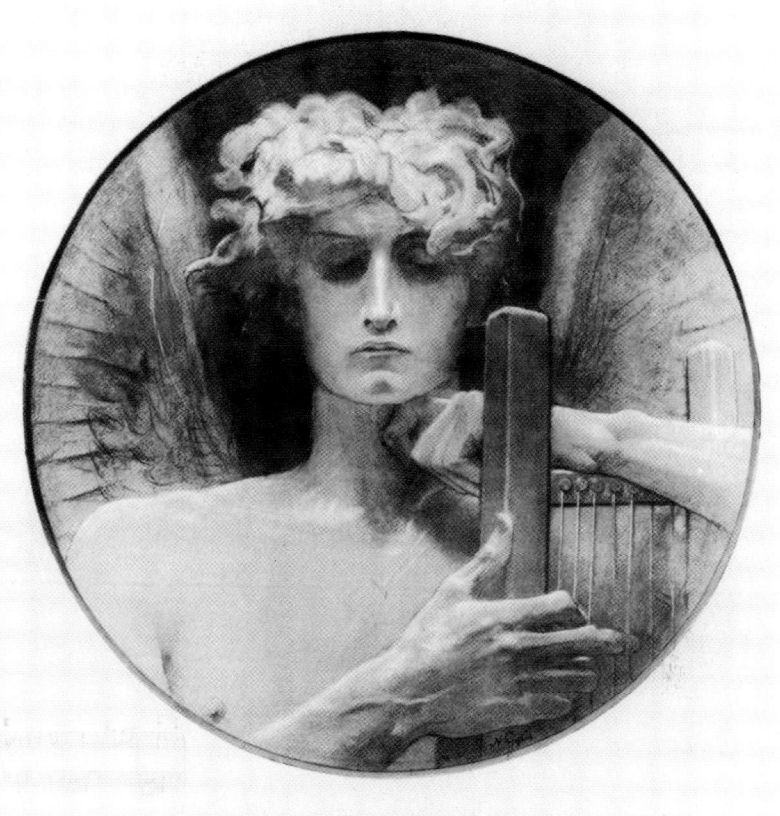

Figure 3.15. Nikolaus Gysis, *Genius with Lyre*, ca. 1888
Colored lithograph.
(Hessisches Landesmuseum, Darmstadt)

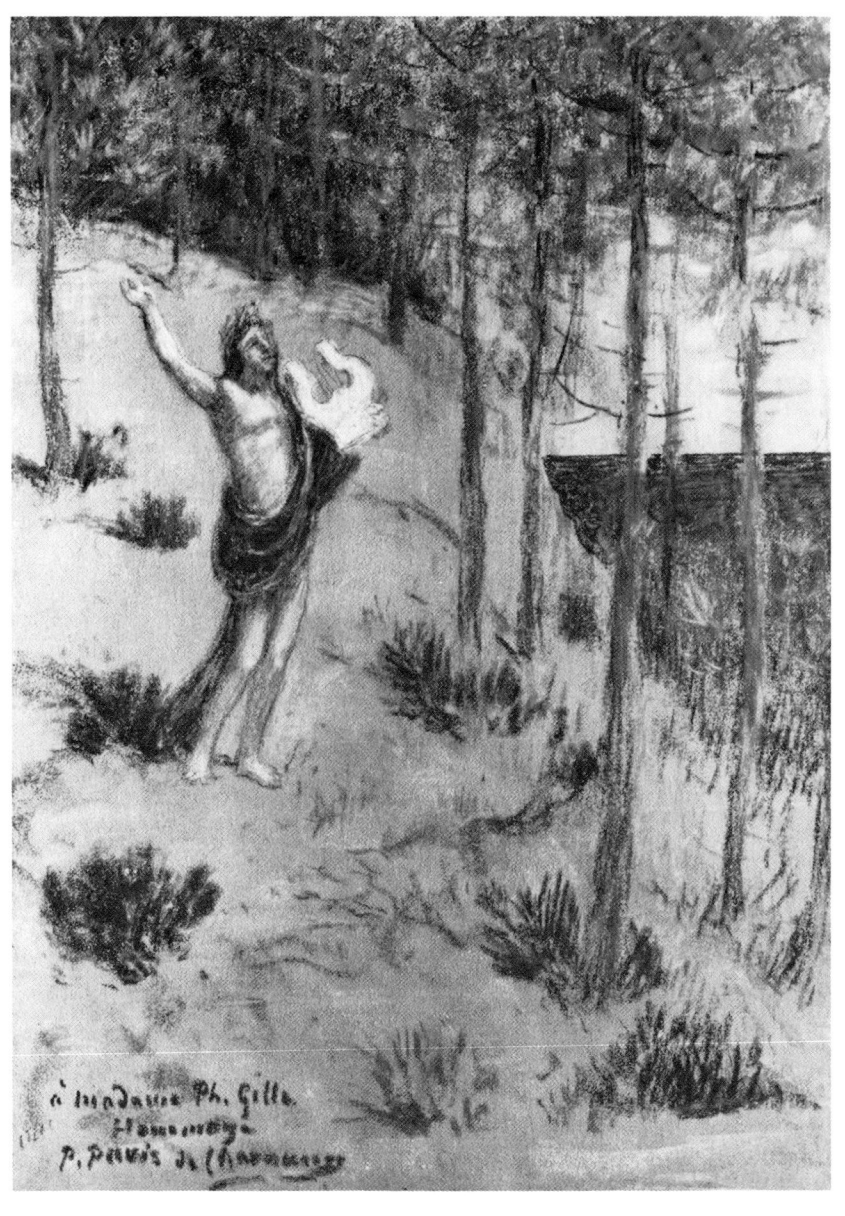

Figure 3.16. Pierre Puvis de Chavannes, *Orpheus (à Madame Ph. Gille—Hommage)*, ca. 1890
Pastel.
(*Private collection, Puteaux; photo: Archive Musée des Arts Décoratifs, Paris*)

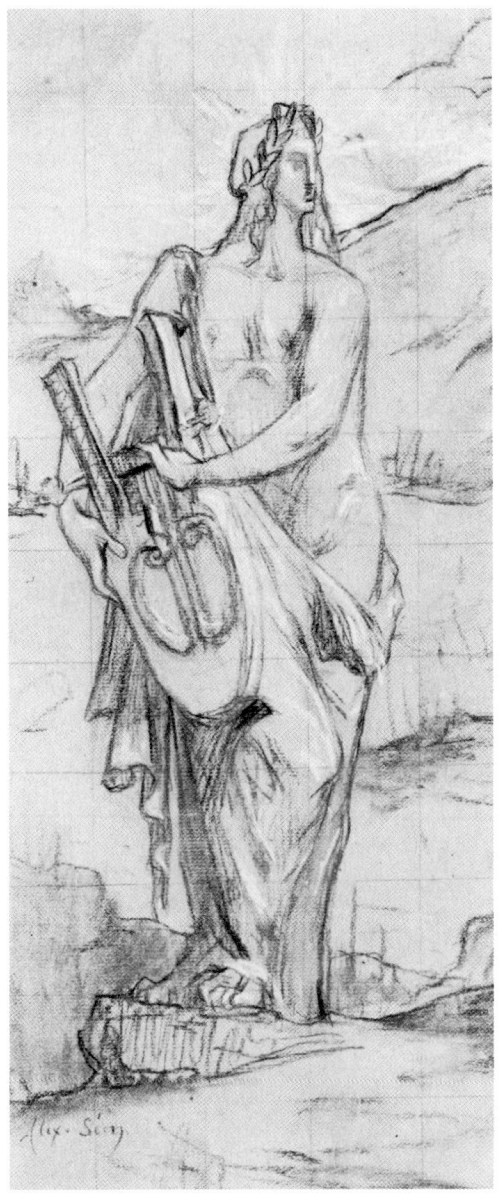

Figure 3.17. Alexandre Séon, *Orpheus*, ca. 1890
Pencil and chalk drawing.
(Private collection, Paris; photo courtesy Galerie Coligny, Paris)

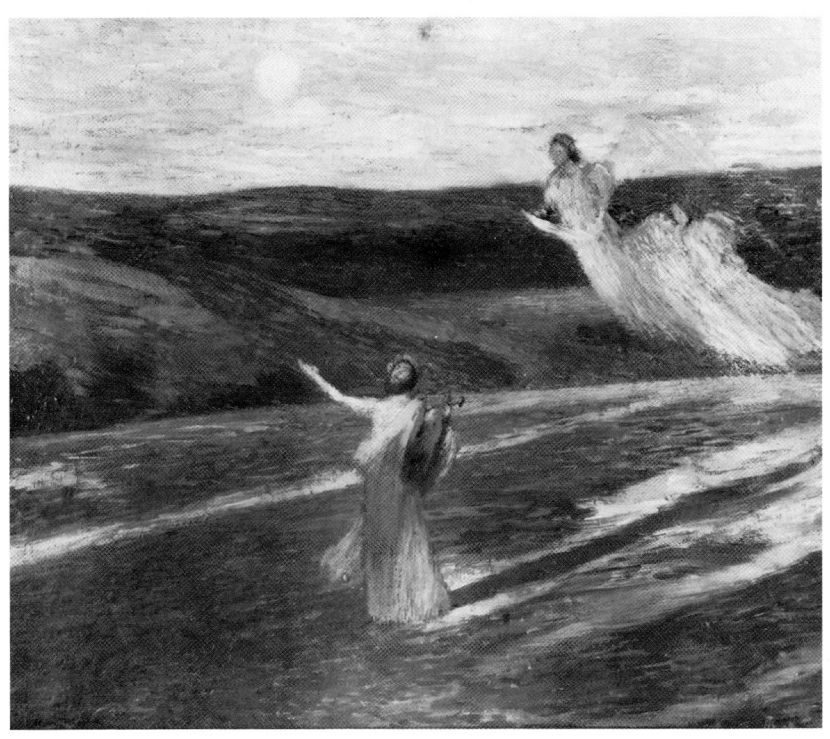

Figure 3.18. Henri Martin, *Orpheus*, ca. 1894
Oil on canvas.
(Musée des Beaux-Arts, Dijon)

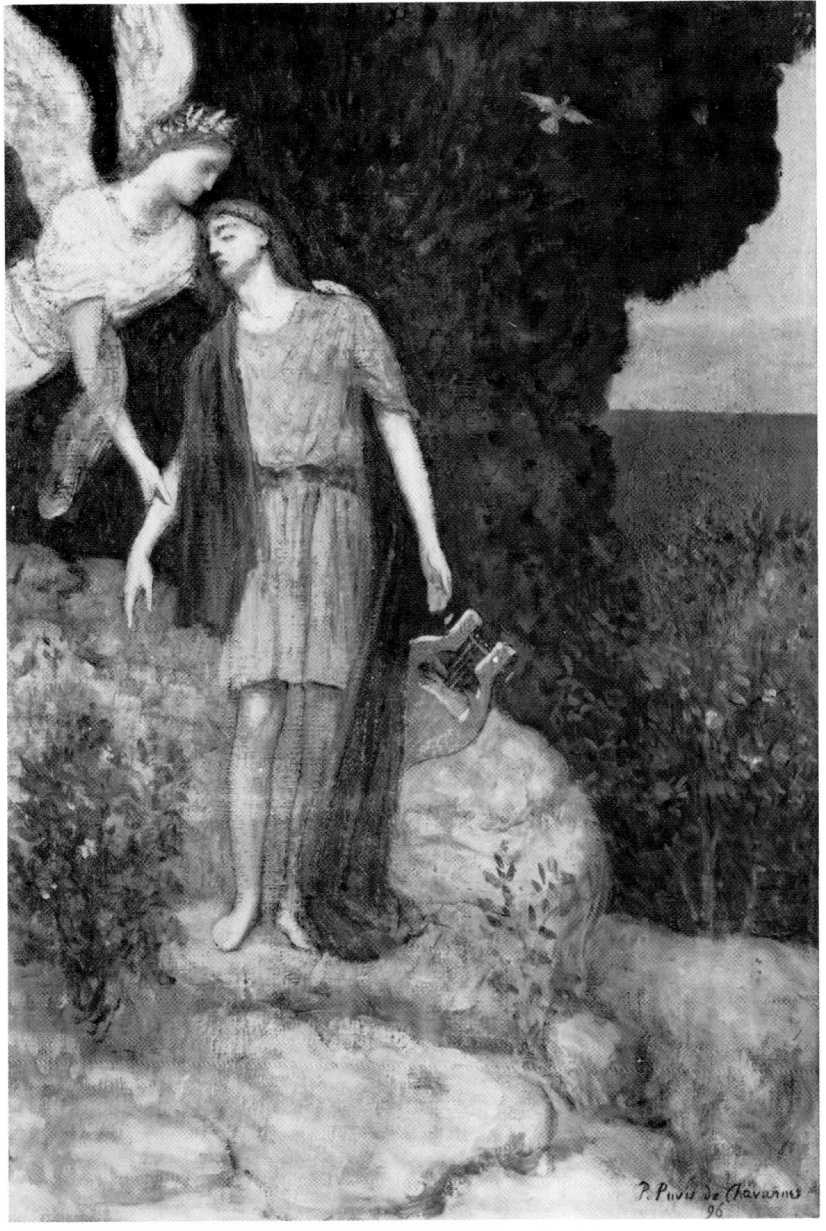

Figure 3.19. Pierre Puvis de Chavannes, *The Poet*, ca. 1896
Oil on canvas.
(Photo courtesy Sotheby's, London)

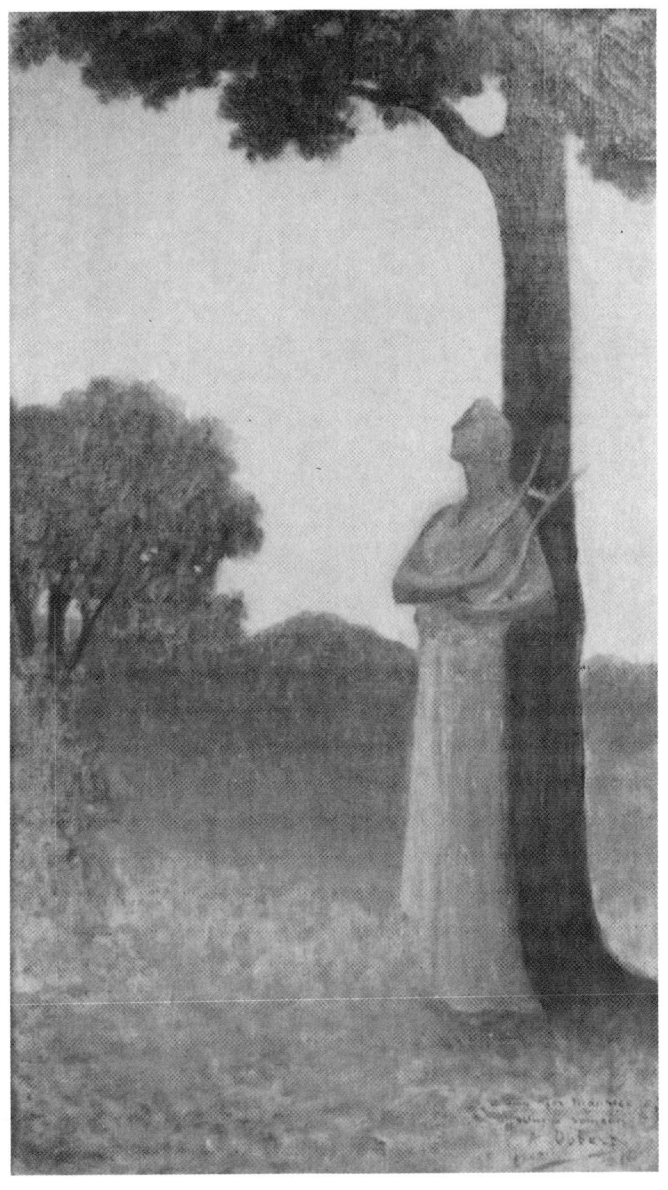

Figure 3.20. Alphonse Osbert, *Orphée*, 1902
Oil on canvas.
(Private collection, Paris)

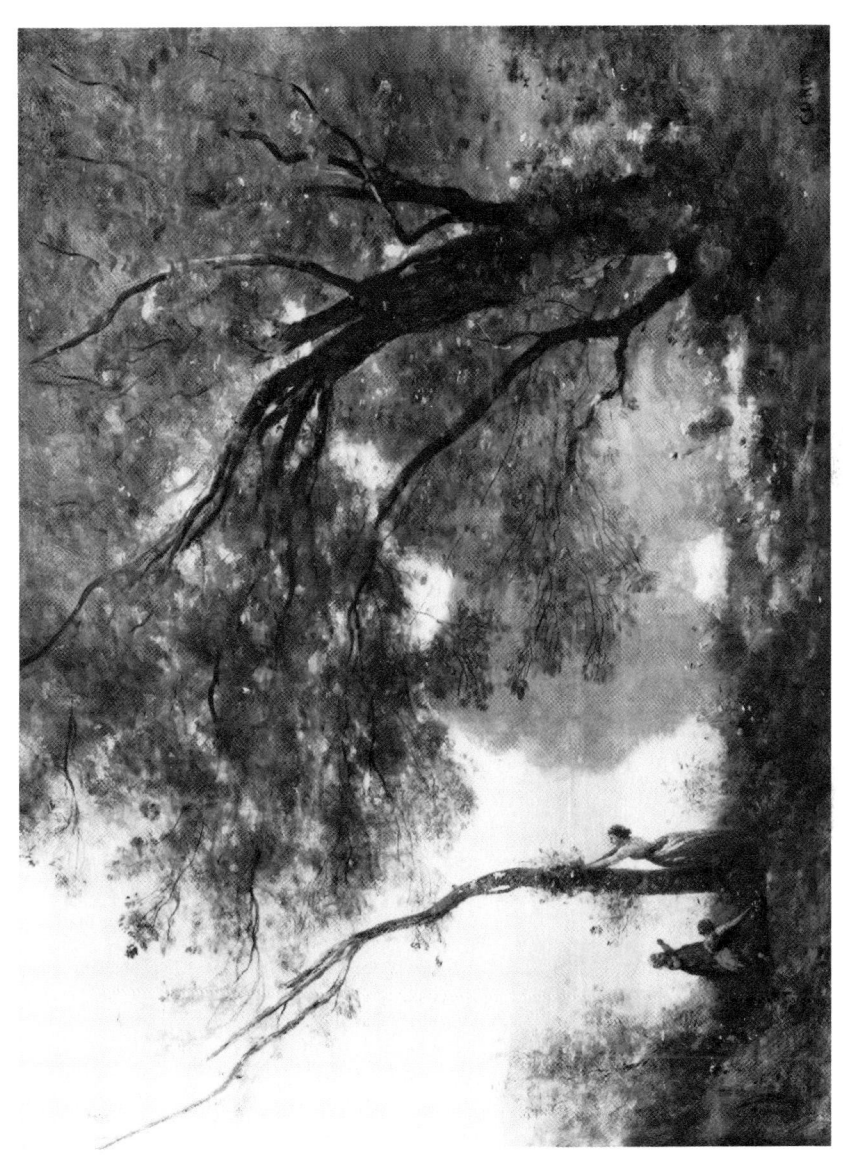

Figure 3.21. Camille Corot, *Souvenir de Mortefontaine*, 1864
Oil on canvas.
(*Louvre, Paris; Cliché des Musées Nationaux, Paris*)

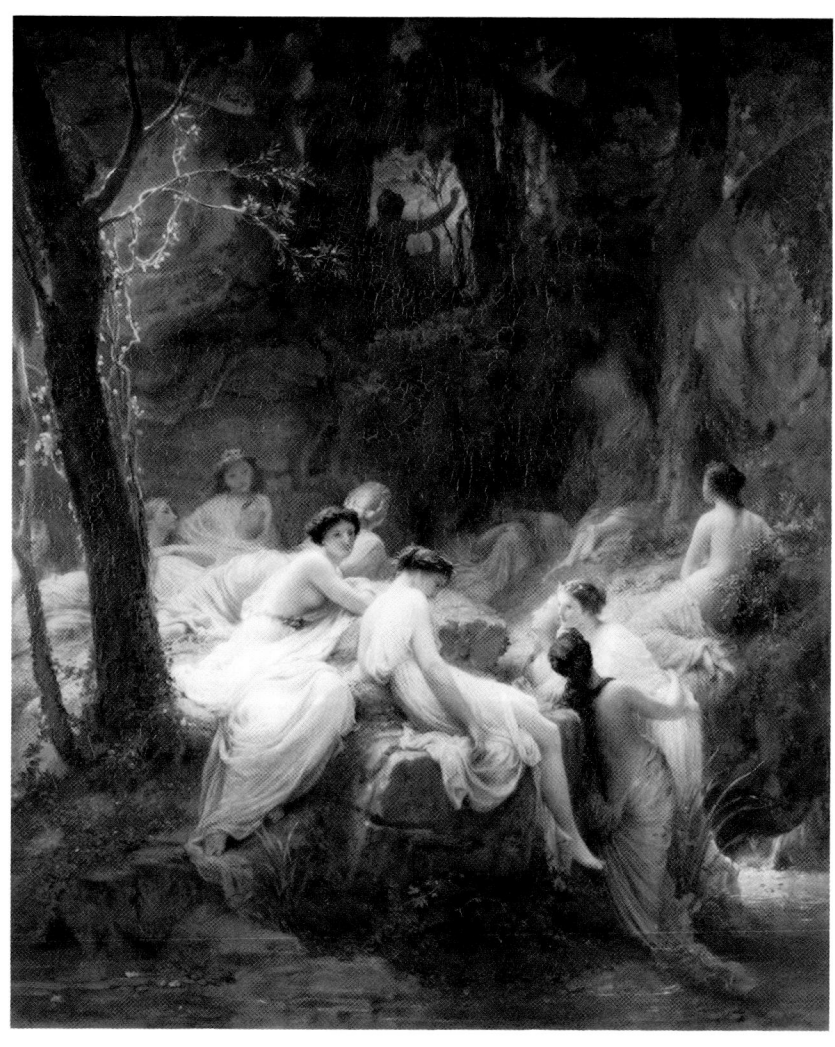

Figure 3.22. Charles François Jalabert, *Orpheus*, 1853
Oil on canvas.
(Walters Art Gallery, Baltimore)

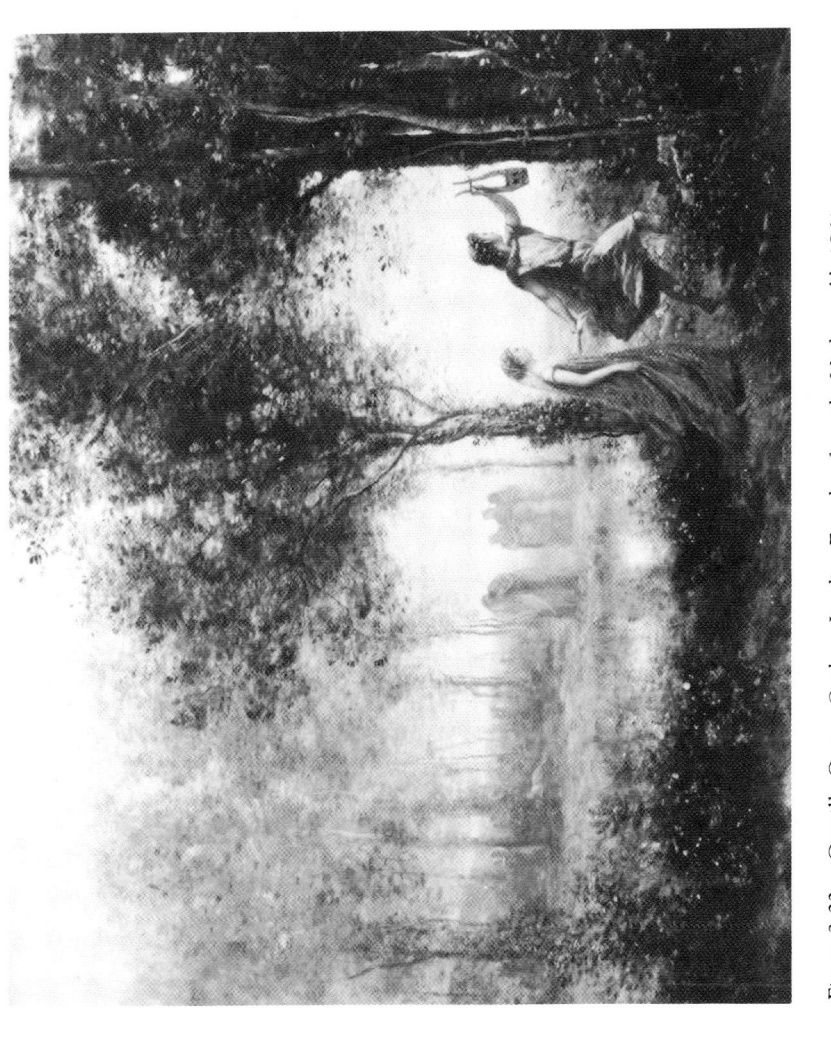

Figure 3.23. Camille Corot, *Orpheus Leading Eurydice from the Underworld*, 1861 Oil on canvas.
(*The Museum of Fine Arts, Houston; Museum purchase with funds provided by the Agnes Cullen Arnold Endowment Fund*)

4

Orpheus and Eurydice: Orpheus in Hades

Eurydice's role is significantly diminished in the Symbolists' interpretations of the myth of Orpheus. There are certainly masterworks in the course of the nineteenth century—by Corot, Feuerbach, and Lord Leighton, for instance—which deal with the high drama surrounding Orpheus' descent into Hades and his ultimately ill-fated attempt to retrieve Eurydice. Nonetheless, it is clear that in the works of the Symbolist artists under discussion here—Moreau, Puvis, Séon, Redon, Rodin, Delville, and von Stuck—this aspect of the mythic narrative is relatively deemphasized. Indeed, the Symbolists appear to intentionally reject the most popular tradition, stemming from Ovid's *Metamorphoses* and Virgil's *Georgics*, which focused on Eurydice's death and Orpheus' subsequent heroism and desperate grief.[1] The Symbolists, in their insistence on Orpheus' sacerdotal role, quite naturally objected to the undue dominance of the romance and the suppression or even elimination of the tragic consequences and religious implications of the myth through the imposition of a happy ending, as, for instance, in the eighteenth-century Gluck/Calzabigi opera, *Orfeo ed Euridice* (fig. 4.1), or culminating in the parody of the myth in the Offenbach/Cremieux *Orphée aux enfers* (fig. 4.2).[2]

Nineteenth-century depictions of this aspect of the myth focus on rather specific moments with distinct psychological or emotionel tenor: Orpheus' impassioned plea to Pluto and the assembled court of the Underworld; Orpheus, still averting his eyes, leading forth Eurydice; his fateful glance itself; or finally, the actual disappearance of Eurydice.

Orpheus Pleads before Pluto

Henri Regnault's *Orphée aux enfers*, revealing his training with Cabanel, is typical of an interpretation popular in the first half of the nineteenth century, which focuses on the hero-poet pleading before a panoramic assemblage of the regal personages of Hades. Orpheus stands before the ruler of the Underworld, his hands sweeping the strings of his massive lyre, enchanting the god and his consort, the three Fates, even Cerberus at his feet (figs. 4.3, 4.4). At the right is an Ingre-inspired Eurydice, clasping her hands, pleading for her liberation (fig. 4.5).[3]

In *Orpheus in Hades*, 1899 (fig. 4.6), Pierre Amédée Marcel-Beronneau's Hades is an environment of incredible macabre detail. The poet's nude body is finely delineated. His wreathed head is thrown back in closed-eyed ecstasy. His figure, as well as his extravagantly carved lyre are bathed in a glowing, unearthly light. In stark contrast to his idealized beauty are the contorted, writhing bodies and the haunted, staring faces of the dead, devoured by a multitude of serpents, nearly enveloped by arching, entangled briars. The cliff in the background seems to ooze, a breathing mass of undulating forms: snakes, lizards, serpent-haired figures, owls, bats, tortured plants. In the midst of this frightening environment sits the impassive Pluto, his figure dominated by a huge white beard, a crown of snakes emerging from his head.

Marcel-Beronneau studied with Gustave Moreau. The dense accumulation of detail is consistent with Moreau's concept of "necessary richness." The mass of bodies and anatomical fragments is, in fact, reminiscent of the victims in Moreau's *Les Lyres mortes* or *Tyrtée*. Marcel-Beronneau's later works, most frequently depictions of Salome, are also characterized by this dense, jewel-like pattern. The poet's androgynous beauty also clearly reflects Moreau's physical ideal. Moreover, Marcel-Beronneau clearly has adopted Moreau's insistent theme of the poet's pathetic heroism. Hermes, other members of the royal entourage, even Eurydice herself, are excluded in order to give full emphasis to the poet's foray into this frightening otherworld. Orpheus is the laurel-wreathed hierophant rather than the distraught lover—a figure of ideal beauty and spiritual strength, whose transport of emotional or artistic ecstasy shields him from the evil and ugliness of the Underworld. However, the grandeur of Orpheus' descent is somewhat diminished by elements of melodrama, such as the flashlight-glare emanating from the eyes of the Michelangelesque figure of Pluto.

Jean Delville's *Orpheus*, 1896 (fig. 4.7), is also a lithe, androgynous figure, of striking beauty. A bit of drapery coils about his legs, resembling an extension of the orange flames that permeate the hellish landscape. Simeon Solomon emphasizes, as well, the horrific aspects of the Underworld, filled with bizarre creatures and frightening terrain. A phantomlike Eurydice floats nearby, in the arms of a winged female, perhaps the figure of death (fig. 4.8).

In *Orpheus Returning from the Shades*, 1900 (fig. 4.9), Sir William Blake Richmond depicts Orpheus entirely alone, his arms thrown up in despair, his chest bursting with anguish, his drapery swept dramatically back by some unearthly force. The sheer cliffs, dark crevices and cracked rocks in Richmond's painting prompt comparison to the dark and ominous landscape in Percy Bysshe Shelley's *Orpheus*:

> On one side of this jagged and shapeless hill
> There is a cave, from which there eddies up
> A pale mist, like aereal gossamer,
> Whose breath destroys all life—awhile it veils
> The rock.[4]

Richmond's figure of Orpheus is comparable to Shelley's description of the poet:

> . . . so Orpheus, seized and torn
> By the sharp fangs of an insatiable grief,
> Maenad-like waved his lyre in the bright air,
> And wildly shrieked 'Where she is, it is dark!'[5]

In comparable fashion, a small drawing by Burne-Jones (fig. 4.10) presents the violin-playing poet, a heroic nude, standing amidst a landscape of sheer cliffs and watery passages. In 1879 Burne-Jones devoted the entire decorative scheme for the "Graham" piano to the myth of Orpheus and Eurydice. He included a depiction of Eurydice's death but also gave special attention to Orpheus' journey to Hades, with separate roundels devoted to the fateful glance and Eurydice swept away (figs. 4.11, 4.12, 4.13).[6]

Orpheus Leads Forth Eurydice

Depictions of Orpheus leading forth Eurydice from the Underworld explore the emotional or psychological tension, the incredible terror or expectant joy of the lovers. Orpheus is sometimes portrayed as unflinching in his resolve, or wavering in confidence. Eurydice is sometimes the model of calm patience or otherwise torn with unrestrained anxiety.

Camille Corot

This episode enjoyed considerable popularity in the 1860s. Corot's *Orpheus Leading Back Eurydice*, 1861 (see fig. 3.23), depicts the wreathed poet holding his lyre aloft in front of him, while leading Eurydice forward with his other hand. She is a young girl, very passive, her arms limp, as though they have not yet regained their life energy. Actually, Orpheus clasps her wrist and her hand hangs loosely in his grasp. Her veiled head is turned with an intense gaze toward her husband. The Elysian fields are evoked in the suggestive, poetic style typical of the artist's late works—a landscape of delicate trees aglow with a gentle light.[7]

Anselm Feuerbach

Corot's delicate poetry contrasts sharply with the severe classicism of Anselm Feuerbach's *Orpheus and Eurydice* (fig. 4.14), dating from eight years later. In this work, the monumental figures of Orpheus and Eurydice, fully draped in the heavy folds of classical garb, fill the entire canvas. There are only minimal indications of the surrounding: the outline of huge boulders at the right and a glowing light penetrating the darkness at the upper left. Orpheus stares intently at that light while leading his wife gently but firmly with an arm around her waist. Feuerbach emphasizes a nobility of spirit: Orpheus' concentration and dedication to purpose and Eurydice's touching humility and compliance. She walks with downcast eyes, clutching her garment to herself.[8] There is no expression of anxiety, weakness or failure in Feuerbach's interpretation. Rather, this work is entirely consistent with the artist's ideal of "truly majestic, forbidding tranquility."[9] The gravity of the moment, the ultimate tragedy of the story, is expressed through the dramatic contrasts of dark and light, the marmoreal quality of the drapery (the figures stand in a rather compressed space, resembling carvings on a bas-relief or frieze), each of the minute folds illuminated with a harsh raking light, and in the airless atmosphere, the sense of eerie stillness that pervades the work. The small figure of flayed Marsyas, carved on Orpheus' lyre, offers a mythical parallel to Orpheus, underscores his link to Apollo and suggests his ultimate doom.[10]

Elie Delaunay

Elie Delaunay's beautiful sketch, ca. 1870 (fig. 4.15), for his painting in the Grand Foyer of the Paris Opéra, portrays Orpheus, under the watchful eyes of Hermes and Cerberus, about to emerge with Eurydice into the light of this world. The poet's eye, though not yet his head, is turned back towards Eurydice, an almost comical indication of his torment and wavering resolve.

Auguste Rodin

Later in the century, ca. 1893, Rodin interprets this episode of the Orpheus myth (fig. 4.16).[11] Here the couple emerges from a mass of roughly hewn marble, a palpable manifestation of the darkness of the Underworld which they are attempting to flee. The stone curls forward to form a wave of solid matter between the lovers. Also, Eurydice is not entirely separated from the stone around her—the darkness and impenetrability of death. Indeed, she seems entrapped by the heavy matter: her hair merges with the flowing mass of rock behind her; her feet are at one with the material upon which they stand. Orpheus walks before her, conscientiously shielding his eyes with one hand.

Orpheus' face is tense with concentration and anguish. Eurydice's visage is inclined toward him imploringly, wracked with desire. Rodin establishes compelling contrast between Orpheus' physical constraint and emotional severity and Eurydice's barely restrained passion. The focus is on the harsh conditions of Eurydice's release, the gods' cruel interdiction that Orpheus must not gaze on his wife until they have reached earth. This demand is the source of intense emotional upheaval, with Orpheus denied the natural joy and ebullient emotions on retrieving his lover, and Eurydice forced to endure long moments of confusion, doubt, and fear, with no explanation for Orpheus' refusal to communicate. While Corot and Feuerbach emphasized the heroic or calm moments of stoic control, Rodin emplores inner conflict with gestures of quiet tension and despair.

Orpheus' Fateful Glance

Lord Leighton

British artists at mid-century—including Lord Leighton, George Frederick Watts, and Charles Ricketts—apparently preferred the moment of highest drama, when restraint crumbles and the fateful glance occurs. Indeed, this episode is ideally suited to the Victorians' penchant for transforming myths into stories of very human love and conflicts. Lord Leighton's 1864 Royal Academy submission, *Orpheus and Eurydice* (fig. 4.17), was exhibited with the text of Robert Browning's poem, "Eurydice."[12] In this painting, Eurydice pulls insistently on Orpheus' clothing with one hand, while drawing his head to her with her other hand. Just as firmly, the poet resists her attention, pushing violently away from her, turning his head away, his face contorted with painful dismay, even anger or disgust. Similarly, the "immortal look,"[13] is the focus of Browning's verse. The poem consists of Eurydice's imploring, insistent plea to Orpheus:

> All woe that was
> Forgotten, and all terror that may be,
> Defied, no past is mine, no future: look at me![14]

In these works, Eurydice is the active agent who openly courts disaster by brazenly dismissing caution.

Similarly, another British poem from mid-century, by a little known poet, Francis William Bourdillon, focuses on Eurydice's role in the tragedy. In this interpretation she is less the willful temptress, and more the weak victim of her own overwhelming emotions. It is Eurydice herself who speaks:

> I followed through the cavern black;
> I saw the blue above.
> Some terror turned me to look back:
> I heard him wail, "O love!
> What hast thou done! What hast thou done!"
> And then I saw no more the sun,
> And lost were life and love.[15]

George Frederick Watts

Between 1869 and 1903, George Frederick Watts painted several versions of *Orpheus and Eurydice* (fig. 4.18). In contrast to Lord Leighton's work, or perhaps in direct response to it, Watts chooses a slightly later moment in the drama, the fateful gaze itself. More significantly, he establishes a different emotional or psychological reading. Here, it is Orpheus himself who turns to his wife who instantly collapses lifeless. The painting is filled with dramatic action, as Orpheus violently turns his entire body, desperately attempting to pull his beloved toward him. The composition is animated with a flurry of brushstrokes, communicating the frenzy of emotion which dominates the scene.

Charles Ricketts

A small bronze by Charles Ricketts, dated 1905–7 (fig. 4.19), similarly depicts Orpheus succumbing to his overwhelming emotions. In this work Orpheus arches over backward in an extraordinary gesture, clasping Eurydice's head to his lips. The lovers' heads are brought together in their embrace, forming a poignant counterpoint to their nude bodies which arch dramatically away from each other.[16]

In the classical texts it is always Orpheus who looks back, while Eurydice is the passive object of the drama. Eurydice's reaction varies significantly, however, her words sometimes imputing no blame, at other times, charged with reproach. This difference is apparent in the texts of Ovid and Virgil. In the *Metamorphoses* there is no anger or recrimination in Eurydice's reaction:

> Dying the second time,
> She had no reproach to bring against her husband,
> What was there to complain of? One thing only:
> He loved her. He could hardly hear her calling
> *Farewell!* when she was gone.[17]

Eurydice's response in Virgil's *Georgics* is harsher:

She cried: "What madness Orpheus, what dreadful madness hath ruined my unhappy self and thee? Lo, again the cruel Fates call me back and sleep veils my swimming eyes. And now farewell! I am swept off, wrapped in uttermost night, and stretching out to thee strengthless hands, thine, alas! no more."[18]

As discussed already in chapter 1, in the medieval period Eurydice played a more active role, one, however, which transforms her into a morally inferior creature, the temptress, an agent of evil. During the nineteenth century, the Victorians are fascinated with Eurydice's role, finding her querulous nature a perfect way of investing the love story with added dramatic tension. The works discussed here focus on the dramatic moment when prudence is overwhelmed by violent emotions of doubt, anxiety and fear. These works explore the interaction of the lovers, assigning weakness and guilt.

Eurydice Swept Away

Ovid's lines capture the poignant drama of Eurydice's final and abrupt disappearance: "Was it he, or she, reaching out arms and trying to hold or to be held, and clasping nothing but empty air?"[19]

Nineteenth-century depictions of this scene are markedly alike as though they follow a similar formula. Paul Baudry includes this motif as the subject of one of the twelve vaults in the Grand Foyer of the Paris Opéra (fig. 4.20).[20] Orpheus is portrayed kneeling with arms outstretched in disbelieving protestation, as the lifeless body of his wife is spirited away by the god, Hermes.

Essentially the same composition is used by Emile Gallé on a crystal vase (fig. 4.21), exhibited at the Exposition Universelle of 1889. Here, Orpheus' sensitively carved outstretched hands are poignant expressions of his horror and grief. Eurydice's body falls backward, her hair and drapery merging with the fluid lines of the landscape behind her.

Gustave Moreau

The Symbolists, and Moreau in particular, preferred to explore the poet's lamentation or death. In Moreau's oeuvre, Eurydice appears in only a few small paintings and drawings (fig. 4.22), the object of Orpheus' depthless grief.[21] In a watercolor and gouache (fig. 4.23), the poet stands over the body of his wife, grieving with upstretched arms and wide open mouth. Eurydice's long, attenuated, Mannerist body is outstretched at his feet. The wounded swan that lies nearby, and the bird that flies away as if escaping from Orpheus' grasp, are clearly intended as symbolic equivalents of the dead wife. (The dead swan suggests comparison with Wagnerian symbolism, especially the dead swan in *Lohengrin*.) The watery, red-dominated landscape is an example of Moreau's exploration of the psychological potency of the landscape, identified by Wyzewa as "Wagnerian."[22] As will be discussed in the next chapter, the landscape becomes increasingly important for Moreau, a symbolic equivalent of intense emotion.

The Role of Eurydice in Occultist Texts

In occultist and mystical texts, Orpheus' quest for Eurydice in Hades is not interpreted as a romantic drama, but rather as the journey of initiation or *katabasis* of the priest. Eurydice, though mentioned only briefly in esoteric literature, is often transformed from lover and wife into an alchemical symbol, subsidiary, always, to Orpheus' priestly role.

Eliphas Lévi elevates the love story to the level of purified, selfless devotion, a concept, as he himself notes, comparable to the notion of Christian chivalric love. Orpheus' descent into Hades is transformed from the desperate quest of a tormented lover and grieving husband into the noble search of the priest for his spiritual counterpart.

> The story of Orpheus is a dogma, a revelation of sacerdotal destinies.... Thus must the pure man create a companion for himself, he must elevate the student to himself by devoting himself to her, and by not coveting her. It is in renouncing the object of passion that one merits to possess that one of true love.[23]

Orpheus' love for Eurydice is the alchemist's search for truth. He leads forth Eurydice with "a magnetic current."[24] Eurydice is the object of pure love, the symbol of the priest's sacerdotal devotion. Orpheus' glance, then, is his succumbing to weak, human passion. It is the abandonment of the role of hierophant.

Charrot's *Dictionnaire des termes hermétiques,* clearly influenced by Eliphas Lévi, also interprets the myth in terms of alchemy. Eurydice is presented as an abstraction—"vision, clarity, mysterious wife or the science of eternal wisdom."[25]

> Orpheus descending into Hades to retrieve Eurydice.... This is the pure man, creating for himself a companion of his own intelligence, that is to say, looking for and studying the true science.[26]

If the hierophant weakens he destroys his work, he is left without his "rod of the sorceress that had to be the wand of the magician."[27] Eurydice is symbolic of the creative act; she *is* the mystery, the hermetic truth which the initiate seeks. Their pure passion is a symbolic equivalent of the process of true science, or alchemy.[28]

For Edouard Schuré, in *Les Grands Initiés*, Orpheus is "pontiff of Thrace, high priest of the Olympian Zeus, and the revealer of the heavenly Dionysus,"[29] revealer of the universal principle of the masculine-feminine to the confusion and division of Greece.

> Far different is the light with which Orpheus shines! He beams throughout the ages with the personal ray of creating genius, whose soul in its masculine depths quivers with love for the Eternal-Feminine. Just as the perfect fusion of the masculine and of the feminine constitute the very essence and mystery of divinity, so the equilibrium of these two principles can alone produce mighty civilizations.[30]

Also, in a section of his discussion of Gustave Moreau in *Précurseurs et révoltés*, 1920, entitled "Le Cycle des grands symboles," Schuré once again discusses the universal of the feminine-masculine, "the Evolution of woman and man rejoining one another above the life of passion in the heroic life, under the inspiration of the poet."[31]

Schuré chooses a vocabulary pertinent to marriage to describe Orpheus' revelation of the universal principle to his disciple:

> The mysteries of the Bridegroom and the Bride are unveiled only to divine men. . . . Jupiter is the divine Bridegroom and Bride. This is the first mystery.[32]

Orpheus' union with Eurydice, but also that of Dionysus and Persephone articulate this principle. In *From Sphinx to Christ*, Schuré explains the heart of the Dionysian mysteries:

> We know that the drama played in the temple ended in the symbolic marriage of Persephone to the resurrected Dionysus. This union was given the name—sacred marriage. It exteriorised, so to speak, the inward phenomenon experienced by the initiates. Each of these had travelled to another world, through plunging into the depths of the subconscious, and in this Hades had found the monsters of Tartary and all the gods—Demeter, the primeval mother; Persephone, the immortal Soul; the Dionysus, the cosmic Self, the transcendent Spirit, evolving towards the truth through all his metamorphoses.[33]

Orpheus and Eurydice unite into a single being. Orpheus explains: "It was at this moment that divine Eros overpowered us, and, by a single look, Eurydice-Orpheus were united forever."[34]

In esoteric literature then, Orpheus' descent into Hades is interpreted as the ritual *katabasis* of the vates, priest, or initiate. Indeed, Schuré correctly emphasizes Orpheus' role as leader of the Orphic cults, in that the poet's quest for Eurydice in Hades is a parallel to the descent of Zagreus-Dionysus, the Orphic god, into the Underworld to retrieve his mother Semele. In like fashion, there exists a parallel between Orpheus' death by dismemberment at the hands of the Maenads, and Dionysus' fate, torn apart by the Titans.[35]

Orpheus' Glance: Meaning and Interpretations

At the heart of this episode of the myth, of course, is the mysterious condition imposed upon Orpheus not to look upon or communicate with Eurydice during their journey from Hades. This type of interdiction is a familiar element in classical mythology, the Bible, and fairy tales. In Genesis, chapter 19, Lot's wife violates the angel's instructions and looks back to see the destruction of Sodom, and is instantly transformed into a pillar of salt. Apuleius' *The Golden Ass*, books 4-6, relates the tale of Psyche. She is forced to wander the earth performing a series of superhuman tasks assigned as punishment by Venus because she disobeyed her lover, Cupid, and looked upon him while he slept. Moreover, curiosity also provokes Psyche to open the casket of beauty which she fetches from Persephone in Hades, only to be enveloped by a deadly sleep.[36] Proscribed vision or blindness as a means of punishment are central aspects of other myths: the man who looks directly at the gorgon, Medusa, is turned to stone; the shepherd Daphnis' infidelity is punished with blindness. In an important way, these taboos relate to the Christian notion of sin symbolized by the forbidden fruit of Paradise.[37] Indeed, Orpheus' transgression is perhaps most intelligible in the context of his role as priest of the Orphic cults. Like another great civilizer, Prometheus, who is punished for giving fire to man, Orpheus is perhaps punished for revealing the secrets or mysteries of the initiate to man.

Orpheus' fateful glance, rife with ambiguity and powerful drama, continues to engender compelling interpretations. In Paul Diel's *Le Symbolisme dans la mythologie grecque*, which seeks to establish the psychological essence of myths, the episode involving Eurydice is understood in terms of Orpheus' essential struggle between the Apollonian and the Dionysian. Eurydice is interpreted as "the sublime side of Orpheus, his force of Apollonian concentration."[38] She is contrasted with or opposed to "the dionysian multiplication of desires, to the Maenads, and, on a concrete plane, to the multitude of women secretly desired."[39] For Diel, then, the myth of Eurydice is essentially the story of the state of Orpheus' soul. Her death is the symbol of the death of his soul, what Diel calls "sa banalisation."[40]

The rule imposed upon his quest for Eurydice is symbolic of the ceding of his soul to banal desires.

> The condition is symbolic: Orpheus' love can be reborn, Eurydice can live again, only if Orpheus is animated only by the sublime regret transformed into the joy of finding Eurydice again.[41]

In the context of Diel's rather contrived and contradictory Freudian interpretation, Orpheus is not capable of true and profound love; his feelings are fraught with ambivalence and sentimental weakness.

> But the sublime regret, love regretted, did not entirely heal Orpheus. Debauchery remains within him in the form of perverse regret. His glance searches for perverse promises of the subconscious which he must leave behind. Orpheus gives in to the temptation to turn around; Eurydice disappears forever.[42]

His death at the hands of the Maenads is the concretization of his struggle between contradictory desires. In the version of the myth that asserts that Orpheus relinquishes his Dionysian weakness and devotes himself to Apollo, his death at the hands of the Maenads must be interpreted as an act of vengeful perversion.

Maurice Blanchot's "The Gaze of Orpheus," was the central essay in a 1955 collection of critical works entitled, *L'Espace littéraire*, a compendium which clearly reflects the allegorizing tendency of his criticism of that period. As opposed to Diel's psychological reading of the myth, for Blanchot, the gaze of Orpheus is central to his analysis of the act of writing, or more generally, the process of artistic creation.

> The act of writing begins with Orpheus' gaze, and that gaze is the impulse of desire which shatters the song's destiny and concern, and in that inspired and unconcerned decision reaches the origin, consecrates the song.[43]

Orpheus' gaze is simultaneously creation and destruction.

> Eurydice is the limit of what art can attain; concealed behind a name and covered by a veil, she is the profoundly dark point towards which art, desire, death and the night all seem to lead. She is the instant in which the essence of the night approaches as the *other* night.[44]

Blanchot defines Orpheus' goal as "the work," in the rarified, metaphysical sense intended by Mallarmé. "His *work* is to bring it (the dark point, Eurydice) back into the daylight and in the daylight give it form, figure and reality." Yet, Orpheus' fate is to destroy that which he seeks.[45] The gaze destroys Eurydice, ruins his work. And yet, it is at the same time, inspiration. It is the act of impatient desire that plunges the artist into the depths of ruin and death, and yet frees the work from the limits of control, concern and law.

> To look at Eurydice without concern for the song, in the impatience and imprudence of a desire which forgets the law—this is inspiration.[46]

The gaze is the artist's confrontation with chance, fate, the unknown, the unconscious, death.

> Inspiration means the ruin of Orpheus and the certainty of his ruin, and it does not promise the success of the work as compensation, anymore than in the work it affirms Orpheus' ideal triumph or Eurydice's survival (p. 102). [Yet] it is also only in this gaze that the work can go beyond itself, unite with its origin and establish itself in impossibility.[47]

The gaze of Orpheus is, then, inspiration, the inherently self-destructive impulse of the creative act. For Blanchot, art, or more specifically, writing, is a result of this incredible contradiction.

> He loses Eurydice because he desires her beyond the measured limits of the song, and he loses himself too, but this desire, and Eurydice lost, and Orpheus scattered are necessary to the song.[48]

In the context of the Symbolists' overriding emphasis on Orpheus' priestly function, Eurydice's role, the poignant tale of undying love and heroic encounter with the terrors of Hades diminishes in importance. The poet's descent into Hades—if submerged, remains, however, important, the *sine qua non* of his priestly powers, his *katabasis*, the passage to initiation.

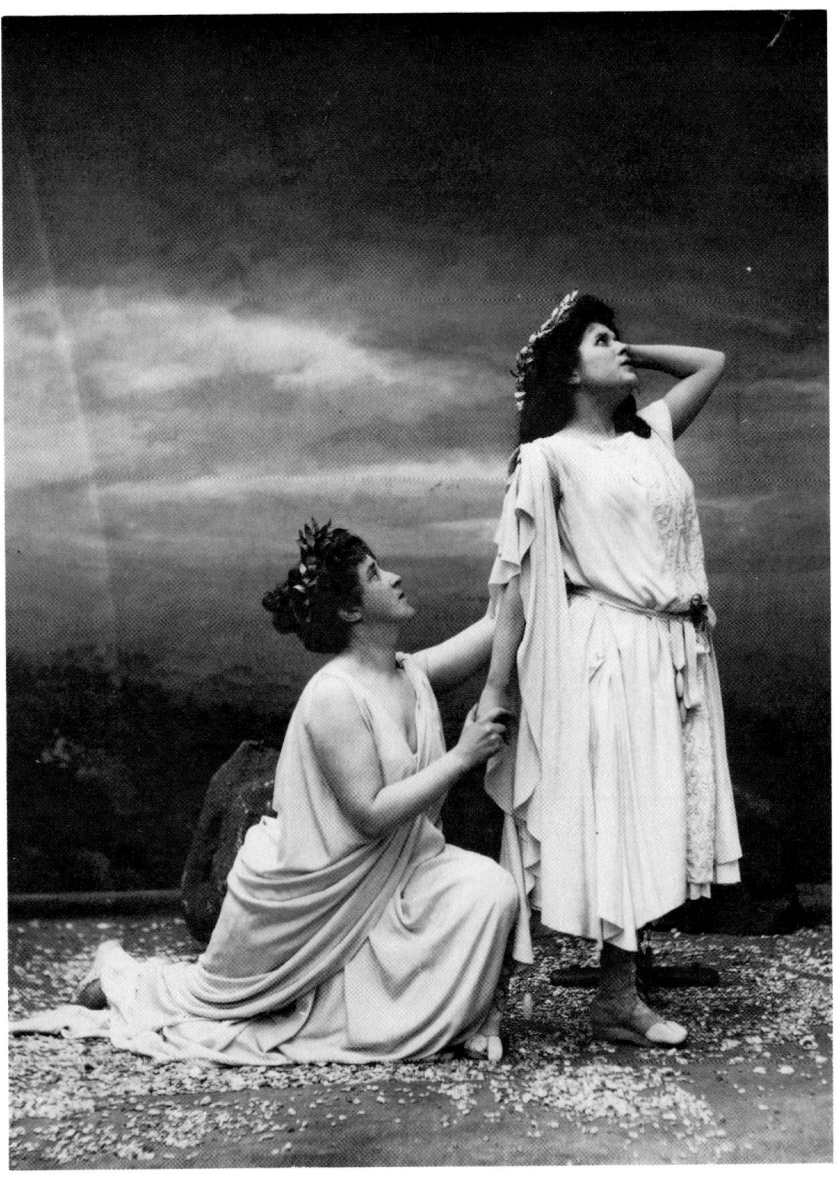

Figure 4.1. Paul Nadar, Photograph of Mmes. Gerville-Réache and Holmstrand as Orpheus and Eurydice in Gluck's *Orphée*, 1900
(Copyright Arch. Phot. Paris/SPADEM; PRO LITTERIS, Zurich)

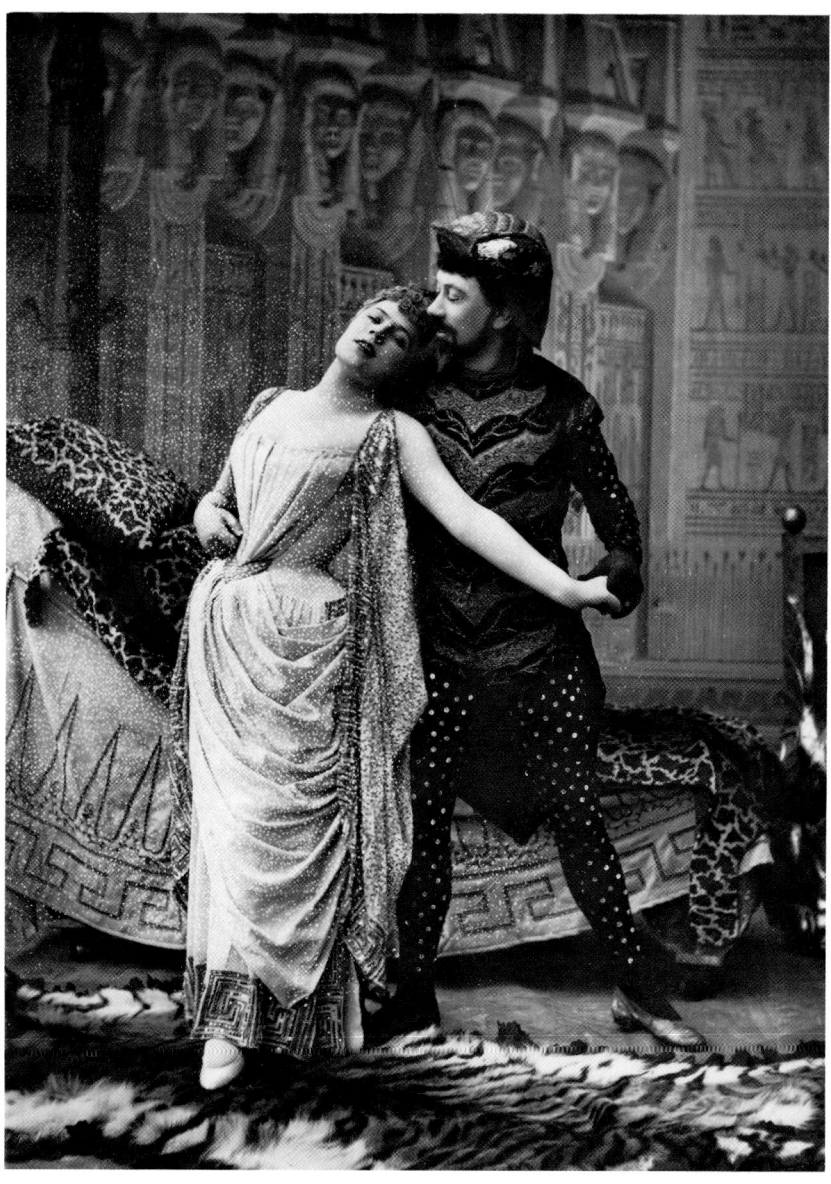

Figure 4.2. Paul Nadar, Photograph of Jeanne Granier and M. Vauthiers as Eurydice and Jupiter in Offenbach's *Orphée aux enfers*, 1887
(Copyright Arch. Phot. Paris/SPADEM; PRO LITTERIS, Zurich)

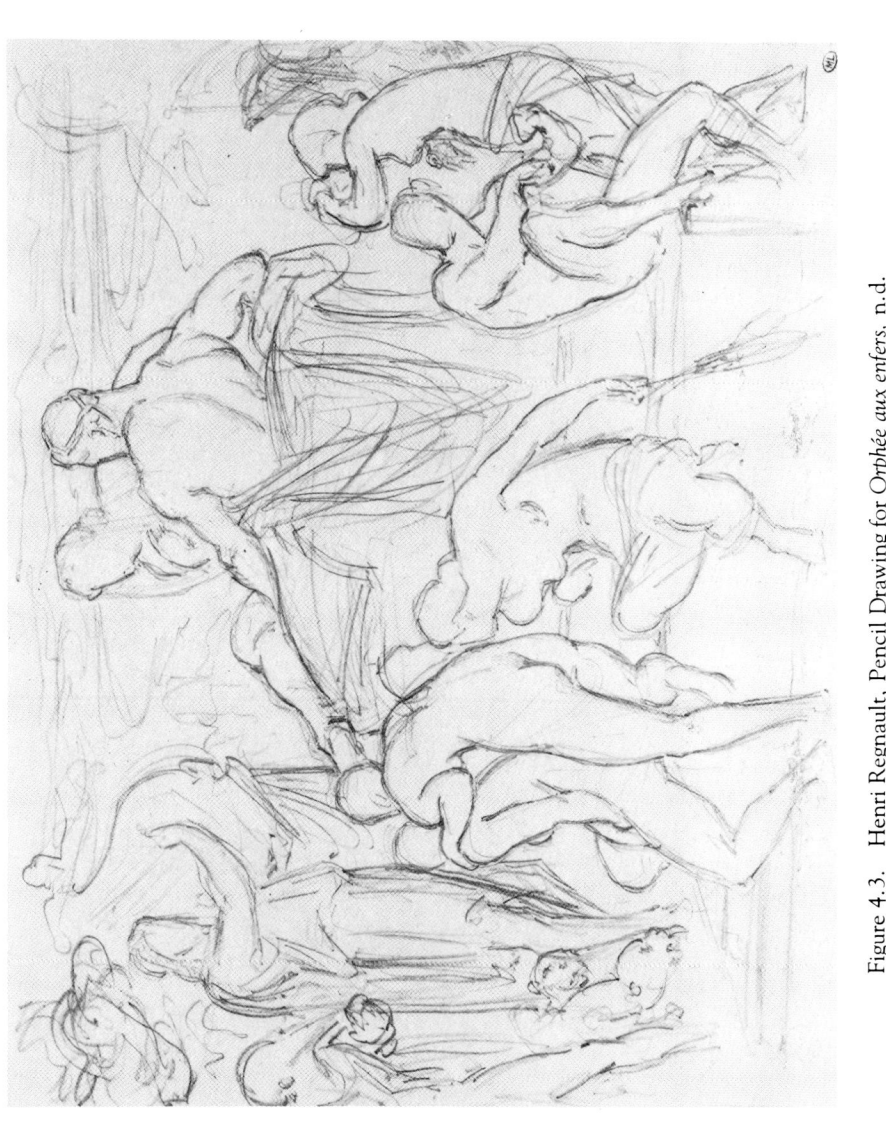

Figure 4.3. Henri Regnault, Pencil Drawing for *Orphée aux enfers*, n.d. (*Cabinet des Dessins, Louvre, Paris; Cliché des Musées Nationaux, Paris*)

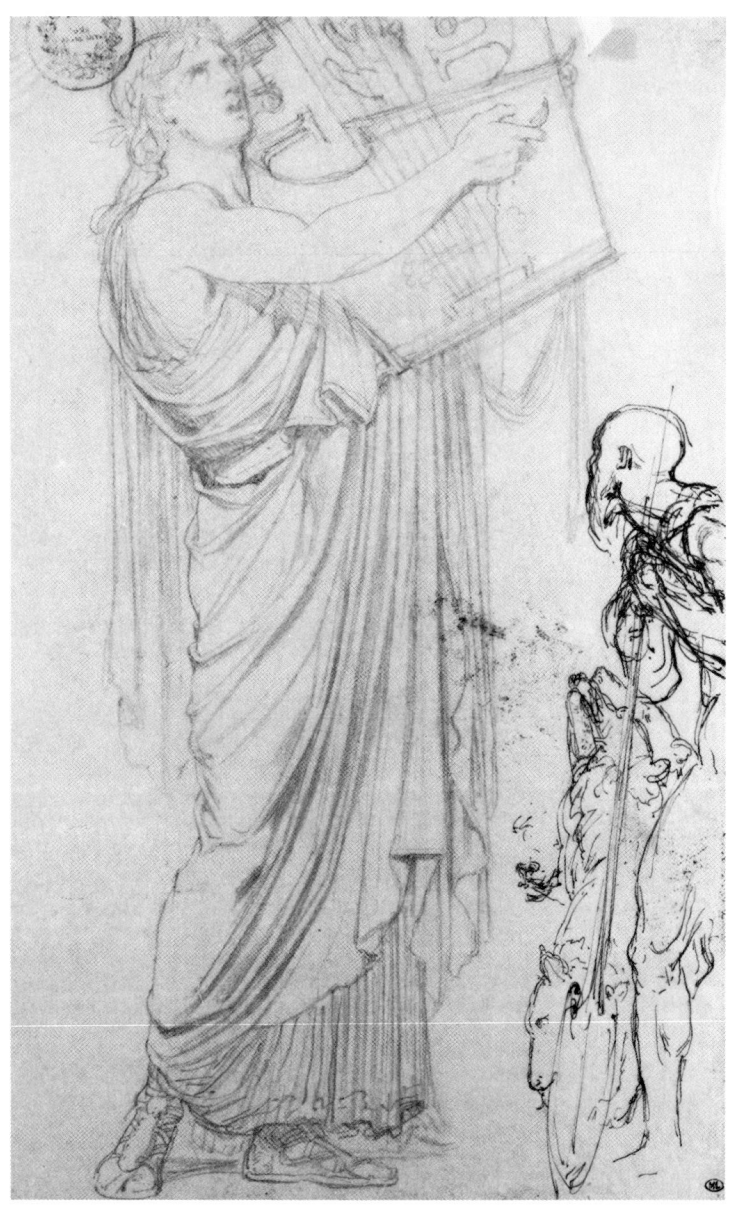

Figure 4.4. Henri Regnault, Pencil and Ink Drawing for *Orphée aux enfers*, n.d.
(*Cabinet des Dessins, Louvre, Paris; Cliché des Musées Nationaux, Paris*)

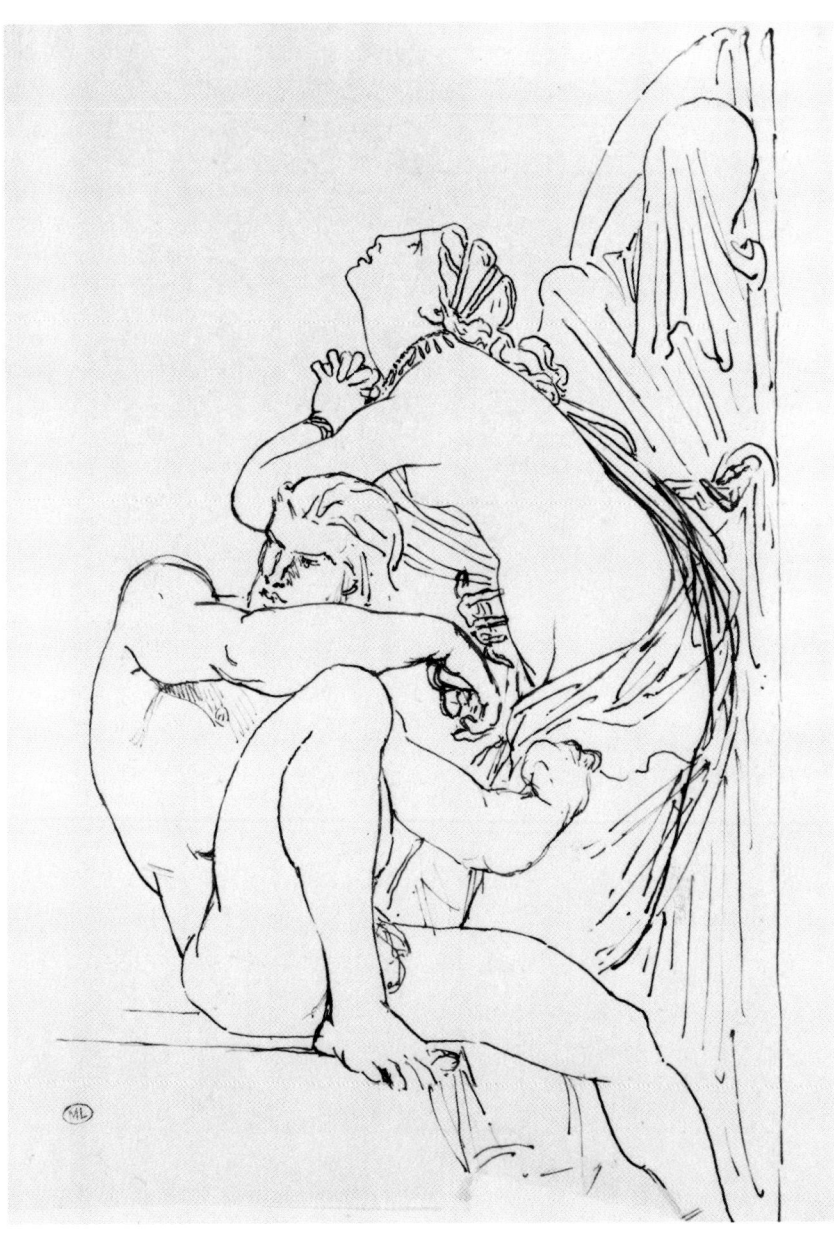

Figure 4.5. Henri Regnault, Ink Drawing for *Orphée aux enfers*, n.d. *(Cabinet des Dessins, Louvre, Paris; Cliché des Musées Nationaux, Paris)*

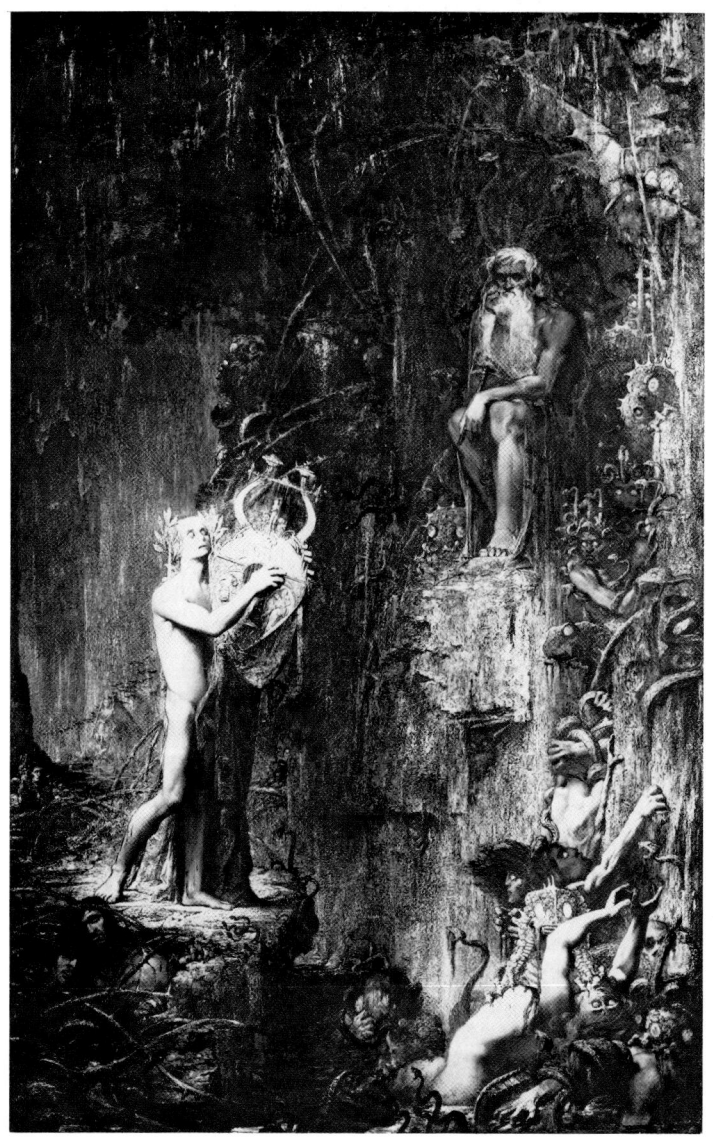

Figure 4.6. P. A. Marcel-Beronneau, *Orpheus in Hades*, 1899
Oil on canvas.
(*Musée des Beaux-Arts, Marseille*; photo: N. D. Roger-Viollet, Paris)

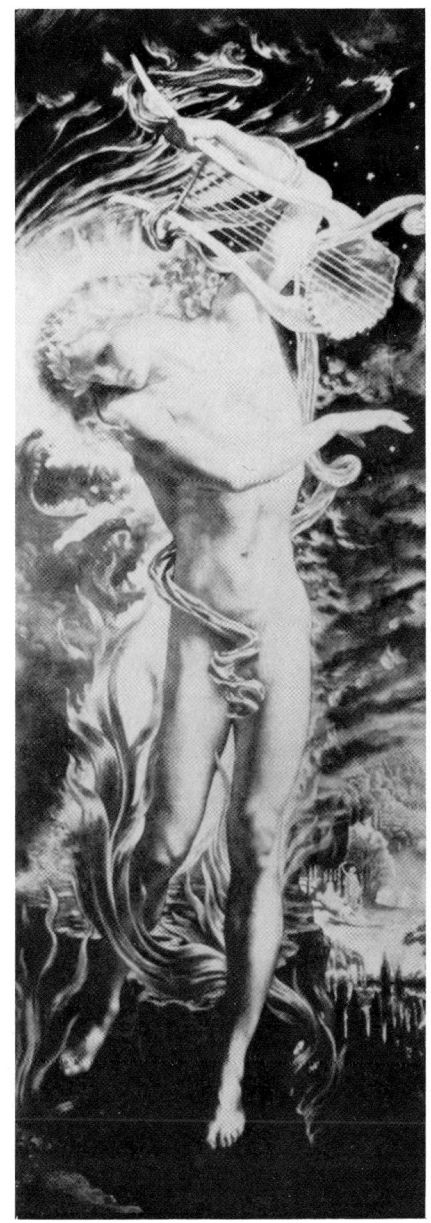

Figure 4.7. Jean Delville, *Orpheus*, 1896 Oil on canvas.
(Photo: Galerie Hasenclever, Munich)

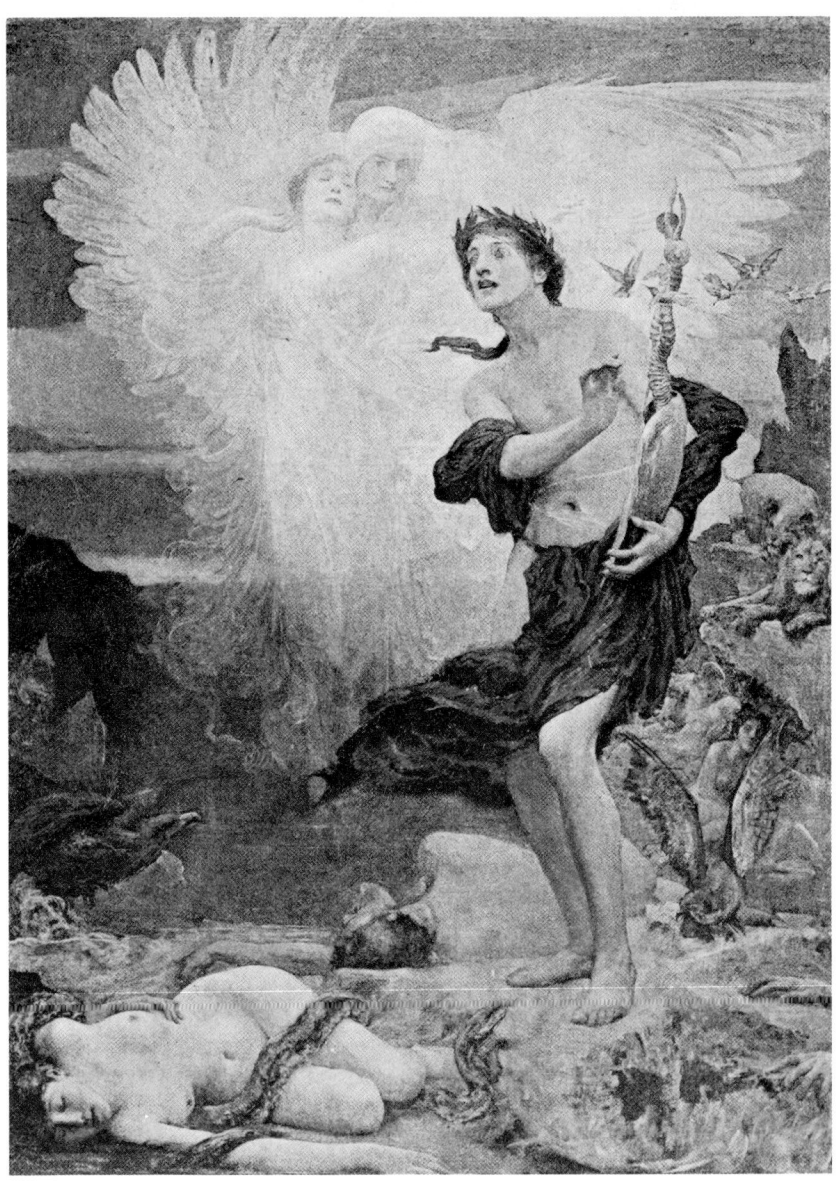

Figure 4.8. Solomon J. Solomon, *Orpheus*, 1892
(*Photo courtesy Frick Art Reference Library*)

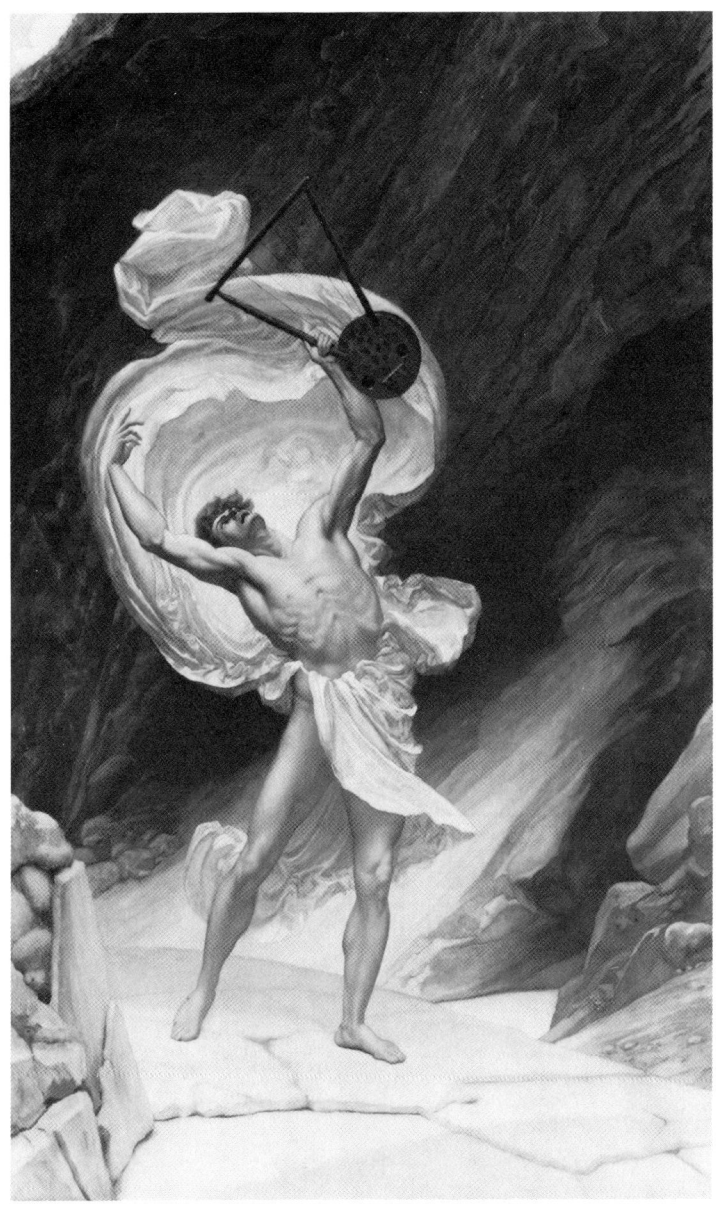

Figure 4.9. Sir William Blake Richmond, *Orpheus Returning from the Shades*, 1900
Oil on canvas.
(Royal Academy of Arts, London)

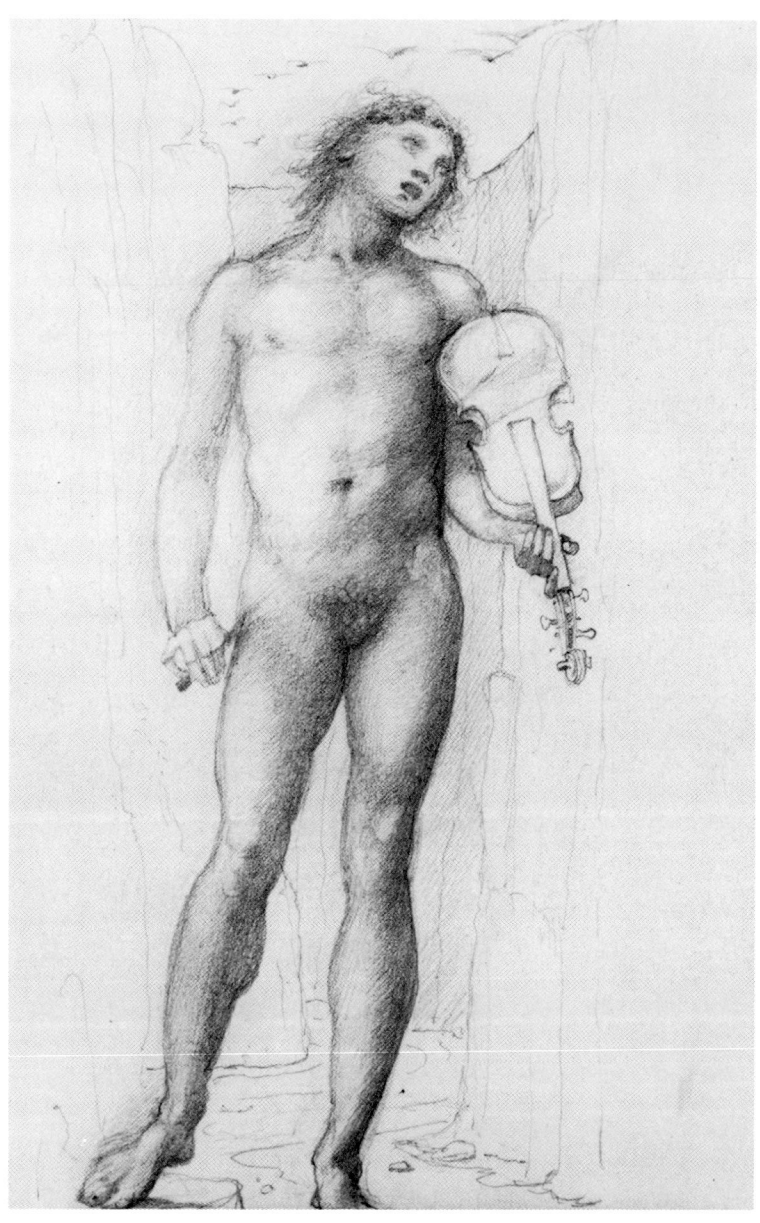

Figure 4.10. Edward Burne-Jones, *Orpheus*, 1870–72
Pencil drawing.
(*Barry Friedman Gallery, New York; photo eeva-inkeri*)

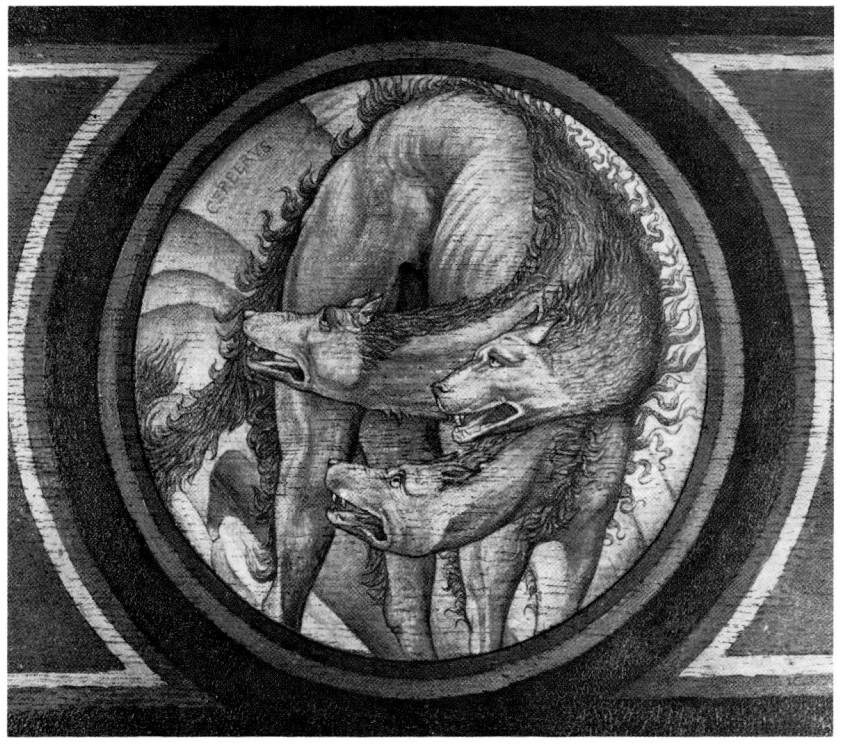

Figure 4.11. Edward Burne-Jones, *Cerberus*
Oil on wood panel on the "Graham" piano, 1879–80.
(*Private Collection; photo: Colin Wilson*)

Figure 4.12. Edward Burne-Jones, *The Death of Eurydice*. Oil on wood panel on the "Graham" piano, 1879–80. (*Private Collection; photo: Colin Wilson*)

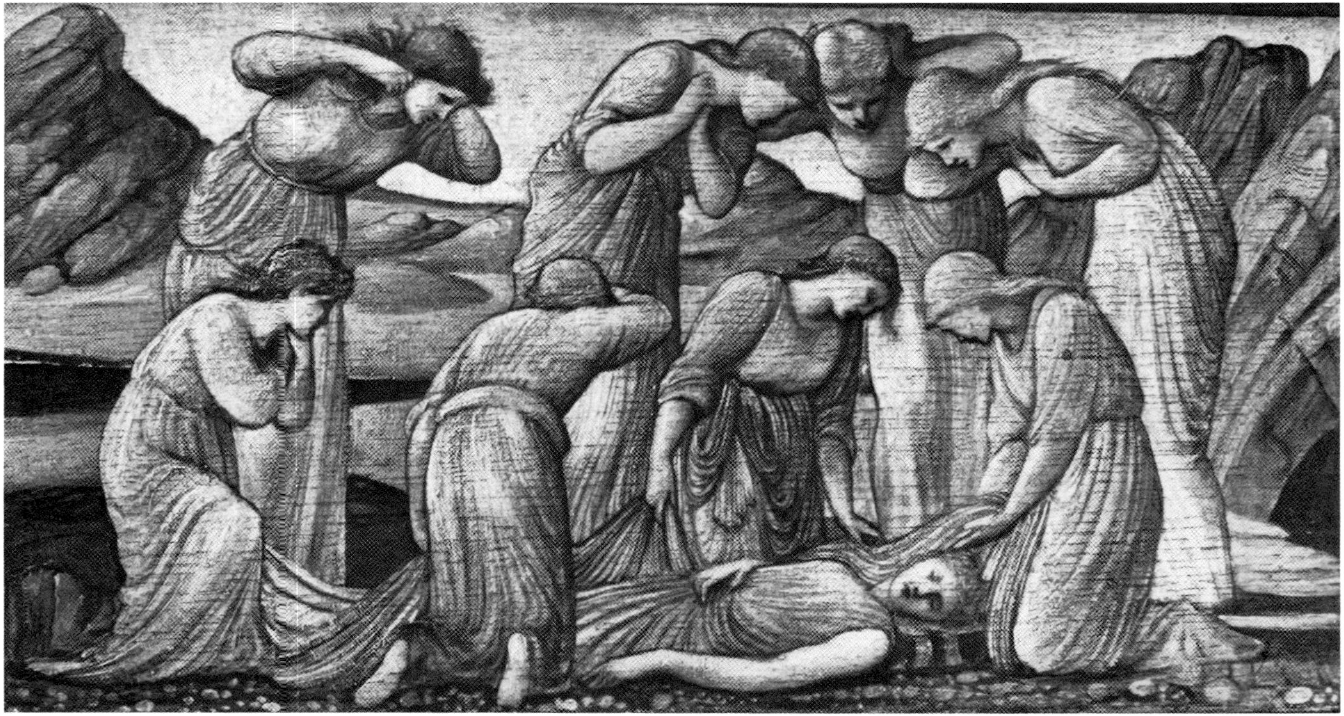

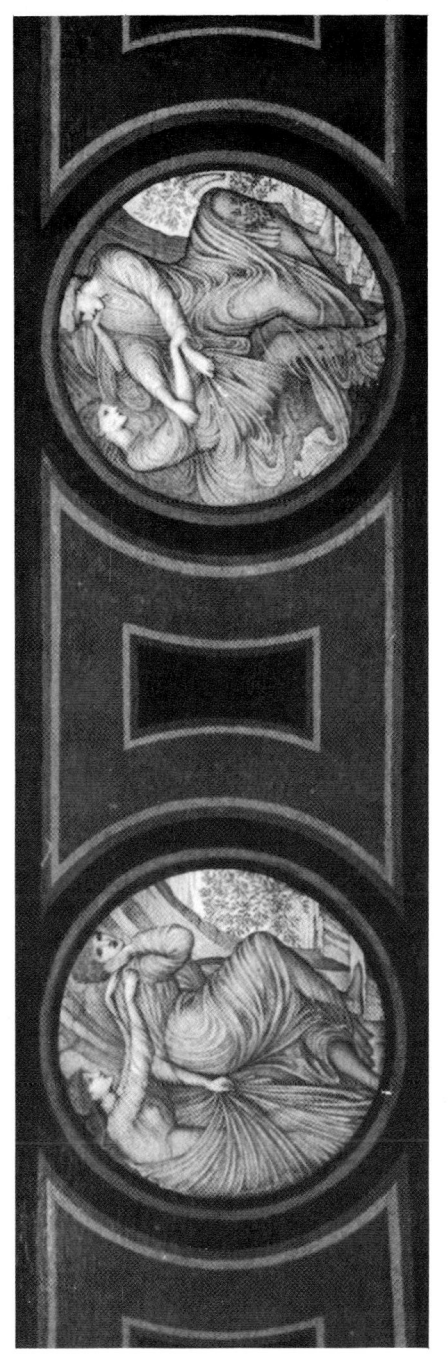

Figure 4.13. Edward Burne-Jones, *Orpheus and Eurydice*. Oil on wood panel on the "Graham" piano, 1879–80. *(Private Collection; photo: Colin Wilson)*

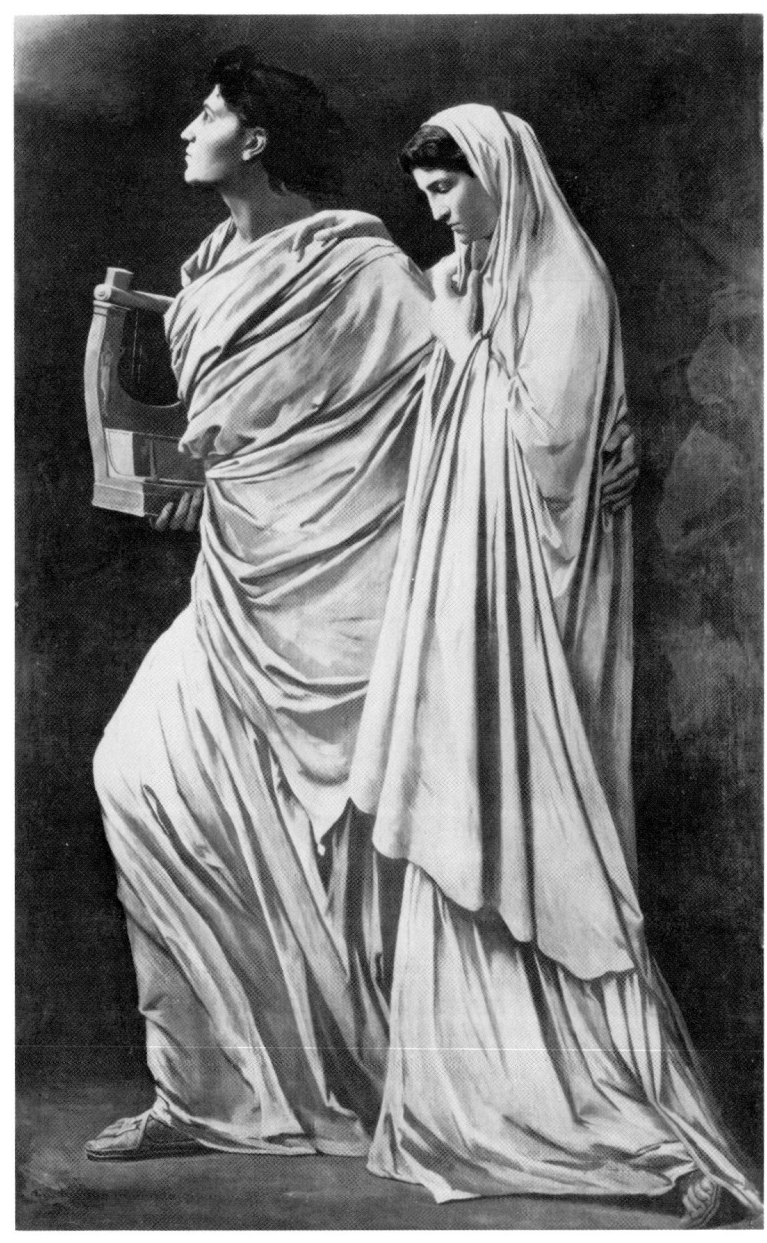

Figure 4.14. Anselm Feuerbach, *Orpheus and Eurydice*, 1869
Oil on canvas.
(Kunsthistorisches Museum, Vienna)

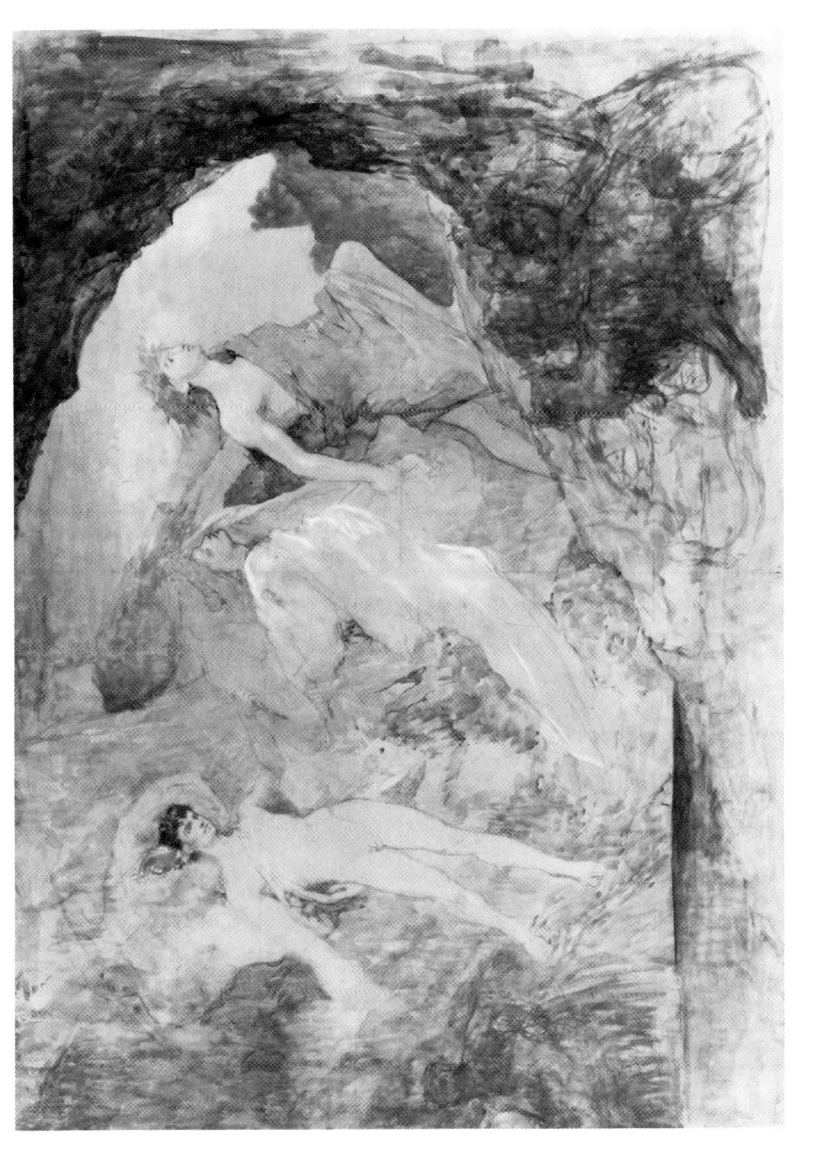

Figure 4.15. Elie Delaunay, *Orpheus and Eurydice*, ca. 1870 Watercolor sketch of painting for the Grand Foyer, Opéra, Paris. *(Shepherd Gallery, New York)*

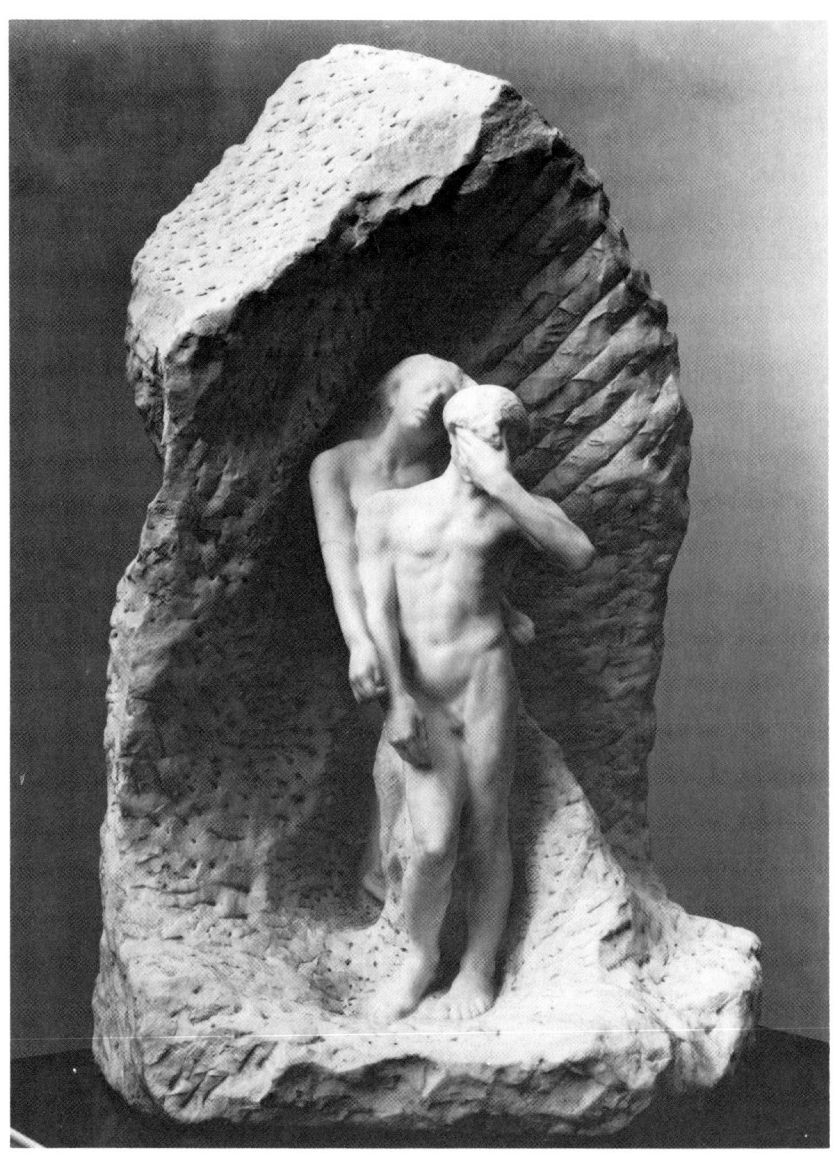

Figure 4.16. Auguste Rodin, *Orpheus and Eurydice, Emerging from the Gates of Hell,* ca. 1893
Marble.
(The Metropolitan Museum of Art; gift of Thomas F. Ryan, 1910, New York)

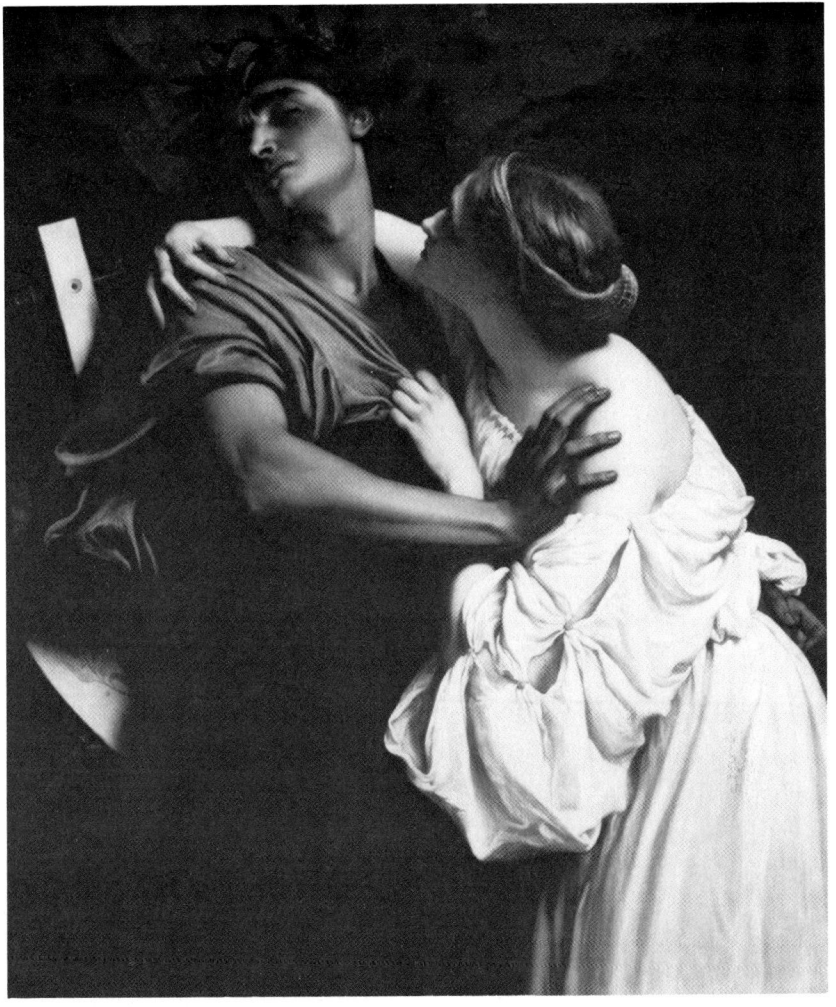

Figure 4.17. Frederic Lord Leighton, *Orpheus and Eurydice*, 1864
Oil on canvas.
(Leighton House Art Gallery and Museum, London)

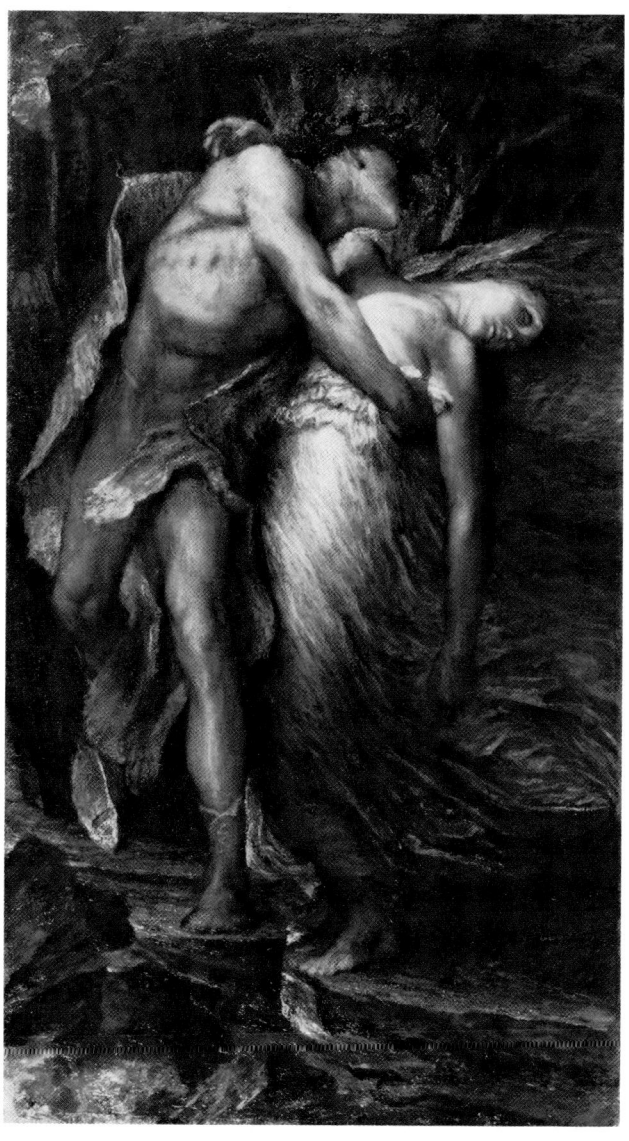

Figure 4.18. George Frederic Watts, *Orpheus and Eurydice*, 1900–1903
Oil on canvas.
(Reproduced by permission of the Trustees of The Watts Gallery, Compton, Near Guildford; photo courtesy Courtauld Institute of Art, London)

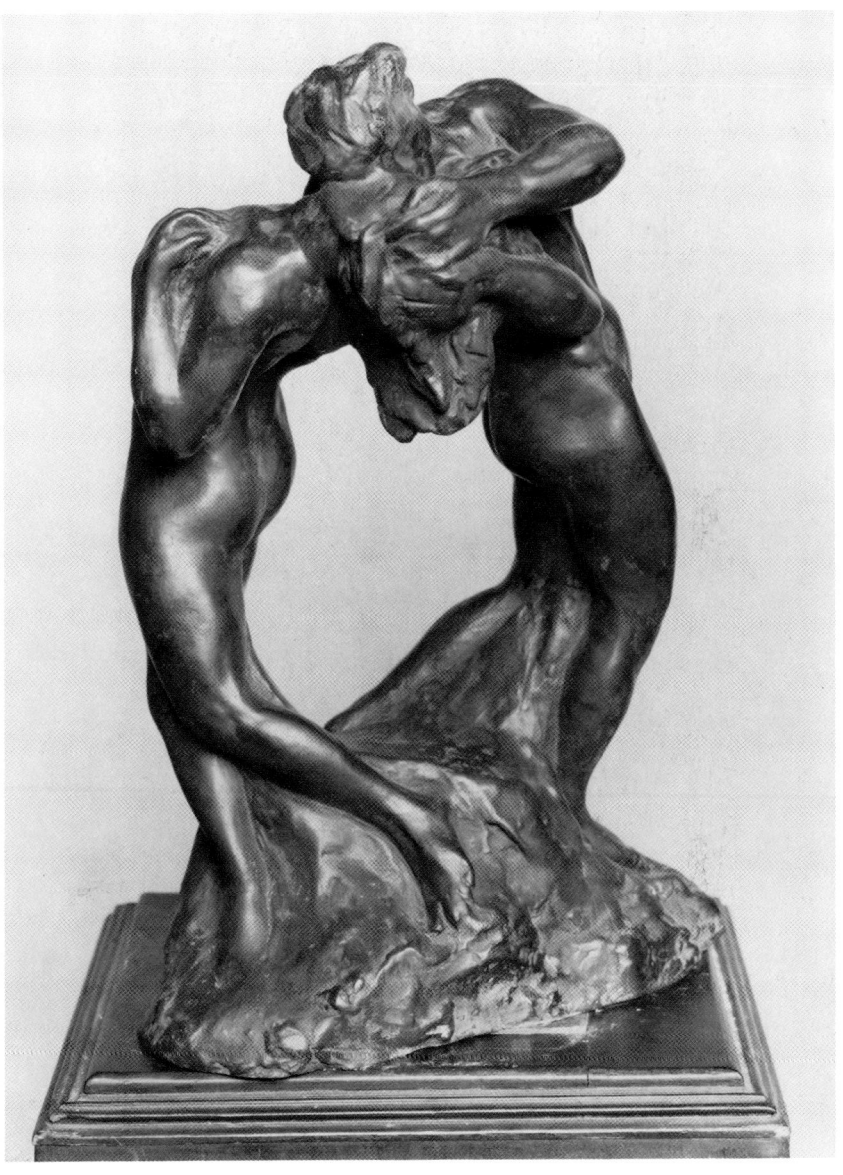

Figure 4.19. Charles Ricketts, *Orpheus and Eurydice*, ca. 1905–7
Bronze.
(Tate Gallery, London)

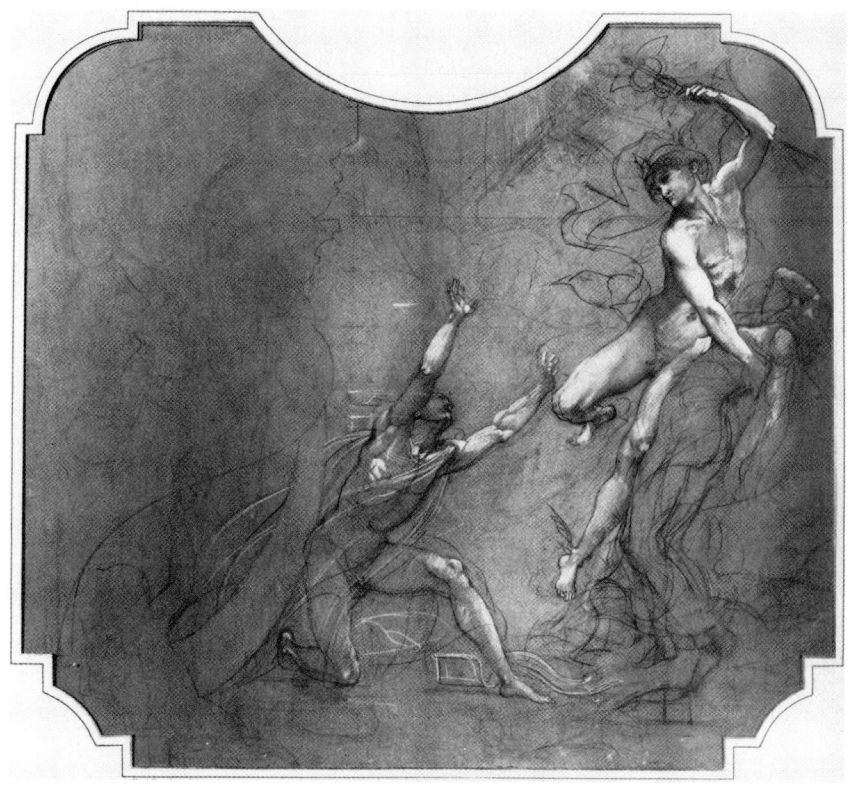

Figure 4.20. Paul Baudry, *Orpheus and Eurydice*, 1865–73 Cartoon for painting, Grand Foyer, Opéra, Paris. (*Bibliothèque et Musé de l'Opéra, Paris; photo: Bibliothèque National, Paris*)

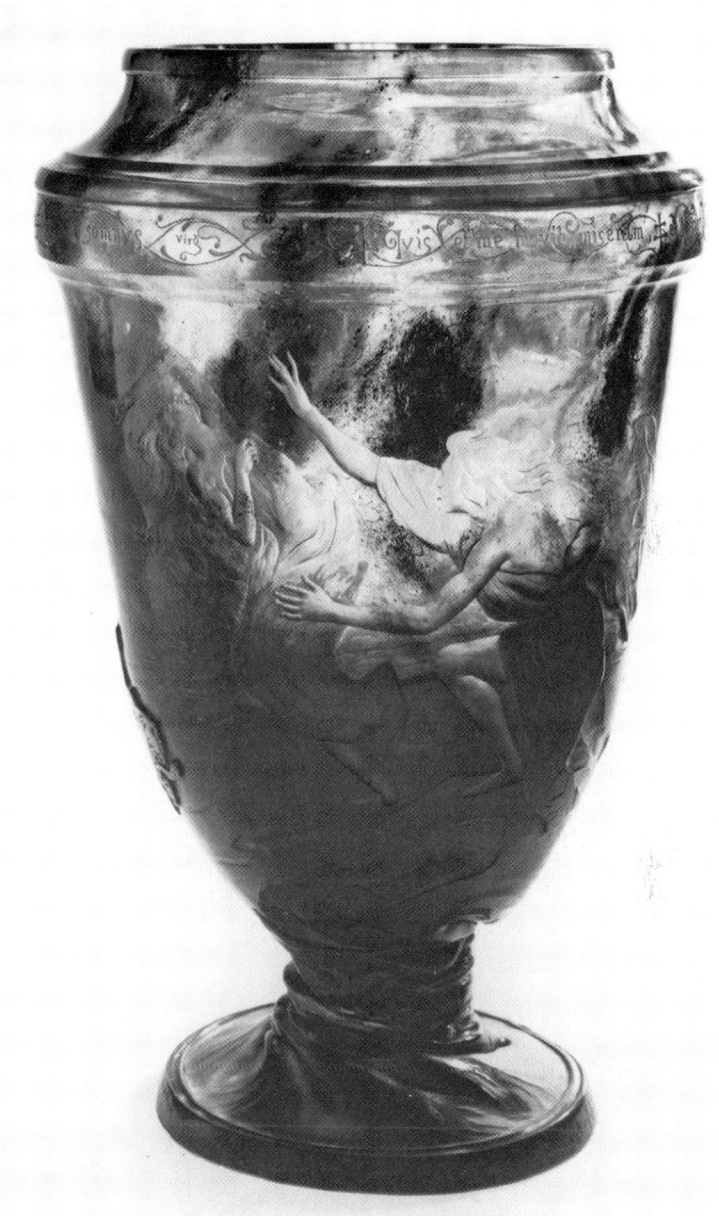

Figure 4.21. Emile Gallé, *Orpheus and Eurydice*, ca. 1888–89 Cameo-engraved crystal vase.
(Musée des Arts Décoratifs, Paris; Photo Giraudon)

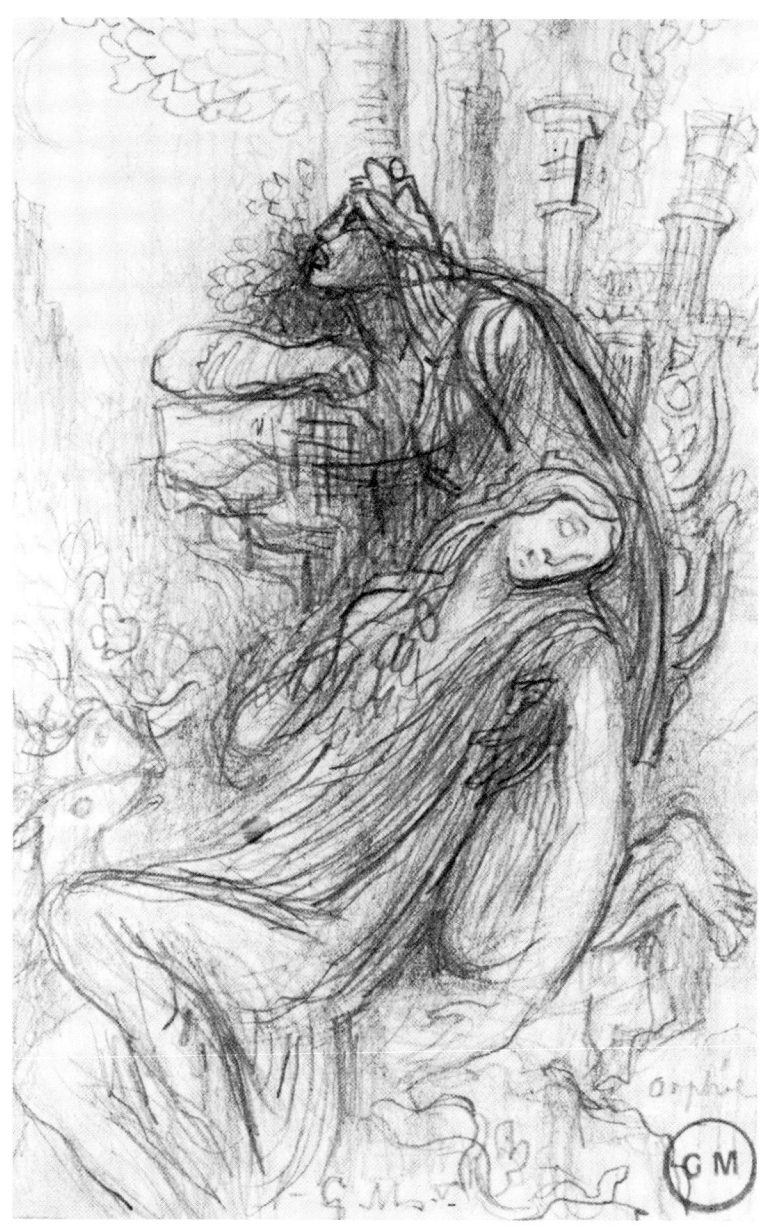

Figure 4.22. Gustave Moreau, *Orphée*, n.d.
Pencil drawing.
(*Musée Gustave Moreau, Paris; MGM 1983, #519;
Cliché des Musées Nationaux, Paris*)

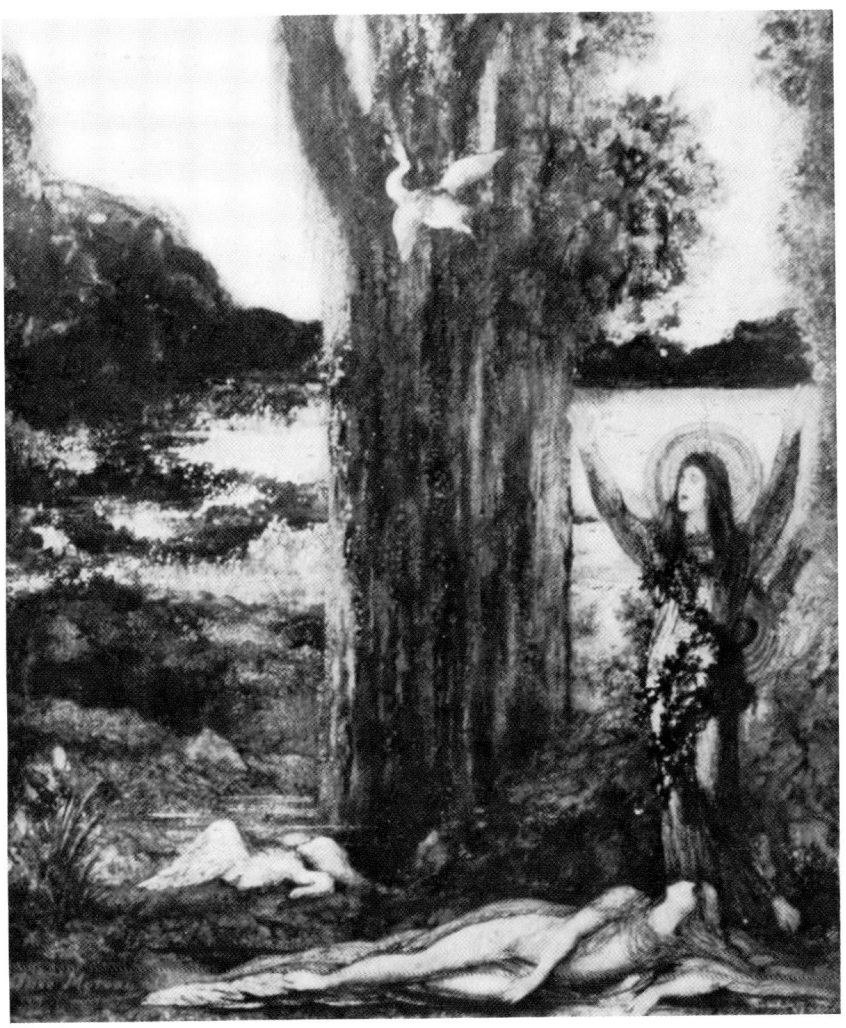

Figure 4.23. Gustave Moreau, *Orpheus*, ca. 1887
Watercolor and gouache.
(Private Collection)

5

Orpheus Lamenting

The poet's plaintive lament, his sensitive spirit yearning for an unattainable ideal, or mourning over happy love forever shattered by death, or consumed with the agony of the creative process, is a central theme of Romanticism. Literature of the late eighteenth and early nineteenth centuries is rife with this subject: the sufferings of Goethe's Werther; the tormented search of Shelley's Alastor for his ideal "vision and love";[1] Lamartine's loss of Elvire (Julie Charles) commemorated in his elegiac *Méditations*; or Alfred de Musset's exploration of the tormented relationship between the poet and his muse in his *Nuits*, inspired by his unhappy love for George Sand. Certainly, Orpheus' despair, captured in Gluck's famous aria, "Che farò senza Eurydice," is another expression of this dominant theme.[2]

For the Symbolists, too, the contorted, solitary figure of Orpheus is the embodiment of spiritual torment, an expression of his own personal emotional or aesthetic struggles: Moreau mourns the loss of his loved ones; Puvis explores the theme of the isolation of creativity; for Rodin, Orpheus' loss of Eurydice is a symbol of the cruel loss of the artist's personal muse. In Orpheus' lamentation, the Symbolists explore emotional depths, depicting rather grim scenes of undisguised anguish rather than moments of quiet reverie or sad introspection. Moreover this intensity of feeling is communicated less with an accumulation of narrative detail than with the evocation of interior states through formal means.

Gustave Moreau

Gustave Moreau's *Orpheus Lamenting at the Tomb of Eurydice*, 1891–97 (fig. 5.1), has been interpreted as an expression of his intense grief at the death, in March 1890, of his companion of 25 years, Adélaïde-Alexandrine Durieux. Having barely recovered from the death in 1884 of his mother, to whom he was extraordinarily attached, the passing of this intimate friend was a crushing blow. He himself described this work as a fitting memorial to those people dear to him who had been cruelly snatched away. He wrote to a friend and companion of his last years, Henri Rupp:

> God is cruel to artists like the bird keeper to the bird, gouging out their eyes so that they might sing better. . . . While renouncing all joy after so many cruel losses, I give in, not only to an imperious need of my soul, but I consider this renunciation like a moral offering that I carry to those disappeared loved ones, proof, an ever perceptible testimony for them of my profound fidelity to their memory. Without that—what a humiliation after having so loved to be so forgotten. There is no doubt that, after a brief period of this revival to life, oblivion is complete.[3]

This painting is a poignant expression of Moreau's own confrontation with death, loneliness, and sadness, and yet transcends the level of personal grief. It is the last in a series of thematically related works, identified by Ary Renan as the "Cycle of the Poet, in which Moreau explores his notion of the priestly function of the poet, the poet as martyr and victim. Indeed, in his descriptive analysis of the painting, Moreau hails Orpheus as "le chantre sacré . . . le Vates."[4] Moreau's personal grief is absorbed into the mytho-heroic proportions of the tragedy of Orpheus' loss of Eurydice; personal loss is transformed into a confrontation with cosmic forces (witness Moreau's own parallel between God controlling the artist as the bird-keeper tames the bird).

Tragic and holy martyrdom is a central and ennobling aspect of Moreau's concept of the poet-artist, enhanced by Moreau's conflation of pagan and Christian imagery, creating a hybrid tragic hero at the center of his imaginative pantheon. The image of Orpheus lamenting, then, is redolent with Christian symbolism; the pose of Orpheus' body reminiscent of the martyred Saint Sebastian as presented in the Renaissance: the torso is nude to the waist, the body crumpled to the knees, one arm extended as though lashed to the blasted tree trunk against which the poet slumps. Within Moreau's own oeuvre, the similarity between lamenting poet and martyred saint is clear (fig. 5.2). This conflation of poet and saint is confirmed, as it were, by a drawing combining the attributes of both—lyre, arrows, halo—in a single figure (fig. 5.3).[5]

The aura of saintly martyrdom permeates the painting. A leaden atmosphere of death and anguish endows the grief and sorrow of the individual with symbolic force. The scene is heavy with silence; all sound squelched by the weight of grief. Moreau writes, "The great voice of beings and objects is extinguished—the sacred singer is quiet for always."[6] Orpheus does not cry out in his anguish but succumbs to his distress in mute sorrow. This is an image of intense physical and emotional suffering turned inward. In fact, silence is one of the major themes of the painting. Moreau writes:

> The soul is alone, having lost all which was its splendor, its force and sweetness, it laments itself, in this complete abandon, in this inconsolable solitude; It laments and its heavy complaint is the only human sound in this deathly solitude. . . . Silence is everywhere, the moon appears above the pavilion.[7]

The ponderous silence permeating this landscape contrasts with Moreau's other interpretations of this episode, in which the poet's anguish is made manifest in loud protestations.[8] For instance, in the beautiful watercolor and gouache illustrated earlier (see fig. 4.22), the haloed poet stands above the lifeless body of Eurydice. His lyre is slung over his back; both arms are thrust upward; his mouth is wide open in a vehement cry.

François Louis Français

François Louis Français' *Orpheus* of 1863 (fig. 5.4) offers an elucidating contrast to the Moreau painting. There are a number of significant similarities between the two works: in each, the poet is absorbed in sad reverie, leaning against a tree; in the background, Eurydice's elaborate sepulcher is visible; the landscape of the earlier work is drenched with moonlight, as that of the latter is dominated by a low hanging white orb. However, the differences between the works are essential. With the delicate, fernlike silhouettes of the trees and the silver tones which bathe the landscape, Français creates the lyrical atmosphere of the classical idyll, revealing the influence of Corot, and bearing comparison in fact with Corot's poetic idylls and souvenirs of the 1850s and 1860s.[9] The 1859 revival of Gluck's *Orphée et Eurydice*, starring Mme. Viardot, was apparently the shared inspiration for both artists.[10]

In contrast to Français' soft, Virgilian poetry, Moreau's landscape is brooding and expressionistic. The tree in the background is afire with red; the foreground is covered with fluid patches of saturated colors, as though made molten by the intensity of the poet's passion. The great poet's voice is silenced, but the landscape seems to flow with his anguish:

> Only the drops of dew, falling from the flowers of water, make their regular and discreet noise, this sound full of melancholy and sweetness, this sound of life amidst the silence of death.[11]

It is informative that, while the critics' point of reference in their discussion of the Français painting is classical poetry—"great poetic sentiment. . . . The ensemble exhales a Virgilian perfume"[12]—Edouard Schuré, for example, discusses Moreau's painting in terms of Wagner:

> Here we see the world from on high, from the point of view of the spirit.... Before such a painting by the Master, we have an intuition of a more homogenous world where more docile and fluid elements assume the forms and colors of our thoughts. Here the landscape plays a role analogous to that of the Wagnerian orchestra. Through its nuances and harmonies, it modulates the emotions of an interior drama and prolongs them back and forth, in a prodigious world outside time and space. It is from the living center of the soul that he creates his world, it is in accordance with the laws of the soul that he models and completes it. His art merits in all regards the name of psychological painting.[13]

Moreau's own commentary, as well as Schuré's elaborate essay, situate the painting at the very heart of the Symbolist aesthetic, resonant with the most significant themes of the period: synaesthesia, color symbolism, Wagnerism, the psychologically potent landscape, the pessimism of decadence. Certainly, correspondences, or the synaesthetic ideal, are inherent in Moreau's commentary in which he "hears" the drops of red. Moreover, this color/sound has a specific emotional significance—"this noise full of melancholy and of sweetness."[14]

Schuré's concept of "la peinture psychique," depending profoundly on concepts of color symbolism and music as the ideal form of the arts, is entirely consistent with contemporary aesthetic theories of Synthétisme or Idéisme. Moreau writes:

> What importance does Nature have by Herself? She is nothing more than an excuse for the artist to express himself.... Art is the never ending search for the expression of internal feelings by means of plastic form.[15]

Certainly Moreau's essential idea is comparable to Gauguin's emphasis of the role of the artist's imagination in his manipulation of the motif in nature. The psychological landscape—the manipulation of the motif in nature in order to describe an inner terrain of emotion—is important in the 1890s, in the works of artists such as Sérusier, Osbert, Munch, Aman-Jean, De Gouve de Nuncques and Hodler.[16] Alphonse Germain's appraisal of Osbert's works emphasizes this concept: "The essays in psychic landscape ... breathe the rhythm of Nature's life."[17]

As explored already in chapter 2, the Symbolist concepts of synaesthesia and color symbolism are inextricably tied to Wagnerism and the idea of the total work of art. Schuré was not the first to discover the Wagnerian quality of Moreau's paintings. Téodor de Wyzewa, cofounder of the *Revue wagnérienne*, wrote in his review of the 1885 Salon of "A painting by Monsieur Moreau, the symphonist of refined emotions."[18] His praise of Redon, Bartholomé, Whistler and Fantin-Latour similarly explores the Wagnerian aspects of their works. It is evident in Wyzewa's discussions, as in Schuré's, that the Wagnerian quality of paintings applies most specifically to the symbolic evocation of emotional states in the landscape. This is clear in Wyzewa's discussion of Redon's "dark landscapes.... Monsieur Odilon Redon attempts to create afresh the empty landscapes of bitterness and fear, and the cruelty of imagery, by which Monsieur Félicien Rops evokes the vicious passions of an age of perversity."[19] Wyzewa's notion of modern painting is based on his vision of Wagner's renewal of the arts: encompassing a synthesis of all the arts (plastic arts, literature, music), an ideal vision of art as the creation of life (not merely the representation of objects but the exploration of the emotional or psychological world, that is, the entire human condition or reality).

The Symbolist landscape swells and reverberates with emotion. It is more than a mere backdrop for human drama, but rather becomes a symbolic or abstract equivalent of those emotions. The Symbolist's infusion of emotion into the landscape (without anecdote or narrative), into the constituent colors, lines and forms themselves, certainly draws upon or parallels the abstraction inherent in Wagner's revolutionary music, which eschewed the traditional operatic form in favor of the "endless melody," the "melodic knot of motifs," the complex interweaving of symbolic themes, the *leitmotifs*.

Wyzewa's synaesthetic ideal and his expansive universal aesthetic is based on a perception of the abstract qualities of art. He strongly disdains descriptive realism in painting, invoking, instead, the abstract truths in art:

> The colors and lines, through the influence of habit, assume for the souls an emotional value, independent of the objects themselves, which they represent.[20]

The differences between Français' and Moreau's Orpheus, between the former's descriptive precision or narrative specificity, and the attempt, in the latter, to communicate profound emotion in the abstract components of the landscape, parallel the contrast between Gluck and Wagner. In 1886, Wyzewa set up a similar contrast, using Gluck, seemingly to represent the traditional Italian operatic form; and, on the other hand, Beethoven, as a representative of "la musique wagnérienne." The former is characterized by a contrived structure, the emotional sphere constricted by insistent specificity of cause, words and situation, while Wyzewa discusses Beethoven in terms of emotions, left as abstract, indefinite forces.[21]

Pierre Puvis de Chavannes

Similarly, Puvis de Chavannes' works were the focus of Wyzewa's praise: "Emotional, symphonic painting must today recognize M. Puvis de Chavannes as its Master, the exemplary poet of modern painting."[22] In this context, Puvis'

Orpheus or *Death of Orpheus* (fig. 5.5), was admired not so much for its exploration of a specific mythological figure or setting, but rather for its penetration of the emotional core of the myth presented in the irreducible elements of the picture—color and line. Orpheus' anguish is embodied in the bizarre contortions of his body—his torso twisted and curled; one arm outstretched rigidly; the other hand gripped convulsively across his face. This intense emotion is echoed, moreover, in the penetrating violet coloration of the desolate and arid surrounding terrain.[23]

In 1895, Marius Vachon associated *Orpheus* with *L'Enfant prodigue*, 1879, and *Le Pauvre Pêcheur*, 1881, as "une trilogie de la misère."[24] Each painting presents an image of psychological and physical torment. The body of each figure is emaciated and contorted with pain. The dominant violet color of the surrounding terrain is somehow oppressively airless. Clearly, these images of torment derive a good deal of their impact from implied association with traditional depictions of Christian martyrdom. For instance, *Le Pauvre Pêcheur*—his hands held as though bound together, his hair matted in the shape of a crown of thorns—evokes comparison with Christ scourged. Similarly, Orpheus' anguish might be compared with Christ in the Garden of Gethsemane, contemplating his cruel fate.[25]

Moreover, *Orpheus* may be compared with *The Dream* (fig. 5.6) of the same year, forming together a dialogue about the vicissitudes of artistic creativity. *The Dream* is an image of inspiration, calmness and buoyancy, the mind eased by the peace of sleep or dream. In contrast, *Orpheus* embodies the difficulty of inspiration, the cessation of creative flow, the anguished confrontation with the void.

Alexandre Séon

Alexandre Séon's works reveal Puvis' influence in a number of ways: theme, compositional formula, incorporation of a powerful landscape setting, expressive of emotional truth in the elemental, abstract components of line and color, even the dry matte surface of his works, which imitate the quality of fresco technique. Séon's 1896 *Lamentation of Orpheus* (fig. 5.7) clearly echoes Puvis' 1883 *Orpheus*. Once again, Orpheus is sprawled horizontally, the lower half of his body concealed with a clinging drapery. The differences, however, are significant: The expressionist intensity of Puvis' Orpheus is transformed by Séon into an image of mannered elegance. The outline of the poet's body is attenuated, a series of flowing lines. The upper body does not arch rigidly upward, but rather the poet's head is cradled in the crook of his arm. Similarly, the face is not covered with the spasmodically clutching hand. Rather, the forearm is held upright, the hand positioned in a graceful, even self-conscious gesture. Despite the clear similarity between Puvis' desolate terrain and Séon's bizarre landscape, Séon replaces Puvis' rocky, arid setting with a weird environment of beach sand and spindly fingers of rock, inspired by the Ile de Bréhat in Paimpol in Brittany.

Actually, Orpheus is a dominant theme in Séon's oeuvre, explored first in 1883, the same year as—and clearly inspired by—Puvis' painting of Orpheus.[26] In this work (fig. 5.8), the poet stands leaning against a massive wall of rock, a glimpse of ocean visible to the right. His body is entirely nude, his hand is clutched to his face in a gesture of despair markedly reminiscent of Puvis' Orpheus. The other arm holds the lyre close to the musician's chest.

Another interpretation of this theme, entitled *The Poet* (fig. 5.9), dates from 1895. Here the poet has abandoned his lyre on the rocks and has climbed to the top of one of the jagged pinnacles, where he gestures beseechingly with both arms towards the brilliant sky which illuminates the watery landscape beyond.

In his Orpheus works painted during the years 1883–96, Séon's effort to clarify or distill the basic components of the picture—pathetic gesture of the androgynous poet, the rock and the sea—is evident. These rather melancholy and lifeless landscapes demonstrate his fascination with Symbolist or Neo-Impressionist theories about the abstract power of line and color. Alphonse Germain proclaims Séon, "un peintre idéaliste-idéiste," and presents an elaborate explanation of Séon's theory of color:

> To give form, *through line,* to a symbol in a type amplified to an archetype; to homogenize this symbol, *by means of colors,* with the character of a being or better its substratum. . . . The idea that creates a gesture, to express succinctly through a concordance of expressive linear directions, and a dominance of pertinent symbolic colorations.[27]

Séon's blue expresses profound melancholy and despair. The reductive landscape, an almost geometric assemblage of broad areas of undifferentiated color, exploits the abstract power of line and form. The similarity of these compositions to a sculptural frieze is intentional, a result of the artist's study of the division of tones.[28] Germain situates Séon's "Symbolisme des teintes," in the broad context of theories of color which evolved throughout the nineteenth century, as well as particularly in the context of Symbolist aesthetic idealism of the 1880s and 1890s:

> Everything ascends toward style, to idealize everything. Style is, as recognized by Charles Blanc, "truth agrandized, simplified, disengaged from all insignificant details, rendered in its original essence, in its typical aspect." The Ideal, as he understands it, and according to the definition of J. Péladan: "the entirely sublimated idea, and its point of supreme harmony, intensity, subtlety."[29]

F. Holland Day

Séon's Orpheus series may well constitute an important link between Symbolist painting and turn-of-the-century Pictorialist photography. Generally, one may compare the arcadian visions drawn from antiquity of Puvis, Alma-Tadema, Feuerbach, or von Marées with the mythologically evocative photographs of F. Holland Day, Baron von Gloeden, George Seeley, Clarence White, or Annie W. Brigman.[30] Specifically, however, the androgynous or homoerotic *tableaux vivants* of von Gloeden or F. Holland Day warrant careful comparison with Séon's works, while in fact, a strong case can be made for Séon's series as the direct inspiration for Day's 1907–8 series of male nudes with lyres. For instance, Séon's *The Sorrow of Orpheus*, 1883, is strikingly similar to Day's *Nude Youth with Lyre* (fig. 5.10) and Séon's 1895 *The Poet* may be compared to Day's *Nude Youth Standing on a Cliff, Arms Raised* (fig. 5.11).[31] Day emphasizes the androgynous physiques of his young, male models. The mood of his compositions may be described as pastoral or elegaic. As in Séon's paintings, the melancholic figures, clutching oversized lyres, pose amidst huge boulders and rock cliffs.[32]

It is reasonable to assume that Day was aware of Séon's work. Though the photographer was not in Paris for the exhibition of *The Poet* at the 1896 Salon Rose + Croix or of *The Lamentation* at the sixth Rose + Croix exhibition, the following year, he had traveled extensively in Europe, first in 1889, then in 1890, 1894, 1900, and 1901. Day's interests would surely have brought him into contact with Péladan's and Séon's Decadent, Symbolist milieu. Day himself may be described as a Decadent aesthete. He was a friend of William Morris and Oscar Wilde; had himself published Beardsley, and was, as well, an enthusiast of Yeats. His avid interest in the occult and spiritism is revealed in his membership in the Boston Monday Nighters Club, in Yeats's Order of the Hermetic Students of the Golden Dawn, as well as in his contributions to Visionist magazines such as the *Mahogany Tree* and the *Knight Errant*. Moreover, in 1895 he became a member of the London photographic association, the Linked Ring Brotherhood. The assumption that Day was familiar with Séon's paintings is further reinforced by the American's presence in Paris during February and March 1901, as he accompanied the extremely successful exhibition of American Pictorialists which toured major European capitals. That same year, Séon's works were exhibited at the avant-garde gallery of Georges Petit, on the rue de Sèze. This exhibition was hailed by Charles Saunier in his "Gazette d'art" in *La Revue blanche:*

> He received the confidences of Orpheus, was present for his dreams and his despairs and recounts them in his works with a lapidary simplicity.[33]

Auguste Rodin

Rodin's *Orpheus*, 1892 (fig. 5.12), relates to a complex of themes within the sculptor's oeuvre. Firstly, it is but one manifestation of his preoccupation with the theme of Orpheus.[34] Furthermore, it must be understood in terms of Rodin's more general preoccupation with the concept of the poet-artist, and situated among such works as his monuments to Hugo, Balzac, Carrière, Puvis, and Whistler. This work may also be viewed in the context of the rather elaborate exploration in his oeuvre, of the dialogue between poet and muse. The anguish of creativity, so eloquently expressed in Orpheus' physical being, is yet another important theme in Rodin's sculptural oeuvre.

The sculpture is an image of torment, expressive of both physical pain and emotional anxiety. The poet's right arm is stretched into the air, as if frozen in the backward motion of the rhythmic strumming of the instrument. The hand seems incredibly heavy, however, an enormous weight for the withered extended arm. Orpheus half kneels, his upper torso rigidly stretched upward, his head thrown back in a gesture of great anguish. The poet's body strikes a precarious balance with his enormous lyre, straining against the crushing weight of the giant boxlike instrument. This is not the only instance of Rodin's use of the grappling with material weight as symbolic of the artist's struggle with creativity. In *The Fallen Caryatid*, ca. 1881 (fig. 5.13), a female body is crushed by the weight of a huge stone. In *Meditation*, 1885 (fig. 5.14), a standing female nude is contorted with the effort of supporting a now-invisible, absent or, one might say, abstract weight. These figures are expressive of Rodin's preoccupation with the crushing burden of creative endeavor, part of the evolution of Rodin's nontraditional, "personalized muse."[35]

Perhaps the most peculiar element of his *Orpheus* is the disembodied hand that extends downward at the top of the back plane of the giant lyre (fig. 5.15). This aspect, however, is not surprising when considered in terms of Rodin's fascination with fragments, parts of the human body, and especially hands. One of the basic principles of his work is the repetition and exploitation of fragments, constantly metamorphosed and renewed in context and meaning. Here, the intrusive hand might be interpreted as a symbol of inspiration, the intervention of some creative force. It may, more specifically, be a remainder of Eurydice, a remembrance of her formerly sustaining presence, a symbolic fragment of Orpheus' beloved, a physical manifestation which makes her absence all the more poignant and palpable. Within the context of earlier versions of this sculpture itself, and other related works, it is clear that Eurydice is Orpheus' muse. His anguish, therefore, is caused by the absence of his beloved and the loss of creative power. Rodin conflates, then, the pathetic romance of the myth with his own personal fixation with the tragic sacrifice and torment of creativity.

A photograph of an earlier plaster version (fig. 5.16) indicates that Eurydice was originally portrayed hovering over the poet's head. Her body was not complete, consisting only of head, upper torso and fragments of arms. In this version, then, Orpheus' uplifted arm does not appear so incredibly heavy, and is rather drawn toward Eurydice, or reaches to her face in a caress. Similarly, Orpheus' violently upraised and thrust-back visage is directed towards her face. One is tempted to interpret this work as a depiction of Eurydice disappearing, already partially enveloped by the shadows of Hades (hence the fragmentary anatomy), at the moment of Orpheus' precipitous glance. However, Rodin once again goes beyond traditional symbolism, and this depiction of Orpheus and Eurydice is part of his rather complex exploration of the theme of the artist and his muse. The awkward position and abrupt abbreviation of Eurydice's body bear comparison to the *Tragic Muse* (fig. 5.17), for instance, from before 1885. Rodin explores, therefore, not only the tragedy of love but also of art, which is at the basis of the myth of Orpheus.

The hovering muse figures, of course, in traditional imagery of the inspiration of the artist or creative genius.[36] Rodin, however, continually renews and distorts this familiar vocabulary. For instance, the inspiring muse is often intentionally unidealized (note the rather grotesque visage of the *Tragic Muse*), or frequently presented in mere fragments or deleted altogether. This evolution is evident, for instance, in the various stages of the Victor Hugo monument. In the earliest studies the poet is surrounded by the traditional winged muses, sirens, and Iris, the messenger of the gods. In the final version, however he is alone, no longer accompanied by these allegorical figures (fig. 5.18). His left arm reaches out in an imperious and powerful gesture, as though to summon the orphic voice, or as if capable of quelling the noise of the world. His right hand is held to his ear as though to facilitate his hearing. There is however, no longer a muse hovering at his ear, and Hugo listens, then, to an interior voice or to some vibration which emanates mysteriously from the world. Rodin eschews the traditional images of poetic greatness and inspiration which depend upon allegory and personification, and introduces instead abstract, even nonexistent, images of the poet's role, of his inspiration. This transformation of traditional symbolism into a more enigmatic and private set of symbols is evident, too, in *Orpheus*, with the reduction or abstraction of Eurydice into the stark fragment of the hand.

Hovering muse and heavy burden of creativity are conflated in *I Am Beautiful*, ca. 1880–82 (fig. 5.19). A male figure struggles to lift above his head, a cumbersome, peculiarly crouched woman. She is apparently a recalcitrant muse, her face turned away, her entire body seemingly curled inward. Rodin's illustrations for Alfred de Musset's "Nuit de mai" elucidate the identification of this crouching female as the muse (fig. 5.20).[37] In one of the drawings, a male nude struggles to grasp a winged muse. In another, inscribed with the first line from Musset's poem, "poète prend [sic] ton luth" (fig. 5.21), the female is not winged, and appears to slump instead, powerless and weighty in the arms of the man. (Here the female figure resembles somewhat the figure in *Meditation*, who is herself crushed by an invisible weight.) As in *I Am Beautiful* then, the winged muse and the painfully weighty female are identified, one to the other, in these drawings. Another drawing, *The Genius of Sculpture*, ca. 1880–82 (fig. 5.22), relates to this transformation of traditional winged muse into cumbersomely lifted burden.[38] In this work, the heroic nude sculptor is depicted with one hand outstretched toward the small sculpture on the stand before him, his other hand clenched to his forehead. A female nude hovers above him, embracing his head and shoulders with her arms. Her position is incredibly distorted, as the lower half of her torso "floats" belly up, involving therefore a physically impossible twist. The symbolic value of this massive and awkward female is ambiguous. She appears to be the palpable manifestation of the artist's thoughts. It is as though the artist's concentration bears the female aloft. And yet, the manner in which she clutches the tortured artist resembles a kind of deadly stranglehold.[39]

Clearly, Rodin identifies the muse with love. The identification of Orpheus' love for Eurydice and his creative power is at the heart of Rodin's interpretation of the myth. In *Orpheus*, the abandoned, mourning poet reaches upward toward the void which was Eurydice, his love and his muse. His body arches upward in the same pose as the figure in *Fugit Amor* (fig. 5.23), who grasps (like Paolo for Francesca, surely) eternally in vain for his love.

Moreover, it is not only emotional love, but also erotic or sexual energy which Rodin connects to artistic creativity. For example, in one of his studies for the Monument to Balzac, he portrays the poet as a gigantic nude grasping his penis. In *The Sculptor and His Muse*, 1890 (fig. 5.24), a female figure crouches on the artist's shoulder (again, of course an image of inspiration as burden), and whispers in his ear while fondling his genitals. The seated artist, pushed to the side by the weight of the muse, holds a hand to his mouth, only partially masking a face that is contorted with ecstasy or anguish. Similarly, the gesture of the figure in *Meditation* (see fig. 5.14), clasping her hand to her breast, which could be interpreted as an allusion to the traditional symbol of the flowing source of creativity, might also be understood as a convulsive gesture of sexual ecstasy. This reading would, in turn, invest the other contortions of the woman's body with sexual overtones.[40]

The myth of Orpheus and Eurydice expresses Rodin's notion of the poet and his muse, his vision of inspiration as crushing burden, his perception of creativity as a tragic or agonzied venture. The importance of Orpheus as the embodiment of the artist, is revealed in Rodin's writings, which make evident a profound personal identification with Orpheus:

> I attend the outstretched beauty like a beloved dead woman; she is hidden in shadows; and like water, some islets of sweet flesh emerge. This sleeping voluptuousness, is the melancholy of the blackest tombs, while the other parts of the body return to the nocturne of the depths. Ah, Eurydice, I find you again and push back the shadows. Ah, is she not perfect, this form which endures the night, one would say eternal! Ah! the reflections of bronze. This form delights my heart and my eyes. Ah! This submerged body, engulfed in shadow, in this bath of shadow.[41]

Understood in this context, *Orpheus* is a kind of self-portrait, or at least a symbolic embodiment of Rodin and his creative mission. Rodin/Orpheus leads forth beauty/sculpture/Eurydice from the bronze/shadows. Eurydice, the sculpture, inflates Rodin's heart and eyes with life. Yet, she is an ideal of unthinkable, timeless beauty, and thus, inherently unattainable, and hence, the source of pain and anguish to the sculptor. Significantly, Rodin illustrated the first poem of *Les Fleurs du mal*, "Bénédiction," with a drawing which is clearly a reprise of his *Orpheus and Eurydice* in the Metropolitan Museum of Art, hence associating his image of the mythic poet (and in the context of the passage quoted here, himself) with Baudelaire's exploration of the theme of the malediction and martyrdom of the poet (fig. 5.25).[42]

Clearly, the lamentation of Orpheus figures prominently in major works by Moreau, Puvis, Séon, and Rodin. It is, moreover, a motif which functions as a profound expression of these artists' own personal emotions, but is allied, at the same time, to some of the most significant issues of the Symbolist aesthetic. In the paintings, the poet's grief permeates the surroundings, forming a psychological landscape analogous to the Wagnerian orchestra. Through nuances and harmonies it modulates emotions of the interior drama, prolonging those feelings in time and space. In these antinaturalist landscapes the Symbolists explore the concepts of synaesthesia and correspondences, using the direct expressive power of color and line to create landscapes expressive of an interior reality. In the case of Rodin, Orpheus' lamentation is an expression of his own perception of the anguish of creativity. Orpheus' painful loss of Eurydice is the powerful symbol of the poet-artist's anguished relationship to his muse.

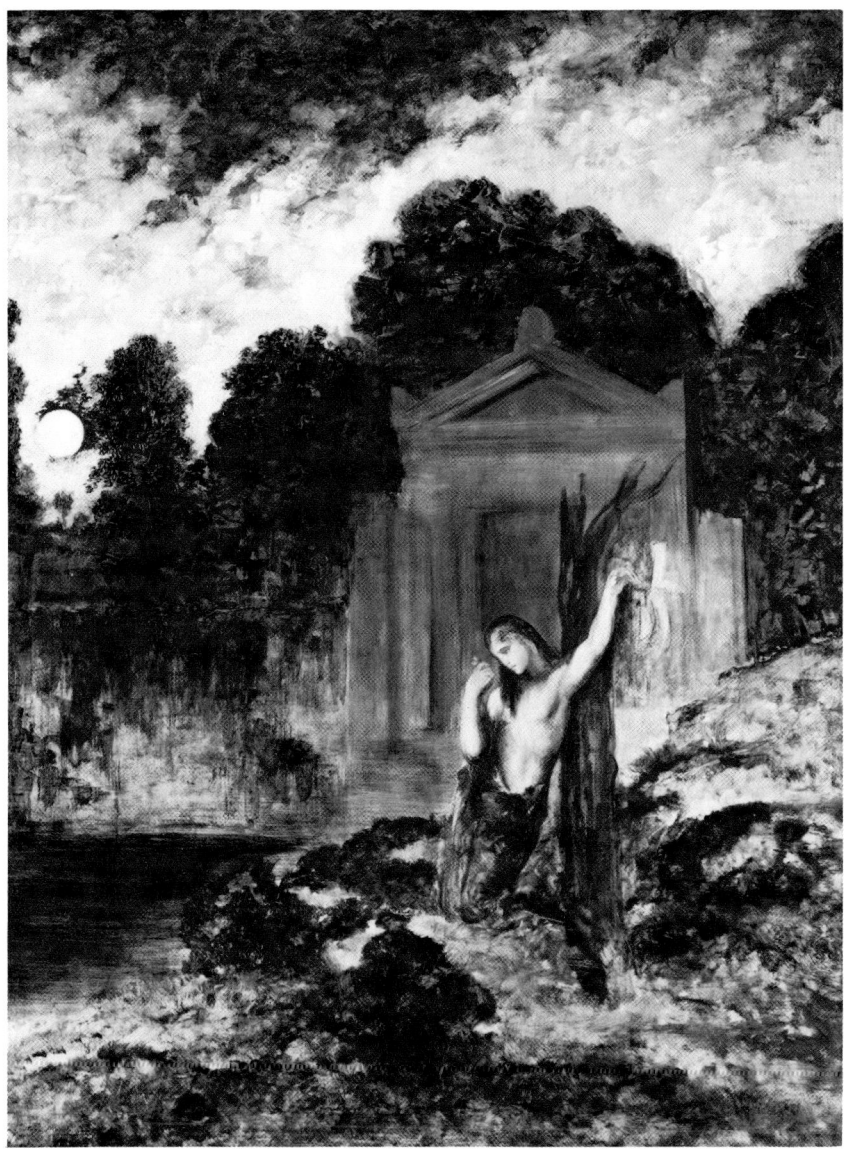

Figure 5.1. Gustave Moreau, *Orpheus Lamenting at the Tomb of Eurydice*, 1891–97
Oil on canvas.
(Musée Gustave Moreau, Paris; MGM 1974, #194; Cliché des Musées Nationaux, Paris)

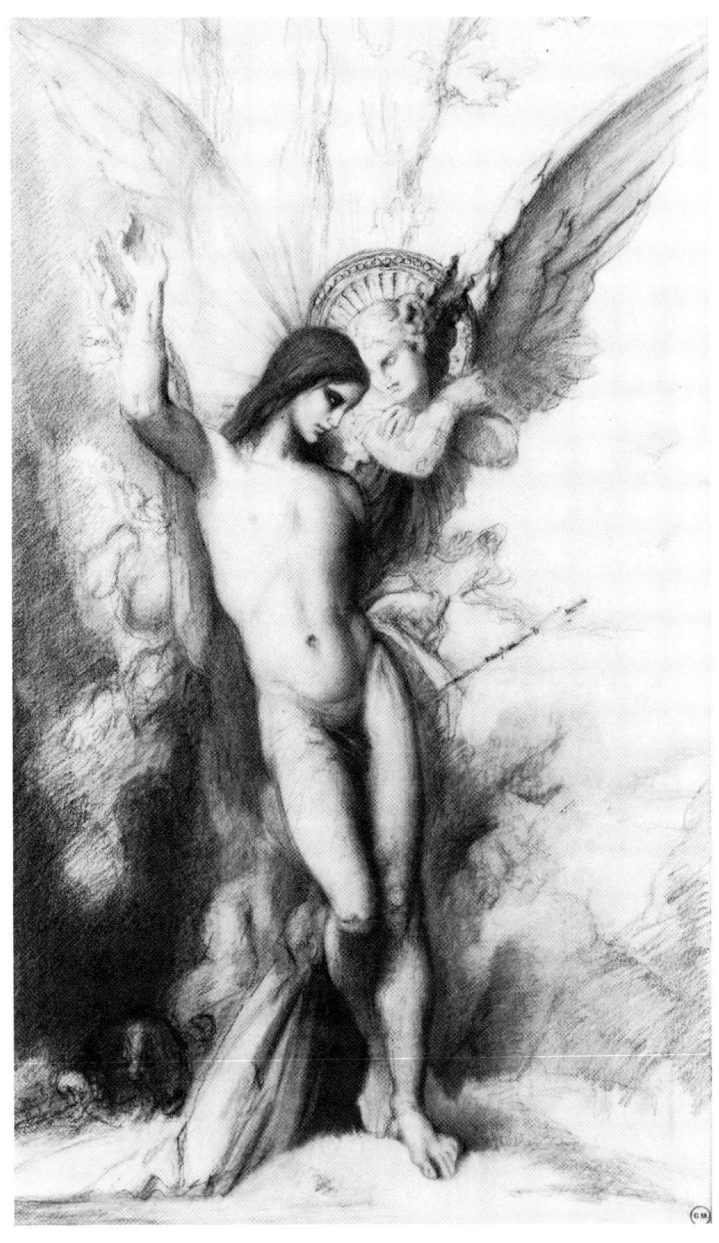

Figure 5.2. Gustave Moreau, *St. Sebastian*, 1876
Pencil, black chalk, and red crayon on paper.
(*Musée Gustave Moreau, Paris; MGM 1983, #827;
Cliché des Musées Nationaux, Paris*)

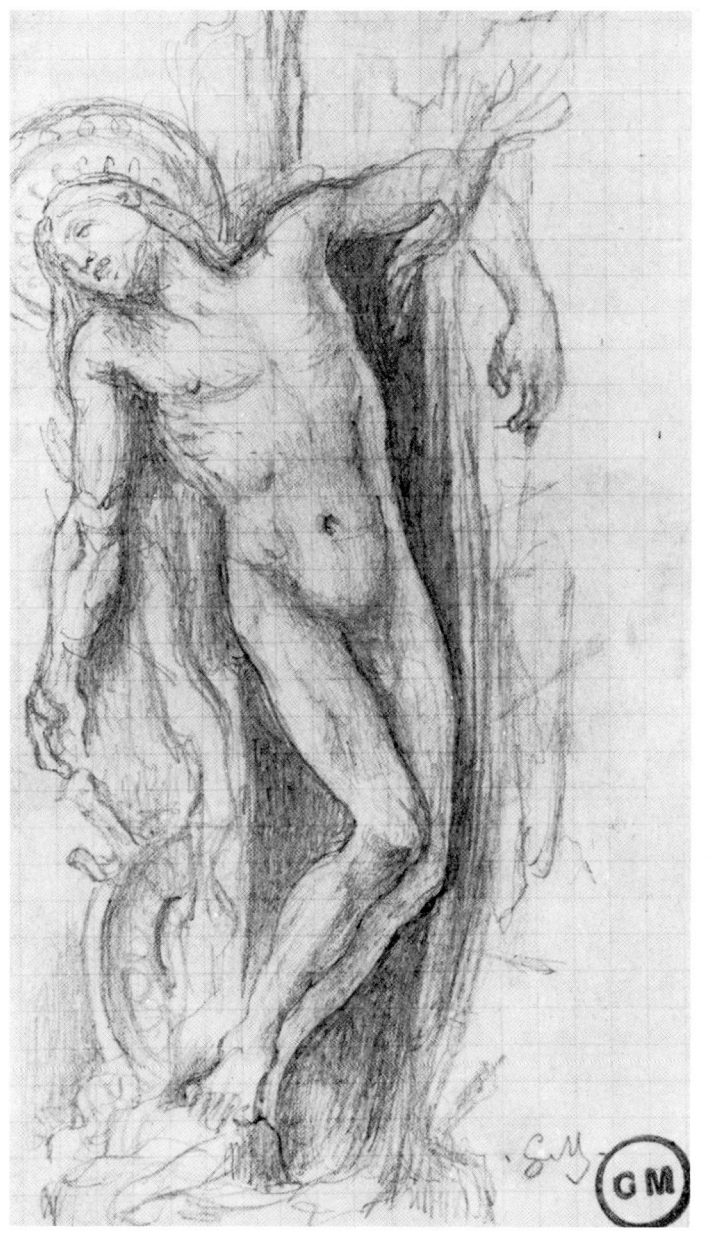

Figure 5.3. Gustave Moreau, *Orpheus/St. Sebastian*, n.d. Pencil drawing.
(*Musée Gustave Moreau, Paris; Cliché des Musées Nationaux, Paris*)

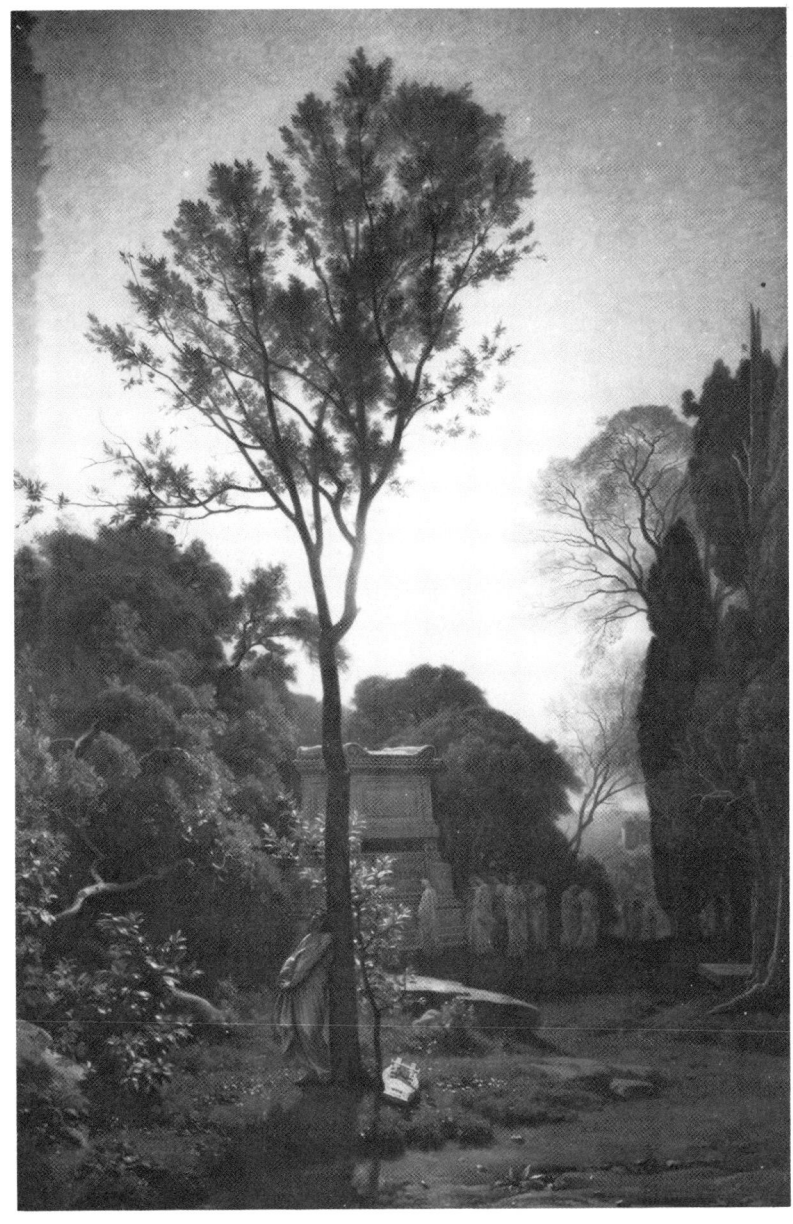

Figure 5.4. François Louis Français, *Orpheus*, 1863
Oil on canvas.
(Louvre, Paris; Lauros-Giraudon)

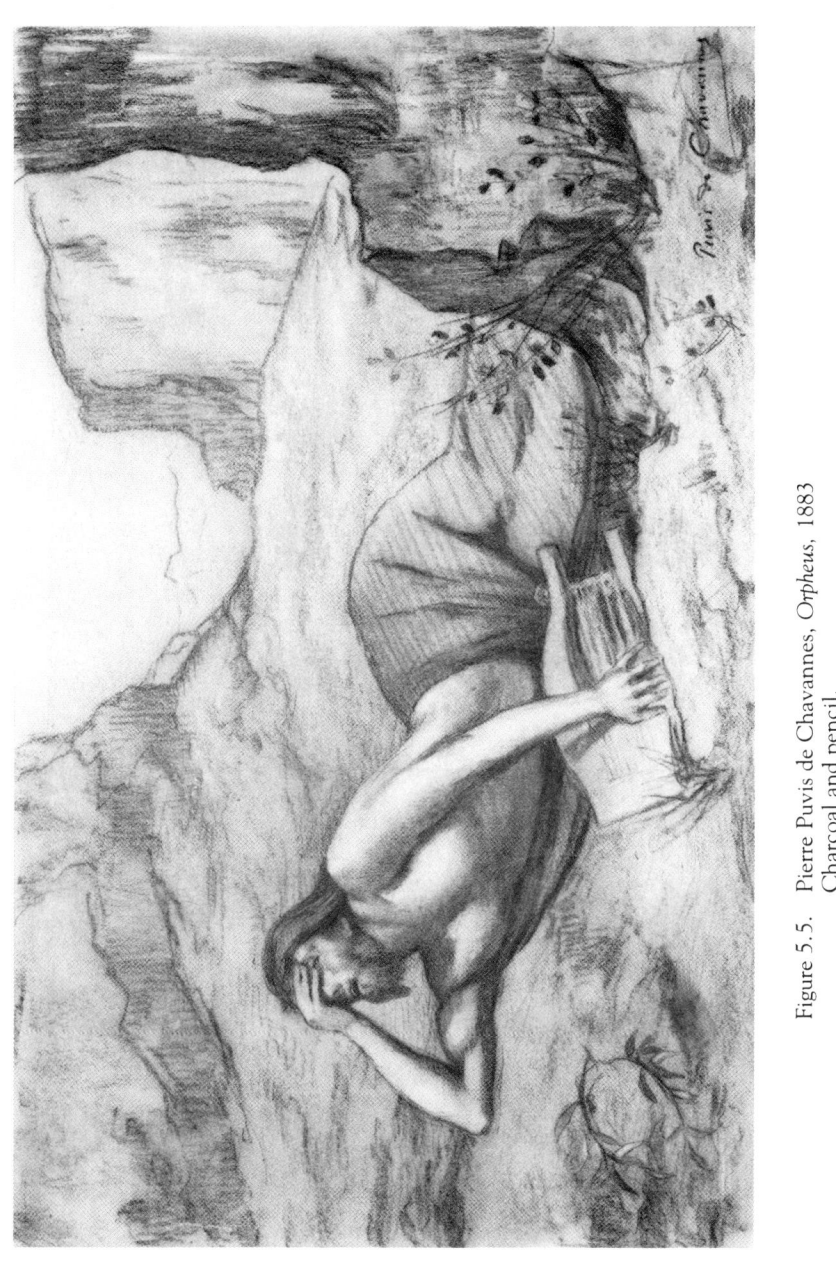

Figure 5.5. Pierre Puvis de Chavannes, *Orpheus*, 1883. Charcoal and pencil. (Yale University Art Gallery, gift of Mr. and Mrs. James W. Alsdorf)

Figure 5.6. Pierre Puvis de Chavannes, *The Dream*, 1883
Oil on canvas.
(Musée d'Orsay, Paris; *Cliché des Musées Nationaux, Paris*)

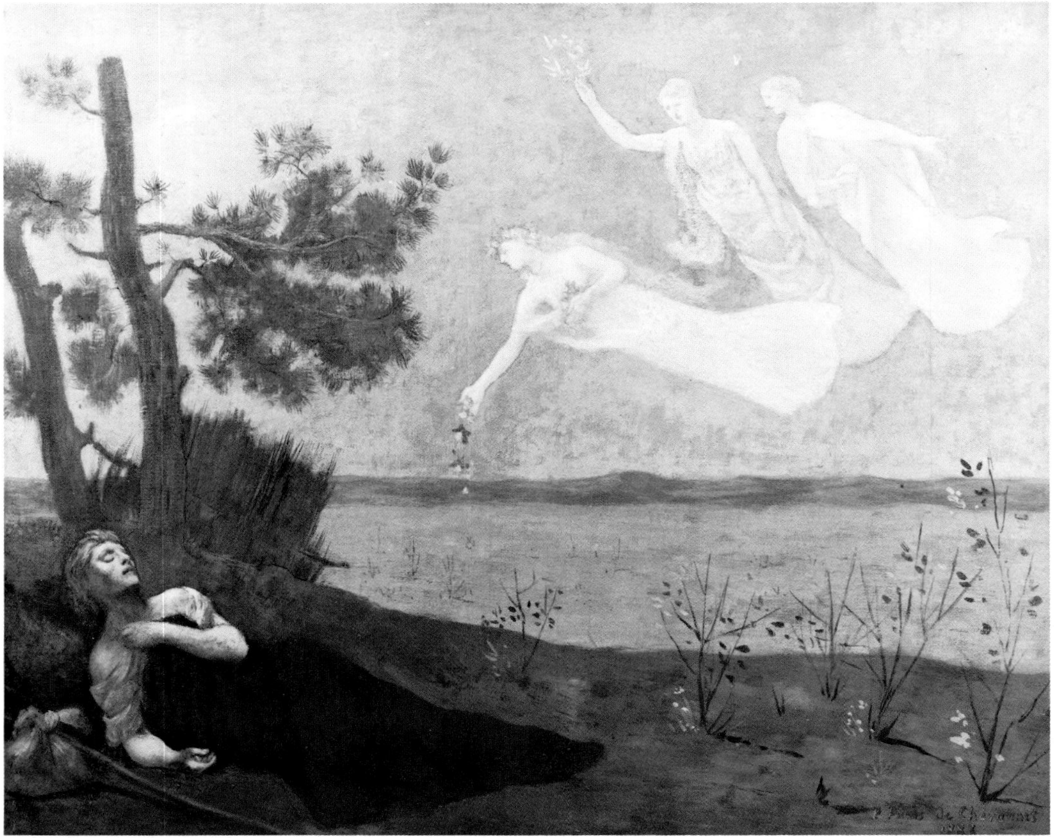

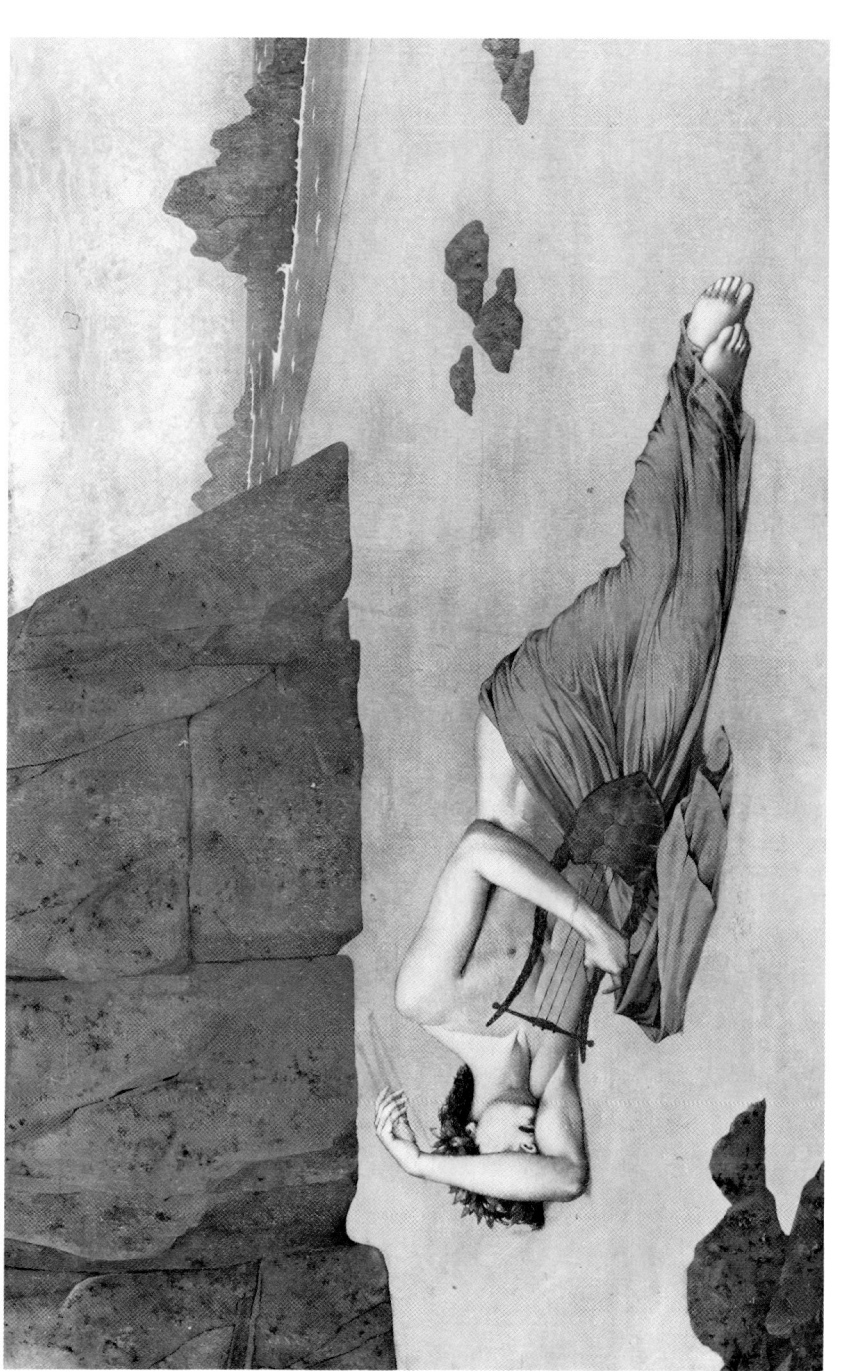

Figure 5.7. Alexandre Séon, *Lamentation of Orpheus*, 1896. Oil on canvas. (Musée d'Orsay, Paris; Cliché des Musées Nationaux, Paris)

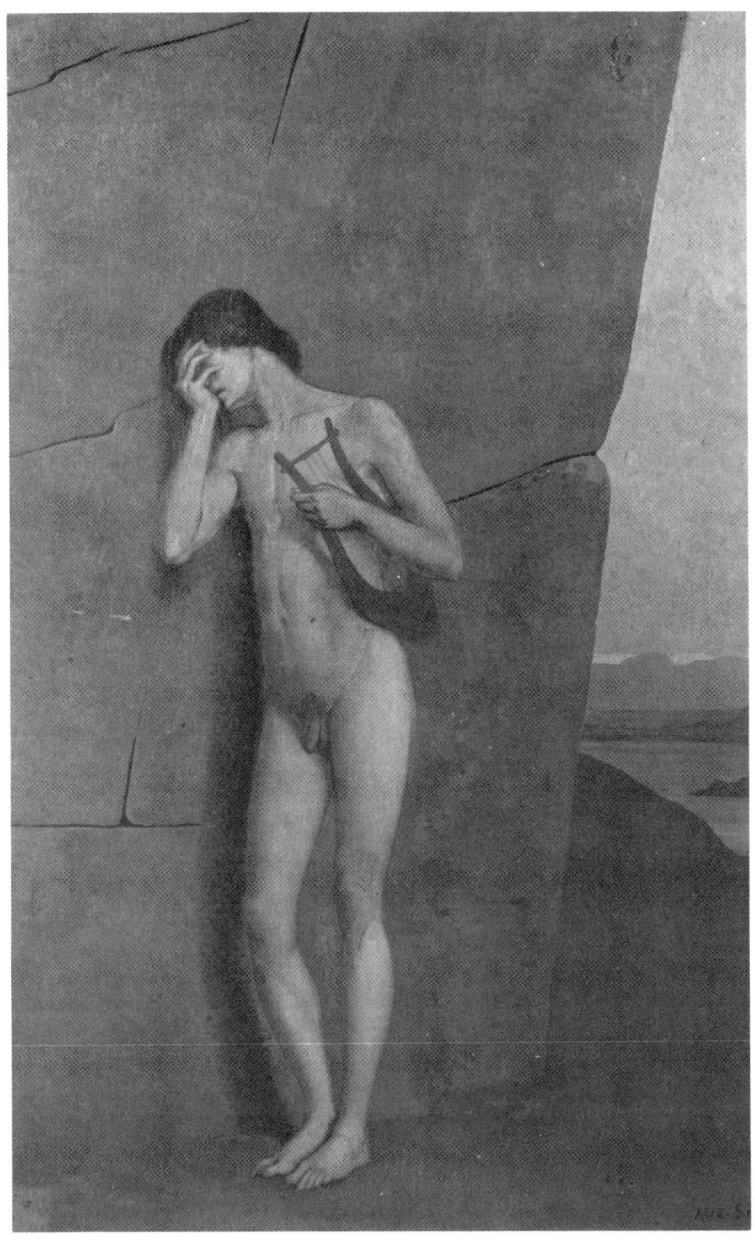

Figure 5.8. Alexandre Séon, *Orpheus*, 1883
Oil on canvas.
(*Musée d'Art et d'Industrie, Saint-Etienne*)

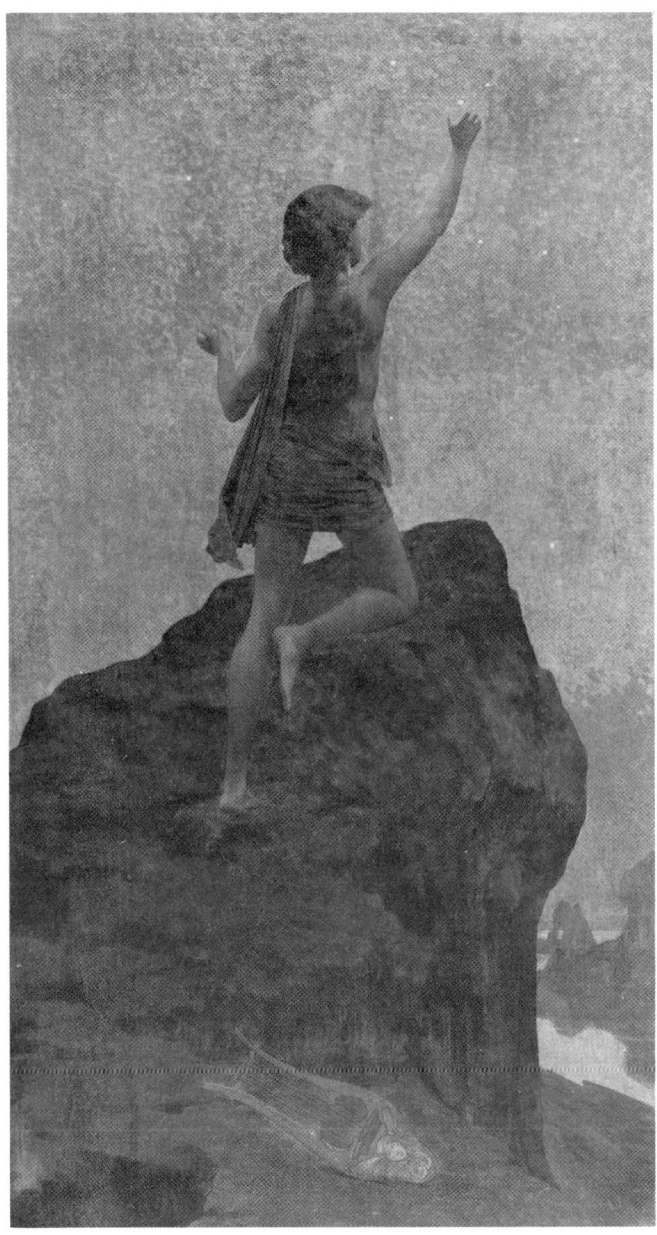

Figure 5.9. Alexandre Séon, *The Poet*, 1895
Oil on canvas.
(Musée d'Art et d'Industrie, Saint-Etienne)

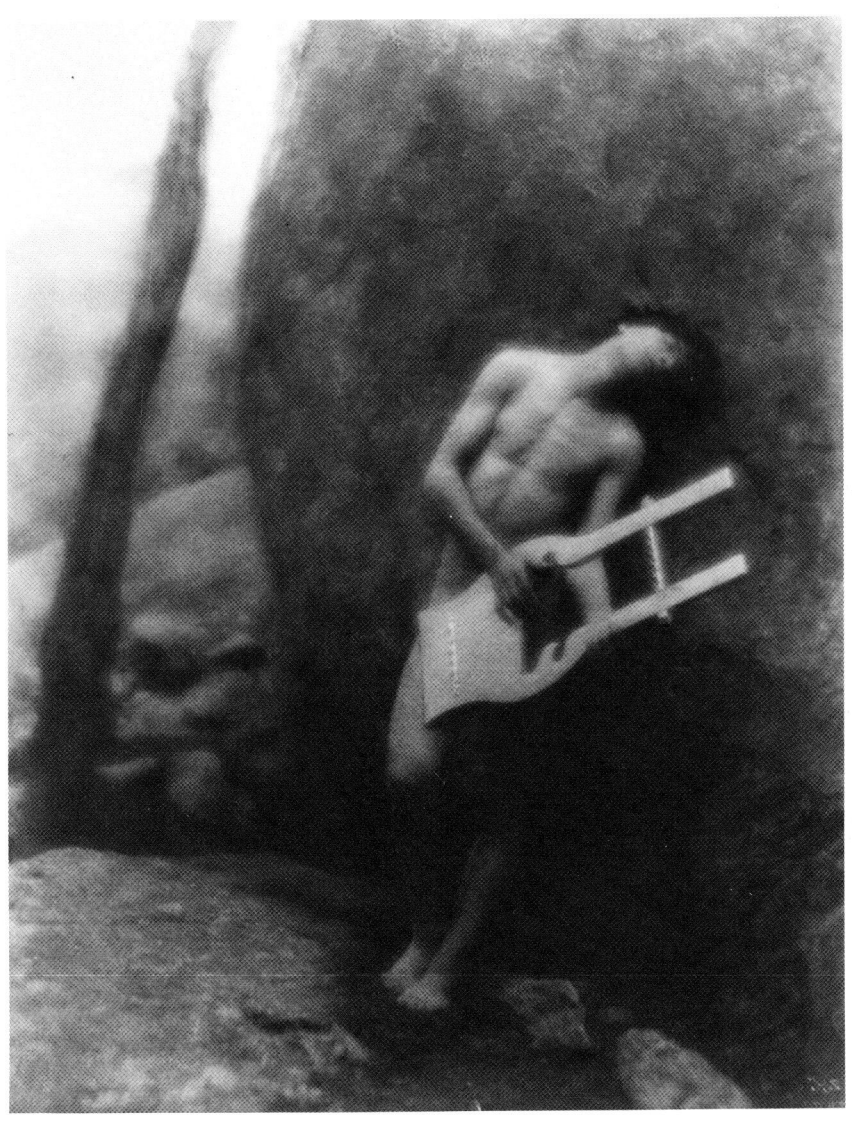

Figure 5.10. F. Holland Day, *Nude Youth with Lyre*, 1907–8 Combination print.
(*Library of Congress, Washington, D.C.*)

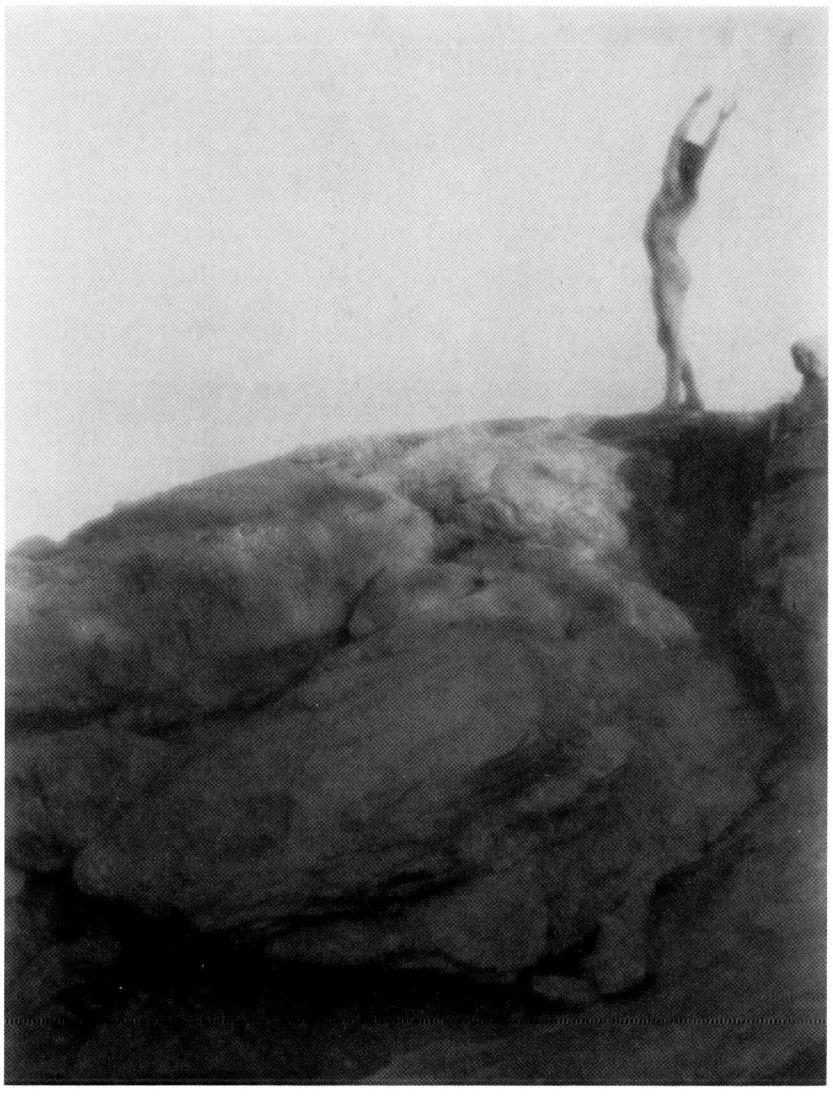

Figure 5.11. F. Holland Day, *Nude Standing on Cliff, Arms Raised*, 1907–8
Photograph.
(Library of Congress, Washington, D.C.)

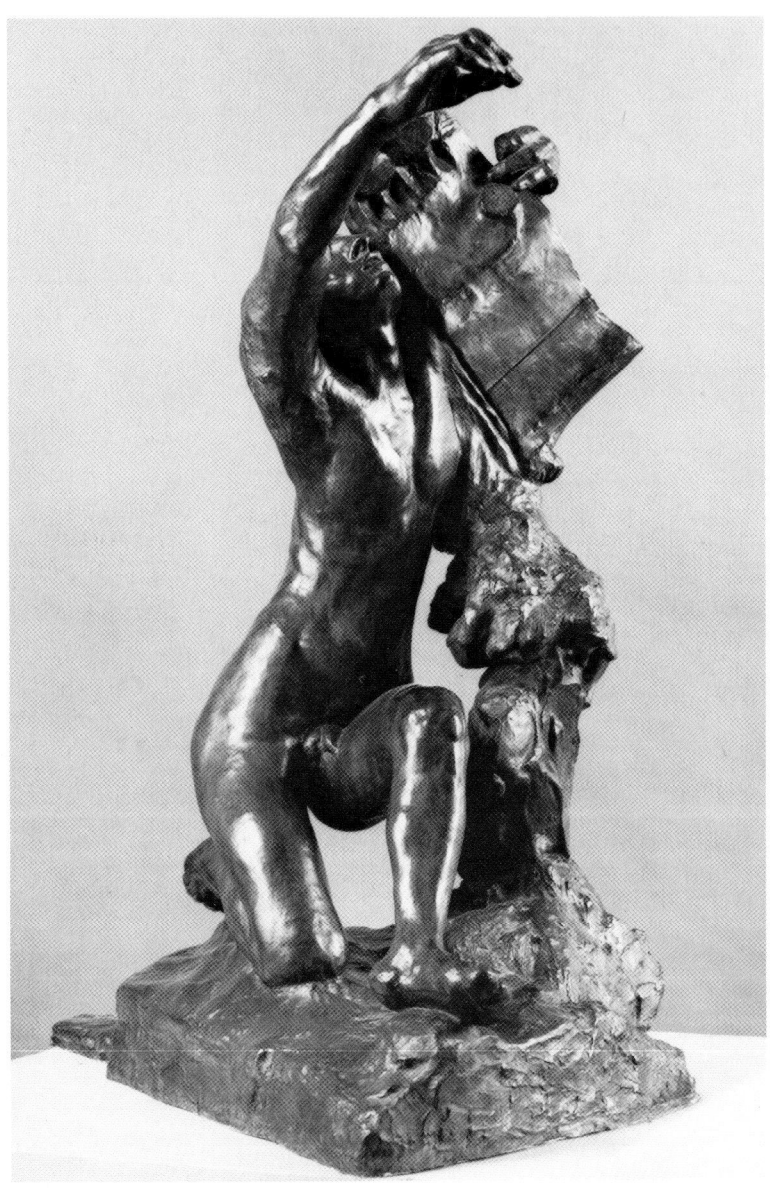

Figure 5.12. Auguste Rodin, *Orpheus*, 1892 Bronze.
(Musée Rodin, Paris; photo: Bruno Jarret; © ADAGP/SPADEM, Paris, and PRO LITTERIS, Zurich)

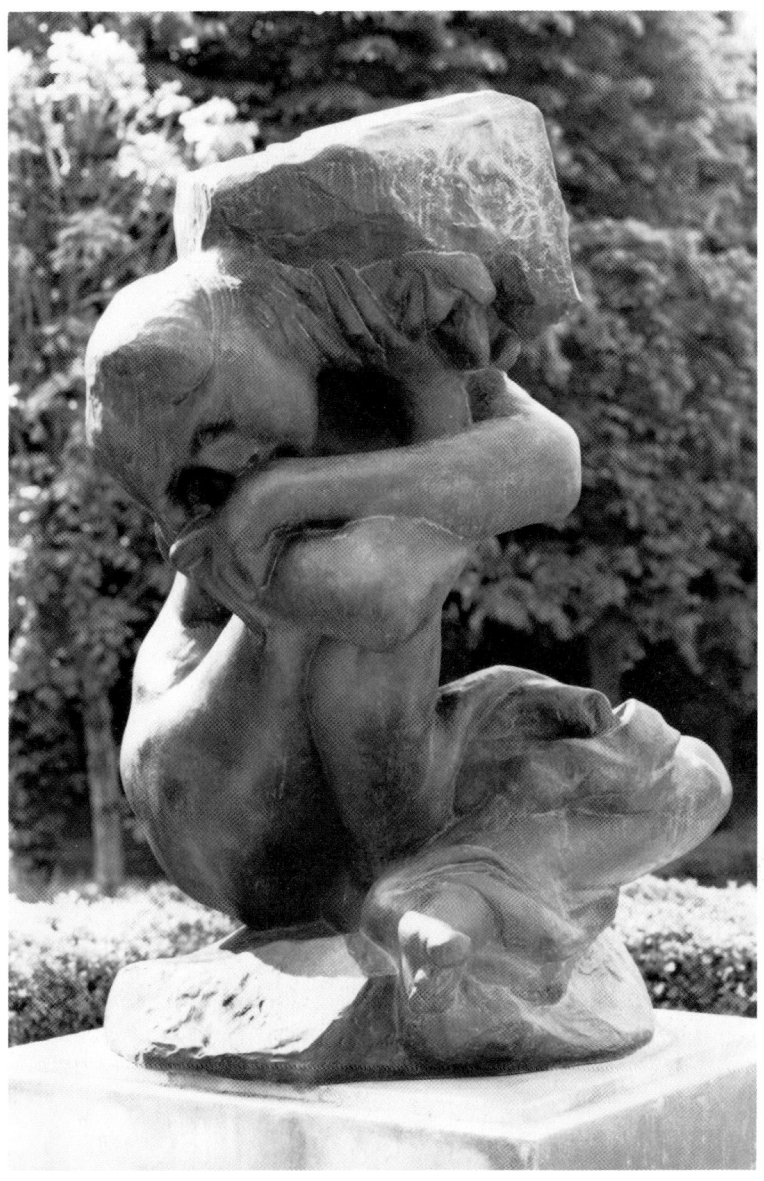

Figure 5.13. Auguste Rodin, *The Fallen Caryatid*, ca. 1881 Bronze.
(Musée Rodin, Paris; photo: Bruno Jarret;
© ADAGP/SPADEM, Paris, and PRO LITTERIS, Zurich)

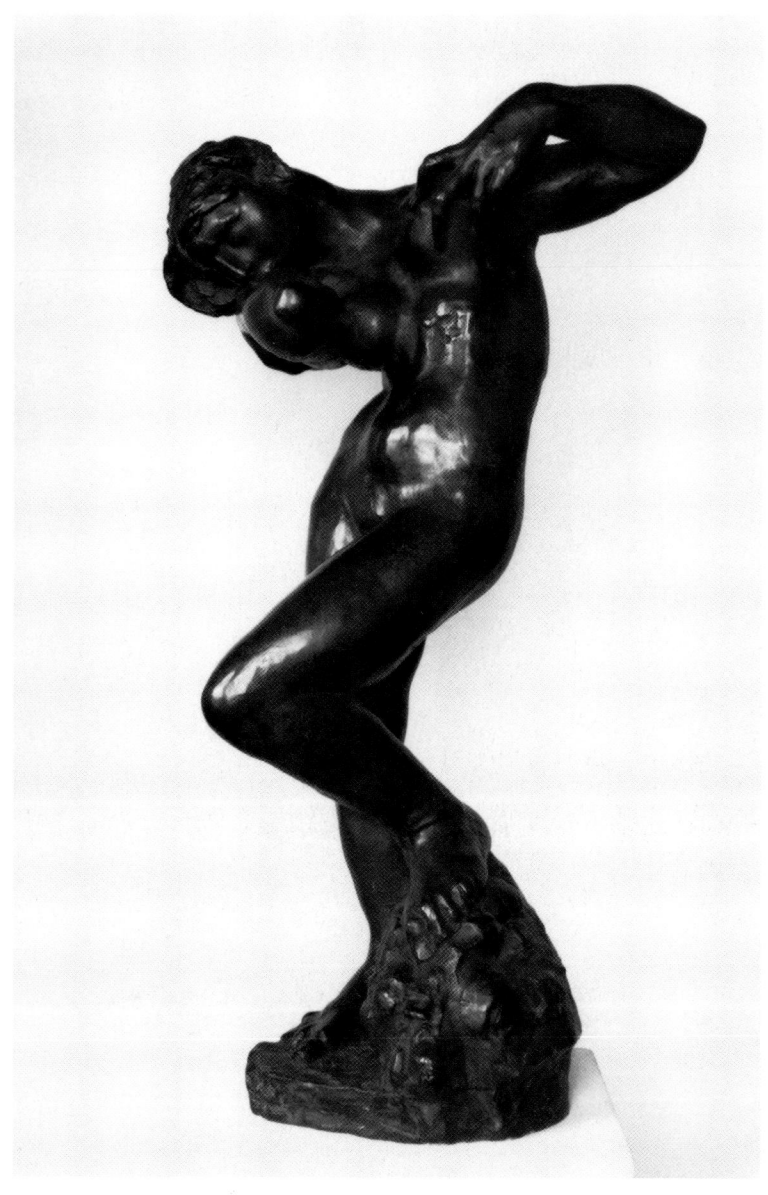

Figure 5.14. Auguste Rodin, *Meditation*, 1885
Bronze.
(Musée Rodin, Paris; photo: Bruno Jarret;
© ADAGP/SPADEM, Paris, and PRO LITTERIS,
Zurich)

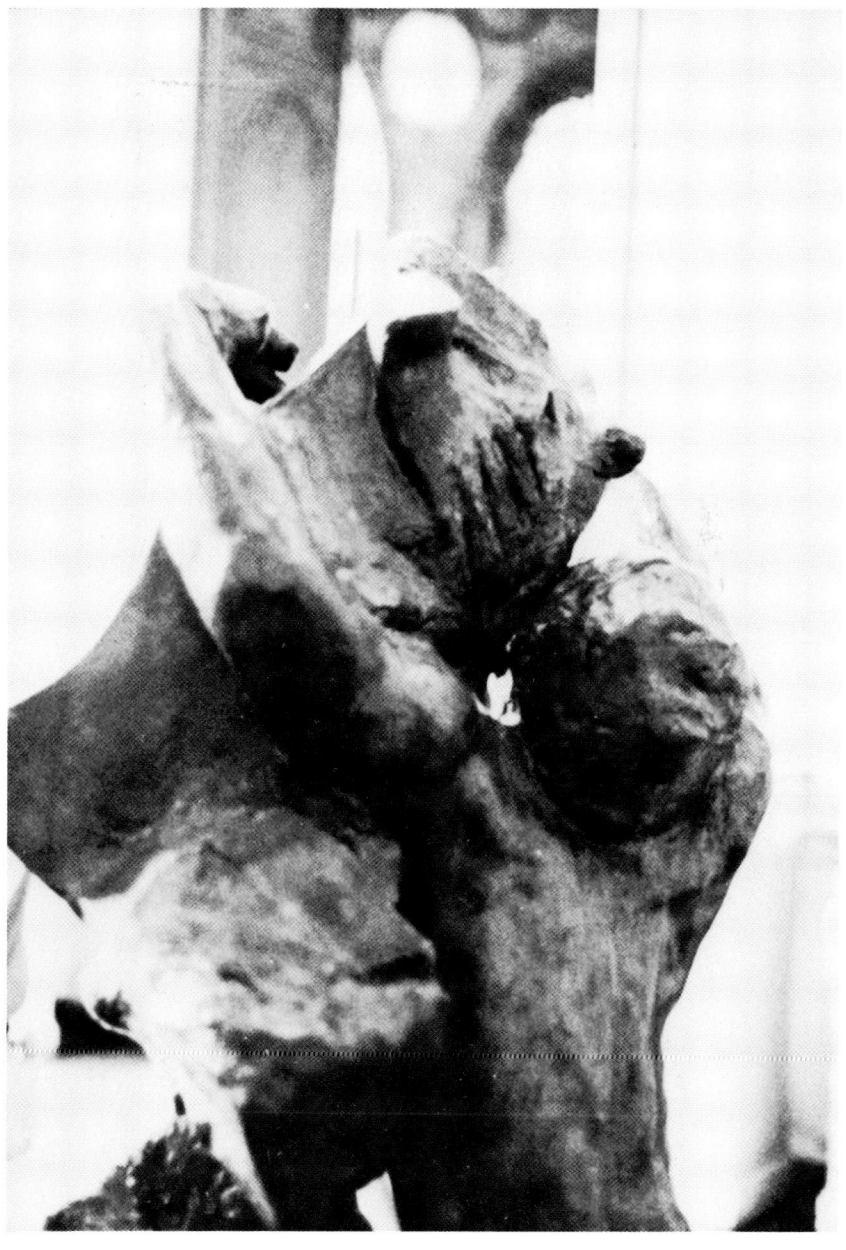

Figure 5.15. Auguste Rodin, *Orpheus* (rear view), 1892
(Musée Rodin, Paris)

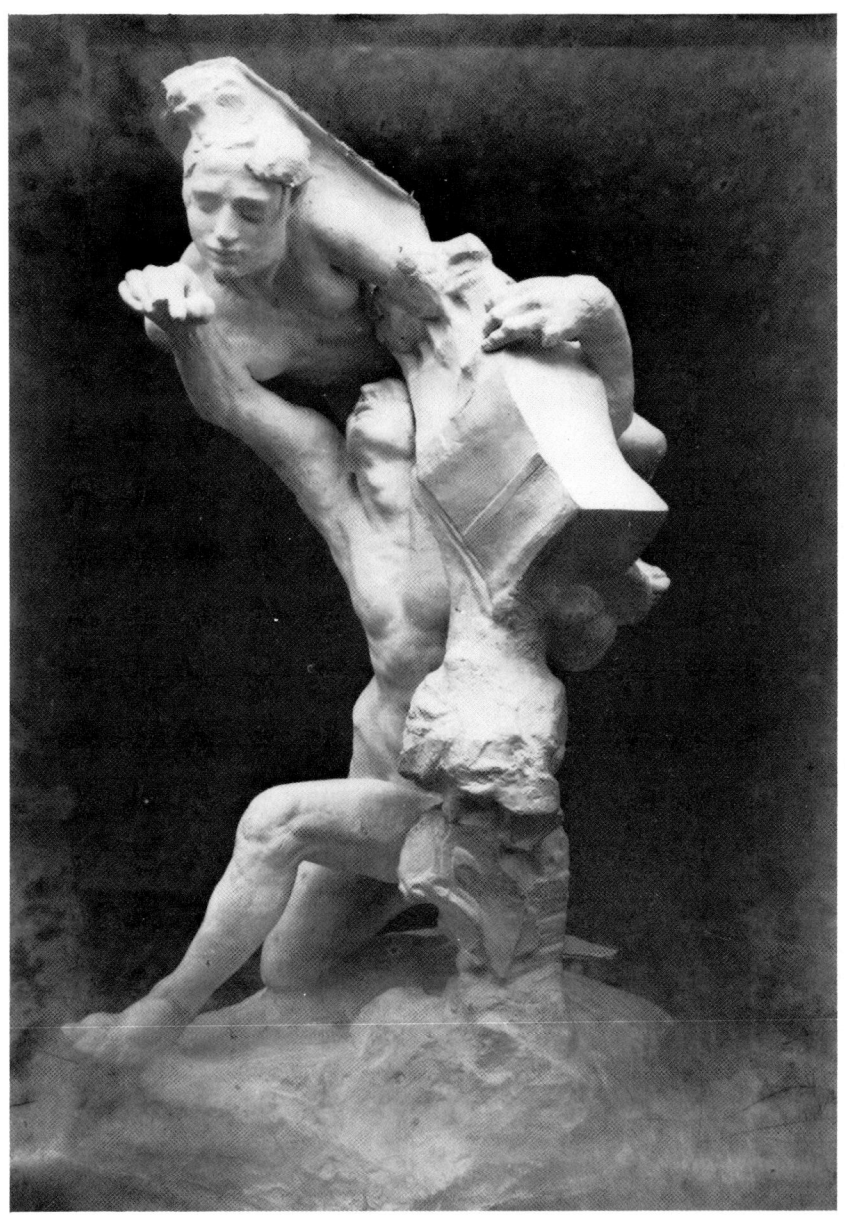

Figure 5.16. Auguste Rodin, *Orpheus, Imploring the Gods*, ca. 1892
Photograph of plaster, now destroyed.
(Musée Rodin, Paris; photo: Bulloz contretype Bruno Jarret)

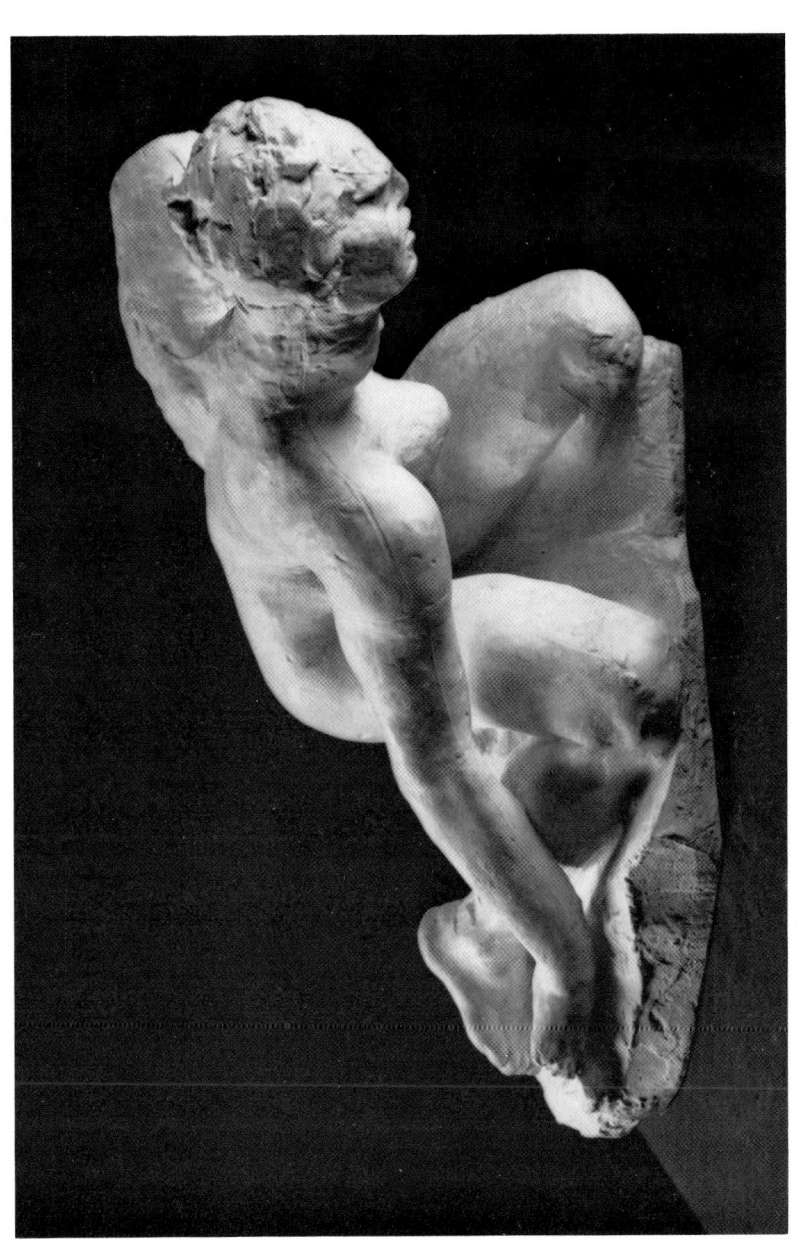

Figure 5.17. Auguste Rodin, *The Tragic Muse*, ca. before 1885
Plaster.
(*Musée Rodin, Paris; photo: Bruno Jarret;* © ADAGP/SPADEM, *Paris, and PRO LITTERIS, Zurich*)

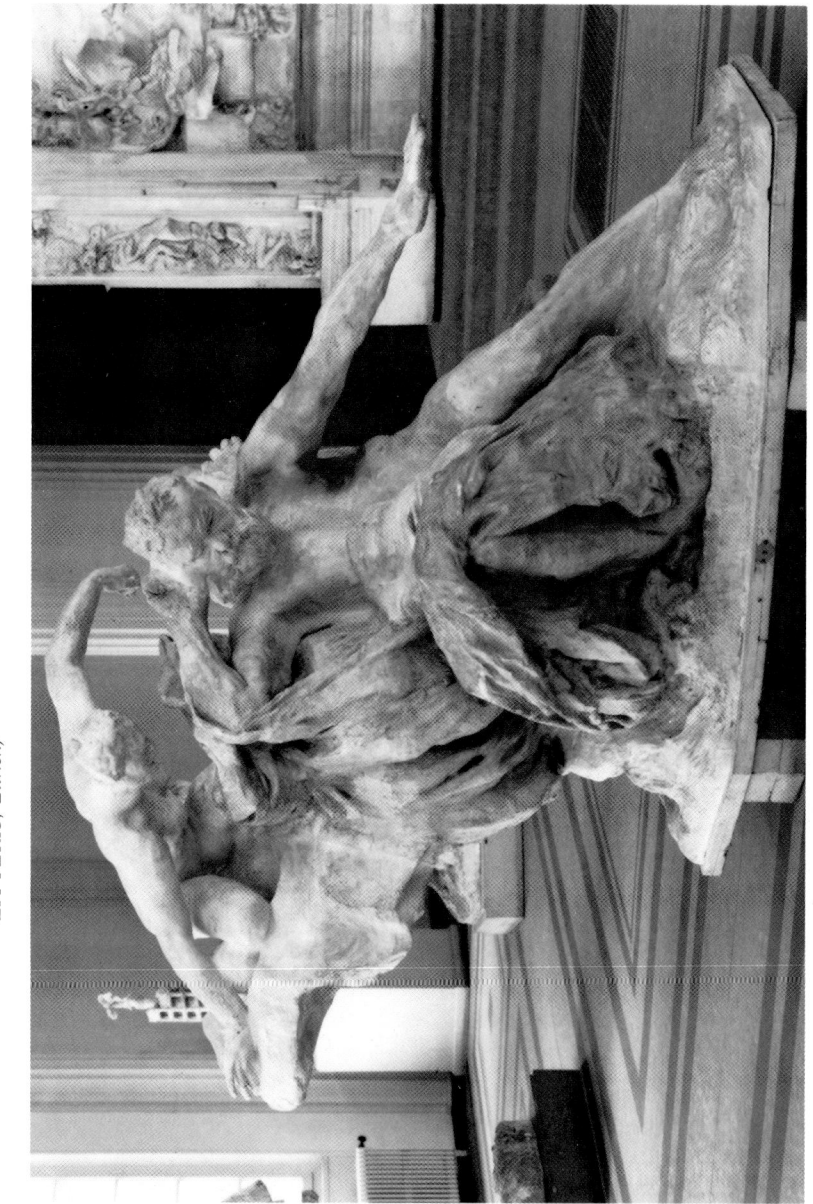

Figure 5.18. Auguste Rodin, *Monument to Victor Hugo*, ca. 1909 Waxed plaster.
(Musée Rodin, Paris; photo: Bruno Jarret; © ADAGP/SPADEM, Paris, and PRO LITTERIS, Zurich)

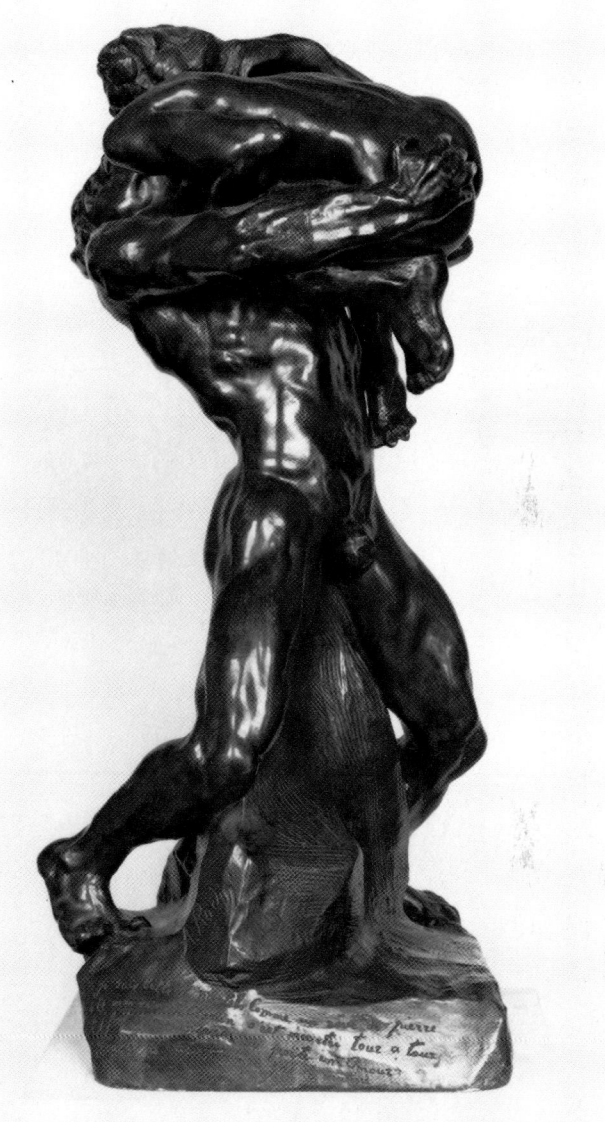

Figure 5.19. Auguste Rodin, *I Am Beautiful*, 1880 Bronze.
(Musée Rodin, Paris; photo: Bruno Jarret; © ADAGP/SPADEM, *Paris, and PRO LITTERIS, Zurich)*

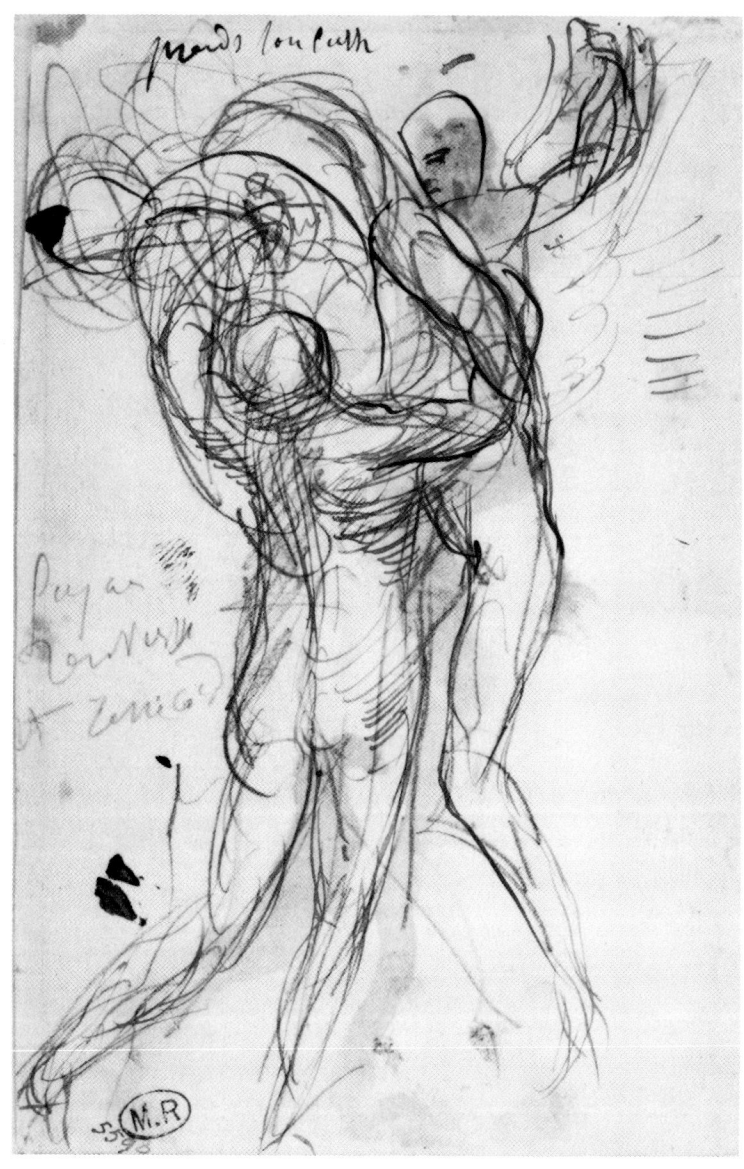

Figure 5.20. Auguste Rodin, *"Prends ton luth,"* n.d. Ink and wash, illustration for Alfred de Musset's, "Nuit de mai."
(Musée Rodin, Paris; photo: Bruno Jarret; © ADAGP/SPADEM, Paris, and PRO LITTERIS, Zurich)

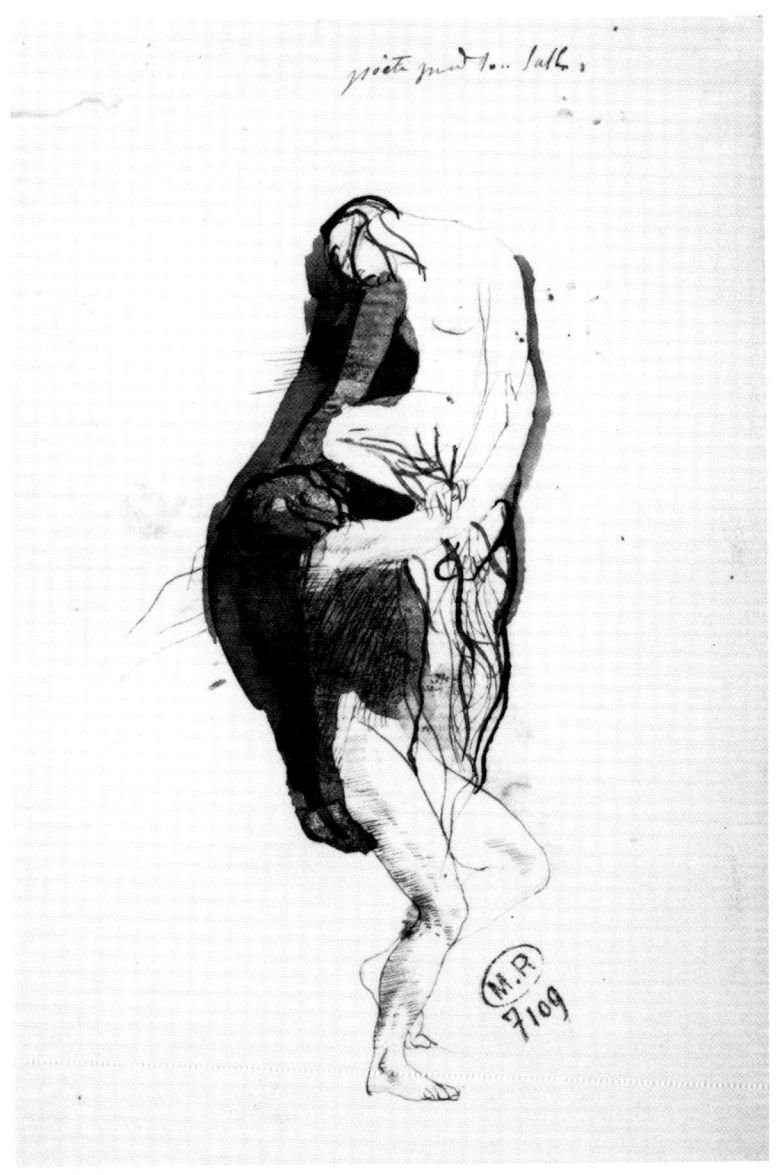

Figure 5.21. Auguste Rodin, *"Poète, prend [sic] ton luth,"* n.d. Violet ink, black wash and gouache, illustration for Alfred de Musset's, "Nuit de mai."
(Musée Rodin, Paris; photo: Bruno Jarret; © ADAGP/SPADEM, Paris, and PRO LITTERIS, Zurich)

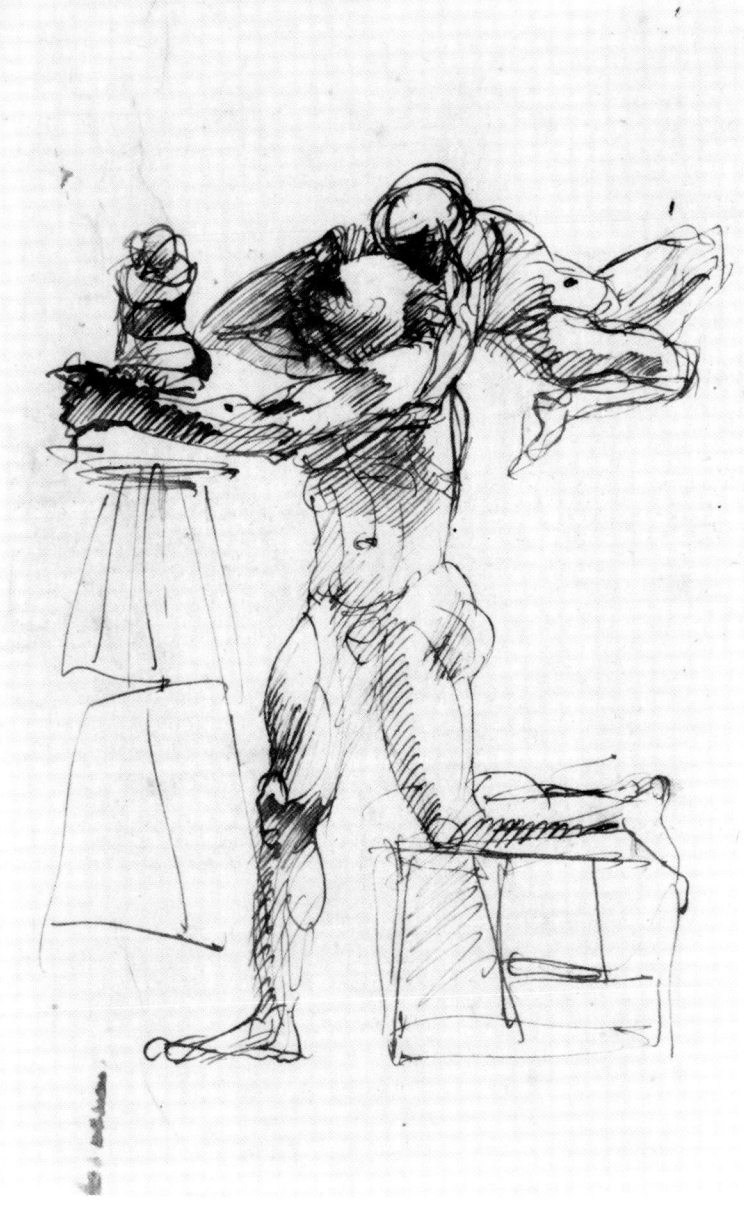

Figure 5.22. Auguste Rodin, *The Genius of Sculpture*, ca. 1880–82 Brown ink and wash on brown transparent paper. (*Collection Mrs. Noah L. Butken, Cleveland*)

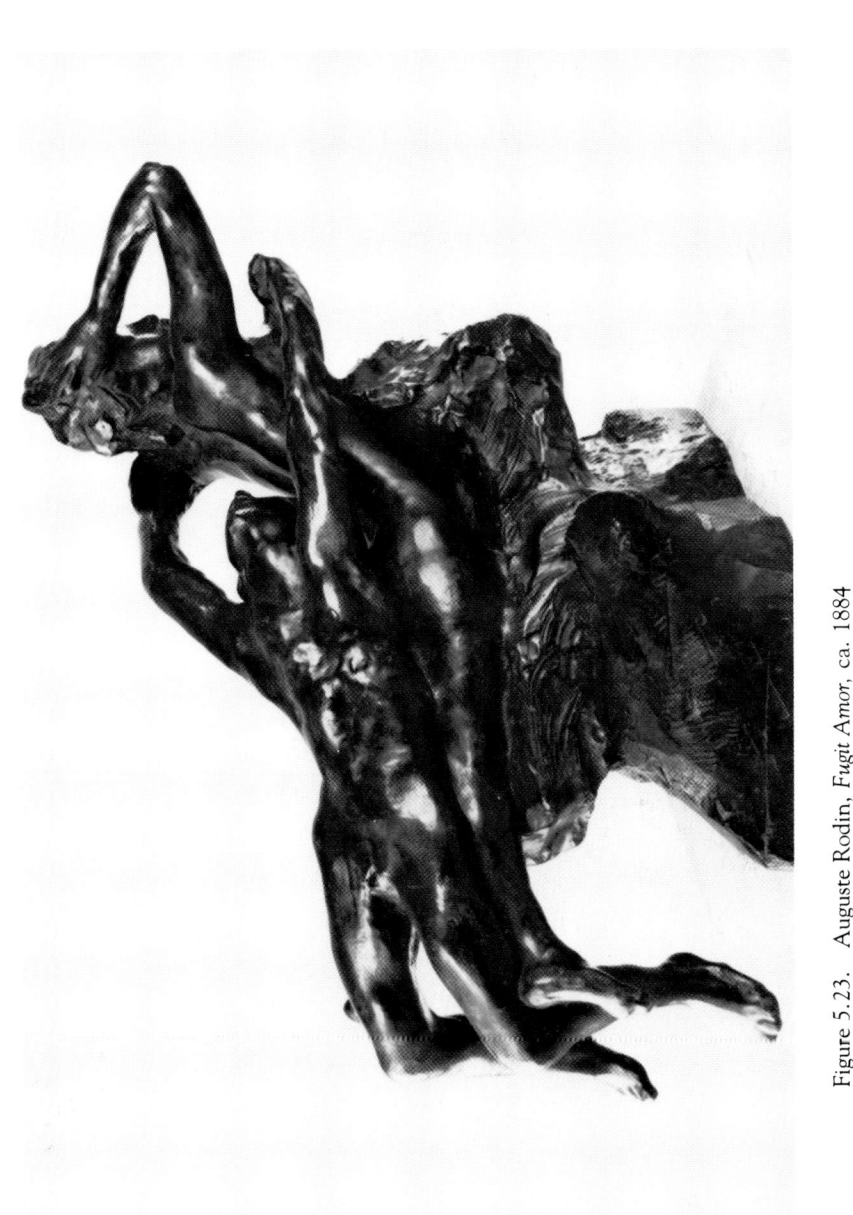

Figure 5.23. Auguste Rodin, *Fugit Amor*, ca. 1884 Bronze.
(Musée Rodin, Paris; photo: Bruno Jarret; © ADAGP/SPADEM, Paris, and PRO LITTERIS, Zurich)

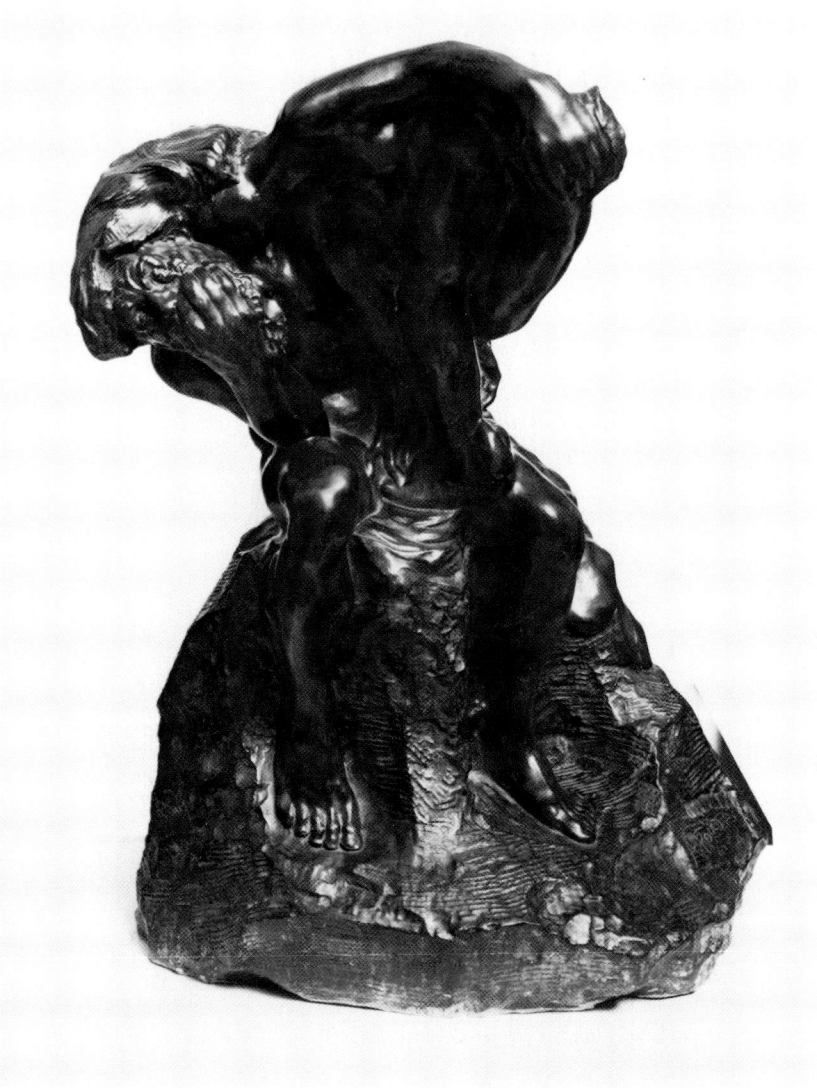

Figure 5.24. Auguste Rodin, *The Sculptor and His Muse*, 1890 Bronze.
(*By permission of The Fine Arts Museum of San Francisco, gift of Alma de Bretteville Spreckels*)

— « Soyez béni, mon Dieu, qui donnez la souffrance
Comme un divin remède à nos impuretés,
Et comme la meilleure et la plus pure essence
Qui prépare les forts aux saintes voluptés !

Je sais que vous gardez une place au Poète
Dans les rangs bienheureux des saintes Légions,
Et que vous l'invitez à l'éternelle fête
Des Trônes, des Vertus, des Dominations.

Je sais que la douleur est la noblesse unique
Où ne mordront jamais la terre et les enfers,
Et qu'il faut pour tresser ma couronne mystique
Imposer tous les temps et tous les univers.

Mais les bijoux perdus de l'antique Palmyre,
Les métaux inconnus, les perles de la mer,
Montés par votre main, ne pourraient pas suffire
A ce beau diadème éblouissant et clair ;

Car il ne sera fait que de pure lumière,
Puisée au foyer saint des rayons primitifs,
Et dont les yeux mortels, dans leur splendeur entière,
Ne sont que des miroirs obscurcis et plaintifs ! »

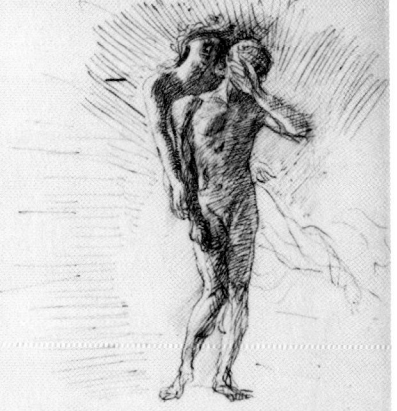

Figure 5.25. Auguste Rodin, Illustration for Baudelaire's "Bénédiction"
Ink and wash drawing for *Les Fleurs du mal*.
(Musée Rodin, Paris; photo: Bruno Jarret;
© ADAGP/SPADEM, Paris, and PRO LITTERIS, Zurich)

6

The Death of Orpheus

The pastoral splendor, infernal drama, and elegaic poignancy of the preceding episodes of the myth culminate in the dramatic crescendo of the poet's death, as Orpheus falls victim to a Dionysian frenzy, and is rendered limb from limb by the maddened Bacchae.[1] Ultimately, however, the poet wrests a victory from fate—his music enduring in the song and oracle emitting from his severed head which is rescued by Apollo and, also, in his instrument, preserved in the constellation Lyra.

His death may be seen as a compelling symbol of man's ultimate confrontation with the gods, his punishment for transgressions against immutable laws of the universe—in this case, Orpheus' revelation of secrets or mysteries to mankind. To probe the explanations for Orpheus' death ultimately brings into focus his position between the gods Apollo and Dionysus. As discussed at length in chapter 1,[2] Orpheus was sometimes even identified as Apollo's son, and his musical talent with the lyre is invariably associated with the sun-god. Sometimes it is Dionysus who brings about Orpheus' death, as punishment for his continuing to praise Apollo and refusing to worship Dionysus himself. Alternatively, however, Orpheus, leader of the Orphic cult, is allied with Dionysus. The Bacchantes' fury, then, may be the result of the poet's refusal to admit them to the mysteries of his religion, or their frustration with his homosexual cult which bore their men away, or jealousy over Orpheus' prolonged loyalty to his dead wife, Eurydice. His murder may simply be the accidental victimization of a priest of Dionysus by the madness of his own followers. Indeed, a central aspect of the Orphic mysteries is the parallel between the life and death of Orpheus and those of the Orphic god, Zagreus-Dionysus. These elements of the Apolline and Dionysian are by no means inconsequential details; but rather, the entire myth of Orpheus resonates profoundly with this dialogue between Apollo and Dionysus.

Orpheus is hunted down and ripped apart by a band of women in a riveting image of horrific slaughter, unleashed primal energy and sexual aggression. The sado-erotic implications of this bloody drama inspired its enduring popularity.

The depictions on fifth-century vases, of the poet, lyre clutched to his breast, fallen helplessly to the ground, surrounded by a group of women, bearing stones, spears or arrows, establishes a compositional formula that endures well into the nineteenth century. What is especially noteworthy, however, in the nineteenth century, are depictions of the severed head, a revival, in effect, of a motif which had been popular in antiquity, but depicted only seldom thereafter.

Emile Lévy

Emile Lévy's compelling *Death of Orpheus*, 1866 (fig. 6.1), might be taken as a prototype for the depiction of the subject. The setting is a nocturnal forest, a herm of Bacchus just visible amidst the shadows. The Maenads approach the limp body of their apparently unconscious victim. The women play timbrels and flutes and carry statues of Satyrs; their bodies are entwined with snakes and adorned with oak leaves. The line of dancing women curls down the hillside to the prostrate body of the poet. Three of the women have already begun their attack, poised over Orpheus' body with thyrsus and sickle, attacking with the same vicious energy as the cat depicted at the left.[3] A Maenad seizes Orpheus' left arm at the wrist with violent power, while another tears at his skin. The beauty of his extraordinarily smooth and attenuated body, sprawled limply at the edge of a glassy pool of water, constitutes a placid foil to the intense energy of the women who dominate the upper areas of the picture.

Paul Baudry

The influence of Lévy may be apparent in *The Death of Orpheus* included in Paul Baudry's decorative scheme for the Grand Foyer at the Opéra (fig. 6.2).[4] Here too the Maenads, carrying thyrsi, timbrels, knives and sickles, swarm down a hillside and surround the prostrate body of Orpheus, which occupies (with his broken lyre) the lower portion of the composition. As in the Lévy painting, one woman attacks Orpheus with a sickle, while another pulls at his limp left arm (in this case tied by a rope). If Baudry was not directly influenced by Lévy's work, it seems likely that both artists were inspired by a common text, perhaps Aeschylus, Euripides, or Ovid.[5]

It is not at all surprising that Baudry's massive project should be the object of considerable critical attention.[6] E. About, in 1874, waxes poetic about the Opéra as "un temple consacré à toute la famille des arts."[7] Camille Renard carefully classifies Baudry's panels into three categories: those concerned with Beauty: *The Judgment of Paris*; those concerned with Dance: *Salome Dancing before Herod; Orpheus and the Maenads; Jupiter and the Corybantes;* and those with the subject of music: *Saint Cecilia's Dream; Saul and David; Orpheus and*

Eurydice; The Shepherds; The Assault; Marsyas. The eight muses are portrayed between these panels.[8]

Indeed, an examination of the paintings which Renard groups under the subject Dance reveals a common theme—the loss of rational control, succumbing to religious or sexual ecstasy, and the release of primal energy. The Bacchantes are mad with Dionysian fury. The wild dance of the Corybantes, the eunuch priests of Cybele or Rhea, is similarly inspired by religious ecstasy. Salome's seductive dance is inspired by her own urges or the insidious demands of her mother, Herodiade. Two of the episodes culminate in destruction—that of Orpheus and Saint John the Baptist; the third in the successful concealing of the crying child Zeus. Taken together, the various subjects depicted in the panels which encircle the ceiling of the Grand Foyer explore an entire range of emotions in the arts: from soothing balm to the mad spirit (Saul and David) to destructive frenzy (Orpheus and the Maenads); from bellicose inspiration (the assault) to pastoral elegy (the shepherds); anguished disappointment (Orpheus and Eurydice in the Underworld) to uplifting dream of a celestial concert (St. Cecilia).

Auguste Rodin

Rodin's depiction, dating from before 1889, has been entitled alternately, *Orpheus and the Maenads*, *Orpheus and the Muses*, or *Orpheus and the Furies* (fig. 6.3). This confusion of Muse and Maenad is hardly surprising, indeed is entirely consistent with Rodin's perception of creativity or the muse as both inspiration and love as well as ponderous weight and crushing burden. The female figures, situated above the poet's head, constitute an awkward and massive weight which Orpheus seems destined either to support or to grapple with.[9]

Gustave Adolf Mossa

Orpheus (fig. 6.4), a 1906 watercolor is entirely consistent with the rather bizarre oeuvre of the later-generation Symbolist, Gustave Adolf Mossa (1883–1971),[10] Mossa reinforces the aggressive sexuality which is central to the confrontation of Orpheus and the Maenads, depicting knife-wielding Bacchantes lurking in the shadows of rocks and trees. The poet, meanwhile, strides nobly and entirely unconcealed in a brightly lit, open plain. The theme of sexual aggression or castration is underlined by the poet's lyre held out in front of his body, its silhouette emphasized by an erect, phallic form. Mossa's eschewal of mythological trappings, dressing the Bacchante in contemporary garb, serves to emphasize the psychological aspect of this brutal sexual encounter.

The castrating, destructive female and her victim, the poet-artist, is a dominant theme in Mossa's work. The femme fatale is represented in the guises of the Sphinx, Salome, Judith, Eve, Pandora, and a variety of other cold, murderous females. The bizarre intensity of Mossa's personal identification with the artist-victim is revealed in a 1905 *Psychological Self-Portrait* (fig. 6.5) in which the artist's self-portrait is dominated by the image of the knife-wielding woman, his neck draped with the serpent, Eve. The artist's desperation is evident in the bloody handprint which stains the wall. The neck of a violin which seems to emerge from the same hand which holds the paint brush (a rather facile allusion to the Symbolist ideal of synaesthesia) serves to identify Mossa the artist with Orpheus the musician.

This self-reflective figure of the artist-victim dominates Mossa's work, in the guise of the poet, Pierrot, Saint John the Baptist, Samson, or Christ. The conflation of Christian martyr and poet victim is, in fact, a significant subtheme in Mossa's work. The columnar, mummified figure in *Resurrection* (fig. 6.6), resembling Mossa's depictions of Christ, is identified as the poet through the golden laurel wreath crown and the broken lyre suspended at his waist. The poet stands erect like the single mournful cyprus tree, on the outskirts of a cemetery, evident in the tiny crosses which dot the horizon. Mossa exploits Christian symbolism, then, to convey the victory of the poet and his art in death. He strides in noble serenity, untroubled by the mass of miniature nude female bodies swarming at his feet. The femme fatale who tortured him and destroyed his life is impotent against his nonmaterial, spiritual self and his art.[11]

Gustave Moreau: The Dead Poet and Themes of Religious Syncretism

Moreau's "cycle du poète"[12] is dominated by the figure of the dead poet (fig. 6.7), a mournful image which, consistent with Moreau's religious and cultural syncretism, reverberates with the solemnity of the Christian pietà. *Wounded Poet and Centaurs*, 1890 (fig. 6.8), for instance, is a scene of Moreau's own invention—a pagan deposition, as it were, which depends upon the traditional Christian iconographic formula for its emotional weight and impact. Similarly, his depictions of Sappho and Prometheus resonate with Christian symbolism (figs. 6.9 and 6.10). Indeed, a central issue in the hostile criticism which greeted the exhibition of *Prometheus* at the 1869 Salon was Moreau's likening of the pagan hero to Christ.[13]

Orphée mort is paradigmatic of this genre within Moreau's oeuvre. The contrast with the preceeding images by Lévy, Baudry, and Mossa is instructive. Moreau is not interested in the sado-erotic implications of Orpheus' death and eschews the aggressive energy of the actual assault in favor of the sorrowful aftermath. Indeed, an inscription on a related drawing (fig. 6.11) makes clear that the figures which crowd around Orpheus' mangled body are not the murderous Maenads but instead his mournful followers.[14] In this context, the upright figure who holds the lyre aloft might be identified as Apollo rescuing Orpheus' lyre and head.

In mood and style this painting is comparable to *Orpheus Lamenting at the Tomb of Eurydice*. In both works, rather than the moment of extraordinary drama, Moreau chooses instead to express intense emotion, a profound sadness which permeates the entire landscape. The fluid application of paint, the fiery pervasive red give the impression that the entire scene—the rough and rocky terrain, the passage of pale blue sky—is awash with the poet's blood. Orpheus' body—sprawled in a pietà pose, his legs hanging downward, the body bent at the waist to the right, one arm hanging limply—is a brutal white patch against the dominant reds and earth tones of the landscape. The analogy with *Orpheus Lamenting* is confirmed, in fact, by the preparatory drawing mentioned above in which Moreau vacillates between the lamentation pose derived from Saint Sebastian and a position reminiscent of the traditional portrayals of the dead Christ.

Moreau's manipulation of the Christian iconographic formula of the pietà in order to invest the image of the poet-martyr with greater solemnity and drama, is another expression of the religious or cultural syncretism which pervades his entire aesthetic. The conflation of Orpheus and Christ is specifically confirmed, by a late painting entitled *Orpheus* (fig. 6.12) which includes both figures—the Christian martyr and the pagan victim—side by side within the same composition. The haloed poet, draped in black, holds an elaborate golden lyre. The figure to the left may be identified as the crucified Christ—his arms extended upward with daubs of red suggesting drops of blood—similar to Moreau's depiction of the crucified Christ in *Christ the Redeemer* (fig. 6.13). A pencil drawing (fig. 6.14), apparently a preparatory sketch for *Orpheus*, clarifies the subject. The religious syncretism is explicit in Moreau's drawing for *Les Lyres mortes* (fig. 6.15) in which the central figure—ascending on a sphere from the watery grave of many poet-martyrs—grasps both cross and lyre.[15]

The Severed-Head Motif

Consistent with Moreau's choice of mournful quietude instead of bloody drama is his fascination with the poet's severed head. It is noteworthy that the Symbolists, including Delville, Séon, and Redon, are the first artists since antiquity to depict the severed head of Orpheus, an indication, perhaps, of how profoundly this image appealed to their antimaterialist and idealist aesthetic. The aura of bloody destruction and fierce sexual aggression which dominates their equally frequent depictions of the severed head of Saint John contrasts strikingly with the ethereal beauty and eerie serenity which characterize the depictions of Orpheus' severed head. These images celebrate Orpheus' Dionysian destruction; representing the disintegration of the poet's physical reality which allows oneness or complete integration with the natural world and the victorious release of the orphic voice in the universe.

Gustave Moreau

Gustave Moreau's *Young Thracian Woman Carrying the Head of Orpheus*, ca. 1865 (fig. 6.16), had a significant influence on subsequent interpretations of the theme, indeed, seemed to function as a kind of talisman for the Symbolists. Upon its exhibition at the 1866 Salon and at the Exposition Universelle of the following year, the painting was the object of biting satire, and most typically, touted as confirmation of the view of Moreau as a painter of ideas, a literary artist.[16]

In the 1860s the painting was praised for its archaeological veracity.[17] Ernest Chesneau, countering the charges that Moreau was essentially a painter of ideas, admires the visual power of the image, especially the brilliant landscape.[18] In the official illustrated catalogue for the 1867 Exposition Universelle, Léon Scribe evokes the profound mythic and mystical sensibility of the work.[19] Théophile Gautier was intrigued by the riveting gaze of the young woman who caressingly holds the poet's head. Gautier explores briefly the parallels between the myth and the biblical story of St. John and Herodiade.[20] It inspired a poem by Armand Silvestre which appeared in *L'Artiste* in 1867.[21]

Moreau's painting continued to capture the attention of artists, poets and critics in the 1880s, 1890s and beyond, who responded to the image as a profound symbol of the eternally alienated artist. In 1889, Paul le Prieur writes:

> Where does the legend of Orpheus take place? In Thrace, in Italy, or everywhere at the same time? Is it still about Orpheus? Isn't it the image of the poet of all countries and all times, martyred, misunderstood and venerated after his death?[22]

Raymond Bouyer, writing in *L'Artiste* in 1897, stresses the relevance of Moreau's "poème antique" to his contemporary world: "Gustave Moreau knows how to combine modern anxiety with antique fable."[23] In 1886, the notorious Decadent poet, Jules La Forgue, published a rhapsodic description of the painting in the periodical, *Le Symboliste*, stressing its rarified quality of refinement.[24]

The major themes which dominate the Symbolists' appreciation of this work are the unearthly atmosphere of penetrating or mournful silence, the hieratic quality of this image of religious martyrdom, and above all, the hypnotic power of the young woman's gaze at the poet's severed head. Jean Lorrain's poem, "La Destinée," dedicated to Moreau, explores the meanings of the mysterious painting. Lorrain evokes the frozen, lifeless silence of the landscape:

> Not a cry, not a bird in the air
> An eternal setting in the distance on the red flood
> And on the sand, at the foot of the rock, nothing moves,
> Roses of salt crystals and of bitter coral.[25]

Similarly, Ary Renan's sensitive analysis of the work emphasizes the crushing silence:

> A mysterious concordance, meanwhile, makes nature sympathetic to this silent drama, to these cold obsequies. A half-day opaline illuminates the confines of the world; a subtle sleep, a malaria-like stagnation enervates things; one only hears a small flute, an ironic refrain, modulated by the shepherds, there, on a rock by the Hebrus.[26]

Renan explores the special role of the artist-martyr in Moreau's work:

> For the painter, for us, for tradition, Orpheus is the first and great poetic victim, the inspired apostle who matures the face of the world. What dies with him is civilizing art.[27]

Similarly, for Edouard Schuré, Orpheus is the priest, one of the great initiates of his theosophical pantheon. Schuré interprets the confrontation of the woman with the poet's severed head in terms of initiation or spiritual metamorphosis. The young woman is a symbol of humanity, who partakes of the martyr's knowledge and discovers a new, transcendent level of consciousness.

> The virgin has trembled with tenderness for the poet torn apart by the Bacchantes. Thus sympathy is for the feminine spirit the first revelation of the universal soul. This comprehensive emotion makes her already live a new life, greater, loftier and more profound. The ocean of passions groans still beneath her feet, but the other ocean calls her, that of human suffering, which she throws herself into, into which she plunges with lost heart, forgetting herself and she is reborn metamorphosed. Passive renunciation is the supreme virtue. Thus the elected woman, renouncing herself, penetrates into the heroic and superhuman epoch.[28]

For both Renan and Schuré then, Orpheus is priest and initiate, solemn martyr, harbinger of civilization and spiritual truth.

It is, however, the powerful conjunction of the woman's face and the delicately featured, almost androgynous visage of the poet which captivates these writers. This hypnotic gaze elicits a very personal response on the part of the viewer. The final verse of Lorrain's poem consists of these lines:

196   The Death of Orpheus

> Mournful offering, she places between my trembling fingers,
> The head, still moist with the kisses of the sword
> And it is myself, which I find in the depths of these white eyes.[29]

The poet, seemingly, is drawn into the reflective quality of the two faces, absorbed by the powerful suggestion of a conflation of Orpheus and Narcissus.[30] Lorrain is simultaneously the humble and awestruck initiate who solemnly holds Orpheus' head and the martyred poet himself. Similarly, Renan attempts to decipher the woman's powerful gaze:

> She carries her sweet funereal burden with slow step, and from her lowered lid falls an indecisive glance, scarcely damp, of ignorant dreaming, charged with a discrete indifference in which the soul sleeps. And, more than hers, it is our melancholy which overflows, all our inexpressable compassion which animates itself and which walks forth while rocking the first relics of an undefined cult.[31]

The hypnotic gaze is the central image in Marcel Proust's evocation of the talismanic power of the painting, which prompts him to make pilgrimage to the Luxembourg Palace where the work hung.

> We go simply, like a woman carrying the severed head of Orpheus, before the *Femme portant la tête d'Orphée*, and we see something in this head of Orpheus that looks at us, the thought of Gustave Moreau painted on this canvas, which looks at us with these beautiful blind eyes which are thought colors.[32]

Proust finds in Moreau's painting an expression of the immortality of the poet's true, interior soul. Similarly, more than fifty years later, in André Breton's commentary on the painting, it is the riveting gaze which is the focus of his analysis. He speaks of the "magic eye" in Gustave Moreau's "somnambulistic world":

> [H]e takes to a high point of exaggeration the eye of the priestess . . . exchanging with Orpheus that ineffable regard between Hegelian death and the human being that receives death's secret.[33]

Moreau, in his studious fascination with the Orpheus myth, would have most surely been aware of the tradition which ascribes Orpheus' murder to his leadership of a homosexual cult. In fact, it is Orpheus' ambiguous sexuality which makes him the perfect expression/symbol of Moreau's androgynous poet-martyr. It has been suggested that Moreau's androgynous hero is a reflection of his own latent homosexuality.[34] Or perhaps it is more the chaste virginal Orpheus who captivates Moreau's imagination. Moreau might well have been aware of the compelling description of the pure, androgynous priest, offered by Eliphas Lévi in *Histoire de la magie:*

> Orpheus is widowed and remains as such in purity; the marriage with Eurydice had not attained consummation, and as the widower of one who was a virgin he rested himself in virginity. The poet is not two-hearted, and children of the race of gods love once and once alone. Paternal inspirations, yearnings for an ideal which shall be found beyond the tomb, widowhood made holy in its consecration to the sacred muse. What a revelation in advance of inspirations yet to come! Orpheus, bearing in his heart a wound that nothing but death shall heal, becomes a doctor of souls and bodies; he dies at length, the victim of his chastity—the death which he suffers is that of initiators and prophets. He perishes proclaiming the unity of God and the unity of love: this at a later period was the root of the Orphic mysteries.[35]

Contrasting Interpretations

The reverential aura, eerie beauty and meditative quality which characterize Moreau's work, as well as the depictions of later Symbolists, may be elucidated by contrast with a number of other late nineteenth-century interpretations whose melodramatic and narrative quality clearly reflects these artists' titillation with the lurid image of the poet's severed head. Abel Boyé, for instance, in *The Immortal Lyre*, 1899 (fig. 6.17), focuses on the nymphs, shepherds, dogs, sheep, and swans who are attracted by the sounds of the lyre which floats in the river Hebrus. Similarly, in John William Waterhouse's *Nymphs Finding the Head of Orpheus*, 1900 (fig. 6.18), two maidens discover the head and lyre of the poet. In this work, melodrama is somewhat mitigated by a quality of emotional or dramatic seriousness and by a delicate aura of Pre-Raphaelite poetry which is typical of Waterhouse's mythological paintings. Ludovic Alléaume, a student of Hébert and L. Olivier Merson, produced *Lamentation on the Death of Orpheus*, 1914 (fig. 6.19), which focuses on the histrionic gestures of two nude women who discover the poet's head and lyre amidst a watery mass of reeds and irises. Their extreme dismay is rendered somewhat comical by the particularly lifeless appearance of Orpheus' head, resembling perhaps, a rather uninteresting plaster.

Henri Léopold Lévy's *Death of Orpheus* (fig. 6.20) is a somewhat unusual interpretation of this subject in that not only the poet's severed head, but also his lifeless body, is depicted. The head, glowing and haloed, is encircled by a group of seagulls and lapped by the waves of an animated sea. The truncated neck of the poet's body is obscured by the lyre, still cradled in the corpse's arms. Unfortunately, the ridiculous intrudes somewhat, as one imagines that the head has rolled down the sharp incline on which the body sprawls, to the water's edge. The depiction of the decapitated body is quite rare. Other examples include a small oil by Moreau, *Orpheus* (fig. 6.21), and Franz von Stuck's *Dead*

198   The Death of Orpheus

Orpheus, 1891. In the von Stuck work, the poet still clutches an enormous, intricately decorated lyre, while blood gushes from his severed neck. In another work, the Munich artist depicts a centaur's discovery of the poet's bloody severed head (fig. 6.22). This work, enclosed in an elaborate original frame, is paired with another painting entitled *Resonance*.[36]

The Impact of Moreau's *Orpheus* on Other Artists

The impact of Moreau's *Young Thracian Woman Carrying the Head of Orpheus* is unmistakably apparent in Jean Delville's *Orpheus,* 1893, Redon's various versions of this theme: *Head of Orpheus Floating in the Waters,* 1881, *Orphée aux enfers,* ca. 1905, *Orpheus,* 1905, *Orpheus with Eyes Closed* probably also ca. 1905, and *Orpheus,* after 1913, as well as Alexandre Séon's *La Lyre d'Orphée,* 1898. None of these works include the Thracian woman, but rather focus attention exclusively on the head and lyre. However, the woman's hypnotic intense gaze, the almost magnetic tension between the two faces remains implicit in many of these images in which the severed head dominates the composition, often pushed forward by a reflective surface of liquid, so that the painter or the observer is in the reverent position of the Thracian woman.

Jean Delville

In Delville's *Orpheus* (fig. 6.23), the head and lyre float on a rippling surface of opalescent blue-green. The fine waves which move diagonally across this surface create a gentle motion, and suggest, as well, the rhythmic sound of the water. One imagines the shells which float nearby, reverberating with this incessant sound or perhaps also with the poet's mournful song. The water is, moreover, flecked with pinpoints of blue-white light, evidently stars reflected from the night sky above. Hence, the blue-green ground is at once the river Hebrus on which the head and lyre float and the sky into which the instrument ascends as the constellation Lyra. The reflective surface of the water intensifies the apparition of the severed head, pushing it uncomfortably close to the picture plane. There is further evidence of the impact of Moreau's painting on the younger artist. The head rests on a similarly elaborate lyre—intricately carved and decorated with jewels and inlays. More significantly, Delville endows Orpheus' face with the same idealized, delicately modeled, vaguely androgynous features that characterize the poet's visage in Moreau's work. In fact, it was Madame Delville who was the artist's model for this painting.

Alexandre Séon

Alexandre Séon's lifelong preoccupation with the theme of Orpheus apparently culminated with *Orpheus' Lyre*, ca. 1898 (fig. 6.24). In this work, the poet's laurel-wreathed head rests on a crude three-stringed lyre, propped precariously amid a few jagged rocks, giving the impression that it has been washed there by the movement of the waves. The cluster of rocks is the only relief in a landscape which otherwise consists of three smoothly painted expanses of sky, water and land. The aura of isolation and desolation is reinforced by the somber, limited range of colors, the thin, dry texture of the paint, and the brittle linear articulation of the head and lyre. The painting is clearly exemplary of Séon's idealist, mural style, discussed in chapter 5. Orpheus' face appears strangely alive, animated with a careworn expression, evident in the knitting of the brow and the parting of the lips. This same pained and weary expression marks the poet's face in Valère Bernard's 1901 relief sculpture of marble and onyx (fig. 6.25).[37] Bernard, a native of Marseille, was, like Séon, a devoted friend and student of Puvis de Chavannes. He might well have been familiar with this particular work by Séon, exhibited at the Salon des Artistes Français in 1898, or in the 1901 exhibition at the Galerie Georges Petit. The severed head figures, moreover, in other aspects of Séon's oeuvre—in the frontispiece he designed for Péladan's "l'Androgyne" and in his illustrations for Edmond d'Haraucourt's *L'Effort*, 1899.[38]

Odilon Redon

At least five depictions of Orpheus can be identified among Odilon Redon's many depictions of disembodied heads. The poet's head dominates these compositions: his eyes closed in contemplation, the faces animated, however, with an aura of psychological awareness. Indistinct, aqueous or flower-filled environments do not distract from but rather intensify this meditative, introspective mood.

The earliest version, *Orpheus' Head Floating on the Waters*, 1881 (fig. 6.26), is perhaps the most unusual. The poet's head—capped with a thick bush of hair—floats upright in the water, the neck and chin submerged beneath the liquid. The brutality of this rather peculiar position is reinforced by the harsh chiaroscuro of the charcoal drawing, the light-bathed background contrasting starkly with the densely shadowed face.

In the other four works, Orpheus' head floats on his lyre—a mandolin in the Cleveland Museum painting (fig. 6.27). In two of the versions the instruments resemble rather massive pedestals for portrait busts which contradict the impression of floating weightlessness (fig. 6.28). An allusion to Moreau's *Orpheus* is evident in the version in the San Francisco Museum (fig. 6.29), in which Redon conflates the poet's head on the lyre and the head of the Thracian woman—an amalgamation achieved through the similarity of profiles, the angle at which the head inclines, the treatment of the hair, and the neckline of the bodice.[39]

The watery expanses or bursts of blossoms which surround the severed heads cannot be accurately described as landscapes as they offer neither a spatially defined setting nor details with reference to the mythic narrative. They could, perhaps, be understood as psychological landscapes which intensify or reverberate with a psychic or emotional activity otherwise masked by the passive visage of the poet. This idea may be clarified by *The Dream*, ca. 1912 (fig. 6.30). Here flowers are not a bouquet placed in a vase, nor do they grow in a landscape setting, but rather they float in the center of the composition amidst flowing passages of blue, gold and white. The blossoms that seem to hover in mid-air through the concentration of the closed-eyed figure at lower left may be, to use Proust's phrase, the "colored thoughts" of that meditating soul.[40]

These images of the poet's severed head floating gently amidst amorphous environments evoke Orpheus' victory. Destroyed and fragmented, the poet achieves complete integration with nature. Released from the confines of the physical being, the Orphic voice merges with the natural world. Orpheus' attainment of oneness with nature was, of course, one of the primary themes in Herbert Marcuse's *Eros and Civilization*. Marcuse claims both Narcissus and Orpheus as embodiments of "the Great Refusal: refusal to accept separation from the libidinous object (or subject)."[41] It is the refusal of the performance principle symbolized in the archetypal hero, Prometheus. Narcissus and Orpheus eschew the limited concept of Eros, a repressive order of procreative sexuality, adopting instead a fuller notion of Eros which allows for a profound unity of the individual with nature or reality outside the self. Narcissus is not the antagonist of love, but the embodiment of a new love which implies a oneness with the universe. He stares enrapt, unknowing, at his own image, is drawn into rest, sleep and death, to be reborn into the flower. Orpheus' song pacifies animals, animates trees and rocks, and thereby liberates nature. Similarly, his espousal of homosexuality may be interpreted as a liberation of man from a rigid notion of love in order to embrace a fuller notion of Eros. In death, Orpheus achieves ultimate oneness with nature.[42] Marcuse himself relates his interpretation of Narcissus and Orpheus to Freud's concept of the primary ego-feeling, a "limitless extension and oneness with the universe . . . a feeling which *embraced the universe* and expressed an *inseparable connection of the ego with the external world.*"[43] Redon's images of Orpheus' head, in serene contemplation, awash in the beauty of nature, seem to embody Freud's "oceanic feeling," or Marcuse's notion of metamorphosis in death, the disintegration of limitations between self and nature.

Of course Orpheus' death—fragmentation and metamorphosis—parallels the demise of the Orphic god, Zagreus-Dionysus. The fragments of Dionysus, torn asunder by the Titans, become part of a vast cycle of rebirth and integration with the world: he endures in mankind (created from the ashes of the Titans); he is born of woman (Semele); he is reunited with god, the creator, Zeus. Marcuse traces this cycle of metamorphosis in his discussion of Narcissus:

> Narcissus and Dionysus are closely assimilated (if not identified) in the Orphic mythology. The Titans seize Zagreus-Dionysus while he contemplates his image in the mirror which they gave him. An ancient tradition (Plotinus, Proclus) interprets the mirror-duplication as the beginning of the god's self-manifestation in the multitude of the phenomena of the world—a process which finds its final symbol in the tearing asunder of the god by the Titans and his rebirth by Zeus. The myth would thus express the reunification of that which was separated, of God and world, man and nature—identity of the one and the many.[44]

Another image of the unity of the poet with nature, the victory of the Orphic voice, may be found in *The Vision*, 1907 (fig. 6.31), by F. Holland Day.[45] Not only does he depict the androgynous poet standing amidst an idyllic landscape; but moreover, he captures the concept of oneness with nature in the more abstract or surreal image of a human head which is superimposed over the outcrop of rock, merged, as it were, with nature.

In Redon's oeuvre, the aqueous environment is clearly associated with themes of generation, growth, and metamorphosis. Water imagery is the common element in many diverse contexts: his fantasies about his own birth; his fascination with the birth of his son, Ari; wonderment with the life-movement of microscopic organisms; contemplation of antediluvian forces which generated the cosmos; the growth and transformation of ideas and images in the artist's personal aesthetic or inner imaginative world. The sea constitutes an important theme in Redon's autobiographical *A soi-même*, becoming the subject of almost incantatory passages.[46]

Images of genesis, metamorphosis or evolution dominate Redon's lithographic series.[47] Forms emerge from murky, swampy settings. The boundaries between man, plant and inanimate material are dissolved as Redon fantasizes about genesis and evolution. The human head floats in a delicate bubble, blossoms forth from the bud of a plant, emerges from the worm-like chrysalis, or the body of a fish. A creature which is half-dog, half-fish struggles from the primeval ooze. A rocky cliff is transformed into a human face. Faces sprout from plants, float like germinating seeds or terminate globular larvae, images, once again, of the integration of man and nature. Balloons, seeds, eyes, heads are continually conflated in Redon's oeuvre, a kind of rhythmic poetry or metamorphosis of floating circular forms which merge and emerge.[48]

202   The Death of Orpheus

Redon's concept of evolution, however, was not based on a sophisticated scientific principle but, rather, was more a poetic, elusive concept inspired by a fascination with the rapports between man and nature, of an all-encompassing spiritual and material unity.[49] One specific inspiration for Redon's images of the primeval swirl of life emerging in murky waters may have been the research of his friend, the biologist Armand Clavaud. An enthusiast of the philosophy of Spinoza and Hindu religion, Clavaud sought to establish direct links between the plant and animal worlds, one great physiological and spiritual unity.[50]

Like his friend Clavaud and so many of his contemporaries, Redon was attracted by a religious or cultural syncretism. His simultaneous fascination with Eastern philosophies, Druid religion and Wagner's Nordic mythology is manifest in his diverse subject matter: Buddha, pagan mythology, as well as Christian subjects.[51] Certainly Redon's sustained interest in Flaubert's *Temptation of Saint Anthony* (he devoted three series of lithographs to this work) derives from the author's hallucinatory descriptions of deities from all religions and cultures, which echo his own syncretic attitude.[52] The range and variety of Redon's images of the severed head—many different martyrs and specters, Orpheus, Christ, Saint John—demonstrate his fluid synthesis of different myths and religions. The comparison of a charcoal, *Profile with Crown of Thorns* (fig. 6.32) and the Orpheus in the San Francisco Museum suggests a specific conflation of Orpheus and Christ. In each composition, the visage—closed-eyed and contemplative—faces downward from the upper right corner of the composition. The thorny branches, extending out from the head, and curling in front of the profiled face, form a shape similar to the silhouette of the lyre in the *Orpheus*. Redon weaves together the thorny branches into the familiar shape of the poet's lyre, in order perhaps to explore his keen sensitivity to the rich intermingling of pagan and Christian iconography, the specific parallels between Orpheus and Christ.[53]

Orpheus versus Saint John the Baptist: Apollonian-Dionysian Dichotomy

The Symbolists' depictions of Orpheus' severed head are characterized by a transcendent aura, a delicate physical beauty, and a haunting quality of consciousness or psychological animation. Moreau's 1865 painting, which may well have established this tenor for subsequent interpretations, is rather exceptional within Moreau's oeuvre in that the Thracian woman is not one of Moreau's typical threatening femmes-fatale. Similarly, the tranquil serenity, (one is tempted to say chastity) of Moreau's Orpheus paintings contrasts dramatically with the bloody, murderous, sexually agressive atmosphere which characterizes his interpretations of the Salome theme (fig. 6.33). Indeed, this contrast is in no way exclusive to Moreau's oeuvre. Presentations of the Baptist's severed head are very frequently tinged with necrophilia and sado-eroticism (fig. 6.34). One interpretation of the severed head of Orpheus, a work by Joseph-Emile Millochau (fig. 6.35), defies this contrast: The Maenad, a luxurious nude in the style of Cabanal, languorously embraces the head of the poet.[54]

The gentle beauty of the Symbolists' depictions of Orpheus' severed head, and especially that peculiar impression of psychological animation—that the eyes will open or that words will emit from the parted lips—may indicate that the Symbolists looked to antique models which emphasized the animated quality of the oracular head.[55] Moreover, the magical or oracular head figures prominently in occult texts; witness, for instance, the many references in Collin de Plancy's *Dictionnaire infernal*.[56]

An ethereally beautiful but nonetheless severed head embodies a profound contradiction between life and death, between transcendent beauty and destruction, between the spiritual and the physical. The poet's severed head is symbolic of Orpheus as the accommodation of the Apollonian and the Dionysian, a meaning which surely would not have escaped the Symbolists who were so profoundly interested in ancient cults and religions, and specifically in the evolution of tragedy in a religious context. Eschewing the tale of hapless lover or desperate hero, the Symbolists focused on the crux of the myth, Orpheus as symbol of Art: Orpheus' physical destruction contains his victory; the Dionysian sacrifice is requisite for the Apollonian apotheosis of his art. (Just as the Dionysian orgia completes Orpheus' initiation—completes the cycle of *katabasis-sparagmos-omophagi*-resurrection—so, Dionysian destruction is necessary for the transcendent release of the Orphic song.)[57]

The Apollonian-Dionysian dichotomy became a dominant theme in the late nineteenth century, most prominently, of course, in Nietzsche's *Birth of Tragedy*.[58] The occultists and Symbolists were similarly intrigued with this theme which emerged so naturally in the context of their study of world religions, ancient mystery cults and, most specifically, the relationship between the development of theater and religion.

Creuzer devoted major sections of his *Symbolik* to the mystery cults; the orphic cults in particular, as playing a crucial role as the conduit of spiritual truths from Egypt and India to Greece. In effect, Creuzer explains the contradictory Apollonian and Dionysian elements of the myth of Orpheus through the crucial role of the orphic cults in the development of religion:

> In combining these different clues, we are led to believe that, around the fourteenth century before our era, the orphic school flourished, in which the reformed doctrine of Dionysus was united with the ancient theory of light, originating from upper Asia, into a great theological system, in which all the sacerdotal science arising from Greece up until this age are collected. That is how one explains, according to us, this apparent contradiction between Orpheus—enemy of the reli-

gion of Bacchus and victim of his bloody zealots, and Orpheus—originator of the mysteries of this religion.[59]

The mystery cults, the dichotomy between the Apollonian and the Dionysian, especially in the context of the correspondence between theater and religion constitute major themes in Edouard Schuré's syncretic Theosophy. The spiritual evolution delineated in *Les Grands Initiés* hinges upon the role of the cults of Dionysus. In *The Genesis of Tragedy and the Sacred Drama of Eleusis* (which at the same time draws upon and argues vehemently with Nietzsche's *Birth of Tragedy*) Schuré emphasizes Orpheus' important role between the Apollonian and the Dionysian.

> The religious organizer of primitive Greece was the Doric Orpheus, son of a priestess of Apollo. His powerful though ultra-sensitive nature was in marvelous accord with his soul,—a tuneful lyre. He blended and fused both deities in his life and work. He elaborated Apollonian thoughts with Dionysian enthusiasm. Orpheus was the founder of the Orphic mysteries, the creator of the myth of Dionysus torn to pieces by the Titans and restored to life by Athene. This myth is a summary of the entire cosmic evolution, i.e., of the dispersion of the deity throughout the visible world and its return to eternal and infinite harmony by the sufferings of incarnation. It is a striking fact that the Greek theatre—and through it, the whole of modern theatre—should owe its birth to the myth of Dionysus ... itinerant dithyramb. The satyrs bewailing the death of Dionysus and then celebrating his resurrection with cries of joy, a god emerging from a vat of crushed grapes in a fume of intoxication—such was the singular origin of tragedy.... With Dionysus there breaks out into Art, Poetry and the Theatre, an idea unknown to India: the idea of the necessity of Grief, of progress by struggle of the purification of the Soul by Suffering.[60]

Schuré's interest in the mystery cults and the religious derivation of theater is not an isolated phenomenon, but figures significantly in the writings of Péladan, Pater (in his noted *Greek Studies*), Maury, and others.[61] For Joséphin Péladan, the connection between esoteric religion and the genesis of tragedy is essential to his concepts of art as initiation and artist as priest. His own theatrical ventures were tied to religious concepts, for instance the three plays—*Terre de Sphinx*, *Terre du Christ* and *Terre d'Orphée*—which were to constitute *Les Idées et les formes*. His writings include, moreover, *Origine et esthétique de la tragédie*, including "Le Mystère d'Eleusis. La religion et le théâtre."[62] The antique mystery cults emerge even as a subject in the visual arts, witness works such as Paul Sérusier's *The Mysteries of Eleusis*, ca. 1895 (fig. 6.36), or *La Fantaisie* (fig. 6.37), by the Finnish Symbolist, Magnus Enckell.[63]

This fascination with the mystery cults of antiquity and with the religious origins of theater are, then, manifestations of that broad-ranging impulse to create an all-encompassing syncretic unity, to discover the underlying spiritual harmony of mankind. It is an expression, as well, of the conviction—inspiration of the Sâr Péladan's exhortation, "Artist, you are priest!," at the heart of Wagner's *Art of the Future* or Schuré's *Théâtre de l'âme*—that art is in its essence religious. Greece itself emerges changed in concept, no longer perceived in terms of Winckelmann's "noble simplicity and calm grandeur," but rather in terms of a profound dialogue between sun-drenched images and the darkest realms of mystery. The complex mythological character of Orpheus—artist as well as priest; adherent of Apollo and promulgator of the Dionysian; initiate and martyr, miraculous oracle—is a profound expression of this complex aesthetic-religious attitude. The Symbolists rediscover the symbolic meaning of Orpheus, finding special meaning in the tragic yet ethereally beautiful image of his severed head—an expression of the pain and transcendence of the creative act, of the orphic victory of the poet in creative harmony with the universe, a symbol of their own antimaterialist, idealist aesthetic.

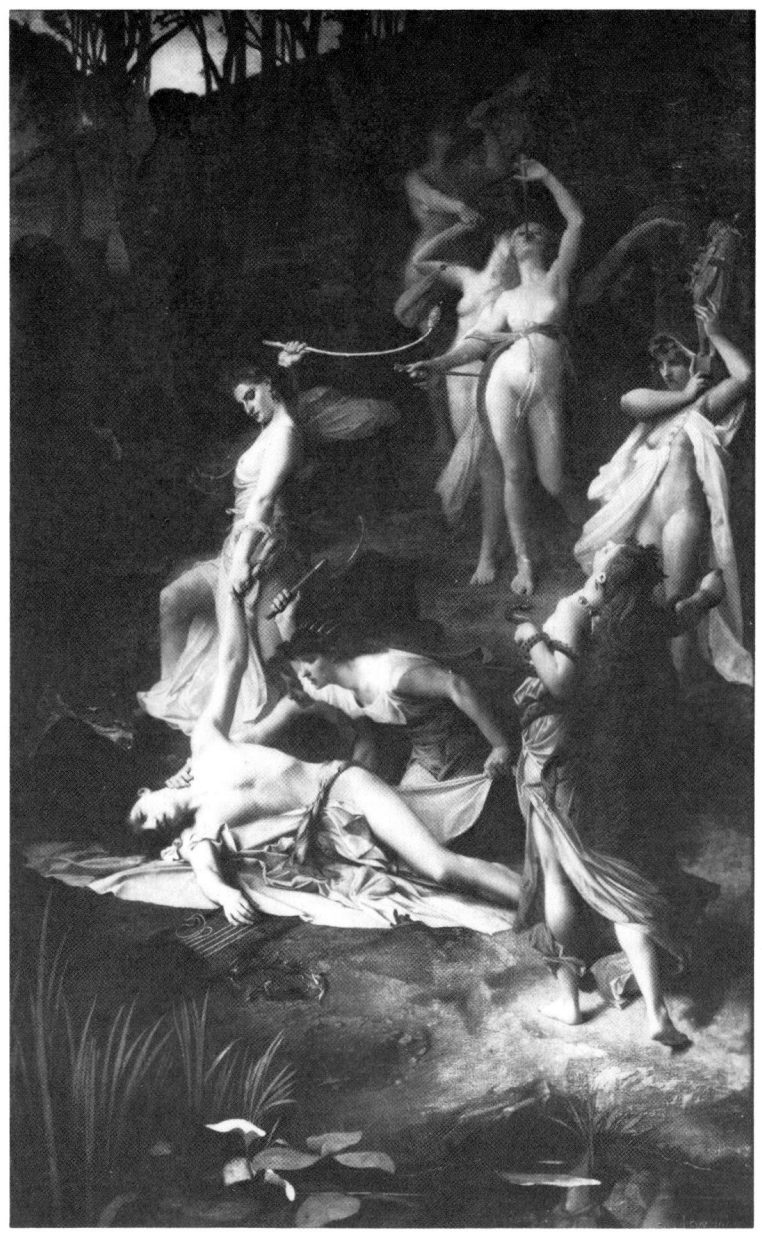

Figure 6.1. Emile Lévy, *The Death of Orpheus*, 1866
Oil on canvas.
(Louvre, Paris; photo: N. D. Roger-Viollet)

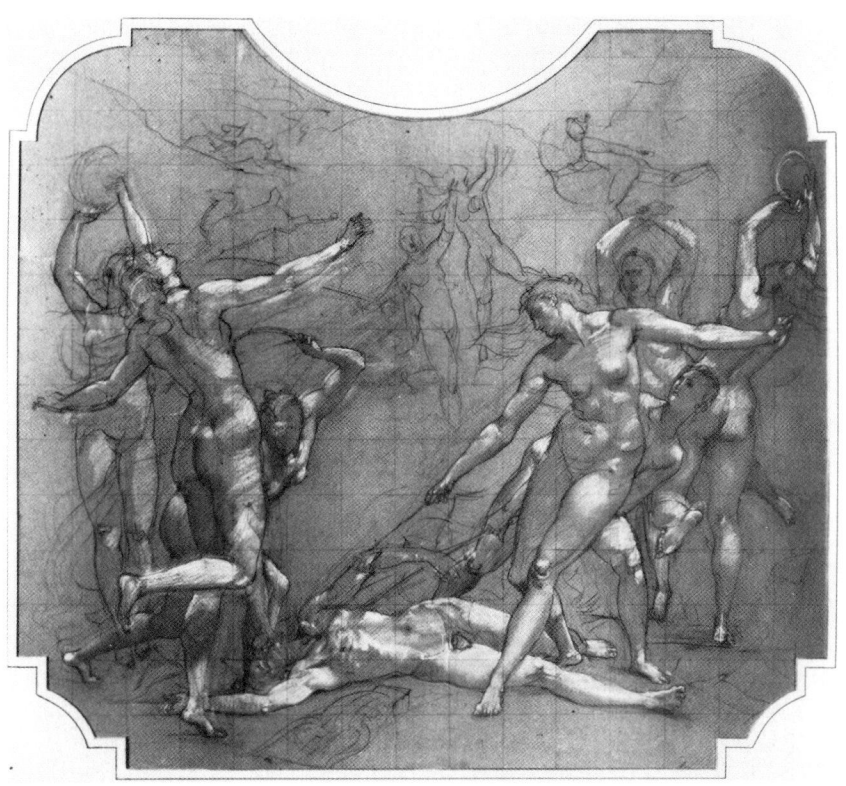

Figure 6.2. Paul Baudry, *The Death of Orpheus*, ca. 1865–73
Cartoon for painting, Grand Foyer, Opéra, Paris.
(*Bibliothèque et Musée de l'Opéra, Paris*; photo:
Bibliothèque National, Paris)

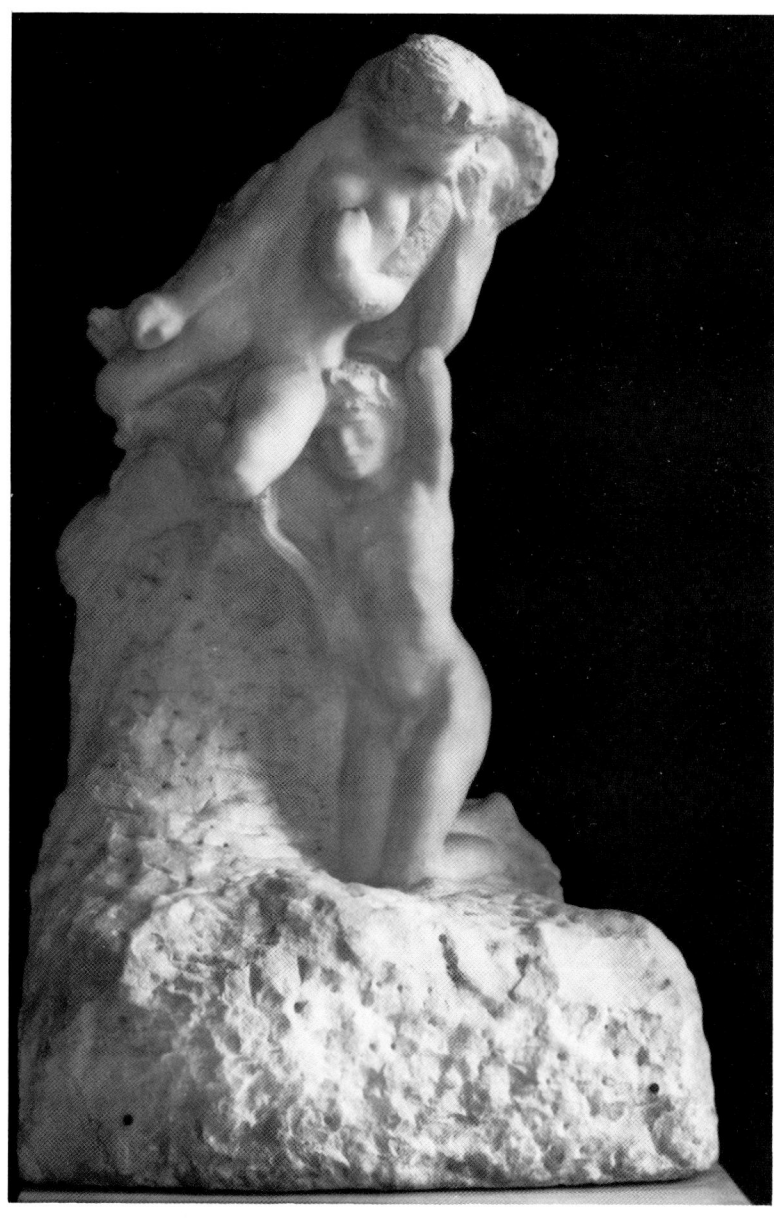

Figure 6.3. Auguste Rodin, *Orpheus and the Maenads*, 1889 Marble.
(Musée Rodin, Paris; photo: Bruno Jarret; © ADAGP/SPADEM, Paris, and PRO LITTERIS, Zurich)

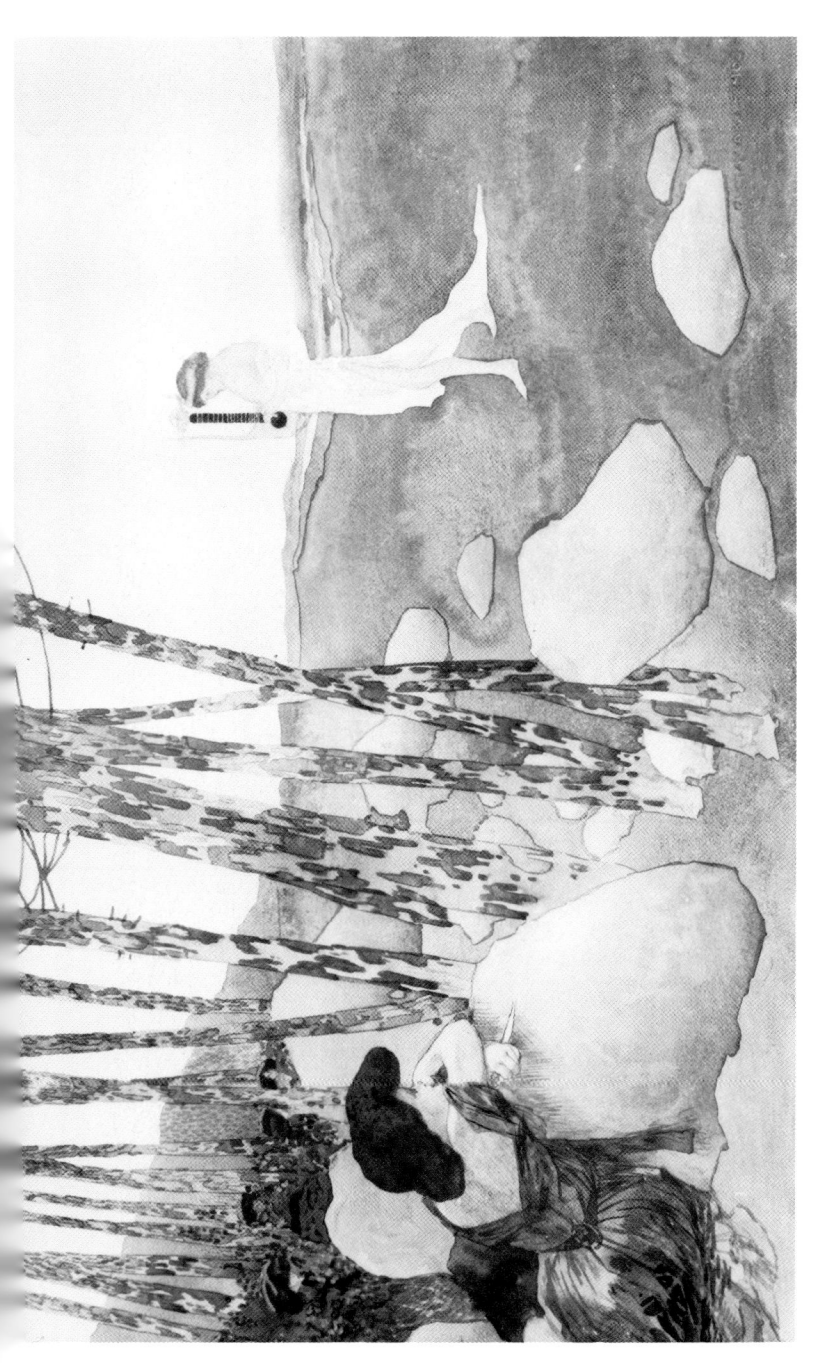

Figure 6.4. Gustave Adolf Mossa, *Orpheus*, 1906 Watercolor, pencil, ink and gouache. *(Private collection, Paris; photo: Michel De Lorenzo; courtesy Musée des Beaux-Arts, Nice)*

Figure 6.5. Gustave Adolf Mossa, *Psychological Self-Portrait*, 1905 (*Private collection, Nice; photo: Michel De Lorenzo; courtesy Musée des Beaux-Arts, Nice*)

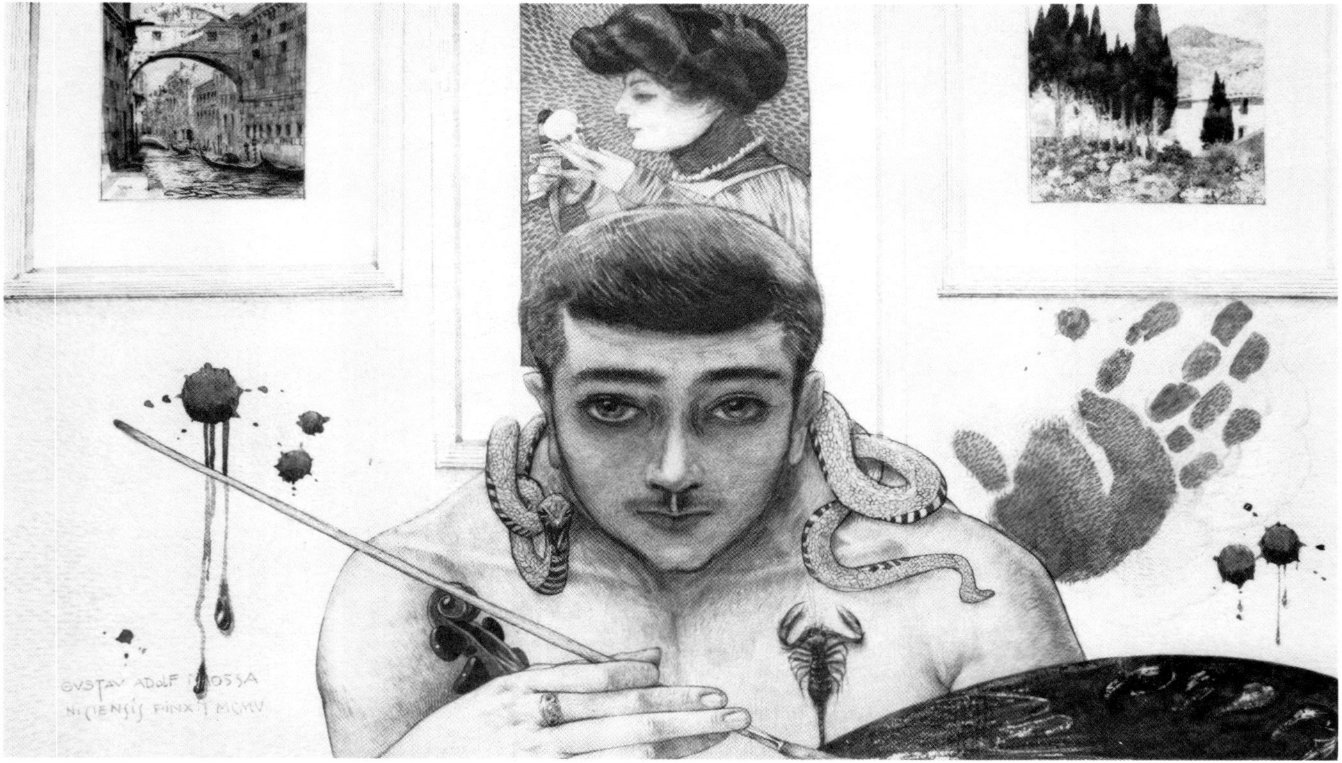

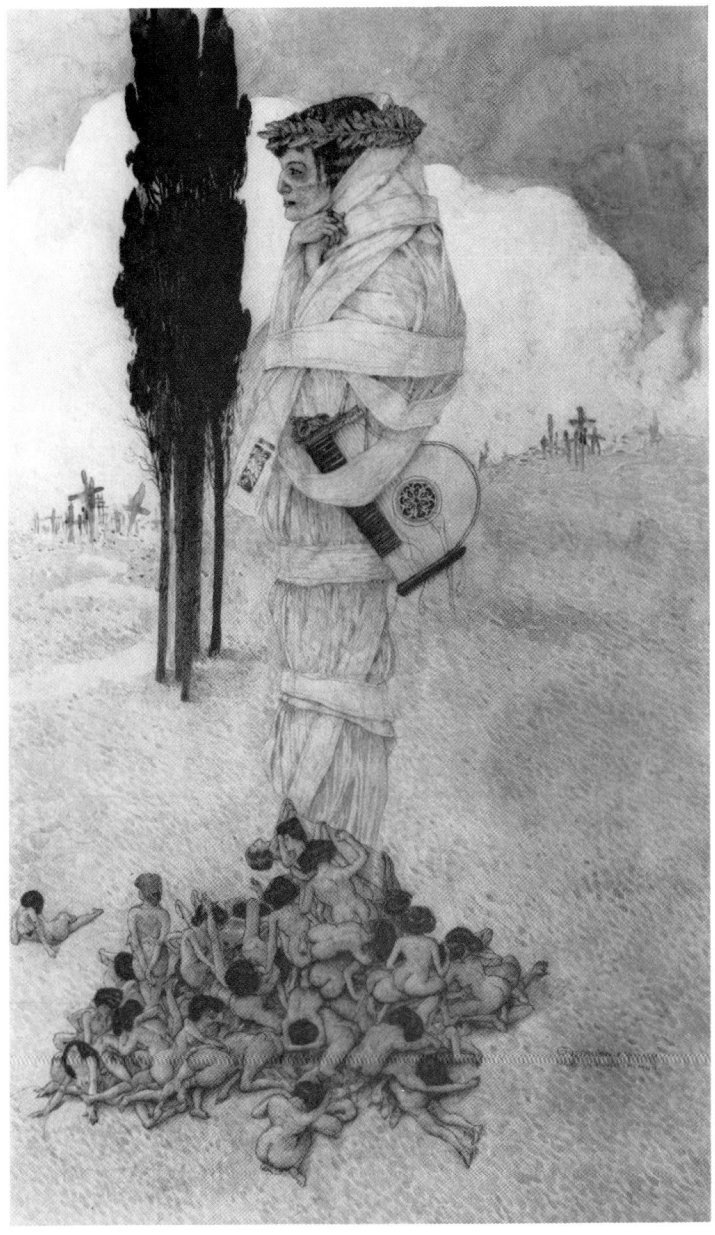

Figure 6.6. Gustave Adolf Mossa, *Resurrection*, 1907 (*Private collection, Tel Aviv; photo: Michel De Lorenzo; courtesy Musée des Beaux-Arts, Nice*)

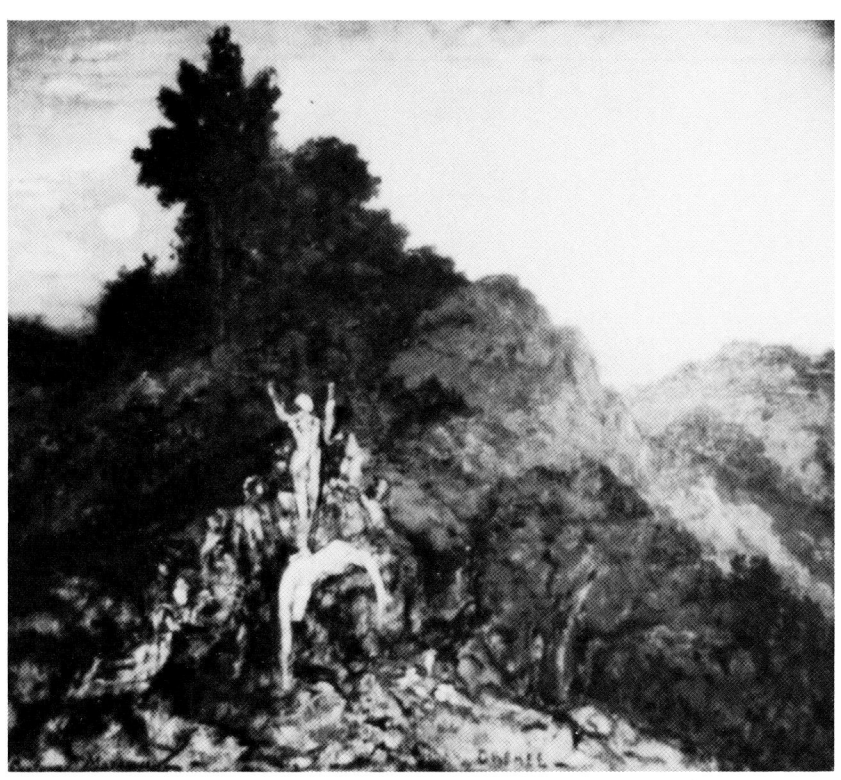

Figure 6.7. Gustave Moreau, *Orphée mort*, n.d.
Oil on canvas.
*(Musée Gustave Moreau, Paris; MGM 1974, #102;
Cliché des Musées Nationaux, Paris)*

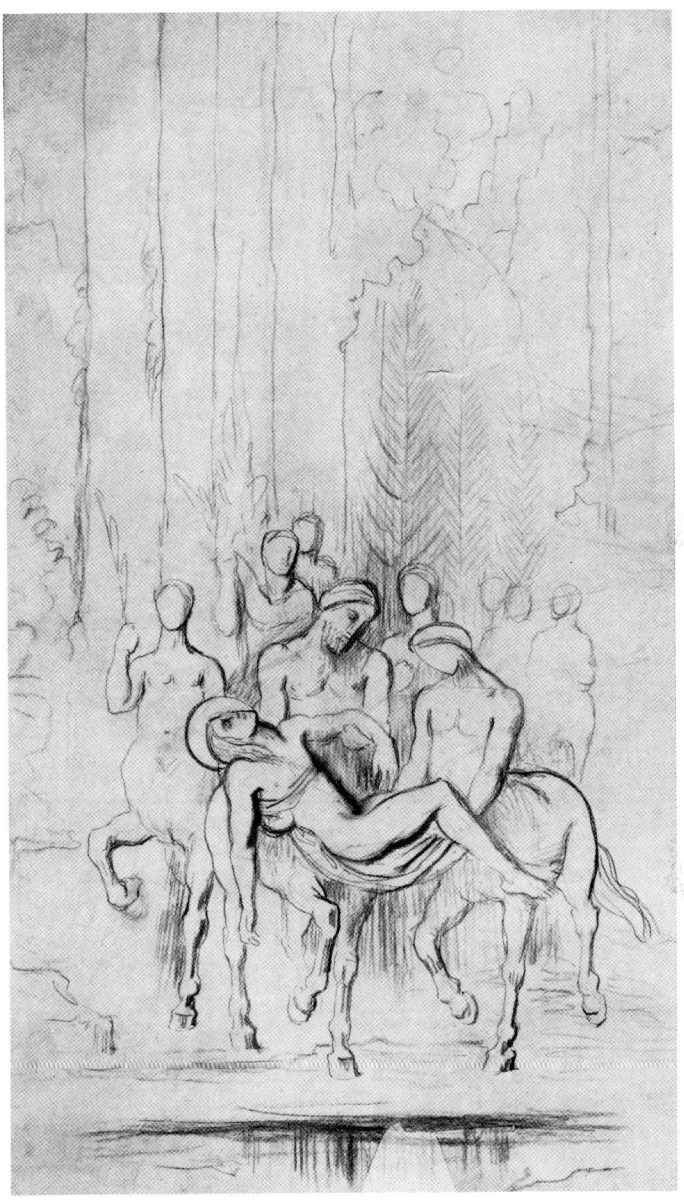

Figure 6.8. Gustave Moreau, *Wounded Poet and Centaurs*, 1890 Cartoon drawing.
(*Musée Gustave Moreau, Paris;* MGM 1974, #981; *Cliché des Musées Nationaux, Paris*)

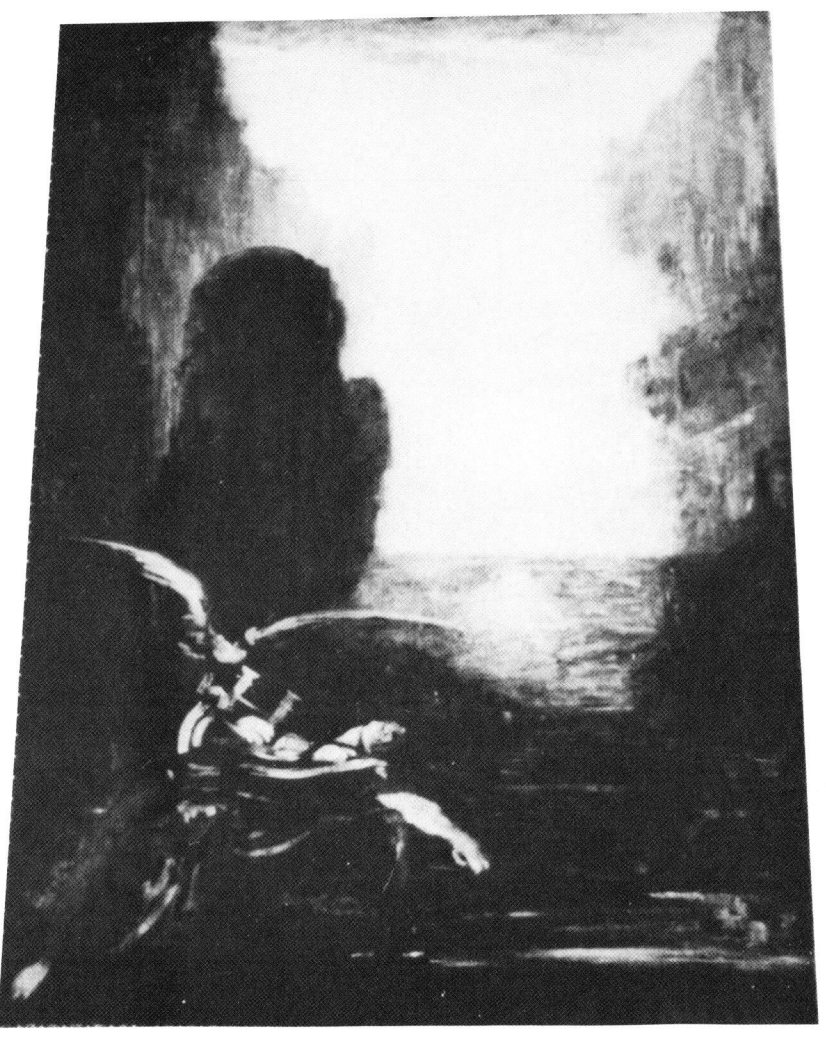

Figure 6.9. Gustave Moreau, *Death of Sappho*, n.d. Oil on canvas.
(Musée Gustave Moreau, Paris; MGM 1974, #71; Cliché des Musées Nationaux, Paris)

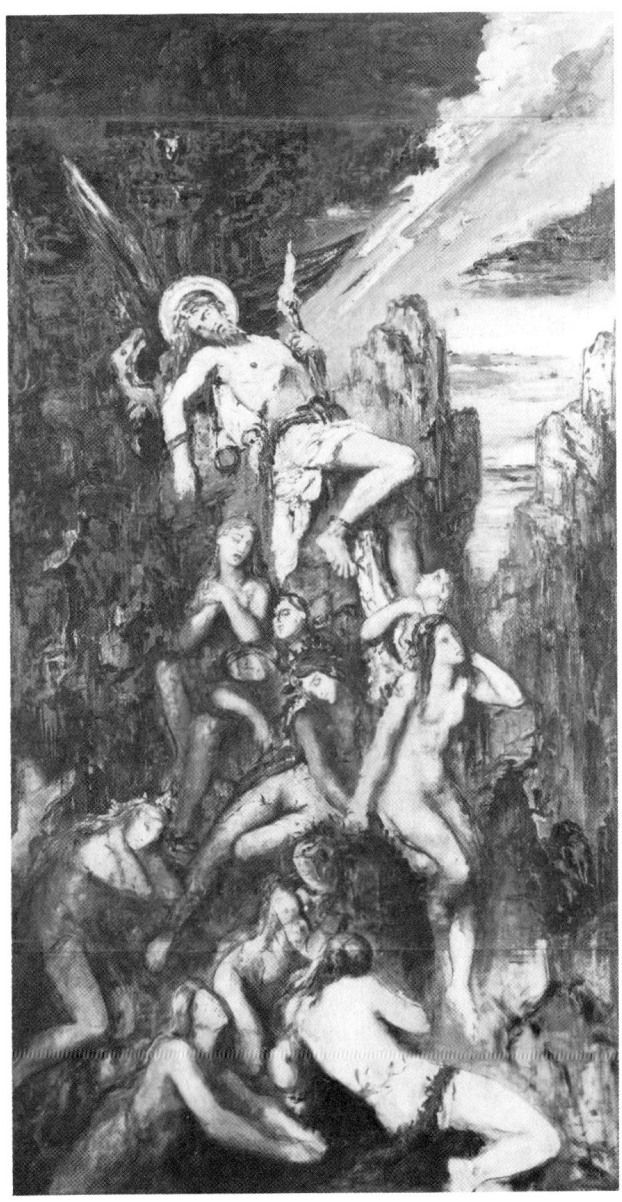

Figure 6.10. Gustave Moreau, *Prométhée foudroyé*, n.d.
Oil on canvas.
*(Musée Gustave Moreau, Paris; MGM 1974, #35;
Cliché des Musées Nationaux, Paris)*

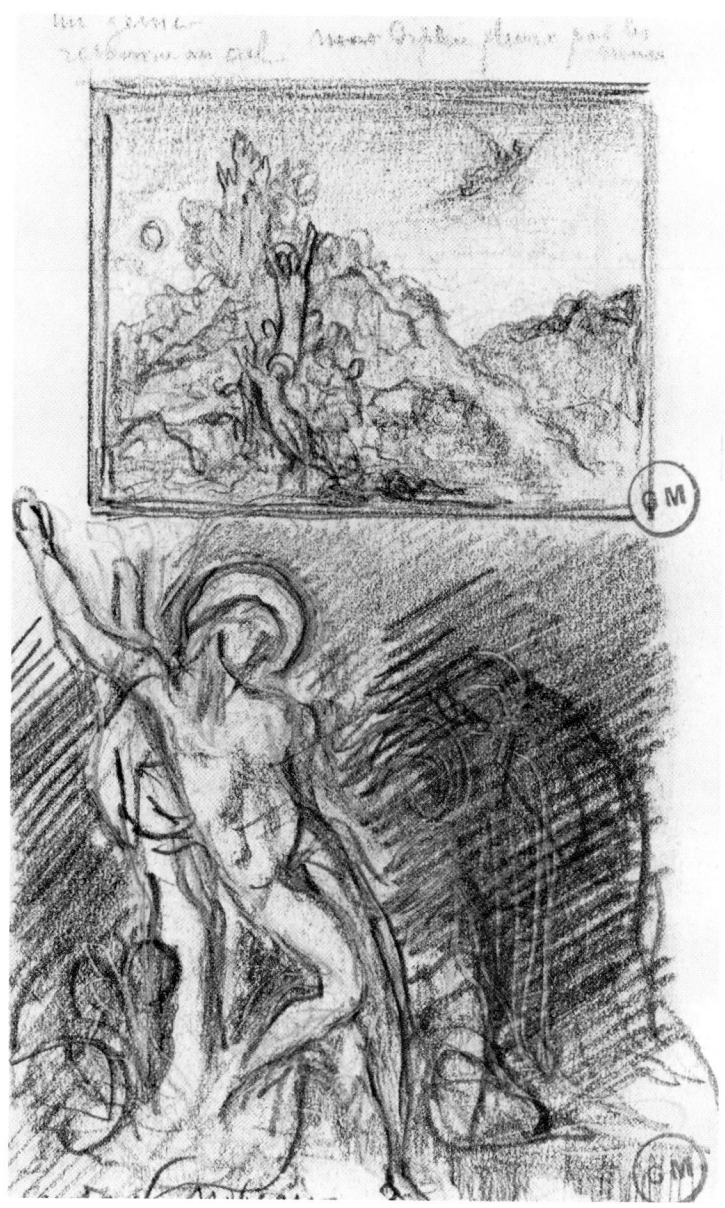

Figure 6.11. Gustave Moreau, *"La Mort d'Orphée pleuré par les muses,"* n.d.
(Musée Gustave Moreau, Paris; MGM 1983, #4013; Cliché des Musées Nationaux, Paris)

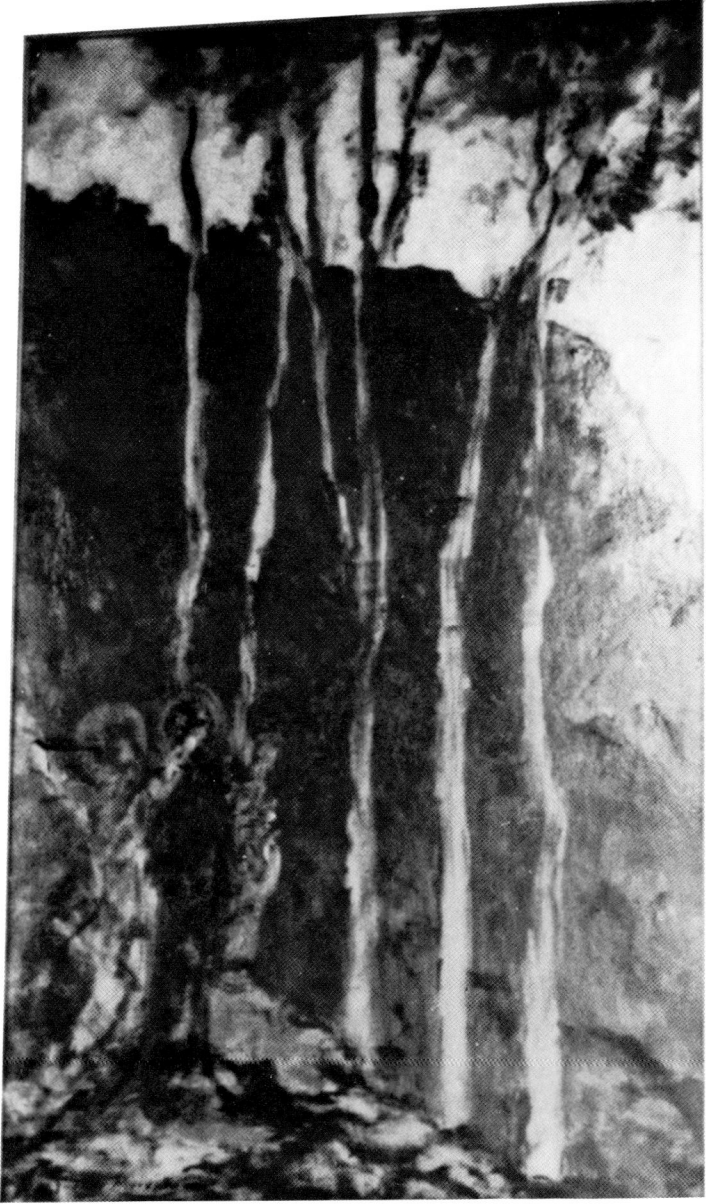

Figure 6.12. Gustave Moreau, *Orpheus*, n.d. Oil on canvas.
(Musée Gustave Moreau, Paris; MGM 1974, #33; Cliché des Musées Nationaux, Paris)

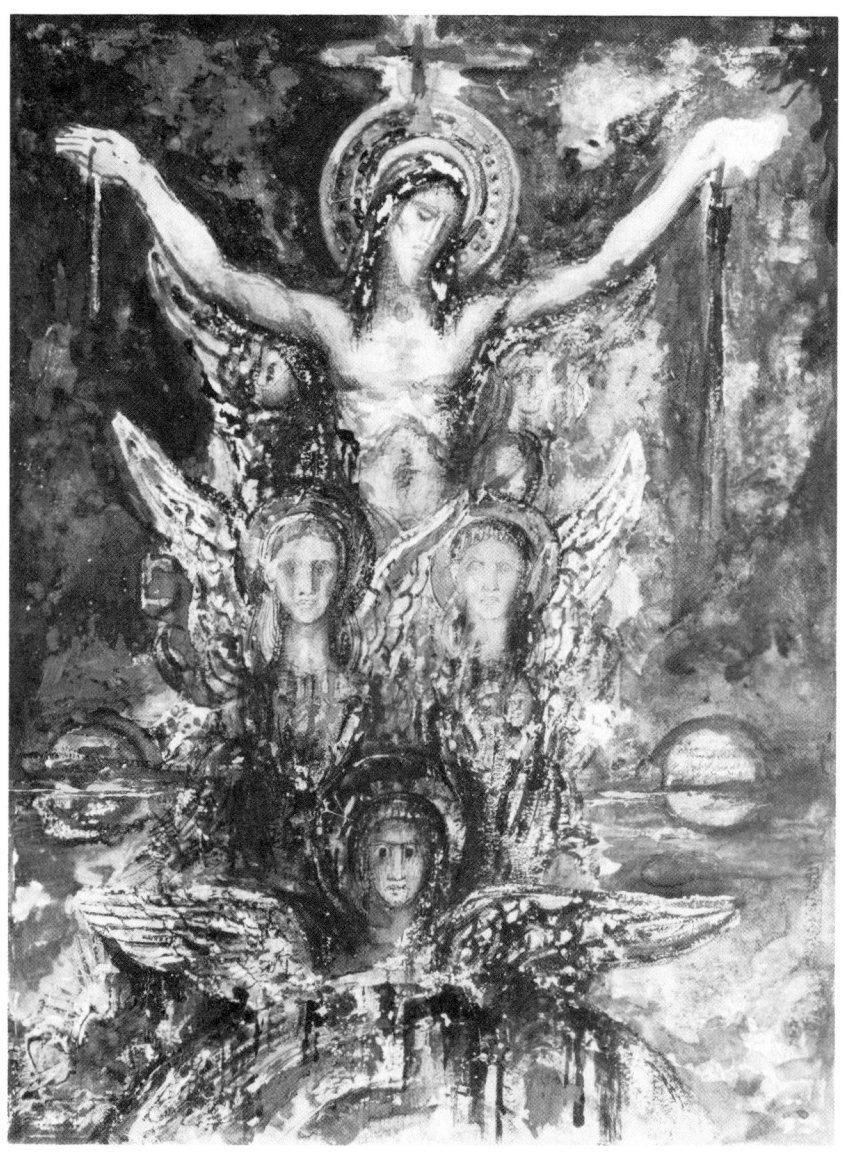

Figure 6.13. Gustave Moreau, *Christ the Redeemer*, n.d. Watercolor.
(*Musée Gustave Moreau, Paris; MGM 1974, #303; Cliché des Musées Nationaux, Paris*)

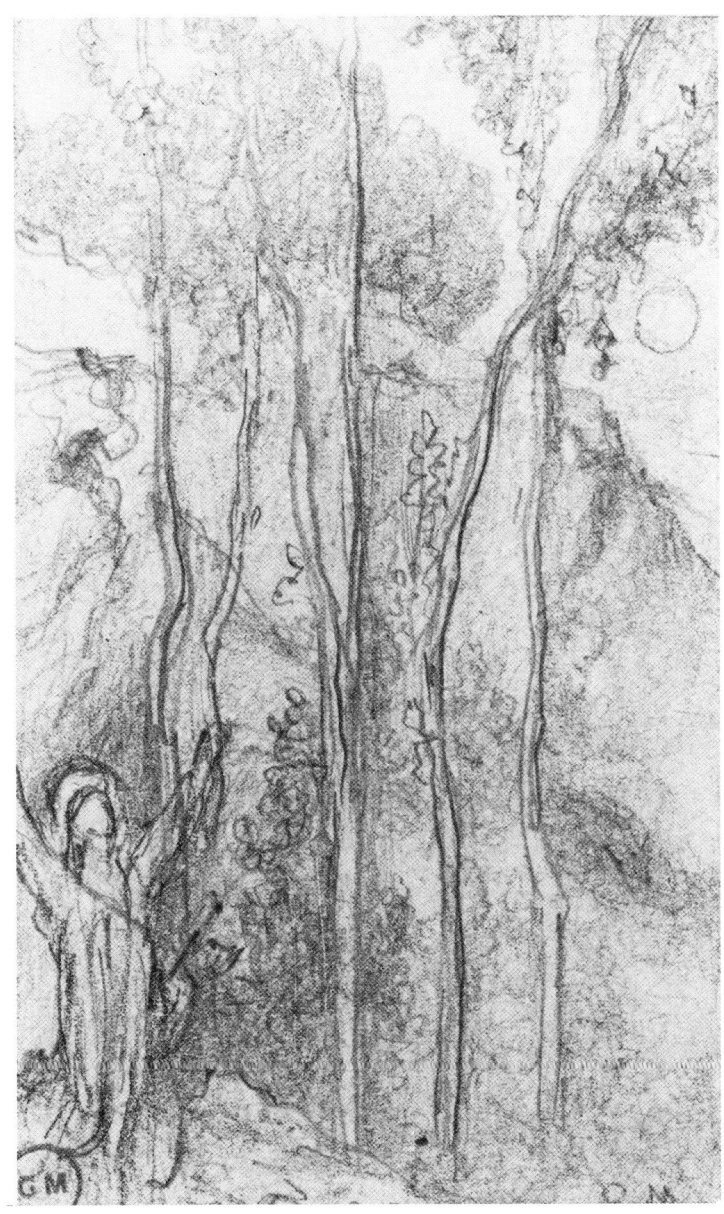

Figure 6.14. Gustave Moreau, *The Sorrow of Orpheus*, n.d. Pencil drawing.
(Musée Gustave Moreau; MGM 1983, #613; Cliché des Musées Nationaux, Paris)

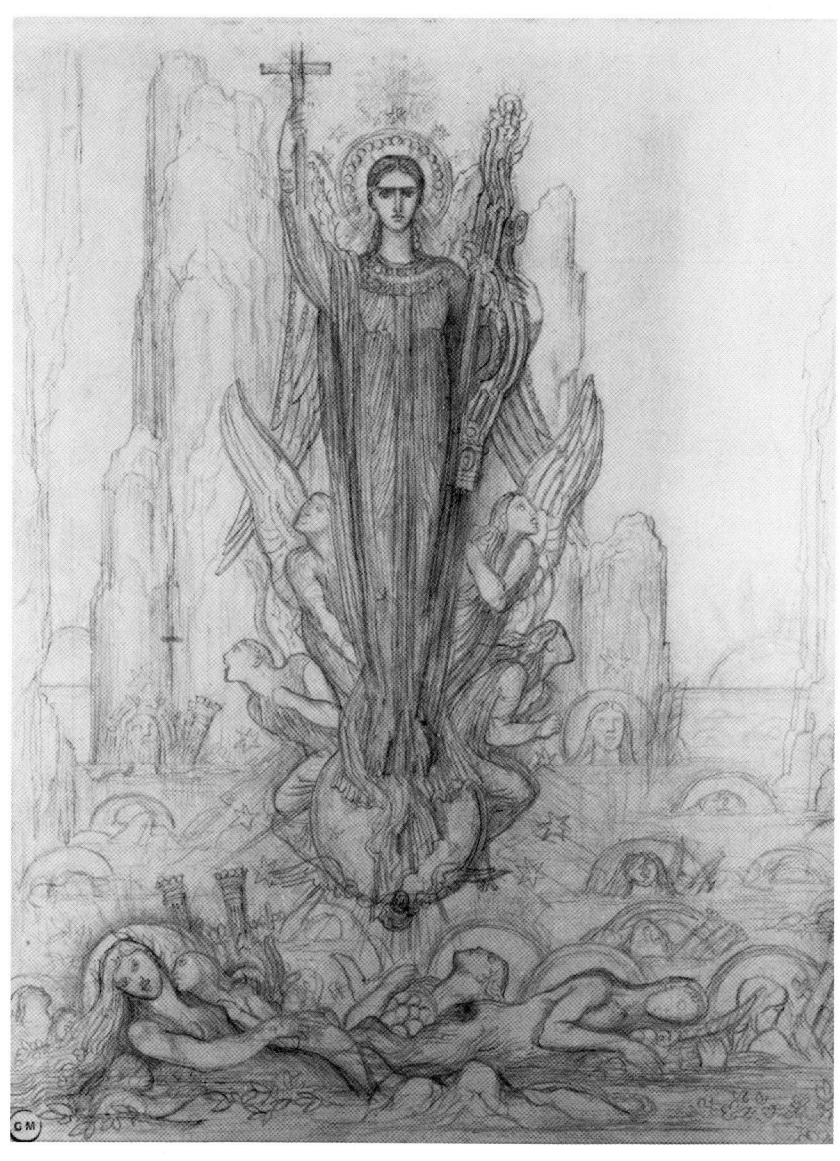

Figure 6.15. Gustave Moreau, *Les Lyres mortes*, 1896
Pencil drawing.
(Musée Gustave Moreau, Paris; MGM 1983, #153; Cliché des Musées Nationaux, Paris)

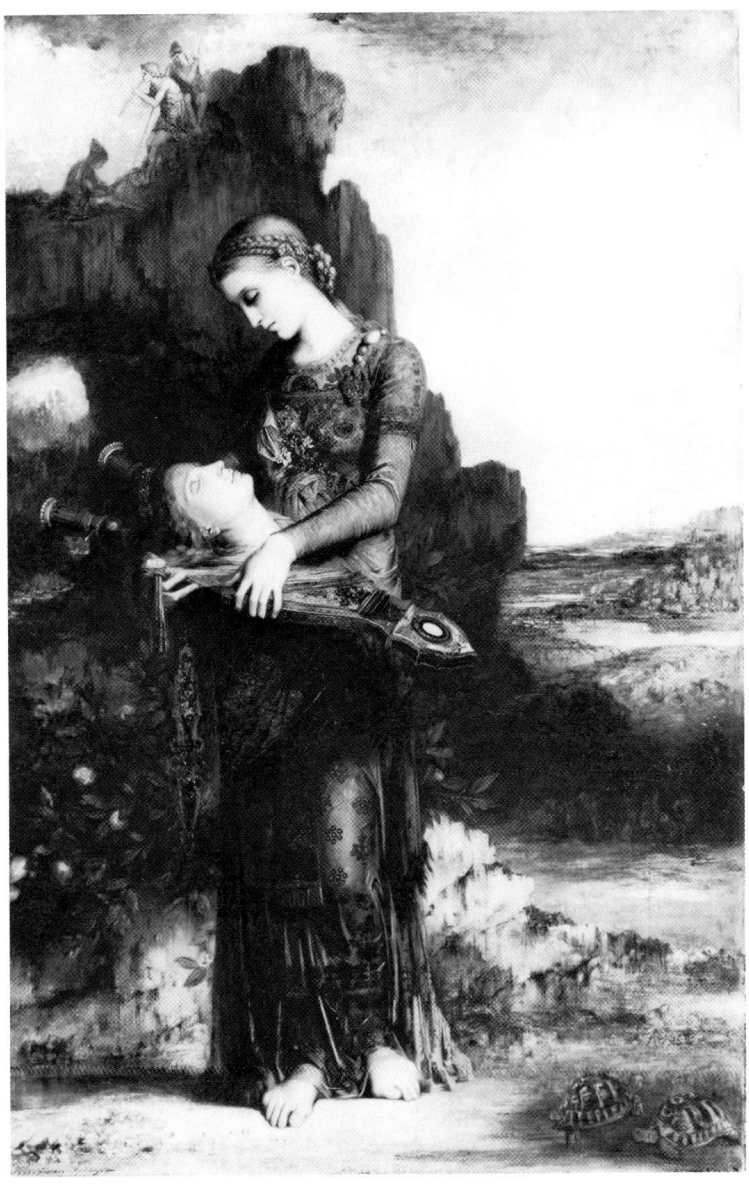

Figure 6.16. Gustave Moreau, *Young Thracian Woman Carrying the Head of Orpheus*, ca. 1865
Oil on panel.
(Musée d'Orsay, Paris; Cliché des Musées Nationaux, Paris)

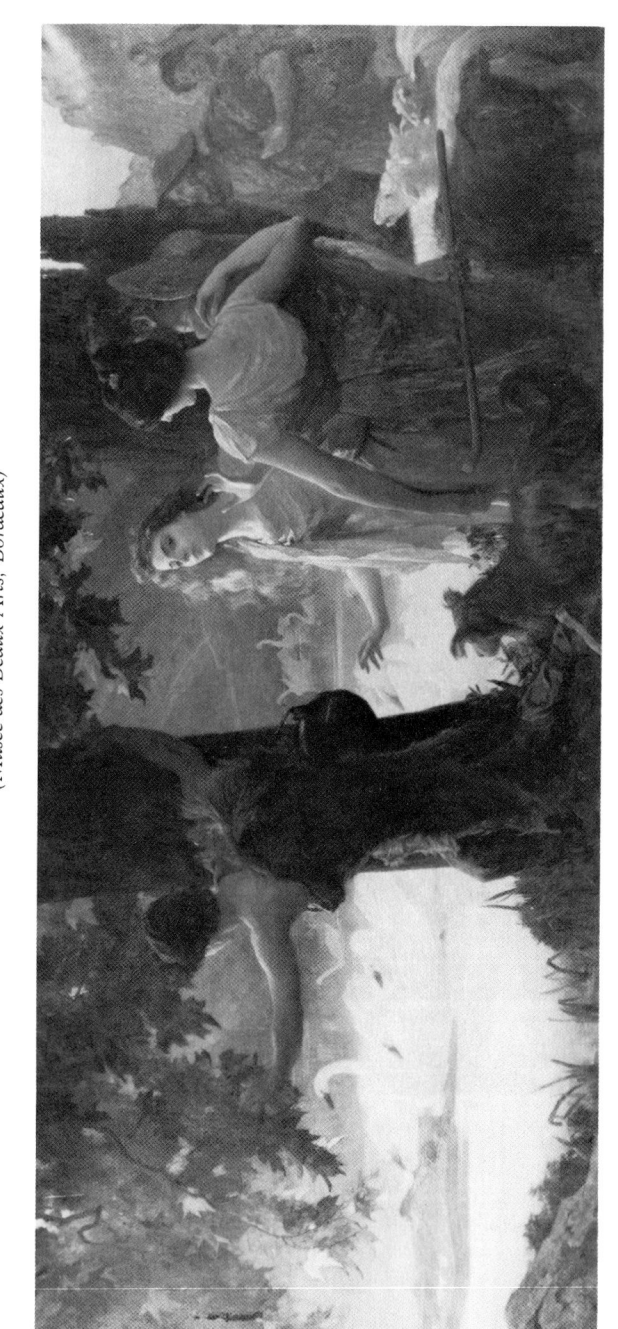

Figure 6.17. Abel Boyé, *The Immortal Lyre*, 1899
Oil on canvas.
(*Musée des Beaux-Arts, Bordeaux*)

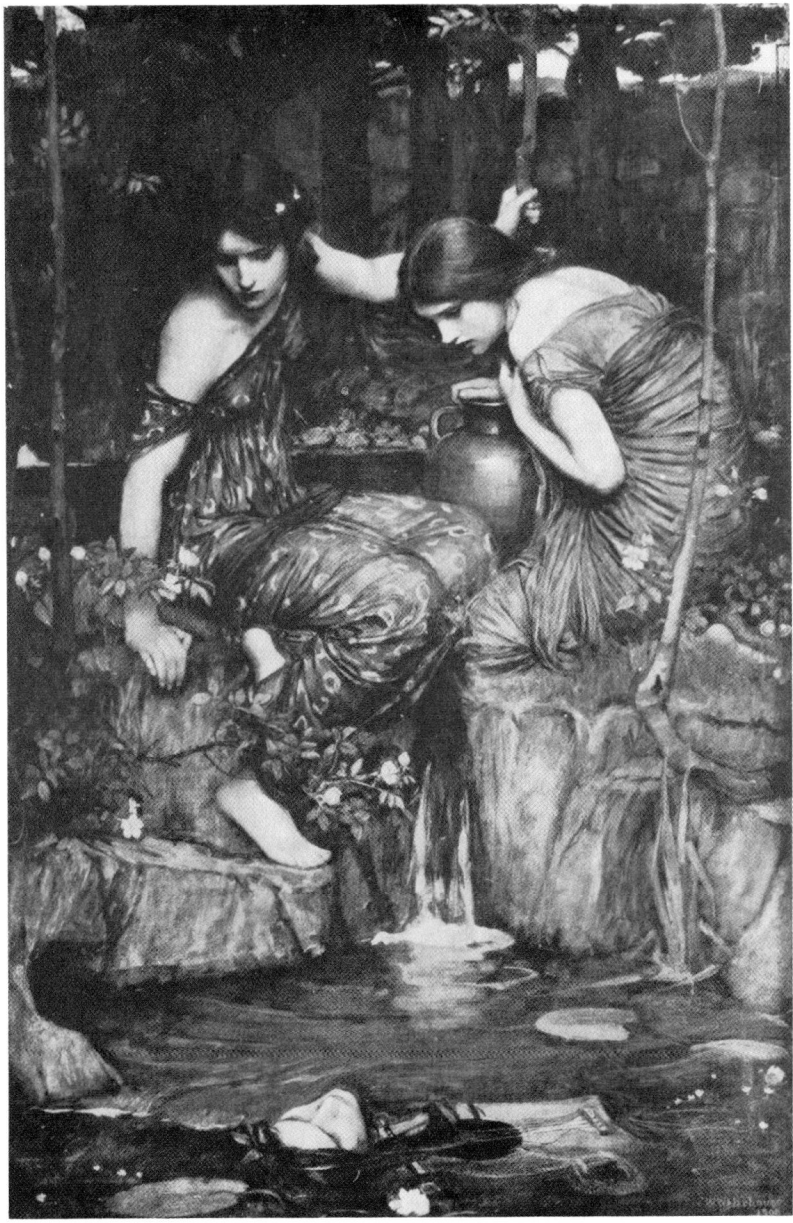

Figure 6.18. John William Waterhouse, *Nymphs Finding the Head of Orpheus*, 1900 Oil on canvas.
(Photo courtesy Courtauld Institute, London)

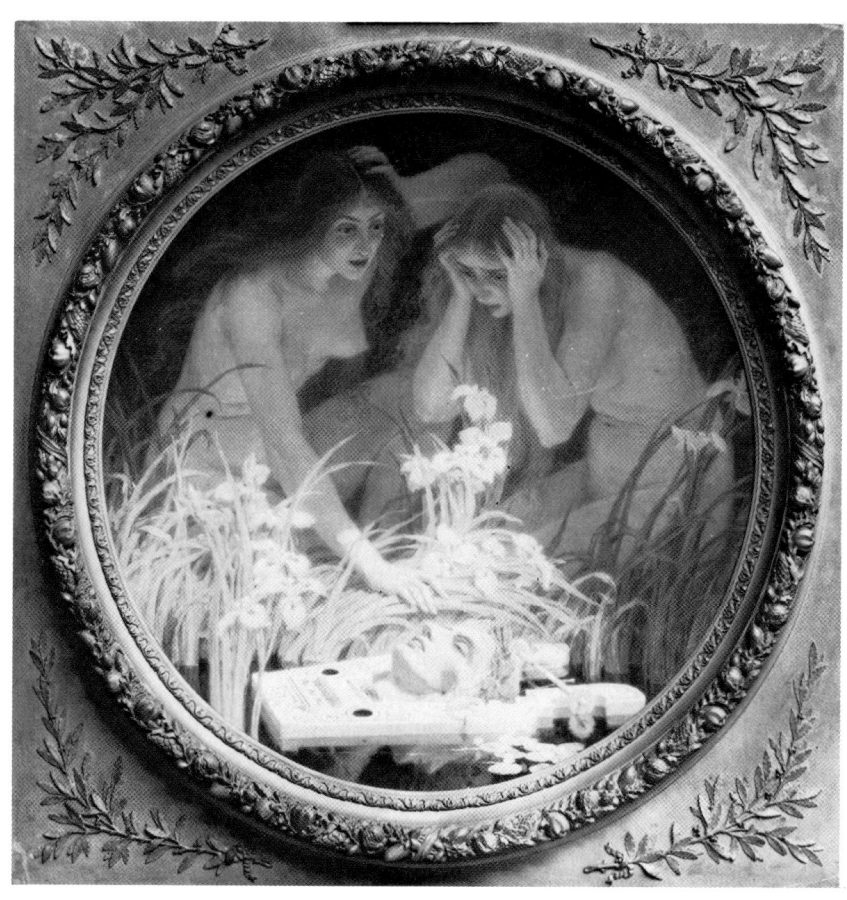

Figure 6.19. Ludovic Alléaume, *Lamentation on the Death of Orpheus*, 1914
Oil on canvas.
(Photo N. D. Roger-Viollet)

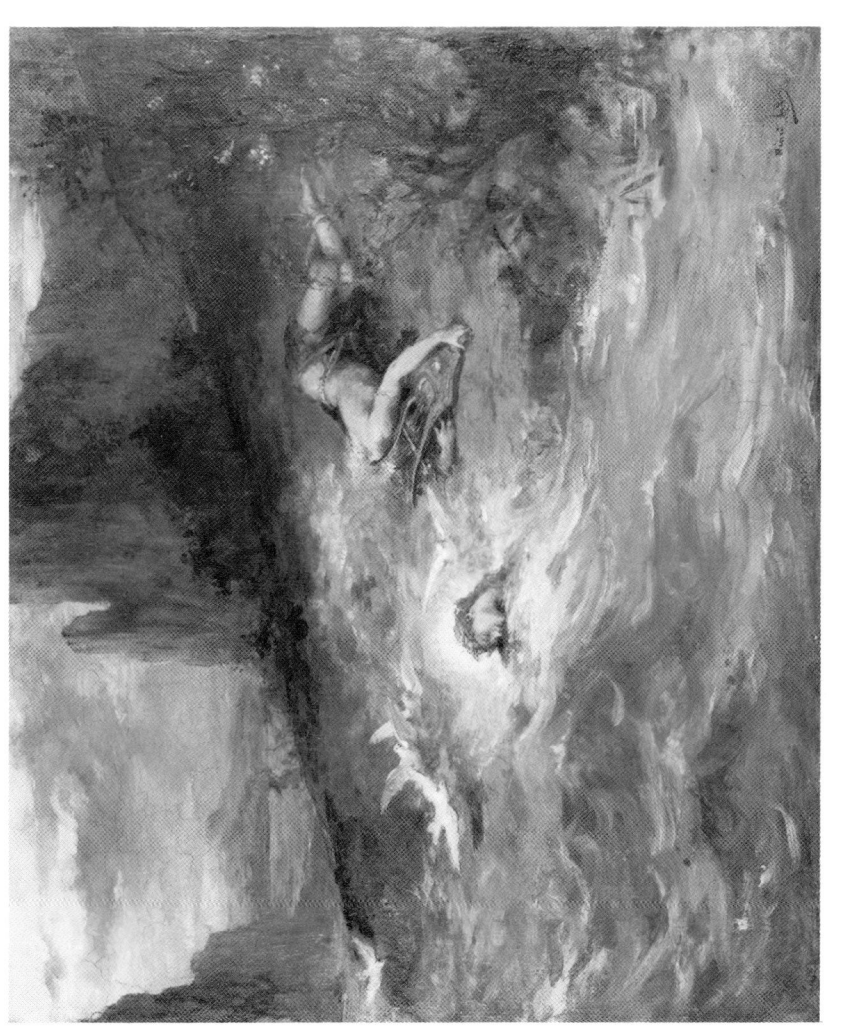

Figure 6.20. Henri Léopold Lévy, *Death of Orpheus*, ca. 1870. Oil on canvas. (The Art Institute of Chicago, The Harold T. Martin Trust)

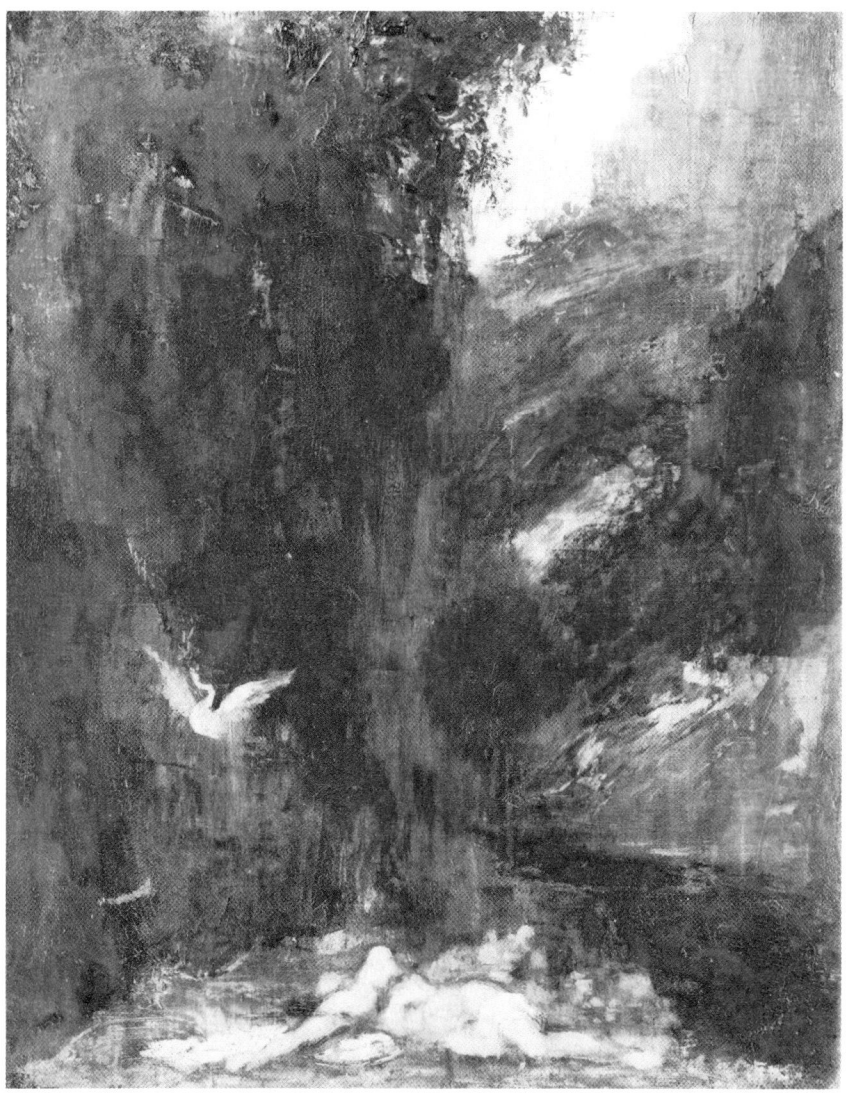

Figure 6.21. Gustave Moreau, *Orpheus*, n.d.
Oil on canvas.
(Musée Gustave Moreau, Paris; MGM 1974, #726;
Cliché des Musées Nationaux, Paris)

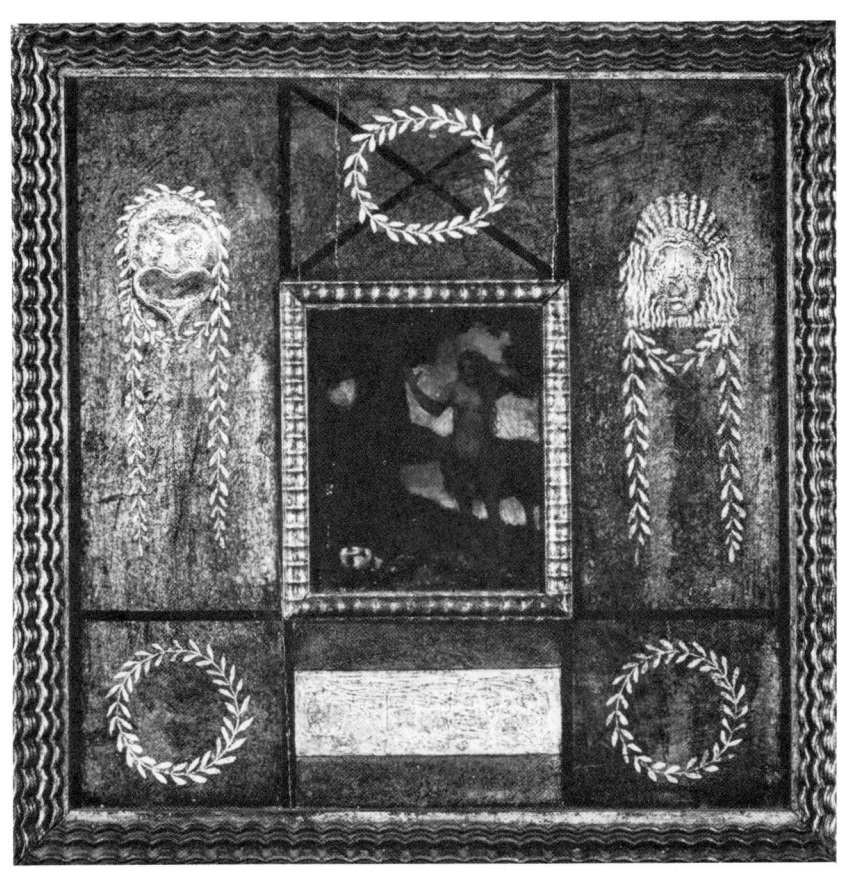

Figure 6.22. Franz von Stuck, *Orpheus*, ca. 1891
Oil on board.
(Collection Hans-Gerd Neef, Cologne)

Figure 6.23. Jean Delville, *Orpheus*, 1893
Oil on canvas.
(Collection Anne-Marie Gillion Crowet, Brussels)

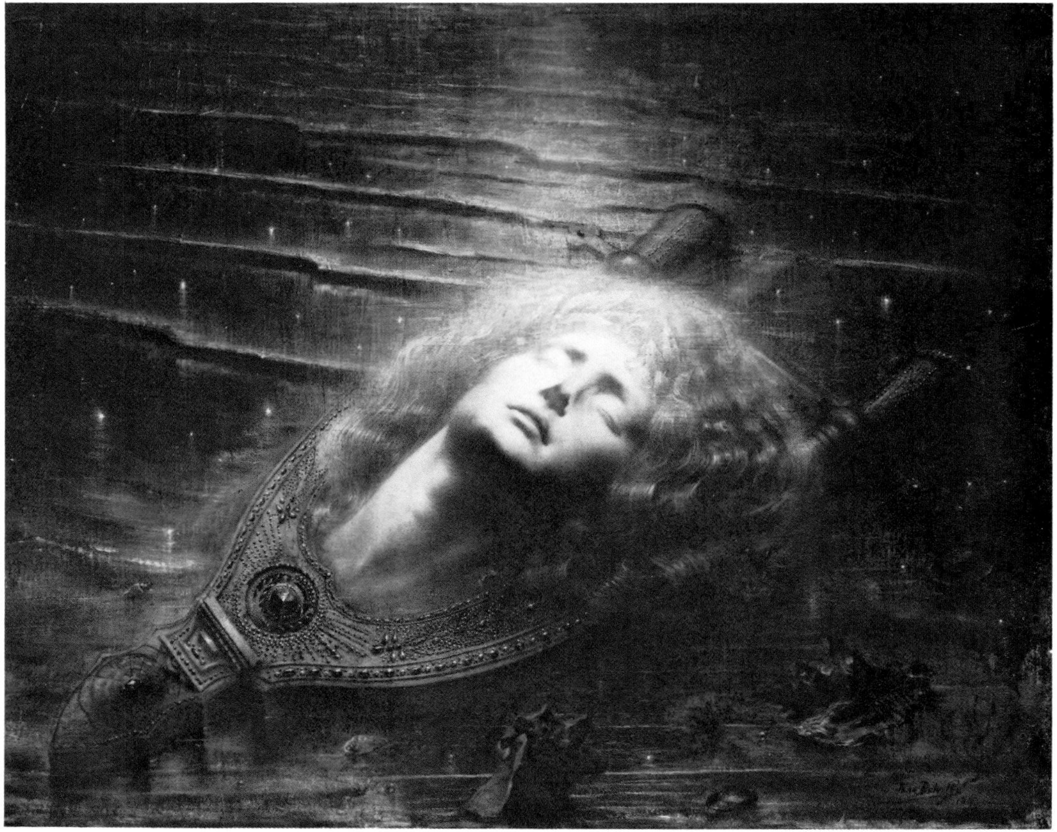

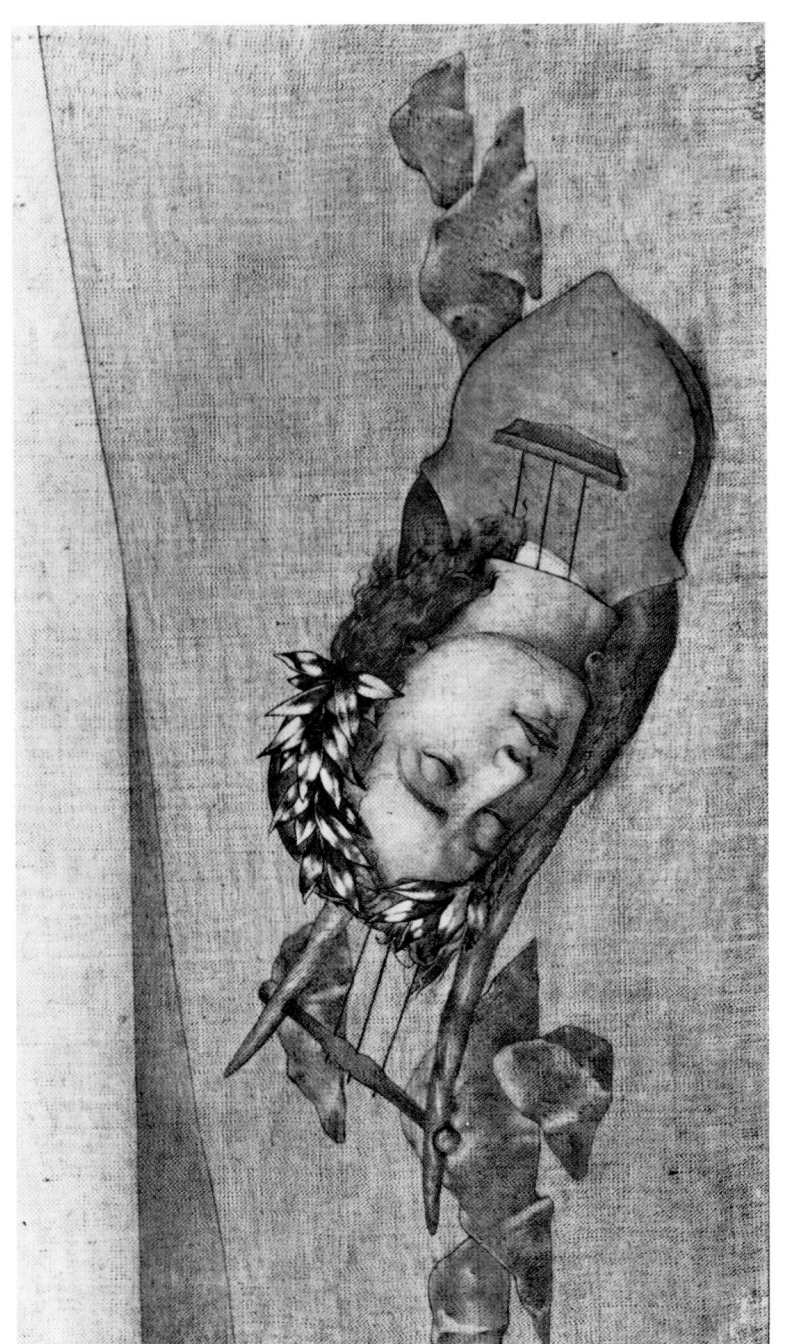

Figure 6.24. Alexandre Séon, *Orpheus' Lyre*, ca. 1898. Oil on canvas. (*Musée d'Art et d'Industrie, Saint-Etienne*)

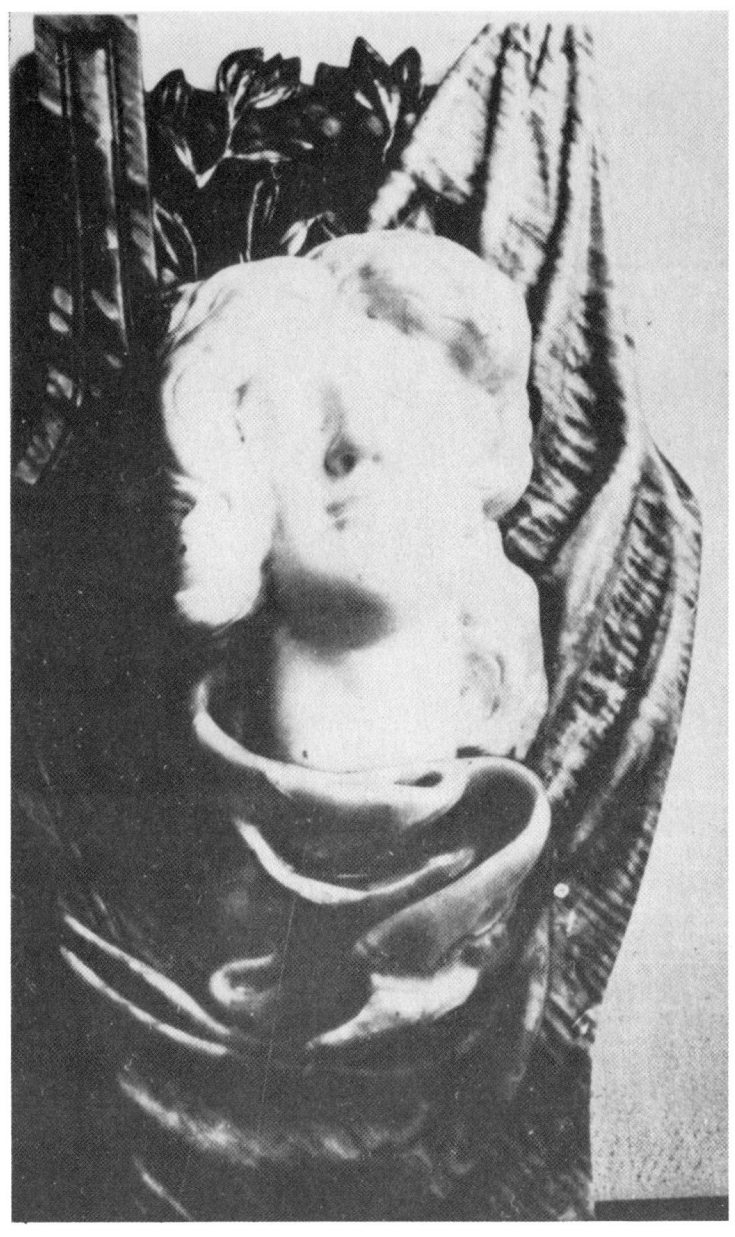

Figure 6.25 Valère Bernard, *Orpheus*, 1901
Marble and onyx.
(Musée des Beaux Arts, Marseille)

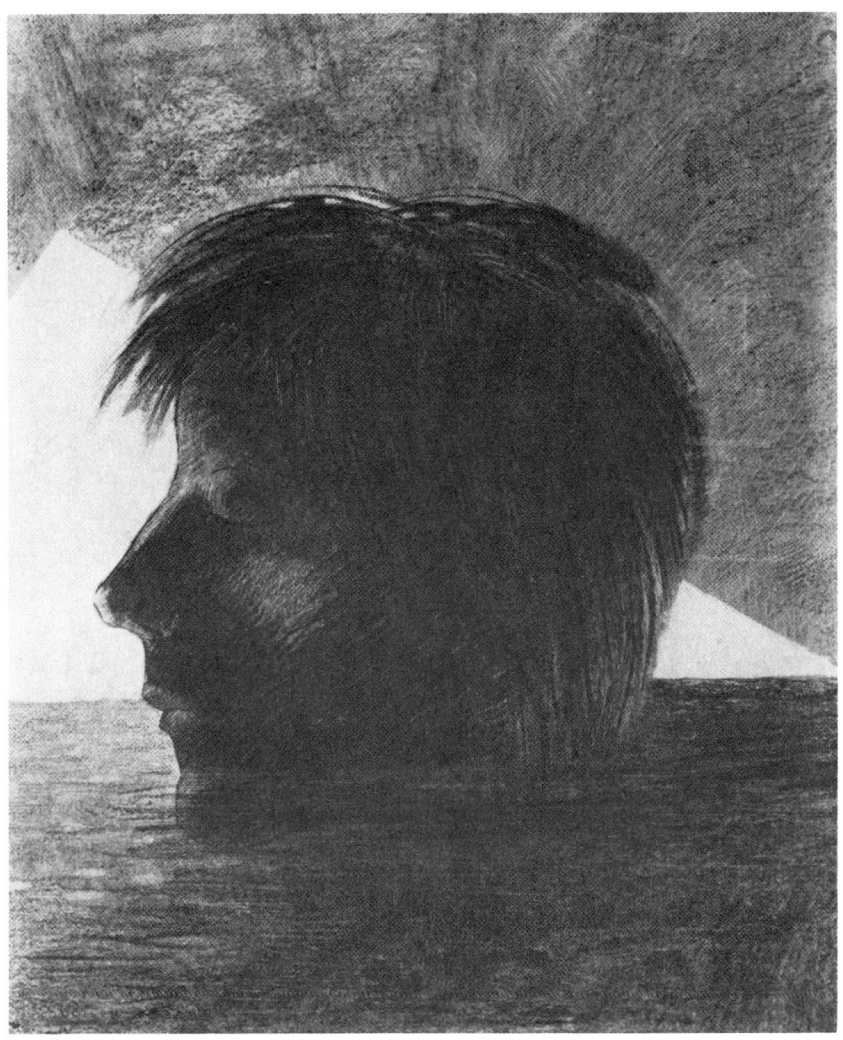

Figure 6.26. Odilon Redon, *Orpheus' Head Floating on the Waters*, 1881
Charcoal drawing.
(Rijksmuseum Kröller-Müller, Otterlo)

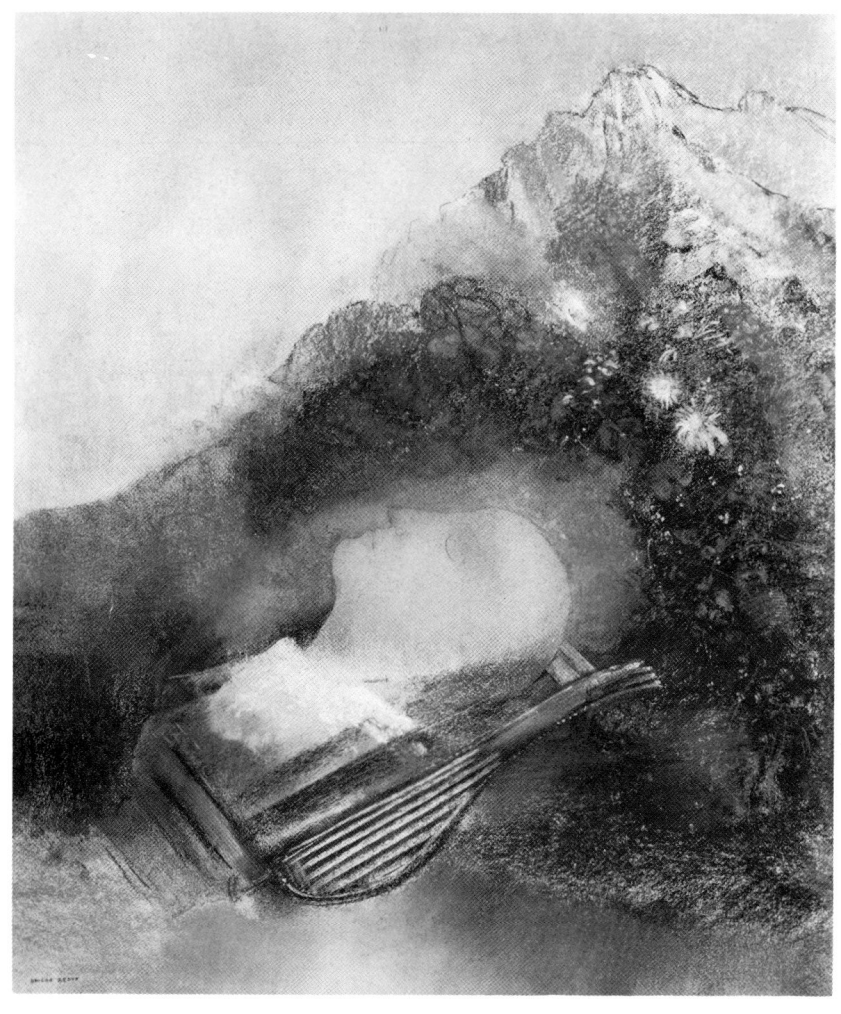

Figure 6.27. Odilon Redon, *Orpheus*, ca. after 1913
Pastel.
(The Cleveland Museum of Art, gift of J.H. Wade)

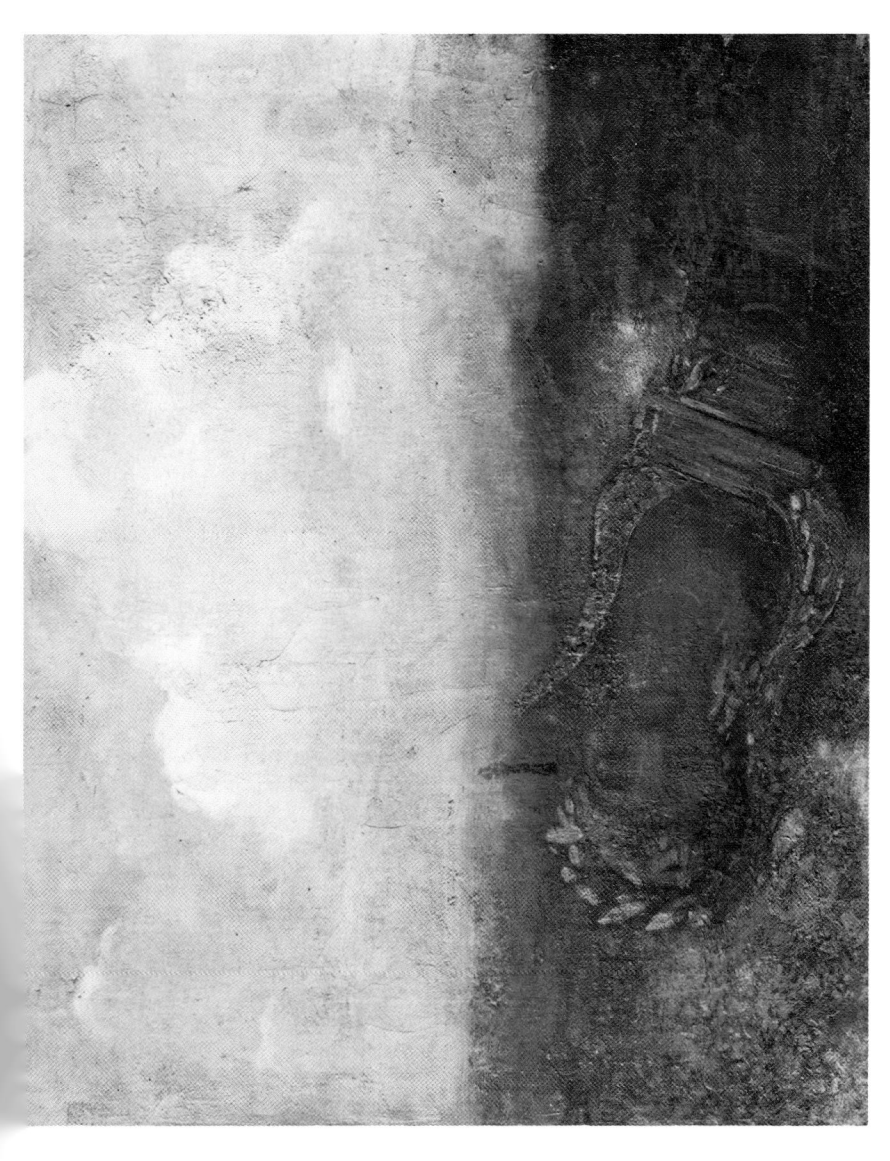

Figure 6.28. Odilon Redon, *Orpheus with Closed Eyes*, ca. 1900 (*Formerly collection Ari Redon, Paris; photo Agraci*)

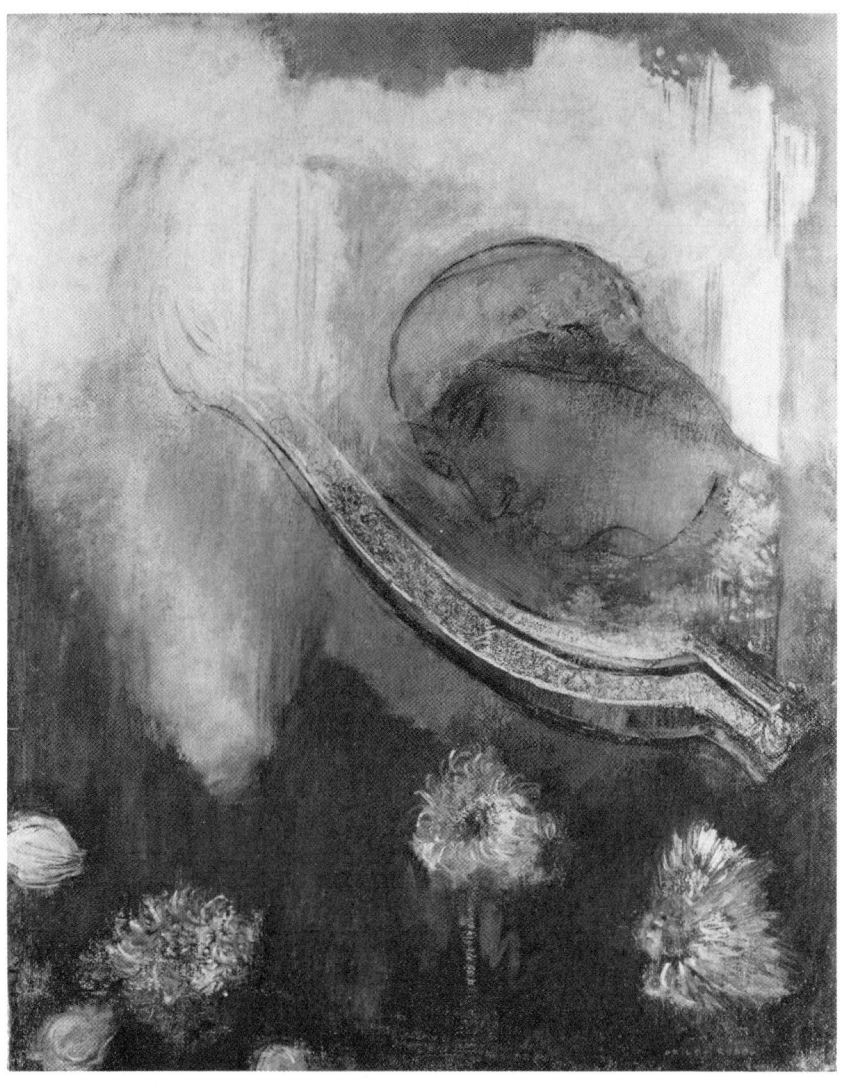

Figure 6.29. Odilon Redon, *Orpheus*, ca. 1905
Pastel on paper fixed to canvas mount.
(The Fine Arts Museums of San Francisco, Achenbach Foundation for Graphic Arts, Bequest of Frederick J. Hellman)

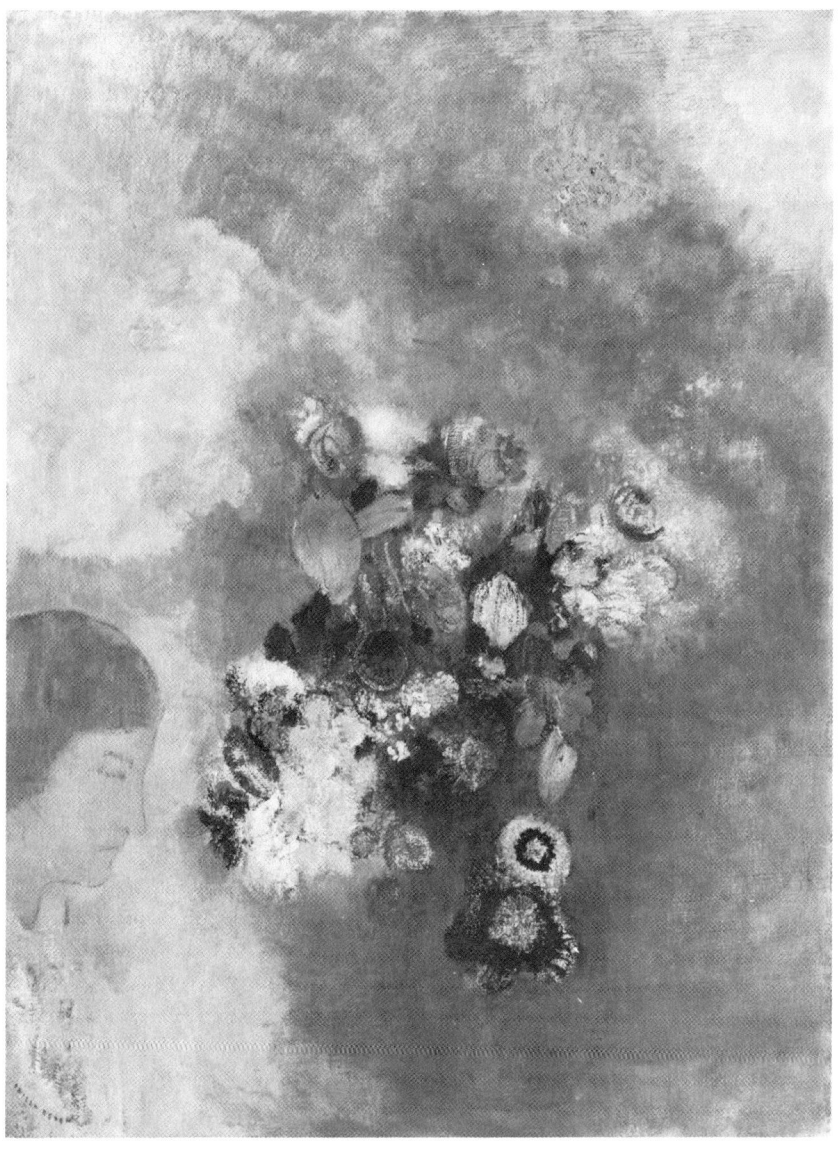

Figure 6.30. Odilon Redon, *The Dream*, ca. 1912
Oil on canvas.
(Hahnloser-Jäggli Stiftung, Winterthur; photo: Schweizerisches Institut für Kunstwissenschaft)

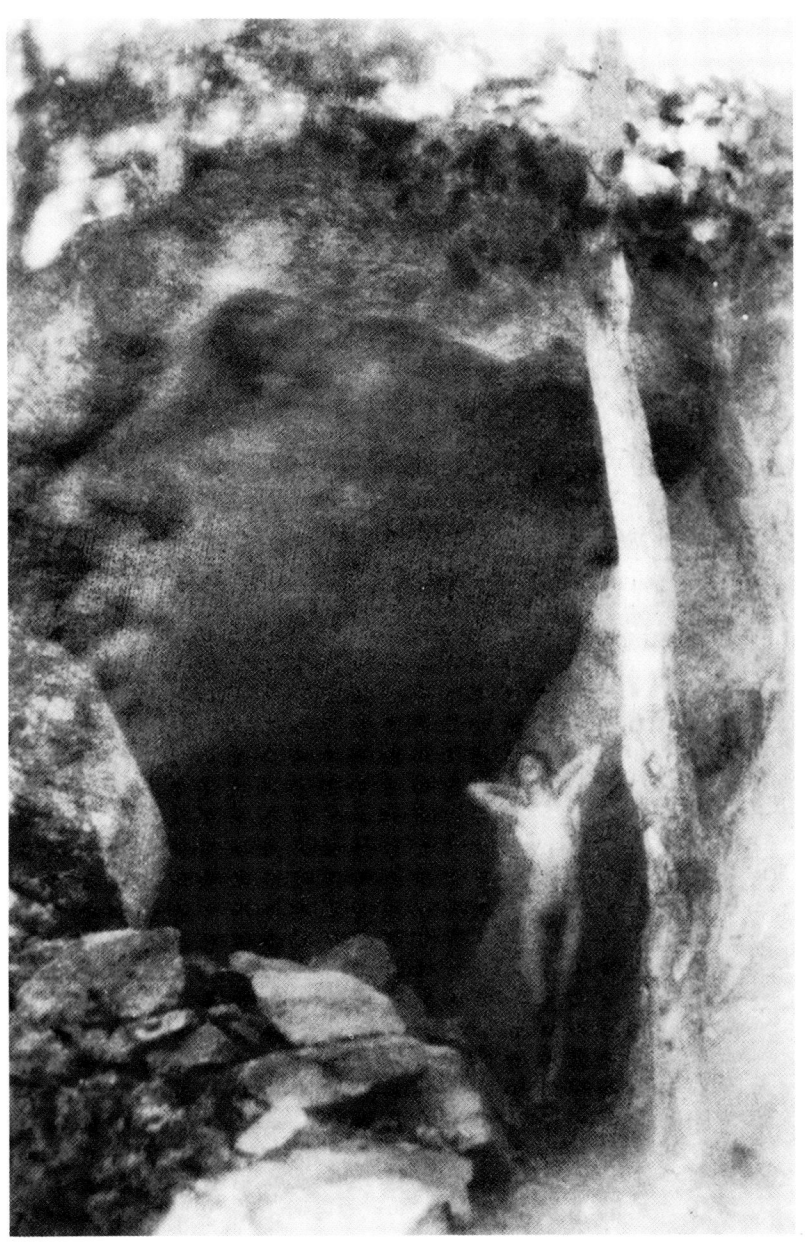

Figure 6.31. F. Holland Day, *The Vision*, 1907
Platinum print.
(Royal Photography Society [?], London)

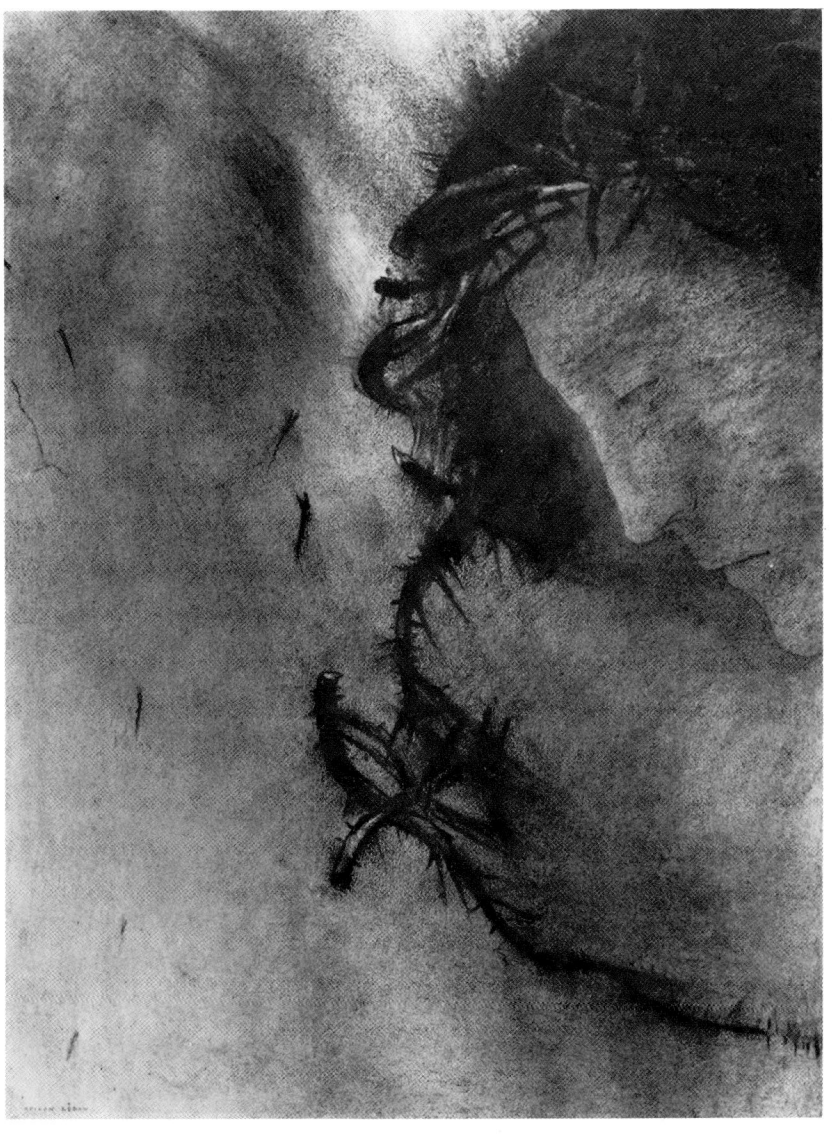

Figure 6.32. Odilon Redon, *Profile with Crown of Thorns*, n.d. Charcoal drawing.
(Photo courtesy Sotheby's, London)

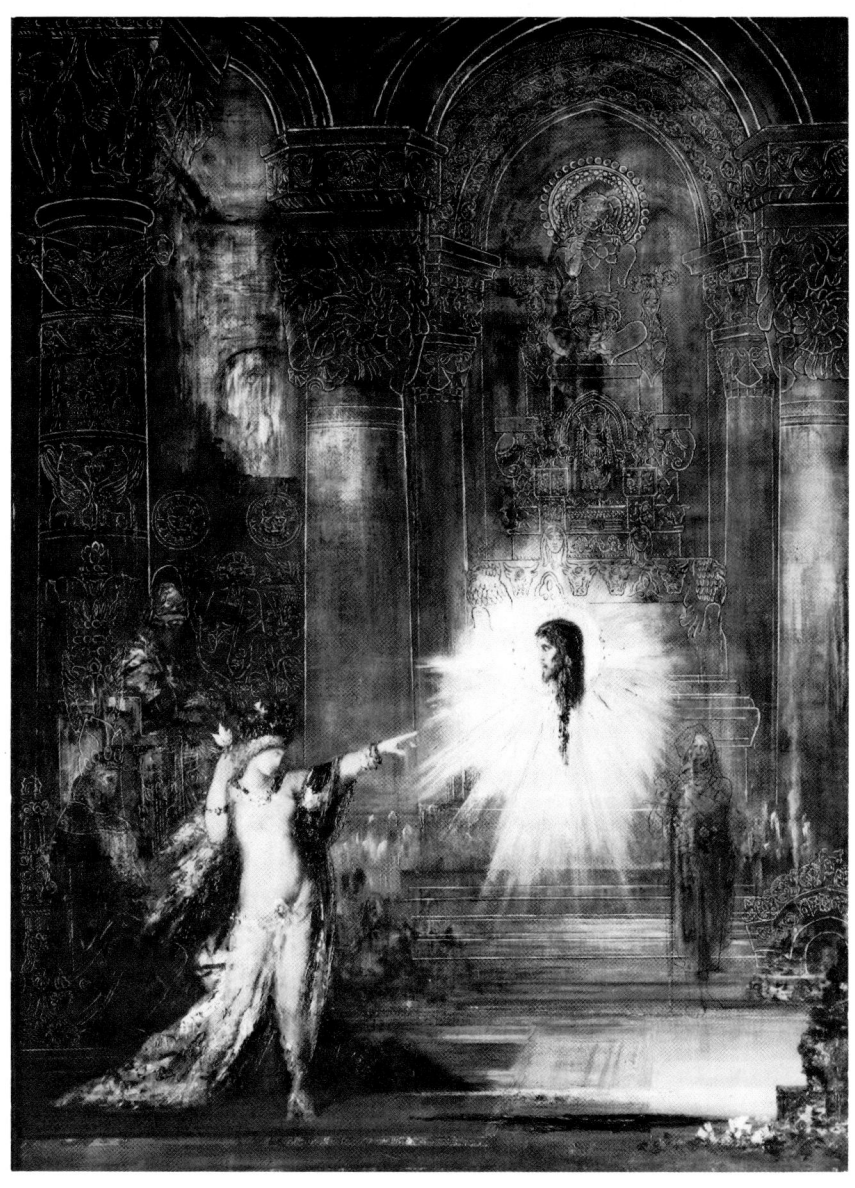

Figure 6.33. Gustave Moreau, *The Apparition*, 1876
Oil on canvas.
(Musée d'Orsay, Paris; Cliché des Musées Nationaux, Paris)

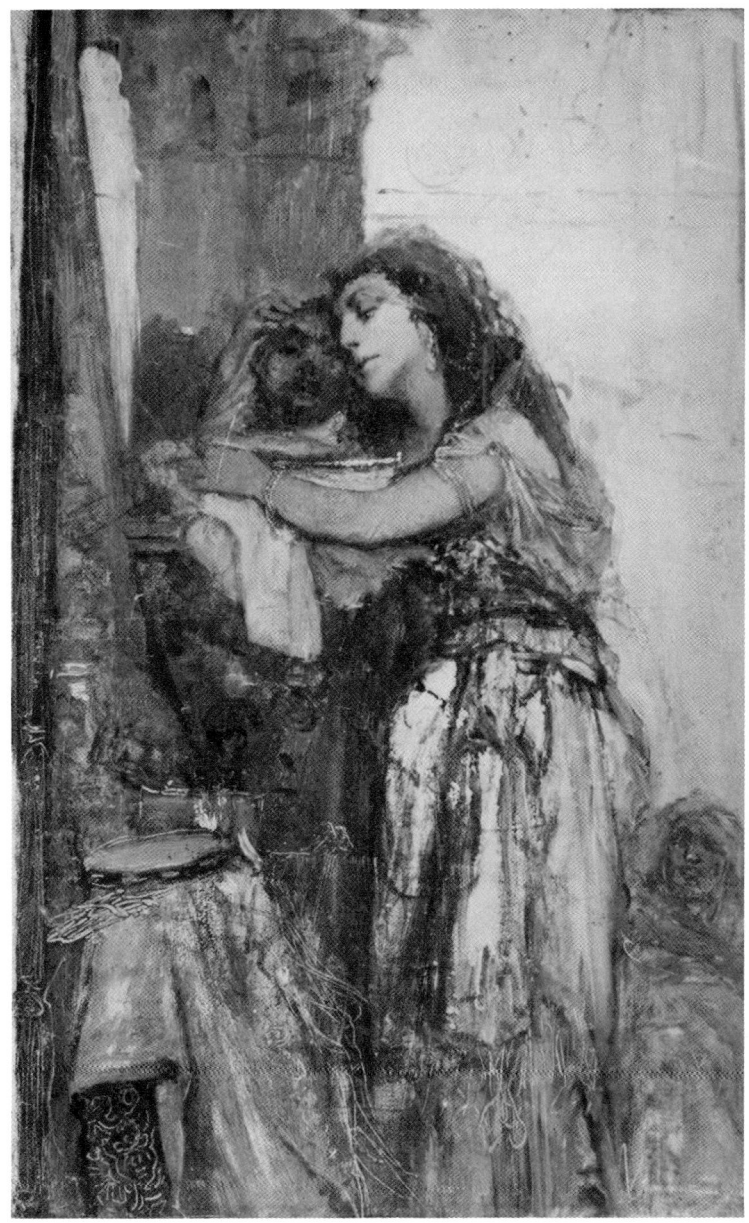

Figure 6.34. Maurycy Gottlieb, *Salome with the Head of John the Baptist*, n.d.
Oil on wood.
(*National Museum of Warsaw*)

Figure 6.35. Joseph-Emile Millochau, *A Maenad Lamenting the Head of Orpheus*, n.d. Oil on canvas.
(Photo: N. D. Roger-Viollet)

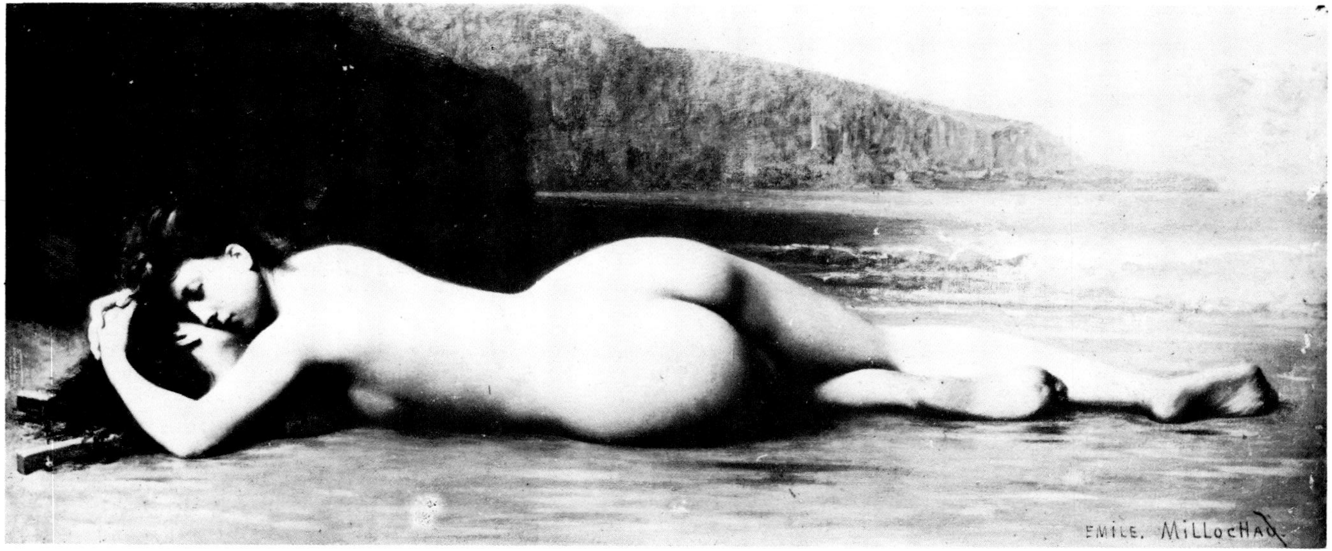

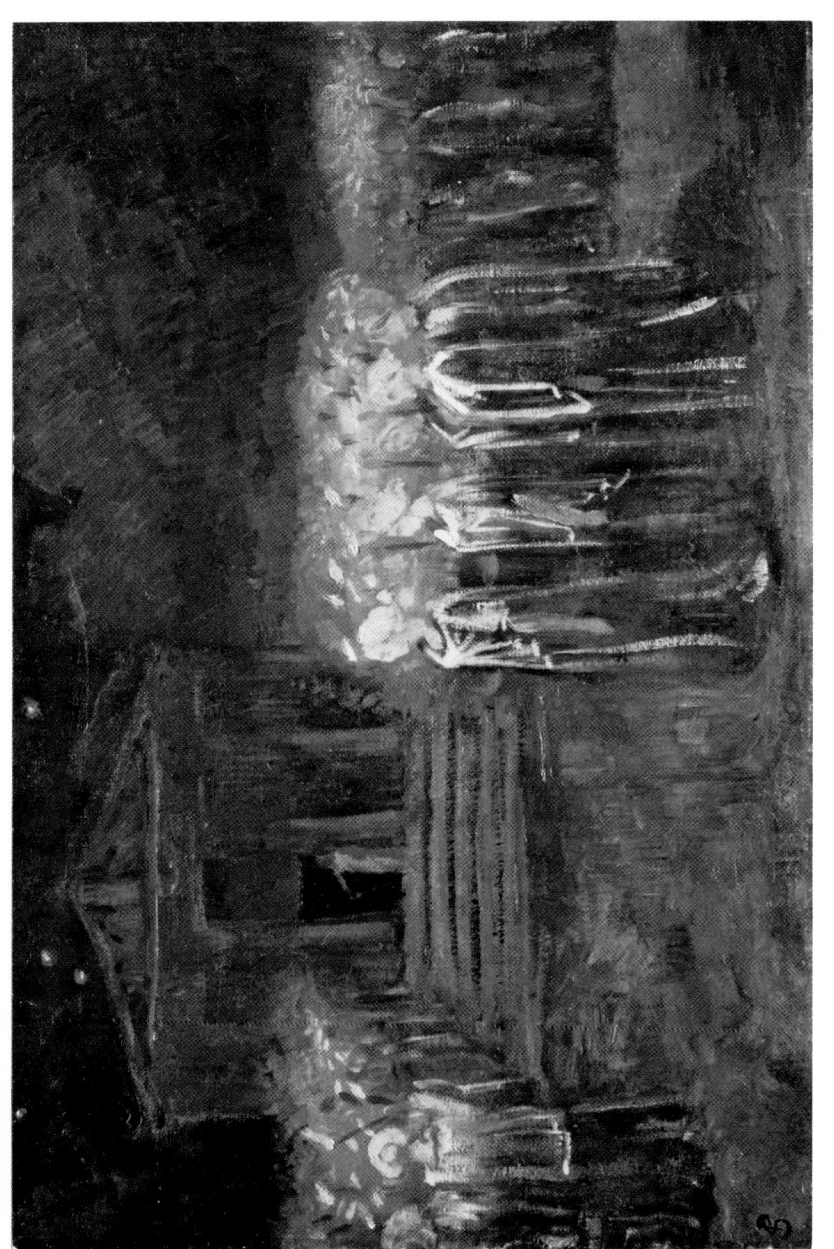

Figure 6.36. Paul Sérusier, *The Mysteries of Eleusis*, ca. 1895
Oil on canvas.
(*Collection Piccadilly Gallery, London*)

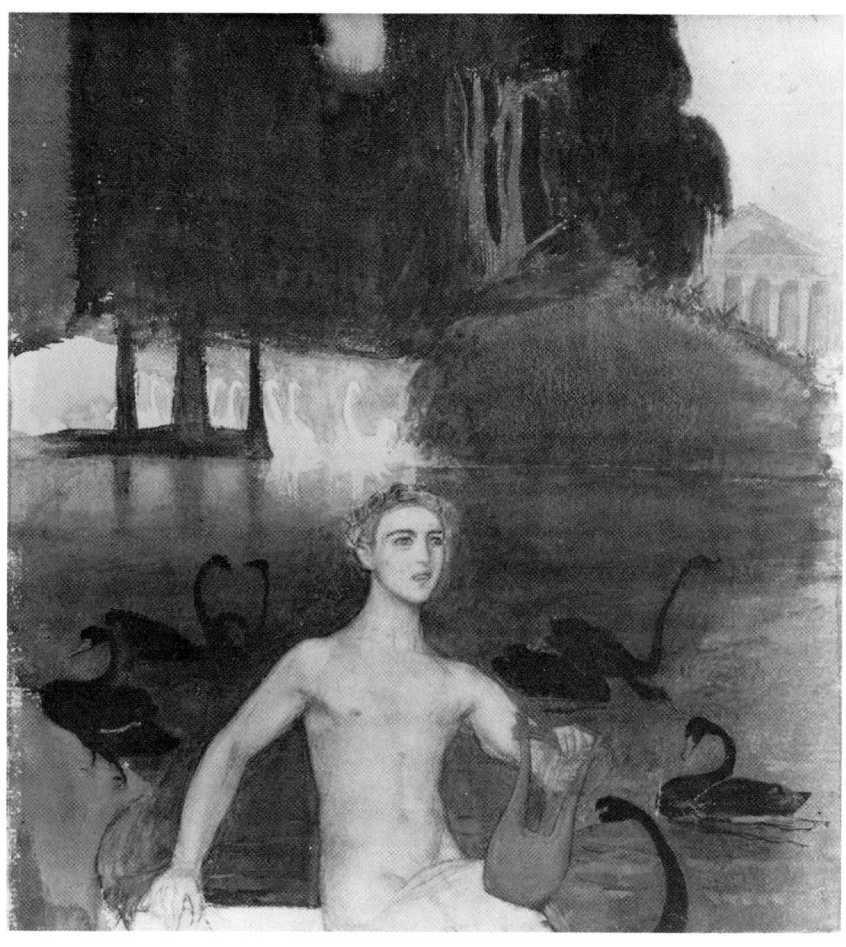

Figure 6.37. Magnus Enckell, *La Fantaisie*, 1894–95
(*Ateneumin Taidemuseo, Helsinki*)

7

Orphic Imagery in the Twentieth Century

The image of Orpheus and the orphic theme survive in the twentieth century, in works by Chagall, Corinth, Racz, Marcks, Marc, Kokoschka, Zadkine, Dufy, Masson, Picasso, Noguchi, Beckmann, Newman, Seuphor, and Fieschi; and in the writings of Mallarmé, Valéry, Apollinaire, Rilke, Cocteau, Divoire, Ségalen, Pierre Jean-Jouve, Pierre Emmanuel, Anouilh, and Saint Pol-Roux; as well as in the music of Stravinsky, Debussy, Milhaud, and Henry.[1] The continued vitality of the myth is bound to a sustained interest in many of the most important aspects of the Symbolist aesthetic: the conviction that art is religion, the art object revelation and the artist-priest or initiate; the aspiration toward an artistic ideal based upon the concepts of synaesthesia, correspondences, *Gesamtkunstwerk*. These crucial themes, which revolve around the figure of Orpheus in the Symbolist milieu, endure to significantly inform the evolving idealist, nonfigurative aesthetic of the twentieth century. Furthermore, of course, the twentieth-century artist derives new meaning from the myth. Aspects of the myth, for instance the relationship between Orpheus and Eurydice, are reinterpreted in the wake of Freud. For many of the artists and writers the myth is exploited as a vehicle for the exploration of their own interior world; the stage for the playing-out of a highly personal, psychological drama.

The Symbolist Aesthetic and the Emergence of Abstraction

Vasily Kandinsky

Recent scholarship has come to acknowledge the importance of mysticism or spiritism to the evolution of abstraction in the first decades of the twentieth century. Kandinsky, Marc, Mondrian, and Kupka, for instance, were drawn to Theosophy and mysticism. Kandinsky perceived in the doctrines of Theosophy a manifestation of the great spiritual epoch which he anticipated. He was thoroughly familiar with Theosophical literature including: Schuré's *Les Grands*

Initiés; Steiner's editions of Goethe's writings on aesthetics and color theory as well as his articles "Theosophica" and "Lucifer Gnosis"; and Helena Blavatsky's *The Secret Doctrine* and *Isis Unveiled*.[2] Moreover, specific illustrations in mystical texts (Besant and Leadbeater's *Thought Forms*, 1901, and Leadbeater's *Man Visible and Invisible*, 1902) may have had an impact on the evolution of his abstract vocabulary.[3] The abstractionists' interest in Oriental philosophy (not unrelated to the fascination with the East which so preoccupied earlier generations in nineteenth-century Germany) significantly informs their nascent aesthetic.[4]

The musical ideal is an underlying principle of Kandinsky's works of art and a pervasive motif in his writings as well. In *On the Spiritual in Art* he explains how the abstract artist must emulate the immaterial quality of music:

> A painter who finds no satisfaction in mere representation, however artistic, in his longing to express his internal life, cannot but envy the ease with which music, the least material of the arts today, achieves this end.[5]

Kandinsky understands the impact of the work of art in terms of sound or resonance. "The work of art must *klingen* or resonate, so that the soul of the viewer vibrates with the same resonance."[6] He likens the artist to a pianist: his color moves the eye which strikes the strings of the soul.[7] This theory of susceptible vibrations may be informed by Theosophical theories or even have a specific basis, for instance, in Besant and Leadbeater's *Thought Forms*:

> [W]hen, for example, a musical note is sounded, a flash of colour corresponding to it may be seen by those whose five senses are already to some extent developed. It seems not to be so generally known that sound produces form as well as colour, and that every piece of music leaves behind it an impression of this nature, which persists for some considerable time, and is clearly visible and intelligible for those who have eyes to see.[8]

Even the titles of his graphic works—*Verses without Words*, 1904; *Xylographie*, 1909; and *Klänge*, 1913—reflect his fascination with the synthesis of all the arts, or *Gesamtkunstwerk*.

These preoccupations were by no means peculiar to Kandinsky, but rather, were shared by other members of the Munich art circle. In 1897, in an article in *Dekorative Kunst*, August Endell describes his aesthetic milieu

> at the beginning of a totally new art, an art with forms, that mean nothing and represent nothing, and remind one of nothing, yet that will be able to move our souls so deeply, so strongly, as before only music has been able to do with tones.[9]

Similarly, Arthur Roessler compares the effect of pure tone, color or line on the soul. Kandinsky's colleague in the Neue Künstler Vereinigung, Alfred Kubin, in his novel, *Die andere Seite,* includes descriptions of abstract color forms.[10]

Franz Marc

Franz Marc, coeditor with Kandinsky of the *Blaue Reiter Almanach,* shares Kandinsky's preoccupation with the spiritual, positing art as a "mystisch-innerliche Konstruktion."[11] Marc's insistence on the religious essence of art and the artist's role as initiate, as well as the pantheism which informs his effort to visualize the beasts' world, reveal his indebtedness to the German Romantic tradition.[12] Like Kandinsky, Marc was interested in Eastern philosophy and religion, especially Indian concepts of second-sight and reincarnation.[13]

Marc believes in a cosmic force, a powerful rhythm which animates and unifies the universe, a concept that bears comparison to the Theosophists' notion of an invisible transcendent reality. This mystical perception of a unifying force in nature is at the base of his pantheism:

> I am attempting to enhance my sensibility for the organic rhythm that I feel is in all things: and I am trying to feel pantheistically the rapture of the flow of "blood" in nature, in the trees, in the animals, in the air. I am trying to create pictures with a new sense of motion and with colors that will mock the easel paintings of the past. . . . I can see no more successful means toward an "animalization" of art, as I like to call it, than the painting of animals. That is why I have taken it up.[14]

This set of attitudes—the mystical perception of art and the artist, the belief in a transcendent reality, the desire to approximate the unconscious pure vision of the animal and thereby achieve oneness with nature—may be described as "orphic." A minor work from 1907, a study for a tapestry (fig. 7.1), which, despite its rather conventional image of a youthful, lyre-playing Orpheus amidst the animals, confirms nonetheless the orphic theme which perhaps underlies Marc's aesthetic mysticism and his often-repeated depictions of animals.[15]

Piet Mondrian

The impact on Mondrian of this Symbolist-occultist milieu of the turn of the century is equally clear. His intense interest in Theosophy is reflected in his membership in the Society as of 1909 and his active involvement until 1916 or 1917. A portrait of Madame Blavatsky hung in the artist's otherwise purely De Stijl studio. He owned a 1908 Dutch edition of Steiner's *Mysticism and Esoterism* and a 1913 Dutch edition of Krishnamurti's *At the Feet of the Masters.*

He was reading Schuré as late as 1934. Not surprisingly, his formulation of Neo-Plasticism appears to have been significantly informed by Schoenmacker, especially his mathematical works, as well as by Indian doctrines popularized by the Theosophists.[16]

Mondrian demonstrated a fascination with the relationship between color and sound, an interest which may, once again, have been inspired by Theosophical texts. He was guided specifically by the Oriental principle of the dual nature of the absolute, in his grouping of tones into two sorts: the first, pure sound or noise, which he associated with noncolors, symbolic of the Spirit and the positive principle; the second, contaminated sound, associated with pure colors, matter, the negative principle.[17]

Frantisek Kupka

Frantisek Kupka looked back to a mediumistic experience as a youth in Bohemia as the beginning of his lifelong interest in mysticism. He was involved with Theosophical circles in Austria and Germany. His reading included the Veda, Plato, Kant, Nietzsche, Schopenhauer, Bergson, Besant, and Leadbeater, as well as works on astrology, alchemy, chemistry, and astronomy. Kupka quotes from H. P. Blavatsky's *The Secret Doctrine,* subscribing to her theory of cyclic evolution of consciousness. Paralleling the Theosophical principle combining art, religion, and science, Kupka's mysticism was enriched by scientific discoveries. Kupka shared the enthusiasm of Kandinsky, Mondrian, and Marc for non-Western art and esoteric religions.[18]

The most significant leitmotif of Kupka's writings and works of art is the synaesthetic ideal. His goal was a "New Reality" of rhythm and harmony, the infusion of music into the painting. Signing himself, "color symphonist,"[19] he frequently assigned musical titles to his works. Kupka describes his endeavor: "I am still groping in the dark, but I believe I can find something between sight and hearing and I can produce a fugue in colors as Bach has done in music."[20] As in the works of Kandinsky and Mondrian, Kupka's fascination with analogies between colors and sounds inevitably propelled his works away from mimesis toward abstraction. In one of his early experiments with these synaesthetic ideas, *Touches de Piano/Lac,* 1909 (fig. 7.2), there is a dynamic tension between the Impressionist-based landscape and the linear patchwork of color representing pure sound, which flutters on the picture surface; an energetic contrast between traditional perspectival space and an abstract passage of color forms, equivalents of sounds.[21] The pictorial equivalent of music is, however, not a goal in itself, but an expression of the artist as clairvoyant, discovering and revealing a hidden transcendent order in the cosmos.

Akseli Gallen-Kallela

A similar balance of abstract color forms within a fairly traditional landscape is found in Waterfall at Mäntykoski, 1892–94 (fig. 7.3), by the Finnish painter, Akseli Gallen-Kallela. Here, superimposed over the realist-impressionist landscape, are five golden strings, symbols of the music in nature, the inner voice of the cosmos. There is a compelling comparison between Gallen-Kallela's image and Mallarmé's dictum that the role of the poet is to summon the orphic voice of the world. Here the artist gives concrete form to that orphic voice. Consonant with the mystical Theosophical notions of the correspondences and the artist's revelatory role, the strings, resting taut on the surface of the painting, between the illusion of nature and the observer's real world space, are the artist's instrument. He plays the strings (his subjective vision), causes them to vibrate, to communicate the essence of a hidden reality. As with Kupka, Gallen-Kallela sees the artist as the clairvoyant, the initiate who can make manifest the orphic mysteries of nature.[22]

These works represent a fascinating transitional stage between Symbolism and abstraction. Eventually the remnants of realistic imagery and overt symbolism of the analogy between color and sound will fall away. The theory of correspondences and synaesthesia, the musical ideal eventually propel the artist toward an aesthetic of pure form and color, a new expression of the spiritual realm. The conceptual basis of abstraction emerges from the Romantic-Symbolist milieu and its constellation of ideas about the religious essence of art, the spiritual role of the artist, an ideal synthesis of all the arts based on a theory of correspondences and synaesthesia. The idealist aesthetic of burgeoning abstraction may be understood, then, as the perpetuation of the orphic theme or orphic voice.

Orpheus as Symbol in the Works of Selected Authors and Artists

Paul Valéry

The aesthetic ideal of the poet, Paul Valéry, of mystical correspondences, of the synthesis of architecture and music is embodied in his "suprême édificateur,"[23] an amalgam between the poet-musician, Orpheus, and the musician-architect, Amphion. Already in 1890, while still in Montpellier, Valéry was formulating his poetic ideal: a tightly composed entity, expressive not merely of the emotional or psychic essence of the individual, but a construction of metaphysical or cosmological significance which reveals a transcendent reality. He wrote to Pierre Löuys:

> I dream of a short verse, a sonnet written by a refined dreamer who would be, at the same time, a judicious architect, a sagacious algebrist, an infallible calculator of the effect to be produced.[24]

It is clear that Mallarmé represents Valéry's poetic ideal, is himself the living embodiment of Orpheus:

> The poets worthy of this name are reincarnations of Amphion and Orpheus. This man (Mallarmé) made us dream of these beings—semi-kings, semi-priests, semi-real, semi-legendary—to which we owe the belief that we are not at all only animal.[25]

Mallarmé is clearly the source for the younger poet's aesthetic mysticism, his fascination with Orpheus, his understanding of correspondences, even for his obsession with the architectural ideal.[26] Mallarmé's famous definition of poetry: "l'explication orphique de la terre," as well as his poetic ideal: "le livre, un livre architectural et prémédité" reverberate quite clearly in Valéry's unpublished "Orphisme":[27]

> At the sound of his lyre, the stones harmonized themselves into temples. The interpretation of the world through poetry, that is the universe explained beyond all syllogism, by Beauty.[28]

The orphic image is also self-reflective as Valéry declares: "Car nous sommes orphiques, constructeurs au son de la lyre de Temples bénis."[29]

"Paradoxe sur l'architecte," published in *L'Ermitage* in March 1891, concludes with the first, prose poem, version of Valéry's Orpheus sonnet.[30] This work is a veritable catalogue of Symbolist themes: the Wagnerian ideal of music; correspondences, analogies; the image of Orpheus itself. With extravagant, mystically redolent prose, Valery evokes his artistic hero, the great creator-constructor, musician-architect who will cleanse a world of aesthetic decadence:

> He will be born, perhaps, to raise up the first tabernacles and the unexpected sanctuaries where the credo of the future will echo through incense. Tomorrow, the supreme constructor will rise up from a people (if this race and the times are not murderous . . .) . . . this far away spirit, and desired by my own soul. . . . I predict he will be a musician, a recluse in the pure solitude of his dream.[31]

The temple and cathedral are his architectural ideals interwoven constantly with music through analogies of perfect mathemetical proportions. Valéry's ideal aesthetic of mystical correspondences results in an inebriating, overwhelming spiritual-sensual experience.

For subtle analogies unite an unreal and fugitive structure of sounds into a solid art, by which imaginary forms are immobilized in the sun, in porphyry.... Thus, an inexpressible correspondence will be manifest, the intimate infinite that one must distinguish under the habitual veils and lies, between two incarnations of art, between the royal façade of Reims, and such a page of Tannhäuser, between the ancient magnificence of the great heroic temple and such a supreme *andante* burning with glorious flames....

For the liturgical organs drive towards the dream of cupolas in saphires and of enormous vaults full of thunder; but the flutes like graceful colonettes soar upward so high that a vertigo crowns them.... A triumphal and total largo explodes finally beneath the final vault; and from all the expressed motifs the secret disengages and wrings itself loose, the glorious absolute love.[32]

This overwhelming sensual experience provokes heroic memories of a long-passed golden age embodied in the figure of Orpheus presented in the prose poem sonnet:

And the god holds the lyre between his silver fingers. The god sings and according to the all powerful rhythm, the fabulous stones rise toward the sun, and one sees growing toward the incandescent azur, the golden harmonious walls of a sanctuary....

He sings! seated on the shores of a splendid sky, Orpheus! His work arrays itself with a vesperal trophy, and his divine lyre enchants the porphyry, because the temple erected by this musician unites the sureness of ancient rhythms with the immense spirit of the great hymn of the lyre.[33]

In three subsequent major works—two dialogues, *Eupalinos ou l'architecte,* and *L'Ame et la danse,* and the melodrama *Amphion,* written in collaboration with the composer Arthur Honegger—Valéry similarly explores the mystical correspondence between music and architecture.[34] The character of the Greek architect, Eupalinos (friend of Phaedra and subject of Phaedra's discussion with Socrates) is clearly another expression of the central Orpheus-Amphion myth. Valéry's choice of Orpheus, Amphion or Eupalinos as the title figure indicates a fluid understanding of the traditional myth—"The myth of Orpheus, that is to say, the animation of everything by a spirit—the fable of mobility and order."[35]—and an essential fixation on his hero, the poet-architect. Indeed, Valéry's collaboration with Honegger on the melodrama, *Amphion,* is the fulfillment of an almost thirty-year dream of creating a work on the theme of Orpheus, which would in its synthesis of speech, song, dance, decor, and modern musical orchestration embody his ideal of the correspondence between the arts.

Guillaume Apollinaire

Guillaume Apollinaire's 1912 designation in *Les Peintres cubistes* of "Orphic Cubism" makes explicit the strong connection between the myth of Orpheus and the sphere of avant-garde painting in the early twentieth century. His various references to Orphism, between October 1912 and March 1913, refer to an ill-defined group of artists including Picasso, Delaunay, Léger, Picabia, and Duchamp, but it is, in fact, an intentionally ambiguous term intended to accommodate Apollinaire's gradually maturing ideas about abstraction:[36] the independence of pictorial structure from visual reality; "non-conceptual" art (art that communicates directly without verbal subject); the analogy between music and painting; the importance of sublime meaning or subject no longer attached to our reality, but evoking a higher level of consciousness.[37] In his commentary on the Salon des Indépendants of 1913, Apollinaire jubilantly celebrates the increasingly significant coloristic and nonfigurative painting: "Du Cubisme sort un nouveau cubisme . . . le règne d'Orphée commence."[38]

The key elements of Apollinaire's Orphism—the theory of correspondence, the ideal of music, a rejection of the traditional mimetic function of painting in favor of a visual art which communicates an inner, universal meaning, corresponding to a higher level of consciousness—are strikingly similar to Kandinsky's aesthetic theories, and may well have been influenced by Apollinaire's reading of *Über das Geistige*.[39] However, what is even more apparent is the evolution of Apollinaire's ideas from the same milieu—Symbolist theory, occult and Theosophical concepts—that informed the aesthetics of Kandinsky, Mondrian, Kupka, and Picabia. Apollinaire frequented the Closerie des Lilas, a favorite haunt of the Neo-Impressionist painters and Symbolist poets; a spot which later attracted a new group including Picasso and Braque. He contributed to the Symbolist journal, *Vers et Prose*, edited by Paul Fort and André Salmon, which included among its contributors: Vielé-Griffin, Marcel Schwob, Henri de Regnier, Verhaeren, Maeterlinck, Stuart Merrill, Yeats, Gide, and Valéry.[40] Apollinaire's poem, "Sur les Prophéties," attests to his exposure to this world of occultism and alternative religions. Apollinaire, as well as Picasso and Max Jacob, had often visited the Sâr Joséphin Péladan during their Montmartre period, and Apollinaire wrote an obituary upon the Sâr's death, June 27, 1918.[41] He was fascinated with the curious mixture of superstition and religion that characterized these enthusiasts of the black arts, and was well acquainted with the basics of Rosicrucianism, the Kabbala, the Neo-Catholic revival, and Theosophy.[42]

In the context of Apollinaire's intimate acquaintance with Symbolism and occultism, it is not at all surprising that he should choose "Orphism" to designate the work of the new abstract artist, nor that the image of the poet musician should appear elsewhere in his poetry and prose. Apollinaire hailed the Symbolist generation with this rallying call: "The new Amphions, the new Orpheuses, the young poets of whom I have been speaking will soon compel your admiration, making the very stones and wild animals sensitive to their tones."[43]

The image of Orpheus figures in Apollinaire's *La Marchande des quatre saisons ou le bestiaire mondain*, published in the June 15 issue of *La Phalange*, and later revised and retitled, *Le Bestiaire ou le cortège d'Orphée* and published in 1911 with woodcuts by Raoul Dufy. In the later edition, there was not only a change of title but added emphasis given to the role of the poet-musician with the addition of two more poems with the theme of Orpheus. Poems 1, 13, 18, and 24 are entitled "Orphée." The first explores the mystical powers of the artist, exalted in the image of metaphysical light. "La Tortue," "Le Cheval," "L'Eléphant," "La Chenille," "Le Lièvre" partake of this glorification of the poet's powers. The second poem portrays Orpheus amidst the insects. The third emphasizes Orpheus' role as prefiguration of Christ (fig. 7.4). The fourth presents Orpheus, protector against various temptations: the female Alcyon, love, the Sirens.[44] Apollinaire's commentary on the poem underlines the focus of his interest: the lyre-bearing Orpheus, master of enchanting song, civilizer, pagan prefiguration of Christ:

> Orpheus was a native of Thrace. The sublime poet played a lyre that Mercury (often confused with Hermes Trismegistus and, with the Greeks, guide of souls to Hades) gave to him. It was composed of a tortoise shell with leather glued around it, two branches, the bridge and cords made from the guts of a sheep. Mercury also gave similar lyres to Apollo and Amphion. When Orpheus played and sang, the wild animals themselves came to listen to his song. Orpheus invented all the sciences and arts. Based in magic, he knew the future and foretold the coming of the Christian SAVIOUR.[45]

Apollinaire invokes the Orpheus-Christ who fascinated the Gnostics, was celebrated by the Renaissance Neo-Platonists and was elaborated once again in the nineteenth century in the context of mytho-religious syncretism. The entire world is God's lyre; Christ is the divine Orpheus, his cross the lyre; his music penetrates men's souls, drawing them to Him. Apollinaire proclaims: "La Poésie c'est la Création."[46] The Orphic voice is linked to the ultimate creative act, the divine creation, Genesis.[47]

The first quatrain invokes the "Pimander" of Hermes Trismegistus in its powerful celebration of the orphic voice of the poet:

> Admire the distinguished power
> And the nobility of the line:
> It is the voice that light makes heard
> And of which Hermes Trismegistus speaks in his Pimander.[48]

Apollinaire probably adopts the association of light and creation from that hermetic text. Light is the primordial form from which all subsequent forms derive, created from the interaction of the shadows and the voice of light. The voice of light is embodied in the word and thence truth is revealed to man. (Light is the symbol of divine creation—primordial form (light) revealed to man in the WORD.) Ballanche may be another source for Apollinaire's hermetic imagery, as he too links Orpheus and Pimander, the orphic voice and light:

> Is there not a voice in all things? I seemed to see a great light which enveloped the immensity of nature . . . and it seemed to be the voice of light. I questioned myself and the voice replied within me.[49]

This original revelatory power of language is exactly that which the Symbolist poets sought to restore. For Mallarmé, "Poetry is the expression of the mysterious consciousness of certain aspects of existence by human language restored to its essential rhythms; it thus endows our stay with authenticity."[50] In addition, Edouard Schuré's association of Orpheus and light in his *Les Grands Initiés*, a passage from Flaubert's *Tentation de Saint-Antoine*, and one of Redon's lithographic illustrations for that book, *Le Profil de lumière*, have been cited as sources for Apollinaire's image of the voice of light, symbol of the poet's vocation and creative power, generally.[51]

Symbolist literature and esoteric and occult texts are the sources, then, for Apollinaire's notion of the poet-priest embodied in Orpheus: the voice of light or artistic creation as revelation of divine truth. This mystical concept of creativity is the foundation of Apollinaire's Orphism and the defining principle of his concept of pure painting. In *La Peinture nouvelle*, April–May 1912, he discusses the new artists:

> The new artists must (create) an ideal beauty which is no longer simply the prideful expression of the species, but the expression of the universe so far as it has become human through light.[52]

Apollinaire's poet is alchemist, dreamer, and initiate. The poet's role is the revelation of the truths of the universe. The poet must draw the reader into

> universes which palpitate ineffably above our heads, into those nearer and yet further away from us which gravitate about the same point of infinity as that which we bear within ourselves.[53]

The myth of Orpheus figures, as well, in other contexts in Apollinaire's oeuvre, manipulated and frequently rather drastically rewritten in a manner which makes clear Apollinaire's emotional and imaginative distance (in contrast to the attitude of the Symbolists). In *Le Poète assassiné*, published in 1916, the hero is Croniamantal, the most famous poet of his day. He ultimately falls victim to an eruption of rabid anti-poetry sentiment: "Like Orpheus, all poets were threatened with a tragic death."[54] Curiously however, Tristouse Ballerinette, Croniamantal's lover (this Orpheus' Eurydice), participates in his death. If Tristouse Ballerinette can be identified with Apollinaire's lost love, Marie Laurencin, his broadly interpreted version of the myth becomes the stage for a highly personal psychological drama of lost love, and on a less conscious level, the transformation of the muse into the castrating monster. In many of the light-hearted poems in *Le Cortège d'Orphée*, Apollinaire's approach verges on parody. The 1910 *L'Hérésiarque et cie*, with the hero Benedetto di Orfei, is overtly antireligious.[55] Apollinaire is fascinated with myth, religion and esoteric knowledge, and particularly appreciates the figure of Orpheus as a powerful expression of the poet's mission. However, Apollinaire is not a mystic and orphism does not constitute a world-view for him nor a compelling definition of his own creative being.

Marc Chagall and Ossip Zadkine

In his roles as friend, critic, impressario and patron, Apollinaire exerted a considerable influence in the circles of Montmartre and Montparnasse. Chagall and Zadkine, both Russian emigrés arriving in Paris within a year of one another, kept studios at La Ruche in the Vaugirard area. They frequented the regular gatherings at the Café du Dôme and the Café Rotonde. Both artists dedicated works to Apollinaire: Chagall in 1911–12, *Hommage à Apollinaire*, and Zadkine in 1937, *Monument à Guillaume Apollinaire*.[56] It is hardly surprising to discover that in 1913–14, Chagall painted *Orpheus* (fig. 7.5). There is a considerable stylistic tension between the cubistic geometricization of the poet's youthful body; and the loosely painted, vibrantly colored passages of paint which constitute the flowering landscape. There is, as well, a related spatial ambiguity between the lyre-playing figure and the surrounding environment.

Though this portrayal of Orpheus appears to be an isolated image in Chagall's oeuvre, in Zadkine's work, in contrast, it is an oft-repeated theme, reworked in six different versions between 1930 and 1960 (fig. 7.6).[57] Moreover, Orpheus is but one of a number of figures from classical mythology or history which figure in Zadkine's work—*Ariane, Astarte, Antiquity, Athena, Clementius, Caryatide, Centaur, Demeter, Diana, Discobolus, Daphne, Ephebe*, the *Three Graces, Hermaphrodite, Laocoon, Leda*, the *Labyrinthe, Menades, Narcissus, Niobe*, the *Birth of Venus, Phoenix, Prometheus, Pomona, Venus*, and *Vestale*.[58] But it was Orpheus who especially fascinated Zadkine.[59] His compulsion to repeatedly rework and perfect his original 1930 Orpheus was inspired by both formal and symbolic reasons. He expressed frustration with the limitations of the post-cubist architectonic stylization of the anatomy. Moreover, he was struck by the inadequacy of the conventional image of lyre-bearing figure to convey the significance of the mythic Orpheus. Zadkine yearned to transcend conventional narrative forms and to construct new forms which symbolically embody the essence of the myth. Gradually, Zadkine succeeds in integrating the conventional attribute of the lyre into the human form: the torso is hollowed out as though forming the sounding-box of the instrument; the strings, like branches, seem to emerge from his innards; his arms are the structural elements of the lyre. Through this dramatic conflation of human form and instrument, Zadkine attempts to create a sculptural embodiment of the mythical creative genius.[60]

Michel Seuphor

The Belgian abstractionist, Michel Seuphor, born Ferdinand Louis Berckelaers, adopted his pseudonym, an anagram of Orpheus, in 1918. His life and career constitute an interesting connection between nonfigurative art and the theme of Orpheus. Seuphor was friends with the Delaunays, Mondrian, and Arp, among other prominent avant-garde artists. With Torres-Garcia he founded the "Cercle et Carré" group in 1929. He wrote extensively on Mondrian and Neo-Plasticism, geometric abstraction and nonfigurative art in general. His own works, "dessins à lacunes," consist of collages and drawings, white voids manipulated against a background of precisely executed parallel lines, finely measured, with modulations achieved through variations in the thickness of the individual lines as well as the overlapping and crossing of the lines. The theme of Orpheus figures in several works including *La Mort d'Orphée*, 1964 (fig. 7.7). This work consists of eight attached panels of ink and collage on cardboard. White fragments and calligraphic elements meander across gently modulated passages of brown, greys, and blacks, forming a fluid pattern which evokes, at once, the broken lyre and fragments of the poet's body floating on the waters of the Hebrus River as well as musical notes on a scale or, more generally, musical patterns and rhythms.[61] Any stylistic similarity with Paul Klee's 1926 *Ein Garten für Orpheus* (fig. 7.8) is merely coincidental. The delicately interwoven linear patterns are typical of Klee's first Dessau pictures. Consistent with his fascination with music and myth, Klee turns to the story of Orpheus in another work as well, *Orpheus*, 1929.[62]

Rainer Maria Rilke

In the work of Rainer Maria Rilke, Orpheus is more than an incidental or even sustained theme. For Rilke, Orpheus is Poetry; Orpheus embodies, moreover, the essential meaning of life and death. Orpheus is the key to Rilke's ontology, a joyous answer to the poet's lifelong anguished struggle with the questions of God, being, existence, the mystery of life and death. The Orpheus myth is not only the central motif in Rilke's *Sonnets to Orpheus*, but is, moreover, a sustained theme throughout the poet's poetry and prose. Already in an early work, *Das Buch der Bilder*, Rilke articulates his cosmic vision of the poet: "On the Border of Night . . . I am a chord stretched on vast rustling resonances."[63] This image (curiously similar to the painting by Gallen-Kallela discussed above) captures Rilke's mystical vision of the poet. Rilke's Poet summons forth the orphic voice of the world, the inner vibration of things; the Poet (Orpheus) moves between our world and the beyond; the Poet's soul resonates with the mysterious rhythms which encompass all; he brings together or orchestrates the melody of death and the harmony of life.[64]

Rilke plumbs the complexities of Orpheus' mythic persona, exploring the various moments of the narrative. In Sonnet I, 1, Orpheus is the poet musician who animates trees and enchants animals, harbinger of religion to mankind:

> There rose a tree. O pure transcendency!
> O Orpheus singing! O tall tree in the ear!
>
> . . . Creatures of stillness thronged out of the clear
> released wood from lair and nesting-place;
>
> . . . And where before
> hardly a hut had been to take this in,
>
> . . . you built temples for them in their hearing.[65]

It is, however, Orpheus' descent into Hades which is crucial to Rilke's perception of the poet. It is that journey, the initiation in the infernal realms, that endows Orpheus with the vision to turn grieving into creativity, to reconcile lament (Klage) and praise (Ruhm). Orpheus bridges the vast, tortured chasm between this world and the other, this reality and the beyond. Orpheus, the initiate or priest who has penetrated the mysteries of life and death is capable of transforming the dreadful duality or opposition into a vision of transformation within a spiritual continuum. Like Kandinsky and Mondrian, Rilke's aesthetic is also informed by spiritism or Theosophy, envisioning our reality as merely a fleeting existence, one moment in a vast succession of spaces and times which are encompassed by a transcendent spiritual reality. Orpheus' Hades journey essentially puts death into perspective. This vision of death as a transformation of life is expressed in Sonnet I, 9:

> Only one who has lifted the lyre
> among shadows too,
> may divining render
> the infinite praise.
>
> Only who with the dead has eaten
> of the poppy that is theirs,
> will never again lose
> the most delicate tone.
>
> Only in the dual realm
> do voices become
> eternal and mild.[66]

The intensity of his objections to the Christian concept of the afterlife, which Rilke saw as a denigration of the value and beauty of this life, may have been the root of his spiritual crisis.[67] In Rilke's philosophy, Orpheus comes to replace Christ or, at the very least, Christ becomes a mere shadow of Orpheus. Rilke's, *The Book of Hours*, 1899–1903, culminates with his proclamation of the advent of a new Poet-Death-Messiah who will render death comprehensible, reveal it as the fulfillment, not the negation of temporal life.[68] Understandably, it is Orpheus, leader of the orphic cults and victim of the Dionysian orgia, who consumes Rilke's imagination. The cycles of reincarnation central to the orphic mysteries correspond to Rilke's vision of life and death, his concept of transformation. It is through his destruction at the hands of the Maenads, the fragmentation of his physical being, his disintegration into thingness, that Orpheus achieves oneness with nature, which allows him to sing the inner voice of things animate and inanimate. His martyrdom transforms the poet, releases the orphic voice, a transcendent song of the truth of life and death. Sonnet I, 26:

> In the end they battered and broke you, harried by vengeance,
> the while your resonance lingered in lions and rocks
> and in the trees and birds. There you are singing still.
>
> O you lost god! You unending trace!
> Only because at last enmity rent and scattered you
> Are we now the hearers and a mouth of Nature.[69]

Walter Rehm perceptively explains the significance of Orpheus' death: "Only by dying does Orpheus become ever-present as a pan-poetic-world-element: as a song. Everywhere 'it' sings . . . *he* is the singer."[70] Rilke's mysticism clearly derives from the tradition of German Romanticism and Symbolism. Rilke's interest in death may specifically stem from his study the works of Alfred Schuler, an archaeologist and student of the antique mysteries, in Munich in 1915. Along with Klage and Wolfskehl, Schuler was a member of a group of Munich cosmologists in the circle of Stefan George. Through Schuler, Rilke would have become familiar as well with the works of J. J. Bachofen, who has been recognized as a major source for Rilke's "Orphic-Theology."[71]

Rilke himself provided substantial explanation of his cosmology, acknowledging his perception of death as a continuation of life as the central theme of the sonnets and elegies. In a 1923 letter to Nanny von Escher, Rilke writes:

> Two inmost experiences were decisive for their production: the determination constantly maturing in me to keep life open towards death, and, on the other hand, the intellectual necessity of instating the transformations of love differently in this wider whole than was possible in the narrower orbit of life (which simply excluded death as the other). It is here that one should, so to say, seek the 'plot' of these poems, and now and then it stands, I believe, simple and strong in the foreground.[72]

Rilke's metaphysical and aesthetic goals: the presentation of the continuity of life and death in a transcendent spiritual unity; the dismissal of the confining measurement of space and time (past, present, future) in favor of infinity, an endless flow; the dismissal, even, of the visible world for the greater reality of the invisible are achieved in the orphic song.[73] Orpheus is a paradigm of pure contradiction. He celebrates the world in all its irreducibly antithetical aspects. Things fall apart, they become invisible, but the poet retrieves and recreates them in the invisible/audible; a more profound form of being.[74] The orphic song reveals and celebrates transformation and metamorphosis, the inexorable movement of everything toward the spiritual, allowing, therefore, simultaneous lament and praise. Death no longer terrifies, decay is not tragic; both are forms of transformation.

Rilke strives to attain the orphic voice by pushing his poetry beyond the usual level of human self-consciousness and preoccupation with destiny, fate or being. Geoffrey Hartman has described Rilke's poetics as the "unmediated vision."[75] Rilke attempts to renew sensation, to perceive life in the object; to feel the objectness of the body. He creates a "new" language which defies normal linguistic or logical expectations; a language which, according to Hartmann, is stripped of an anthropomorphic, self-reflective overlay, in which words' power of concreteness is rediscovered.[76] To a great extent, this immediacy seems to be achieved through a powerful synaesthetic imagery. In Sonnet I, 1, space and music, the acoustic and the visible are energetically interchanged: "O tall tree in the ear!"[77] The immediacy of his poetics creates a celebration in Sonnet I, 15:

> Wait . . . , that tastes good . . . It's already in flight
> . . . Just a little music, a stamping, a humming-:
> Girls, you warm, you silent girls,
> dance the taste of the fruit experienced!
>
> Dance the orange. . . .[78]

Some of Rilke's own commentaries on contemporary artists are revelatory in regard to his poetics. For instance, his admiration of Cézanne's "Sachlichkeit," his treatment of fruit, the ordinary subject, the human form, all with the same matter-of-fact vision, is related to Rilke's concept of the "pure physical fruit." Rilke speaks of fruit's heaviness, its state of perpetual rest. He uses active verbs to describe the "being" of fruit.[79] Similarly, Rilke's fascination with gesture as a kind of pure speech of the body is confirmed in or related to his knowledge of Rodin's sculpture.[80]

Rilke's poetry resonates with his joyful confidence in the complementary nature of life and death. He sings/celebrates the eternal metamorphosis, the transformation of all life in the context of a transcendent spiritual reality. Confident of Orpheus' knowledge, gained through his initiation in descent to Hades, Rilke does not fear death. Rilke is at one with nature, absorbed in Nature like the scattered fragments of Orpheus' body. He conjures the lifeness of objects, the natural thingness of human form like magical Orpheus charmed the beasts and animated rocks and trees.

Max Beckmann

The following statement by the German painter Max Beckmann reveals perhaps an underlying mysticism comparable to his compatriot Rilke's mystical cosmology:

> Always art has been side by side with religion and science, the helper and freer of the path of mankind. It resolves through form the many paradoxes of life, and allows us sometimes to glimpse behind the dark curtain, which hides the unknown space in which we shall one day be whole.[81]

Beckmann's implied messianic role of art, the function of the artist in resolving the "paradoxes of life," in revealing the greater unity beyond present-day reality, could well serve as commentary on Rilke's sonnets.

Indeed, Beckmann was interested in Theosophy and read extensively in the more encompassing areas of myth and religion. The esoteric and occult theories so popular during the 1890s may have had a profound impact on his formation, informing his concept of painting as a "magic operation." Indeed, many scholars have emphasized the mystical-cosmological essence of Beckmann's work and thought.[82] F. W. Fischer, pointing to passages in Beckmann's diary, identifies his attitude as a marriage of Existentialist anxiety with Gnostic leanings:

> To be sure, something really earth solving is hardly to be hoped for, but a the least there remains for us protest against the "apparent" craziness of the cosmos.[83]

Gert Schiff, noting Beckmann's "indifference to the letter of the myth" warns against using myth or religion and mysticism as central points in any analysis of his painting.[84] In this way Schiff differentiates Beckmann's anxiety, his quest for self, for meaning in the world, from the mysticism of Beckmann's friend Frommel and other members of the circle of Stefan George.[85] Schiff, for instance, suggests that the scene in the right panel of *The Departure*, 1932–33 (fig. 7.9), his first triptych, can be read as a parody of the Orpheus myth:

> The bellhop who delivers messages, hands out telegrams and calls the hotel guests to the telephone, was to Beckmann the modern Hermes, messenger of Fate. This one carries a fish, sacred to those divinities who lead mortals from the shadows of death back to life. With this in mind, one might read the scene as a parodistic inversion of a myth: a *blind* Hermes *follows* a *living* Eurydice who abducts a dead Orpheus from Hades. Even the loathsome 'Cupid' fits into the parody; it seems questionable whether these figures will find their way out into the light.[86]

Beckmann's own explanation of this panel stresses a theme of universal psychological significance:

> Here you see yourself as you try to find your way in the dark; you illumine the hall and stairs with a miserable lamp and you drag along, tied to you as part of yourself, the corpse of your memories, mistakes and defeats, the murder everybody commits once in his life—you can never rid yourself of your past, you must carry the corpse along, and Life beats the drum.[87]

Surely this supposed reference to the Orpheus myth seems to demonstrate what Schiff has called Beckmann's indifference to the letter of the myth. Yet, Beckmann's psychological interpretation and his manipulation or reversal of traditional mythic roles seem to reveal the artist's sensitivity to that perplexing and crucial moment of the myth during which magically gifted Orpheus stumbles, looks back and becomes the instrument of Eurydice's ultimate death. He is haunted forever by this failure (whether a result of his own weakness or the unfolding of inexorable laws of Fate) which leads, ultimately, to his own destruction. A parallel is established between Orpheus' tragedy and the psychological burden, the corpse of memories, regrets, past events unfulfilled, of everyman. Beckmann penetrates this perplexing moment of the myth and discovers in Orpheus' troublesome failure a shadow, an allegory or prefiguration of the psychological or moral anguish which haunts modern man.

In the *Argonauts* triptych, 1949–50 (fig. 7.10), one of the male youths in the central panel has been identified as Orpheus. According to his diary entry, Beckmann painted the left panel, *The Painter and His Model*, first.[88] Later, he referred specifically to that panel, as well as to the triptych as a whole, as "The Artists." A dream apparently led to Beckmann's change of the title, to *The Argonauts*, adopted in December 1950.[89] The choice of titles apparently has an autobiographical basis. His friend, the poet Wolfgang Frommel, who called his group of writers and artists in Amsterdam "The Argonauts," once suggested that Beckmann abandon his "chthonian" themes of the Amsterdam underworld, and instead paint his Amsterdam Argonaut group. Beckmann gave Frommel a photo of his 1905, *Young Men by the Sea* (closely related to the central panel of *The Argonauts*) inscribed: "In remembrance of the Argonauts conversation." In addition, Göpel points to a "Wertheresque" portrait of Frommel by Beckmann (reworked in 1949), in which Frommel holds a book inscribed "OR-U," thus identifying the poet Frommel with his archetype. Apparently also, Beckmann had read with great interest Frommel's discussion of the Argonaut myth as one of the basic themes of the West.[90]

There are compelling contrasts and complex interrelationships between the three panels. The left panel portrays the painter at his easel and his model (whom Beckmann identifies as Medea). The right panel portrays a group of seated women musicians. (Beckmann described them as the chorus of a Greek tragedy. Frommel interprets them as the companions of Sappho who continued the song of Orpheus.) The intensity of the painter's demeanor is answered by Medea's ferocious appearance, holding an oversized sword, her scanty theatrical costume revealing her breasts and an expanse of thighs, which seem somehow frighteningly hard. She sits on a huge mask which resembles a severed head, evoking the physical violence of Medea's infanticide and murder of her husband, and suggesting indirectly, perhaps, Orpheus' brutal murder. Her pose, clutching the sword, her buttocks pressed on the "face" of the mask, creates a psychologically powerful image of the castrating female. In contrast, the women musicians in the right panel (Frommel's followers of Sappho), present a pacific image of elegantly dressed and coiffed females, their bodily forms interlocked with the curves and curls of their musical instrument. Even the plants in the two panels reflect this contrast: in the left panel is a spiky, angular plant which resembles a cactus; while in the right panel long elegant leaves are graced with white and red blossoms. Schiff interprets this contrast as Dionysian and Apollonian.[91] Meanwhile Frommel speculates about the impact of J. J. Bachofen, especially his concept of "mother right," on Beckmann's portrayal of women in this triptych.[92] The two side panels bring together painting and music, the theme of the unity of the arts, familiar in the context of Symbolism. Orpheus, the archetypal poet-musician, appropriately is positioned in the center panel.

The two side panels, though they do include floors and walls of a similar bluish-grey color, still cannot be read as a single space or room. These interior spaces form together a remarkable contrast with the wide open, outdoor space of the central panel. There is a curious spatial disparity in the scene. Orpheus and Jason stand on a high plain (Jason leans on huge red boulders reminiscent perhaps of Beckmann's Colorado journey).[93] Orpheus' lyre rests on the ground. From a vast lower area emerges an older giant figure on a tremendous ladder. The expanse of pink sky, with purple sun (eclipsed), red planets and sliver of black moon, reinforces the feeling of vast expanses of space.[94]

There are various and contrasting identifications of the old man. Frommel interprets him as Glaucus, the original builder and pilot of the Argo, transformed into a god after the battle with the Tyrrhenians. Frommel claims that Beckmann would have been familiar with the story of Glaucus' appearance to Orpheus and Jason, giving prophecy, from Philostratus' *Imagines*, retold in Frommel's own manuscript about the myth.[95] Gert Schiff identifies the old man as either Glaucus or possibly another mythical prophet, Phineus, a blind Bithynian.[96] For Fischer, the old man is generally a figure of prophecy and metamorphosis. He climbs the ladder which is a symbol of perpetual transition and is thereby associated with the overall theme of initiation. Citing Helena Blavatsky, Fischer understands the bird as a symbol of magic and wisdom, of the enduring and unchanging knowledge of the world.[97]

In the traditional myth of the Argonauts, Orpheus' role is magical and religious. His singing calms the wandering rocks; his singing overwhelms the dangerous voices of Sirens and lulls to sleep the dragon that guards the Golden Fleece. Throughout, though, he is the priest who incessantly makes sacrifices to the gods and initiates the Argonauts into the mysteries of Samothrace. In Beckmann's painting, the golden bodies of Jason and Orpheus are majestic and statuesque. Orpheus' erect posture—his muscular back, the solid balance of his stance—is appropriate to his spiritually powerful role. It is also perhaps significant that Orpheus' head is situated amidst the stars. For Fischer, who emphasizes the themes of initiation, cycles of rebirth, perpetual transition, Orpheus reveals Beckmann's preoccupation with the mysteries of the orphic cult.[98]

In the end it is probably impossible or irrelevant to attempt to decipher Beckmann's use of the myth and to assign specific allegorical significance to individual elements in the triptych. Rather, the traditional myth seems to float in and out of focus, absorbed by Beckmann into a realm of personal experience. Moreover, the very manner in which Beckmann manipulates the triptych form, exploiting a feeling of synthesis-antithesis-resolution between the wings and the central panel; a sense of spatial, temporal or psychological simultaneity (perhaps absorbed from contemporary experimental theater) reinforces a sense of ambiguity in regard to the artist's precise attitude toward the myth.[99] Clearly, in contrast to Rilke, for whom the figure of Orpheus is central to his mystical aesthetic and cosmology, myth does not constitute the center of Beckmann's work. Beckmann freely fuses and amalgamates the myth with his personal themes.

André Masson

In the 1930s, André Masson executed several works with the theme of Orpheus. A series of drawings and etchings entitled *Sacrifices of the Gods*, including an image of the death of Orpheus, were completed in 1932–33 and published in 1936 with a text by Georges Bataille.[100] Between 1932 and 1934 Masson painted a series of mythological works, including *Orpheus* (fig. 7.11).[101]

Yet another manifestation of Masson's interest in the Orpheus theme is the series of portraits of his Surrealist friends and colleagues as severed heads. Executed at the behest of his friend, Jacques Doucet, they were published in *La Revue Européenne*, as illustrations for "Le Paysan de Paris," by Aragon, and later published in *Une Oeuvre, un portrait*. The series included portraits of Breton, Artaud (fig. 7.12), Desnos, Eluard, Leiris (fig. 7.13) and Péret. The portraits of Breton and Artaud recall the floating severed heads in many of Odilon Redon's works.[102] In particular the peculiarly upright position of the head in Michel Leiris' portrait is strikingly similar to the presentation of Orpheus in Redon's 1888 charcoal. Masson had professed his admiration for Redon more than once, describing telluric pictures which evolve into metabiological fantasies worthy of Redon.[103] In his 1957 article on Redon, Masson specifically argues against viewing Redon either as a proto-Surrealist or as an illustrator of the Symbolists, praising the lack of narrative in Redon's work and acknowledging as well the impact on his own work of Redon's manipulation of color and texture. Specifically pertinent in regard to Masson's own use of the severed-head motif is his discussion of Redon's vocabulary and subjects, which takes note especially of "decapitated heads in full flight," "the figuration of the eye in Redon . . . orbicular shells . . . orbicular eyelids . . . the single eye shining with innocence or dark with guilt."[104] The segmentation of the body, with juxtaposition of plant forms and elements of the human anatomy, becomes a leitmotif in Masson's own work.[105] But perhaps the clearest evidence of Redon's impact on these portrait drawings is the pervasive sense of serenity and the aura of peaceful introspection, a quality which contrasts markedly with the aggressive violence, even sadism, that accompanies the segmentation of anatomical parts (and representation of death) in much of Masson's work in the 1920s and 1930s, indeed, throughout his career.[106]

More typical of the themes of aggression, sex, and violence is the image of Orpheus, one of five illustrations in Les Sacrifices.[107] The first plate in Les Sacrifices is Mithra. Here, the masked god, physically strong, his genitals prominent, straddles the bellowing bull, and plunges his knife deep into the animal's chest. The blood gushes forth, falling in huge droplets to the ground where branches and plants burst forth. The Death of Orpheus (fig. 7.14) is the subject of the second plate. The wreathed poet is completely surrounded and overcome by a pack of horse-headed females. Once again, the sexual aspect of the attack is stressed. One animal rips at the poet's breast. Orpheus' legs are pinned, wide-apart, the fanged mouth of one of the attackers about to plunge into his genitals. The poet's tear-streaked profile is sad and poignant amidst the crush of fiercely snarling heads, madly ripping limbs and claws. The poet's hand grows into the curling form of his stringed lyre. The third plate is The Crucified. Here, a horse-headed human is pinned to a cross placed on a high promontory, adorned with horses' skulls. The dramatic background includes eclipsed moons, blazing plummeting suns, hovering planets. Horse-headed winged creatures are seemingly substituted for the putti familiar to Christian crucifixions. Three women attend to the crucified, collecting the blood from his gaping wound in a cup; touching their lips to the wound on his chest and feet. These are, in fact, ambiguous gestures, expressive less of grief-stricken adoration, than themselves part of the ritualized sacrifice.[108] The fourth image, Le Minotaure, shows the coupling of the beast and a woman, floating within a great abyss, a cosmic setting of jagged rocks adorned with skulls, and erupting volcanoes. The fifth image portrays Osiris. Clearly these etchings are inspired by Masson's fascination with the darker side of myth, with the underlying connection between love and death.

The choice of the particular subjects of this series (for instance, the bull which figures in three of the five plates: Mithra, Minotaur and Osiris) was undoubtedly nourished by Bataille's fanatic preoccupation with ritual sacrifice, death and murder.[109] Masson, like Bataille, is drawn to the Dionysian, somber side of myth. This preoccupation determines the aspect of the Orpheus myth which interests him—not the noble singer of magical power, nor the ill-fated lover—but rather the priest of the orphic cults who falls victim to the Dionysian orgia. This furious, Dionysian, orgiastic aspect of the Orpheus myth is in marked contrast to the aura of calm transcendence implied with the reference to Orpheus in the severed-head portraits of the twenties. This shift in focus in Masson's interpretation of the myth of Orpheus may be attributed to Bataille's influence.

Jean Cocteau

The myth of Orpheus was a lifelong fixation for Jean Cocteau. Well versed in every aspect of the myth and its historical metamorphosis, he freely manipulates the mythic narrative, varying his emphasis of symbolic significance, using the myth, essentially, as a vehicle for the exploration of personally compelling issues: the role of the artist; the mystery of death; unresolved feelings toward his dead father; his own homosexuality; feelings of alienation or persecution at the hands of critics or fellow artists; his own misogynist tendencies. In the wake of Freud, the myth becomes a process of self-examination, a means of exorcising personal psychological demons. The Orpheus myth is essentially absorbed by Cocteau into a process of self-mythification. Cocteau is Orpheus.

Cocteau's works, from over a 35-year period, dealing explicitly with the theme of Orpheus include: *Orphée*, the play, 1925 (first performed 17 June 1926); *La Douleur d'Orphée*, poésie plastique (exhibited December 1926); *Orphée*, ballet, 1944; a series of lithographs published by Editions Rombaldi, 1944; *Orpheé*, the film, 1950; a series of paintings, including *La Tête d'Orphée* and *Orphée attaqué*, 1951; Cocteau's epée d'Académicien, 1955; paintings for the Salle des Mariages de l'Hôtel de Ville de Menton, 1957–58 (fig. 7.15); and *Le Testament d'Orphée*, 1959, film (fig. 7.16).[110]

Several major themes emerge in Cocteau's manipulation of the myth. Cocteau's strong personal identification with Orpheus, Creator par excellence, is clear in the 1959 film, *Le Testament d'Orphée*. The film was a dubious artistic success—an awkward, self-directed, confessional treatment of his own psychological and emotional conflicts, in which Cocteau himself plays the role of the poet. Actually, Cocteau's identification with Orpheus is stated quite explicitly already in the 1925 play, in the context of the police commissioner's burlesque interrogation of Orpheus' severed head:

> COMMISSIONER: As you can tell me your place of birth, perhaps you'll no longer refuse to tell me your name. You're called . . .
> ORPHÉE'S HEAD: Jean
> COMM.: Jean what?
> ORPHÉE'S HEAD: Jean Cocteau.
> COMM.: Coc . . .
> ORPHÉE'S HEAD: C.O.C.T.E.A.U.[111]

One of the important themes of *The Testament* is the aging poet's anxiety about being pushed aside by a new generation of writers and artists. This concern was already apparent in the earlier film, *Orphée*, as well as in the play. The renowned, established poet is treated with contempt by the new generation at the Café des Poètes, and is finally killed by the Bacchantes, champions of the new poet hero, Cégeste. Critics and writers, hostile to Cocteau, play themselves in the film. Cocteau had been consistently haunted by charges of dilettantism and was especially sensitive about his exclusion from the circle of the Surrealists. Cocteau exploits Orpheus, avatar of the misunderstood artist, to express his own feelings of alienation.

Orpheus-martyr, prefiguration of Christ, fascinated Cocteau as well. A small drawing depicting the laurel-wreathed poet in profile with his lyre is inscribed: "Saint Orphée, martyr de la poésie et de la musique." Cocteau uses the traditional conjunction of Orpheus and Christ to inflate further his own myth, pointing, for example, to his own initials "J. C." as an indication of his role as artist-martyr. Further evidence of Cocteau's association of Orpheus and Christ is found in the evolution of his conception of the 1925 play. His original idea, involving the Christian nativity, was subsequently radically altered: "Je lui substituai le thème orphique ou la naissance inexplicable des poèmes remplacerait celle de l'Enfant Divin."[112] This fluid syncretism might well reflect Cocteau's familiarity with the avant-garde circles in Montmartre and especially his friendship with Apollinaire and his familiarity with that author's synthesis of pagan and Christian themes in his *Bestiaire*. It was probably Apollinaire who introduced Cocteau to Orpheus' role in Theosophical texts.[113] Rilke may have also had a significant influence on Cocteau's syncretic manipulation of Greek myth and Christian themes. Beyond the general theme of Orpheus, there are more specific images and themes which might derive from Rilke's poetry: angels, mirrors, the general preoccupation with death, and especially the vision of death as a realm parallel to this world.[114]

One of Cocteau's most important themes is the nature of artistic inspiration. In the play Orpheus transcribes messages pounded out by the hoofs of a mysterious horse. In the film, the horse is replaced with a Rolls Royce, the princess' (La Mort d'Orphée) car. Orpheus is completely fascinated with the messages (actually the poems of the young avant-garde poet), Cégeste, now assistant to the princess (La Mort d'Orphée), transmitted by the radio. These devices indicate Cocteau's vision of the poet as a passive mouthpiece, conduit or medium, translating mysterious messages from the beyond. In *Le Secret Professionnel* Cocteau writes: "The poet's role is a humble one—he is at the orders of his night."[115] The poet's passive role is further explained in *Journal d'un inconnu*:

> It is true that any poet is the recipient of orders. But these have come from a tenebrosity which centuries have piled up in him, and of which he is but the humble vehicle . . . tenebrosity into which he cannot go.[116]

This "tenebrosity" or "night," that is, death or afterlife, constitutes one of Cocteau's major preoccupations. In the 1950 film, *Orphée*, the major narrative focus is the love between Orphée and La Princesse, La Mort d'Orphée. The princess is a pivotal character. The angel Heurtebise and the young poet, Cégeste (killed at the beginning of the film at the Café des Poètes), are her assistants. Like Cégeste, Eurydice is run down by black-leather-garbed motorcyclists. Later, she dies again because of Orpheus' careless, or, as Cocteau seems to suggest, intentional glance. Cocteau's most fascinating cinematic tricks are devised to communicate the fluid connection between this world, life, and a parallel realm of death. Mirrors are the portals to the beyond. Cocteau uses a vat of mercury to give the impression of the characters' passage through this doorway. The "Zone" is the dense but airless area between life and death. Identical horizontal sets allow Cocteau to create the impression of the characters floating in this curious environment.[117]

Love and Death are inextricably tied in Cocteau's imagination. Orphée's love for La Mort d'Orphée is the source of his inspiration. While in the other world to retrieve Eurydice, he confesses his love for the princess, La Mort d'Orphée. It is the love of La Mort d'Orphée which grants him Eurydice once again, and reestablishes the reality of their bourgeois home. The love between Orphée and La Mort d'Orphée is the determining factor, the key to all of the events in the film.[118]

The self-referential or autobiographical meaning of Cocteau's association of love, death, and creativity has been explored in Freudian-based interpretations. The poet's night, the tenebrosity, is not only the other world, death, but also the dark side of his own brain, his unconscious. Cocteau's overwhelming fixation with death has been linked to his traumatic experience of a series of losses. When he was eight years old his father committed suicide. His friend, Roland Garros, was killed during World War I. The young writer, Radiguet, died eighteen months before the play, *Orphée*, was completed. The Orpheus myth is the vehicle, then, for the exorcism of Cocteau's grief over the loss of his friends, his desire to recapture the love of his dead father.[119]

In addition, in the context of Cocteau's own sexual orientation, the tradition which presents Orpheus as leader of a homosexual cult would have contributed to his fascination with the myth. A certain misogynist intention may be detected in Cocteau's trivialization of the traditionally exalted relationship between Orpheus and Eurydice. Eurydice may symbolize the death wish; or, she is the castrating female. Alternatively, the descent into Hades is a psychological journey into the Self, the quest for Eurydice a journey into the depths of one's own heart.[120]

Psychoanalytic Interpretation: The Role of Eurydice

Clearly, the interpretation of the myth in the age of Freud exploits the sexual antagonism inherent in the story of Orpheus' homosexuality and his death at the hands of the enraged Thracian women. Eurydice, painted as the evil temptress, pulling Orpheus away from his pure, artistic endeavors, parallels her presentation in medieval commentaries on Ovid as an avatar of Eve, the serpent, the temptress. The beautiful pas-de-deux in the Stravinsky-Balanchine ballet (discussed at length below) clearly emphasizes Eurydice's role in her own demise. She is the temptress who crumbles Orpheus' resolve. She clings to, caresses, and pulls at him, interrupting their steady forward progress. Finally, overwhelmed with fear and frustration, Orpheus tears the protective mask from his eyes. Eurydice instantly falls dead, swept beneath a wavering curtain into the realm of the dead.

Another instance in which the myth is manipulated in a highly personal and psychologically charged fashion is Oskar Kokoschka's 1915 drama, *Orpheus and Eurydice,* a play written when the wounded artist was returning from the Russian Front in a hallucinatory state (fig. 7.17). The most striking alteration of the traditional love story is the introduction of Eurydice's abortion of a child by Orpheus. This reinterpretation apparently stems from the abortion of his child by Alma Mahler. The psychological basis of this manipulation of the myth is confirmed in a letter to Mahler's widow calling the play, "the only child we have."[121] The play was one step in the artist's attempt to purge himself of his bitter resentment of his lover, which culminated in his "murder" of Alma in the form of a fetish or bizarre doll.

A misogynist overtone might be identified as well in Victor Ségalen's *Dans un monde sonore,* 1907, and *Orphée-roi,* 1921, in which Eurydice symbolizes fleshly temptation, the distractions of the material world. In the play, *Or-phée-roi* (created in collaboration with Debussy), for instance, Eurydice's love interferes with Orpheus' receptivity to the music of the spheres. Her love weakens him, transforms him into a pitiable lover. Eurydice is finally destroyed by the purity of the music.[122]

Anouilh's play, *Eurydice,* 1941, focuses (as the title indicates) on the love relationship, here, of Orpheus, a traveling musician and Eurydice, a minor actress. Typical of the psychologically oriented interpretations of the myth, there is a turning away from the poet's role of priest, initiate and musician, which had so preoccupied the Symbolists. Like Cocteau, Anouilh replaces the traditional aura of mythic grandeur with a prosaic atmosphere of unheroic characters and an unimpressive setting. Their love is marred by Eurydice's shame over her past, including a liaison with M. Dulac, the director of the actor's troupe. She flees Orpheus and is killed in an automobile crash. However, M. Henri, the angel of death, revives her. The pathetic tragedy continues. Orpheus, already poisoned with jealousy by the insinuations of Dulac, intentionally kills Eurydice with his glance. It is only in death that Orpheus and Eurydice are united in perfect love, free from the negative emotions of this world. In Anouilh's play, the myth is stripped of its idealistic core. Orpheus is no longer the creative, priestly archetype; but rather is a pathetic figure, crippled by the human emotion of jealousy.[123]

His fascination with Freud and his conversion to Catholicism are the sources for Pierre Jean Jouve's insistent exploration of eroticism and mysticism. Jouve draws upon the Orpheus myth in *Dans les années profondes*. In this work, he draws upon a traumatic episode in his life—his illicit love for the already married Lisbe and her tragic death from cancer. These episodes are transformed, in the work, into the adventures of Léonide and Hélène de Sannis. Jouve suggests that Léonide secretly desired the death of the older Hélène because she was an avatar of his mother, who had to die in order that he achieve manhood. Hélène is idealized, mythologized. She comes to dominate Léonide's mind, becomes absorbed into his inner being.

The poems in *Matière céleste*, 1937, elaborating upon this myth of Hélène, relate the anguish of the poet's desolate search for self-knowledge. Four poems in the last part of this work are devoted to Orpheus: "Orphée," "Orphée agonisant," "Orphée," "Les Adieux d'Orphée." At first, Orpheus rails against Eurydice's death. He is ultimately tempted by and finally becomes the victim of the vicious sexuality of the Maenads. He emerges from these trials, however, resigned to Eurydice's death, in a state of greater self-knowledge and inner serenity.[124]

The impact of Jouve on Pierre Emmanuel is evident in *Le Tombeau d'Orphée*, 1941, and *Orphiques*, 1942. In these works, the myth is reinterpreted in terms of psychoanalytical symbols. Orpheus and Eurydice are two parts of a single personality. This perception of Orpheus and Eurydice as constantly struggling aspects of a single being, though drawing upon modern psychoanalytic theory, also seems to relate to the concept of the primordial androgyne which fascinated the Romantics and Symbolists. Emmanuel finds a resolution of this conflict between Orpheus and Eurydice, between man and woman, between two aspects of the Self, in Christian salvation. Christ, at once body and spirit, offers the perfect unity in his crucifixion and resurrection.[125]

The myth of Orpheus is obviously rich in psychological truth. Many of the same aspects of the myth which fascinated previous generations are reexplored in these twentieth-century interpretations, but now articulated in modern psychoanalytic terms and categories. At their weakest, these works involve liberal deformations of the myth in pursuit of personal psychological truths, and lose sight of the essential, universal meaning of the myth.

Orpheus and Twentieth-Century Music

In the twentieth century, the theme of Orpheus is the subject of several important musical compositions including: Milhaud's 1924, *Les Malheurs d'Orphée*; Igor Stravinsky's *Orpheus* of 1948; and Pierre Henry's *Tombeau d'Orphée*, 1958.

In addition, Orpheus was the subject of collaborations between composers and writers: Valéry and Debussy; the aborted collaboration between Ségalen and Debussy between 1906 and 1916 on *Orphée-roi*; Honegger and Valéry; and Jean Cocteau's use of César Franck's music in 1944.[126]

Igor Stravinsky, Isamu Noguchi, Georges Balanchine

Stravinsky's Orpheus was commissioned by the Ballet Society of New York in 1948, the theme and basic narrative chosen by Georges Balanchine and Lincoln Kirstein. The sets and costumes were designed by Isamu Noguchi. Though there was, apparently, a close collaboration between composer and choreographer, Noguchi, on the other hand, seems to have worked more independently.[127]

Balanchine describes the ballet as "a contemporary treatment of the ancient myth of Orpheus."[128] It opens with Orpheus' lamentation at the grave of Eurydice, the solace offered by his friends, the distraction of the satyrs' and wood sprites' dance leaving his grief unrelieved. He is subsequently led into Hades by the Angel of Death. Their pas-de-deux is focused on the Angel's black coil which passes around and through the hands of the grief-paralyzed poet; the lyre which he insistently thrusts into Orpheus' hands; and the mask which will enable Orpheus to descend into the Underworld. The landscape of the passage to and from Hades is dramatically suggested by a wind-swept, white silk curtain, fluttering as though moved by the swirling currents of hot air from Hades and the cool drafts from the world above. Glowing red and orange rocks levitate, transformed thereby into radiant planets or suns. Their rising accentuates, by contrast, the descent of Orpheus into Hades. Noguchi explains further their symbolism: "Rocks levitate—give sense of sinking . . . transition of levels and consciousness into another state . . . a state of dream."[129]

In Hades, huge red flames and white bones protrude from left and right on the stage. Orpheus and the Angel of Death are confronted by the grey, spiky Furies, whose bodies literally bristle with fear and anger at Orpheus' intrusion.[130] They also meet the tortured souls of the dead, grey, pathetically bent creatures, bearing huge boulders in Sisyphus-like fashion. The Angel exhorts Orpheus to play and sing to calm the inhabitants of Hades and to charm Pluto. A huge, boulderlike shape turns slowly to reveal the ruler of the Underworld, clasping Eurydice. His body is clad in black, adorned with white pendulous protrusions. Charmed by Orpheus' music, he joins the poet's and Eurydice's hands, releasing her. A blue, teardrop shape descends suddenly from above, marking the rent of the darkness of the Underworld, the opening to the light of the world above.[131]

The white, fluttering curtain descends again, providing a dynamic backdrop for the upward passage of the couple, led by the Angel of Death, bearing the lyre. This pas-de-deux between Orpheus and Eurydice is, undoubtedly, the dramatic highlight of the ballet (fig. 7.18). Orpheus, wearing his golden mask, leads Eurydice forward. She echoes his steps. The passage is especially arduous because of the psychological burden caused by the interdiction against Orpheus looking at Eurydice. Balanchine explains: "Eurydice is tormented momentarily by the fact that, although they are really together once again, they are actually remote to each other: Orpheus because he cannot see; Eurydice, because she cannot be seen by the man she loves."[132] Eurydice caresses, pleads, seemingly seduces Orpheus with gestures of her entire body. Finally, and dramatically framed by four beats of silence, Orpheus rips the protective mask from his face. Eurydice immediately falls dead and is snatched away beneath the fluttering curtain. The lyre, held by the Angel of Death, is brutally snatched from Orpheus' grasp. Orpheus, hence, is bereft of Eurydice and also deprived of the power of his music.

Upon his return to this world, Orpheus is set upon by a vicious group of Bacchantes, with long streaming red and yellow hair. As he attempts to repulse their lascivious advances, they fall upon him ripping off, first one arm, then another, then finally severing his head. The segments of his body are disguised by a small green hillock at the rear of the stage.

The final scene functions as an epilogue. The music returns to the initial harp theme. Apollo appears and solemnly approaches the hillock, Orpheus' grave. He holds a huge golden mask, a combination of the traditional oracle head, the lyre which continued to emit song and the blinder used earlier in the ballet. Apollo strums invisible strings, summoning forth music from the head/lyre. Finally, Orpheus' lyre rises slowly, tethered to a blossoming garland, clearly symbolizing the apotheosis, the resurrection of the poet and his art.

The movement of the ballet, from poignant lamentation, through arduous descent, intensified grief, death and, finally, resurrection, is consonant with the Symbolists' interpretation of the myth. The ballet does not impose a facile happy ending in the tradition of Gluck, but rather, must be considered, along with works by Milhaud and Henry, as part of a musical tradition which renews the magic and power of the myth. The initial scene of Orpheus grieving in a desolate landscape, in fact, evokes comparison to depictions of the inconsolable poet by Moreau, Séon, or F. Holland Day.[133]

The Angel of Death was a character apparently conceived by Balanchine to lend continuity to the passages to the Underworld and back again. The invention of this character clearly relates to Hermes' role in the traditional myth. Moreover, in twentieth-century works it is hardly unusual: Rilke includes angels; angels and the figure of death are crucial in Cocteau's works; Anouilh also introduces an angel of death.

Orpheus and Eurydice's pas-de-deux as they ascend from Hades is tremendously powerful. Eurydice's bewilderment with Orpheus' remoteness is poignant. Her attempts to make Orpheus look at her range emotionally, from playful coaxing to powerful seduction. Orpheus is torn between Eurydice—carnal, intuitive—and the gleaming lyre, the lofty purity of the artistic ideal. The pas-de-deux may be read in psychological terms, an inner struggle between aspects of Orpheus' own psyche. Noguchi, in fact, discusses the psychological overtones of the ballet. Orpheus' descent to Hades is a descent "to another state of consciousness—a state of dream."[134] The mask is important because this is a "story of the artist blinded by his own vision."

> (Orpheus) leads Eurydice earthward, but, alas, he is now beset by doubts of material possession. He tears off his mask and sees Eurydice as she really is, a creature of death. . . . Eurydice has become more symbolic, not a character the way Orpheus is, but symbolic of his vision, yes, part of his imagination and his dream.[135]

Noguchi succeeds in transforming the stage and creating the illusion of movement through vast, cosmic spaces. The undulating curtain, which descends during the passages between this world and Hades, is a simple but powerfully suggestive device, conveying a sense of undefined space and movement. The glowing translucent rocks which rise during these passages similarly suggest heat, as well as providing an appropriately unearthly, cosmological setting. The huge white bones and red flames which project onto the stage, left and right, during the poet's moments in Hades, effectively create a dangerous and eerie environment. Light animates and energizes Noguchi's essentially simple objects. A specifically Greek setting was intentionally avoided:

> For it was no dubiously archaeological Greece that was desired but rather a time-less climate in which the three dimensional movement would be enhanced by the formal solidity of hand-hewn ritual appurtenances—masks, bones, flames, lyres, shaped as independent sculptural objects.[136]

Noguchi's sculptural objects are woven into the choreography, seemingly inspiring the powerful gestures which, in turn, correspond to the expressive rhythm of the music. The objects are important as symbols, but moreover function organically with the dance movement and music.[137]

The manner in which the decoration becomes a "partner" of the dance parallels the organic relationship between the structure of the music and the dance. In this regard, Ingolf Dahl has analyzed Stravinsky's use of "one-levelled monochromatic music."

> He was aware of the problem that such a subjugation to the Apollonian principle would impose on him. But, while rejecting all Dionysian temptation, he has developed a non-dynamic variety of musical means, as subtle as it is convincing. . . . The music evolves in closed forms: variation, pas d'action, pas de deux, interlude,

and so on, the composer seeking a strict musical structure to parallel the action rather than follow it. The unity of this structure forms a counterpoint to the progressive plot development, thereby anchoring but not explaining it.[138]

Hence, just as the settings were designed to avoid creating a Greek-inspired tableau, similarly the music does not follow or explicate the mythic narrative in any conventional manner.

Composer, choreographer and designer were all sensitive to the ritualistic, even religious, nature of the theater. Stravinsky's music has been described in terms of its speaking quality:

> Stravinsky thinks of his music in terms of its speaking quality and as giving voice to the inflection of the figures and their story. It is not the language of everyday life, but rather a hieratic speech, intoned by the orchestra and by the instrument individually.[139]

Noguchi conceives of sculpture as ritualistic and religious like theater: "Probably it has a ritual basis because most sculpture had a religious beginning . . . a primitive meaning."[140]

> There is a joy in seeing sculpture come to life on the stage in its own world of timeless time. Then the very air becomes charged with meaning and emotion, and form plays its integral part in the reenactment of a ritual. Theatre is a ceremonial; the performance is a rite. Sculpture in daily life should or could be like this. In the meantime, the theatre gives me its poetic, exalted equivalent.[141]

Epilogue

Stravinsky's ballet constitutes a suitable conclusion to this discussion of the image of Orpheus in the nineteenth and twentieth centuries. The clarity with which the ballet defines the moments of the myth provides an elegant recapitulation of the essential aspect of the mythic narrative. The marriage of music, dance, and sculpture is consonant, moreover, with the crucial concepts of synaesthesia and correspondences associated with the myth. The participants' awareness of theater as ritual can be linked to the Symbolists' appreciation of the sources of art in theater and religion, and the original connection between theater and cult. The ballet explores with great seriousness, as well, the essential symbolism of the myth—Orpheus the initiate, the priest, martyr to an exalted artistic ideal.

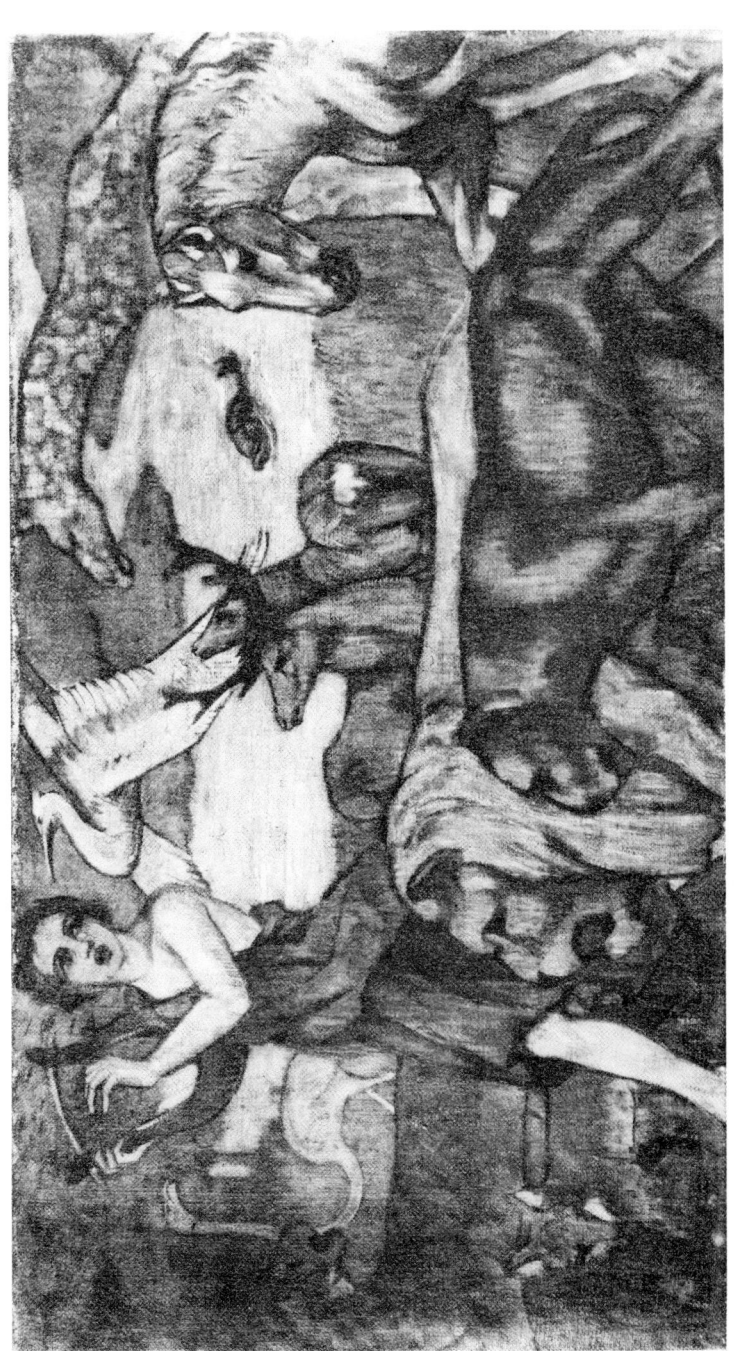

Figure 7.1. Franz Marc, *Orpheus and the Animals*, 1907. Oil on canvas. (Städtische Galerie im Lenbachhaus, Munich)

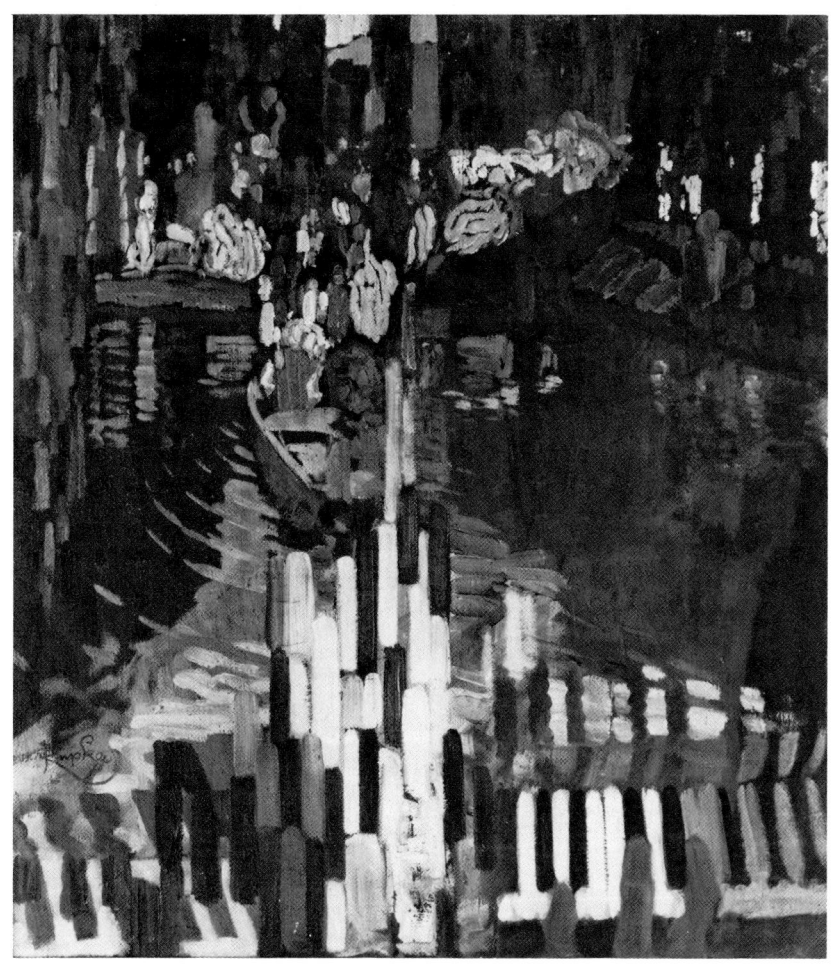

Figure 7.2. Frantisek Kupka, *Touches de Piano/Lac*, 1909
Oil on canvas.
(National Gallery, Prague)

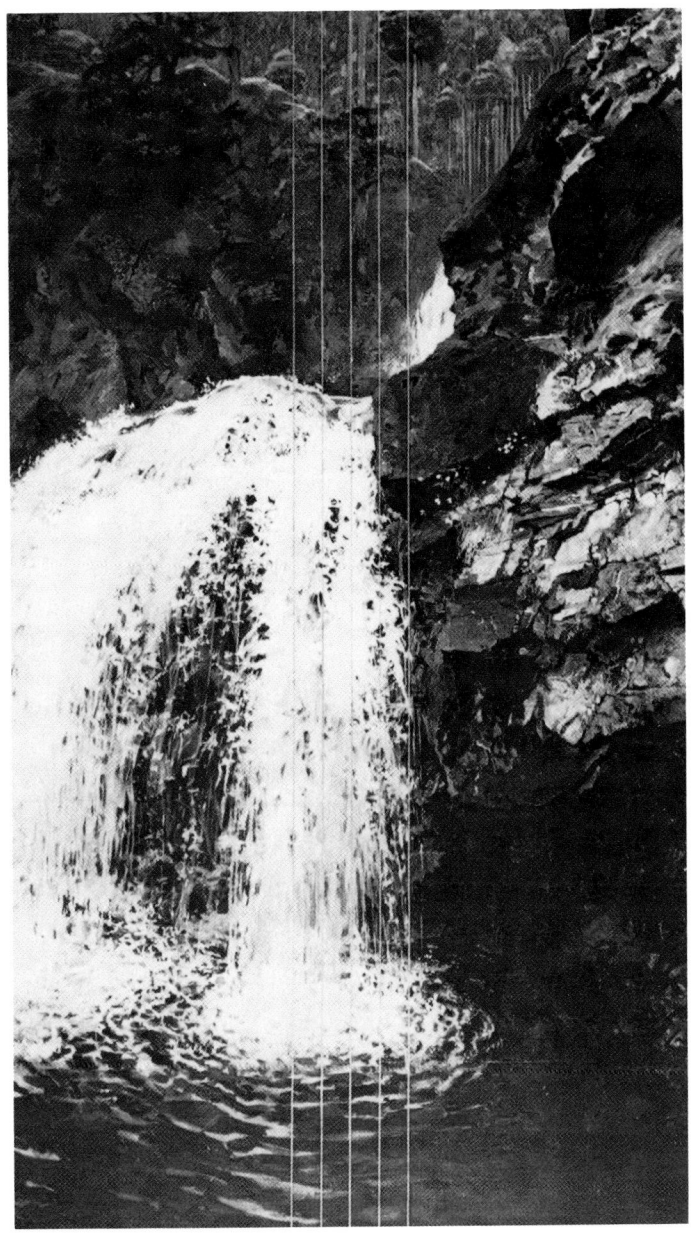

Figure 7.3. Akseli Gallen-Kallela, *Waterfall at Mäntykoski*, 1892–94
Oil on canvas.
(*The Jorma Gallen-Kallela Family Collection, Lugano*)

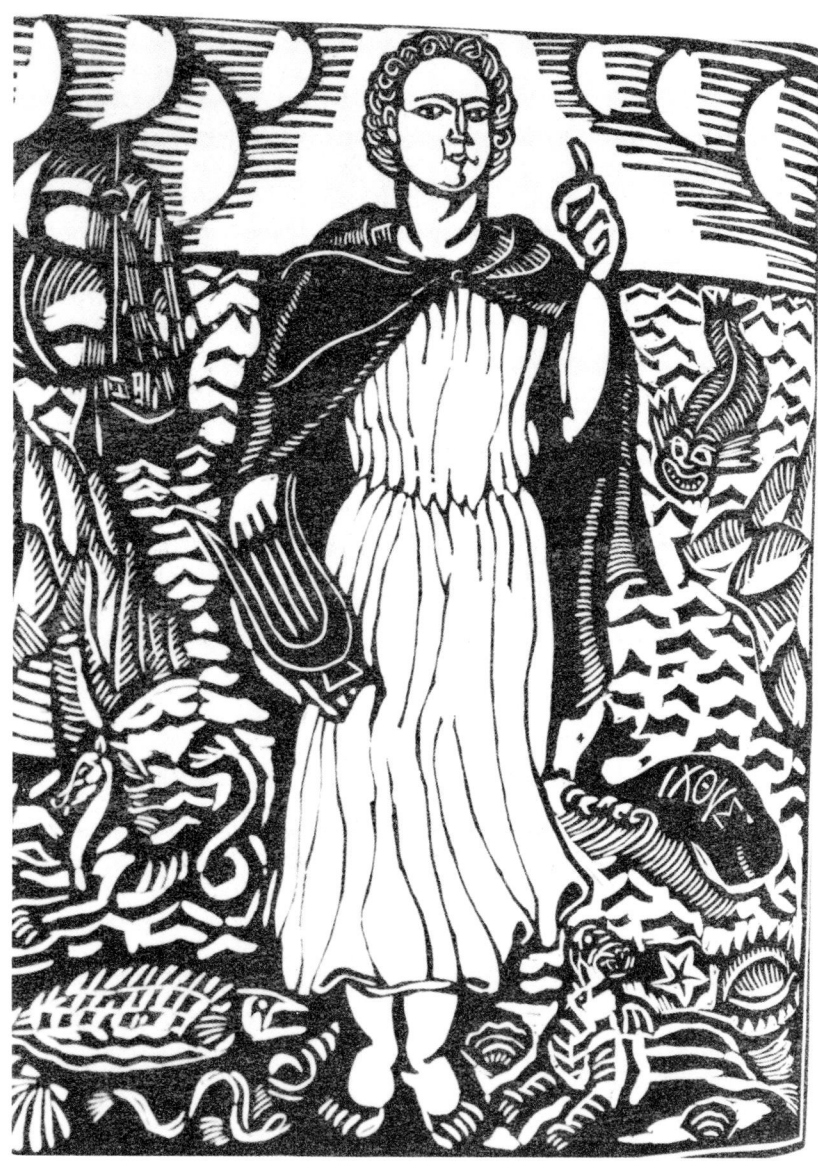

Figure 7.4 Raoul Dufy, *Orphée*, 1911
Wood block print illustration for Apollinaire's *Le Bestiaire ou le cortège d'Orphée*.
(Department of Prints and Photographs, Metropolitan Museum of Art, New York, Harris Brisbane Dick Fund, 1926)

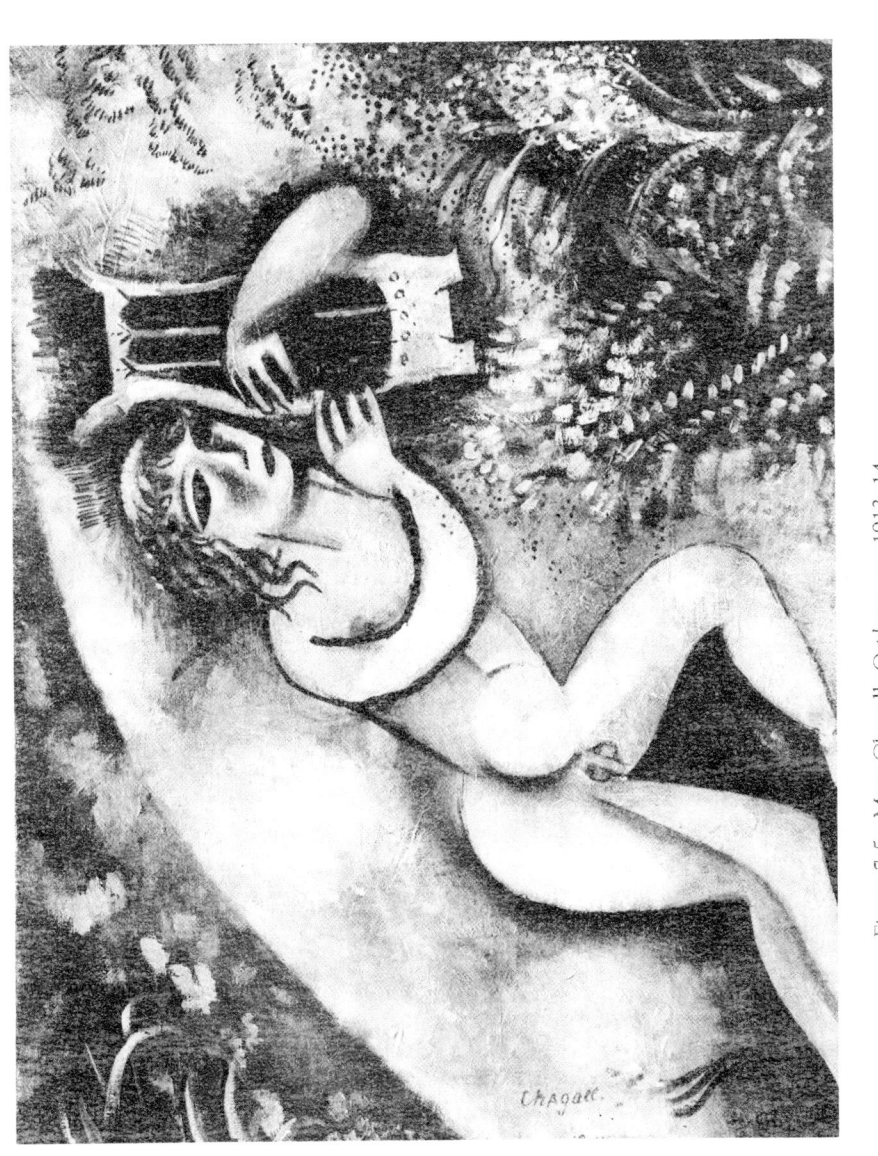

Figure 7.5 Marc Chagall, *Orpheus*, ca. 1913–14
Oil on canvas.
(Formerly The Solomon R. Guggenheim Museum, New York)

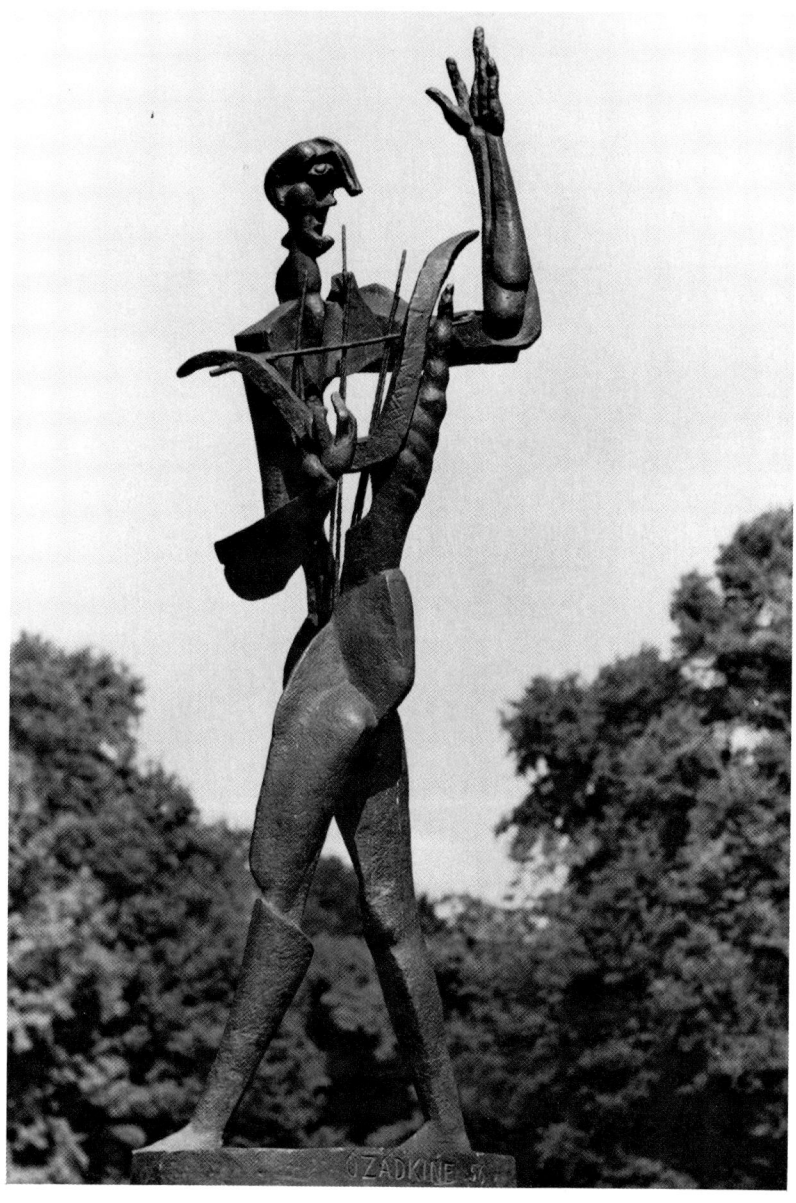

Figure 7.6. Ossip Zadkine, *Orpheus*, 1956
Bronze.
(Open Air Museum of Sculpture, Middelheim, Antwerp; photo: Jean De Maeyer, Antwerp)

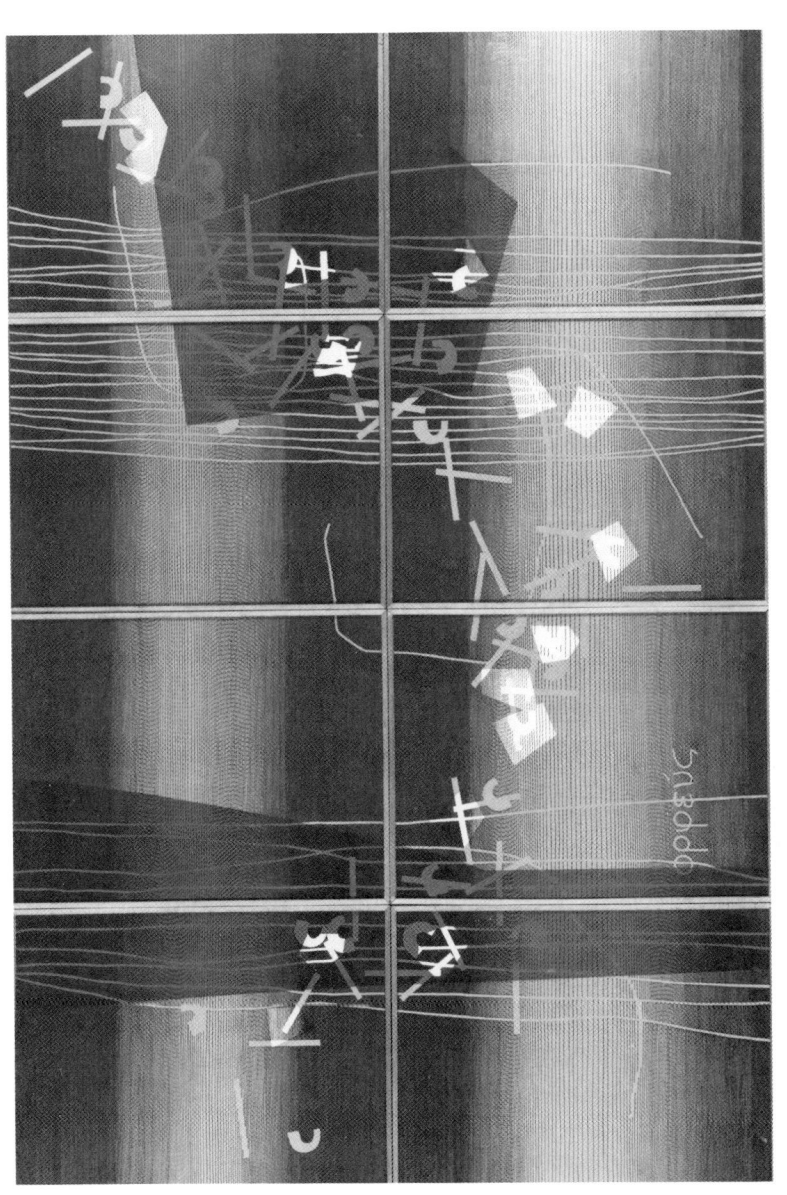

Figure 7.7. Michel Seuphor, *La Mort d'Orphée*, 1964. Ink and collage on cardboard. (*Musée National d'Art Moderne, Centre Georges Pompidou, Paris; Cliché Musée National d'Art Moderne*)

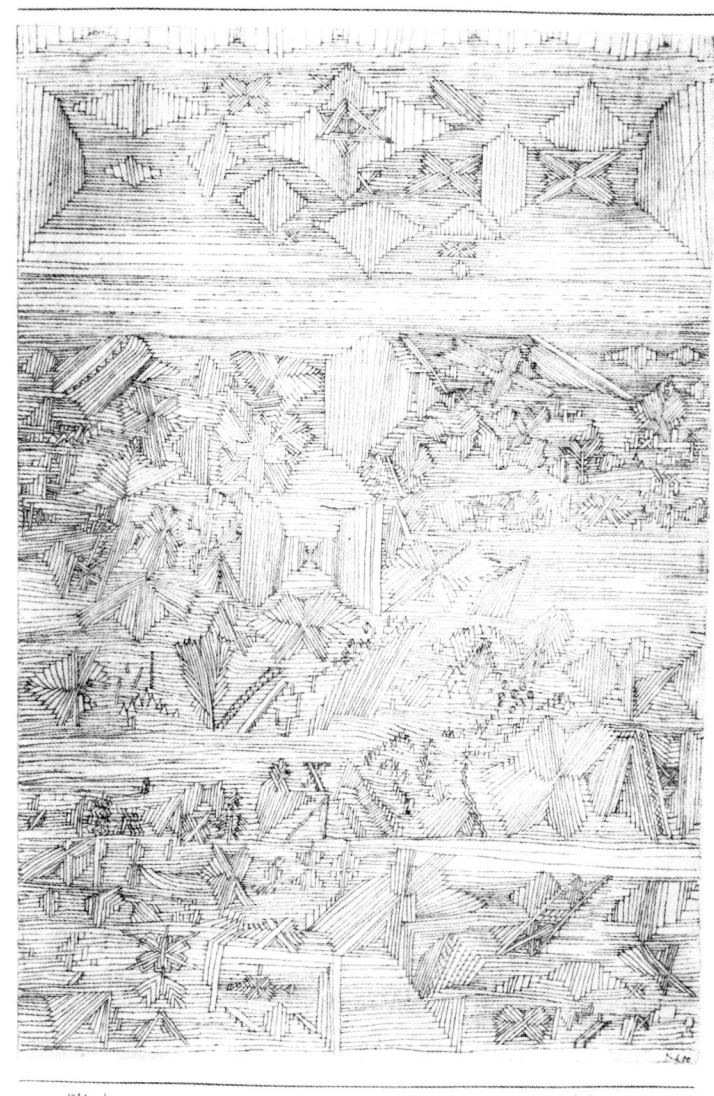

Figure 7.8. Paul Klee, *Ein Garten für Orpheus*, 1926.3
Ink drawing.
(Paul Klee Foundation, Museum of Fine Arts, Berne,
Copyright by COSMOPRESS, Geneva)

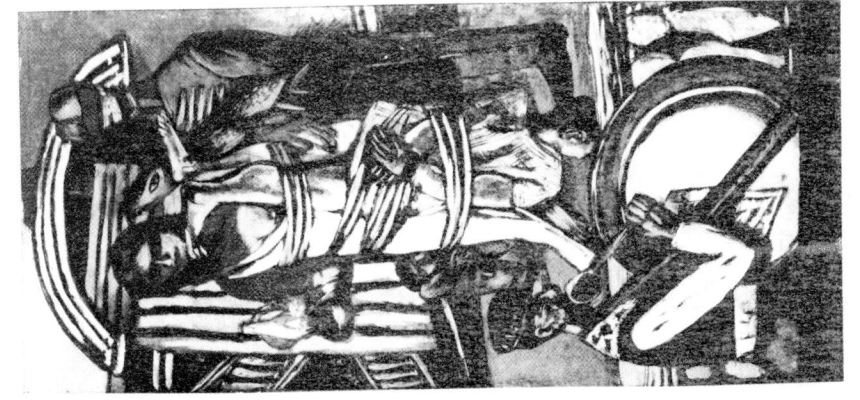
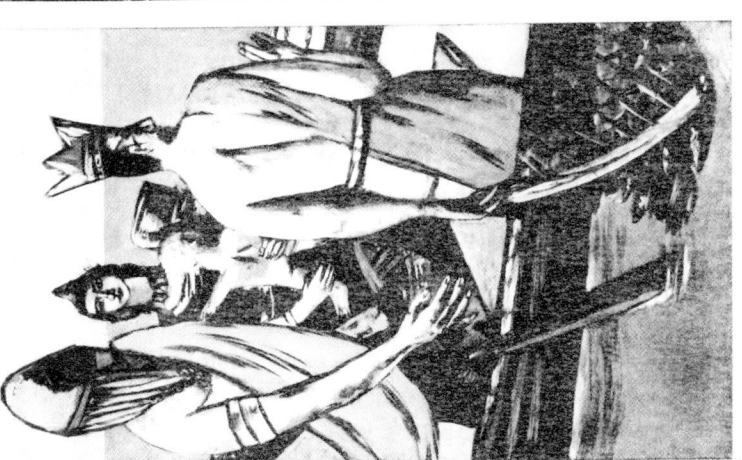
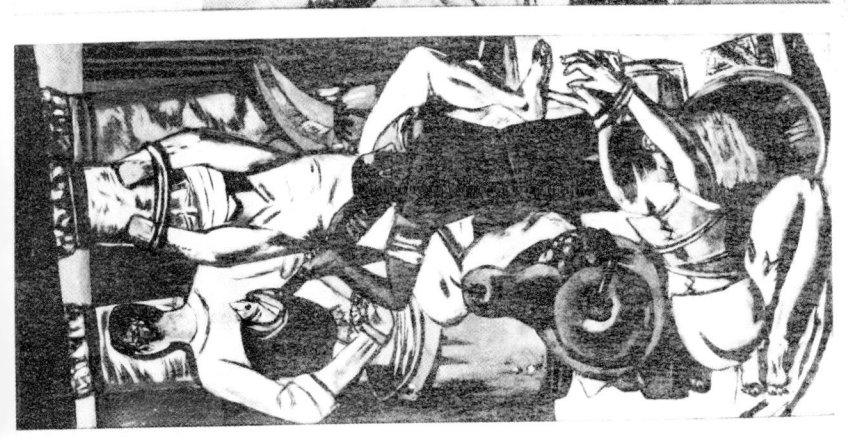

Figure 7.9. Max Beckmann, *The Departure*, 1932–33
Oil on canvas.
(Collection The Museum of Modern Art, New York. Given anonymously [by exchange])

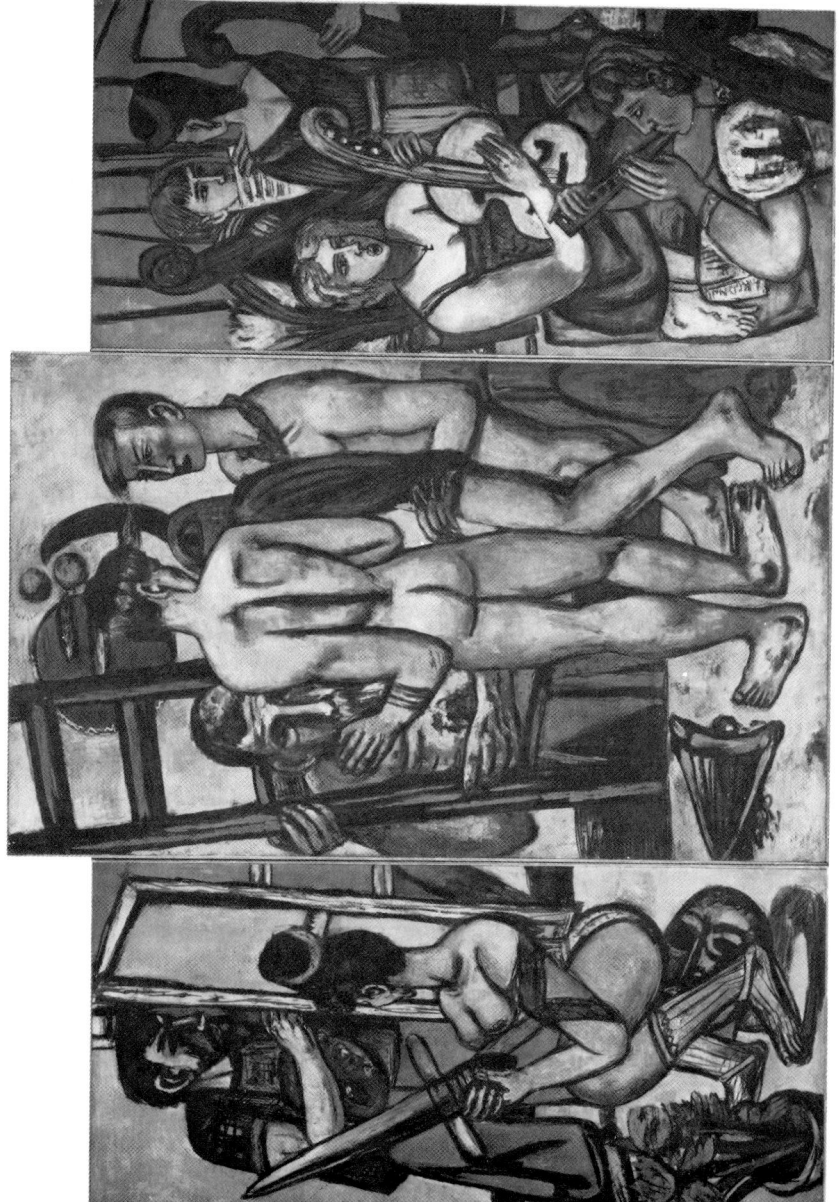

Figure 7.10. Max Beckmann, The Argonauts, 1949–50
Oil on canvas.
(The National Gallery of Art, Washington, gift of Mrs. Max Beckmann)

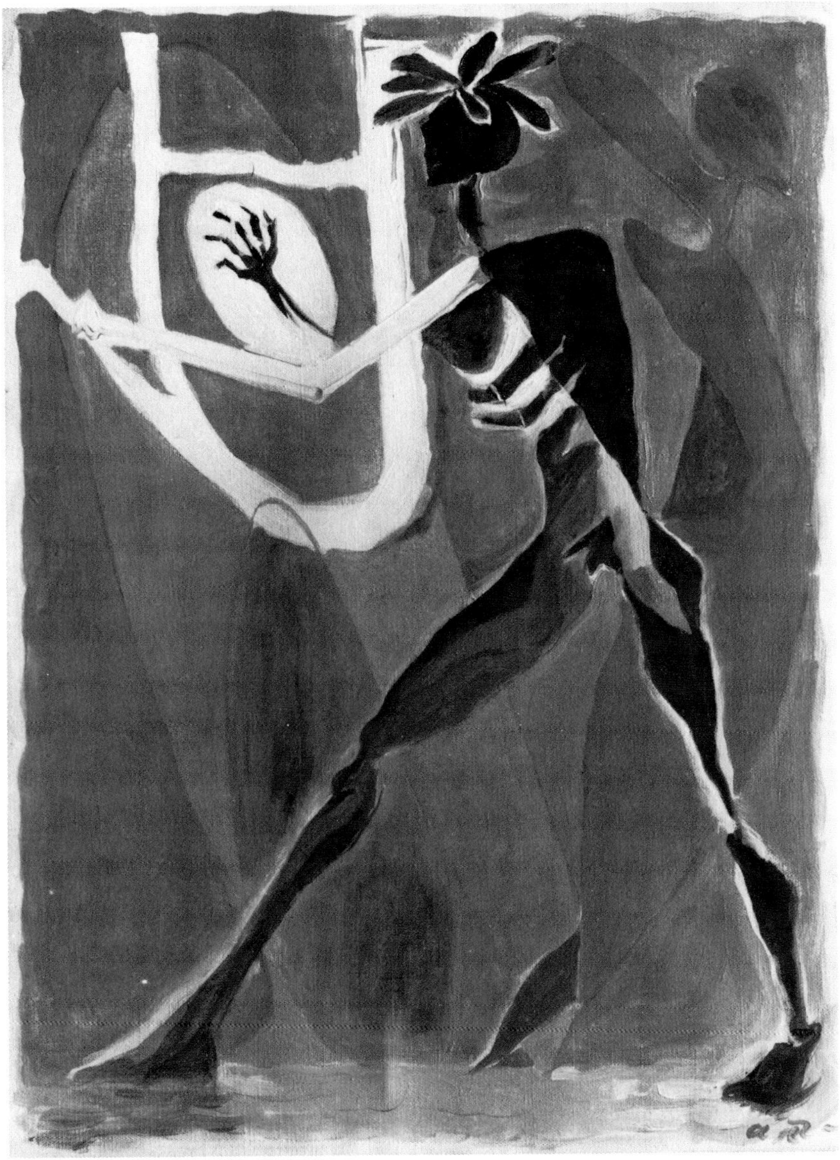

Figure 7.11. André Masson, *Orpheus*, 1934
Oil on canvas.
(Photo courtesy Galerie Louise Leiris)

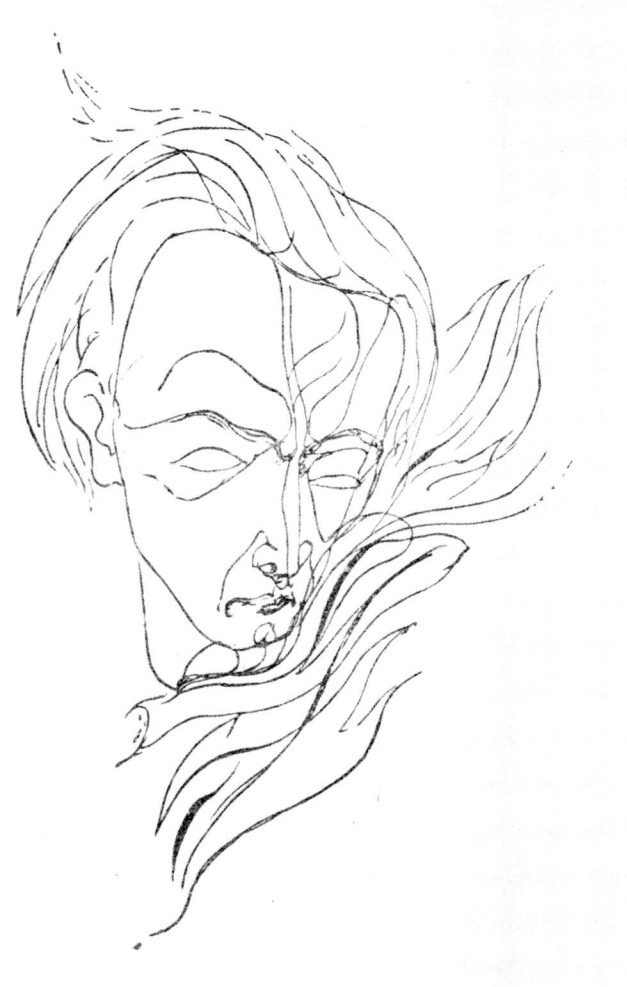

Figure 7.12. André Masson, *Portrait of Antonin Artaud*, 1925. Ink drawing.
(Private collection, Paris; photo courtesy Galerie Louise Leiris)

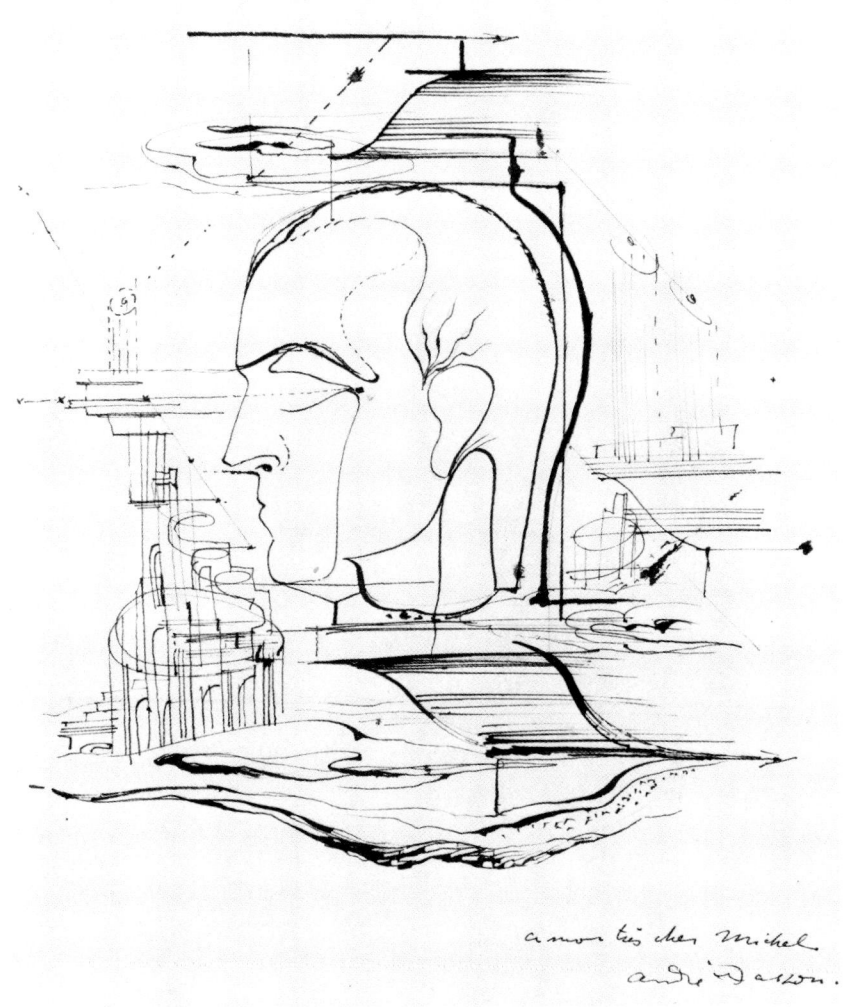

Figure 7.13. André Masson, *Portrait of Michel Leiris*, 1925
Ink drawing.
(Private collection, Paris: photo courtesy Galerie Louise Leiris)

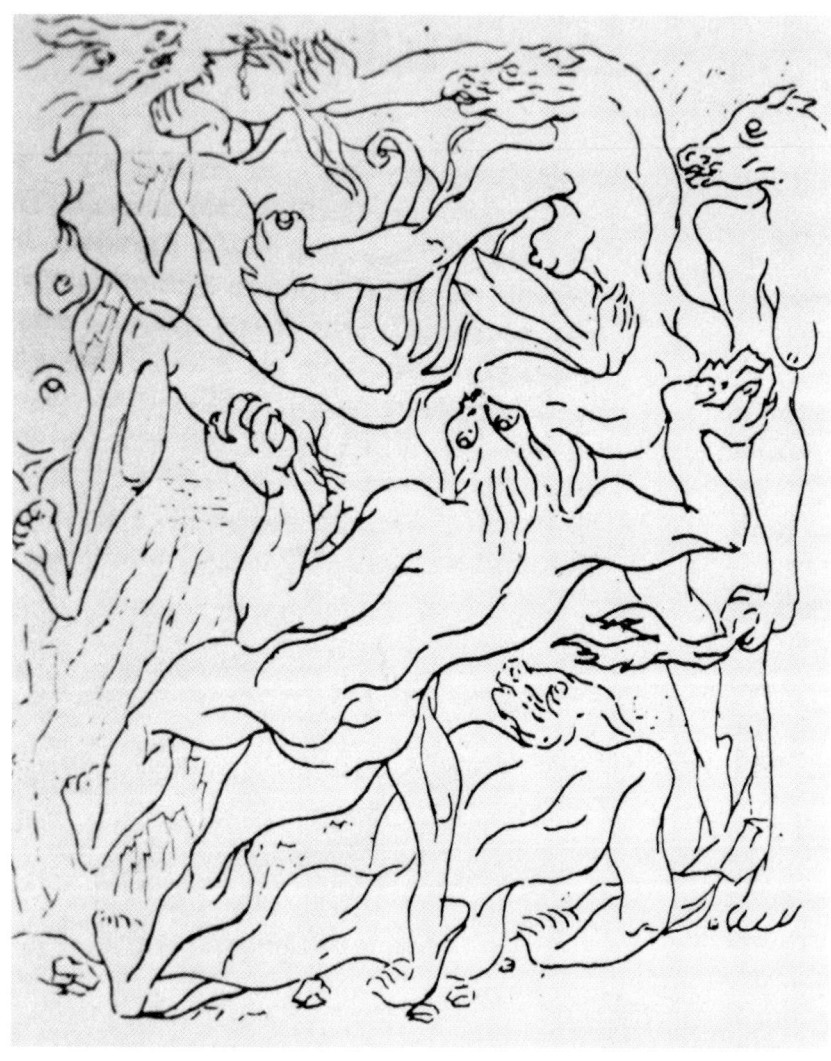

Figure 7.14. André Masson, *The Death of Orpheus*
Engraving for *Sacrifices of the Gods*, 1936.

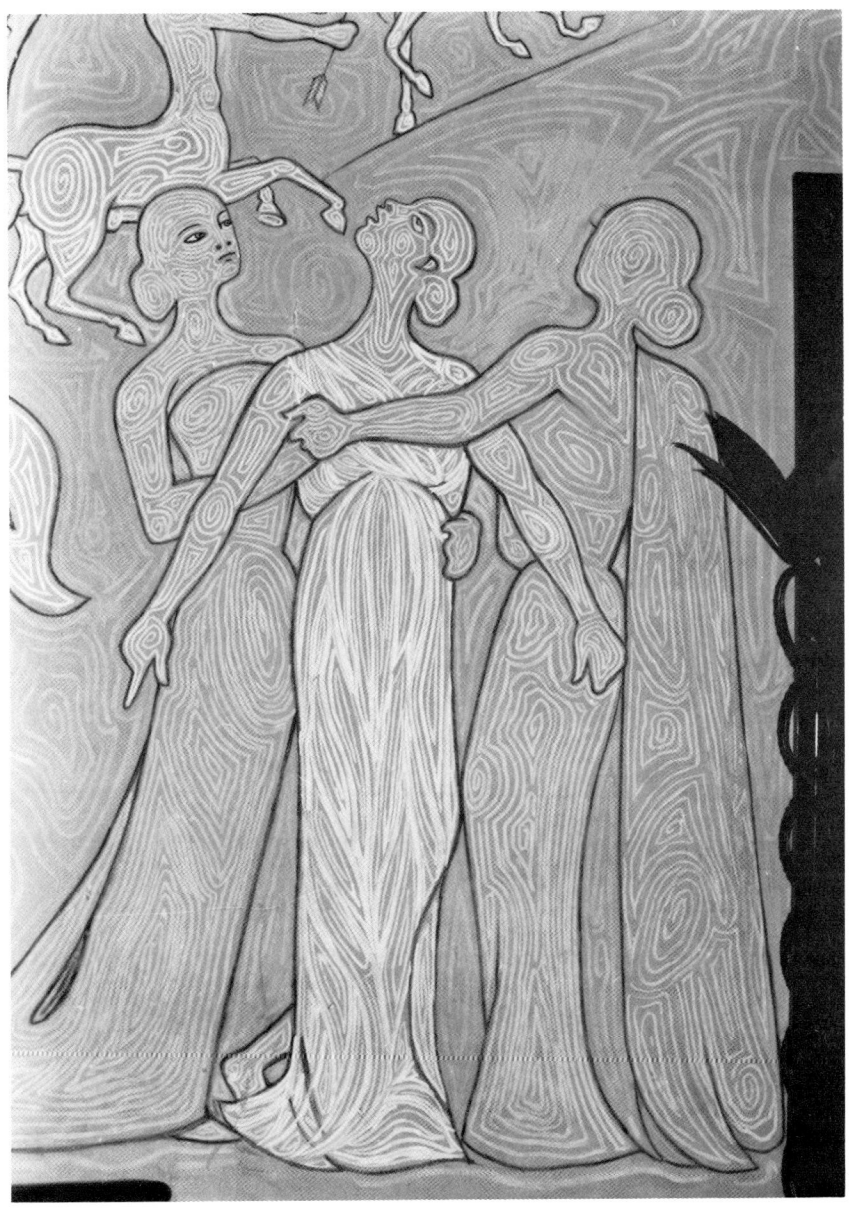

Figure 7.15. Jean Cocteau, *Death of Eurydice*, 1957–58
Fresco.
(Salle des Mariages, Hôtel de Ville, Menton)

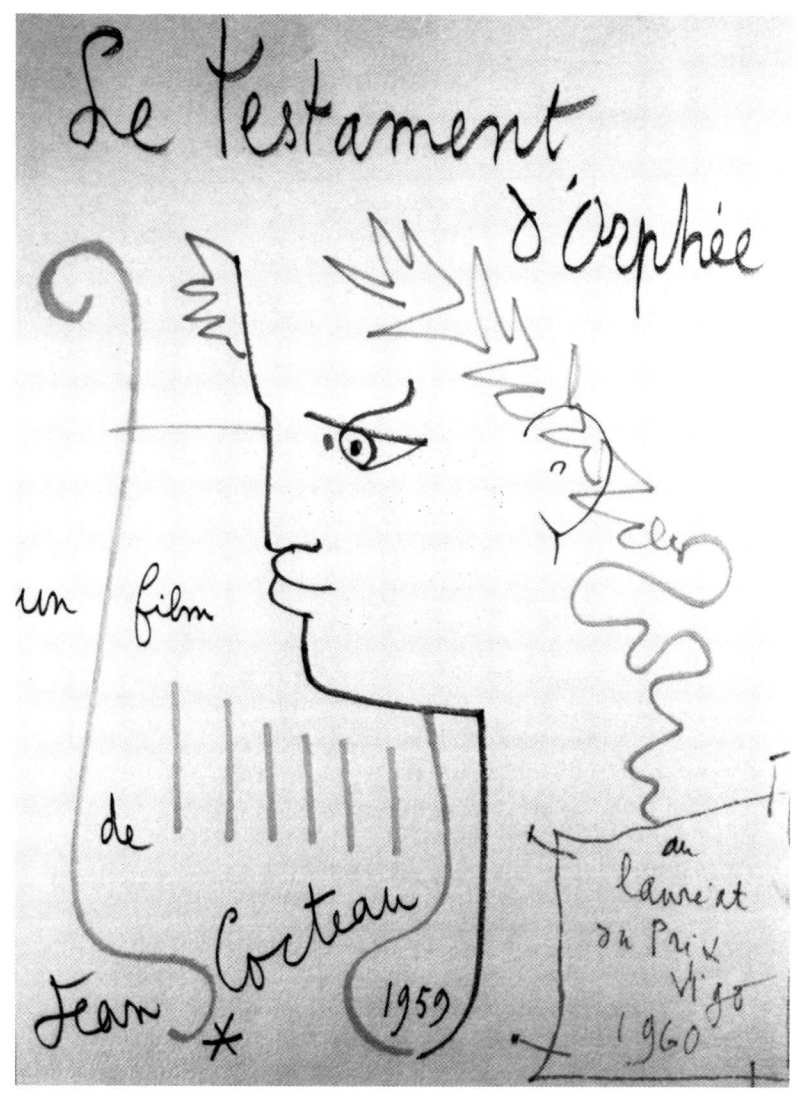

Figure 7.16. Jean Cocteau, *Le Testament d'Orphée*, 1959 (Galerie Proscenium, Paris; photo: Michel Petit)

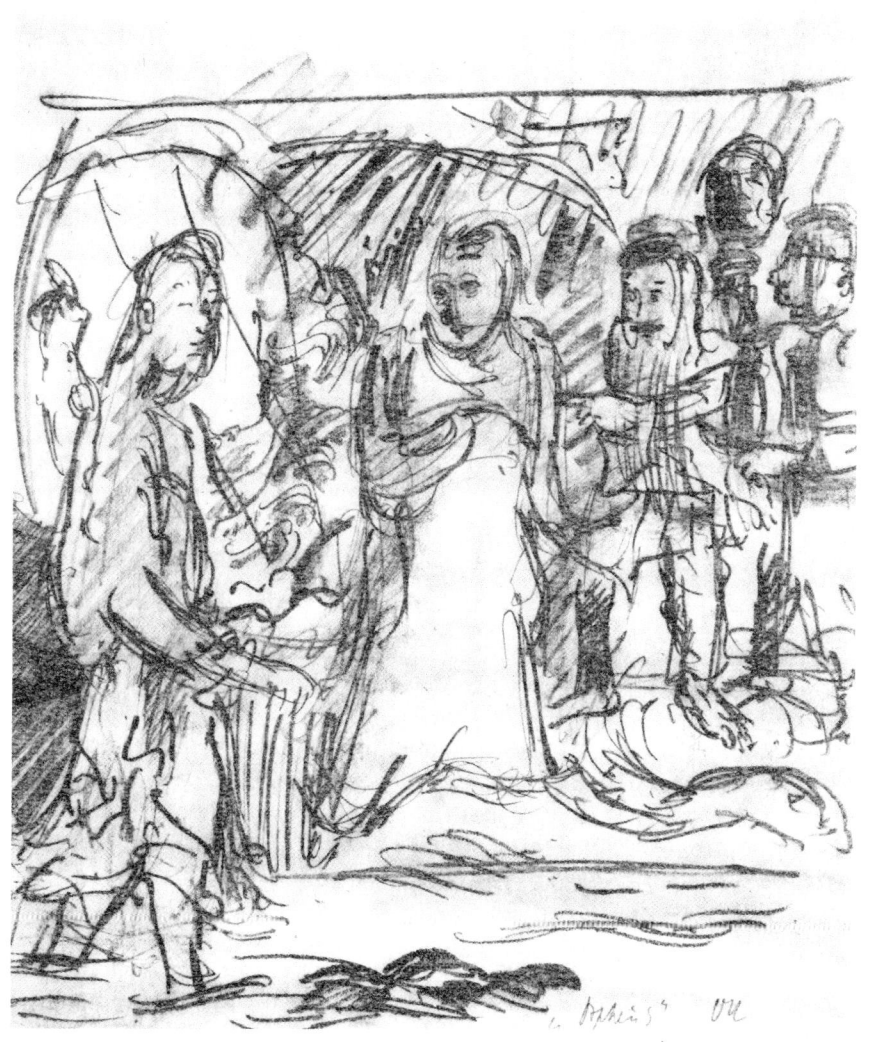

Figure 7.17. Oskar Kokoschka, *Orpheus*, 1918
Pencil drawing.
(Kunsthalle, Bremen)

Figure 7.18. Kay Mazzo and Mikhail Baryshnikov in Pas-de-deux from *Orpheus*, 1948 Ballet with music by Igor Stravinsky, choreography by Georges Balanchine. (*Photo:* © *1978 Martha Swope, New York*)

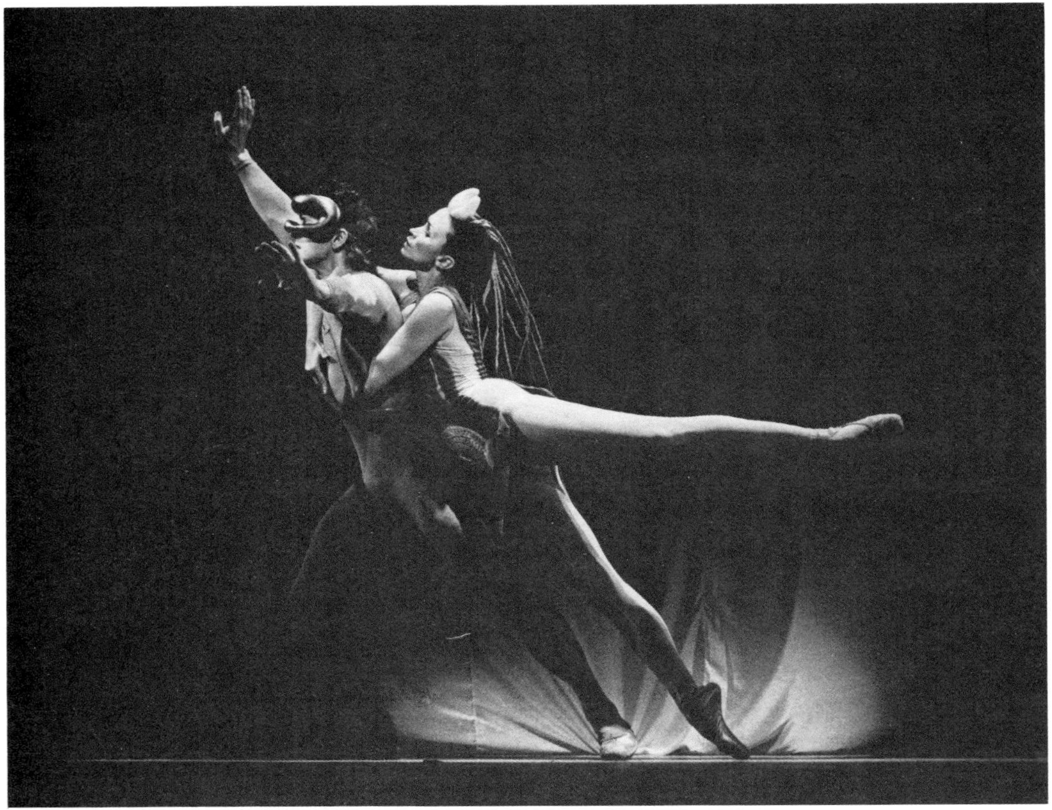

Notes

Chapter 1

1. There is a sizeable literature dealing with Orpheus, Orphism, and the religions of antiquity. Among the most significant or helpful works are: Larry J. Alderink, *Creation and Salvation in Ancient Orphism*, No. 8, American Classical Studies (Chico, Calif., 1981); André Boulanger, *Orphée: Rapports de l'orphisme et christianisme* (Paris, 1925); F. M. Cornford, *From Religion to Philosophy* (London, 1912); E. R. Dodds, *The Greeks and the Irrational* (Berkeley, 1951); Robert Eisler, *Orpheus the Fisher, Comparative Studies in Orphic and Early Christian Cult Symbolism* (London, 1921); Robert Eisler, *Orphisch-dionysische Mysterien-Gedanken in der christlichen Antike* (Hildesheim, 1922–23; 1966); Mircea Eliade, *Histoire des croyances et des idées religieuses* (Paris, 1976); W. K. Guthrie, *Orpheus and Greek Religion and Their Gods* (London, 1935); June Harrison, *Prolegomena to the Study of Greek Religion* (Cambridge, 1922); Karl Kerenyi, *Pythagoras und Orpheus* (Zurich, 1950); Otto Kern, *Orpheus: Eine religionsgeschichtliche Untersuchung* (Berlin, 1920); Ivan M. Linforth, *The Art of Orpheus* (New York, 1973); Vittorio D. Macchioro, *From Orpheus to Paul: A History of Orphism* (New York, 1930); G. R. S. Meade, *Orpheus* (New York, 1965); Louis Moulinier, *Orphée et l'Orphisme à l'époque classique* (Paris, 1955); Martin P. Nilsson, *A History of Greek Religion* (Oxford, 1925); Martin P. Nilsson, *The Dionysiac Mysteries of the Hellenistic and Roman Age* (Lund, 1957); Martin P. Nilsson, "Orpheus," and "Orphisme," in *The Oxford Classical Dictionary* (Oxford, 1964 ed.); Walter F. Otto, *Dionysus: Myth and Cult*, trans. with introduction by Robert B. Palmer (Bloomington and London, 1965); A. Provoost, *Orpheus* (Leuven, 1974); Salomon Reinach, *Orpheus: A History of Religions*, trans. Florence Simmonds (New York, 1930); Ronald Watmough, *Orphism* (Cambridge, 1934); Walter Wili, "The Orphic Mysteries and the Greek Spirit," in *The Mysteries: Papers from the Eranos Yearbooks*, ed. Joseph Campbell, Bollingen Series 30, vol. 2 (Princeton, 1955); Konrad Ziegler, "Orphische Dichtung," *Realencyclopedia der classischen Altertumswissenschaft*, vol. 18, part 2; cols. 1321–1417, ed., Pauley, Wissowa, Kroll (Stuttgart, 1942).

2. The Orphic cosmogony begins with Chronus (Time) who produces Aether, Chaos, and Erebus. From Aether, the primordial egg, emerges the god, Phanes

(Eros), creator and ruler of all the gods. Phanes and Night beget Uranus, Gaea, the Titans, etc. Zeus swallows Phanes and thus produces the world again. Zeus and Demeter beget Kore Persephone. Zeus and Persephone in turn produce Dionysus. It is his birth, death, and rebirth that are the focus of this theogony and anthropogony. Dionysus is torn apart and eaten by the Titans, incited by the jealous wife, Hera. The goddess Athena saves his heart, which is swallowed by Zeus, and hence preserved. The god is conceived by Zeus and Semele, daughter of Cadmus and Harmonia. Semele's destruction is engineered, once again, by the jealous Hera, who tempts her to ask to see Zeus in his overwhelming Olympian splendor. Dionysus is reborn, finally, from Zeus' own thigh. Later, Dionysus retrieves Semele from Hades, and she is accepted among the Olympian gods as immortal. There are compelling parallels between the myth of Orpheus and the story of the god Zagreus-Dionysus: Orpheus' descent into Hades and his death by dismemberment recall the god's *katabasis* and *sparagmos*.

A fourth-century B.C. papyrus fragment from Deverni naming Zeus, "the beginning, the middle, the end of all things," is attributed to Orpheus. (See Eliade, 1980, pp. 183–84.) However, many of the cosmogonic hymns attributed to Orpheus are probably the works of Neo-Platonic writers from the Hellenistic or early Christian periods. (See John Block Friedman, *Orpheus in the Middle Ages* [Cambridge, 1970], p. 7.) The description of the departure of the Argo in Apollonius of Rhodes' *Argonautica* includes Orpheus' song about the evolution of the cosmos, the power of the gods, and the naming of Zeus as the primary force in the universe. (*Argonautica*, trans. R. C. Seaton [London, 1921] book 1, lines 490–520, p. 37.)

3. See bibliography provided in n. 1, especially Boulanger, Eisler and Macchioro.

4. Vegetarianism was part of the Orphic regimen. After the ritual omophagia, partaking of the flesh of a bull (to commemorate Dionysus' death, and to symbolically express the divine aspect of man's being), the initiate forever abstained from meat. Even the wearing of wool cloth was forbidden in the temple.

5. See discussion in chapter 6 about the importance of Orpheus' Apolline-Dionysian identity in the nineteenth century. Walter A. Strauss' *Descent and Return: The Orphic Theme in Modern Literature* (Cambridge, 1971) focuses on this issue in nineteenth- and twentieth-century literature. The introduction offers an especially intelligent discussion of the subject.

6. There is no single consistent explanation of Orpheus' lineage and country of origin. Without exception, his mother is named the muse of epic poetry, Calliope. His father, however, is most often named as the river god or king, Oeagrus, but alternatively as the god Apollo himself.

Apollonius of Rhodes, *Argonautica* (London and New York, 1921), book 1, p. 5, lines 23–34, and Virgil, fourth *Georgic*, vol. 1 of Loeb Classical Library Edition, trans. H. R. Fairclough (Cambridge and London, ca. 1974), p. 233, for example, name Oeagrus as Orpheus' father. On the other hand, Pindar, in his brief allusion to Orpheus' role with the Argonauts, links Orpheus to the race of Apollo (*The*

Odes of Pindar, The Loeb Classical Library, trans. John Sandys [Cambridge, 1961], fourth Pythic Ode, pp. 216–17, line 177).

7. A frieze on the Sikyonian treasure house at Delphi dating from shortly before the mid-sixth century B.C., depicts Orpheus holding his zither, with the Dioskouroi, on the ship Argo. See Felix M. Schoeller, "Darstellungen des Orpheus in der Antike" (Freiburg, Inaugural Dissertation, Albert Ludwigs Universität, 1969) fig. I.1,2, and A. Provoost, *Orpheus* (Leuven, 1974), fig. 11. Schoeller's text and "De Antieke Orpheusvoorstellingen," by Carlo Heyman and Arnold Provoost, in *Orpheus*, pp. 29–48, offer the most concise discussions of depictions of Orpheus in the antique.

8. Concerning these examples of Orpheus' dedication to Apollo, see Apollonius of Rhodes, 1921, book 1, p. 41, lines 535–44; book 2, p. 149, lines 682–94, p. 165, lines 925–29; book 4, p. 399, line 1547.

9. Ibid., 1921, book 1, p. 5, lines 23–34.

10. Ibid., book 4, p. 390, lines 1409–25.

11. Ibid., book 4, p. 357. lines 904–7.

12. Ibid., book 1, p. 67, lines 914–22. See also Diodorus Siculus, another Hellenistic author, concerning the Argonaut Orpheus' roles as initiate and priest. *Diodorus Siculus*, vol. 2, trans. C. H. Oldfather (Cambridge and London, 1925), book 4, p. 477, line 43, 1–2.

13. *Aristophanes*, vol. 2, trans. B. Rogers, including *The Frogs* (London, 1961), p. 393, line 1032. Horace, *Satires, Epistles and Ars Poetica*, trans. H. R. Fairclough (London and New York, 1929), p. 483, lines 391–407. Pindar, *Olympiques, Pythiques*, Paris, 1922–23 (2, Olympic, 4). Diodorus Siculus, 1925, book 3, p. 301, 65, 6.

14. See Schoeller, 1969, p. 10, pp. 75–76.

15. Ibycus, quoted in *Lyra Graeca*, vol. 2, trans. J. M. Edmonds (Cambridge and London, 1958), p. 91.

16. Orpheus' precedence over Homer becomes an important concept in the nineteenth century. See chapter 2.

17. In *Rhesus*, Rhesus' mother, condemning Athena for the death of her son, invokes her sister muses and Rhesus' own cousin, Orpheus, instructor in rites and mysteries. See: *Euripides*, vol. 2, ed. David Grene and Richmond Lattimore, including *Rhesus*, trans. R. Lattimore (New York, 1958), p. 395, lines 943–45. See also Pausanias, *Description of Greece*, vol. 4, *Boeotia*, book 9, trans. W. H. S. Jones (Cambridge and London, 1935), vol. 30, p. 301, lines 4–5.

18. Aristophanes, 1961, p. 393, lines 1030–35.

19. Horace, 1929, *Ars Poetica*, p. 483, lines 391–407.

294   Notes for Chapter 1

20. Boccaccio, *Genealogia deorum gentilium,* book 2, pp. 702–3, xiv, 8, as quoted in Friedman, 1970, p. 138.

21. ". . . et par la douceur de ses discours, qu'il leur fit suivre une manière de vivre plus courtoise et plus humaine, les assemblant en corps de villes, leur apprenant à faire des bâtiments, leur enseignant à se ranger et obéir aux loix publiques, et garder les ordonnances des mariages."

    in Natalis Comes, *Mythologie,* 1627 Paris edition, trans. Jean Baudouin (New York, 1976), p. 783.

22. George Sandys, *Ovid's Metamorphoses Englished,* 1632 Oxford edition (New York and London, Garland facsimile reprint, 1976), p. 387. Also, on page 355 Sandys cites Horace's linking of Orpheus and Amphion.

23. Ovid, *Metamorphoseon,* trans. Samuel Garth, Dryden, et al., 1732 Amsterdam edition (New York and London, Garland facsimile edition, 1976), p. 329. Herodotus, *Histories,* vol. 1, book 2, p. 367, 81, Diodorus Siculus, 1925, book 4, p. 425, 25, 4.

24. Ovid, *Metamorphoseon,* 1732, p. 329.

25. Ibid., p. 329.

26. *Aeschylus,* vol. 1: *Oresteia,* trans. Richmond Lattimore, including *Agamemnon* (Chicago, 1953), p. 88, lines 1629–30.

27. *Euripides,* vol. 3, ed., David Grene and Richmond Lattimore, including *Iphigenia in Aulis,* trans. Charles R. Walker (New York, 1958), p. 176, lines 1211–14.

28. *Euripides,* vol. 5, ed. David Grene and Richmond Lattimore, including *The Bacchae,* trans. Wm. Arrowsmith (Chicago, 1959), p. 179, lines 560–64.

29. Simonides quoted in *Lyra Graeca,* vol. 2 (Cambridge and London, 1958), p. 311, no. 51. See Schoeller, fig. VI.1 and Provoost, fig. 2, illustrating a Boeotian ceramic of this period (the end of the sixth or the beginning of the seventh century B.C.) depicting Orpheus amidst the animals. The bearded poet is shown in profile, seated on a primitive chair, playing a phorminx, an ancient Greek stringed instrument. He is surrounded by a semicircle of birds and beasts portrayed with a quick, almost calligraphic style. Pindar, in the fourth Pythic Ode, lines 176–77, names Orpheus' instrument as the phorminx.

30. Orpheus amidst the animals is an image favored by writers and artists in the Hellenistic period or the late antique. See for example: *Diodorus Siculus,* vol. 2 (Cambridge and London, 1925), book 4, p. 425, 25; or Antipater of Sidon in *The Greek Anthology,* vol. 2, trans. W. R. Paton (London and New York, 1925), book 7, p. 7, Epigram 8. See also Epigram 9 by Damagetus and Epigram 10 by an anonymous author, on p. 9, which also describe Orpheus surrounded by the beasts.

31. See Virgil's fourth and sixth Eclogues as well as Damoetas' description of two cups by Alcimedon in the third Eclogue: Virgil, vol. 1: *Eclogues, Georgics, Aeneid, 1–6,*

trans. H. R. Fairclough (Cambridge and London, 1974), pp. 33, 45, and 21. See Ovid, *Metamorphoses*, trans. Rolfe Humphries (Bloomington, 1960), book 10, p. 237, lines 86–109, and book 11, p. 259, lines 740–41.

In his description of *Boeotia*, Pausanias writes of sculptures of poets and famous musicians including Thamyris, Arion, Sacades, Hesiod and Orpheus: Pausanias, *Description of Greece*, vol. 4, *Boeotia*, trans. W. H. S. Jones (Cambridge and London, 1935), vol. 30, p. 301, 4.

32. Philostratus, *Imagines* and Callistratus, *Descriptions*, trans. A. Fairbanks (London and New York, 1931), Philostratus the Younger's "Orpheus," p. 311, no. 6.

See as well, Callistratus' description of a statue of Orpheus on Helicon: ibid., Callistratus' *Description*, 7, "On the Statue of Orpheus," p. 403.

33. Schoeller, fig. V.2 and Provoost, fig. 9. See also fig. 12 in Henri Stern, "Un nouvel Orphée-David dans un mosaïque du VIe siècle," *Académie des Inscriptions et Belles-Lettres, comptes rendus* (Paris, 1970), pp. 63–79. Stern notes the coincidence of the reappearance of this theme in Greco-Roman art and Psalm 151 (about Orpheus and David) in the last century B.C.

34. See Schoeller and Provoost for a broad selection of these images.

35. See Schoeller, p. 33, and Provoost, p. 45, regarding Varro's *De Re Rustica*, 3, 13, 3.

36. The Orpheus attributed to Giovanni Bellini is an unusual image. The poet is accompanied by three figures not normally related to this mythological tale—Circe, Luna, and Pan. See Fern Rusk Shapley, "Giovanni Bellini and Cornaro's Gazelle," *Gazette des beaux-arts*, ser. 6, vol. 28 (July–December 1945), pp. 27–30; *The Summary Catalogue of European Painting and Sculpture* (Washington: National Gallery of Art, 1965), cat. no. 598, maintains the attribution to Bellini; Fritz Heinemann, *Giovanni Bellini e I Belliniani* (Venezia, 1962), cat. no. 487, attributes the work to Andrea Previtali.

Prints by Marcantonio Raimondi are to be found in *The Illustrated Bartsch*, 26 (formerly vol. 14, part 1), ed. Konrad Oberhuber (New York, 1978), Pl. 315, 314 (236).

Concerning Giulio Romano's paintings in the Sala di Ovidio, see Frederick Hartt, "Giulio Romano and the Palazzo del Tè" (New York: Institute of Fine Arts, New York University, Ph.D., 1949), pp. 24–25. Egon Verheyen, "Correggio's Amori de Giove," *Journal of the Warburg and Courtauld Institutes* 29 (1966): 160–92; Verheyen, "Die Sala di Ovidio im Palazzo del Tè," *Römisches Jahrbuch für Kunstgeschichte* 12 (1969): 161–70; Verheyen, *The Palazzo del Tè in Mantua: Images of Love and Politics* (Baltimore, 1977).

Illustrated editions of Ovid are significant sources for artists' interpretations of mythological themes. Padovanino's *Orpheus Enchanting the Animals* seems to draw upon the 1606 edition of the *Metamorphoses* illustrated by Antonio Tempesta. Also, the painting may be compared to the illustration in Julius Wilhelm Zincgreff's *Emblemata Ethicopoliticorum Centuria*, published in 1619. In this regard see C. M. Kauffmann, "Orpheus: The Lion and the Unicorn," *Apollo* 98 (September 1973): 192–96; Karla Langedijk, "Baccio Bandinelli's Orpheus: A Political Message," *Mitteilungen des Kunsthistorischen Instituts in Florenz* 20, part 1, (1976): 33–52.

37. See André Chastel, *Art et humanisme en Florence au temps de Laurent le Magnifique* (Paris, 1959), pp. 272–74, plate LXV,d. Earlier, Robert H. H. Cust, "On Some Overlooked Masterpieces," *Burlington Magazine* 4 (1904): 252–58, had attributed this work to G. B. Sozzini.

38. Further evidence of the interest in this theme in the humanist circle of Lorenzo are three medals executed by Bertoldo di Giovanni (ca. 1420–91). These medals treat the three major elements of the myth: Orpheus charming the beasts with his lyre (fig. 11); Orpheus in the Underworld; and Orpheus killed by the Maenads. The detailed scene of Orpheus playing his music includes not only animals but trees, rocks, rivers, and people. See Wilhelm von Bode, *Bertoldo und Lorenzo dei Medici* (Freiburg im Breisgau, 1925), pp. 38–40.

    The fifteenth-century Florentine painter, Jacopo dell Sellaio, executed three cassone panels dealing with the theme of Orpheus. One depicts the poet attired in the long robes and pointed cap of an Eastern mage, playing his violin amidst an amazing array of 45 animals, real and fantastic (note the dragon fighting to the left). Orpheus stands in front of a natural arch of stone, which is perhaps itself assembled through the magical powers of his music. The landscape beyond is similarly complex, including vast waterways, mountains, and forests. See Paul Schubring, *Cassoni* (Leipzig, 1915), p. 304, cat. no. 357, plate 85. Chastel, 1959, 18, relates these works to Poliziano's *Orfeo*, noting their theatrical settings and artifical juxtaposition of scenes. See the section on Poliziano below for a further discussion of the significance of Orpheus to Ficino and the circle of Lorenzo the Magnificent.

39. In an interesting variation on this type, Aelbert Cuyp manipulates the same formula, but, renewing the clarity and prominence of Orpheus, transforms the mythical poet into a portrait of a musician from Dordrecht, thus elegantly attributing legendary powers and talents to this contemporary artist. See Wilfrid Blunt, "Exhibitions in Edinburgh," *Burlington Magazine* 91 (1949): 256–58, illus. 23.

40. Langedijk, in her discussion of Bandinelli's statue of Orpheus as an image of the prince of peace, relates the Zincgreff emblem, the Roemer, Angelo Bronzino's portrait of Cosimo I as Orpheus, to a conflation of the image of Orpheus enchanting the animals to the Christian image of David soothing Saul's spirit, and Christ as the prince of peace. See discussion below concerning the evolution of this conflation of Orpheus-David-Christ.

41. Examples of this conflation of Orpheus and David include a painting in a Jewish catacomb from the third century; paintings in the fourth-century synagogue of Doura-Europas; sixth-century mosaics in synagogues in Gaza and Jerusalem. See Henri Stern, "Orphée dans l'art paléochrétien," *Cahiers Archéologiques* 23 (1974): 1–16; Eisler, 1966, pp. 3ff.

    The lyre-playing Orpheus appears in miniatures of the Homily of Sancta Lumina with homilies by Gregory of Nazianus and illustrations by the Pseudo-Nonnus. See Kurt Weitzmann, *Greek Mythology in Byzantine Art* (Princeton, 1951), pp. 67–68, who points to an illustrated mythological handbook such as the *Bibliotheke* of Apollodorus, as a source for the Pseudo-Nonnus illustrations.

42. Concerning David see 1 Samuel 16:12–15; 2 Samuel 22; Genesis 49; Jeremiah 23:5–6; 1 Chronicles 25; Micah 5:1–9; Isaiah 9:5–6; Isaiah 11:1–10; Ezekiel 34:23, 24, 27; Zachariah 2:9–10 and 9:9–10.

43. Henri Stern, 1970, pp. 70 and 76.

44. Quoted in Friedman, 1970, pp. 14–16, and discussed on pp. 16–28; See also Stern, 1974, pp. 8–9.

45. Tatian and Theophilus were the earliest Christian Apologists to stress this identification of Orpheus and Christ. At the end of the second century or beginning of the third century, Clement of Alexandria associates Orpheus and Christ through David. He names Orpheus, the Theologian, who prefigures Christ (*Protreptique*, vol. 1, 3–6). In the fourth century, Eusebius was clearly influenced by Clement's espousal of this tradition (*Laudatio Constantine*, book 14, and his *Preparatio Evangelica*). This association of Orpheus-David-Christ continues to figure in Christian tracts through the thirteenth century as well as in works of art well into the Renaissance. The conflation of David and Orpheus is mentioned in Sandys' 1632 edition of the *Metamorphoses*. The 1732 Garth/Dryden edition, citing Justin, mentions the tradition of Orpheus the monotheist, who learned the mysteries from the Hebrews. See Ovid, *Metmorphoseon*, 1632, p. 356; Ovid, *Metamorphoses*, 1732, p. 329. For further discussion, see Friedman, pp. 148ff; Stern, 1970, pp. 70, 89; Stern, 1974, pp. 9, 13–14; and D. P. Walker, "Orpheus the Theologian and Renaissance Platonists," *The Journal of the Warburg and Courtauld Institutes* 16 (1953): 110.

46. The Thracian Orpheus is sometimes identifiable through his hat and boots. The conflation of Orpheus and Christ is clear in a fresco in the catacomb of Callixtus; the wild beasts are substituted with a flock of sheep.

47. Friedman, 1970, discusses the Nisibene hymns of St. Ephraim of Syria, fourth century, based on the apocryphal gospel of Nicodemus, recounting the dialogue of Death and Satan, connecting Orpheus' victory over the beasts and his venture into Hades with Christ's victory over death. See also Elaine Pagels, *The Gnostic Gospels* (New York, 1979) and *The Nag Hammadi Library*, ed. James M. Robinson (New York, 1977).

48. See page 13ff.

49. C. de Boer, ed., *Ovide moralisé* (Amsterdam 1915–38), book 11, pp. 177–84, quoted in Friedman, p. 125.

50. Quoted in Friedman, pp. 130–31.

51. See Ficino's *Theologica Platonica*, 13: 2; Agrippa's *De occulta philosophia*, 3: vii; Steuco's *De Perenni Philosophia*, 1: xxviii; and Pico's *Examen vanitatis doctrinae gentium*, which quote portions of the Testament, Chastel, 1959, p. 273; Chastel, *Marsile Ficin et l'Art* (Travaux d'Humanisme et Renaissance, 14, Geneva, Droz, Lille, 1954), pp. 175–78. Ficino's free Latin translation of the Testament or *Falmode*, is based on George of Trebizond's translation of Eusebius' version in *Praeparatio Evangeliza*, which was available in the Laurentian library by 1462. Ficino's presentation of Christ as Orphic Shepherd parallels Dante's characterization, which in turn is informed with the attitudes of the moralized *Metamorphoses*: "Le Sage, par sa voix, adoucit et rend humbles les coeurs cruels et meut à sa volonté ceux qui n'ont point une vie de science et d'art et ceux qui n'ont pas une vie de raison et sont comme des pierres," from Dante, *Convivio*, 2:1,3, as quoted in Chastel, 1959, p. 272. This conflation of Orpheus and Christ remains significant well into the seventeenth century. Note for example Milton's elegiac "Lycidas," 1638, and Calderon's autosacramentale, "El Divino Orfeo." See Langedijk, p. 49, concerning Augustin Chesneau's 1657–67 *Emblemes Sacrez sur le Très-Saint et Très-Adorable Sacrement de l'Eucharistie* (based on Clement of Alexandria's *Protreptikos I*) which interprets Orpheus as the image of Christ's love, attracting diverse followers.

52. Ficino's *De Immort. Anim.*, 17:i, p. 386 as quoted in Meade, 1965, p. 15. Ficino also lists the ancient thinkers in *De Christiana Religione*, cf. xxii, as quoted in Walker, p. 105.

53. See Walker, 1953, p. 107, concerning the Neo-Platonists who adopted Ficino's line of great thinkers: the two Picos, Symphorien Champier, Amaury Bouchard, Agrippa of Nettesheim, Agostino Steuco, La Boderie, Duplessis-Mornay, Walter Raleigh, Cudworth, Thomas Taylor.

54. See Meade, 1965, p. 15, concerning De Mirville's *Pneumatologie*, 3: 70, which discusses the sacred science of ancient Khem which was transmitted via the Columns of Hermes to Orpheus, Hesiod, Pythagoras, and Plato.

55. Ch. Picard, "Orphée: Les Fontaines et les tombes," in "Notes et Correspondance," *Revue Archéologique* 1 (January 1960): 120.

56. In *L'Altercazione*, 2:4–6, Lorenzo describes Ficino: "I believed that Orpheus had returned to the earth." See Walker, p. 105, n. 1; Chastel, 1954, p. 48.

57. Walker, p. 100, quotes Ficino's *In Convivium Platonis . . . Comm.* Ficino's concept of the *furores* obviously derives from Plato's *mania* presented in *Phaedrus*: "that of prophets and seers; authors of rites and initiations; poets; and lovers." See *Phaedrus*, in *The Collected Dialogues of Plato*, ed. Edith Hamilton and Huntington Cairns, Bollingen Series 71 (Princeton, 1961), p. 491. See also the *Apology* and *Ion*, in which Plato compares the divine power of poets to that of the prophets and korybants.

58. Ficino relates medicine, music, and theology. Music is the medicine of the soul, soothing it, driving out madness. See P. O. Kristeller, "Music and Learning in the Early Italian Renaissance," in *Renaissance Thought and the Arts* (Princeton, 1980), p. 157.

59. See Rudolf Wittkower, *Architectural Principles in the Age of Humanism* (London, 1962), pp. 124–25, and Langedijk, p. 42, concerning the many treatises which reflect the importance of the Pythagorean-Platonic principle. There are significant similarities between the Orphic and the Pythagorean religions: the conviction that the soul is trapped in the prison of the human body; a belief in reincarnation or the transmigration of the soul; an adherence to an ascetic regimen. Both Orpheus and Pythagoras are linked to Apollo. The legend of Pythagoras of the Golden Thigh names Pythagoras as a son of Apollo, and in another parallel to the myth of Orpheus, he descends into Hades. In this regard see Guthrie, 1935, pp. 215–20; Kerenyi, 1950.

Orpheus was first associated with the spheres in Lucian's *Treatise on Astrology*. See *Lucian*, vol. 5, ed. A. M. Harmon, including *On Astrology* (London and Cambridge, 1962), pp. 354–57. Lucian's treatise is cited in the 1627 edition of Natalis Comes' *Mythologie* (1976), p. 779, and in the 1732 Garth/Dryden edition of Ovid, p. 329. Ficino's concept of the medicinal or tranquilizing power of the sound of Orpheus' lyre derives apparently from Byzantine and medieval sources. See Friedman, pp. 155–56.

A thirteenth-century image of the harmony of the spheres portrays Orpheus, Pythagoras, and Arion listening to the *musica mundana* transmitted through the central figure, Air. Actually a number of figures, including Apollo, Hermes, Pan, the Muses, and David, are associated with the harmony of the universe. See Charles de Tolnay, "The Music of the Universe," *The Journal of the Walters Art Gallery* 6 (1943), figs. 5, 6, 7. The focus of de Tolnay's discussion is the figure of David as a symbol of harmony in Bicci di Lorenzo's *Annunciation* in the Walters Art Gallery.

Orpheus and Eurydice by the fifteenth-century Scottish poet, Robert Henryson, describes Orpheus' quest for Eurydice, beginning with his ascent through the spheres and followed by his descent into Hades. Clearly, the journey among the planets is a type of initiation, the secrets of which allow him to enter the otherwise forbidden Underworld. See Friedman, pp. 201–2.

60. Concerning Nicholas Trivet's identification of Orpheus with "sapientia" and "eloquentia" see Friedman, ibid., pp. 89 and 113.

61. See Fraunce, *The Third Part of the Countess of Pembroke's Yvychurch* (London, 1592; New York: Garland, 1976), p. 50. Fraunce's work, one of the most important sixteenth-century English mythographies, is based on Boccaccio, Comes, and Georgius Sabinus. He names Orpheus as "wise and eloquent" while Eurydice is "Appetitum."

See as well Baudouin, *Recherches touchant la mythologie, recueillis des anciens auteurs*, published in his 1627 edition of Comes' *Mythologie*, 52, who emphasizes the poet's eloquence. The extensive commentary on book 10 in Sandys' edition of the *Metamorphoses* stresses the harmony and eloquence of Orpheus' music, its profound effect on the soul. Ovid, *Metamorphoses*, 1632, p. 356. The commentary on books 10 and 11 in the Garth/Dryden edition, including an extensive overview of pagan and Christian authors, similarly identifies Orpheus as a symbol of Eloquence. Ovid, *Metamorphoses*, 1732, p. 329.

Similarly, in the various editions of Ripa's *Iconologia*, Orpheus' music is associated with Harmony, with the symbol of Music, itself, and with Eloquence. See for instance: Cesare Ripa, *Iconology*, ed. George Richardson (London, 1779; New York: Garland, 1979), p. 70.

62. Ovid, 1960, book 11, p. 236, line 61.

63. Virgil, *Georgics*, 1974, book 4, p. 231, lines 495–500. See as well *Euripides*, vol. 1, ed. David Grene and Richmond Lattimore, including *Alcestis*, trans. R. Lattimore (Chicago, 1955), p. 20, lines 357–63; Isocrates, *Busiris*, vol. 3, trans. L. van Hook (Cambridge and London, 1961), p. 107, line 8; Athenaeus, *Deipnosophistae*, vol. 6, trans. C. B. Gulick (Cambridge and London, 1937), book 13, p. 219, line 597; Seneca, *Tragedies*, trans. F. J. Miller (Chicago and London, 1907), *Hercules Furens*, p. 138, lines 569–89 and *Hercules Oetaeus*, pp. 253–54, lines 1031–50; and Pausanias, *Boeotia*, 1935, vol. 30, p. 301, line 4. In this vein, the 1627 Baudouin edition of Comes (p. 782) and the 1732 Garth/Dryden edition of Ovid mention Orpheus' journey to Thesprotia. The English text explains that this journey was to learn the arts of necromancy. Orpheus is, however, deceived by a ghost and subsequently withdraws from mankind. This is presented as the basis of the story of Orpheus' descent into Hades.

64. A Roman coin, dated 238–44 A.D. (Provoost, fig. 21), from the period of Gordianus Pius, is clearly modeled on this earlier relief sculpture. A fresco from the first century B.C. (Provoost, fig. 17) shows Eurydice and Orpheus flanking the snarling figure of Cerberus. Orpheus approaches the beast with a dignified, determined air. Eurydice is seated, her body violently twisted as she looks behind her, her arms thrust out in an expression of surprise or violent emotion.

65. Virgil, *Georgics*, 1974, book 4, pp. 229–31, lines 467–85.

66. Ovid, *Metamorphoses*, 1960, book 10, p. 235, 40–47.

67. Early nineteenth-century portrayals of Orpheus in Hades closely resemble the images on these fourth-century B.C. vases. See for example paintings by Le Boullenger or Mongez exhibited at the 1808 Salon or Regnault's *Orphée aux enfers* represented here with figures 4.3–4.5.

68. Friedman, chapter 5; Kenneth R. R. Gros Louis, "Robert Henryson's Orpheus and Eurydice and the Orpheus traditions of the Middle Ages," *Speculum* 41 (1966): 643–55, esp. p. 650.

69. Boethius' *Consolation*, quoted in Friedman, p. 92.

70. As quoted in Friedman, p. 111.

71. As quoted in Friedman, p. 115.

72. As quoted in Friedman, p. 120. This strict moral interpretation informs later presentations of the myth. In Natalis Comes' *Mythologie*, 1627 ed., the central moral of the myth is that man must suppress emotions and desires. In this interpretation, however, Orpheus symbolizes the body or carnal desires, and Eurydice embodies the spiritual. See Natalis Comes, *Mythologie*, ed. Jean Baudoin, p. 784. Fraunce's 1592, *The Third Part of the Countess of Pembroke's Yvychurch*, draws on Boccaccio, Comes and Georgius Sabinus. Eurydice is *Appetitium*, the coveting faculty of man. The serpent symbolizes *affectium* and concupiscence. Orpheus is the eloquent or wise man who civilizes the ignorant. See Fraunce, p. 50.

73. Friedman, p. 116. Euripides, in *Alcestis* and Isocrates in *Busiris* as well as Athenaeus in *Deipnosophistai* seem to claim a victorious ending for Orpheus' quest for Eurydice in Hades. See above, n. 63.

74. Friedman, pp. 165–66.

75. A Latin elaboration of Martianus Capella's *De nuptiis*, dated ca. 1450, underlines the transformation of Orpheus of classical myth into medieval lover. "Orpheus, whose habit was to reach into the spirit of the sun, the monthly orbit of the moon, the numerically established course of the stars in heaven, now led to a pursuit of another kind, his studies modified, and speaks of kissing, of embracing, and follows his beloved." In Friedman, p. 168.

76. Eurydice's story is similarly emphasized in the 1632 Sandys edition of the *Metamorphoses* and in the 1732 Garth/Dryden edition. In the latter, "The Death of Eurydice" serves as the subtitle to book 10. The accompanying illustration portrays her flight from the snake and death in the arms of one of her companion Dryads.

77. Niccolo dell'Abate's *Aristaeus and Eurydice*, 1557, emphasizes a vast panorama including distant cities, forests, waterways and a cloud-filled sky. Poussin's version balances the mythic drama with a richly detailed landscape. Other seventeenth-century depictions include works by Richard van Orley (Museum Fodor, Amsterdam) and J. Glauber (Glasgow Art Gallery).

78. Pieter Brueghel's depiction of Hades is also a vision of Gothic horrors. Other more typical depictions of Orpheus pleading before the enthroned divinities of the Underworld include works by Rubens, in the Paintings Gallery, Sanssouci, Potsdam (see Adolf Rosenberg, *The Work of Rubens* [New York, 1913], illus. p. 394); Jean Restout's 1763 *Orpheus Reclaiming Eurydice in Hades* (see Pierre Rosenberg, *Jean Restout* [Rouen, 1970], Pl. L.); and Franz Anton Maulbertsch (see illus. 285 and 286 in Klara Garas, *Maulbertsch* [Graz, 1960]).

79. Depictions of Orpheus' confrontation with Cerberus include Marcantonio Raimondi's print (*The Illustrated Bartsch*, 26, formerly vol. 14, part 1, 1978) and the painting by Corrado Giaquinto (Marchese de Luca di Melpignano, Molfetta) in the robust style of the Roman Rococo. Additional sculptural versions include

works by Baccio Bandinelli (Palazzo Medici-Riccardi, Florence); Cristoforo Stati (Metropolitan Museum of Art, New York); de Keyser; and Ferdinand Tietz. See chapter 4 concerning the sustained popularity of certain types, well into the nineteenth century.

80. Among the many interpretations of Orpheus' fateful glance at Eurydice are works by Marcantonio Raimondi (see *The Illustrated Bartsch*, 26 [formerly vol. 14, part 1], ed. K. Oberhuber [New York, 1978], no. 282 [216], p. 267, and no. 295 [223], p. 285); Heinrich Aldegrever (see *The Illustrated Bartsch*, 16 [formerly vol. 8, part 3], *Early German Masters*, ed. Robert A. Koch [New York, 1980], no. 100 [394]); Agostino Carracci (*The Illustrated Bartsch*, 39 [formerly vol. 18, part 1]); Annibale Carraci, fresco in Villa Farnese, Rome; and Rubens' painting in the Prado, Madrid. The editions of Ovid's *Metamorphoses* include, of course, illustrations of this dramatic scene. See, for example, the 1606 Tempesta edition or Sandys 1632 edition. In the former, the depiction is presented with almost comic literalism. Orpheus, with his violin casually cast over his shoulder, seems to glance carelessly behind him. The startled Eurydice, theatrically thrusts out her arms, struggling against the ominous, glowing-eyed devil that clutches at her wrist, pulling her back into the flames of Hades.

An attribution of blame for Orpheus' failure is very often at issue. The medieval understanding of Eurydice as a symbol of evil or moral weakness, of course, exercised a profound impact on interpretations of this scene. (John R. Martin, *The Farnese Gallery* [Princeton, 1965], pp. 98–99, contrasts Caracci's presentation with a description by Bellori which is clearly infused with a medieval moralizing tone.) The interpretation of this episode continues to fascinate artists in the nineteenth and twentieth centuries. For example, in the Ballanchine/Stravinsky ballet, *Orpheus*, Eurydice is portrayed as the seductress or temptress, compelling Orpheus to look at her.

81. Anonymous author, in *The Greek Anthology*, no. 617, p. 331. The 1732 Garth/Dryden edition of Ovid cites Hyginus and Apollodorus concerning this explanation.

82. Pausanias, *Boeotia*, 30:2–9, pp. 302–3. The 1627 edition of Comes, ed. Baudoin, and the 1732 Garth/Dryden Ovid similarly offer the three explanations of Orpheus' death.

83. Isocrates, *Busiris*, p. 125, lines 38–42.

84. Conon, *Fragments of Greek History*, fragment 45, in F. Jacoby, *Fragmente der griechischen Historiker*, 1923.

85. In one of Aeschylus' surviving tragedies, *The Bacchae*, Pentheus is the victim of Dionysus' punishment. Like Orpheus, he is torn apart by the Bacchae, including Agave, his own mother.

86. As quoted in Friedman, p. 8.

87. Friedman, pp. 120 and 131.

88. Friedman, p. 9.
89. Ovid, *Metamorphoses*, 1960, book 10, p. 236, lines 82–85.
90. Pausanias, p. 301.
91. See Friedman, p. 123, concerning Giovanni del Virgilio's presentation of woman as a symbol of flesh, or carnal temptation. The 1632 George Sandys edition of Ovid interprets the homosexuality of Orpheus, Jupiter and Ganymede, Apollo and Hyacinthus, as expressions of simplicity and innocence, a result of the abhorrence of the flesh (pp. 358–59). Love of women, furthermore, is a hindrance to the study of philosophy and the administration of civil affairs (p. 387).
92. For the seventeenth-century Northern artist, the death of Orpheus, like the other episodes of the myth, is an excuse for depictions of vast and panoramic landscapes such as *Thracian Women Killing Orpheus* by A. Keirincx (Collection Duke of Northumberland). The *Death of Orpheus* by N. Knupfer (Dial Index) is quite unusual in that it depicts the actual dismemberment and mutilation of the poet, rather than merely the threatening approach of the women. The stiff, wooden body of Orpheus covered with gashes and cuts, is stretched out, among the crazed women, in a position distinctly resembling the crucified Christ.
93. An illustration by Colard Mansion in the 1484 edition of the *Ovide moralisé*, brings together, in a single image, as a type of continuous narrative, a homosexual encounter and the death of Orpheus. To the left, Orpheus and a young man embrace; while at the center of the composition, he lies dead, his lyre floating away on the river. To the right of the composition are two rather bourgeois looking women, dressed in contemporary fifteenth-century garb, who throw the stones that kill the poet. See Erwin Panofsky, *Albrecht Dürer* (Princeton, 1948), vol. 1, p. 32; André Chastel, 1954, pp. 178–79.
94. Panofsky, 1948, vol. 2, cat. no. 928, p. 95, explains the inscription. The word "puseran," is used for "pederast," a garbled form of the Italian word, "buggerone."
95. Edgar Wind, " 'Hercules' and 'Orpheus': Two Mock-Heroic Designs by Dürer," *Journal of the Warburg and Courtauld Institutes* 2 (July 1938–April 1939): 206–18. Wind understands the homosexual theme in the two drawings as a derisive device intended to mock or undermine the popularity of these figures as symbols of Eloquence with the humanists. Wind judges the inscription, the suspended book, the fleeing child and stripped tree to be "distinctly ludicrous" (p. 214). He concludes, "His point was intended to be rude. . . . Clearly Dürer intended to say: the lofty ideals embodied in Hercules and Orpheus are desecrated by some of their modern would-be successors (p. 215). Concerning Hercules' homosexual liaisons, Wind cites Gyraldus' "Herculis Vita," *Opera*, ed. 1696, vol. 1, pp. 578ff. and Aristotle and Ptolemy as cited by Pico della Mirandola, *Opera*, ed. 1601, vol. 1, p. 327. Dürer had indeed admired the Orphism of Poliziano and Pico but is, in these drawings, expressing his extreme disillusionment with the excessive stylish humanism that had evolved in the following twenty years. If Dürer intended a critical statement on Orpheus' homosexuality, he was not apparently alone in

this judgment. Pico della Mirandola's nephew, Gian Francesco Pico, condemned Orpheus' "unnatural vice," and connected it to Orpheus' espousal of Polytheism. Other followers of Ficino accused Plato of pederasty and heresy. Agrippa, in *De Vanitate*, in the context of a critique of Orphism, Ficino and Pio, refers to Orpheus's pederasty, asserting that it was Orpheus' powerful but feminizing music that seduced the Thracian men (see Walker, pp. 114–15). There were, apparently, many connections between Dürer's circle and Pico della Mirandola's heirs, nephews, and the executors of his estate, Gian Francesco Pico and Alberto Pio. See Pico, *Opera*, 1601, vol. 2, p. 880, for letter by Gian Francesco Pico to Pirckheimer. There are recorded visits of Alberto Pio to Germany. He became Maximilian's ambassador to the papal court. In this regard, see Wind, p. 215, n. 2.

96. Karl Kerenyi, "Orfeo Simbolo Dionisiaco," *Umanesimo e Simbolismo* (Padova, 1958), pp. 183–92, appears to date Poliziano's *Orfeo* as 1480, commissioned as part of the celebration of the double engagement of Clara Gonzaga and Gilberto Montpensier and Francesco Gonzaga and Isabelle d'Este (hence subsequent to Mantegna's decoration of the Camera degli Sposi in 1473).

97. See also Carl Giehlow, "Poliziano und Dürer," *Die graphischen Künste*, No. 2 (1902): 25–26.

98. Politian and Tasso, *Orpheus and Aminta*, trans. Louis E. Lord (London, 1931), pp. 98–99. Karl Kerenyi sees *Il Favolo di Orfeo* as a reflection of the depth of the Neo-Platonist's understanding of the myth and of Greek tragedy. (Kerenyi, 1958, pp. 183–92). His Orpheus is a Dionysian symbol and the drama is a descendant of Greek tragedy. Kerenyi links the *Favola* to Euripides *Bacchantes*, Aeschylus' *Pentheus*, Tespi's *Pentheus*, and Aeschylus' *Bassarae*, which all focus on the frenzied ritualistic murder of the hero. Each hero's death is a representation of Dionysus' *sparagmos*. Each play is a reenactment of the tragedy—the act of suffering and pathos—that was at the heart of the Dionysian festival, the "megala Dionysia," inducing terror, purification, and finally release in the hearts of the spectators. "Dionisio soffre in Penteo, soffre in Orfeo—simbolo dionisiaco in questo senso—egli soffre in tutti gli eroi, la sofferenza dei quali fa risonare il teatro tragico greco" (Kerenyi, pp. 189–90). Kerenyi contrasts this rebirth of Greek tragedy with the generally light spirit of works which mark the three phases of development of the Italian opera: (1) Rinuccini, Corsi and Peri, 1547, *Favola de Dafne*; (2) Rinuccini, Peri, and Caccini, 1600, *Eurydice*; and (3) Monteverdi, Striggio, 1607, *Orfeo*. Monteverdi initially included the Bacchic demise of Orpheus, but then, bowing to popular taste, retreated to a lighter version. *Eurydice*, with its happy ending, can be considered a forerunner of the extremely influential Gluck/Calzabigi *Orpheus and Eurydice*.

99. Concerning the popularity of the image of Orpheus in the circle of Giorgione see Otto Kurz, "Holbein and others in a XVIIth Century Collection," *Burlington Magazine* 83 (1943): 279–82. In his discussion of the inventory of the Imstenradt family collection in the seventeenth century (*Iconophylacium sive Artis Apelleae*

Thesaurarium), Kurz notes the following entries: Orpheus in the Underworld (1654 inventory), Arundel Collection; a cassone in Bergamo; A half-figure now preserved only in a copy of David Teniers; the Widener collection Bellini (attributed by G. M. Richter to Giorgione's early oeuvre).

100. Erik Fischer, "Orpheus and Calais. On the Subject of Giorgione's 'Concert Champêtre,'" in *Liber Amicorum Karel G. Boon* (Amsterdam, 1974), pp. 71–77.
101. Quoted in Fischer, p. 72.
102. Quoted in Friedman, p. 9.
103. Lucian, *On Astrology*.
104. Conon, *Fragments of Greek History*, fragment 45, in F. Jacoby, *Fragmente der griechischen Historiker*, 1923.
105. Philostratus, *The Life of Apollonius of Tyana*, quoted in Friedman, p. 10.
106. See Schoeller and Provoost for other illustrations.
107. Boccaccio as quoted in Friedman, p. 141.
108. Natalis Comes, *Mythologie*, 1627, ed. Jean Baudoin, p. 781.
109. Ovid, *Metamorphoses*, 1632, p. 387.
110. Ovid, *Metamorphoses*, 1732, pp. 329 and 363.

Chapter 2

1. Religious syncretism is a dominant theme of the German Romantics. Novalis' fifth "Hymn to the Night" of 1797 celebrates a conflation of religions from various cultures. See Novalis (Friedrich von Hardenberg), *Hymnen an die Nacht*, 5, in *Werke*, ed. Hans-Joachim Mähl and Richard Samuel, vol. 1 (Munich, Vienna: Carl Hanser Verlag, 1978), pp. 149–55. Novalis often links the Christian tradition and Indian religions. Hölderin's cult of nature is consonant with an inclusive vision of world religions. See his poem "The Only One," in which Christianity is accomodated to the Greek pantheon, and Christ is named "Hercules' brother." See Hölderlin, *Poems*, trans. Michael Hamburger (New York, Pantheon, ca. 1952). It seems hardly necessary to mention the importance of myth in the works of Winckelmann, Lessing, Herder, Goethe or Heine. Note specifically, however, Herder's studies in comparative philology, religion and mythology. Johann Gottfried Herder's *Ideen zur Philosophie der Geschichte der Menschheit*, translated by Edgar Quinet in 1827, had a profound influence, not only on Quinet but on Jules Michelet and many others.

2. Friedrich Creuzer, *Symbolik und Mythologie der alten Völker* . . . (Heidelberg, 1810). See also J. J. von Görres, *Mythengeschichte der asiatischen Welt* (Heidelberg, 1810); and Friedrich Majer, *Allgemeines mythologisches Lexicon* (Weimar, 1803). Additional volumes followed in 1811–13; however, this encyclopedic work was

never completed. Note also the theme of India in Majer's *Brahma, oder die Religion der Indier als Brahmaismus* (Leipzig, 1818). See as well the following: J. J. Wagner, *Ideen zu einer allgemeinen Mythologie der alten Welt* (Frankfurt a.M., 1808); J. A. Kanne, *Erste Urkunden der Geschichte oder allgemeine Mythologie* (Bayreuth, 1808).

3. Schopenhauer's *The World as Will and Representation*, which deals with the religion of the Upanishads, is permeated with Indian themes. The fascination with India is shared by Goethe (who studied with Schopenhauer and Majer in Weimar), Wagner, and Nietsche.

4. August Wilhelm von Schlegel, who had, with his brother Friedrich, studied Sanskrit in Paris under Alexander Hamilton, went on to establish and chair one of the first departments of Sanskrit in Bonn in 1818. Note the theme of India in Friedrich Schlegel's *Ages of the World*, 1800; *Athenäum*, and of course, *Über die Sprache und Weisheit der Indier*, 1808. Friedrich Bopp's *Comparative Grammar: Sanskrit, Zend and Greek*, appeared in Paris, 1833–52. The noted linguist, Eugène Burnouf, published his *Commentaire sur le Yacna (Avestan)* in 1833 and *L'Introduction à l'histoire du Buddhisme indien* in 1844. A chair of Sanskrit was established at the Collège de France in 1814, and subsequently in Berlin and Vienna. See in this regard, *The Rise of Modern Mythology, 1680–1860*, Burton Feldman and Robert D. Richardson, eds. (Bloomington and London, 1972), pp. 267ff, and Olga Amsterdamska's Ph.D. dissertation (New York, Columbia University, Department of Sociology), "The Sociology of Linguistics: Schools of Thought in Nineteenth-Century Germany." See also Raymond Schwab, *La Renaissance Orientale* (Paris, 1950); A. Leslie Willson, *A Mythical Image: The Ideal of India in German Romanticism* (Durham, N.C., 1964); Rene Gerard, *L'Orient et la pensée romantique allemande* (Paris, 1963); Edward W. Said, *Orientalism* (New York, 1979).

5. Müller was named Taylorian Professor of Modern Languages at Oxford in 1850. His failure to gain the chair of Sanskrit in 1860 (awarded instead to Monier-Williams) apparently shattered his life.

6. George W. Cox, *A Manual of Mythology in the Form of Questions and Answers* (London, 1867), pp. 106, 107. See also, Cox's, *The Mythology of Aryan Nations* (London, 1870), vol. 2, pp. 239 and 240, in which he discusses the linguistic origin of the names Orpheus and Eurydice, crediting Müller as his source.

7. Or, les doctrines orphiques, ce sont, au fond, selon le témoignage du père de l'histoire, des doctrines égyptiennes. A ses yeux, dogmes orphiques, appelés encore bachiques, dogmes égyptiens et pythagoriques, c'est tout un.

In J.D. Guigniaut, *Religions de l'antiquité, considerées principalement dans leurs formes symboliques et mythologiques* (Paris, 1825–51), vol. 3, 1, pp. 96–97.

8. Friedrich Creuzer, *Symbolik und Mythologie der alten Völker, besonders der Griechen* (Leipzig/Darmstadt, 1810–12), as quoted on p. 396, *The Rise of Modern Mythology, 1680–1860* (from book 1, iii).

9. Ibid., p. 391 (from Creuzer, book 1, vi).

10. Note Voss's articles in the *Gazette littéraire d'Iéna*, 1821, and *Anti-Symbolique* (Stuttgart, 1824); G. Hermann Lobeck's *Aglaophamus*, 1829; Schelling's *Einleitung in die Philosophie der Mythologie* (in Schelling's *Werk*, ed. M. Schröter [München, 1928], vol. 6, 4, *Vorlesung und Passion*); K.O. Müller's *La Terre mère: Doriens/Minyeurs/Etrusque*; and additional works by Welcker, Preller, Buttmann, Voelcker, Schwenck, Gerhard, and Panofka. Concerning this controversy over Creuzer's *Symbolik*, see Ernst Howald, *Der Kampf um Creuzers Symbolik* (Tübingen, 1926); Otto Gruppe, *Geschichte der klassischen Mythologie und Religionsgeschichte* (Leipzig, 1921), especially pp. 133–39; F. Cumont, *Recherches sur le symbolisme funéraire des Romains* (Paris, 1942); Pinard de la Boullaye, *L'Etude comparée des religions* (2 vols., Paris, 1922), vol. 1, pp. 261–68.

11. For a presentation of Guigniaut's major ideas, see his entry, "Mythologie," in the *Encyclopédie des gens du monde* (Paris, 1843), vol. 18, pp. 325–38, and his lecture to the Institut Impérial de France, "Notice historique sur la vie et les travaux de George-Frédéric Creuzer," 31 July 1863 (Paris, 1863).

12. Germany had an enormous impact on Benjamin Constant's career. He studied in Weimar in 1804 and produced a translation of Schiller's *Wallenstein*. See his *De la religion considerée dans sa source, ses formes, ses développements*, 1826–31.

13. Quinet was undoubtedly influenced by Herder's *Ideen zur Philosophie der Geschichte der Menschheit*, 1784–91, which he translated in 1827. Herder was an important influence, also, on the development of Quinet's associate, Jules Michelet. See, for example, Michelet's *Bible de l'humanité*, 1864. Michelet's interest in Herder's notion of historical development is closely associated with his enthusiasm for Vico. He translated *La scienza nuova*. See below a discussion of Quinet's manipulation of these Viconian notions of historical development as the basis for a utopian-socialist vision of society, in connection with Ballanche and Chenavard.

14. "L'erreur principale de M. Creuzer était écrite dans le titre de son livre. Il est trop *symbolique*." See Ernest Renan, "Des religions de l'antiquité et de leurs derniers historiens," *Le Revue des deux mondes* (May 15, 1853): 831–33. See also pp. 836 and 838 for Renan's defense of the independent importance of Hellenic culture.

15. "Ce fut un grand enseignement et comme une révélation que de voir ainsi pour la première fois réunis dans un *panthéon* scientifique tous les dieux de l'humanité, indiens, égyptiens, perses, phéniciens, étrusques, grecs, romains." Ibid., p. 826.

16. Also note Renan's emphasis on the importance of the mystery cults, their role in the development of monotheism: ibid., pp. 840–41 and pp. 843 and 846. The Hellenist, Louis Ménard, was devoted to the mystery cults and viewed the development of Christianity and monotheism as the advent of decadence. The polytheism of the Greek religion was his ideal which he identified with democracy; monotheism with corrupt political states.

17. La mythologie grecque, envisagée dans son premier essor, n'est que le reflet des sensations d'oranges jeunes et délicats, sans rien de dogmatique, rien de

308   Notes for Chapter 2

>   théologique, rien d'arrêté. . . . La nature entière se reflétait ainsi dans ces consciences primitives en divinités encore innommées. Le langage elle-même, comme dit M. Creuzer, fut une mine féconde de dieux et de héros. La mythologie est un second langage, née comme le premier de l'écho de la nature dans la conscience, aussi inexplicable que le premier par l'analyse, mais dont le mystère se révèle a qui sait comprendre les forces cachées de la spontanéité, l'accord secret de la nature et de l'âme, cet *hiéroglyphisme* perpétuel sur lequel se fond l'expression de tous les sentiments humains. Chaque dieu nous apparaît ainsi comme un cycle achevé, une région d'idées, un ton de l'harmonie des choses.

> In ibid., pp. 826–28.

18. Comte Eugène Félicien Albert Goblet d'Alviella, "La migration des symboles," *Revue des deux mondes*, année 60, 3eme per., vol. 99 (May 1890); ibid., p. 140.

19. "On pourrait définir le symbole—une représentation qui ni vise pas à être une reproduction." Ibid., p. 121.

20. > On peut concevoir un état religieux où tous les cultes deviendraient purement symboliques. Rien ne les empêcherait de conserver avec un soin pieux les rites et les traditions de leur héritage; seulement ils en feraient surtout les symboles des vérités communes à toutes les religions, et, par suite, ils pourraient se traiter les uns les autres,—comme on le voit entre les rites de certaines églises,—en formes locales et également légitimes de la religion universelle . . . un pareil syncrétisme semble, à première vue, fort éloigné de nous.

    In ibid., p. 144. See also p. 122 concerning his emphasis of the religious context of the symbol.

21. Brunetière explains his notion of symbolism in "Le symbolisme contemporain," in "La Revue littéraire," *La Revue des deux mondes* 104 (1891): 684–85:

    > Voilà l'origine et le fondement de tout le symbolisme: La nature a des dessous dont aucun naturaliste, n'ayant jamais saisi que les dehors, il n'en a donc aussi représenté que la plus vaine apparence. Mais nous voulons pénétrer plus avant; nous voulons déchirer le voile; et nous voulons atteindre enfin l'essence dont les manifestations se jouent à la surface des choses. . . .

22. "[P]our expliquer, par des symboles de plus en plus généraux, l'énigme du monde, celle de l'homme, les lois de l'univers." J. D. Guigniaut, *Mythologie*, 1843, vol. 18, p. 329.

23. "[U]ne religion n'est qu'une symbolique. . . . Pareillement, tout art n'est qu'une symbolique . . . une langue n'est qu'une symbolique." Brunetière, 1891, pp. 685–86.

24. "Tout symbole est en ce sens une espèce de révélation." Ibid., p. 686.
25. "L'origine du symbole, fils de la religion . . . jusqu'à nos jours chaque religion revêtit de symboles les idées primordiales de son culte." Georges Vanor, *L'Art symboliste* (Paris, 1889), pp. 38–40.
26. Dans ce sens, le Symbolisme date de toujours, puisqu'il est le fond même de toute poésie. C'est précisément parce que le symbole joue ce role synthetique, aliment aux sens, à l'âme, à l'esprit, qu'il est d'essence supérieure à la comparaison et à l'allégorie, lesquelles distinguent et séparent ce que le symbole unit et joint ensemble pour en faire une seule et même chose.

    In Jean Thorel, "Les Romantiques allemands et les symbolistes francais," *Entretiens politiques et littéraires* (September 1891): 95–109.
27. Ibid.:

    Les romantiques allemands cherchaient les plus riches symboles aussi bien dans la nature que dans les légendes, les contes ou les mythes de partout qu'ils étudiaient sans relâche. C'est ce mouvement qui a déterminé Creuzer à écrire sa "Symbolique" où il analyse tous les mythes des peuples de l'antiquité.
28. Cette simple et sublime religion de la nature révélant la divinité à l'homme par ses oeuvres . . . qui est tout ensemble un culte, une philosophie, une poésie, et que l'on entrevoit au berceau de toutes les croyances païennes, de tous les systemes religieux comme de toutes les mythologies de l'antiquité depuis l'Inde jusqu'à la Grèce et l'Italie, et de la Scandinavie ou de la Celtique, jusqu'à l'Egypte, l'Assyrie et la Bactriane.

    In J. D. Guigniaut, 1843, p. 338.
29. Among these many syncretic histories of civilization, note Benjamin Constant, *De la religion considérée dans sa source, ses formes, ses développements*, 1826–31; J. D. Guigniaut, *Le Polythéisme romain considéré dans ses rapports avec la philosophie grecque et la religion chrétienne*, 1833–36; Jules Michelet, *Bible de l'humanité*, 1864; Edgar Quinet, *De l'origine des dieux*, 1828 and *Le Génie des religions*, 1842; Alfred Maury, *Histoire des religions de la grèce antique*, 1857–59; *The Distribution and Classification of Tongues*, 1857; *Croyances et légendes de l'antiquité . . . d'histoire et de mythologie . . . Inde, Perse, Grèce, Gaule, Christianisme*, 1868; Thales Bernard, 1858 translation of Jacobi's *Dictionnaire, mythologie universel. Grèce, Italie, Egypte, Inde, Chine, Japon, Scandinavie, Gaule, Amérique, Polynésie*; E. Goblet d'Alviella, *Introduction a l'histoire générale des religions*, 1887; *Migration des symboles*, 1891; Jacques Paul Migne, *Encyclopédie théologique*.
30. See Herbert J. Hunt, *The Epic in Nineteenth Century France* (Oxford, 1941), pp. 23–24, for an excellent analysis of the Romantics' preoccupation with the past—illuminism, theosophy, mysticism, philology, comparative mythology, comparative religious studies, the fascination with ancient or Eastern religions:

The net result of all this will be the almost unquestioning acceptance of half a dozen "humanitarian" convictions, of capital importance in the orientation of French Romantic poetry: the idea that the past offers not only a means of escape from the present but also a source of instruction for the future, the assumption that the whole of humanity is but one great family, all the branches of which have inherited their languages, myths and religious beliefs from one original stock, and that theology and myth, inseparably related to one another, and sooner or later fused in the crucible of the national epic, are subject to a continuous development as each race, more enlightened than its immediate precursor or rival, works upon them; finally, the certainty that this continuity is not purposeless, implies enrichment and a steady conquest over the domain of the unseen, and shows man as moving forward (or backward, in the illuminist sense) to a state of completion and unity which whither he was created to achieve or from which he had fallen away through his initial "prevarication."

31. J. D. Guigniaut's *Religions de l'antiquité* was dedicated to Cousin. Guigniaut was friends, as well, with both Quinet and Michelet.

32. Quinet, *De l'origine des dieux*, 1828, as quoted in Sloane, *Paul Marc Joseph Chenavard* (Chapel Hill, 1962) pp. 426–37.

33. Quinet, *Le Génie des religions*, quoted in Joseph C. Sloane, 1962, p. 102.

34. Jules Michelet, *Bible de l'humanité* (3rd ed., Paris, 1864), pp. i–iv, as quoted by Sloane, 1962, p. 100.

35. Michelet, 1864, as quoted by Sloane, 1962, p. 101. Vico's *Scienza nuova* and Herder's *Ideen zur Philosophie der Geschichte der Menschheit* are important sources for the notions of universal histories. Michelet translated Vico's book in 1827. Quinet produced a translation of Herder's work.

36. See Sloane, 1962, pp. 74, 81–82. Additionally see p. 110.

37. Ballanche's theories are elaborated in baffling and confused form throughout his works: *Essais de palingénésie sociale*; *Essais sur les institutions sociales*; *La Vision d'Hébal, chef d'un clan écossais*; and *Palingénésie sociale ou Théodicée de l'Histoire*. This last work, intended as the author's magnum opus, was to have several parts: "Orphée, Formule générale," "La Ville des expiations," and "Elégie." Only "Orphée" was completed. See Pierre Simon Ballanche, *Oeuvres complètes*, Paris, 1830.

38. Genesis 5:2—"Male and female he created them, and blessed them and called their name Adam in the day they were created."

39. Albert Joseph George, *Pierre Simon Ballanche: Precursor of Romanticism* (Syracuse, 1945), pp. 96–97; Brian Juden, "Particularités du mythe d'Orphée chez Ballanche," CAIEF, congrès (24 juillet 1969), pp.137–52; Joseph C. Sloane, *French Painting between the Past and the Present: Artists, Critics, and Traditions from 1848*

to 1870 (Princeton, 1951); idem, "Paul Chenavard," *Art Bulletin* 33 (1951): 240–58; idem, *Paul Marc Joseph Chenavard: Artist of 1848* (Chapel Hill, 1962).

40. For a discussion of Ballanche's Christianity, see Victor de Laprade, "Ballanche, sa vie et ses écrits," Mémoire, Lyon, Académie des Sciences, Belles-Lettres et Arts, Classe des Lettres, 1850, vol. 2, pp.176–78.

41. See Ballanche, *Oeuvres complètes* (cited n. 37), vol. 3, pp. 90, 135, 136, 142 especially.

42. Ibid., p. 82. Ballanche speaks of "la poésie de la pensée."

43. Ibid., vol. 4, p. 6. Ballanche claims that "la religion est l'histoire allégorique de la nature." He also states: "La mythologie est une histoire condensée."

44. See Sloane, "Chenavard," 1951, pp. 246–50, and *Chenavard*, 1962, especially pp. 44–60 (both cited n. 39). Chenavard's commission was a product of the liberal government installed in 1848. By 1852, under the encouragement of the conservative government of Napoleon III, the Pantheon was returned to the Church. Of course, Chenavard's pantheistic, anticlerical program was canceled. Neither the conservatives nor the liberals viewed the paintings merely as a decorative scheme; both factions perceived the political and philosophical implications of the plan. Indeed, Chenavard and some of the most important members of his circle were actively involved in politics. Chenavard's last work, *The Divine Tragedy*, 1869, also deals with the theme of relgious syncretism. The frenzied image portrays the destruction of all religions. Divinities from Norse legend, and Greek, Roman and Egyptian mythology, Old and New Testament figures, even the Christian Trinity meet the same destruction. The skulls interspersed with the cherubim above Christ's head, indicating the destruction of Christianity, too, reflects Chenavard's anti-clericalism. Amidst this scene of universal catastrophe, the only possible glimmer of hope is the figure of Venus, carried away by Love and Bacchus. Also, in the upper left corner, a hermaphrodite bearing a lyre, seated on a hippocamp, appears untouched by the havoc below. The trio of Venus, Love, and Bacchus may indicate the artist's confidence in the immortality of love, beauty and genius, their independence from religious dogma. The hermaphrodite may allude to Ballanche's philosophy, an image of man's restoration to the perfection of the primordial androgyne.

45. Concerning the concept of "hommes spontanés," see Ballanche, *Prolégomènes pour Orphée*, in *Oeuvres complètes*, vol. 4, p. 6.

46. See Sloane, *Chenavard*, 1962 (cited n. 39), chapter 4, "Theory of History," pp. 70–71, 81–83. See also Herbert J. Hunt, *The Epic in Nineteenth-Century France* (Oxford, 1941).

47. An investigation of the bibliographies of figures such as Quinet, Michelet, or Maury reveals their interest in esoteric religions and magic, as well as myth and history: Quinet, *Merlin enchanteur*, 1869; Jules Michelet, *La Sorcière*, 1862; *De l'ésotérisme dans l'art*, 1890; V. E. Michelet, *La Rédemptrice*, 1890; and *Les Com-*

pagnons de la hiérophanie, 1897; L. F. Alfred Maury wrote not only about Greek religions, archaeology, and mythology but also *Les Fées du moyen-âge*, 1843; *Des hallucinations hypnagogiques*, 1848; *Nouvelles observations sur les analogies des phénomènes du rêve et l'aliénation mentale*, 1853; *De certain faits observés dans les rêves et dans l'état intermédiaire entre la veille et le sommeil*, 1857; *Magie*, 1869; *Le Sommeil et les rêves*, 1861; *La Magie et l'astrologie dans l'antiquité et le moyen-âge*, 1864; and *Croyances et légendes du moyen-âge*, 1896.

The Hellenic mystery cults were an important theme in esoteric literature including the writings of Guigniaut, Ménard, Maury, Regon de Battignies, Dupuis, Matter, H. Delaage, Péladan and Schuré. Jacques Matter was a member of Allan Kardec's spiritist circle in Lyon, along with Camille Flammarion. His publications, largely devoted to gnosticism and the Alexandrian philosophies, include *Histoire de l'école d'Alexandrie*, 1820; *Histoire critique du gnosticisme et son influence*, 1826; *Schelling ou la philosophie de la nature*, 1842; *St. Martin, le philosophe inconnu*, 1862; *Swedenborg*, 1863; *Le Mysticisme en temps de Fénélon*, 1864. Other important esoteric literature includes: Adolphe Franck's *La Kabbale*, 1845; Delaage's *Le Monde occulte*, 1851; Alex Erdan, *La France mystique*, 1853; Ragon de Battignies, *La Maçonnerie occulte*, 1853; L. Figuier, *L'Alchimie et l'alchimiste*, 1854; and *L'Histoire du merveilleux*, 1860.

48. Eliphas Lévi's works include *Bible de la liberté* (Paris, 1841); *Doctrines religieuses et sociales* (Paris, 1841); *La Mère de dieu* (Paris, 1844); *Des origines cabalistiques du christianisme, de la kabbale considérée comme source de tous les dogmes* (Paris, 1855); *Dogme et rituel de la haute magie* (Paris, 1856); *Histoire de la magie* (Paris, 1860); *La Clef des grands mystères* (Paris, 1861); *Fables et symboles en philosophie occulte* (Paris, 1862); *La Science des esprits* (Paris, 1865); *Le Livre des splendeurs* (Paris, 1868). Concerning Lévi, see Frank Paul Bowman, *Eliphas Lévi: Visionnaire Romantique* (Paris, 1969); Christopher McIntosh, *Eliphas Lévi and the French Occult Revival* (New York, 1974); Alain Mercier *Eliphas Lévi et la pensée magique au XIXème siècle* (Paris, 1974); Thomas A. Williams, *Eliphas Lévi: Master of Occultism* (University, Alabama, 1975).

49. "Tout l'univers n'est qu'un temple sublime, n'ayant qu'un rôle, qu'un soleil et qu'un Dieu." Lévi, *Fables et symboles*, "Sixième Grand Symbole, Le Temple de l'avenir," p. 467.

50. Les vrais poètes sont des envoyés de Dieu sur la terre. Le grand initiateur de la Grèce et son premier civilisateur en fut aussi le premier poète. . . . La fable d'Orphée est tout un dogme, c'est une révélation des destinés sacerdotales, c'est un idéal nouveau issu du culte de la beauté. On a dit que le beau est la splendeur du vrai. C'est donc à cette grande lumière d'Orphée qu'il faut attribuer la beauté de la forme révélée pour la première fois en Grèce.

In Eliphas Lévi, *Histoire de la magie* (Paris, 1869, ed. de la Maisnie, La Roche-sur-Yon, Vendée, 1974), pp. 90 and 93.

51. Lévi, *La Clef*, p. 33

52. Certainly, Lévi's all-encompassing occult philosophy inspires Péladan. But more specifically Péladan's curious association of Cain and Abel with Orpheus and Eurydice may derive from Lévi. In *Histoire de la magie* Lévi compares Medea and Cain. Cain and Abel play symbolic roles in *La Clef des grands mystères*. See *La Clef*, pp. 24–25, 33, and 202.

    Péladan wrote about his fellow Lyon natives, Séon, Chenavard, Janmot, and Puvis in *La Revue forézienne* in 1902. "Les grands méconnus," MS.13.214, Fonds Péladan, Bibliothèque de l'Arsenal, Paris. See also his article, "Paul Chenavard," *L'Artiste*, No.9, n.s. (1895): 356–62.

53. Stanislas de Guaïta was, along with his fellow Lyonnais, Papus, Péladan, and Paul Adam, one of the founders of the Rose + Croix in 1887. His writings include *Au Seuil de mystère*, 1886 and *La Clef de la magie noire*, 1897. In this regard see Paul Leutrat, *La Sorcellerie lyonnais* (Paris, 1977). Péladan was, in fact, one of de Guaïta's disciples, but broke away in 1890 to form, in 1891, his own splinter Rosicrucian group, the Rose + Croix Esthétique. His followers included Gary de Lacroze, Léonce de Larmandie, de La Rochefoucauld, Elémir Bourges, St. Pol Roux, Erik Satie, and Samas.

54. "Artiste; tu es prêtre: l'art est le grand mystère ... chef d'oeuvre ... rayon du divin descend comme sur un autel ... artiste tu es roi ... l'art est l'empire véritable ... artiste, tu es mage; l'art est le grand miracle et prouve notre immortalité." Joséphin Péladan, *Salon de la Rose + Croix* (10 mars–10 avril, Paris: Galerie Durand Ruel, 1892); "Geste esthétique de 1892," pp. 7–11.

55. Péladan's works include *La Décadence latine*, 1884–1906, 21 volumes; *L'Amphithéâtre des sciences mortes*, 1891–1911, 7 volumes; *Les Idées et les formes*, 1900–1901; *La Décadence esthétique*, 1888–1910, ca. 17 volumes. Concerning Péladan, see Robert Pincus-Witten, *Occult Symbolism in France: Joséphin Péladan and the Salon Rose + Croix* (New York, 1976).

56. "Dieu, n'a pas plus ni moins parlé à Moïse qu'à Orphée, à Manou, qu'à Zoroastre, à Cakya à Mouni qu'à Méni, à Rama qu'à Krisnah." Joséphin Péladan, *La Terre du Sphinx*, pp. 5–6, MS.13.155, Fonds Péladan, Bibliothèque de l'Arsenal, Paris, p. 10. See Gisèle Marie, *Elémir Bourges, ou l'éloge de la grandeur, correspondances inédits avec Armand Point* (Paris, 1962), p. 44, for an apt description of Péladan's syncretism: "Péladan se voulait être la Coryphée, le melodieux Orphée donnait la main à Saint François, *le poverello*."

57. Joséphin Péladan, "Projets de pièces de théâtre," MS.13.204, Fonds Péladan, Bibliothèque de l'Arsenal, Paris. These manuscripts include five versions of the play *Terre d'Orphée*, each differing somewhat in structure.

58. The Fonds Péladan also includes a small watercolor sketch by Péladan showing the dolmens and menhirs of the tomb of Oleagre, Orpheus' father.

314 Notes for Chapter 2

59. Péladan rabidly condemns the excesses of the women priestesses and Maenads who cause Orpheus' death. The theme of misogyny is apparent in "A la jeune femme contemporaine," *Amphithéâtre des sciences mortes*, MS.13.205, Fonds Péladan, Bibliothèque de l'Arsenal, Paris, p. xxi:

> Quand Orphée, ce Kaldéen civilisateur des Aryas, obéissant à la propension ethnique, instaura des mystères feminins, il te donna l'empire de la sensibilité et tu prêtas serment d'éternelle vassale à l'art et mystère.
>
> Ménades, le sang d'Orphée coule encore sous votre fureur sacrilège: parjurés, vous avez même oubliés le pacte grandiose. Eh bien, descendant de cette race et sacerdote de ce rite, digne ou indigne, mais légitime, puisque seul je pleure encore le grand Aède, je viens ruiner le rite d'Ionie.
>
> On a parlé de religion a fonder; il y en a une a détruire, la tienne, femme, et ce livre commence ta ruine.

60. Lyon had been a center of occult and spiritist learning since the Medieval and Renaissance period. See Leutrat, *La Sorcellerie lyonnaise*. Concerning Papus in particular and occultism in general, see Filiz Eda Burhan, "Vision and Visionaries: Nineteenth-Century Psychological Theory, the Occult Sciences, and the Formation of the Symbolist Aesthetic in France" (Ph.D. diss., Princeton University, 1979); Alain Mercier, *Les Sources ésotériques et occultes de la poésie symboliste, 1870–1914* (Paris, 1969); Jean Pierrot, *L'Imaginaire décadent* (Paris, 1977).

Papus' occultist colleagues include Vintras (1807–75), Boullan (1824–93), Péladan (1859–1918), and Allan Kardec (H.L.D. Ricail) (1804–69). Papus was the disciple of the Maître Philippe. His other masters include Saint Yves d'Alveydre, Fabre d'Olivet, Wronski, Eliphas Lévi, Lacuria, and Louis Lucas.

Papus joined the Theosophical Société Isis in 1887. That same year he joined the Rose + Croix. In 1888 he began the influential occultist review, *L'Initiation*, which published material by Chamuel, Lejay, Barlet, Sedir, Villiers de l'Isle Adam, Catulle Mendes, Emile Goudeau and Jules Lermina. In 1888 he formed a new organization, Hermes. His noted *Traité élémentaire de la science occulte* was published in 1888. In 1890 he formed Le Group Indépendant d'Études Esotériques, which later became the Université des Hautes Etudes. From June 1890 until November 1898, along with Chamuel, Papus edited another important occult revue: *La Voile d'Isis*. His publications include: *Traité méthodique de la science occulte*, 1891; *Traité élémentaire de la magie pratique*, 1893; and *Le Diable et l'occultisme*, 1896.

61. Papus, "La Vie de Christ," MS.5491.I.26, Fonds Papus, Bibliothèque Municipale, Lyon, p. 23. See also: "Alchimie," MS.5491.I.7, and "Alchimie au XIXème siècle," MS.5491.I.2.

62. Papus, "L'Etat social de l'homme," MS.5491.I.8, Fonds Papus, Bibliothèque Municipale, Lyon, p. 13.

63. Papus, "Occultisme contemporaine," MS.5491.I.17, Fonds Papus, Bibliothèque Municipale, Lyon, p. 46:

Il suffit de citer Lycurgue, Solon, Numa, Minos, Pythagore, Platon, d'une part, puis, Orphée, Moïse, d'autre part, pour voir l'importance de cette Université centrale, nommée Hermes, dont tous les temples de l'occident n'étaient que des écoles secondaires.

64. Ibid., p. 25:

Pour atténuer l'acte de sa créature, le Créateur, utilisant le Temps et l'Espace qui étaient corollaires du plan physique, créa la Différenciation de l'Etre collectif: chaque cellule d'Adam devint un être humain individuel et ainsi a devint le Principe de la vie universelle et de la forme plastique: Eve. L'homme dut, dès lors, épurer les principes inférieurs qu'il avait ajoutés à sa nature, par la souffrance, la résignation aux épreuves et l'abandon de sa volonté entre les mains de son Créateur. Les reincarnations furent le principal instrument de salut et, comme tous les hommes sont les cellules d'un même Etre, le salut individuel ne sera total que lorsque le salut collectif sera accompli.

65. Papus, "L'Analogie," MS.5491.I.3, Fonds Papus, Bibliothèque Municipale, Lyon.

66. H. P. Blavatsky, *An Abridgement of the Secret Doctrine* (London, 1966), p. xxiii. Besides *The Secret Doctrine*, first published in 1888, Madame Blavatsky's writings also include *Isis Unveiled*, 1877; *The Theosophist*, 1879; *Lucifer*, 1887.

67. Edouard Schuré, *The Great Initiates* (London, 1913), vol. 1, p. xxxiii. His works include: *Les Grandes Légendes de France*, 1891; *Précurseurs et révoltés*, 1920 and *L'Evolution divine*, 1928.

68. Ibid., p. 346. See as well pp. 8, 299, 300, 314, 332, 346.

69. Edouard Schuré, "The Hellenic Miracle" in *L'Evolution divine*, translated as *From Sphinx to Christ* (Philadelphia, 1928), p. 203. See also p. 202 and 204 for this emphasis on the Dionysian cults.

70. See Alain Mercier, *Les Sources ésotériques et occultes de la poésie symboliste*, Paris, 1969, for a good overview of the extensive body of occult literature of this period.

71. See Filiz Eda Burhan, "Vision and Visionaries: Nineteenth Century Psychological Theory," 1979, and George L. Mauner, *The Nabis: Their History and Their Art, 1888–1896* (New York, 1978) concerning the impact of the occultists on Post-Impressionism.

72. Dès les premiers âges de la Grèce, la Poésie consacrée aux services des autels ne sortait de l'enceinte des temples que pour l'instruction des peuples: elle était comme une langue sacrée dans laquelle les prêtres, chargés de présider aux mystères de la religion, traduisaient les volontés des Dieux.... On donnait à cette langue sacrée le nom de Poésie.

In Fabre d'Olivet in *La Voile d'Isis*, no. 43. See Mercier, 1969, p. 231. Other writings by Fabre d'Olivet that were published in *La Voile d'Isis* include a commentary on *Les Vers dorés* (no. 13, 25 February 1891) and "Discours sur l'essence et la forme de la poésie," (no. 41 and following, 23 September 1891).

73. Le Verbe est l'existence de l'Etre, l'Evidence de son identité, la Providence de sa Perfection, Dieu même engendré de lui-même—le Verbe est l'Eternel Présent en Présence de l'Eternel, son objectivité créatrice en personne, le génie générique du génie divin, le Formateur de ses Especes, l'Archétype, le Poète-Dieu, Dieu parlant.

In Saint-Yves d'Alveydre, MS. 5493, Fonds Papus, Bibliothèque, Lyon.

74. ... un livre qui soit un livre, architectural et prémédité, et non un recueil des inspirations de hasard fussent-elles merveilleuses. ... J'irai plus loin, je dirai: le Livre, persuadé qu'au fond il n'y en a qu'un, tenté à son insu par quiconque a écrit, même les Génies. L'explication orphique de la Terre, qui est le seul devoir du poète et le jeu littéraire par excellence: car le rythme même du livre, alors impersonnel et vivant, jusque dans sa pagination, se juxtapose aux équations de ce rêve, ou Ode.

In Stéphane Mallarmé, "Proses Diverses," in *Oeuvres complètes* (Paris, 1945), pp. 662 and 663.

Mallarmé's language in his celebration of the poet Théodore de Banville in 1864 *Symphonie littéraire* (Paris, 1945), pp. 264–65, clearly reveals his rarified concept of the Poet. His praise of de Banville is extravagant: "c'est le divin Théodore de Banville, qui n'est pas un homme, mais la voix même de la lyre." Mallarmé traces the poet's noble, even godly, lineage back to Orpheus and Apollo:

il marche en roi à travers l'enchantement édénéen de l'âge d'or, célébrant à jamais la noblesse des rayons et la rougeur des roses, les cygnes et les colombes, et l'éclatante blancheur du lis enfant,—la terre heureuse! Ainsi a dût être celui qui le premier reçut des dieux la lyre et dit l'ode éblouie avant notre aïeul Orphée. Ainsi lui-même, Apollon.

75. L'oeuvre pure implique la disparition élocutoire du poète, qui cède l'initiative aux mots, par le heurt de leur inégalité mobilisés; ils s'allument de reflets réciproques comme une virtuelle traînée de feux sur des pierreries, remplaçant la respiration perceptible en l'ancien souffle lyrique ou la direction personnelle enthousiaste de la phrase.

In Mallarmé, "Variations sur un sujet," 1945, p. 366.

Note a similar presentation of the sacred role of the poet-artist in Saint Pol-Roux, 1891 letter to Jules Huret, as quoted by Huret, *Enquête sur l'évolution littéraire* (Paris, 1891) p. 148.

76. A quoi bon la merveille de transposer un fait de nature en sa presque disparition vibratoire selon le jeu de la parole, cependant; si ce n'est pour qu'en émane, sans la gêne d'un proche ou concret rappel, la notion pure.

Je dis: une fleur! et, hors de l'oubli où ma voix relègue aucun contour, en tant que quelque chose d'autre que les calices sus, musicalement se lève, idée meme et suave, l'absente de tous bouquets.

In Mallarmé, "Variations," p. 368. See as well p. 378 of this work which was first published in *La Revue blanche* in 1895.

77. Les sciences occultes constituent un des principaux angles fondamentaux de l'art. Tout vrai poète est d'abord un initié. La lecture des grimoires éveille en lui des secrets dont il avait eu toujours la connaissance virtuelle.

In Charles Morice as quoted in Alain Mercier, 1969, p. 252.

78. Il faut aux disciples de Mallarmé des allégories et toute l'ésotérisme des antique théurgies. Point de poésie sans un sens caché. . . . Ne leur reprochez pas trop, Monsieur, d'être des mystiques et de s'éprendre de l'ésotérisme des antiques théurgies. Qu'ils cherchent par-delà tout Evangile précis—à cette heure où tous les évangiles tombent en ruine—une religion qui satisfasse à la fois leur coeur et leur raison dans le fond commun de toutes les religions et de toutes les métaphysiques, dans le frisson du mystère, dont certaines questions ont toujours fait frémir l'humanité, dans les hiéroglyphes de l'ancienne Egypte, dans les grimoires de Paracelse et dans les méditations de Spinoza—ne les condamnez pas si vite—êtes-vous bien sûr qu'ils aient tort?

In Charles Morice, *Demain, questions d'esthétiques* (Paris, 1888) pp. 9 and 25. See as well *La Littérature de toute à l'heure* (Paris, 1889); *L'Esprit belge* (Brussels, 1899), especially pp. 154 and 156; and *Tristan Corbière* (Paris, 1912) p. 25.

79. Richard Wagner, *Relgion and Art*, in vol. 6 of *Richard Wagner's Prose Works*, trans. Wm. Ashton Ellis (London, 1897), p. 213. See also pp. 216, 261–62.

80. Ibid., p. 247. See also p. 216.

81. See Mauner, *The Nabis: Their History and Their Art*, 1978.

82. Nos aspirations, notre mysticisme n'étaient pas, à la vérité, toujours très orthodoxes. Nous faisons un singulier mélange de Plotin, d'Edgard Poe, de Baudelaire, et de Schopenhauer. Les petites revues théosophiques étaient florissantes. Il y avait Mme. Blavatsky, Péladan, les expositions de la Rose-Croix. Enfin nous subissions l'influence de la philosophie allemande qu'on nous avait enseignée au collège.

In Maurice Denis, *Nouvelles Théories sur l'art moderne et l'art sacré, 1914–1921* (Paris, 1921), p. 172. See also p. 178 concerning Denis' invoking of Bergson in regard to his mystical notion of art.

83. Delville spent many years in England, teaching at the Glasgow School of Art for over six years. See Marian Burleigh-Motley, "George Russell (AE): The Painter of the Irish Renaissance" (New York University, Institute of Fine Arts, Ph.D. diss., 1978), p. 156.

84. Jean Delville, *The New Mission of Art, A Study of Idealism in Art*, trans. Francis Colmer, introduction and notes by Clifford Bax and Edouard Schuré (London, 1910), p. 11. See as well pp. 32, 70, 94 concerning his religious concept of art; religious syncretism, pp. 88 and 91–92; and pp. 34, 53–54, 61, 147, 159–60, 175, concerning his occultist view of the marriage of art and science.

85. Wackenroder, *Phantasien über der Kunst*, 1799, "in the mirror of sound, the human heart recognizes itself," as quoted by George P. Mras, *Eugène Delacroix's Theory of Art* (Princeton, 1966), p. 41. Mras also quotes Schiller, *Upon the Aesthetic Culture of Man in a Series of Letters:* "Plastic art in its highest consummation must become music," p. 41.

86. Swedenborg, *La Nouvelle Jerusalem*, trans. Hermann (Paris, 1889), p. 203, as quoted by Françoise Cachin, *Gauguin* (Paris, 1965), p. 280.

87. "Le sentiment des harmonies extérieures fait les poètes. / L'intelligence des harmonies intérieures fait les prophètes." In A. Constant de Baucour (Eliphas Lévi), "Les Correspondences," *Les Trois Harmonies* (Paris, 1845).

88. Alphonse Louise Constant. "Allégorie," in *Dictionnaire de la littérature chrétienne* (Paris, 1851), vol. 12 of *La Nouvelle Encyclopépide théologique*, translation here quoted from Thomas A. Williams, *Eliphas Lévi: Master of Occultism*, 1975, p. 45.

89. L'homme a dans son âme des sentiments innés, que les objets réels ne satisferont jamais, et c'est à ces sentiments que l'imagination du peintre et du poète sait donner une forme et une vie. Le premier des arts, la musique, qu'imite-t-il?

In Madame de Staël, *De l'Allemagne*. as quoted by Eugène Delacroix, in his Journal, 8 October 1822, and as cited by Mras, 1966, p. 42.

90. The themes of correspondences and synaesthesia are important in Baudelaire's discussion of Delacroix in *Curiosités Esthétiques*, and in his *Salon of 1859*.

91. Charles Baudelaire, "Richard Wagner and Tannhäuser in Paris," quoted in *The Painter of Modern Life and Other Essays* (London, 1965), p. 116: "What would be truly surprising would be to find that sound *could not* suggest color, that colours *could not* evoke the ideas of a melody."

92. Note especially the 35 issues of *La Revue wagnérienne*, published between 8 February 1885 and 11 November 1887. Writing in 1923, Dujardin described the profound connection between the Symbolists and Wagner; "La revue musicale," as quoted by Elga Duval, *Théodor de Wyzewa: Critic without a Country* (Paris, 1961), p. 31.

Wagner était l'un des maîtres du Symbolisme et on n'allait pas tarder a s'en apercevoir; sa conception de l'art, sa philosophie, sa formule même est à l'origine du Symbolisme et il était impossible d'aller au fond du Wagnérisme, sans y rencontrer le Symbolisme.

93. Richard Wagner, "Opera and Drama," in *Literary Works*, trans. W. A. Ellis, (London, 1899), vol. 2.

94. "La poésie, proche l'idée, est Musique par excellence ne consent pas d'infériorité." In Stéphane Mallarmé, "Variations sur sujet," 1945, p. 381. See also, "La Musique et les lettres," 1945, pp. 648 and 649. Consonant with Mallarmé's dream of "un mythe pur . . . le type innommé ou abstrait," the image of Orpheus does not figure in his works of poetry or prose, but rather, the essential meaning of the myth informs his works in a subliminal or nonspecific manner. Indeed, Mallarmé's exploration of mythic significance, without recourse to specific figural images (in this instance, the fascination with the orphic voice without representation of the traditional mythic figure of Orpheus), is comparable to the continued importance of the Symbolist orphic theme in the aesthetic realm of the abstractionists of the early twentieth century.

95. . . . servants de l'Evangile des Correspondances et de la Loi de l'Analogie, donneront selon les forces de leur esprit et la bonne foi de leur coeur, en de vastes synthèses, une explication mélodieuse et lumineuse des mystères glorifiés dans la Réalité des Fictions.

    In Charles Morice, "De la vérité et de la beauté," in *Pages choisies, vers et proses* (Paris, 1912), p. 71. See Rookmaaker, *Synthetist Art Theories* (Amsterdam, 1959), pp. 166 and 210–20, concerning the importance of the concept of synaesthesia in Morice's works generally.

96. See also Rookmaaker, *Gauguin and Nineteenth Century Art Theory* (Amsterdam, 1972), pp. 194–96 regarding Aurier's synthetist theories or p. 167 in *Synthetist Art Theories*. Rookmaaker cites Aurier's criticism of Salons of 1891 in *Mercure de France* 3 (1891): 37.

97. See Maurice Denis, *Nouvelles Théories*, "Le Symbolisme: sur l'art moderne et l'art sacré et l'art religieux moderne" (Paris, n.d.), pp. 175–76 and 189–91; Denis (p. 179) cites Aurier's entry in *Revue encyclopédique* 1, no. 32 (April 1892).

98. Concerning this theme of "audition colorée," see Andrew George Lehmann, *The Symbolist Movement in France, 1885–1895* (Oxford, 1950), especially p. 209 and his bibliography; Thomas Munro, "Suggestion and Symbolism in the Arts," *The Journal of Aesthetics and Art Criticism* 15, no. 2 (December 1956): 152–80; George L. Mauner, 1978, pp. 77–81, cites Alfred Binet's article, "Audition colorée," *Revue des deux mondes* (1 October 1892).

99. Edmond Astruc, "Jeunesse de Valère Bernard, discours de réception à l'Académie de Marseille," 1913, as quoted in the "Biographie," *Valère Bernard, "Symboliste" 1860–1936* (Marseille: Musée des Beaux Arts [July–December 1981]):

    Le Père-Castel avait déjà tenté un clavecin des couleurs et l'abbé Tardiff avait fait construire un orgue aux travées de lampes électriques de couleurs différents. Les danses de la Loïe Fuller en montèrent une application. Ensuite des Américains inventèrent un instrument composé de plaques de mica colorées. Un marseillais, M. Louche a réalisé un piano des couleurs en utilisant toute la gamme du clavier qui commande autant d'ampoules électriques de couleurs différentes, tons et demi-tons, mélanges en accords ou séparés en chants, avec la cadence adaptée à la symphonie, danse ou chant que l'on veut faire voir. Avec Valère Bernard, ni verres, ni écrans, ni liquides colorés. Son invention est basée sur la décomposition de lumière blanche et le jeu des interférences. Après des difficultés sans nombre venant de la source de la lumière, qui, en principe, aurait dû être le soleil, donnant à l'origine les couleurs du spectre, puis les difficultés venant des couleurs complémentaires qui, en se superposant, se décomposaient et redonnaient du blanc, il arriva enfin, avec neuf touches, à donner les septs couleurs de prisme, plus le blanc et un vert jaune, les pédales servant à intensifier ou diminuer la valeur des couleurs, à modeler l'harmonie complète. C'est la grande Art de la lumière, disait Valère-Bernard, le mécanisme donne la maîtrise parfaite des couleurs du spectre dans toute leur pureté.

100. The notion of original sin is crucial to the Orphic cults. Man contains both good and evil because he is born from the ashes of the Titans, the evil giants who had killed and devoured Dionysus-Zagreus, thus containing the god's divinity and their own evil natures.

101. "Parce que l'intelligence et la poésie sont bien mieux personnifiées dans ces époques tout entières d'art et d'imagination [l'antiquité païenne] que dans la bible toute de sentiment et de religiosité." In *L'Assembleur de rêves: Ecrits complets de Gustave Moreau*, ed. Pierre-Louis Mathieu (Fontfroide, 1984), p. 104.

102. Earlier scholarly literature on Moreau does not attempt to explain the curious juxtaposition of mythological legend and Christian story in the painting. Ary Renan, "Gustave Moreau" (Paris, 1900), barely makes reference to the work. The Abbé Loisel, *L'Inspiration chrétienne du peintre Gustave Moreau* (Paris, 1912), p. 7, in his general insistence on the importance of Christian themes in Moreau's oeuvre, seems intentionally to ignore the unorthodox inclusion of Orpheus in the context of Genesis. Pierre-Louis Mathieu, *Gustave Moreau* (Boston, 1976), p. 167, who cites the Bible and Hesiod's *Works and Days* as sources for the work, acknowledges the "syncretic order" of the composition. See also p. 168 concerning Moreau's positive appraisal of Michelangelo's inclusion of the Sibyls among the prophets of the Old Testament on the Sistine Ceiling, perhaps a specific inspiration for his own syncretism.

103. André Boulanger, *Orphée-Rapports de l'Orphisme et du Christianisme* (Paris, 1925), pp. 157–63. In the early Christian era, depictions of the crucifixion were considered violent and eschewed in favor of nonnarrative emblems and symbols (the cross, the lamb, the fish, etc.) or for idyllic scenes (Christ the Good Shepherd, David, Daniel between the Lions, Moses, Adam in Paradise).

104. This fresco was included in Antonio Bosio, *Roma sotteranea* (Rome, 1632), p. 239. It was frequently illustrated during the nineteenth century. It is number CLXXII bis, 645a in A. L. Millin's re-edition of the 1811 Galerie Mythique, *Nouvelle Galerie mythique* (Paris, 1859) which included a part of Guigniaut's

translation of Creuzer's *Symbolik* and a commentary on the relationship between art and religion by Alfred Maury; fig. 230 in René Ménard, *La Mythologie dans l'art ancien et moderne* (Paris, 1878); and fig. 35 in André Pératé, *L'Archéologie chrétienne* (Paris, 1892), p. 66.

105. "Cristo, il non favoloso Orfeo, veramente richiamo l'uomo dalla vita animalesca ad una vita ragionevole e gl'insegno la vita della virtù e della felicità." See P. R. Garucci, *Storia dell'arte cristiana* (Prato, 1873), vol. 2, p. 29, pl. 25.

106. See George L. Hersey, "Delacroix's Imagery in the Palais Bourbon Library," *Journal of the Warburg and Courtauld Institutes* 31 (1968): 383–403. See above, n. 35.

107. P. S. Ballanche, *Prolégomènes pour Orphée: Oeuvres complètes* (Paris, 1830), vol. 3., p. 136. See Moreau quotation cited in n. 101.

Chapter 3

1. See other works by Moreau, including *Orphée* (no. 566 catalogue Musée Gustave Moreau, 1974).

2. George de Forest Brush, an American who studied with Gérôme at the Ecole des Beaux Arts produced *Orpheus*, 1890, a rather ludicrous, even stolid image of the poet serenading a group of rabbits. Brush is best known for his Indian subjects and idealized treatments of family scenes. See Thieme-Becker, 5: 149; and *An American Perspective* (Washington: National Gallery of Art, 1982 [John Wilmerding, Linda Ayres, Earl A. Powell]), illus. p. 73.

3. Like de Forest Brush, Swan had studied with Gérôme, as well as with Bastien-Lepage, Dagnan-Bouveret, and the sculptor Fremiet. For basic biographical information see Thieme-Becker, 32: 337. See also, *Lord Leverhulme: A Great Edwardian Collector and Builder, Paintings—Sculpture—Ceramics—Furniture—Architecture* (London: Royal Academy of Arts, 12 April—25 May 1980), pp. 77–78. Apparently Swan also exhibited a silver statuette of Orpheus at the Royal Academy exhibition of 1895. On the basis of this sculpture, he reworked the 1894 painting, redated 1896. A bronze version of the statue is in the collection of the Manchester City Art Gallery. A contemporary of Swan, the noted British animal painter Briton Riviere, similarly used historical subjects, especially biblical subjects, as the excuse for elaborate naturalistic depictions of animals. Riviere's *Daniel in the Lion's Den* is an example of this historical-*animalier* painting. Riviere's 1874 *Apollo*, which depicts a figure seated at the foot of a tree, a variety of wild animals sprawled at his feet or approaching from every corner of the forest, follows so closely the traditional image of Orpheus taming the beasts that one is tempted to suggest an error in the title.

4. See Thieme-Becker, 32: 264. Styka was trained by his father, Jan Styka, as well as by Jean Jacques Henner. He was best known for his portraits of noted individuals including Tolstoy, Henner, Caruso, Shaliapin, Paderewski.

See also Louis Henri Foreau's *La Douleur d'Orphée* exhibited at the Salon of 1892. See Bénézit, vol. 4, p. 435 (illustrated in 1892 Salon catalogue). A gouache, watercolor, and pencil sketch is in the Louvre, Cabinet des Dessins. Foreau, primarily a landscapist, studied with J. Lefèbvre, Henry Lévy, L. O. Merson, and Harpignies. See chapter 6 concerning Lévy's *Death of Orpheus.*

Foreau's Orpheus declaims with a dramatic gesture heavenward, comparable to the stances of Orpheus in Moreau's *Vie de l'humanité,* Eugène Guillaume's Orpheus, or Rodin's *Orpheus* of 1892 (discussed in chapter 5). Eugene Guillaume, 1822–1905, who had studied with Pradier, was an academician of great prestige. He was named Directeur of the Ecole des Beaux Arts in 1864 and Directeur Général in 1879. His work consists of portraits and mythological subjects. A plaster sketch of *Orphée* is in the Louvre. A bronze version can be seen today on the roof of a building opposite St. Germain des Près in Paris.

5. De Groux was a member of L'Essor and Les XX until 1890. He shared a studio with Degouve de Nuncques. After 1892 he spent much of his time in Paris, leading a fairly isolated existence. He did not exhibit in the Rose + Croix Salons. His most famous work was *Christ Reviled,* 1888. Works such as *Lohengrin,* 1908, and *Siegfried,* as well as the frontispiece to Rémy de Gourmont's *Le Fantôme,* 1893, are evidence of his enthusiasm for Wagner. See Delevoy, *Symbolists and Symbolism* (New York, 1978); *Peintres de l'imaginaire: Symbolistes et Surréalistes Belges* (Paris: Galeries Nationales du Grand Palais, 4 February–8 April 1972); and *Il sacro e il profano* (Turin: Galleria Civica d'Arte Moderna, June–August 1969).

6. Fabry collaborated with Horta in the Hôtel Solvay, 1894, the Hôtel Aubecq, 1899, and the Maison Braecke, 1901. In 1905 (?) he collaborated with another Belgian Art Nouveau architect, Pierre Hankar, in La Hulpe, on the Villa of his friend, the sculptor Philippe Wolfers. Between 1905 and 1925 he executed works for the Hôtels de Villes of Saint-Gilles, Laeken, Woluwe-Saint Pierre, as well as six mosaics for the Musée de l'Art et de l'Histoire in Brussels in 1919. See *Peintres de l'imaginaire,* 1972, p. 55; *Horta* (Saint-Gilles, Bruxelles: Musée Horta, 1973); *Belgian Art 1880–1914* (Brooklyn, N.Y., 23 April–29 June 1980), p. 98.

7. *Le Poète, panneau décoratif,* was exhibited in 1895; *La poésie lyrique, panneau décoratif,* in 1898; and *Orphée* in 1899.

8. In *Pélerinage à l'Isle de Delos,* 1898, Collection Bertrand Fried, Paris, Orpheus is presented in his role as priest of Apollo, the sun-god, his music accompanying the dance of the vestal maidens on the island of Apollo's birth. Presumably, the statuesque figure with upraised arms, draped in red, standing at the center of the composition is the Delian Apollo himself. The pastoral scene, especially the dancing maidens, and also the artist's muted palette attest to the significant influence of Puvis de Chavannes. It is tempting to find also the impact of the Swiss Symbolist Hodler in Fabry's dramatic treatment of the mountains and sky, but especially in the peculiar gesture of Apollo. The solemn, ritualistic grandeur of the scene prompts comparison with Homeric hymns, invocations to Apollo. Hymn 21 proclaims, "And of you, the sweet-tongued minstrel, holding his high

pitched lyre, always sings, both first and last." See Hesiod, *The Homeric Hymns and Homerica*, English translation, Hugh G. Evelyn-White (Cambridge and London, 1959), p. 447, Homeric Hymn 21 "To Apollo," lines 3–4.

Hymn 3 is addressed to Delian Apollo:

> And you, O Lord Apollo, god of the silver bow, shooting afar, now walked on craggy Cynthus, and now kept wandering about the islands and the people in them. Many are your temples and wooded groves, and all peaks and towering bluffs of lofty mountains and rivers flowing to the sea are dear to you, Phoebus, yet in Delos do you most delight your heart; for there the long robed Ionians gather in your honour with their children and shy wives, mindful, they delight you with boxing and dancing and song, so often as they hold their gatherings. See ibid., Homeric Hymn 2 "To Delian Apollo," pp. 335–37, lines 141–65.

Callimachus' Hymn 4 apostrophizes the Isle of Delos itself: see Callimachus, *Hymns and Epigrams, Lycophron, Aratus* (Cambridge and London, 1955), p. 111, Hymn 4 "To Delos," lines 317–20.

9. The mural *War and Peace* is dedicated to Belgian heroism and also to the welcome offered by the British to Belgian refugees during World War I. Jean Delville and his family also fled to England (Scotland) during this period. See *Les Heures harmonieuses*, 1897, p. 198, in Delevoy; *Les Parques*, 1898, illus. no. 23; and *Les Gestes*, 1895, illus. no. 24 in *Les Peintres de l'imaginaire*, 1972.

10. Concerning the images of Blake and Fuseli, see *Peintres de l'imaginaire*, 1972, p. 24. See also Burne-Jones's *Merlin and Vivien*, 1870–74, illus. 19, Martin Harrison and Bill Waters, *Burne-Jones* (London, 1973).

11. *La Musique* and *Depths of the Sea* share the following characteristics: the accentuated musculature, the mermaid figure, the silent or muffled underwater environment, complete with minute details of shells. The tense exaggerated musculature is also apparent in Burne-Jones's *Car of Love*, 1870 (Harrison/Waters illus. 237) and *Wheel of Fortune*, ca. 1882, illus. 190. In addition, the female figures in Fabry's *Pelerinage to the Isle of Delos* may be compared to the dancers in Burne-Jones's *Lyric Poetry*.

12. An earlier work, a gouache, dated 1913, perhaps intended as a poster maquette uses the same composition.

13. See the Rodin drawing, *The Genius of Sculpture*, discussed in chapter 5, concerning the role of the hovering female figure in Rodin's works.

14. See Heinrich Voss, *Franz von Stuck, 1863–1928* (München, 1973), cat. no. 51/270, dated 1891; 572/269, dated ca. 1924. The paintings in the Music Room in the Villa Stuck date from 1897–98. See chapter 6 concerning von Stuck's images of Orpheus' death, Voss cat. nos. 44/268 and 53/186. In the 1891 version, Orpheus is portrayed as a muscular nude, his short cropped hair bound by a filet. His figure, articulated with dramatic chiaroscuro, is flanked by four animals. The

primitivizing, linear stylization with which the animals are depicted is consistent with von Stuck's art in 1891–92 and reflects specifically his interest in Greek red-figured vases. See, Voss, p. 39. The flatness of the composition is reinforced by the linear pattern formed by the curves of the scarf which entwines the poet's arms and billows out from his body, rhyming with the curved structure of the massive lyre as well as the thin arched neck of the flamingo. The compositional flatness and archaic stylization is further emphasized by the inclusion of the inscription "ORPHEUS."

15. See Fritz von Ostini, *Villa Franz Von Stuck* (Darmstadt, 1909), pp. 21 and 32, for photographs of the music room including the marble archaic statue of Diana placed directly below the image of Orpheus.

16. Voss, p. 30. For other subjects in the music room, see Voss cat. nos.: 185/118 (*Die Wippe*, 1898); 33/14 (*Belauschung*, 1890); 101/217 (Der Tanz, 1894); 192/218 (*Ringetanz*, 1899); 12/204 (*Neckerei*, ca. 1889).

17. The inscriptions read:

> Wenn Orpheus sang
> Dann kamen
> Die Thiere der Erde
> Die Vögel in der Luft
> Die Fische im Wasser
> und lauschten
>
> Der Mann der nicht Musik hat
> in sich selbst
> Den nicht die Eintracht
> süsser Töne rührt
> taugt zu Verrat zur Räuberei
> und Tücken
> Trau keinem solchen!
>
> Sieh wie die Himmelflur ist
> eingelegt mit Scheiben lichten
> Goldes
> Auch nicht der kleinste Kreis den
> du da siehst
> Der nicht im Schwung wie ein
> Engel singt.

From *The Merchant of Venice*, act 5, scene 1.

18. The importance of the harmony of the spheres was discussed in chapter 1. Charles de Tolnay, "The Music of the Universe," *The Journal of the Walters Art Gallery* 6 (1943): 83–104, illustrates a thirteenth-century miniature of the harmony of the spheres.

19. Charles Baudelaire, "Correspondances," *Les Fleurs du mal* (Paris, 1961), p. 13, line 1.

20. Ibid., line 8.

21. Ibid., line 2.

22. See also the title page for Jean Paul's *Ein Studenbuch fuer Seine Verehrer*, 1900 (published by and with an introduction by Stefan George und Karl Wolfskehl), in which the poet's elegant lyre is the dominant motif, silhouetted against a frieze of thin tree trunks and star-filled sky, reminiscent of the background in *Orpheus* (illus., p. 19). See Peg Weiss, *Vassily Kandinsky in Munich: The Formative Jugendstil Years* (Princeton, 1979), p. 85, concerning Lechter's 1900 mural designs for the Pallenberg Hall in the Cologne Arts and Crafts Museum. The central figure is Stefan George as a knight at the "mystical source."

23. This painting by Martin Brandenburg was very kindly brought to my attention by Mr. Hans Neef of Cologne.

24. See *Budapest, 1890–1919: L'Anima e le forme* (Milano: Electa, 1981), cat. 92. See also cat. no. 62, *Orpheus* by Karoly Ferenczy.

25. Coudray won the Rome prize in 1893 for a bas-relief of *Orpheus Entering the Underworld*. See Thieme-Becker, 7: 569.

26. See Thieme-Becker, 15: 379–80; *Plakate um 1900* (Darmstadt: Hessisches Landesmuseum, 1962), no. 49.
    The poet-musician is a dominant theme in Bourdelle's work. Note, for example, *The Dying Centaur*, 1911; *Sappho; Apollo*; the Orpheus frieze from the Théâtre des Champs Elysées, 1912; the Beethoven series. A small gouache entitled *The Genius of Beethoven* (pl. 7 in *Antoine Bourdelle* [Ottowa: National Gallery of Canada, and New York, 1961]) is comparable to a small pen and ink drawing in the Bourdelle Museum, Paris, which depicts the poet's face as a dark mask accented with a laurel wreath like a crown of fingerlike flames.

27. Concerning the flying muse figures, see *Puvis de Chavannes, 1824–1898* (Paris: Grand Palais, November 1976–February 1977, and Ottawa, National Gallery of Canada, March–May 1977 [Paris, 1976]); *The Dream*, 1883, cat. no. 160, here fig. 5.6; *Le Bois sacré*, 1884–89, cat. no. 174. These flying figures are also present in the Boston Public Library murals, 1895–96; *Physics*, as illustrated in Aimee Brown, "L'Allégorie réelle chez Pierre Puvis de Chavannes," *Gazette des beaux-arts*, ser. 6, vol. 89, 119e année (January 1977): 27–40, fig. 13. The winged muse assisting the poet is the central image of *Le Poète*, Puvis' frontispiece to *Interrupta*, ca. 1896, dedicated "A la mémoire de Paul Guigou," reproduced in *La Revue encyclopédique*, no. 262. This leitmotif of the flying muse in Puvis' work can ultimately be traced to Delacroix. The flying figures appear in Delacroix's *Daniel in the Lion's Den*, 1853; one of the pendentives as well as in the Hemicycle of Peace in the Library of the Deputies in the Palais Bourbon, 1838–47; in the Library in the Luxembourg Palace, 1840–46; as well as in *Christ in the Garden of*

Olives, 1826 (Robaut nos. 176, 177, 178) and *St. Jérôme* (Robaut no. 1102). Donald Rosenthal, in his discussion of Puvis, in *The Second Empire: Art in France under Napoleon III* (Philadelphia: Philadelphia Museum of Art, 1978), p. 347, mentions Puvis' adaptation of the flying figures from Delacroix. Puvis' interest in the myth of Orpheus may well stem from his teacher's treatment of the theme in the two libraries as well as in a painting of *Orpheus and Eurydice*. The close similarity between Delacroix's *Hesiod and the Muses* and Puvis' *Dream* reflects a shared approach to the themes of poetry and inspiration. Also, Puvis' interest in monumental mural paintings may well be inspired by Delacroix's large-scale public decorative cycles. Puvis' Boston Public Library murals may well be compared to Delacroix's works in the Palais Bourbon, in terms of themes and scope. As mentioned in chapter 1, Puvis' *Les Bûcherons* may be considered in the context of interpretations of the Ages of Man, treated in enormous complexity by Chenavard, Delacroix, and Moreau.

28. *La Muse du peintre*, ca. 1900, is in the Collection of Michel Perinet, Paris; *Sérénité*, 1898, is in the Collection of the Musée de Nantes. Other appropriate titles include *L'Inspiration* and *Bucolique*.

29. *Artistes de l'âme*, 1896, Paris, Théâtre de la Bodinière, checklist found in the Archives of the Atelier Osbert.

30. *Orphée*, 1902, oil on canvas, was brought to the author's attention by Mlle. Yolande Osbert, the artist's daughter. It is in the collection of a relative of Osbert, Mme. David, Paris. The work was painted for the marriage of Osbert's cousin. It is inscribed on the reverse: "A. Osbert 1902 20 fev." The stretcher is also inscribed in the artist's hand: "Orphée/24 février 1902, A. Osbert. no. 189." This work is unpublished and this constitutes the first mention of the myth of Orpheus in the context of Osbert's work.

31. See Corot's *Morning, Dance of the Nymphs*, 1859; *Dance of Nymphs*, 1860–65; *Souvenir de Montefontaine*, 1864, here fig. 3.21.

32. In Jean Leymarie, *Corot* (Geneva and New York, 1979), pp. 107–8.

33. See Alfred Robaut, *Corot, Catalogue raisonné et illustré* (Paris, 1965). Orpheus subjects include *Orphée charmant les fauves*, IV, n. 3198; *Orphée charme les humains*, II, n. 195; III, n. 1713; *Orphée entrainant Eurydice*, IV, n. 3197; *Orphée ramenant Eurydice*, Salon 1861, III, n. 1622; *Orphée salue la lumière*, III, n. 1634; *Orphée salue la lumière*, III, n. 1632; *Orphée salue la lumière*, IV, n. 2978.

34. Leymarie, 1979, p. 100.

35. The first six Osberts listed here were exhibited in the exhibition *Alphonse Osbert* (Paris: Galerie Coligny, 17 April–24 May 1980), cat. nos. 7, 8, 13, 18, 4, and 6, respectively. The last five works listed here were exhibited in the Osbert Atelier, *Hommage à Alphonse Osbert*, organized by Les Amis du Peintre Alphonse Osbert, 18 May–22 June 1974, numbered in the checklist 1, 6, 7, 9, and 25, respectively.

36. See chapter 5 for more about the theme of the psychological landscape in Symbolism. The important theme of synaesthesia discussed in chapter 2 will be explored further in chapter 7.

Chapter 4

1. Plato, "The Symposium," in *The Collected Dialogues*, ed. Edith Hamilton and Huntington Cairns, Bollingen Series 71 (Princeton, 1961), pp. 533–34, paragraph 179d. Ovid, *The Metamorphoses*, trans. Rolfe Humphries, 1960, book 10, pp. 234–36. Virgil, *Georgics*, trans. H. R. Fairclough (London and Cambridge, 1974), vol. 1, book 4, pp. 229–33.

2. The Gluck/Calzabigi opera was presented in Paris at the Académie Royale de Musique in 1774. Berlioz's version of the opera premiered in Paris in 1859 with Pauline Viardot-Garcia in the title role. It was revived at the Opéra Comique in 1899 and 1900.

    For Nadar's photographs of the Offenbach parody, see, *L'Atélier Nadar et l'art lyrique* (Paris: Direction des Musées de France, 1975–76), pp. 14, 29, 30. Gustave Doré apparently designed the costumes for the 1858 presentation of Offenbach's *Orphée aux enfers*. He also painted a version of the opera's final orgy scene. In this regard see Mary Tompkins Lewis, "Literature, Music and Cézanne's Early Subjects," p. 39, n. 3, in *Cézanne, The Early Years* (London: The Royal Academy, 1988). In regard to other works by Doré on the theme of Orpheus, see below, chapter 6, n. 5.

3. The 1808 submissions to the Salon by Le Boullenger and Mongez are clearly inspired by Ovid's text. In these works, the hero-poet, playing his giant lyre, addresses his plea to the enthroned Pluto and Persephone. The onlookers include the three Fates and Hermes. The shallow, stage-like space of these compositions is characteristic of the Neo-Classical period. The figures in each work are draped in classical garb. The differences between the two paintings are, in fact, minor. In Le Boullenger's work, the setting is a lotus-columned hall, while in Mongez's painting, the setting is an underground cavern with a columned passage visible only in the background to the right. In Le Boullenger's composition, Amor assists the poet strumming his cithara. In Mongez's painting the poet kneels, playing his tortoise-shell lyre without assistance. Le Boullenger portrays Hermes poised, awaiting his instructions. Mme. Mongez depicts Hermes already leading forth Eurydice at the left. She also includes an enchained Cerberus who snaps ferociously at the heels of the poet.

    Machard's 1865, prize-winning *Orphée aux enfers* is a Romantic transformation of this basic formula. The statuesque poet stands at the center of the composition, his right arm stretched out in eloquent supplication toward Pluto and Persephone who sit on a raised throne, arely visible in the general gloom. At the left, white-veiled Eurydice is led forward by Hermes. Emerging from the darkness at Orpheus' feet are the writhing bodies and agonized faces of the Shades.

4. Shelley, *Poetical Works*, ed. Thomas Hutchinson (London, 1970), pp. 628–30, lines 18–21. "Orpheus" was written in 1820; published by Dr. Garnett in 1862, *Relics of Shelley*; revised and enlarged by Rossetti, *Complete Poetical Works of P. B. Shelley*, 1870.

5. Ibid., lines 50–53.

6. The Graham piano (owned by William Graham) was designed in 1879–80 with grisaille decorations of the theme of Orpheus and Eurydice. See cat. no. 30 in *Fantastic Illustration and Design in Britain, 1850–1930* (Rhode Island School of Design, 1979).

7. See chapter 3, for discussion of Corot's Orpheus compositions.

8. Concerning clutching the garment as a symbol of death, see Karl Sittl, *Die Gebärden der Griechen und Römer* (Hildesheim/New York, 1970), reprint of Leipzig 1890 edition.

9. Fritz Novotny, *Painting and Sculpture in Europe, 1780–1880* (Harmondsworth, Middlesex: Penguin, 1960), p. 181.

10. See Herbert von Einem, "Anselm Feuerbach's *Orpheus und Eurydike*," *Wallraf-Richartz Jahrbuch* 36 (1974): 295–310, concerning the figure of Marsyas on Orpheus' lyre. See also *Anselm Feuerbach: 1829–1880, Gemälde und Zeichnungen* (München-Berlin, 1976), pp. 181–82. Feuerbach's painting echoes earlier neoclassical depictions of Orpheus and Eurydice. For instance, Angelica Kauffmann's depiction of the lovers' journey from the Underworld, though in a more delicate style and lighter emotional tenor, including a cupid lighting the way with a torch, nonetheless constitutes a very similar compositional prototype for the Feuerbach.

11. See below, chapter 5, for discussion of other works by Rodin.

12. Lord Leighton was a close friend of Browning, serving as a pallbearer at the poet's funeral in 1889. Earlier, in 1856, Leighton had submitted to the Royal Academy another painting with the theme of Orpheus, *The Triumph of Music, Orpheus by the Power of His Art, Redeems His Wife from Hades*, whereabouts now unknown.

13. Robert Browning, *The Complete Poetic and Dramatic Works* (Cambridge, 1895), p. 395, line 6.

14. Ibid., lines 6–8.

15. *A Victorian Anthology 1837–1895*, ed. Edmund Clarence Stedman (Boston and New York, 1895), p. 533.

16. Stephen Calloway, *Charles Ricketts: Subtle and Fantastic Decorator* (London, 1979), p. 70, cat. no. 76.

17. Ovid, *The Metamorphoses*, 1960, book 10, p. 236, lines 60–64.

18. Virgil, *Georgics*, 1974, vol. 1, book 4, p. 231.

19. Ovid, *Metamorphoses*, 1960, book 10, p. 236, lines 58–60.

20. Orpheus is included in two other contexts in Baudry's paintings in the Opéra. Orpheus' death at the hands of the Maenads is one of three compositions devoted to the dance. Also, Orpheus is included in the painting decorating the western end of the foyer devoted to the civilizing poets. Moreover, Orpheus is portrayed in the paintings by Delaunay which decorate the small room extending the east end of the foyer. Delaunay portrays Orpheus leading forth Eurydice attended by Hermes. Moreover, Orpheus and Eurydice are one of four mythological couples portrayed in the adjoining front foyer, in mosaics designed by Curzon and the Venetian, Salviati. (The other couples are Artemis and Endymion, Aurora and Cephalus, and Hermes and Psyche.) In addition see chapter 6 concerning Baudry's paintings.

Ludwig Thiersch's painting, *Orpheus and Eurydice*, ca. 1909, utilizes essentially the same compositional format as the Baudry. Thiersch's work, however, lacks the dynamism of Baudry's interpretation—the gestures are stripped of emotional truth, becoming instead empty melodramatic expressions. It is interesting to note the similarity of the paintings by Baudry and Thiersch to Lord Leighton's *The Return of Persephone*. See *Victorian High Renaissance* (The Minneapolis Institute of Arts, 1978), cat. no. 58. Another comparable work is Drolling's *Orpheus and Eurydice*, found in an engraving from René Ménard's *La Mythologie*, 1878.

Moreover, depictions of Apollo's beloved nymph, Daphne, who escapes from his grasp, metamorphosed into a bay tree, are often comparable to these interpretations of Eurydice slipping from the grasp of Orpheus. For instance, Chasseriau's 1846, *Apollo and Daphne*, Louvre, Paris, has even occasionally been incorrectly identified as a representation of Orpheus and Eurydice. An extremely similar composition can be found amidst the many drawings in the Gustave Moreau Museum. In this drawing, a nude woman seems to evaporate upward, out of the grasp of Moreau's familiar, haloed, lyre-bearing poet. The drawing is inscribed, *Orpheus and Eurydice*, but the transformation of the woman's feet into the roots of a tree, and also the branches and leaves which surround her head and body, clearly indicate some sort of conflation with the theme of Daphne and Apollo (MGM 1983, drawing #523). Paul Eugène Breton's 1902 marble sculpture, *Enlèvement d'Eurydice*, can be considered a variation of this basic formula. In this work, Orpheus is entirely deleted, as the focus turns to Hermes spiriting away the limp body of Eurydice. Breton, 1868–1933, was the student of Falguière, Margueste, and F. Charpentier. In a work by the American sculptor, Joseph Maxwell Miller, it is the poet who reaches desperately towards Eurydice, struggling against Hermes, who holds her limp body in his grasp. Maxwell Joseph Miller was a native of Baltimore who studied with Raoul Charles Verlet.

21. A similar composition is found in a drawing (MGM 1983, #97). Here the poet kneels over the outstretched body of his dead wife, his arms stretched upward. The swan hovers nearby. This is clearly a preparatory drawing for a small painting (MGM 1974, #272). Orpheus grieves in exactly the same pose, however, Eurydice is no longer included in the composition. The landscape is a desolate vista of greys and browns, hardly relieved by a faint suggestion of a thin, ghostly tree. See also MGM 1983, #259, entitled *Orpheus*, in which the couple is surrounded

by a group of rather concerned-looking animals. Orpheus' rather boyish face gazes questioningly. In drawing #259, inscribed with a partially illegible title, ". . . and Eurydice," Orpheus gazes longingly at Eurydice's face.

Apparently, Moreau's works include only one representation of Orpheus in Hades, a small drawing.

22. Concerning the notion of the "Wagnerian" landscape articulated by both Wyzewa and Schuré, see chapter 5.

23. La fable d'Orphée est tout un dogme, c'est une révélation des destinées sacerdotales, c'est un idéal nouveau issu du culte de la beauté. C'est déjà la régénération et la rédemption de l'amour. . . . Ainsi l'homme pur doit se créer une compagne, il doit l'élever l'élève à lui en se dévouant à elle, et en ne la convoitant pas. C'est en renonçant à l'objet de la passion qu'on mérite de posséder celui du véritable amour.

In Eliphas Lévi, *Histoire de la Magie* (Paris, 1860; rpt. La Roche-sur-Yon, Vendée, 1974), pp. 90 and 91.

24. "le courant magnétique," in Eliphas Lévi, *La Clef des grands mystères* (Paris, 1861), pp. 131–32. See also: Eliphas Lévi, *Fables et symboles*, vol. 1 of *La Philosophie occulte* (Paris, 1862), p. 293:

Nous représentons ici l'initié sous la figure d'un poète. En effet, poésie veut dire création et l'initié est un véritable créateur. Il donne la lumière et conserve la vie à ceux mêmes qui le persécutent, il ne se venge que par des bienfaits. Ses enchantements sont des chants en l'honneur de Dieu et de la nature.

25. "vision, clarté, épouse mystérieuse ou la science de la sagesse éternelle," in Charrot, *Dictionnaire des termes hermétiques*, Fonds Papus, Bibliothèque de Lyon, MS 5836. Entry entitled "Eurydice," in vol. 2.

26. Orphée descendant aux enfers chercher Eurydice. . . . C'est l'homme pur, se créant une compagne de son intelligence, c'est-à-dire, cherchant et étudiant le vrai science.

In ibid., "Orphée," in vol. 4.

27. "verge de sorcière qui devait être la baguette du mage," in ibid.

28. See Eliphas Lévi's *Histoire de la magie* (MS.13.388, in the Fonds Péladan, Bibliothèque de l'Arsenal, Paris, pp. 7–8) which presents Orpheus as mystic, initiate, or hierophant in a fashion similar to Lévi's entry in *La Clef des grands mystères*.

29. Edouard Schuré, *The Great Initiates*, trans. Red. Rothwell (London, 1913), p. 314.

30. Ibid., pp. 308–9.
31. "L'Evolution de la femme et de l'homme se rejoignant au-dessus de la vie passionnelle dans la vie héroïque, sous l'inspiration du poète," from Edouard Schuré, *Précurseurs et révoltés* (Paris, 1920), p. 367. See p. 332, where Schuré identifies Moreau with Orpheus: "Le jeune Moreau . . . auprès des orgies picturales de Delacroix, il demeurait pensif comme Orphée devant les rondes des Bacchantes."
32. Schuré, 1913, p. 318.
33. Edouard Schuré, *From Sphinx to Christ* (*L'Evolution divine*), trans. Eva Martin (Philadelphia, 1928), p. 208.
34. Schuré, 1913, p. 353. See also pp. 355–56, 360, 361, 362. Schuré significantly rewrites the traditional myth of Orpheus and Eurydice. Eurydice is the victim of the Thessalian, Aglaonice, priestess of evil Hecate. She is bewitched by a Bacchante into drinking a cup of poison. Eurydice is tempted by the promise of the knowledge of the mysteries, and, hence, is a victim of curiosity like Pandora or Psyche (p. 354). Orpheus' descent to retrieve Eurydice is unavailing. Yet, Schuré seems to diminish the importance of Orpheus' failure. The fateful glance is not mentioned at all. Rather, Eurydice appears in a dream to Orpheus, in order to reveal the Truth. She explains:

> For me thou hast braved the infernal regions, seeking me among the dead. Here I am at the call of thy voice; it is not in the bosom of the earth I inhabit, but rather the region of Erebus, the cone of Shade between earth and moon. Sorrowing like thyself, I continually whirl round and round in this limbo. If thou wilt deliver me, save Greece by giving her light. Then I, finding my wings once more, shall rise to the stars, and thou wilt find me again in the light of the Gods. Until then, I must move in a circle of grief and trouble.

Orpheus must accept the role of prophet, indeed, martyr to the true religion. He confronts the Bacchantes and Thracians, attempting to seduce them with his Apollonian music. At the incitation of Aglaonice, Orpheus is killed. Schuré's description of Orpheus' death resonates with biblical overtones: "Holding out his hands to his disciple, he said: 'I die, but the Gods live forever!'" Indeed, Orpheus' head continues to sing, even after death. "The Tradition of Orpheus, his science and mysteries, were there perpetuated and spread throughout all the temples of Jupiter and Apollo."

Schuré offers an explanation for his unusual version of the myth. He defends its authenticity and dismisses the more commonly accepted version as a later version, an apology on the part of Orpheus' murderers, the Thracians, after they did finally accept him as their prophet.

> At a later date the Thracians, converted to the religion of Orpheus, related that he had descended into hell to seek the soul of his spouse, and that the Bacchantes, jealous of his eternal love, had torn him to pieces, but that his

head, though flung into the Ebro [sic], and carried off by the stormy waves of the river, still uttered the plaintive moan: "Eurydice! Eurydice!"

In Alfred Maury's *La Magie et l'astrologie* (Paris, 1860; 1864 edition cited here), there is a possible explanation for Schuré's unusual association of Orpheus and the moon-goddess Hecate. Maury points out that, "Hecate joue en effet un grand rôle dans les poèmes orphiques" (p. 55, n. 1, citing Orph. *Argon.*, 974; Lith. 45, 47). Orpheus plays an important role in Maury's history of alchemy: "Orphée fut donné comme l'inventeur de l'alchimie et du grand oeuvre" (p. 65, n. 3 cites Fabric. *Biblioth. graec.* t. xii, p. 695).

35. See the discussion in chapter 1. See also *The Nag Hammadi Library in English*, James M. Robinson, ed. (San Francisco, 1977). See The Gospel of the Egyptians 3:2 and 4:2; The Concept of Our Great Power 6:4; The Paraphrase of Shem 7:1; The Second Treatise of the Great Seth 7:2; The Teachings of Silvanus 7:4; Melchizedek 9:1.

36. Apuleius, *The Golden Ass*, trans. Robert Graves (New York, 1951), books 4–6.

37. Concerning the theme of the forbidden object or action, see Joseph Campbell, *The Masks of God: Occidental Mythology* (Middlesex, England, 1964). Also, the 1732 Garth/Dryden translation of Ovid's *Metamorphoses* relates the story of the Shepherd turned to stone by Cerberus' glance; and the fable of Olenus and Lethaea who were transformed into stones (book 10, p. 2).

38. "Le côté sublime d'Orphée, sa force de concentration apollonienne," in Paul Diel, *Le Symbolisme dans la mythologie grecque* (Paris, 1966), p. 137.

39. "La multiplication dionysiaque des désirs, aux Ménades et, sur le plan concret, à la multitude des femmes secrètement desirées," in ibid., p. 137.

40. Ibid., p. 137.

41. La condition est symbolique: l'amour d'Orphée peut renaître, Eurydice peut revivre, uniquement si Orphée n'est plus animé que par le regret sublime transformé en joie de retrouver Eurydice.

    In ibid., p. 138.

42. Mais le regret sublime, l'amour regretté, n'a pas entièrement guéri Orphée. La débauche reste en lui sous forme de regret pervers. Son regard recherche des promesses pervers du subconscient qu'il doit quitter. Orphée cède à la tentation de se retourner; Eurydice disparaît à jamais.

    In ibid., p. 139.

43. Maurice Blanchot, *The Gaze of Orpheus*, trans. Lydia Davis, ed. P. A. Sitney (Barrytown, New York, 1981), p. 104.

44. Ibid., p. 99.

45. Ibid., pp. 99 and 100.

46. Ibid., p. 101.
47. Ibid., p. 102.
48. Ibid., p. 101.

Chapter 5

1. Percy Bysshe Shelley, *Selected Poetry and Prose* (New York, 1966), p. 138, line 366.
2. See chapter 4, n. 2, concerning the productions of Gluck's opera in the nineteenth century.
3. Dieu est cruel avec les artistes, comme l'oiseleur avec l'oiseau, il crève les yeux pour qu'ils chantent mieux. . . . En renonçant à toute joie après tant de pertes cruelles, je cède non seulement à un besoin impérieux de mon âme, mais je considère ce renoncement comme une offrande morale que j'apporte à ces chers êtres disparues, une preuve, un témoignage toujours sensible pour eux de ma fidélité profonde à leur souvenir. Sans cela quelle humiliation après avoir tant aimé de tant oublié. Et qu'on ne s'y trompe pas, après peu de temps de cette reprise à la vie, l'oublier est complet.

   Moreau, as quoted in Jean Paladilhe, *Gustave Moreau* (Paris, 1971), pp. 50–56.

4. Gustave Moreau Museum, Cahier rouge, handwritten notes by the artist, p. 65, entry dated 10 August 1897.
5. Other depictions of Saint Sebastian by Moreau include the following illustrated in Mathieu, *Gustave Moreau,* catalogue raisonné (Boston: New York Graphic Society, 1976): 114, 115, 120, 126, 165, 166, 167, 168, 326, 369. Another work, *Martyr* (Musée Gustave Moreau, *Catalogue* . . . [Paris, 1974], no. 46), portraying a figure slumped on a gnarled tree similarly resonates with both pagan and Christian symbolism. The subject of the martyr, Saint Sebastian, was especially popular in bronzes of the late Renaissance and Mannerist period.
6. "La grande voix des êtres et des choses est éteinte . . . le chantre sacré se tait pour toujours." Gustave Moreau Museum, Cahier rouge, p. 65.
7. L'âme est seule, elle a perdu tout ce qui était la splendeur, la force et la douceur, elle pleure sur elle-même, dans cet abandon de tout, dans sa solitude inconsolée, elle gémit et sa plainte lourde est le seul bruit humaine de cette solitude de mort. . . . Le Silence est partout, la lune apparaît au-dessus de l'édicule.

   In ibid., p. 65.

8. More conventional presentations of Orpheus and Eurydice include the following drawings: (Musée Gustave Moreau, 1983), nos. 97, 259, 519 (fig. 4.22 here), and a small oil (Musée Gustave Moreau, 1974), no. 272.

9. See chapters 3 and 4 concerning a discussion of Corot's paintings with the theme of Orpheus. Français briefly studied with Corot, as well as with Jean Gigoux. In this work, Français appears to exploit a genre which Corot had made popular.
10. Paul Mantz, "Salon de 1863," *Gazette des beaux-arts* 4 (1863): 40.
11. Seules les gouttes de rosée, tombant des fleurs d'eau, font leur bruit régulier et discret, ce bruit plein de mélancolie et de douceur, ce bruit de vie dans ce silence de mort.

    In Gustave Moreau Museum, Cahier rouge, handwritten notes by the artist, p. 65.
12. "grand sentiment poétique.... L'ensemble exhale un parfum virgilien," in Paul Mantz, 1863, p. 40.
13. Ici, nous voyons le monde d'en haut, par le côté de l'Esprit.... Devant tel tableau du maître, nous avons l'intuition d'un monde plus homogène, ou les éléments plus dociles et plus fluides revêteraient les formes et les couleurs de nos pensées. Le paysage joue ici un rôle analogue à celui de l'orchestre wagnérien. Par ses nuances et ses harmonies, il module les émotions du drame intérieur et les prolonge en arrière et en avant, dans un prodigieux au-delà du temps et de l'éspace.... C'est du centre vivant de l'âme qu'il crée son monde, c'est selon les lois de l'âme qu'il le modèle et qu'il l'achève. Son art mérite donc à tous égards le nom de peinture psychique.

    In Edouard Schuré, "La Peinture psychique et le symbolisme transcendant," in *Précurseurs et révoltés* (Paris, 1920), p. 340. This article originally appeared in *Revue de Paris* (1 December 1900): 587–622; *Précurseurs et révoltés* was originally published in 1904.
14. "ce bruit plein de mélancolie et de douceur," in Gustave Moreau Museum, Cahier rouge, p. 65
15. Gustave Moreau as quoted by Philippe Jullian, *The Symbolists* (Oxford and New York, 1973), p. 50.
16. A list of "psychological landscapes" from the 1890s might include Sérusier, *Melancholy*, ca. 1890; Maillol, *Prodigal Son*, ca. 1890; Osbert, *Reverie in Moonlight*, ca. 1890; Munch, *Separation*, ca. 1893; Aman-Jean, *Girl with Peacock*, 1895; De Gouve de Nuncques, *Night in Bruges*, 1897; Hodler, *The Chosen One*, 1893–94.
17. Alphonse Germain on Osbert, as quoted by Philippe Jullian, *The Symbolists*, p. 50.
18. Téodor de Wyzewa, "Salon de 1885," as quoted by Robert L. Delevoy, *Symbolists and Symbolism* (Geneva and New York, 1982), p. 47.

19. Téodor de Wyzewa, in Delevoy, ibid., p. 47.

20. C'est que les couleurs et les lignes, sous l'influence de l'habitude, sont également revêtu pour les âmes d'une valeur émotionnelle, indépendante des objets même qu'elles représentaient.

    In Téodor de Wyzewa, "Notes sur la peinture wagnérienne et le Salon de 1886," *La Revue wagnérienne* 2 (8 May 1886) (Geneva: Slatkine reprints, 1968, vols. 1–3 [1885–88]: 106).

21. Téodor de Wyzewa, "Notes de la musique wagnérienne (suite)," *La Revue wagnérienne* 8 (8 September 1886): 264–65 (Geneva: Slatkine reprints, 1968). Wyzewa praises Beethoven's emotionally powerful music: "Un quatuor de Beethoven nous suggère des émotions définies; mais le maître nous a laissé libre de choisir à ces émotions les causes, le siège, les accompagnements notionnels qui nous paraissent les plus propres" (p. 264).

22. La peinture émotionnelle, symphonique, doit reconnaître aujourd'hui pour maître Monsieur Puvis de Chavannes. . . . Le poète exemplaire de la peinture moderne.

    In Téodor de Wyzewa, "Notes sur la peinture wagnérienne et le Salon de 1886," pp. 110–11.

23. Other works by Puvis with the theme of Orpheus are discussed above in chapter 3. Extreme sadness or creative paralysis is the theme of the 1896 painting, *Le Poète, Orpheus or The Dream of The Poet*. The poet's lyre is abandoned on the ground. He stands limply, his shoulder supported by a winged muse who lifts his right arm as though to infuse it, once again, with creative energy, the strength to take up the lyre again. This image was used, as well, as the frontispiece for Paul Guigou's *Interrupta*. The catalogue entry in *Puvis de Chavannes* (Ottawa and Paris, 1976), mentions other related drawings but gives no provenance or bibliographical sources, cat. no. 163, p. 181.

24. Marius Vachon, *Puvis de Chavannes* (Paris, 1895).

25. For comparable lamentation poses see Delacroix's *Christ in the Garden of Olives*, 1826 (Robaut nos. 179–83) or Millet's *Hagar and Ishmael*, 1849.

26. See chapter 3 concerning Séon's priestly *Orpheus*. In addition, see chapter 6 for a discussion of the severed head in Séon's work. The Museum at Saint-Etienne has another drawing inscribed "à J. L. Majola" which might have been a study for the 1896 painting.

27. Corporéiser, par *les lignes*, un symbole dans un type amplifié à l'archétype; homogénéiser ce symbole, *au moyen des teintes*, avec le caractère d'un être ou mieux son substratum. . . . L'Idée que suscite un geste, *l'explétiver* par une concordance de directions linéaires *expressives*, et une dominante de colorations pertinent symboliques. . . .

In Alphonse Germain, "Un peintre idéaliste-idéiste—Symbolisme des teintes—Alexandre Séon," *L'Art et l'idée*, No. 2 (February 1892): 109–10.

28. Germain notes, "Toute uniforme division du ton nuisait à la structure des reliefs." See ibid., p. 108.

29. Tout monter au style, idéaliser tout. Le style, c'est, reconnaît-il avec Charles Blanc, "la vérité agrandie, simplifiée, dégagée de tous les détails insignifiants, rendue à son essence originelle, à son aspect typique." L'Idéal, il le comprends, selon la définition de J. Péladan, "toute idée sublimée, à son point suprême d'harmonie, d'intensité, de subtilité."

   In ibid., p. 109.

30. Ellen Fritz Clattenburg, *The Photographic Work of F. Holland Day* (Wellesley, College Museum, 21 February–24 March 1975); Charles Leslie, *Wilhelm von Gloeden: Photographer* (New York, 1977); Jean-Claude de Magny (preface), *Photographs of the Classical Male Nude: Baron Wilhelm von Gloeden* (New York, 1977); Margaret Florence Harker, *The Linked Ring—The Secession Movement in Photography in Britain, 1892–1910* (London, 1979); Gert Schiff, "The Sun of Taormina," *Print Collector's Newsletter* 9, no. 6 (January–February, 1979): 198–201; Estelle Jussim, *Slave to Beauty: The Eccentric Life and Controversial Career of F. Holland Day, Photographer, Publisher, Aesthete* (Boston, 1981). See also, the following numbers of *Camera Work*: 15, 23, 25.

31. Similarly, Day's *The Prodigal* (Jussim #54) may be compared to Puvis' *The Prodigal Son*, 1879. In addition, Day's *Nude Youth Standing on a Cliff*... bears comparison with Max Klinger's 1898 illustration for *Death II*, Bl. 8. cat. no. 284, illus. 266 in Philip von Zabein's *Max Klinger* (Hildesheim, 1984).

32. Though Estelle Jussim (pp. 175–78) cites an English critic's identification of the subject of Day's series as Orpheus, she nonetheless prefers to read these photographs as concerning Apollo. She cites Day's prolonged enthusiasm for Keats, specifically Keats' "Hymn to Apollo," as well as the impact of Poussin's *The Inspiration of the Poet*, on Keats' imagery. She cites Ian Jack, *Keats and the Mirror of Art* (Oxford, 1967). A recent Sotheby's, New York, sales catalogue included one of Day's photographs and identified the subject of the series as Orpheus.

33. Il a reçu les confidences d'Orphée, assisté à ses rêveries et à ses désespérances et les raconte dans ses oeuvres avec une simplicité lapidaire.

   In Charles Saunier, "Gazette d'Art," *La Revue blanche* 25 (1901): 304. Of course, one may also assume that Day would have been aware of Séon through his knowledge of Puvis. This prominent Bostonian could not help but be aware of Puvis' decorative scheme in the Boston Public Library, executed between 1891 and 1896.

34. See chapter 4 concerning Rodin's 1894 *Orpheus and Eurydice*, and below, chapter 6 concerning his *Orpheus and the Maenads*.

35. See Rosalyn Frankel Jamison, "Rodin's Humanization of the Muse," pp. 105–25, in *Rodin Rediscovered* (Washington: National Gallery of Art, 1981). Jamison analyzes Rodin's transformation of the relationship between poet and muse, from traditional formulas involving the bestowal of accolades, wreaths, palms, the granting of fame and glory—to the more ambiguous, indeed a quite private level of symbolism involving Rodin's perception of the anguished travail of creativity. She discusses Rodin's manipulation of various figural types: the burdened figure: *Caryatid*, ca. 1881, *I Am Beautiful*, 1880, *Meditation*, 1885; hovering figures: *Tragic Muse*, before 1885, *Sculptor and His Muse*, 1890, the monument to Victor Hugo, 1909. Rodin's emphasis, throughout, is on the cumbersome, anguished process of creation.

36. In the nineteenth century, the theme of the artist and his muse appears in works such as Ingres' *Portrait of Cherubini*; Delacroix's *Hesiod and the Muse*, 1838–47; Puvis' *The Dream* (fig. 5.6 here), 1883; and Henri Martin's *Orpheus* (fig. 3.18 here), ca. 1894. See Rodin's *The Poet and Love*, ca. 1896, in which the muse has only one wing and no head; or a bronze study for the Carrière monument in which the muse is similarly truncated, very different from the figure in the plaster for the monument in which the muse places a laurel wreath on the poet's head.

37. See Claudie Judrin, *Rodin et les écrivains de son temps* (Paris, 1976), p. 118. Judrin quotes the inscription, "Le poète et la muse. Prends ton luth poète, et me donne un baiser" from de Musset.

38. Jamison, in *Rodin Rediscovered*, p. 106.

39. A small relief from the lower right section of *The Gates of Hell*, which has been identified by Albert Elsen as God or a self-portrait, depicts a nude, bearded male, with a hand held to his forehead in contemplation. His ear is approached by a floating or crouching female nude, resembling somewhat *Iris, Messenger of the Gods*. See Albert E. Elsen, "The Gates of Hell; What They Are About and Something of Their History," *Rodin Rediscovered*, pp. 63–79. Note specifically p. 65, fig. 3.6.

40. Jamison, in *Rodin Rediscovered*, 1981, pp. 108–9, concerning Rodin's linking of erotic energy and creativity.

41. Je veille la beauté étendue comme une chère morte; elle est enfouie dans l'ombre; et, comme de l'eau, émerge quelque îlot de douces chairs. C'est la mélancolie des plus noirs tombeaux cette volupté couchée, tandis que les autres points du corps retournent au nocturne des fonds. Ah! Eurydice, je te retrouve et je repousse les ombres. Ah! est-elle parfaite cette forme que soutient la nuit, on dirait éternelle! Ah! Ces reflets de bronze! Cette forme rejouit mon coeur et mes yeux. Ah! ce corps échoué, enlisé dans l'ombre, dans ce bain d'ombre!

In Rodin's Album as quoted in Gustave Coquiot, Rodin à l'Hôtel de Biron et à Meudon (Paris, 1917), pp. 68–69. Also note on p. 75 Rodin's statement, "modeler l'ombre, c'est de faire surgir de pensées."

42. See Claudie Judrin, Rodin et les écrivains de son temps, 1976, pp. 41–42. Judrin's illustrations 33 and 34 similarly relate to this theme of the muse/burden.

Chapter 6

1. See chapter 1, for a discussion of the various explanations for Orpheus' death: destruction by Zeus' lightning; suicide; wasting away from sadness; or torn apart by the Maenads, enraged by his faithfulness to Eurydice's memory or by his seduction of their husbands into a homosexual cult.

2. Concerning Orpheus' position between Apollo and Dionysus, see chapter 1 as well as below in the present chapter.

3. Lévy's depiction of Orpheus' death is very similar to Euripides' description of Agave's attack on her son, Pentheus. See Euripides, The Bacchae, in Euripides, The Complete Greek Tragedies Series, vol. 5, ed. D. Grene and R. Lattimore, trans. Wm. Arrowsmith (Chicago, 1959), p. 204, lines 1122–37.

4. See chapter 4 for a discussion of the other Orpheus paintings in the Grand Foyer. Baudry received the commission for the decoration of the Grand Foyer in 1865 and devoted his energies to this enormous project for eight years. See G. Lacambre's entries, VI-2 and VI-3, pp. 250 and 251 and Arlette Serullaz's entry VII-4, p. 364, concerning Baudry in The Second Empire, Art in France under Napoleon III (The Philadelphia Museum of Art, 1978). Serullaz dates Baudry's drawing of Melpomene as ca. 1868. If, as Madame Lacambre indicates, Baudry began his preparations for the project with trips to Rome and London to study Michelangelo and Raphael (Bénézit dates those trips 1864 and 1868, respectively), Baudry's conception for his painting might well have been influenced by Lévy's popular 1866 Salon painting. Certainly, Baudry's finished work does not date until ca. 1870–71. Baudry's drawings for these works were exhibited at the Salon of 1882 and in 1886 at the exhibition at the Ecole des Beaux Arts.

5. Gustave Doré's painting of the Death of Orpheus, exhibited at the Salon in 1879 (no. 1027), also bears comparison to Lévy's and Baudry's earlier works. Note as well the similarity of the central motif in Bouguereau's 1884 Childhood of Bacchus, to Lévy's, Baudry's, and Doré's works. Also, note Charles Gleyre's Pentheus Pursued by Maenads (see New York: Grey Art Gallery, 1980 cat. no. 64), which investigates a related theme.

6. Camille Renard, Etude sur les peintures de Paul Baudry au Foyer du nouvel Opéra de Paris (1874); C. Ephrussi, Paul Baudry, sa vie et son oeuvre (Paris, 1887) (Ephrussi quotes Renard); E. About, Paul Baudry, peintures décoratives exécutées pour le foyer public de l'Opéra par Paul Baudry (Paris, 1874); E. About, Peintures décoratives du grand foyer de l'Opéra par Paul Baudry (Paris, 1876).

7. E. About, 1874, p. 7.

8. In addition, the two ends of the long room are decorated with (west) *Homer and the Poets of Antiquity*, and (east) *Parnassus with Apollo, the Graces and the Muses and Famous Composers*. This latter work included Meyerbeer, Rossini, Herold, Auber, Boieldieu, Méhul, Mozart, Beethoven, Gluck, Haydn, Rameau, Lulli as well as Charles Garnier, Ambroise Baudry and Paul Baudry himself. Also, the ceiling of the room is decorated with a large rectangular painting of *The Union of Melody and Harmony between Poetry and Glory*, flanked by two smaller circular paintings of (west) *Comedy* and (east) *Tragedy*. See chapter 4 concerning Delaunay's Orpheus and Eurydice in one of the three panels by that artist in the small chamber beyond the imposingly ornate Carrière-Belleuse fireplace at the east end of the grand foyer. The other works portray the zodiac, Apollo receiving the lyre, and Amphion. The west end is decorated with paintings by Barrias of the Olympian gods and pastoral and dramatic poetry.

9. See chapter 5.

10. Mossa produced Symbolist works until ca. 1919. The death of his mother and the breakup of his marriage in that year apparently provided him with some sort of psychological release which, in turn, stripped his works of their intensity. His work of the next fifty years or so is decidedly banal in contrast to his earlier production. See Jean-Roger Soubiran, *G. A. Mossa et les symboles* (Nice, 1978).

11. In *L'Invitation au voyage*, 1907, Mossa identifies himself with an ideal poet, an amalgam of Baudelaire's poet and Goethe's Werther.

12. Ary Renan, *Gustave Moreau* (Paris, 1900), chapter 7, pp. 99ff.

13. See Paul de Saint-Victor, "Le Salon de 1869," *La Presse* (1869); Ary Renan, 1900, pp. 88 and 74; and Henry Marcel, *La Peinture française aux XIXeme siècle* (Paris: A. Picard & Kahn Ed., 1906), p. 252. Moreau may well have been familiar with Louis Ménard's epic poem, *Prométhée délivré*, 1843, or Quinet's *Prométhée*. In this regard, see Donald Charlton, *Secular Religions in France 1815–70* (London/New York, 1963) and Henri Peyre, *Louis Ménard* (New Haven/London, 1932).

14. The partially indecipherable drawing is inscribed: "Mort Orphée pleuré par les [muses?]."

15. Note the following related works in the Musée Moreau: Musée Gustave Moreau, *Catalogue des dessins . . .*, 1983, *La Douleur d'Orphée*, no. 339, *La Douleur d'Orphée*, no. 505, and *Orphée*, no. 635. In addition see the following works which relate to the lyre-bearing figure: Musée Moreau, 1983, *Orphée*, no. 634; and Musée Moreau, *Catalogue . . .*, 1974, *Orphée*, no. 162; *Orphée*, no. 1001; and *Sans titre*, no. 1135.

Ary Renan, 1900, p. 100, acknowledges the importance of the image of Orpheus in Moreau's work and frames it within the context of Orpheus' significance in early Christian art: "C'est surtout Orphée . . . rappelons nous que les premiers

Chrétiens l'adoptèrent comme image messianique." Moreau, through his studies of the ancient mystery cults, would certainly have been aware of the profound parallels between Orphism and Christianity. (To summarize these parallels, discussed at length in chapter 1: the son of god [Christ, Zagreus-Dionysus], who experiences a violent death, only to be reborn or resurrected. The members of these religious communities are initiates who share a belief in original sin, the duality of body and soul, good and evil, a concept of afterlife and rebirth. There is, of course, a compelling parallel between the Christian sacrament of the Eucharist, and the Dionysian omophagia, by which man partakes of the divine.)

There is an interesting image from the Early Christian period (though probably not one which Moreau would have known), reflecting the religious syncretism of that era, which brings together the images of the Orphic god Dionysus and Christ. The cylinder seal from the third century depicts a crucified figure surmounted by seven stars and a silver moon and labeled Orpheus-Bakkikos. This image may have been produced by a newly converted Christian, and is hence one of the first images of the crucifixion; or, the seal may be a pagan image referring to an obscure tradition of the martyrdom of the orphic god himself, or his enemy Lycurgos, or, of course, Orpheus. In this regard see Robert Eisler, *Orphisch-dionysische Mysteriengedanken in der christlichen Antike* (Hildesheim, 1966), pp. 334ff., illus. p. 338.

The apocalyptic vision in the study for Moreau's last painting, *Les Lyres mortes* (Musée Moreau, 1983, no.153) may be compared to the theories of degenerative cycles of history of Ballanche and Chenavard, specifically to Chenavard's last painting, *The Divine Tragedy*.

16. The caricaturist Cham printed a satirical commentary: "Il n'ya pas qu'Orphée pour avoir perdu la tête et ce pauvre M. Moreau donc! Espérons qu'on la lui retrouvera aussi," Cham, *Salon de 1866 photographié par Cham* (Paris, 1866), p. 4.

17. The chronicler in *L'Artiste* stressed the archaeological accuracy of Moreau's work: "Parmi les peintres qui se sont révélés depuis quelques années, Gustave Moreau est certes le plus original, le plus savant, le plus styliste. Il a traversé la Renaissance, il a traversé le Moyen Age: mais il s'est arrêté dans l'Antiquité, les poèmes qu'il nous a rapportés sont des chefs-d'oeuvre de sentiment." See Marc de Montifaud, "Salon de 1866 I and 2," *L'Artiste* (15 May 1866): 169–78; (15 June 1866): 196–205; The work was illustrated in an engraving by A. Lamy in the 1 January 1867 issue, opposite p. 66. Also note the entry in 15 August 1866, p. 264 of *L'Artiste*, describing the engraving of Lévy's *Orphée:*

> La mort d'Orphée
> Il n'y a de jeune que ce qui a vieilli, dit le poète anglais Chaucer. Rien n'est plus jeune qu'Orphée; les poètes, les peintres, les sculpteurs rejeunissent tous les jours Orphée. La musique elle-même oublie Apollin pour Orphée, et les quarante mille chanteurs populaires de la France s'appellent des orphéonistes. On a beau peindre la mort d'Orphée, le dieu n'est pas mort: frappez seulement son nom, la jeunesse en sortira. Elle en sortira avec toutes les autres muses et avec le talent, si c'est M. Lévy qui a fait le tableau,

comme il a fait celui-ci. M. Lévy a été à Rome: on dirait qu'il revient de la Thrace; il a vu Orphée, Linus et les muses.

In contrast, Léon Scribe, in the official illustrated catalogue of the World Exposition of 1867, objects to this archaeological quality: "Wenn schon eine Fälschung, dann lieber eine, die nicht im Widerspruch zur Archaeologie steht. . . . Es ist ein schwerer Irrtum, im Jahre 1867 so zu tun, als könnte man noch auf ehrliche Weise zu der naiven Manier der Meister von 1467 kommen," as quoted by Hahlbrock, *Gustave Moreau* (Berlin, 1976).

18. "Je demande instamment qu'on me désigne au Salon un paysage plus grandiose, un ciel plus féerique que celui de *l'Orphée*, une figure mieux rythmée que celle de la jeune fille et une plus belle tête que celle de l'amant d'Eurydice dans le même tableau . . . oeuvres de peintre et non d'écrivain." Ernest Chesneau, review of the 1867 Exposition Universelle, in *Le Constitutionel*, 10 September 1867.

19. "Ein Hauch von Mystizismus umschwebt dieses Bild, wie er immer gefällt, selbst wenn er aus zweiter Hand kommt," Léon Scribe, in the official catalogue of the Exposition Universelle (Paris, 1867); as quoted by Hahlbrock, *Gustave Moreau* (Berlin, 1976).

20. Théophile Gautier in *Le Moniteur universel*, 15 May 1866.

21. The poem by Armand Silvestre appeared in *L'Artiste*, No. 5 (February 1867): 114:

> La mort d'Orphée
> C'est ta mort que j'envie, o doux fils de Linus,
> Quand les vierges de Thrace aux crinières tragiques
> Sous leurs pieds bondissants, comme aux fêtes bacchiques,
> Effroyable vendange! écrasaient des flammes nues!
>
> Quand, aux chansons du cuivre, effroyable vendange!
> Elles foulaient ton coeur et que leurs beaux pieds blancs
> Buvaient, sur ta poitrine, une rosée étrange;
> Et que ta chairs *volait* sous les thyrses sanglants!
>
> Le regret te vint-il des chastes promenades
> Ou ta lyre endormait l'écho silencieux?
> —A quoi bon de tes chants heurtés des creux maussades?
>
> Mieux vaut jeter son âme aux désirs furieux,
> Tendre sa gorge nue aux ongles des Menades,
> Et faire de son corps la pâture des Dieux!

22. Où se passe la légende d'Orphée? En Thrace, en Italie ou partout à la fois? S'agit-il même encore d'Orphée? N'est-ce pas l'image du poète de tous les pays et de tous les temps, martyrisé, incompris, et qu'on vénère après sa mort?

In Paul LePrieur, "Gustave Moreau et son oeuvre," *L'Artiste* 59, no. 1 (1889): 180.

23. Raymond Bouyer, "Les Artistes aux Salons de 1897," L'Artiste (1897): 349:

> Oeuvre unique qui, après les Plafonds herculéans d'un Delacroix, son instigateur, a su faire resplendir une grande âme en un petit cadre; poème orphique, aux chants diversifiés, qui greffe l'érudition sur le sentiment, qui rechauffe l'archéologie par la couleur, qui incarne l'intellectualité dans la forme, poème consciencieux et conscient que traverse un grand émoi: l'âme actuelle, ou plutôt l'éternel frisson de la vie y palpite obscurement sous la cuirasse limpide des pierres précieuses; le symbole est sans date, comme le coeur. Gustave Moreau sait unir la moderne inquiétude à la fable antique.

24. *La Jeune fille à la tête d'Orphée* de M. Gustave Moreau. Conception digne des larmes des meilleurs de ce temps-ci. Technique s'arrêtant au respect de la toile ou même du panneau de bois. Compositions moins hiératique qu'immortellement inébranlable dans la dignité de sa tenue. Ton de Léonard et sa suprême distinction par un pinceau du temps d'Ingres, mais modèle d'amour et en décor d'émail stagnant et corse d'ailleurs par tous les tons décoratifs, figés (niellés, historiés, damasquinés) en une dureté autorisée des chers Primitifs. Mais, je vous en prie! nulle gravure ne donnera le profil de cette immortelle jeune fille, cette Cordélia si jeune de tissus et d'inviole, si mure d'expression compatissante et supérieure.

Jules Laforgue, "A propos de toiles, ça et là," *Le Symboliste* (ed. Gustave Kahn), no. 4 (30 October–6 November 1886).

25. Lines 5–8 of "La Destinée," published in *La Revue indépendante* 2 (November 1884–April 1885): 393, is quoted in its entirety below. Lorrain, the author of *M. de Phocas*, used a reproduction of Moreau's painting as the frontispiece for his first book of poetry, *Le Sang des Dieux*, 1882. In regard to Lorrain's general fascination with the severed head, one tale relates that he kept a wax model of a severed head on his table, which may have inspired Beardsley's *Salome*. See Robert L. Delevoy, *Symbolists and Symbolism* (New York, 1982), p. 142.

> La Destinée pour G.M.
> C'était au pied creusé d'une haute falaise
> En bloc pale, ou saignaient, lavés par l'eau de mer,
> De longs coraux de pourpre et des roses de chair.
> A l'horizon sinistre ardait un ciel de braise.
>
> Apre lieu. Pas un cri, pas un oiseau dans l'air
> Un éternel couchant au loin sur le flot rouge
> Et sur le sable, au pied du roc, où rien ne bouge.
> Les roses de sel gemme et de corail amer.
>
> Portant dans ses bras nus une tête coupée,
> Une forme bleuâtre et d'ombre enveloppée,
> Surgit, flotte et m'aborde auprès des flots sanglants.
> Morne offrande, elle pose entre mes doigts tremblants

>   La tête humide encore des baisers de l'épée,
>   Et c'est moi que je trouve au fond de ces yeux blancs.

26. Une mystérieuse concordance, cependant, fait sympathiser la nature à ce drame silencieux, à ces froides obsèques. Un demi-jour opalin éclaire ces confins du monde; un sommeil subtil, une stagnation de malaria engourdissent les choses; on entend seulement une petite flûte, un refrain ironique, modulé par des bergers, là-bas, sur une roche de l'Ebre.

    In Ary Renan, 1900, p. 58ff.

27. Pour le peintre, pour nous, pour la tradition, Orphée est la première et la grande victime poétique, l'apôtre inspiré qui mûra la face du monde. Ce qui meurt avec lui, c'est l'art civilisateur.

    In ibid., p. 58.

28. La vierge a frémi de tendresse pour le poète déchiré par les Bacchantes. Ainsi la sympathie est pour l'âme féminine la première révélation de l'Ame Universelle. Cette émotion compréhensive la fait vivre déjà d'une vie nouvelle, plus vaste, plus haute et plus profonde. L'océan des passions gronde encore sous ses pieds, mais un autre océan l'appelle, celui des douleurs humaines, qu'elle s'y jette, qu'elle s'y plonge à coeur perdu en s'oubliant elle-même et elle renaîtra métamorphosée. Le renoncement passif est le suprême vertu. Ainsi la femme élue et s'élisant elle-même pénètre au stade héroïque et surhumaine.

    In Edouard Schuré, *Les Précurseurs et révoltés* (Paris, 1904), pp. 350–51 (Section on Moreau originally published in *La Revue de Paris*, [1 December 1900]: 587–622).

29. Lorrain, "La Destinée," lines 12–14, quoted above in n. 25.

30. See below, concerning Herbert Marcuse's analysis of the myths of Orpheus and Narcissus.

31. ... elle emporte à pas lents son doux fardeau funèbre, et de sa paupière abaissée tombe un regard indécis, humide à peine d'ignorante songerie, chargé d'une tiédeur discrète où l'âme dort. Et, plutôt que la sienne, c'est bien notre melancolie qui déborde, toute notre compassion inexprimable qui s'anime et qui promène en les berçant les premières réliques d'un culte indéfini.

    In Ary Renan, 1900, p. 56.

32. Nous allons simplement, comme une femme portant la tête morte d'Orphée, devant *La Femme portant la tête d'Orphée* et nous voyons dans cette tête d'Orphée quelque chose qui nous regarde, la pensée de Gustave Moreau peinte sur cette toile, qui nous regarde de ces beaux yeux d'aveugle que sont les couleurs pensées.

    Marcel Proust, "Notes sur le monde mystérieux de Gustave Moreau," ca. 1898–1900, in *Contre Sainte-Beuve* (Paris, 1971), p. 671. In addition, Proust writes:

> C'est ainsi que les poètes ne meurent pas tout entiers et que leur âme véritable, cette âme, la plus intérieure qui était la seule ou ils se sentissent eux-mêmes, nous est dans une certaine mesure gardée. Nous croyions le poète mort, nous allions faire un pélérinage au Luxembourg comme on va simplement devant une tombe.

Proust also alludes to the Moreau painting in an autographed dedication in one of twelve deluxe printings of *Du côté de chez Swann* by Grasset in 1913:

> A. M. René Blum
> Cher René, je veux que vous receviez le premier exemplaire un peu élégant que m'a adressé Grasset. Ainsi vous revient le livre que vous lui aviez apporté, avec ce geste si noble, consacré par un grand artiste, et qui portait la tête d'Orphée.

33. André Breton, "Gustave Moreau," in *Le Surréalisme et la Peinture* (Paris, 1965).

34. It has been suggested that Moreau's androgynous hero is a reflection of his own latent homosexuality: See G. Schiff, *Die seltsame Welt des Malers Gustave Moreau* (Zurich: Du Atlantis, 1965). See also Françoise Cachin, "M. Vénus et l'Ange Sodom—l'Androgyne au temps de Gustave Moreau," *Nouvelle Revue de psychanalyse* 7 (Spring 1973): 65. See for example, Valdina de Koenisgberg, "Gustave Moreau's 'The Young Man and Death': The Image of the Woman as the Femme Fatale" (Qualifying paper for M.A., New York University, Institute of Fine Arts, 1981).

35. Eliphas Lévi, *The History of Magic,* trans. Arthur Edward Waite (New York, 1973), p. 89.

36. Musée Gustave Moreau, *Catalogue* . . . (Paris, 1974), no. 726.

37. See cat. no. 53 in Jean Roger Soubiran, *Valère Bernard, "Symboliste" 1860–1936* (Marseille: Musée des Beaux-Arts, July–December 1981). In this entry, Soubiran quotes M. Penchinat at Valère Bernard's reception into the Académie of Marseille on 22 March 1903. Penchinat notes the peculiar facial expression of Valère Bernard's Orpheus:

> Contrairement à la verité physiologique, le masque qu'a taillé votre ciseau n'a pas repris la sérénité que la mort imprime toujours. Deux plis verticaux persistent sur l'adorable figure, comme si la douleur morale d'avoir succombé dans le débat pour l'idéal contre l'ivresse grossière l'avait suivi au-delà du trépas. Là, le symbole est tellement clair, tellement expressif qu'il se traduit de lui-même. La matière et la force brutale seront toujours vaincues, même après des apparences de victoire: Prométhée est enchaîné, Orphée mis en morceaux, mais le feu bien-faisant et pour jamais dérobé au despote céleste, et quand le poète a chanté son dernier vers, l'art et la poésie planent sur son cadavre, invincibles parce qu'ils sont immortels.

38. The frontispiece of "L'Androgyne" (part 8 of *L'Ethopée* or *La Décadence latine*) consists of a head with eyes and mouth wide open, floating in the sky over a

rocky, sea-lashed cliff, typical of Séon's Isle de Brehat landscapes discussed in chapter 5. The severed head is the leitmotif in Séon's illustrations for part 4 of *L'Effort*, Paris, 1899, "La Fin du monde " (the story of the artist-martyr in the midst of the cataclysmic destruction of the world). This book also contains the following sections: part 1, La Madone—L'Effort est une douleur, lithographs by Alex. Lunois; part 2, L'Antéchrist—La Compréhension des hommes n'est pas la récompense de l'effort, illustrations by Eugène Courboin; part 3, L'Immortalité— Le Souvenir des hommes n'est pas la récompense de l'effort. Illustrations by Carlos Schwabe.

39. See Sven Sandstrom, *Le Monde imaginaire d'Odilon Redon* (Lund/New York, 1955), pp. 47–48.

40. Concerning Téodor de Wyzewa's notion of the psychological landscape see chapter 5, n. 19ff. See as well *Closed Eyes*, 1890, in which the amorphous watery environment serves to intensify the pensive, introverted expression. See Brooks Adams, "The Poetics of Odilon Redon's Closed Eyes," *Arts Magazine* (January 1980): 130–34. Fernand Khnopff's *Mon Coeur pleure d'autrefois*, 1889, warrants discussion as it transforms a watery landscape into a reflective mirror, the focus for narcissistic self-absorption. See Jeffrey W. Howe, *The Symbolist Art of Ferdinand Khnopff* (Ann Arbor, Mich.: UMI Research Press, 1979), chapter 6.

41. Herbert Marcuse, *Eros and Civilization* (New York, 1955), p. 154. See in entirety, chapter 8, "The Images of Orpheus and Narcissus," pp. 144–56.

42. Ibid., pp. 150–51 and 156.

43. Ibid., p. 153, quoting Freud, *Civilization and Its Discontents*, pp. 13 and 14. (Marcuse's italics.)

44. Ibid., pp. 151–52, n. 14, citing Friedrich Wieseler, *Narkissos: Eine kunstmythologische Abhandlung* (Göttingen, 1856), p. 89; Marcuse also cites Erwin Rhode, *Psyche* (Freiburg, 1898); Otto Kern, *Orpheus* (Berlin, 1920); and Ivan M. Linforth, *The Arts of Orpheus* (New York, 1973). Note also the prominence of the theme of Narcissus in the works of Gide and Valéry.

45. See chapter 5 and also Margaret Harker, *The Linked Ring: The Secession Movement in Photography in Britain, 1892–1910* (London, 1979).

46. Odilon Redon, *A soi-même* (Paris, 1922), p. 88 ("O mer, o grande amie!") and p. 11. Brooks Adams, 1980, pp. 130–34, in regard to *Closed Eyes*, posits a connection between Redon's water imagery, his fantasies about his own birth and that of his son, with a psychological rebirth in release from depression and an artistic renewal in his exploration of color ca. 1890.

47. A few specific examples from these series include "Blossoming," from *In Dream* (1879), Hobbs, *Odilon Redon* (Boston, 1977), illus. 19, p. 29; "When life was awakened in the depths of Obscure Matter," from *Origins* (1883), Hobbs, illus. 25, p. 43; "The Marsh Flower, human and sad head," from *Homage to Goya* (1885), Hobbs, illus. 29, p. 47; "The chimera looked at everything with terror,"

346   Notes for Chapter 6

from *Night* (1886), Hobbs, illus. 33, p. 51; "The sinister command of the spectre is fulfilled, the dream has ended in death," from *The Juror* (1887), Hobbs, illus. 41, p. 63; "Next there appears a curious being having a man's head on a fish's body" from the 1888 edition of Flaubert's *Temptation of Saint Anthony*, Hobbs, illus. 47, p. 68; "Oannes: I, the 1st consciousness in chaos, rose from the abyss to harder matter, to determine forms," from the 1896 edition of Flaubert's *Temptation of Saint Anthony*, Hobbs, illus. 67, p. 105; "A long Chrysalis, the color of blood," from *To Gustave Flaubert* (1889), Hobbs, illus. 66, p. 104; "The beasts of the sea, round like water-skins," from the 1896 edition of Flaubert's *Temptation of Saint Anthony*, Hobbs, illus. 68, p. 106; "And then fell a great star from heaven, burning as it were a lamp," from the *Apocalypse of Saint John* (1899), Hobbs, illus. 87, p. 127.

48. Verhaeren, "The Idol," is a specific source for Redon's transformation of cliff into human face. See Hobbs, p. 61, citing a letter of 3 February 1887; Ari Redon, *Lettres de Gauguin, Gide, Huysmans, Jammes, Mallarmé, Verhaeren . . . à Odilon Redon* (Paris, 1960), p. 170. Hobbs, p. 65, also suggests the impact of Gilkin's, "Le Preneur des rats." See as well Rosaline Bacou, *Odilon Redon* (Geneva, 1956), vol. 1, pp. 100ff, concerning Iwan Gilkin's "Fleurs humaines" as a source for Redon's flower-human imagery.

49. Jerome Viola, "Redon, Darwin, and the Ascent of Man," *Marsyas* 11 (1962–64): 42–57 (derived from Masters thesis, New York University, Institute of Fine Arts, June 1961).

50. Clavaud's microscopic studies may have been the inspiration for Redon's images of life emerging from primeval, swirling waters. See Odilon Redon, 1922, pp. 19ff; See also Redon's 18 July 1894 and 2 January 1909 letters to Bonger, in *Lettres d'Odilon Redon, 1878–1916* (Paris and Brussels, 1923), pp. 20ff and 84. Odilon Redon, 1922, p. 28, concerning the association of ideas and forms. In contrast, Redon's frontispiece for André Mellerio's essay *L'Art idéaliste*, 1896, seems to oppose the spiritual and the physical. Here the severed head, the brow, as usual, furrowed with care and anxiety, is surrounded by a thick black worm-like creature. The worm coils threateningly around the head and neck as though strangling it. Two tiny eyes peer out with manic intensity; small black fingers touch the skull, as though the creature prepares to devour the head. This image is not unlike *Chimera*, 1902 (Hobbs, 118), in which a closed-eyed figure whose visage resembles that of Christ is surrounded by a coiling serpent or worm. See Robert Goldwater, *Symbolism* (New York, 1979), pp. 120–23.

51. For example note Redon's *Buddha*, pastel, ca. 1905; Hobbs; color 5, p. 137; entitled *Buddha*, with a caption from Flaubert: "I was taken to schools. I knew more than the scholars." Hobbs, illus. 64, p. 103; *Cyclops*, 1898–1900, Hobbs, illus. 90, p. 132; *The Chariot of Apollo*, 1909, Hobbs, illus. 92, p. 134; *Red Sphinx*, 1910–12, Hobbs, color 4, p. 96; *Pandora*, ca. 1910, Hobbs, color 6, p. 140; *Angel and Demon*, ca. 1875, Hobbs, illus. 10, p. 20; *The Sacred Heart*, ca. 1895, Hobbs, illus. 93, p. 135; *Saint Sebastian*, 1910, Hobbs, illus. 91, p. 133; *Druid Priestess*,

1891, Hobbs, illus. 57, p. 90; *Parsifal*, 1892, Hobbs, illus. 34, p. 53; *Brunhilde*, 1885, Hobbs, illus. 35, p. 53. Redon's syncretism is especially clear in the charcoal and pastel, *Mystic Knight or Oedipus and the Sphinx*, Hobbs, illus. 56, p. 87; begun as early as 1869 but completed only in 1890, and exhibited in the spring of 1893 at the fifth exhibition of the Peintres-Graveurs. This work presents an extremely ambiguous image which merges the story of Oedipus with that of Salome and Saint John the Baptist. Or perhaps, Redon concocts a narrative inspired by Moreau's influential *Young Thracian Woman Carrying the Head of Orpheus*, 1866. This hermetic symbolism was championed by the Rosicrucian and mystical adherents of the publication *Le Coeur*. It inspired, even, an interpretive poem by the magazine's editor, Jules Bois. See Hobbs, pp. 85–87.

52. Hobbs, pp. 100ff, especially p. 110. Concerning The Temptation of Saint Anthony series see especially Jean Seznec, "The Temptation of Saint Anthony in Art," *Magazine of Art* 40, no. 3 (March 1947): 87–93, and Jean Seznec, "Odilon Redon and Literature," in *French Nineteenth-Century Painting and Literature*, ed. U. Finke (New York, 1972).

53. The half-lyre which appears in Redon's frontispiece to Iwan Gilkin's *La Damnation de l'artiste*, 1890, seems to confirm the interpretation of this thorny shape as an allusion to the poet's lyre.

54. The theme of Salome and Saint John the Baptist was popular throughout the nineteenth century, embodying for the Symbolists the contrast between the spiritual and material or physical, the conflict between the artist-martyr and the femme fatale. The theme figures in the works of Delacroix, Puvis, Baudry, H. L. Lévy, Henri Regnault, Cordier, Daux, Toudouze, Fabry and Moreau, to name just a few examples. Moreau's preoccupation with Salome—ranging from a demoniacal seductress to a coy, flirtatious woman—is an indication of his obsession with the femme fatale. Two of Moreau's works were, of course, the object of Huysmans' extravagant description in *A rebours*. Moreau's *Apparition*, 1876, inspired subsequent works by Redon, Rouault, Piot, Marcel-Beronneau, and Bernard. The sado-erotic implications of the biblical story are explored more and more explicitly for instance, in the illustrations by Beardsley for the English translation (1894) of Wilde's *Salome*; and works by Mossa, Klinger, von Stuck, Klimt, Marcel-Beronneau, Lévy-Dhurmer. The Americans, Robert L. Newman, Henry O. Tanner, and Claude Buck, executed Salomes. Certainly there is a well-established tradition for the emphasis of Salome's role as seductress as well as the bloody details of the Saint's death. See for instance works by Bernardino Luini, Bachiacca, Francesco del Cairo, Guido Reni, and Andrea Solario.

55. See chapter 1 concerning Greek vase paintings and concerning the depiction of Orpheus' severed head in illustrated editions of Ovid's *Metamorphoses*.

56. J. Collin de Plancy, *Dictionnaire infernal* (Bruxelles, 1845). See also Waldemar Deonna, "Orphée et l'oracle de la tête coupée," *Revue des études grecques* 38 (1925): 44–69, including extensive bibliographical information on this subject; See also Jean-Pierre Reverseau, "Pour une étude du thème de la tête coupée dans

la littérature et dans la peinture dans la seconde partie du XIXᵉ siecle," *Gazette des beaux-arts* (September 1972): 173–84.

57. See chapter 1 for a thorough discussion of the various interpretations of Orpheus' death presented in Greco-Roman literature.

58. Friedrich Nietzsche, *The Birth of Tragedy and The Case of Wagner* (New York, 1967), p. 86: Orpheus does not figure significantly in Nietzsche's analysis. Naming Socrates as an opponent of Dionysus, Nietzsche calls him the "new Orpheus who rose against Dionysus."

59. En combinant ces divers indices, nous sommes amenés à penser que, vers le milieu du quatorzième siècle avant notre ère, florissait cette école orphique, dans laquelle la doctrine réformée de Dionysus s'unit avec l'antique théorie de la lumière, originaire de la Haute-Asie, en un grand système théologique, où se trouvait receuillie toute la science sacerdotale parvenue en Grèce jusqu'à cette epoque. Voilà comment s'explique, selon nous, cette contradiction apparente d'un Orphée ennemi de la religion de Bacchus et victime de ses sanglants zélateurs, et d'un Orphée instituteur des mystères de cette religion.

From Guigniaut's translation of Creuzer's *Religions de l'antiquité considérées principalement dans leurs formes symboliques et mythologiques*, 4 vols. (Paris, 1825–51), vol. 6, book 3, part 1; book 7, p. 117, "Religion de Bacchus." On p. 122 Guigniaut notes a work which indicates the fusion of the cults of Apollo and Bacchus. Satyrs, and even Bacchus himself, are portrayed bearing lyres.

60. Edouard Schuré, *The Genesis of Tragedy and the Sacred Drama of Eleusis* (London, 1936) (1925 lectures at the Société de Géographie, Paris), pp. 11, 14, 24–25, concerning the relationship of tragedy and religion. Schuré criticized Nietzsche for his failure to penetrate the mysterious roots of tragedy in Greek esoteric religion, in the mysteries of Eleusis. Schuré of course knew Nietzsche and his work well. He had met him first at the premier of the *Ring of the Nibelungen* at Bayreuth in 1876. It was Malvida von Meysenberg, the devoted admirer and friend of the philosopher, who, in 1870, in Florence, introduced Schuré to his "muse," Margherita Albana Miguaty. Of course, Schuré includes Nietzsche in *Précurseurs et révoltés* (the edition quoted here, Paris: Perrin, 1920). The philosopher and Ada Negri are described as "Les Souffrants." Schuré's only criticism of Nietzsche's masterpiece, *The Birth of Tragedy*, is, once again, the failure to trace the roots of tragedy to Eleusis:

On ne fit pas a Nietzsche la seule critique légitime qu'on pouvait lui adresser. S'il y a un point faible dans son essai d'ailleurs si remarquable, c'est de n'avoir pas éclairé la tragédie grecque par les mystères d'Eleusis, c'est de confondre le Dionysus morale de la vie terrestre avec le Libérateur de la vie céleste et de prendre le plongeon dans les éléments pour l'union mystique de l'âme regénérée et ressuscitée avec l'Esprit divin. (pp. 136–37)

But, in this work, it is clear that Schuré attributes Nietzsche's "suicide spirituel" (p. 182), his "athéisme féroce et son suicide intellectuel" (p. 131) to his rupture with Schuré's beloved Wagner. (Schuré's *Richard Wagner, Son oeuvre et son idée*, appeared in 1875.) Schuré points to Nietzsche as a prime example of the intellectual anarchism of the latter part of the nineteenth century. In the introduction to *Précurseurs et révoltés* he states:

> Nietzsche, dont l'individualisme effréné aboutit à un athéisme épileptique et à sa propre destruction, est le père sinistre et grave de tous les anarchistes de la pensée. Le cas de cette nature puissante mais dévoyée est, à mes yeux, l'un des exemplaires les plus frappant de la maladie intellectuelle que le XIXe siecle legue au XXe, j'entends de la conception matérialiste de l'homme et de l'univers. (pp. ii-iii)

Wagner figures prominently in Schuré's *Genesis of Tragedy* as an example of *The Initiatory Theater*.

61. Walter Pater, *Greek Studies* (London, 1908). "A study of Dionysus" and "The Myth of Demeter and Persephone" were both published originally in the *Fortnightly Review*. Alfred Maury was powerfully influenced by Creuzer in his conception of the development of world religions. It is not surprising, then, that the mystery cults figure significantly in his *Histoire des religions de la Grèce antique* (Paris, 1857–59). Note as well Camille Mauclair, *Eleusis, Causeries sur la cité intérieure* (Paris, 1894) and Henri Delaage, *Le Monde occulte ou mystères du magnétisme dévoilés par le somnabulisme*, 1851, in which the author likens the true magnetic experience with initiation in antique mysteries. See in this regard Alain Mercier, *Les Sources ésotériques et occultes de la poésie symboliste, 1870–1914* (Paris, 1969), who notes the significance of the ancient cults in the Symbolists' study of occultism and esoterica. Note especially pp. 40 and 57. See also Filiz Eda Burhan, "Vision and Visionaries, Nineteenth-Century Psychological Theory. The Occult Sciences and the Formation of the Symbolist Aesthetic" (Ph.D. thesis, Princeton, 1979).

62. See Joséphin Péladan, *Origine et esthétique de la tragédie* (Paris, 1905). Péladan's manuscripts now preserved in the Fonds Péladan, Bibliothèque de l'Arsenal in Paris, include MS.13.204, *Terre d'Orphée*; MS.13.378, *Conférence sur le génie grec*; MS.13.162, *Le Mystère d'Eleusis*; MS.13.233, *L'Art idéaliste et mystique*; MS.13.173, *L'Art dionysiaque*. Note especially, *La Revue bleue* (p. 310, Fonds Péladan MS.13.162):

> Si on veut pénétrer le secret de l'Hellade, on considérera d'une manière parallèle, le courant Dyonisique et l'Eleusianien et réunissant par analogie des contraires, la douleur de Demeter et la joie de Dyonisos; on verra leur confluent.... A un point indéterminable mais positif, Demeter chante le Péan et Dyonisos le thrène: ce sont vraiment deux masques pour une seule face.

63. Concerning *La Fantaisie*, 1895, by Magnus Enckell, see *Le Symbolisme en Europe* (Brussels: Les Musées Royaux des Beaux-Arts de Belgique, 1976), entry 43: "cette 'fantaisie' centrée sur la figuration de Bacchus,—principale divinité des mystères d'Eleusis—, et de son temple, le bois ombragé et les cygnes blancs, forment autant de liens avec la vision de Böcklin."

Works by American Symbolist painters such as Charles Curran and Charles Stetson reveal their interest in the mystery cults. Stetson's works include a Dionysian series, "In Praise of Dionysus" and "Pagan Procession." In this regard see Charles Eldredge, *American Imagination and Symbolist Painting* (New York: Grey Art Gallery, 1979), pp. 104–5:

> For the subjectivist painters of the later period, the appeal of the pagan past was to the life of the senses, as symbolized to them by Dionysus or Bacchus. In lieu of the Apollonian perfection sought early in the century, the *fin-de-siecle* artists painted paeans "in praise of Dionysus," . . . an international group of artists whose resort to the instinctual life of the imagination found reflection in varied pagan rites, arcadian idylls and bacchic revels. . . . Other reversions to ancient motifs made more specific references to bacchic rites and pagan poets popularly associated with the vanished cultures of Greece and Rome.

Chapter 7

1. The myth of Orpheus is a central motif in Ihab Hassan's post-modernist critical work, *The Dismemberment of Orpheus, Toward a Postmodern Literature* (Wisconsin, 1982). Hassan discusses four major figures: Hemingway, Kafka, Genet, and Beckett, "who exemplify in some hieratic order of despair, the sovereignty of the void" (p. xvii). Hassan writes, "Literature does not suffice. Men of letters know this. They seek to transcend themselves in a complex silence. The modern Orpheus sings on a lyre without strings. . . . Orpheus consents to dismemberment. This is the true meaning of the avant-garde" (p. xvii).

2. Kandinsky praises Blavatsky and the Theosophical Society in *On the Spiritual in Art:* "This was the starting point of one of the greatest spiritual movements, which today unites a large number of people and has even given material form to this spiritual union through the Theosophical Society" (p. 143 in Vasily Kandinsky, *Complete Writings on Art* [Boston, 1982]).

3. Sixten Ringbom, "Art in the Epoch of the Great Spiritual," *Journal of the Warburg and Courtauld Institutes* 29 (1966): 386–418; S. Ringbom, *The Sounding Cosmos, A Study in the Spiritualism of Kandinsky and the Genesis of Abstract Painting* (Abo, 1970).

4. Laxmi P. Sihare, "Oriental Influences on Wassily Kandinsky and Piet Mondrian, 1909–1917" (Ph.D. dissertation, New York University, Institute of Fine Arts, 1967). Sihare is careful to underline the differences between Kandinsky's and Mondrian's approaches to Theosophy, characterizing Kandinsky's as more "a mat-

ter of intellectual inquiry" (p. 20), and Mondrian's as absolute faith in doctrines. Peg Weiss, *Kandinsky in Munich: The Formative Jugendstil Years* (Princeton, 1979), approaches this issue of the impact of Theosophical ideas on Kandinsky with considerable caution, focusing instead on the dual importance of Jugendstil stylistic tendencies toward abstract ornamentation and what she prefers to call more generally, "a symbolist striving for inner significance and *geistige* revolution" (p. 10).

5. Kandinsky, *Ueber das Geistige in der Kunst* (New York, 1947), p. 40, quoted by Rose-Carol Washton Long, "Vassily Kandinsky's Abstract Style: The Veiling of Apocalyptic Folk Imagery," *Art Journal* 34, no. 3 (Spring 1975): 217–28.

6. Peg Weiss, "Kandinsky in Munich: Encounters and Transformations," in *Kandinsky in Munich* (New York: Guggenheim Museum, 1982), p. 51.

7. Ibid., p. 52. See also Peter Selz, *German Expressionist Painting* (Berkeley and Los Angeles, 1957), pp. 231–32. Also, L. Sihare, 1967, pp. 109–11, discusses Kandinsky's preoccupation with the synthesis of the arts and the importance of this idea in Hindu aesthetic theories.

8. Leadbeater and Besant, *Thought Forms*, 1961, pp. 58–59, as quoted by Ringbom, 1966, p. 399. Ringbom also notes Kandinsky's description of his synaesthetic response to *Lohengrin*, reported in *Rückblicke*: "Ich sah alle meine Farben im Geiste, sie standen vor meinen Augen. Wilde, fast tolle Linien zeichneten sich vor mir" (p. 398).

9. August Endell, "Formen, Schönheit und Dekorative Kunst," *Dekorative Kunst* 1, no. 2 (November 1897): 75–76, as quoted by Peg Weiss, 1979, p. 26.

10. Arthur Roessler, *Neu Dachauer*, p. 119, as quoted by Weiss, ibid., p. 26: "Just as certain sequences of tones, without being music, can exercise an effect on us— and a similar effect of colour on our souls has been recognized, so too the line . . . exercises a strong effect." See as well Alfred Kubin, *Die andere Seite, phantastischer Roman* (München: G. Müller, 1923).

11. Franz Marc, "Geistige Güter," in *Blaue Reiter Almanach* (New York, 1974), p. 3. A similar idea is expressed on pp. 55–60. Marc discusses the works of El Greco and Cézanne: "Today the works of both mark the beginning of a new epoch in painting. In their views of life both felt the *inner mystical construction*, which is the great problem of our generation" (p. 59). "The epoch of great spirituality," was, of course, the focal theme of Kandinsky's and Marc's "Editors' Preface" to the *Almanac*, pp. 250–51 in the 1974 edition. For further discussion of this crucial idea see Marc, "Two Pictures," pp. 65–69, and "The 'Savages' of Germany," pp. 61–64.

12. Marc read Schiller, Schelling and, of course, Goethe. In this regard see Robert Rosenblum, *Modern Painting and the Northern Romantic Tradition* (New York, 1975), especially chapter 5, "The Pastoral and the Apocalyptic: Nolde, Marc, Kandinsky," pp. 129–48. See also Ringbom, 1966, pp. 409 ff.

13. Ringbom, 1966, p. 409.
14. Franz Marc, in a letter to Reinhard Pieper in December of 1908, as quoted by Frederick S. Levine, "The Image of the Animal in the Art of Franz Marc," p. 39, in *Franz Marc*, exhibition catalogue (Berkeley, Calif., 1979). See also Carla Schulz-Hoffmann, "Franz Marc und die Romantik—Zur Bedeutung romantischer Denkvorstellungen in seinen Schriften," pp. 95–111 in *Franz Marc*, exhibition catalogue (Munich, 1980).
15. See Peg Weiss, "Kandinsky in Munich: Encounters and Transformations," p. 46, in *Kandinsky in Munich*, 1982 (cat. no. 172).

    There are other examples of Orpheus amidst the animals in German twentieth-century art: Lovis Corinth, *Orpheus with Lyre*, 1919, an etching from his portfolio of Legends from Antiquity, issued by the Marées Gesellschaft; Gerhard Marcks, *Orpheus*, a woodcut from a portfolio with verses by Ovid. In addition, one might cite an etching and engraving by the Rumanian-born American artist, André Racz, *Orpheus*, 1954.
16. See Sixten Ringbom, 1966, pp. 413ff and Laxmi Sihare, 1967, pp. 39, 45, 46 especially.
17. See L. Sihare, 1967, pp. 242–43 and 258. Note especially Mondrian's article, "La manifestation du néo-plasticisme dans la musique et les bruiteurs futuristes italiens," *La Vie des lettres et des arts* (Paris, 1922), especially pp. 133 and 134, which originally appeared in Dutch in *De Stijl* 4, no. 8 (August 1921).
18. For discussions of the Symbolist-occultist influences on Kupka see the essays by Meda Mladek and Margit Rowell in *Frantisek Kupka, 1871–1957: A Retrospective* (New York: The Solomon R. Guggenheim Museum, 1975), pp. 24, 28, 76, and Virginia Spate, *Orphism, The Evolution of Non-Figurative Painting in Paris, 1910–1914* (Oxford, 1979), pp. 84ff.
19. See Meda Mladek, "Central European Influences," in *Frantisek Kupka*, 1975, p. 26.
20. The Czech poet, Richard Weiner, wrote in 1912, "Kupka wants painting to sound like music." In ibid., p. 31.
21. Mladek, ibid., pp. 22–25, discusses various possible influences on Kupka's desire to fuse painting and music, including the illustrations for folk songs by Mikulas Ales, which synthesized the musical and the pictorial; the theories of Czech Professor of Music, Eduard Hanslick; Austrian and German Theosophists and through them, the Nazarene Karl Diefenbach.
22. See Kirk Varnedoe, *Northern Light, Realism and Symbolism in Scandinavian Painting 1880–1910* (New York: The Brooklyn Museum, 1982), cat. no. 25, p. 117. Originally the painting included a water nymph playing a harp to a human listener. These allegorical figures were eliminated and replaced with the five golden harp strings. In his essay, "Nationalism, Internationalism and the Progress of Scandinavian Art," pp. 13–32, Varnedoe stresses the international impact of

Scandinavian art. In this regard see also Peg Weiss, 1979, pp. 84–94. Weiss explores especially the impact of Gallen-Kallela on Kandinsky. The Finnish artist and Albert Weisgerber were the stars of the 1902 Phalanx IV exhibition. Weiss further explores the issue of Gallen-Kallela's fame in Germany in her contribution to the 1982 Guggenheim catalogue, *Kandinsky in Munich*, pp. 47–48.

In this context one might cite *Sonata of the Stars*, 1908, by the Lithuanian, Mikaloius Ciurlionis, which presents a huge stringed instrument emiting vibrations in ribbons of color. Ciurlionis was also influenced by Theosophical and occult texts and was himself a musical prodigy. See Edward Lucie-Smith, *Symbolist Art* (New York/London, 1972), pp. 160 and 162, and Edouard Roditi, "The Spread and Evolution of Symbolist Ideals in Art," pp. 499–518, in *The Symbolist Movement in the Literature of European Languages*, ed. Anna Balakian (Budapest, 1982). Roditi claims that because Ciurlionis' works were only available in Russian museums his musicalist-abstractions could not have influenced other artists. Only Henry Valensi, the post-Cubist French painter who founded the musicaliste school in Paris, may have seen Ciurlionis' work during his visit to Russia before 1914 (pp. 507–8).

23. Paul Valéry, "Paradoxe sur l'architecte," in *Valéry, Collected Works*, Bollingen Series 45-4 (New York, 1956), p. 180, trans. Wm. McCausland Stewart.

24. Je rêve une poésie courte, un sonnet écrit par un songeur raffiné, qui serait, en même temps, un judicieux architecte, un sagace algébriste, un calculateur infaillible de l'effet à produire.

Paul Valéry, as quoted by Antonin Fabre, "Le Rôle de la musique dans l'oeuvre poétique de Paul Valéry," *Académie de Vaucluse, Mémoires* (Avignon, 1938), ser. 3, vol. 3, p. 42.

25. . . . les poètes dignes de ce grand nom reincarnent ici Amphion et Orphée. Cet homme (Mallarmé) faisait songer à ces êtres—semi-rois, semi-prêtres, semi-réels, semi-légendaires, auxquels nous devons de croire que nous ne sommes point tout animaux.

Paul Valéry, in *Oeuvres complètes*, Paris, vol. 1, p. 651.

26. In 1890, 20th October, he wrote to Mallarmé of his ideal: "short poems, concentrated with a view to a final 'éclat,' in which the rhythms are like the marble steps of an altar which the last verse crowns," as quoted on p. 505 of William Stewart, "Style, Form and Myth: The Orpheus Sonnet of Paul Valéry," *Stil und Formproblem der Literatur* (Heidelberg, 1959).

27. Stéphane Mallarmé, "Proses diverses," in *Oeuvres Complètes* (Paris, 1945) p. 663.

28. Au son de la lyre, les pierres s'harmonisaient en Temples. L'explication du monde par la poésie, c'est-à-dire au-dessus de tout syllogisme l'univers expliqué . . . par la Beauté.

354 Notes for Chapter 7

Paul Valéry, "Orphisme," quoted by William McCauland Stewart, "Peut-on parler d'un 'orphisme' de Valéry," *Cahiers d'association internationale d'études françaises* (24 July 1969): 187.

29. It is in a letter to Vielé-Griffin, thanking him for a positive reaction to the *Orpheus* sonnet, that Valéry identifies himself as well as Mallarmé as "orphic." See Paul Valéry, *Entretiens politiques et littéraires*, June 1981, as quoted by William M. Stewart, 1969, p. 187.

30. This work was dedicated to Claude Moreau and Bernard Durval (pseudonyms for Pierre Loüys and André Gide) whom Valéry had met in Montpellier in 1890. Later the poem was published in Loüys' journal *La Conque*. Later, Valéry revised the poem and it was added to *Album de vers anciens*, 1926.

31. Il naîtra, peut-être, pour élever les premiers tabernacles et les sanctuaires imprévus ou le Crédo futur, à travers l'encens, retentira. Demain, le suprême édificateur surgira d'un peuple, si ce peuple et le temps n'en sont pas les meurtriers ... cette âme lointaine et par mon âme désirée—Je la devine musicienne, et longtemps recluse dans la pure solitude de son rêve.

Paul Valéry, *Collected Works*, 1956, pp. 178 and 180.

32. Car de subtiles analogies unissent irréelle et fugitive édification des sons à l'art solide, par qui des formes imaginaires sont immobilisées au soleil, dans le porphyre. ... Ainsi, se manifestera l'indicible correspondance, l'intime infinite qu'il faut discerner, sous des voiles habituels et mensongers, entre deux incarnations de l'art, entre la façade royale de Reims, et telle page de Tannhäuser, entre l'antique magnificence d'un grand temple héroïque et tel suprême andante brûlant de flammes glorieuses.

... car les orgues liturgiques creusent pour le rêve des coupoles dans des saphirs et d'énormes dômes pleins de tonnerre; mais les flûtes s'élancent comme de graciles colonnettes, si hautes qu'un vertige les couronne. ... Un largo triomphal et total éclate enfin sous l'ultime voûte; de tous les motifs exprimés se dégage et s'essore le secret, le glorieux amour absolu.

Ibid., pp. 178, 180, 182 and 185–86. Valéry speaks of "la basilique ... l'antiphone de pierre."

33. ... et le dieu tient la lyre entre ses doigts d'argent. Le dieu chante, et selon le rythme tout-puissant, s'élèvent au soleil les fabuleuses pierres, et l'on voit grandir vers l'azur incandescent, les murs d'or harmonieux d'un sanctuaire.

Il chante! assis au bord du ciel splendide, Orphée! Son oeuvre se revêt d'un vespéral trophée, et sa lyre divine enchante les porphyres, car le temple érigé par ce musicien unit la sûreté des rythmes anciens, à l'âme immense du grand hymne sur la lyre!

Ibid., p. 186. For the final (1942) version of the poem, see J. R. Lawler, "The Technique of Valéry's Orphée," *AUMLA, Journal of the Australian University Language and Literature Association* (Christchurch, New Zealand), No. 5 (October

1956): 54–64. Note especially p. 60 concerning the sonnet form as a marriage of music and architecture, the coincidence of underlying movement and subject.

It is interesting that Frantisek Kupka's articulation of mystical correspondences also involves musical and architectural imagery. In this regard see Meda Mladek, "Central European Influences," p. 31; and Margit Rowell, "Frantisek Kupka: A Metaphysics of Abstraction," p. 49, in *Frantisek Kupka* (New York: Guggenheim Museum, 1975).

34. *Amphion* was performed in 1931 at the Paris Opéra and subsequently at Covent Garden.

35. "Le mythe d'Orphée, c'est-à-dire l'animation de toute chose par un esprit,—la fable même de la mobilité et de l'arrangement." Paul Valéry, as quoted by Stewart, 1959, p. 508. Amphion is a primitive man who suddenly receives his lyre, his inspiration, his mission from the god, Apollo. This hero, however, remains limited, merely a mouthpiece for the divine creative force which has animated him. Concerning Valéry's enthusiasm for Gluck's *Orphée* see a letter quoted by Stewart, ibid., p. 508; see as well Paul Valéry, *Lettres à quelques-uns*, p. 123, as quoted by Stewart, 1969, p. 189. In this article Stewart notes references to Orpheus in other poetic works by Valéry.

36. Indeed, the ambiguity of the term troubled many of the artists to whom this label was applied. Kupka clearly wished to differentiate his "Orphism" from that of Apollinaire's Cubist artists. Similarly, by the end of 1912, Delaunay persuaded Apollinaire of the independence of his orphist works from Cubism. In this regard see Virginia Spate, 1979, p. 39.

37. As early as 1908 in "Les Trois Vertus plastiques," Apollinaire spoke of pure painting. By February of 1912 this notion is explicitly tied to the analogy between painting and music (in *Les Peintres cubistes*, p. 50). Apollinaire elaborates upon the transcendent focus of the new painting: "The Fourth Dimension has found its place in art, just as in science. Painters are forsaking the old art of optical illusions and local proportions in order to express the magnitude of metaphysical forms." Quoted by Cecily Mackworth, *Guillaume Apollinaire and the Cubist Life* (London, 1961), p. 86. Also, see Spate, 1979, pp. 74–75.

38. Guillaume Apollinaire, as quoted by Spate, 1979, p. 39.

39. Delaunay introduced him to Kandinsky's book. See Spate, pp. 34 and 76.

40. Cecily Mackworth, 1961, pp. 93–94.

41. Apollinaire's obituary for Josephin Péladan appeared in the *Mercure de France*, 16 July 1918, pp. 372–73.

42. Concerning Apollinaire's interest in Gnosticism, the Pythagoreans and Freemasons, see Mackworth, 1961, pp. 124–27. See also, Scott Bates, *Guillaume Apollinaire* (New York, 1967), pp. 93–94.

43. The lecture was published the same year as "La Phalange nouvelle," in *La Poésie symboliste, trois entretiens sur les temps héroïques (période symboliste) au Salon des Artistes Indépendants,* by P.-N. Roinard, V.-E. Michelet, G. Apollinaire (recueil de conférences données en 1908 au Salon des Indépendants) (Paris, 1908), pp. 133–37, here as quoted by Marcel Adema, *Apollinaire,* translated by Denise Folliot (New York, 1955), p. 95.

44. Moreover, in the second poem, entitled "La Tortue," the theme is the power of the poet's lyre constructed from a tortoise shell. Poem five, entitled "La Serpent," mentions Eurydice as well as Eve and Cleopatra, as victims of serpents' cruelty. However, Apollinaire seems to dismiss Eurydice's role with this flippant line: "Eve, Eurydice, Cléopatre; J'en connais encore trois ou quatre." See Maria Luisa Bellelli, "Ricchezza di temi nel Bestiaire di Guillaume Apollinaire," in *Apollinaire* (Turin and Paris, 1970), pp. 37–107.

45. Orphée était natif de Thrace. Le sublime poète jouait d'une lyre que Mercure (souvent confondu avec Hermes Trimégiste et, chez les Grecs, conducteur des âmes aux Enfers) lui avait donné. Elle était composée d'une carapace de tortue de cuir collé à l'entour, de deux branches, d'un chevalet et de cordes faites avec des boyaux de brebis. Mercure donne également de ces lyres à Apollon et à Amphion. Quand Orphée jouait en chantant, les animaux sauvages eux-mêmes venaient écouter son cantique. Orphée inventa toutes les sciences, tous les arts. Fondé dans la magie il connut l'avenir et prédit chrétiennement l'avènement du SAUVEUR.

Guillaume Apollinaire, Notes to *Le Bestiaire* . . . , 1979, n.p.

46. Guillaume Apollinaire, as quoted by Claudine Frank, "Orpheus and Prometheus, A Study in Apollinaire, Mayakovsky, and the Visual Arts" (Senior essay, Princeton University, 1978), p. 8; See also Philippe Renaud, *Lecture d'Apollinaire* (Lausanne, 1969).

47. See Robert Couffignal, *L'Inspiration biblique dans l'oeuvre de Guillaume Apollinaire* (Paris, 1966), especially pp. 129ff.

48. Admirez le pouvoir insigne
Et la noblesse de la ligne: . . .
Elle est la voix que la lumière fit entendre
Et dont parle Hermes Trismégiste en son Pimandre.

Guillaume Apollinaire, Notes to *Le Bestiaire.* . . . Apollinaire was probably familiar with Louis Ménard's 1867 translation of the "Pimander."

49. P. S. Ballanche, "Orphée," in *Oeuvres,* 1839, book 2, pp. 148–50, as quoted by Virginia Spate, 1979, p. 65.

50. Stéphane Mallarmé, *Correspondance,* ed. H. Mondor and L. J. Austin, 1965, vol. 2, p. 266, as quoted by Spate, 1979, p. 65.

51. Spate, ibid., pp. 63–65. Spate points to the following passage from the *Tentation de Saint-Antoine:* "Sur les ténèbres le rayon du Verbe descendit et un cri violent

s'échappa, qui semblait la voix de la lumière" (Flaubert, *La Tentation de Saint-Antoine*, 1967 ed., p. 115). Spate (p. 350) also notes that Apollinaire wrote about Redon in *Chroniques d'art*, p. 60.

52. Guillaume Apollinaire, *Les Peintres cubistes*, p. 66, originally published in *Soirées de Paris*, May 1912, here as quoted by Spate, ibid., p. 74.

53. Apollinaire's 1917 lecture, "L'Esprit nouveau et les poètes," at the Vieux Colombier, as cited by Margaret Davies, *Apollinaire* (Edinburgh and London, 1964), p. 154. See also Apollinaire's letter to Louise de Coligny, 23 April 1915, from *Lettres à Lou*, ed. Michel Decaudin, 1969, p. 315, here as quoted by Spate, 1979, p. 66.

54. "Comme Orphée, tous les poètes étaient près d'une malemort." Guillaume Apollinaire, *Le Poète assassiné*, Paris, 1979.

55. Concerning the difference between Apollinaire's attitude to myth and religion (as opposed to that of the Symbolists) see Pascal Pia, *Apollinaire par lui-même* (Paris, 1962), p. 47. In this regard see also, Michel Decaudin, "Deux aspects du mythe Orphique au XXe siècle," *CAIEF*, 24 July 1969. Decaudin actually offers an alternative title for this study of the Orpheus image in the works of Cocteau and Apollinaire: "Contributions à l'étude de l'absence du myth d'Orphée chez deux poètes du XXe siècle" (p. 217). About Apollinaire, in fact, he concludes: "Orphée ne joue donc pas, malgré les apparences, un rôle déterminant dans l'oeuvre d'Apollinaire.... C'est qu'Apollinaire n'est pas de ceux qui forcent le destin et traversent l'Acheron. Il reste sur le pont Mirabeau, il ne plonge pas.... Apollinaire reste presque toujours en deçà de la grande aventure cosmique ou chthonienne que pourtant il semble avoir entrevu" (p. 221). Decaudin's judgment is based on a precise definition of the literary myth: It must be based on a sense of the new significance of the traditional myth, not limited to personal experience of the author, but responding to a desire or disposition in society which receives the myth.

56. See Cecily Mackworth, 1961, pp. 158–65. It is interesting that Zadkine had vacationed in 1897 with his uncle in Chagall's native Vitebsk. In 1912, Apollinaire visited Chagall's studio, declaring his works (ca. 1908–12) "sur-naturel." See *Marc Chagall* (Paris: Musée des Arts Décoratifs, 1959), p. 26. Chagall's work is dedicated to four individuals: Apollinaire, Blaise Cendrars, Canudo (the editor of *Montjoie*), and H. Walden (to whose attention Apollinaire brought Chagall, leading to that artist's exhibit at Der Sturm). Apollinaire's appreciation of Chagall is documented, moreover, in his poem, "A travers l'Europe" (published in *Soirées de Paris*, 15 April 1914, no. 23, under the better-known title, "Rotsoge"). It was reprinted in *Der Sturm*, Chagall exhibition catalogue (Nos. 210–11, May 1914) and in *Caligrammes* (*Oeuvres poétiques* [Paris, 1956], pp. 210ff). See Franz Meyer, *Marc Chagall* (New York, 1957), p. 146. Note also pp. 154–62 concerning the primordial androgyne as evidence of Chagall's interest in mystical or cosmological notions of the universe and artistic creation. Note also Apollinaire's criticism of the 1914 Salon des Indépendants. Zadkine's 1937 *Monument to Apollinaire* was one of four projects dedicated to writers. The others are dedi-

cated to Rimbaud, Jarry, and Lautréamont. In this regard, note a Ph.D. dissertation in progress at Columbia University, by Michael Fitzgerald, on Picasso's monument to Apollinaire. See also chapter 5 above, concerning Rodin's monuments to writers and artists. Zadkine completed a *Monument to Rodin* in 1945.

57. It could be argued, however, that this image of Orpheus fits into a broader context of images in Chagall's oeuvre: frequent portrayals of David holding a lyre; depictions of musicians, especially violinists in his works with Jewish themes; musicians in his decorations of operas and concert halls. Also, see Franz Meyer, *Marc Chagall*, 1957, p. 201, who quotes Chagall concerning the choice of Orpheus as subject: "Just then I wanted to test myself against tradition and renew a connection with it."

58. See Ionel Jianou, *Zadkine* (Paris, 1979), p. 45.

59. Edouard Roditi, "Orpheus as a Lyre," *The Observer* (London), 8 May 1960, quoted in Jianou, ibid., p. 47.

60. In this regard see Zadkine's statements quoted by E. Roditi, ibid., quoted in *Hommage à Zadkine* (Paris: Musée Moderne de la Ville de Paris and the Musée Rodin, 1972), cat. no. 20, especially *Le Maillet et le ciseau*, quoted on pp. 181–83, cat. no. 90. See also Ionel Jianou, *Zadkine* (Paris, 1964), Orpheus cat. entry, n.p. Jianou, 1979, p. 46, notes "Cette nouvelle conception du symbole, partie intégrante de la structure de l'objet, fut le résultat d'une longue évolution." A similar integration of human anatomy and the structure of the musical instrument is an important element in his cycle of works on musical themes, for instance *Nature morte musicale; Hommage à Bach; Le Compositeur; Le Violoncelle*. Note as well *The Poet*, 1954, which integrates musical instrument with human anatomy along with a poem by Paul Eluard. See Jianou, 1964, *The Poet* entry, n.p.; and Jianou, *Zadkine*, 1979, p. 48.

61. Seuphor's oeuvre also includes a version of *Orpheus* executed on a Sèvres porcelain vase. Note also *La lyre cassée*, 1965.

62. See Will Grohmann, *Paul Klee* (New York, n.d.), p. 87 and p. 400, illus. 131.

63. Rainer Maria Rilke, *Das Buch der Bilder*, as quoted by Federico Olivero, *Rainer Maria Rilke: A Study in Poetry and Mysticism* (Cambridge, 1931), p. 120. In this regard, Walter Rehm, *Orpheus: Der Dichter und die Toten Selbstdeutung und der Totenkult bei Novalis, Hölderlin, Rilke* (Düsseldorf, 1950), p. 515, speaks of Rilke's intuition of the "acoustic nature of the soul." These concepts are surely related to Mallarmé's mystical and synaesthetic notion of the poem, "De scintillations sitôt le septuor." In this regard see Cecil Maurice Bowra, *The Heritage of Symbolism* (London, 1962), p. 11, "Mallarmé dreamed of something like the spheres, a harmony audible to the spiritual ear in forms of ideal beauty."

64. See Olivero, ibid., pp. 120ff.

65. Da stieg ein Baum. O reine Uebersteigung!
O Orpheus singt! O hoher Baum ihm Ohr!
Und alles schwieg. Doch selbst in der Verschweigung
ging neuer Anfang, Wink und Wandlung vor.

Tiere aus Stille drangen aus dem klaren
gelösten Wald von Lager und Genist;
und da ergab sich, dass sie nicht aus List
und nicht aus Angst in sich so leise waren,

sondern aus Hören. Brüllen, Schrei, Geröhr
schien klein in ihren Herzen. Und wo eben
kaum eine Hütte war, dies zu empfangen,

ein Unterschlupf aus dunkelstem Verlangen
mit einem Zugang, dessen Pfosten beben,
da schufst du ihnen Tempel im Gehör.

Sonnet, I, 1, Rainer Maria Rilke, *Sonnets to Orpheus*, trans. M. D. Herter Norton (New York, 1942), pp. 16 and 17. Rilke may have been inspired by a specific visual source: Orpheus playing amidst trees, animals and birds by the fifteenth-century Italian artist, Cima da Conegliano. This hung in his room in the castle at Muzot where the sonnets were written. See Luigi Coletti, *Cima da Conegliano* (Venice, 1959), cat. no. 59.

66. Nur wer die Leier schon hob
auch unter Schatten,
darf das unendliche Lob
ahnend erstatten.

Nur wer mit Toten vom Mohn
ass, von dem ihren,
wird nicht den leisesten Ton
wieder verlieren.

Mag auch die Spieglung im Teich
oft uns verschwimmen:
Wisse das Bild.

Erst in dem Doppelbereich
werden die Stimmen
ewig und mild.

Sonnet I, 9, Rainer Maria Rilke, *Sonnets to Orpheus*, 1942, pp. 32–33.
"Death is not annihilation but transformation; it gives meaning to life and should be desired with the same intensity of feeling as love that has renounced reciprocation," in M. Schmidt-Ihms, "Rilke's Conception of Poetry with Special Reference to the Sonnets." *Theoria: A Journal of Studies* (Pietermaritzburg), No. 4 (1952): 64.

67. The vehemence of his feelings against Christianity is evident in a rather vicious poem to his mother containing a sarcastic attack on her piety. Cited by Jean Rodolphe von Salis, *Rainer Maria Rilke: The Years in Switzerland* (Berkeley and Los Angeles, 1964), p. 135.

68. See M. Schmidt-Ihms, 1952, p. 61. See also, Hans Egon Holthusen, *Portrait of Rilke*, trans. W.H. Hargreaves (New York, 1971), p. 85, who discusses how Orpheus comes to supplant the figure of St. Francis from *The Notebooks of Malte Laurids Brigge* and the angel of *The Duino Elegies*. Walter Rehm, 1950, discusses Rilke's secularization of Christianity through the figure of Orpheus, pp. 562–571.

69. Du aber, Göttlicher, du, bis zuletzt noch Ertöner,
 da ihn der Schwarm der verschmähten Mänaden befiel,
 hast ihr Geschrei übertönt mit Ordnung, du Schöner,
 aus den Zerstörenden stieg dein erbauendes Spiel.

 Keine war da, dass sie Haupt dir und Leier zerstör',
 wie sie auch rangen und rasten; und alle die scharfen
 Steine, die sie nach deinem Herzen warfen,
 wurden zu Sanftem an dir und begabt mit Gehör.

 Schliesslich zerschlugen sie dich, von der Rache gehetzt,
 während dein Klang noch in Löwen und Felsen verweilte
 und in den Bäumen und Vögeln. Dort singst du noch jetzt.

 O du verlorener Gott! Du unendliche Spur!
 Nur weil dich reissend zuletzt die Feindschaft verteilte,
 sind wir die Hörenden jetzt und ein Mund der Natur.

 Sonnet, I, 26, Rainer Maria Rilke, *Sonnets to Orpheus*, 1942, pp. 66–67.

70. Walter Rehm, 1950, p. 515. The preoccupation with death may stem from the premature death of the young Vera Ouckama Knoop. In this regard see ibid., p. 521. In addition, see M. Schmidt-Ihms, 1952, pp. 61 and 68 concerning Rilke's vision of the unity that transcends the dualism of life and death. Schmidt-Ihms discusses Sonnet II, 1, specifically in regard to Rilke's identification with the Death-Messiah-Poet: "Rilke identifies himself with the Death-Messiah-Poet in whose poetry the dualism of the here and beyond, the fleeting and the enduring, life and death, subject and object is transcended" (p. 68). See also Rilke's letter to Nancy Wunderly-Volkart about the horrors of pain and illness as initiation, a privilege, as quoted in Jean Rodolphe von Salis, 1964, p. 139. In this regard one might examine Sonnet I,25, in which sickness seems to quicken, enrich the flow of life force: "Sickness was near. Already overcome by the shadows, / her blood pulsed more darkly, yet as if fleetingly / suspect, it thrust forth into its natural spring" (R.M. Rilke, 1942, p. 65).

71. See Egon Schwarz, *Poetry and Politics in the Works of Rainer Maria Rilke* (New York, 1981), p. 95, who quotes in n. 20, Rudolf Kramer-Badoni, "Rilke und Bachofen," *Berliner Hefte 3*, 1949, 156: "And indeed almost the whole symbolism of Rilke's late poetry stems from Bachofen, mainly from his later work on 'orphic

theology.'" Rilke himself wrote of feeling "attracted to and divided from," Schuler, who, "from an intuitive understanding of old imperial Rome, undertook to give an explanation of the world which presented the dead as the real beings, the world of the dead as a single incredible existence, but our little life's-respite as a sort of exemption from it" (from a letter to Princess Marie von Thurn und Taxis Hohenlohe, 18 March 1915).

Eight years later, on Schuler's death, Rilke wrote to his wife: "In the *Sonnets to Orpheus* there is much that even Schuler would have admitted; indeed, who knows whether the expressing of so much of it opening and at the same time mysteriously does not derive from the contact with him" (from a letter to his wife, 23 April 1923). Both of these letters are quoted on p. 144 in the notes to the first part of the *Sonnets to Orpheus*, trans. M. D. Herter Norton, 1942.

See also Hans Egon Holthusen, 1971, pp. 132–35, who discusses how Rilke's mysticism, his acceptance of a smoothly flowing spiritual reality, including life and death, found strong confirmation in Schuler's cosmological interpretation of Roman cults and customs. Schuler's "pagan" bias would have been especially appealing to the anti-Christian Rilke.

Note also p. 147, where Holthusen mentions that Princess Taxis was a member of the International Society for Psychic Research. One may presume Rilke's familiarity with this organization and with occult and Theosophical doctrines.

72. Rainer Maria Rilke, letter to Nanny von Escher, 22 December 1923, quoted in the notes, *Sonnets to Orpheus*, 1942, p. 130. See as well Rainer Maria Rilke, letter to Witold von Hulewicz, 13 November 1925, quoted in notes, R. M. Rilke, *Sonnets to Orpheus*, pp. 132–33.

73. M. Schmidt-Ihms, 1952, p. 63, in analyzing the *Duino Elegies*, notes that for Rilke there are three forms of intensified human existence that step out of the three-fold division of time into timeless being—lovers, youthful dead, the hero. Fitting all three categories, it is clear why Orpheus was such a compelling figure for Rilke.

74. Walter Rehm, 1950, p. 530. Rilke's philosophy is stated most clearly in Sonnet I, 3: "Gesang ist Dasein." In this regard see Frank Wood, *The Ring of Forms* (Minneapolis, 1958), pp. 184–85, where he discusses Orpheus as a symbol of all experience and the ordering or forming of this experience through music, that is art, poetry.

See also M. Schmidt-Ihms, 1952, p. 66 for a discussion of Sonnet I, 19, and this theme of the transformation of song from the transient to the permanent.

75. Geoffrey H. Hartman, *The Unmediated Vision: An Interpretation of Wordsworth, Hopkins, Rilke and Valéry* (New York, 1966). See page 141: "Rilke affirms the invincible concreteness of things, submitting himself to a fate and will unperceived through any mediate sense, residing in the body as such, as realized by the simple fact of being present in the same way that the earth, the stars, and nature in general are present."

76. Ibid., pp. 79 and 80.
77. Rilke, *The Sonnets to Orpheus*, 1942, p. 17.
78.   Wartet . . . , das schmeckt . . . Schon ists auf der Flucht.
    . . . Wenig Musik nur, ein Stampfen, ein Summen :
    Mädchen, ihr warmen, Mädchen, ihr stummen,
    tanzt den Geschmack der erfahrenen Frucht!

    Tanzt die Orange. Wer kann sie vergessen,
    wie sie, ertrinkend in sich, sich wehrt
    wider ihr Süssein. Ihr habt sie besessen.
    Sie hat sich köstlich zu euch bekehrt.

    Tanzt die Orange. Die wärmere Landschaft,
    werft sie aus euch, dass die reife erstrahle
    in Lüften der Heimat! Erglühte, enthüllt

    Düfte um Düfte! Schafft die Verwandtschaft
    mit der reinen, sich weigernden Schale,
    mit dem Saft, der die glückliche füllt!

Sonnet I, 15, in ibid., pp. 44 and 45. See also p. 79.

79. Hartman, 1966, p. 86. In this regard note Sonnet I,13, which celebrates with incredible immediacy the nature of the fruit: "Full round apple, pear and banana."
80. Ibid., p. 95. Hartman comments:

"Just as the mouths fashioned by Rodin express the mouths of the body, so his own words aim to render the physical rather than historical, social, emotional, or religious connotations. Rilke attempts to create a new idiom which would neglect the anthropomorphic for the physical bias of language. The common place sense of words is neglected for their seeming origin as signs signifying weight, direction, and invisibly oriented gesture."

81. Max Beckmann, Address to Friends and Philosophical Faculty of Washington University, 6 June 1950, as quoted by Margot Clark, "Beckmann and Esoteric Philosophy," p. 33, in *Max Beckmann, The Triptychs* (London: The Whitechapel Gallery, 1980).
82. Clark speaks of Beckmann's understanding of "painting as a magical operation which could result in secret wisdom or gnosis." Ibid., p. 36 and pp. 33–34 generally. Also in this regard see Charles S. Kessler, *Max Beckmann's Triptychs* (Cambridge, 1970), p. 94. Kessler notes the impact of Bachofen via Frommel and Schuler, both followers of Stefan George. Frommel was a member of Beckmann's circle in Amsterdam. See Beckmann's "On my Theory of Painting," as quoted by S. Lackner, "Memories of a Friendship," *Arts Yearbook 4* (New York: Arts Digest, 1961), p. 49. See for instance: F. W. Fischer, *Max Beckmann: Symbol und Weltbild—Grundriss zu einer Deutung des Gesamtwerkes* (Munich, 1972); Wolfgang Frommel, "Max Beckmann: Die Argonauten, Aus einem Brief," *Castrum Peregrini*

33 (1957–58); Erhard Göpel, *Max Beckmann—Die Argonauten, Ein Triptychon* (Stuttgart, 1957); Erhard Göpel and Barbara Göpel, *Max Beckmann, Katalog der Gemälde* (Bern, 1976).

Fischer's analysis of the *Mühle*, pp. 180–81, stresses Beckmann's notion of the martyrdom of the soul, and his knowledge of orphic doctrines. See page 184 and Chapter 14 generally, concerning Beckmann's dependence on Madame Blavatsky's *Secret Doctrine*. Earlier, p. 148, concerning the *Temptation* triptych, Fischer identifies the magic bird as Simorgh Anke from Blavatsky's *Secret Doctrine* and notes the underlining in Beckmann's notebook of "even religious" in the phrase, "Ein wunderbarer Vogel, verständig, viele Sprachen sprechend und sogar religiös."

83. Gewiss, etwas wirklich Erder lösendes ist kaum zu erhoffen, aber wenigstens blieb uns der Protest gegen den "scheinbaren" Wahnsinn des Kosmos.

In Max Beckmann, *Tagebuch*, 17 July 1950, as quoted by Fischer, 1972, p. 232. Also, Beckmann speaks of grasping "the unutterable things of this world" from the *Creative Credo*, 1918, as quoted in *Voices of German Expressionism*, ed. Victor H. Miesel (Englewood Cliffs, N.J., 1970), pp. 107–9.

84. Gert Schiff, "The Nine Finished Triptychs of Max Beckmann, Marginalia for their Interpretation," in *Max Beckmann, The Triptychs* (London: The Whitechapel Gallery, 1980), p. 21; and Gert Schiff, "Max Beckmann: Die Ikonographie der Triptychen," *Munuscula discipulorum, Kunsthistorische Studien Hans Kauffmann zum 70 Geburstag, 1966* (Berlin, 1968), pp. 265–66.

85. Gert Schiff, 1980, p. 18.

86. Ibid., p. 14.

87. Max Beckmann as quoted by Gert Schiff, ibid., p. 14.

88. Max Beckmann, *Tagebuch*, entry 19 April 1949, as quoted by Fischer, 1972, p. 221.

89. See Beckmann, *Tagebuch*, 9 December 1950. He completes the work on the painting on 26 December 1950, and dies the following day.

90. Charles S. Kessler, 1970, p. 90.

91. See Gert Schiff, 1980, p. 21.

92. Ibid., p. 21. In this regard, Charles S. Kessler, 1970, pp. 95–96 speculates about the impact of J. J. Bachofen, through Frommel and his article on the Argonauts, on Beckmann. Bachofen's psychology of the sexes (see his 1932, *Man and Woman*) may have influenced Beckmann's segregation of the sexes in the Argonaut panels, as well as the fact that all of the women are seated while the men stand.

According to Bachofen, the epic of the Argonauts preserves the dim memory of a prehistoric cultural and spiritual revolution. Before this revolution, woman was the repository of all culture, and the female sex shaped the ethos

364   Notes for Chapter 7

of mankind. During the time when 'mother right' held dominion, all human institutions—legal, social and religious—reflected the supremacy of the 'female principle.' In this era man lived in greater harmony with nature and with his own instinctual being. But by the same token it was an era of inferior spiritual and intellectual achievement. The new age and the new order, symbolized in the triumphs of the Argos, was one of male dominance, conjugal father right, individualism, and Promethean striving. The Aphroditean-Demeterian culture and chthonian worship of the primordial matriarchate were succeeded by a high solar religion and a more disciplined, spiritualized civilization. (pp. 94–95)

93. Gert Schiff, 1980, p. 21.

94. Apparently Beckmann read a great deal about astronomy at this time and specifically knew of Humboldt's red spots. In this regard see Kessler, p. 96, and Schiff, ibid., p. 21. Schiff, 1968, p. 284, identifies the constellation as a reflection of the conjunction of lunar Medea—chthonian principle and solar Jason the energetic hero. Göpel (referred to by Kessler on p. 97) sees the celestial bodies as the transfigured state of the spiritual heroes in eternity.

Fischer emphasizes the cosmological significance of the spatial arrangement of the celestial configuration (pp. 223–27). Specifically, he relates the planets and the ladder to cycles of reincarnation, the concept of perpetual transition important in Blavatsky's *Secret Doctrine*. The theme of the central panel, and therefore of the entire triptych, is initiation. The quest for the fleece is a symbol of the ideal "grosse Werk." Art is a means to enlightenment. Frommel, in fact, spoke of the Golden Fleece as a Holy Grail (noted by Kessler on p. 94).

The first to point to the passage in Humboldt was Armin Kesser, *Blick auf Beckmann* (München, 1962), p. 33.

95. Kessler, 1970, p. 92.

96. Schiff, 1980, p. 21.

97. Fischer, 1972, pp. 228–29.

98. See Schiff, 1980, p. 21; and Fischer, p. 224 and section 14 generally. One might interpret in the figure of Orpheus a certain conflict or ambivalence: his lyre is idle on the ground, his hand moves to the left while his head is turned to the right. Could these elements indicate Orpheus' position between the Apollonian and the Dionysian?

99. See Claude Gandelman, "Max Beckmann's Triptychs and the Simultaneous Stage of the Twenties," pp. 26–32 in *Max Beckmann, The Triptychs* (London: The Whitechapel Gallery, 1980) and Clifford Amyx, "Max Beckmann: The Iconography of the Triptych," *The Kenyon Review* 13 (1951): 610–23.

100. Georges Bataille, *Sacrifices* (Paris, 1970).

101. The other mythological paintings include *Silenus*, 1932; *Bacchanal*, 1933; *Daphne and Apollo*, 1933; *Horses of Diomedes*, 1934. Note the similarity between the

vibrant colors of the Masson and the bright colors and fluid biomorphic linear passages in Barnett Newman's automatist drawing, *The Song of Orpheus*, 1944–45. Other subjects in this series include *The Slaying of Osiris; The Blessing; Gea*. Newman shared Masson's interest in Redon, as well.

102. For a discussion of the severed-head motif in *Les Soupiraux* and *The Man in the Tower* see Carolyn Lanchner, "André Masson: Origins and Development," in *André Masson* (New York: The Museum of Modern Art, 1976), p. 107. See chapter 6 above concerning Redon's severed heads.

103. William Rubin, *André Masson* (New York: The Museum of Modern Art, 1976), p. 57. Concerning Masson's interest in Redon see an interview with Georges Bernier, "Le Surréalisme et après: Un entretien au magnétophone avec André Masson," *L'Oeil* (Paris), 15 May 1955, p. 14. See also Carolyn Lanchner's essay, specifically p. 107, in *André Masson*, 1976; William Rubin, *Dada and Surrealist Art* (New York, 1969), pp. 125–27; Deborah Rosenthal, "Interview with André Masson," *Arts Magazine* (November 1980): 88–94, especially 91.

104. André Masson, "Mystic with a Method, Odilon Redon," *ARTnews*, No. 55 (January 1957): 62.

105. Note especially *Orage*, 1938, which juxtaposes the images of the eyelid and the shell. This is illustrated in René Passeron, *André Masson et les puissances du signe* (Paris, 1975).

106. Concerning the theme of violence see works from 1926, *The Battle of Fishes* or *Horses Attacked by Fishes*. Masson shared the Surrealists' general fascination with the sado-erotic implications of the praying mantis. Note especially works such as *Betrothal of Insects*, 1934 or *Summer Divertissement*, 1934. Note the Eros-Thanatos connection in a small 1931 ink drawing portraying a man violating a lion. The themes of sex and violence are linked as well in a 1928 drawing for *Justine* or in a series of works such as the *Abattoirs, Combats, Massacres,* or *Migrations*.

Masson's fascination with violence and sex is part of a broader, pervasive vision: in the mineral, vegetable or animal realms, he is fascinated with change, metamorphosis, growth, mutation, resulting from energy generated by gentle forces in nature or by violent release of force or aggression. Hence, themes of germination, birth, hatchings, are at one extreme of a spectrum including murder and dissections. These themes are absorbed into Masson's work, in which eyes are pulled from their sockets, torsos are presented without heads, vaginas and faces grow into flowers. In other words, objects and parts of organic systems are torn apart. Their objectness is reinforced. The objects are charged with new energy, transformed and metamorphosed into new subjects.

This coincidence of segmentation and the objectifying of objects with germination and metamorphosis, also figures significantly in Redon's work (see chapter 6 above). In this aspect, also, then, Redon may constitute an important influence. In this regard note Masson's statement about Redon: "Redon operates with a sort of alchemy of fields, like a magician who is simultaneously minerologist, botanist and an expert anatomist" (André Masson, 1957, p. 42). Moreover, in contrasting Redon's technique with that of the Surrealists, Masson uses words such as "grafting" as opposed to "collage." Grafting seems highly appropriate, implying a natural process, the expectation of growth or metamorphosis. Similarly, later in this same article, Masson praises Redon's "lyrical chromatics . . . he invented color as metamorphosis" (p. 61).

107. Masson provided illustrations for Bataille's *Histoire de l'oeil*, 1928, *L'Anus solaire*, 1931, and after *Les Sacrifices*, was the sole illustrator for the four issues of the journal *Acéphale*, 1936–37, with contributions by Caillois, Klossowsky, Monnerot and others.

Bataille's *Histoire de l'oeil* is a sado-masochistic saga involving a series of murders, rapes, the gouging of eyes and castrations. From this surfeit of violence emerges a constellation of orbicular objects—eyes, eggs, testicles—which constitute the dominant theme of the work. The sense of segmentation, reassociation and metamorphosis of the object in Bataille's prose bears comparison with similar themes in Masson's work.

The bullfight is also an important theme in *Histoire de l'oeil*. It is not surprising that in 1913, Bataille and Masson urged Tériade and Skira to entitle their new review, *Minotaure*. Masson's illustrations for *Acéphale*, 1936–37 as well as his *Pasiphae* works, 1943–45, confirm his interest in this theme. The myth of the minotaur—as an expression of man's darker instincts and drives, in its emphasis on aggressive sexuality and mutation of human form—could not help but appeal strongly to Bataille, Masson, and the other Surrealists. In this regard, see Masson's statement in *Mythologie d'André Masson*, ed. Jean Paul Clébert (Geneva, 1971), p. 37: "Mais Bataille et moi, qui nous occupions des mythes grecs les plus sombres, en particulier les mythes dionysiaques et celui du labyrinthe de Crète, avons souligné que notre époque était tout à fait 'minotauresque,' et nous l'avons emporté." And about the Corrida: "Moi, je trouvais normal que ce ne soit pas toujours le taureau qui meurt. Il y a comme le reflet de *sacrifices humaines*. Ce n'est pas très aimable, mais je suis obligé de le dire. Le sacrificateur pouvait devenir le sacrifié. C'est ce qui donnait à la course sa valeur entière. De là à dire que je suis *un cannibale*" (p. 47). The journal *Acéphale*, subtitled, *Religion, Sociologie, Philosophie*, devoted a significant amount of space to Nietzsche and the Dionysian myths. Articles in *Documents*, between 1929–30, are devoted to sacrifices and religious ritual.

108. Françoise Will-Levaillant, *Mythographies masquées d'André Masson* (Paris, 1977), p. 43, recalls K. Mayo's description of the sacrifices of chevreaux in Calcutta, in *Documents*. ("Kali," *Documents*, 1930 (O.C.), p. 243.) Extrait de Katherine Mayo, *L'Inde avec les anglais* (trad. Theo Varlet): "Une femme s'est précipitée en avant et jetée à quatre pattes pour laper le sang avec sa langue."

109. The cult of Mithra proclaims that all good things come from the deity's sacrifice of the sacred bull. The minotaur is half-man and half-bull. The myth of Osiris also involved a bull—his soul inhabited Apis, the Bull of Memphis. See Françoise

Will-Levaillant, 1977, pp. 43–50. She cites an anthropological text: Mauss, "Essai sur la nature et la fonction du sacrifice," *L'Année sociologique*, 1897–98.

110. The Orpheus myth appears in veiled form, moreover, in a variety of other works by Cocteau, before 1925 and also thereafter. See, for instance, *Le Potomak*, 1913–14; *Le Cap de bonne-espérance*, 1916–19 (poem); *Discours du grand Sommeil*, 1916–18; *Le Secret professionnel*, 1922; *Plain-chant* (poem), 1923; *Opéra* (recueil de poèmes), 1925; *Pauvre matelot*, 1927 (livret de l'opéra, D. Milhaud); *Le Livre blanc*, 1928; *Le Mystère de Jean l'oiseleur*, 1925 (31 autoportraits); *Les Enfants terribles*, 1935; *Le Jeune Homme et la mort*, 1946. See Milorad, "Le Mythe Orphique dans l'oeuvre de Cocteau," in *Jean Cocteau—Cocteau et les mythes*, ed. J. J. Kihm, *La Revue des lettres modernes*, Nos. 298–303 (1972) (3) for a discussion of the veiled orphic imagery in these works and others.

111. Jean Cocteau, "Orphée," *Five Plays*, trans. Carl Wilman et al. (New York, 1961), p. 44. In this regard see Arthur B. Evans, *Jean Cocteau and his Films of Orphic Identity* (Philadelphia, 1977), p. 66.

112. Jean Cocteau, from *Journal d'un inconnu* (Paris, 1953), p. 48. See as well, Jean Cocteau, from *Entretiens avec André Fraigneau*, Bibliothèque, 10/18, 1955, p. 53.

113. Concerning the impact of Theosophical texts, especially Schuré, see n. 11, pp. 49–52 in *Orpheus, the Play and the Film* (Oxford, 1976), ed. E. Freeman.

114. Cocteau would certainly have known of Rilke from his stay at Rodin's Hôtel Biron in 1912. See Jean Cocteau, in *Professional Secrets* (New York, 1970), p. 58, talks of "burning his wings" in the light of Rilke's lamp. See also Arthur B. Evans, 1977, pp. 79–82. Though Cocteau never explicitly acknowledged the impact of Rilke, he did, however, express profound pleasure at the congratulatory telegram which the poet sent him upon the production of the play *Orphée* in Germany in 1926. Jean Cocteau, as quoted by Arthur B. Evans, p. 80, "Rilke knew of my play *Orphée*, produced in Berlin by Reinhardt and . . . he sent to Mme. K. this moving telegram: 'Tell Jean Cocteau that I love him. He is the only one whom poetry admits to the realm of myth, and he returns from its radiance aglow, as from a seashore.'" Evans goes on to note, "According to accurate documentation, however, the contents of Rilke's telegram was 'make Cocteau feel how warmly I admire him . . . ,'" but the differing message à la Cocteau shows, once again, to what extent he wanted and needed to be liked by his respected peer, Rilke.

Cocteau was fascinated with Catholicism, following his friend Max Jacob, in converting to that religion. Another work which involves a mixture of pagan and Christian themes is the 1933 play, *Les Chevaliers de la table ronde*. See also, the poem, "La Crucifixion," 1946, which focuses on the theme of the suffering of the soul and the flesh. Wallace Fowlie, *Jean Cocteau: The History of a Poet's Age* (Bloomington, 1966), p. 79, notes the angel Heurtebise's role in the play as a glazier and Cocteau's letter to his friend Jacques Maritain (also instrumental in Cocteau's conversion to Catholicism), in which Cocteau refers to Maritain as a creature of glass.

115. Jean Cocteau, from *Le Secret professionnel*, p. 186, as quoted by Arthur B. Evans, 1977, p. 32.

116. Jean Cocteau, from *The Hand of a Stranger*, trans. Alec Brown (London, 1956), p. 5, quoted by Arthur B. Evans, ibid., pp. 32–33.

117. Concerning Cocteau's film techniques, see *Cocteau on the film*, conversations recorded with André Fraigneau, trans. Vera Traill (New York, 1972).

118. See Arthur B. Evans, 1977, p. 65, who discusses *Le Sang d'un poète*, 1932, in terms of the entire plot development as only a pretext for an in-depth study of death versus the poet. Wallace Fowlie, 1966, pp. 102–3, discusses *Le Sang d'un poète* as the "inner life of a poet." The poet dives through a mirror where he finds the myths of his subconscious. The various episodes: the death of a Mexican, a flying lesson, an opium smoker, an hermaphrodite, are examined through the eye of a keyhole.

119. Milorad's analysis is Freudian in approach. Cocteau's preoccupation with Orpheus is connected with Cocteau's father's death. See Milorad, in "Jean Cocteau, Cocteau et les mythes," 1972, p. 134; and "La Clé des mythes dans l'oeuvre de Cocteau," in *Cahiers de Jean Cocteau*, No. 2 (Paris, 1971), p. 124.

   According to Milorad's analysis, Cocteau is fixated on his unresolved love for his dead father. Love and death are inextricably bound together, and tied, moreover, to Cocteau's creative and sexual identity. Milorad's analysis of the play, *Orphée*, focuses on the Christian virgin birth (p. 122):

   > Orphée, c'est le poète par excellence, donc, par excellence, l' "homme-mère," auteur de chants divins comme l'enfant divin. D'ou viennent les poèmes? Cette question correspond à celle des enfants: "D'ou viennent les enfants??" Si Cocteau est "le mère" de ses poèmes, qui en est le père? Le mythe de la Vierge répond: Dieu le Père, l'habitant par excellence de l'au-delà. Or, pour Cocteau, l'habitant par excellence de l'au-delà est son propre père mort. S'identifiant à la Mère, Cocteau conçoit donc avec le Père mort, et les fruits de cette union sont les poèmes.

120. Milorad, ibid., pp. 114–19, analyzes the women in Cocteau's work as symbols of his resentment of Princesse Natalie Paley, with whom he unsuccessfully tried to normalize his relationship with women. See as well Eva Kushner, *Le Mythe d'Orphée dans la littérature française contemporaine* (Paris, 1961), p. 23.

121. Jaroslaw Leshko, "Oscar Kokoschka's *Still Life with Cat, Rabbit and Child,*" *Arts Magazine* (January 1980): 84–88, specifically p. 87; See also Josef Paul Hodin, *Oscar Kokoschka, The Artist and His Time* (Greenwich, Conn., 1966), pp. 148–49. Kokoschka produced a number of drawings and prints which relate to the theater piece. See the etchings (four in total) in H. Wingler, *Oscar Kokoschka: Das Druckgraphische Werk* (Salzburg, ca. 1975), pp. 116–21; also note the painting with the same figure, illus. no. 48, cat. no. 117 in H. M. Wingler, *Oscar Kokoschka* (Salzburg, 1956).

122. Victor Segalen, *Orphée-Roi*, Paris, 1921. Eva Kushner, 1961, p. 23, sees Eurydice and Orpheus as two parts of the human psyche. See also Pierre Albouy, *Mythes et mythologies dans la littérature française* (Paris, 1969), pp. 191–92. Albouy cites an earlier novel, *Equipée:* "Le réel m'a paru toujours très femme. La femme m'a paru toujours très 'réel.' La matière est femme."

123. Jean Anouilh, *Eurydice* (Paris, 1958). See Pierre Albouy, ibid., pp. 195–96.

124. Pierre Albouy, ibid., pp. 196–201.

125. Ibid., pp. 199–201.

126. See Jacqueline Bellas, "Orphée au XIXe et au XXe siecle: Interférences littéraires et musicales," *CAIEF* (24 July 1969): 229–46; Annemie Schuermans, "Orpheus in de Musiek," in *Orpheus,* ed. A. Provoost (Leuven, 1974), pp. 133–47.

127. *Apollo,* 1928, *Orpheus,* 1948 and *Agon,* 1957, are conceived as a kind of triad. In Nancy Goldner, *The Stravinsky Festival of the New York City Ballet* (New York, 1973), p. 168, Lincoln Kirstein is quoted: "On that night of our first Stravinsky Festival, April 27, 1937, we begged a sequel. The composer confirmed this must inevitably involve Orpheus, Apollo's Thracian scion, whose claim was eloquent Calliope." Also note: Stravinsky's Orpheus was performed in 1948 at the Festival of Contemporary Music in Venice, with choreography by Aurel Milloss, and scenes and costumes by Fabrizio Clerici.

128. Georges Balanchine, *New Complete Stories of the Great Ballets* (Garden City, N.Y., 1968), p. 284.

129. Isamu Noguchi, in interview with Tobi Tobias, New York Public Library Dance Collection, Oral History Archives (January/February 1979), p. 44.

130. Isamu Noguchi, ibid., p. 49. Noguchi relates the costume designs to other balsa wood pieces from this period, including *Cronos,* in which pieces of wood and bone float in a frame.

131. Isamu Noguchi, ibid., p. 52. Balanchine, 1968, p. 287, describes the blue teardrop shape: "A blue stalactite descends from on high to symbolize the reunion."

132. Balanchine, ibid., p. 288.

133. See above, chapter 5. Isamu Noguchi, in Interview, 1979, p. 43, is unclear as to how the initial scene of Orpheus at the tomb of Eurydice evolved. He assumes that the conception was Balanchine's.

134. Isamu Noguchi, ibid., pp. 44–45.

135. Ibid., p. 45.

136. Lincoln Kirstein, quoted in Nancy Goldner, 1973, p. 169.

137. May Clarke and Clement Crisp, *Design for Ballet* (New York, 1978), p. 278, discuss how the decoration becomes a partner of the dance.

Perhaps the least successful elements of Noguchi's designs are the costumes—the bushy attire of the Nature Spirits; the spiky grey suits of the Furies; the entwining elements of the costumes worn by the Bacchantes and Orpheus, as well. In fact, the awkward nature of these costumes may be attributable to the use of new and ill-suited materials used when these works were manufactured for the 1972 revival of the piece at the New York State Theatre. Noguchi himself criticized the execution of the costumes. He found that the entwining ropes of some of the costumes resembled sausages or balloons, while they were "supposed to be part of the leotards, just sewn onto the leotards so that it didn't really stick out" (Isamu Noguchi, 1979, p. 41). Noguchi similarly criticizes the use of polyurethane foam for the rocks in Hades instead of the original papier maché. The new material squeaked during handling.

138. Ingolf Dahl, "The New Orpheus," *Dance Index* 6 (1947): 286.

139. Ibid., p. 285.

140. Isamu Noguchi, 1979, p. 46.

141. May Clarke and Clement Crisp, 1978, p. 277.

Bibliography

General Reference Works, Art History and Methodology, General Studies of the Image of Orpheus

Bénézit, Emmanuel. *Dictionnaire des peintres, sculpteurs, dessinateurs et graveurs.* Paris: Librairie Grund, 1976.
Cabañas, Pablo. *El Mito de Orfeo en la literatura española.* Madrid: Consejo Superior de Investigaciones Cientificas, 1948.
Durand, Gilbert. "Les Chats, les rats et les structuralistes: Symbole et structuralisme figuratif." *Cahiers Internationale de Symbolisme* 17–18 (1969): 13–38.
———. "Les Gnoses, structure et symboles archétypes." *Cahier Internationale de Symbolisme* 8 (1965): 15–34.
———. *L'Imagination Symbolique.* Paris: Presses Universitaires de France, 1968.
———. "L'Occident iconoclaste." *Cahier Internationale de Symbolisme* 2 (1963).
———. "Les Structures anthropologiques de l'imaginaire." *Introduction à l'archétypologie générale.* Paris/Brussels/Montreal: Bordas, 1969.
———. "Les Trois niveaux de la formation des symbolisme." *Cahier Internationale de Symbolisme* 7 (1962).
Freud, Sigmund. *Civilization and Its Discontents.* Trans. James Strachey. New York: W. W. Norton, 1961.
———. *On Creativity and the Unconscious.* New York: Harper & Row, 1958.
Johnson, J. Theodore, Jr. "Orpheus and the Orphic Mode in Literature and the arts." *The Register of the Spencer Museum of Art* (University of Kansas, Lawrence) 5, no. 9 (Fall 1981).
Johnson, Paul. *A History of Christianity.* New York: Atheneum, 1980.
Jung, Carl Gustav. *Answer to Job.* Trans. R. F. C. Hull. London: Routledge & Paul, 1954.
———. *Collected Works.* Ed. Herbert Read, Michael Fordham, Gerhard Adler. New York: Pantheon, 1953.
———. *Man and His Symbols.* New York: Dell (Laurel), 1964.
———. *The Portable Jung.* Ed. and intro. Joseph Campbell. Trans. R. F. C. Hull. New York: Penguin Books, 1971.
———. *Psyche and Symbol.* New York: Doubleday/Anchor, 1958.
———. *Psychology and Religion.* New Haven: Yale University Press, 1945.

———. *Two Essays on Analytical Psychology.* Trans. R. F. C. Hull. Cleveland and New York: Meridian Books/Bollingen, 1958.

Larousse. *Encyclopedia of Mythology.* Intro. Robert Graves. London: Batchworth Press, 1959.

Lockspeiser, Edward. *Music and Painting: A Study in Comparative Ideas from Turner to Schoenberg.* New York, Evanston, San Francisco, London: Icon (Harper & Row), 1973.

Marcuse, Herbert. *Eros and Civilization: A Philosophical Inquiry into Freud.* New York: Vintage Books, 1955.

Mayerson, Philip. *Classical Mythology in Literature, Art and Music.* Waltham, Massachusetts: Xerox, 1971.

"Le Mythe d'Orphée au XIXe et au XXe siècle." *Cahiers de l'Association Internationale des Etudes Françaises* (Paris), No. 22 (May 1970). Including seven essays: B. Juden, "Particularités du mythe d'Orphée chez Ballanche," pp. 137–52; A. Fairlie, "Le Mythe d'Orphée dans l'ouevre de Gérard de Nerval," pp. 153–68; L. J. Austin, "Mallarmé et le mythe d'Orphée," pp. 169–80; W. McC. Stewart, "Peut-on parler d'un 'orphisme' de Valéry?" pp. 181–96; E. Kushner, "Orphée et l'orphisme chez Victor Ségalen," pp. 197–214; M. Decaudin, "Deux aspects du mythe orphique au XXe siècle: Apollinaire, Cocteau," pp. 215–28; J. Bellas, "'Orphée' au XIXe et au XXe siècle: interférences littéraires et musicales," pp. 229–46.

The Oxford Classical Dictionary. Oxford: Clarendon Press, 1964 ed.

Praz, Mario. *Mnemosyne: The Parallel Between Literature and the Visual Arts.* Princeton: Princeton University Press, 1970.

Shakespeare, William. *Twenty-three Plays and Sonnets.* Madison, Wisconsin: Charles Scribner, 1938.

Thieme-Becker (Ulrich Thieme and Felix Becker). *Allgemeines Lexikon der Bildenden Künstler, von der Antike bis zur Gegenwart.* Leipzig: Verlag von E.A. Seemann, 1907–50.

Washington, D.C. *The Summary Catalogue of European Painting and Sculpture.* The National Gallery of Art, 1965.

Mythological Source Texts, Mythological Studies, Orpheus and Orphism

Aeschylus. Vol. 1: *Oresteia.* Trans. and intro. Richmond Lattimore. Chicago: University of Chicago Press, 1953.

Aeschylus. *Oresteia (Agamemnon, Libation Bearers, The Eumenides).* Trans. Richmond Lattimore. Chicago and London: Phoenix Books, The University of Chicago Press, 1969.

Alderink, Larry J. *Creation and Salvation in Ancient Orphism.* American Classical Studies 8. Chico, Calif.: American Philological Association/Scholars Press, 1981.

Apollodorus. *The Library.* Trans. Sir James George Frazer. London and New York: William Heinemann and G. P. Putnam's Sons, 1921; Cambridge and London: Harvard University Press and William Heinemann, 1954.

Apollonius Rhodius. *Argonautica.* Trans. R. C. Seaton. London and New York: William Heinemann and G. P. Putnam's Sons, 1912.

Apuleius. *The Transformations of Lucius, Otherwise Known as the Golden Ass.* Trans. Robert Graves. New York: Farrar, Strauss, Giroux, 1951.

Aristophanes. *The Peace, The Birds, The Frogs.* Trans. B. Rogers. Cambridge and London: Harvard University Press and William Heinemann, 1961. Vol. 2.

Athenaeus (Hermesianax van Colphon). *The Deipnosophists.* Trans. C. B. Gulick. Cambridge and London: Harvard University Press and William Heinemann, 1937. Vol. 6.

Avery, Catherine B., ed. *The New Century Handbook of Greek Mythology and Legend.* New York: Appleton, Century, Crofts, Meredith, 1972.

Batman, Stephen. *The Golden Book of the Leaden Gods.* London, 1577; New York: Garland, 1976.

Baudouin, I. *Recherches touchant la mythologie: Recuellis des anciens auteurs.* Paris, 1627; New York: Garland, 1981.

Boethius. *The Theological Tractates, The Consolation of Philosophy.* Trans. H. F. Stewart. London and Cambridge: William Heinemann and Harvard University Press, 1936.

Böhme, Robert. *Orpheus: Der Sänger und seine Zeit.* Bern: Francke, 1970.

Boulanger, André. *Orphée: Rapports de l'orphisme et christianisme.* Paris: F. Rieder, 1925.

Bulfinch, Thomas. *Mythology.* New York: Avenel Books, 1978.

Callimachus. *Hymns and Epigrams, Lycophron, Aratus.* Cambridge and London: Harvard University Press and William Heinemann, 1955.

Campbell, Joseph. *The Masks of God: Creative Mythology.* New York: Penguin Books, 1968.

———. *The Masks of God: Occidental Mythology.* New York: Penguin Books, 1964.

———, ed. *The Mysteries, Papers from the Eranos Yearbooks.* Trans. Ralph Manheim. Bollingen Series 30, vol. 2. Princeton: Princeton University Press, 1955.

Chesneau, Augustine. *Orpheus eucharisticus.* Paris: Apud Florentinum Lambert, 1657.

Chevalier, Jean. *Dictionnaire des symboles.* Paris, 1969.

Ciaceri, Emmanuele. "Orfismo e pitagorismo nei loro rapporti politico-sociali." *Reale accademizi di archeologia lettere e belle arti.* (Atti, Napoli) n.s., 12 (1933): 207–23.

Cicero. *De Natura Deorum.* Trans. H. Rackham. London and New York: William Heinemann and G. P. Putnam's Sons, 1933.

Comes, Natalis. *Mythologii.* Trans. Jean Baudouin. [Paris, 1627] New York: Garland, 1976.

Cornford, F. M. "Plato and Orpheus." *Classical Revues* (London) 17 (1903): 433–45.

———. *From Religion to Philosophy.* London: E. Arnold, 1912.

Cumont, Franz. *After Life in Roman Paganism.* New Haven: Yale University Press, 1922.

Deutsch, Helene. *A Psychoanalytic Study of the Myth of Dionysus and Apollo: Two Variants of the Son-Mother Relationship.* New York: International University Press, 1969.

Diel, Paul. *Le Symbolisme dans la mythologie grecque, étude psychanalytique.* Pref. Gaston Bachelard. Paris: Payot, 1966.

Diodorus Siculus. Trans. C. H. Oldfather. Cambridge and London: Harvard University Press and William Heinemann, 1933.

Dodds, E. R. *The Greeks and the Irrational.* Berkeley, Los Angeles, London: University of California Press, [1951] 1971.

Dyson, George Wilfred. "Orphism and the Platonic Philosophy." *Speculum religionis* (Oxford) (1929): 19–48.

Eisler, Robert. *Orpheus the Fisher: Comparative Studies in Orphic and Early Cult Symbolism.* London: Watkins, 1921.

———. *Orphische-dionysische Mysteriengedanken in der christlichen Antike.* Hildesheim: Georg Olms Verlagsbuchhandlung, [1925] 1966.

Eliade, Mircea. *Forgeries et alchimistes.* Paris: Flammarion, 1952.

———. *Histoire des croyances et des idées religieuses.* Paris: Payot, 1976.

———. *Images et symboles: Essais sur le symbolisme magico-religieux.* Paris: Gallimard, 1952.

———. *Initiations, rites, sociétés secrètes, naissances secrètes . . . essai sur quelques types d'initiation.* Paris: Gallimard, 1976.

———. *Le Mythe de l'éternel retour: Archétypes et répétition.* Paris: Gallimard, 1949.

———. *Mythes, rêves et mystères.* Paris: Gallimard, 1957.

———. *The Sacred and Profane: The Nature of Religion.* Trans. Willard R. Trask. New York and London: Harcourt Brace Jovanovich, 1959.

Euripides. *Four Tragedies.* Vol. 1: *Alcestis.* Intro. Richmond Lattimore. Chicago and London: University of Chicago Press, 1955.

———. *Tragedies.* Vol. 2: *Rhesus.* Trans. Richmond Lattimore. New York: Modern Library, Random House, 1958.

———. *Tragedies.* Vol. 3: *Iphigenia in Aulis.* Trans. Charles R. Walker. New York: Modern Library, Random House, 1959.

———. *Three Tragedies.* Vol. 5: *The Bacchae.* Trans. William Arrowsmith. Chicago and London: Phoenix Books and University of Chicago Press, 1959.

Farnell, Lewis Richard. *Greek Hero Cults and Ideas of Immortality.* Oxford: The Clarendon Press, 1921.

Fraunce, Abraham. *The Third Part of the Countess Pembroke's Yvychurch, Amintas Dale.* [London, 1592] New York: Garland, 1976.

Freden, Gustaf. *Orpheus and the Goddess of Nature.* Göteborg: Elanders Boktryckeri Aktiebolag, 1958.

Gide, André. "Considérations sur la Mythologie Grecque Fragment de Traîté des Dioscure." In *Oeuvres complètes.* Ed. L. Martin Chauffrer. Vol. 4. Paris, 1932–39.

Godwin, Joscelyn. *Mystery Religions in the Ancient World.* London: Thames & Hudson, 1981.

Goodenough, Erwin R. *Religious Tradition and Myth.* New Haven: Yale University Press, 1937.

Graf, Fritz. *Eleusis und die Orphische Dichtung Athens in vorhellenistischer Zeit.* Berlin/New York: Walter de Gruyter, 1974.

Graves, Robert. *The Greek Myth.* New York: George Braziller, 1957.

The Greek Anthology. Trans. W. R. Paton. London and New York: William Heinemann and G. P. Putnam's Sons, 1925. Vol. 2.

Gropengiesser, H. "Sänger und Sirenen: Versuch einer Deutung." *Aarch. Anzeiger* 4 (1977): 582–610.

Gruppe, Otto. *Geschichte der klassischen Mythologie und Religionsgeschichte.* Leipzig: 1921.

Guthrie, W. K. C. *Orpheus and Greek Religion.* London: Methuen & Co., 1935.

Harrison, June. *Prolegomena to the Study of Greek Religion.* Cambridge: Cambridge University Press, 1922.

Hatch, Edwin. *The Influence of Greek Ideas on Christianity.* New York: Harper & Row, 1957.
Hauser, Friedrich. "Orpheus und Aigisthus." *Archäologisches Institut Jahrbuch* (Berlin) 29 (1914): 26–32.
Herodotus. *Histories.* Trans. A. D. Godley. London and New York: William Heinemann and G. P. Putnam's Sons, 1920. Vol. 1.
Hesiod. *The Homeric Hymns and Homerica.* Trans. Hugh G. Evelyn-White. Cambridge and London: Harvard University Press and William Heinemann, 1959.
Heurgan, Jacques. "Orphée et Eurydice avant Virgile." *Ecole française de Rome. Mélanges d'archéologie et d'histoire* (Paris) 49 (1932): 6–60.
Homer. *The Odyssey.* Ed. Richmond Lattimore. New York, Evanston, London: Harper-Torchbooks, 1968.
Horace. *Satires, Epistles and Ars Poetica.* Trans. H. R. Fairclough. London and New York: William Heinemann and G. P. Putnam's Sons, 1929.
Isocrates. *Busiris.* Trans. Larue van Hook. Cambridge and London: Harvard University Press and William Heinemann, 1961. Vol. 3.
Jacoby, F. *Fragmente der griechischen Historiker.* 1923.
Jonas, Hans. *The Gnostic Religion.* Boston: 1970.
Jung, C. G. and Carl Kerenyi. *Essays on a Science of Mythology: The Myth of the Divine Child and the Mysteries of Eleusis.* Trans. R. F. C. Hull. Bollingen Series 22. Princeton: Princeton University Press, 1963.
―――. *Introduction to a Science of Mythology, the Myth of the Divine Child. . . .* Trans. R. F. C. Hull. London: Routledge & Paul, 1951.
Kerenyi, Karl. "Orfeo simbolo Dionisiaco." *Umanesimo e simbolismo.* Ed. Enrico Castelli. Padova: CEDAM, 1958.
―――. "Pythagoras und Orpheus." *Aufsätze zur Geschichte der Antike und des Christentums.* Berlin: Die Runde, 1937.
―――. *Pythagoras und Orpheus.* Amsterdam: Pantheon, Akademische Verlagsanstalt, 1940.
Kern, Otto. *Orpheus, eine religionsgeschichtliche Untersuchung.* Berlin: Weidmansche Buchhandlung, 1920.
―――. *Orphicorum fragmenta.* Berlin: Weidmannos, 1963.
Kris, Ernst and Otto Kurz. *Legend, Myth, and Magic in the Image of the Artist.* New Haven and London: Yale University Press, 1979.
La Boullaye, Pinard de. *L'Etude comparée des Religions.* 2 vols. Paris: 1922.
Linforth, Ivan Mortimer. *The Arts of Orpheus.* New York: Arno Press, 1973.
Lobeck, C. A. *Aglaophamus.* Königsberg: Borntraeger, 1829.
Loisy, Alfred. "Dionysus and Orphée." *Revue d'histoire et de la littérature religieuse* (Paris), n.s., 4 (1913): 130–54.
Lucian V. Ed. A. M. Harmon. Including *On Astrology.* London and Cambridge: William Heinemann, 1962.
Lynche. *The Fountaine of Ancient Fiction (Cartari, Imagini delle dei degli antiche).* [London, 1599] New York: Garland, 1976.
Lyra Graeca. 3 vols. Trans. J. M. Edmonds. Cambridge and London: Harvard University Press and William Heinemann, 1958.

Macchioro, Vittorio D. *From Orpheus to Paul: A History of Orphism.* New York: Henry Holt & Co., 1930.
Marolles, Michel de. *Tableaux du temple des muses.* [Paris, 1655] New York: Garland, 1976.
Mauss, Marcel. "Essai sur la nature et la fonction du sacrifice." *L'Année Sociologique* (1897–98).
Meade, G. R. S. *Orpheus.* New York: Barnes & Noble, 1965.
Moulinier, Louis. *Orphée et l'orphisme à l'époque classique.* Paris: Belles-lettres, 1955.
Murray, Sister Charles. "The Christian Orpheus." *Cahier archaeologique* 26 (1977): 19–28.
The Nag Hammadi Library in English. Ed. James M. Robinson. San Francisco: Harper & Row, 1977.
Nilsson, Martin P. *The Dionysiac Mysteries.* Series: Ancient Religion & Mythology. New York: Arno Press, 1975.
———. *A History of Greek Religion.* Oxford: Clarendon Press, 1925.
———. "Orpheus" and "Orphisme," *The Oxford Classical Dictionary.* Oxford: Clarendon Press, 1964.
Otto, Walter F. *Dionysus: Myth and Cult.* Trans. and intro. by Robert B. Palmer. Bloomington and London: Indiana University Press, 1965.
Ovid. *Metamorphoses.* Trans. Rolfe Humphries. Bloomington: Indiana University Press, 1960.
Pagels, Elaine. *The Gnostic Gospels.* New York: Vintage, 1981.
Pausanias. *Description of Greece.* Trans. W. H. S. Jones. Cambridge and London: Harvard University Press and William Heinemann, 1935. Vol. 4.
Philostratus, The Elder. *Imagines* and Callistratus, *Descriptions.* Trans. Arthur Fairbanks. London and New York: William Heinemann and G. P. Putnam's Sons, 1931.
Pindar. *Olympiques, Pythiques, Isthmigues et fragments.* Trans. Aimé Puech. Paris: Société d'Edition des Belles Lettres, 1922–23.
Pindarus. *The Odes, Including the Principal Fragments.* Trans. Sir John Sandys. London and New York: William Heinemann and G. P. Putnam's Sons, 1927.
Plato. *Collected Dialogues.* Ed. Edith Hamilton, Huntington Cairns. Bollingen Series 71. Princeton: Princeton University Press, 1961.
Rahner, Hugo, S. J. *Greek Myths and Christian Mystery.* New York and Evanston: Harper & Row, 1957.
Reinach, Salomon. *Cultes, mythes et religions.* Paris: E. Leroux, 1923.
———. *Orpheus: Histoire générale des religions.* Paris: Alcide Picard, ed. 1909.
———. *Orpheus: A History of religions.* Trans. Florence Simmonds. New York: Horace Liveright, 1930.
Reitzenstein, R. and H. H. Schaeder. *Studien, an antikem Synkretismus aus Iran und Griechenland.* Berlin: B. G. Teubner, 1921.
Ripa, Cesare. *Iconologia or Moral Emblems.* [London, 1709] New York and London: Garland, 1976.
———. *Iconology.* Ed. George Richardson. [London, 1779] New York: Garland, 1979.
Sabinus, Georgius. *Metamorphosis Seu Fabulae Poeticae.* [Frankfurt, 1589] New York, London: Garland, 1976.

Seneca. *Tragedies, Hercules Furens, Hercules Oetaeus.* Trans. Frank Justus Miller. Chicago and London: University of Chicago Press and T. Fisher Unwin, 1907.

―――. *Four Tragedies and Octavia (Thyestes, Phaedra, The Trojan Women, Oedipus).* Trans. and ed. E. F. Watling. Harmondsworth: Penguin, 1966.

Virgil. *The Aeneid.* Trans. Rolfe Humphries. New York: Charles Scribners, 1951.

―――. *Eclogues, Georgics, Aeneid 1–6.* Trans. H. R. Fairclough. Cambridge and London: Harvard University Press and William Heinemann, 1974.

Warden, John, ed. *Orpheus: The Metamorphoses of a Myth.* Toronto: University of Toronto Press, 1982.

Watmough, Ronald. *Orphism.* Cambridge: Cambridge University Press, 1934.

Wili, Walter. "The Orphic Mysteries and the Greek Spirit." *The Mysteries, Papers from the Eranos Yearbooks.* Ed. Joseph Campbell. Bollingen Series 30–2. Princeton: Princeton University Press, 1955.

Ziegler, Konrad. "Orphische Dichtung." In *Realencyclopedia der classischen Altertumwissenschaft.* Ed. Pauley, Wissowa, Kroll. Vol. 18, part 2, cols. 1321–1417. Stuttgart: J. B. Metzler, 1942.

The Visual Tradition: Depictions of Orpheus Prior to the Nineteenth Century

Alciati, Andrea. *Emblematum libellus.* [Paris, 1542] Darmstadt: Wissenschaftliche Buchgesellschaft, 1967.

Allen, Don Cameron. *Mysteriously Meant Rediscovery of Pagan Symbolism.* Baltimore: Johns Hopkins Press, 1970.

Alpers, Svetlana L. "Manner and Meaning in Some of Rubens Mythologies." *Journal of the Warburg and Courtauld Institute* 30 (1967): 272–95.

Avery, C. H. F. "Hendrick de Keyser as a Sculptor of Small Bronzes Including His Orpheus and Cerberus Identified." *Bull. Rijksmuseum Amsterdam* 21 (April 1973): 3–24.

Bardon, Henry. "Les Peintures de sujets antiques au XVIIIe siècle, d'après les livrets des Salons." *Gazette des beaux-arts.* pp. 217–49.

Barksdale, A. B. "Some Musical Sidelights of Tietz's *Orpheus*." *Cleveland Museum Bulletin* 59 (September 1972): 212–14.

[Bartsch, Adam.] *The Illustrated Bartsch.* Vol. 16 (formerly vol. 8, pt. 3). Ed. Robert A. Koch. New York: Abaris, 1980.

―――. *The Illustrated Bartsch.* Vol. 26 (formerly vol. 14, p. 1). Ed. Konrad Oberhuber. New York: Abaris, 1978.

Béguin, Sylvie. *Mostra di Nicolo dell'Abate.* Bologna: Edizioni Alfa, 1969.

Bellonci, Maria, ed. *L'Opera completa del Mantegna.* Milan: Rizzoli, 1967.

Bigi, Emilio. *La cultura del Poliziano e altri studi umanistici.* Pisa: Nistri-Lischi, 1967.

Bikerman, E. "The Orphic Blessing." *The Journal of the Warburg and Courtauld Institutes* (London) 2 (July 1938–April 1939): 368–74.

Blunt, Anthony. *Art and Architecture in France, 1500–1700.* Harmondsworth, Middlesex and Baltimore, Md.: Penguin, 1953.

Blunt, Wilfred. "Exhibitions in Edinburgh." *Burlington Magazine* 91 (1949): 256–58.

Bode, Wilhelm von. *Bertoldo und Lorenzo dei Medici.* Freiburg im Breisgau: Pontos-Verlag, 1925.
Bosio, Antonio. *Roma sotterranea.* Rome: L. Grignani, 1650.
Bousquet, Jacques. *Mannerism. The Painting and Style of the Late Renaissance.* New York: George Braziller, 1964.
Buck, August. *Der Orpheus: Mythos in der italienischen Renaissance.* Krefeld: Scherpe, 1961.
Cartari, Vicenzo. *Imagini delle dei degli antichi.* Lione: Stefano Michele, 1581; Graz: Akademische Druck u., Verlagsanstalt, 1963.
Cartier, E. *Etude sur l'art Chrétien.* Paris: Librairie de Firmin-Didot Frères, 1875.
Chastel, André. *Art et humanisme en Florence au temps de Laurent le Magnifique.* Paris: 1959.
―――. *Marsile Ficin et l'art.* Travaux d'Humanisme et Renaissance, vol. 14. Geneva, Droz, Lille: Giard, 1954.
Chiario, Model. "New Orpheus Mosaic in Yugoslavia." *American Journal Archaeology* 76 (April 1972): 197–200.
Coletti, Luigi. *Cima da Conegliano.* Venice: Neri Pozza Ed., 1959.
Collignon, L. M. *Mythologie figurée de la Grèce.* Paris: Bibliothèque de l'Enseignements des Beaux-Arts, 1883.
Cumont, Franz. *Recherches sur le symbolisme funéraire des romains.* Paris: 1942.
Cust, Robert H. Hobart. "On Some Overlooked Masterpieces." *Burlington Magazine* 4 (1904): 256–58.
Deonna, Waldemar. "Orphée et l'oracle de la tête coupée." *Revue des études grecques* (Paris) 38 (1925): 44–69.
Donati, Lamberto. "A comment on the 'Death of Orpheus' in Italian Engraving of the Quattrocento." *Libri* (Copenhagen) 5, no. 1 (1954): 17–19.
D'Orsi, Mario. *Corrado Giaquinto.* Rome: Arte della stampa, 1958.
Dynes, Wayne. "Orpheus without Eurydice." *Gai Saber* 1, no. 3 (1978).
Essen, Carl Claudius van. *Did Orphic Influence on Etruscan Tomb Painting Exist?* Amsterdam: H. J. Paris, 1927.
Ferrari, Oreste, and Giuseppe Scavizei. *Luca Giordano.* 3 vols. Florence: Edizione Scientifiche Italiane, 1966.
Finney, Paul Corby. "Orpheus-David: A Connection in Iconography between Greco-Roman Judaism and Early Christianity." *Journal of Jewish Art* 5 (1978): 6–15.
Fischer, Erik. "'Orpheus and Calais': On the Subject of Giorgione's 'Concert Champêtre,'" *Liber Amicorum Karel G. Boon* (Amsterdam) 5 (1974): 71–77.
Florence, Istituto nazionale di studi sul Rinascimento. *Mostra del Poliziano nella Biblioteca medicea laurenziana* (23 September–30 November 1954).
Friedman, John Block. *Orpheus in the Middle Ages.* Cambridge, Mass.: Harvard Univerity Press, 1970.
Garas, Klara. *F. A. Maulbertsch.* Graz: Akademische Druck und Verlagsanstalt, 1960.
Garte, E. "The Theme of Resurrection in the Dura-Europos Synagogue Paintings." *Society of Architectural Historians Journal* 28 (October 1969): 213.
Garucci, P. Raffaele. *Storia della Arte Cristiana nei primi otto secoli della chiesa.* Prato: Giachetti, 1873–81.

———. *Sculture non cimiteriali*. Rome, 1880.
Giehlow, Carl. "Poliziano und Dürer." *Die Graphischen Künste* 1 (1902): 25–26.
Gordon, R. K., trans. *Anglo-Saxon Poetry*. New York and London: Dutton and Dent, 1970.
Gros Louis, Kenneth R. R. "Robert Henryson's 'Orpheus and Eurydice' and the Orpheus Traditions of the Middle Ages." *Speculum* 41 (1966): 643–55.
Hartt, Frederick. *Giulio Romano*. New Haven, Conn.: Yale University Press, 1958.
———. "Giulio Romano and the Palazzo del Tè." Ph.D. thesis, New York University, Institute of Fine Arts, 1949.
Heinemann, Fritz. *Giovanni Bellini e I Belliniani*. Venice: Pozza, 1962.
Held, J. S. "Edward Hicks and the Tradition." *Art Quarterly* 14 (1951): 121ff.
Henkel, Arthur and Albrecht Schöne. *Emblemata-Handbuch zur Sinnbildkunst des XVI. und XVII. Jahrhunderts*. Stuttgart: J. B. Metzlersche Verlags-Buchhandlung, 1967.
Henryson, Robert. *Orpheus and Eurydice*. [Edinburgh: Walter Chapman and Andrew Myllar, 1580] Edinburgh: The Chapman and Myllar prints, 1950.
Hoffmann, H. "Orpheus unter der Thrakern." *Jahrbuch Hamburger Kunstsammlungen* 14–15 (1970): 31–44.
Janot, Paul. "L'Inspiration du Poète par Poussin." *Gazette des beaux-arts*. 2eme sér. 53 (1911): 177–92.
Joukovsky-Micha, Françoise. *Orphée et ses disciples dans la poésie française et néo-latine du XVIe siecle*. Geneva: Droz, 1970.
———. *Poésie et mythologie au XVIe siècle. Quelques mythes de l'inspiration chez les poètes de la Renaissance*. Paris: Nizet, 1969.
Kauffmann, C. M. "Orpheus: The Lion and the Unicorn." *Apollo*, No. 98 (September, 1973): 192–96.
Kristeller, P. O. "Music and Learning in the Early Italian Renaissance." In *Renaissance Though and the Arts*. Princeton: Princeton University Press, 1980.
Kurz, Otto. "Holbein and Others in a Seventeenth Century Collection." *Burlington Magazine* 83 (1943): 279–82.
Landgedijk, Karla. "Baccio Bardinelli's *Orpheus*. A Political Message." *Mitteilungen des Kunsthistorischen Instituts in Florenz* 20, pt. 1 (1976): 33–52.
Leclercq, Dom H. *Manuel d'archéologie chrétienne*. Paris: Letouzez Editions, 1907.
Lee, M. O. "Mystic Orpheus: Another Note on the Three Figure Reliefs." *Hesperia* 33 (October 1964): 401–4.
Levkoff, Mary. "Christoforo Stati's 'Orpheus,' A Sculpture of the Late Maniera." M.A. thesis, New York University, Institute of Fine Arts, 1978.
Malamani, Vittorio. *Canova*. Milan: Ulrico Hoepli.
Martin, John Rupert. *The Farnese Gallery*. Princeton: Princeton University Press, 1965.
Marucchi, O. *Monumenti del Museo Lateranense*. Rome: 1890.
Meyer-Baer, Kathi. *Music of the Spheres and the Dance of Death*. Princeton: Princeton University Press, 1970.
Michaelis, A. *A Century of Archaeological Discoveries*. London: John Murray, 1908.
Morassi, Antonio. "Some 'modelli' and Other Unpublished Works by Tiepolo." *Burlington Magazine* 97 (1955): 4–12.

Mossakowski, Stanislaw. "Raphael's 'St. Cecelia.' An Iconographical Study." *Zeitschrift für Kunstgeschichte* 31 (1968): 1–26.
Ovid. *Metamorphoseos*. [Bersuire, Lyon, 1518] New York and London: Garland, 1976.
Ovid. *Metamorphoses*. Trans. Garth, Dryden, et al. [Amsterdam, 1732] New York and London: Garland, 1976.
Pallucchini, Rodolfo. *La giovinezza del Tintoretto*. Milan: Edizione Daria Guarnati, 1950.
———. *Tiziano*. 2 vols. Florence: Sansoni, 1969.
Panofsky, Erwin. *Albrecht Dürer*. Princeton: Princeton University Press, 1943.
———. *Dürer's Stellung zur Antike*. Vienna: Oesterreichische Verlagsgesellschaft, Eduard Hölzel, 1922.
———. "The Early History of Man in a Series of Paintings by Piero di Cosimo." *The Journal of the Warburg and Courtauld Institute* 1 (1937–38): 12–30.
———. *Studies in Iconology*. New York: Oxford University Press, 1939.
Peraté, André. *L'Archéologie chrétienne*. Paris: Alcide Picard and Koan, 1892.
Picard, Charles. "Orphée, les fontaines et les tombes." *Revue archéologique* 1 (January 1960): 118–20.
Pirrotta, Nino. *Li due Orfei da Poliziano a Monteverdi*. Turin: Einandi, 1975.
Politian, Angel. Translation of *Orpheus* and Torgilato Tasso, *Aminta*. Intro. Louis E. Lord. London: Oxford University Press, Humphrey Milford, 1931.
Poliziano, Angelo. *Le stanze per la giostra d'Orfeo*. Milan: Signorelli.
Provoost, A., ed. *Orpheus*. Leuven: Acco, 1974.
Reinach, Salomon. "La Mort d'Orphée." *Revue Archéologique*, sér. 3, 41: 242–79.
———. *Peintures de vases antiques recueillies par Millin (1808) et Millingen (1815)*. Paris: F. Didot, 1891.
———. *Répertoire de peintures grecques et romaines*. Paris: Ernest Leroux, 1922.
———. *Répertoire de reliefs grecques et romaines*. Paris: Ernest Leroux, 1909–12.
———. *Répertoire de la statuaire grecque et romaine*. Paris: Ernest Leroux, 1920–30.
[Ripa, Cesare. *Iconologia*.] *Baroque and Rococo Pictorial Imagery: The 1758–60 Hertel Edition of Ripa's "Iconologia."* Ed. Edw. A. Maser. New York: Dover, 1971.
Rosenberg, Adolf. *Rubens*. New York: Brentanos, 1913.
Rosenberg, Pierre and Antoine Schnapper. *Jean Restout*. Rouen: Musée des Beaux-Arts, 17 June–15 September 1970.
Rossi, Giovanni Battista de. *Inscriptiones Christianae urbis Romae septimo saeculo antiguiores*. Rome: Ex, officina Libraria Doct. Befani, 1922.
———. *La Roma sotterranea cristiana*. Rome: Cromo-litografia pontificia, 1864–79.
Sandys, George. *Ovid's Metamorphoses Englished*. [Oxford, 1632] New York, London: Garland, 1976.
Schmidt, M. "Ein Neues Zeugnis Zum Mythos vom Orpheushaupt." *Antike Kunst* 15, no. 2 (1972): 128–37.
Schoeller, Felix M. "Darstellungen des Orpheus in der Antike." Inaugural dissertation, Albert-Ludwigs Universität, Freiburg, 1969.
Schubring, Paul. *Cassoni, Truhen und Truhenbilder der italienischen Frührenaissance*. Leipzig: K. W. Hiersemann, 1915.
Schuster, Peter Klaus. "Zu Dürers Zeichnung 'Der Tod des Orpheus' und verwandten Darstellungen." *Jahrbuch der Hamburger Kunstsammlungen* 23 (1978): 7–24.

Seznec, Jean. *The Survival of the Pagan Gods: The Mythological Tradition and Its Place in Renaissance Humanism and Art.* Trans. Barbara F. Sessions. Bollingen Series 38. Princeton: Princeton University Press, 1972.

――――. "The Temptation of Saint Anthony in Art." *Magazine of Art* 40, no. 3 (March 1947): 87–93.

Shapiro, M. L. "Widener Orpheus." *Studies in the History of Art* (1974): 23–26.

Shapley, Fern Rusk. "Giovanni Bellini and Cornaro's Gazelle." *Gazette des beaux-arts*, sér. 6, 28 (July–December 1945): 27–30.

Sittl, Karl. *Die Gebärden der Griechen und Römer.* [Leipzig, 1890] Hildesheim/New York: 1970.

Solerti, Angelo. *Musica, Ballo e Drammatica alla Corte Medicea.* New York and London: Benjamin Blom, 1968.

Stern, Henri. "Un Nouvel Orphée-David dans un mosaïque du VIe siècle," *Académie des Inscriptions et Belles-lettres, comptes rendus* (Paris) (1970): 63–79.

――――. "Orphée dans l'art paléochretien." *Cahiers archéologiques* 23 (1974): 1–16.

――――. "Orpheus in the Synagogue of Dura Europos." *Journal of the Warburg and Courtauld Institutes* 21 (January 1958): 1–6.

Strauss, Walter A. *The Complete Drawings of Albrecht Dürer.* New York: Abaris Books, 1974.

Suida, W. *Le Titien.* Paris: A. Weber, 1935.

Tempesta, Antonio. *Metamorphoseon . . . Ovidianarum.* [Amsterdam, 1606] New York and London: Garland, 1976.

Tervareut, Guy de. *Attributs et symboles dans l'art profane.* Geneva, 1958–59.

Tietze-Conrat, E. *Mantegna.* London: Phaidon, 1955.

Tolnay, Charles de. "The Music of the Universe." *The Journal of the Walters Art Gallery* 6 (1943): 83–104.

Valentin, Marius. *Orpheus und Herakles in der Unterwelt.* Berlin: G. Reiner, 1865.

Verheyen, Egon. *The Palazzo del Tè in Mantua: Images of Love and Politics.* Baltimore: Johns Hopkins, 1977.

――――. "Correggio's Amori de Giove." *Journal of the Warburg and Courtauld Institutes* 29 (1966): 160–92.

――――. "Die Sala di Ovidio im Palazzo del Tè." *Römisches Jahrbuch für Kunstgeschichte* 12 (1969): 161–70.

Vermeule, Emily. *Aspects of Death in Early Greek Art and Poetry.* Berkeley and Los Angeles: UCLA Press, 1979.

Walker, D. P. "Le Chant orphique de Marsile Ficin." Communication au 5e Colloque International du Centre de la Recherche Scientifique (Sciences Humaines). *Musique et Poésie au XVIe siècle.* Ed. Centre National de la Recherche Scientifique, Paris, n.d.

――――. "Orpheus the Theologian and Renaissance Platonists." *Journal of the Warburg and Courtauld Institutes* 16 (1953): 100–120.

Washington, D.C. *Dürer in America: His Graphic Work.* Ed. Charles W. Talbot. National Gallery of Art, 1971.

Weitzmann, Kurt. *Greek Mythology in Byzantine Art.* Princeton: Princeton University Press, 1951.

Wilkins, Ernest H. "Descriptions of Pagan Divinities from Petrarch to Chaucer." *Speculum* 32 (1957): 511–22.
Wilput, J. *Die Malereien der Katakomben Roms.* Fribourg, 1903.
Wind, Edgar. "'Hercules' and 'Orpheus': Two Mock-Heroic Designs by Dürer." *The Journal of the Warburg and Courtauld Institutes* 2 (July 1938–April 1939): 206–18.
Winternitz, Emanuel. "Orpheus before Opera." *Opera News* 32, no. 15 (10 February 1968): 8–13.
Wittkower, Rudolf. *Architectural Principles in the Age of Humanism.* London: Alec Tiranti, 1962.
Wittkower, Rudolf and Margot. *Born under Saturn: The Character and Conduct of Artists—A Documented History from Antiquity to the French Revolution.* New York, London: W. W. Norton, 1969.
Wril, Julius. *Orpheus in der englischen Literatur.* Wiener Beiträge zur Englischen Philologie. Vol. 40. Wien: W. Braumüller, 1913.
Yates, Frances A. *Giordano Bruno and the Hermetic Tradition.* New York: Vintage Books, 1969.
———. *The Rosicrucian Enlightenment.* London and Boston: Routledge and Kegan Paul, 1972.
Ziegler, Konrad. "Orpheus in der Renaissance und Neuzeit," pp. 248ff. *Form und Inhalt: Studien für Otto Schmitt.* 1950.

Nineteenth-Century Mythographies, Mysticism, Syncretic Histories, Alternative Religions, Occultism

Amadou, Robert. *Anthologie littéraire de l'occultisme.* Paris: R. Julliard, 1950.
———. *Eloge de la lâcheté.* Paris: R. Julliard, 1951.
———. *Les Grands Médiums.* Paris: Denoel, 1957.
———. *Louis-Claude de Saint Martin et le Martinisme.* Paris: Édition du Griffon d'Or, 1946.
———. *Trésor martiniste.* Paris: Villain & Belhomme, 1969.
Amsterdamska, Olga. "The Sociology of Linguistics: Schools of Thought in Nineteenth-Century Germany." Ph.D. thesis, Columbia University, 1983.
Apollinaire, Guillaume. "La Mort de Joséphin Péladan." *Mercure de France* (16 July 1918): 372–73.
Ares, Jacques d'. *Mythologies.* Paris: Editions du Jour, 1974.
Aubrun, René Georges. *Péladan.* Paris: E. Sansot, 1904.
Bachofen, Johann Jacob. *Myth, Religion and Mother Right: Selected Writings.* Trans. Ralph Manheim, pref. George Boas, intro. Joseph Campbell. Bollingen Series 84. Princeton: Princeton University Press, 1973.
———. *Der Mythos von Orient und Occident.* Munich: C. M. Beck, 1956.
Barres, Maurice. *Le Départ pour la vie.* Paris: Plon, 1961.
———. *Un Rénovateur de l'occultisme, Stanislas de Guaïta.* Paris: Chamuel, 1898.
Benichou, Paul. *Le Temps des prophètes: doctrines de l'âge romantique.* Paris: Gallimard, ca. 1977.

Berenger, Henry. "Le Théâtre d'Edouard Schuré." *Revue d'art dramatique* (Paris) 9 (1900): 481–529.

Berlet, C. *Stanislas de Guaïta*. Paris: B. Grasset, 1936.

Bernard, Thalès. *Dictionnaire mythologique universel* (Ouvrage composé sur un plan entièrement neuf, par le Dr. E. Jacobi, Traduit de l'Allemand, refondu et complété). Paris: Librairie de Firmin Didot Frères, 1854.

———. *Histoire de la poésie*. Paris: Dentu, 1864.

Bertholet, Edouard. *La Pensée et les secrets du Sâr Joséphin Péladan*. Neuchâtel: Editions Rosicruciennes, 1952-58.

Bignan, Anne. "Orphée, Homère, Hésiode." *La France littéraire* 1 (1832): 13ff.

Blavatsky, Helena P. *An Abridgement of the Secret Doctrine*. Ed. Elizabeth Preston and Christmas Humphreys. Wheaton, Ill., Madras, London: The Theosophical Publishing House, 1966.

———. *Complete Works*. 10 vols. London: Rider, 1933–64.

———. *Isis Unveiled: A Master-key to the Mysteries of Ancient and Modern Science*. 2 vols. New York: Theosophical Publishing Company, 1877.

———. *The Secret Doctrine*. 3 vols. London: Theosophical Publishing Company, 1888–97.

———. *The Theosophical Glossary*. Los Angeles: Theosophical Publishing House, 1918.

Bois, Jules. *Les Petites Religions de Paris*. Paris: Ancienne Librairie Kolb-Léon Chailley, Successeur, 1894.

Bowman, F. P. *Eliphas Lévi, visionnaire romantique*. Paris: Presses Universitaires Françaises, 1969.

Broussais, Emile. *Régénération du monde*. Paris, 1842.

Buche, Joseph. *L'Ecole mystique de Lyon, 1776–1847*. Pref. Edouard Herriot. Paris: F. Alcan, 1935.

Buchez, Philippe Benjamin. *Introduction à la science de l'histoire*. Paris, 1842.

Burhan, Filiz Eda. "Vision and Visionaries: Nineteenth-Century Psychological Theory. The Occult Sciences and the Formation of the Symbolist Aesthetic." Ph.D. thesis, Princeton University, 1979.

Cahel, Etienne. *Refutation ou examen de tous les écrits ou journaux contre ou sur la communauté. Refutation des trois ouvrages de l'Abbé Constant*. Paris: Prevost, 1841.

Chacornac, Paul. *Eliphas Lévi, rénovateur de l'occultisme en France*. Paris: Chacornac Frères, 1926.

Charlton, Donald G. *Secular Religions in France, 1815–1870*. London and New York: Oxford University Press, 1963.

Charrot. *Dictionnaire des termes hermétiques*. Lyon: Bibliothèque Municipale, MS.5836 (Fonds Papus).

Chenevier. *Le Bien et le mal*. Fonds Papus, Bibliothèque Municipale, Lyon.

Christian, Pierre. *Histoire de la magie*. [Paris: Furne, Gouvet, 1870] English version: London: Forge Press, 1952. MS.13.388 Fonds Péladan. Paris: Bibliothèque de l'Arsenal.

Collin de Plancy, J. *Dictionnaire Infernal*. Brussels: Chez Tous les Librairies, 1845.

———. *Dictionnaire des sciences occultes*. Paris: Chez l'Éditeur aux Ateliers Catholiques du Petit Montrouge, 1848.

Constant, Alphonse Louis (pseud. Eliphas Lévi). *Aphorisme et pensées d'Eliphas Lévi* (choix de Christiane Buisset). N.p., 1972.

―――― . *L'Assomption de la femme; ou le livre de l'amour*. Paris: A. le Gallois, 1841.

―――― . *Le Catéchisme de la paix, suivi de quatrains sur la Bible et de la Bible de la liberté* (extraits). Paris: Chamuel, 1896.

―――― . *La Clef des grands mystères, suivant Menoch, Abraham, Hermès, Trismégiste, et Salomon*. [Paris: G. Ballière, 1861] Paris: La Diffusion Scientifique, 1976.

―――― . *La Dernière Incarnation. Légendes évangéliques du XIXeme siècle*. Paris: Librairie Sociétaire, 1846.

―――― . *Dictionnaire de la littérature Chrétienne*. Nouvelle Encyclopédie Théologique. Paris: J. P. Migne, 1851 (including "Allégorie").

―――― . *Doctrines religieuses et sociales*. Paris: A. le Gallois, 1841.

―――― . *Dogme et rituel de la haute magie*. Paris and New York: G. Ballière, 1856.

―――― . *Le Grand Arcane; ou, L'occultisme dévoilé*. [Paris: Chamuel, 1898] Wellingborough: Thorsons, 1975.

―――― . *Histoire de la magie, avec une exposition claire* . . . (Eliphas Lévi). Paris: G. Baillière; London and New York: H. Baillière, 1860; La Roche-sur-Yon: Vendée, 1974.

―――― . *The History of Magic*. Trans. A. E. Waite. New York: Samuel Weiser, 1973.

―――― . *The Last Incarnation*. Ed. Charles H. Kohlman. Boston: R. G. Badger, 1914.

―――― . *Le Livre des larmes; ou Le Christ consolateur*. Paris: Paulier, 1845.

―――― . *Le Livre des sages; oeuvres posthume*. Paris: Librairie Générale des Sciences Occultes, 1911.

―――― . *Le Livre des splendeurs, contenant le soleil judaïque, la glorie chrétienne, et l'étoile flamboyante; Etudes sur les origines de la Kabbali, avec des recherches sur les mystères de la franc-maçonnérie, suivies de la profession de fois et des élément de kabbale*. Paris: Chamuel, 1894.

―――― . *Le Livre d'or, révélations des déstinées humaines au moyen de la chiromancie transcendante, le nécromancie, la physionomancie, la géomancie, la christallomancie, et toute les sciences divinatoires* (Hortensus Flamel). Paris: Lavigne, 1842.

―――― . *The Magical Ritual of the Sanctum Regnum Interpreted by the Tarot Trumps*. Ed. W. Wynn Westcott. London: G. Redway, 1896.

―――― . *La Mère de Dieu, épopée religieuse et humanitaire*. Paris: C. Gosselin, 1844.

―――― . *The Mysteries of Magic: A Digest of the Writings of Eliphas Lévi*. [London: G. Redway, 1886] Secaucus, N.J.: University Books, 1974.

―――― . *The Mysteries of the Qabalah: The Occult Agreement of the Two Testaments as Contained in the Prophecy of Ezekiel and the Apocalypse of St. John*. Wellingborough: Thorsons, 1974.

―――― . *The Paradoxes of the Highest Science, in Which the Most Advanced Truths of Occultism Are for the First Time Revealed*. Adyar, Madian: Theosophical Publishing House, 1922.

―――― . *Philosophie occulte. Première série: Fables et symboles. Deuxième série: La Science des Esprits*. Paris: Baillière, 1862 and 1865.

―――― . *La Science des esprits: révélation du dogma secret des Kabbalistes*. Paris: F. Alcan, 1894.

———. *La Seigneur de la Devinière; deuxième extrait des chroniques du joyeux curé de Meydon.* Paris: Librairie Phalanstérienne, 1850.
———. *Le Sorcier de Meudon.* Paris: Librairie Nouvelle, 1861.
———. *Transcendental Magic: Its Doctrine and Ritual.* London: W. Rider & Son, Ltd., 1923.
———. *Les Trois Harmonies, chansons et poésies.* Paris: Fellens et Dufour, 1845.
———. *Les Trois Malfaiteurs; légendes orientale.* Paris, Librairie Phalanstérienne, 1847.
Constant de Rebecque, Henri Benjamin. *Oeuvres.* Paris: Gallimard, 1957.
———. *Polythéisme romain considéré dans ses rapports avec les philosophies grecques et la religion chrétienne.* Intro. J. Matter. [Paris: Bechet, 1833] New York: Arno Press, 1978.
———. *De la religion considérée dans sa source, ses formes, et ses développements.* 5 vols. Paris: A. Leroux & C. Chautpie, 1826–31.
Cotte, Roger. *La Musique maçonnique et ses musiciens.* Braine-le-Comte: Editions du Braucens, 1975.
Cox, George W. *An Introduction to the Science of Comparative Myth and Folklore.* London: C. K. Paul & Co., 1881.
———. *A Manual of Mythology in the Form of Questions and Answers.* London: Longmans, Green, 1867.
———. *The Mythology of the Aryan Nations.* [London: Longmans, Green, 1870] Port Washington, N.Y.: Kennikat Press, 1969.
Creuzer, Georg Friedrich. *Symbolik und Mythologie der alten Völker.* 6 vols. Leipzig and Darmstadt: Heyer and Leske, 1819–26.
———. *Religions de l'antiquité, considérées principalement dans leurs formes symboliques et mythologiques.* Trans. J. D. Guigniaut. 4 volumes in 10. Paris: Treuttel & Würtz, 1825–1841.
Crowley, Aleister. *Orpheus: A Lyric Legend.* 2 vols. Botekine: Society for the Propagation of Religious Truth, 1905.
Dautinne, Emile. *L'Oeuvre et la pensée de Péladan; la philosophie rosicrucienne.* Brussels: Office de Publicité, 1948.
Delaage, Henri. *Le Monde occulte ou les mystères du magnétisme devoilés par le somnambulisme.* Paris: E. Dentu, 1856.
Delisle de Salès. *Histoire d'Homère et d'Orphée.* Paris: A. Bertrand, 1808.
Dictionnaire des antiquités grecques et romaines Ed. Daremberg and Saglio. Paris: Hachette, 1907.
Dornis, Jean. "Un Celte d'Alsace: Genèse de l'oeuvre d'E. Schuré." *Revue Mondiale*, sér. 7, 150 (Paris, 1922): 47–61, 164–75.
Doyon, René Louis. *La Douloureuse Aventure de Péladan.* Paris: La Connaissance, 1946.
Drougard, E. "Villiers de l'Isle-Adam et Eliphas Lévi." *Revue belge de philologie et d'histoire* (Brussels) 10 (1931): 505–30.
Encyclopédie des Gens du Monde. Paris: Librairie de Treuttel et Würtz, 1833–44.
Erdan, Alexandre. *La France mystique.* Paris: 1885.
Fabre d'Olivet, Antoine. *The Golden Verses of Pythagoras.* Trans. Nayan Louise Redfield. New York and London: G. P. Putnam's Sons, [1917] 1925.
———. *Hermeneutic Interpretation of the Origin of the Social State of Man and the Destiny

of the Adamic Race. (L'Histoire philosophique du genre humain.) Trans. Nayan Louise Redfield. New York: G. P. Putnam's Sons, 1915.

———. Histoire philosophique du genre humain. Paris: Chacornac, 1910.

———. "Un Manuscrit inédit de Fabre d'Olivet—Dissertation sur le rhythme et la prosodie des anciens et des modernes." Revue d'histoire littéraire de la France (Paris) 31 (1924): 261–93, 457–82.

———. La Musique expliquée comme science et comme art—et considérée dans ses rapports avec les mystères religieux la mythologie ancienne et l'histoire de la terre. Paris: L'Emancipatrice, 1928.

———. Les Vers dorés de Pythagore . . . et précédés d'un discours sur l'essence et la forme de la presse chez les principaux peuples de la terre. Trans. A. Dacui. Paris: L. Bodin, 1907.

Fagiolo, Maurice. "Il Revival Rose and Croix Nel Periodo Simbolista." In Il Revival. Milano: Gabriele Mazzotta, 1974.

Flat, Paul. "M. J. Péladan." Revue politique et littéraire (Paris) 55 (1917): 325–29.

Frainnet, Gaston. Essai sur la philosophie de P.S. Ballanche. Paris: A. Picard, 1903.

Franck, Adolphe. La Kabbale. Paris: Hachette, 1889.

George, Albert Joseph. P. S. Ballanche, Precursor of Romanticism. Syracuse, N.Y.: Syracuse University Press, 1945.

Gerard, René. L'Orient et la pensée romantique allemande. Paris: 1963.

Gilkin, Iwan. Stances dorées. Commentaire sacerdotal du Tarot. Paris and Brussels, 1893.

Girard, Meuri. "La Pensée religieuse des romantiques à propos d'un livre récent." Revue d'histoire littéraire de la France (Paris) 32 (1925): 79–97.

Goblet d'Alviella, E. Croyances, Rites, Institutions. 3 vols. Paris: Librairie Paul Geuthner, 1911.

———. Introduction à l'histoire générale des religions. Paris: 1887.

———. "La Migration des Symboles." La Revue des deux mondes 60 (May 1890): 121–44.

Görres, J. J. von. Mythengeschichte der asiatischen Welt. Heidelberg: 1810.

Guaïta, Stanislas de. Au seuil du mystère. Paris: Chamuel, 1896.

———. De la théogonie d'Hésiode. Dissertation de philosophie ancienne. 8 vols. Paris, 1835.

———. Essais de sciences maudites. Paris: Chamuel, 1895–97.

———. Lettres inédites . . . au Sâr Joséphin Péladan. Ed. E. Dantinne. Neuchâtel: Editions Rosicruciennes, 1952.

———. Le Temple de Satan. Paris, 1891.

Guigniaut, Joseph David. "Mythologie." In Encyclopédie des gens du monde, vol. 18. Paris: Librairie de Treuttel et Würtz, 1843.

———. "Notice historique sur la vie et les travaux de George-Frédéric Creuzer." Paris: Institut Impérial de France, 31 Juillet 1863.

———. La Nouvelle Galerie mythologique comprenant la galerie mythologique de A. L. Millin. 2 vols. Paris: 1850.

———. Le Polythéisme romain considéré dans ses rapports avec la philosophie grecque et la religion chrétienne. Paris, 1833–36.

Hall, Manly Palmer. Twelve World Teachers: A Summary of Their Lives and Teachings. Los Angeles: Philosophical Research Society, 1974.

Herder, Johann Gottfried. *Ideen zur Philosophie der Geschichte der Menschheit.* Trans. Edgar Quinet. Ripa and Leipzig, 1787–91 (1827).
Holler, Helmuth Peter. "The Theomonistic Art of the Future as Foreshadowed by the Theories and Productions of the German Composer Richard Wagner and the Belgian Painter Jean Delville." *Oriental University Progressive Studies,* No. 3. Washington, D.C.: Oriental University, 1921.
Howald, Ernst. *Der Kampf um Creuzers Symbolik.* Tübingen, 1926.
Howe, Elizabeth. *The Magicians of the Golden Dawn.* London, 1972.
Huit, Charles. *La Vie et les oeuvres de Ballanche.* Lyon: E. Vitte, 1904.
Hunt, Herbert J. *The Epic in Nineteenth-Century France: A Study in Heroic & Humanitarian Poetry from Les Martyrs to les Siècles Morts.* Oxford: Basil Blackwell, 1941.
Huysmans, Joris Karl. *Against Nature.* Trans. Robert Baldick. Baltimore, Md.: Penguin Books, 1959.
Jacobi, E. *Dictionnaire mythologique, ou biographie mythique des dieux et des personnages fabuleux de la Grèce, de l'Italie, de l'Egypte, de l'Inde, de la Chine, du Japon, de la Scandinavie, de la Gaule, de l'Amérique, de la Polynésie, etc.* Trans. Th. Bernard. Paris, 1863.
———. *Handwörterbuch der griechischen und römischen Mythologie.* Leipzig: Verlag Gustav Brauns, 1847.
Jeanclaude, Georgette. *E. Schuré, auteur des "Grands Initiés."* Paris: Fischbacher, 1968.
Kanne, J. A. *Erste Urkunden der Geschichte oder allgemeine Mythologie.* Bayreuth, 1808.
King, Charles. "Orpheus, Prophet of God." *Occult Review* (London) 58 (1933): 149–59.
Laprade, Victor D. "Ballanche, sa vie et ses écrits." Académie des sciences, belles-lettres et arts de Lyon, Classe des lettres, Mém. Lyon, 1850.
Laureut, A. *La Magie et la divination chez les Chaldéo-Assyriens.* Paris: Librairie de l'Art Indépendant, 1894.
Lazare, Bernard. *Le Miroir des légendes.* Paris, 1892.
Leutrat, Paul. *La Sorcellerie Lyonnaise.* Paris: R. Laffont, 1977.
Lévi, Eliphas (See: Alphonse Louis Constant).
MacIntosh, Christopher. *Eliphas Lévi: A French Occult Revival.* London: Rider, 1972.
Majer, Friedrich. *Allgemeines Mythologisches Lexicon.* Weimar, 1803.
———. *Brahma, Oder die Religion der Indier als Brahmaismus.* Leipzig, 1818.
Mauclair, Camille. *Eleusis: Causeries sur la cité intérieure.* Paris, 1894.
Maury, Louis Ferdinand Alfred. *Croyances et légendes de l'antiquité . . . d'histoire et de mythologie . . . Inde, Perse, Grèce, Gaule, Christianisme. . . .* Paris: Didier, 1868.
———. *The Distribution and Classification of Tongues.* 1857.
———. *Exposé des progrès de l'archéologie.* Paris: L'Imprimerie Impériale, 1867.
———. *Les Fées.* Paris: Ladrange, 1943.
———. *Histoire des religions de la Grèce antique.* Paris: Librairie de Ladrange, 1857–59.
———. *Magie.* Paris, 1860.
———. *La Magie, et l'astrologie dans l'antiquité et au moyen âge, ou Etude sur les superstitions païennes qui se sont perpétuées jusqu'à nos jours.* 3rd edition. Paris: Didier, 1864.
———. *Le Sommeil et les rêves.* Paris, 1861.
Ménard, Louis. *Du Polythéisme hellénique.* Paris, Charpentier, 1863.
———. *Prologue d'une révolution.* Paris, 1849.

———. *Prométhée délivré*. 1843.
———. *Rêveries d'un païen mystique*. Pref. Maurice Barres. Paris: A. Durel, 1909.
Menard, René J. *La Mythologie dans l'art ancien et moderne*. Paris: Ch. Delagrave, 1878.
Mercier, Alain. *Eliphas Lévi et la pensée magique au XIXe siècle*. Paris, 1974.
———. *Les Sources ésotériques et occultes de la poésie symboliste, 1870–1914*. Vol. 1: *Le Symbolisme français*. Paris: Editions Nizet, 1969.
Michelet, Jules. *Bible de l'humanité*. 3rd edition. Paris: F. Chamerot, 1864.
———. *La Sorcière*. Paris: Les Belles-Lettres, 1862.
Michelet, Victor Emile. *De l'esotérisme dans l'art*. Paris, 1891.
———. *Les Compagnons de la hiérophanie*. Nice: Reproductions Monaco, 1977.
Migne, Jacques Paul. *Dictionnaire universel de mythologie ancienne et moderne*. Paris: J. P. Migne, 1855.
———. *Encyclopédie théologique, ou série de dictionnaires sur toutes les parties de la science religieuse*. Paris: Migne, n.d.
Millin, A. L. *Nouvelle galerie mythologique*. Paris: Librairie de Firmin Didot Frères, 1859 (orig. 1811).
Müller, F. Max. *Comparative Mythology*. London: G. Routledge and Sons, 1909.
———. *A History of Ancient Sanskrit Literature, So Far as It Illustrates the Primitive Religion of the Brahmans*. London: Williams & Norgate, 1860.
———. *India: What Can It Teach Us? Lectures at the University of Cambridge*. London: Longmans, Green, 1883.
———. *Introduction to the Science of Religion*. London: Longmans, Green, 1873.
———. *Lectures on the Science of Language, Royal Institute of Great Britain, 1861, 1863*. London: Longmans, Green, Roberts, 1861–64.
Munnik, Gerrit. *The Influence of H. P. Blavatsky on Modern Art*. Wheaton, Ill.: Virginia Hanson, 1971.
The Mystical Hymns of Orpheus. Invocations Which Were Used in the Eleusinian Mysteries. Trans. T. Taylor. Chiswick: R. Triphook, 1824.
Papus (Dr. Gérard Encausse). *Alchimie au XIXe siècle*. MSS. 5491.I.1 and 2. Fonds Papus. Lyon: Bibliothèque Municipale.
———. *L'Analogie*, MS.5491.I.3 Fonds Papus. Lyon: Bibliothèque Municipale.
———. *L'Etat social de l'homme*. MS.5491.I.8 Fonds Papus. Lyon: Bibliothèque Municipale.
———. *Occultisme contemporaine*. MS.5491.I.17 Fonds Papus. Lyon: Bibliothèque Municipale.
———. *Traité élémentaire de science occulte*. Paris: Chamuel, 1893.
———. *La Vie de Christ*. MS.5491.I.26 Fonds Papus. Lyon: Bibliothèque Municipale.
Pater, Walter. *Greek Studies*. London: Macmillan, 1908.
———. *Marius the Epicurean, His Sensations and Ideas*. Ed. and with an intro. by Harold Bloom. New York: Signet Classics, 1970.
Paulhan, Frédéric. *Le Nouveau Mysticisme*. Paris: Alcan, 1891.
Péladan, Joséphin. "A la jeune femme contemporaine." *Amphithéâtre des sciences mortes*. MS.13.205 Fonds Péladan. Paris: Bibliothèque de l'Arsenal.
———. *Albert Dürer, graveur*. Paris: Fontemoiny, 1914.
———. *L'Androgyne (Couverture de Séon)*. Paris: E. Dentu, 1891.

———. *L'Art dionysique*. MS.13.173 Fonds Péladan. Paris: Bibliothèque de l'Arsenal.

———. *L'Art idéaliste et mystique, doctrine de l'ordre et du salon annuel des Rose+Croix*. Paris: Chamuel, 1894, MS.13.233 Fonds Péladan. Paris: Bibliothèque de l'Arsenal.

———. *Conférence sur le génie grec*. MS.13.378 Fonds Péladan. Paris: Bibliothèque de l'Arsenal.

———. *Dossier concernant la Rose+Croix*. MS.13.205 Fonds Péladan. Paris: Bibliothèque de l'Arsenal.

———. "Geste esthétique de 1892." *Salon de la Rose+Croix*. Paris: Galerie Durand Ruel, 1892.

———. "Les Grands Méconnus." *La Revue forézienne*, sér. 2, 12, no.49 (January 1902). MS.13.214 Fonds Péladan. Paris: Bibliothèque de l'Arsenal.

———. *Istar* . . . . Paris: G. Edinger, 1888.

———. *Le Mystère d'Eleusis*. MS.13.162 Fonds Péladan. Paris: Bibliothèque de l'Arsenal.

———. *Origine et esthétique de la tragédie*. Paris: Bibliothèque Internationale d'Edition, 1905.

———. *Projets de pièces de théâtre*. MS.13.204 Fonds Péladan. Paris: Bibliothèque de l'Arsenal.

———. *Semiramis: Tragédie en quatre actes*. Paris: Société du Mercure de France, 1904.

———. *Terre d'Orphée*. MS.13.204 Fonds Péladan. Paris: Bibliothèque de l'Arsenal.

———. *La Terre du Sphinx*. MS.13.155 Fonds Péladan. Paris: Bibliothèque de l'Arsenal.

———. *Le Théâtre complet de Wagner*. Paris, Geneva: Slatkine, 1981.

———. *Théâtre de la Rose+Croix. Le Prince de Byzance. Drame romanesque en 5 actes*. Paris: Chamuel, 1896.

Peyre, Henri. *Louis Ménard*. New Haven, Conn.: Yale University Press, 1932.

Pierrot, Jean. *L'Imaginaire décadent (1800–1900)*. Paris: Presses Universitaires de France, 1977.

———. "Merveilleux et fantastique: une histoire de l'imaginaire dans la prose française du romantisme à la décadence 1830–1900." Thesis, University of Lille, 1975.

Pincus-Witten, Robert. *Occult Symbolism in France: Joséphin Péladan and the Salons de la Rose+Croix*. New York: Garland, 1976.

———. *Les Salons de la Rose+Croix 1892–1897*. London: Piccadilly Gallery, 1968.

Piper, F. *Mythogie der Christlichen Kunst*. Weimar, 1847.

Quinet, Edgar. *Oeuvres complètes*. Paris: Pagnerre Librairie, 1857.

Redgrave, H. Stanley. "A Master of Magic: Alphonse Louis Constant," *Occult Review* (London) 37 (1923): 227–33.

Renan, Ernest. "Des religions de l'antiquité et de leurs derniers historiens." *Revue des deux mondes* (15 May 1853): 821–50.

———. *Essais de morale et de critique*. Paris, 1859.

———. *Etudes d'histoire religieuse*. Paris, 1857/1897.

———. *Oeuvres complètes*. Paris: Calmann-Lévy, 1949.

———. *Les Origines de christianisme*. Paris, 1863–83.

———. *Souvenirs d'enfance et de jeunesse*. Paris, 1883.
———. *Studies of Religious History and Criticism*. Trans. O. B. Frothingham. New York: Carleton Publishers, 1864.
———. *Vie de Jésus*. Paris, 1863.
Richepin, Jean. *Les Blasphèmes*. Paris, 1884.
———. *Les Morts bizarres*. Paris: Décaux, 1896.
———. *Nouvelle mythologie illustrée*. Paris: Editions de l'Art et de Vulgarisation F. Sant'Andrea and L. Marcerou, n.d.
The Rise of Modern Mythology, 1680–1860. Ed. Burton Feldman and Robert D. Richardson. Bloomington and London: Indiana University Press, 1972.
Rich, Annett C. *Christ or Buddha?* Oceanside, Calif.: The Rosicrucian Fellowship, 1914.
Rollinat, Maurice. *Les Apparitions*. Paris: Charpentier, 1896.
Roman, Jean. *Paris, Fin-de-Siècle*. Paris: Robert Delpire, 1958.
Ronieuf, Louis de. *Edouard Schuré*. Paris: E. Sanset, 1908.
Roos, Jacques. *Aspects littéraires du mysticisme philosophique et l'influence de Boehme et de Swedenborg au début du romanticisme: William Blake, Novalis, Ballanche*. Strasbourg: P.H. Heitz, 1951.
———. *Les Idées philosophiques de Victor Hugo: Ballanche et V. Hugo*. Paris: Nizet, 1951.
Roux, Alphonse and R. Veyssie. *Edouard Schuré: son oeuvre et sa pensée*. Paris: Perrin, 1914.
Said, Edward W. *Orientalism*. New York: Vintage, 1979.
Schelling, F. W. J. von. *Philosophie der Mythologie*. In *Werke*. Ed. Manfred Schröter. Beck und Oldenbourg, 1928.
Schneider, Camille. "E. Schuré, sa conception de la femme inspiratrice." *Revue Mondiale* (Paris) (1 August 1929): 286–98.
———. *Edouard Schuré*. Freiburg, ca. 1971.
Scholem, Gershom. *Die jüdische Mystik in ihren Hauptströmungen*. Zurich, 1957.
Schuré, Edouard. *L'Ame celtique et le génie de la France*. Paris: Perrin, 1921.
———. *L'Ange et la sphinge*. Paris: Perrin, 1921.
———. *Le Double*. Paris: Perrin, 1921.
———. *Le Drame musical*. 2 vols. Paris: Sandoy et Fischbacher, 1875.
———. *La Druïdesse*. 3rd edition. Paris: Perrin, 1914.
———. *Les Enfants de Lucifer, La soeur gardienne*. Paris: Perrin, 1922.
———. *L'Evolution divine*. Paris: 1928.
———. *Femmes inspiratrices et poètes annonciateurs*. Paris: Perrin & Co., 1909.
———. *From Sphinx to Christ (L'Evolution divine)*. Trans. Eva Martin. Philadelphia: D. McKay, 1928.
———. *The Genesis of Tragedy and the Dreams of Eleusis*. Trans. Fred Rothwell. London: R. Steiner, 1936; New York: Anthropological Press, 1936.
———. *Les Grandes Légendes de France*. Paris, 1891.
———. *Les Grands Initiés*. Paris: Perrin, [1889] 1931.
———. *The Great Initiates*. London: Wm. Rider and Son, 1913.
———. *The Great Initiates. A Study of the Secret History of Religions*. Trans. Gloria Rasberry, intro. Paul M. Allen. San Francisco: Harper & Row, 1961.

———. *Hermes and Plato*. Trans. F. Rothwell. London: W. Rider, 1909.
———. *Histoire du Lied ou la chanson populaire en Allemagne*. Paris: Librairie Internationale, 1868.
———. *Krishna and Orpheus, The Great Initiates of the East and West*. Trans F. Rothwell. Chicago: Yogi Publications, 1908. (See also, London: Wm. Rider and Son, 1919.)
———. *Merlin l'Enchanteur. Légende dramatique*. Paris: Perrin, 1924.
———. *La Prêtresse d'Isis. Légende de Pompeii*. Paris: Perrin, 1920. (See also Rothwell translation, London: Wm. Rider and Son, 1910.)
———. *Pythagoras and the Delphi Mysteries*. Trans. F. Rothwell. New York: The Theosophical Publishing Co., 1912.
———. *Rama and Moses, the Aryan Cycle and the Mission of Israel*. Trans. F. Rothwell. London: W. Rider, 1923.
———. *Sanctuaires d'Orient: Egypte, Grèce, Palestine*. Paris: Perrin, 1907.
———. *Le Théâtre de l'âme*. Paris: Perrin, 1900–1902.
———. *La Vie mystique*. Paris: Perrin, 1894.
Schwab, Raymond. *La Renaissance oriental*. Paris: Payot, 1950.
Smith, William, ed. *A Dictionary of Greek and Roman Bilgraphy and Mythology*. London: John Murray, 1876.
Starr, Meredith. "A Visit to Eliphas Lévi." *Occult Review* (London) 34 (1921): 261–67.
Strauss, D.F. *Life of Christ*. 1835.
Thomas, Jules. *Procès de la bible de la liberté*. Paris: Pelout, 1841.
Turner, Frank M. *The Greek Heritage in Victorian Britain*. New Haven and London: Yale University Press, 1981.
Ventori, Franco. *L'Antichità Svelata e l'idea del progresso in N. A. Boulanger*. Bari: G. Laterya & Figli, 1947.
Viatte, Auguste. *Les Sources occultes du romantisme; illuminisme, théosophie, 1770–1820*. Paris: H. Champion, 1928.
Vinson, Julien. *Les Religions actuelles*. Paris: Adrien Delahage and Emile Lecrosnier, 1888.
Voss, J. H. *Anti-symbolique*. Stuttgart, 1824–26.
———. *Gazette littéraire d'Iéna*. 1821.
Wagner, J. J. *Ideen zu einer allgemeinen Mythologie der alten Welt*. Frankfurt am Main, 1808.
Waite, Arthur Edward. "Illuminations of Eliphas Lévi." *Occult Review* (London) 34 (1921): 35–40.
Waldo-Schwartz, Paul. *Art and the Occult*. New York: George Braziller, 1975.
Webb, James. *The Occult Establishment*. La Salle, Ill., 1976.
———. *The Occult Underground*. La Salle, Ill., 1974.
Williams, Thomas. *Eliphas Lévi: Master of Occultism*. Alabama: University of Alabama Press, 1975.
———. *Mallarmé and the Language of Mysticism*. Athens: University of Georgia Press, 1970.
Willson, A. Leslie. *A Mythical Image: The Ideal of India in German Romanticism*. Durham, N.C., 1964.

Nineteenth-Century Literature, Aesthetics, Philosophy

Abrams, M. H. *The Mirror and the Lamp: Romantic Theory and the Critical Tradition.* London, Oxford, New York: Oxford University Press, 1953.
Adolf, Helen. "The Essence and Origin of Tragedy." *Journal of Aesthetics and Art Criticism* 10, no. 2 (December 1951).
Albouy, Pierre. *La Création mythologique chez Victor Hugo.* Paris: Librairie Jose Corti, 1963.
Allison, David B., ed. and intro. *The New Nietzsche: Contemporary Styles of Interpretation.* New York: Delta, 1977.
Aurier, G. Albert. *Commentaire d'un livre futur.* Paris, 1889.
―――. *Oeuvres posthumes.* Paris: Edition Mercure de France.
Austin, L. J., ed. *Studies in French Literature Presented to P. Mansell Jones.* Includes "The Mystical Paganism," by Garnet Rees and Eugene Vinarer. Manchester: Manchester University Press, 1961.
Autin, Albert. "Un Grand Humaniste: Elémir Bourges." Société Scientifique et Littéraire des Basses-Alpes. *Bulletin annales des Basses-Alpes* (Digne) 21 (1926): 14–24.
Balakian, Anna. *The Symbolist Movement.* New York: Random House, 1967.
―――, ed. *The Symbolist Movement in the Literature of European Languages.* Budapest: Akademiai Kiado, 1982.
Banville, Théodore de. *Oeuvres.* Geneva: Slatkine Reprints, 1972.
Barrère, J. B. *Le Regard d'Orphée ou l'échange poétique Hugo/Baudelaire/Rimbaud/Apollinaire.* Paris: Société d'Education et d'Enseignement Supérieur, 1977.
Baudelaire, Charles. *Curiosités esthétiques, l'art romantique, et autres oeuvres critiques.* Intro. Henri Lemaître. Paris: Editions Garnier Frères, 1962.
―――. *Les Fleurs du mal.* Intro. Antoine Adam. Paris: Editions Garnier Frères, 1961.
―――. *Oeuvres complètes.* Paris: Club du Meilleur Livre, 1955.
―――. *The Painters of Modern Life and Other Essays.* Trans. and ed. Jonathan Mayne. London and New York: Phaidon, 1965.
Bays, Gwendolyn. *The Orphic Vision: Seer Poets from Novalis to Rimbaud.* Lincoln: University of Nebraska, 1969.
Bergson, Henri. *Selections.* Ed. Harold A. Larrabee. New York: Appelton, Century, Crofts, 1949.
Bourges, Elémir. *Le Crépuscule des dieux.* Paris: Stock, 1923.
―――. *La Nef.* Paris: Librairie Stock, 1922.
―――. *Les Oeuvres complètes d'Elémir Bourges, 1852–1925.* Paris: F. Bernouard, 1929.
―――. *Les Oiseaux s'envolent et les fleurs tombent.* Ed. Gisèle Marie. Paris: Mercure de France, 1964.
[Bourges, Elémir]. *L'Hommage à E. Bourges.* (Articles by Comtesse de Noailles and others). *Divan* (Paris) 15 (1923): 147–252.
Bowie, Malcolm et al., eds. *Baudelaire, Mallarmé, Valéry: Essays in Honour of Lloyd Austin.* Cambridge: Cambridge University Press, 1982.
Browning, Robert. *The Complete Poetic and Dramatic Works.* Cambridge: Riverside Press, 1887.

———. *The Complete Poetic and Dramatic Works*. Boston and New York: Houghton Mifflin, 1895.
Brunetière, F. "Le Symbolisme contemporain." *Revue des deux mondes* 104 (1891): 681–92.
Buzzini, Louis. *Elémir Bourges, histoire d'un grand livre, "La Nef."* Paris: Au Pigeonnier, 1951.
Byron, George Gordon Nöel. *Cain. A Dramatic Mystery in Three Acts*. Trans. into French with a series of remarks by Fabre d'Olivet (1823); trans. into English by N. L. Redfield. New York and London: G. P. Putnam's Sons, 1923.
———. *Complete Works*. Paris: Bauday's European Library, 1835. Vol. 3.
Carlyle, Thomas. *Sartor Resartus: The Life and Opinions of Herr Teufelsdröckh*. Ed. Charles Frederick Howard. New York: The Odyssey Press, 1937.
Carter, A. E. *The Idea of Decadence in French Literature, 1830–1910*. Toronto: University of Toronto Press, 1958.
Cattaui, Georges. *Orphisme et prophétie chez les poètes français 1850–1950. Hugo, Nerval, Baudelaire, Mallarmé, Rimbaud, Valéry, Claudel*. Paris: Librairie Plon, 1965.
Cellier, Léon. "Le Romantisme et le mythe d'Orphée," *CAIEF*, No.10 (May 1958): 138ff.
Christian, John. *Symbolistes et décadents*. Trans. Inès Hengel. Paris: Editions du Chêne, 1977.
Coeuroy, André. *Appels d'Orphée: Nouvelles études de musique et de littérature comparées*. Paris: La Nouvelle Revue Critique, 1929.
Danto, Arthur C. *Nietzsche as Philosopher*. London and New York: Collier-Macmillan, 1965.
Delsemme, Paul. *Un Théoricien du symbolisme: Charles Morice*. Paris: Nizet, 1958.
Delvaille, Bernard, ed. *La Poésie symboliste*. Paris: Seghurs, 1971.
Desonay, Fernand. *La Rêve hellénistique chez les poètes parnassiens*. Paris: Librairie Ancienne Honoré Champion, 1928.
Dhaenens, Jacques. *Le Destin d'Orphée "El Desdichado" de Nerval*. Paris: Lettres Modernes Minard, 1972.
Diet, Emmanuel. *Nietzsche et les métamorphoses de divin*. Paris: Les Editions du Cerf, 1972.
Dujardin, Edouard. "Les Oeuvres Théoriques de Richard Wagner." *La Revue wagnérienne* 1 (April 1885): 72.
Duval, Elga. *Téodor de Wyzewa, Critic without a Country*. Paris, 1961.
Ferrero, Guglielmo. *Les Lois psychologiques du symbolisme*. Paris: Alcan, 1895.
Fowlie, Wallace. *Mallarmé* (with drawings by Henri Matisse). Chicago and London: University of Chicago Press, 1973.
Gautier, Judith. *Richard Wagner et son oeuvre poétique*. Paris, 1882.
Glaser, Hermann, ed. *The German Mind of the Nineteenth Century, A Literary and Historical Anthology*. New York: Continuum, 1981.
Goethe, Johann Wolfgang. *The Sorrows of Young Werther*. New York: New American Literary Library of World Literature, 1962.
Goudeau, Emil. *Dix ans de Bohème*. Paris, 1885.

Grandmougin, Charles. *Orphée, Drame antique en quatres actes.* Paris: Calmann-Lévy, 1882.

Haraucourt, Edmond. *L'Effort.* Paris: Les Sociétaires de l'Académie des Beaux-Livres, 1899.

———. *Mémoires de jour et des gens.* Paris: Flammarion, 1946.

———. *Oeuvres.* Paris: Lemerre, 1899.

Hautecoeur, Louis. "Le Symbolisme et la peinture." *Revue de Paris* 1 (1 July 1936): 143–62.

Hölderlin, Friedrich. *Poems.* Trans. Michael Hamburger. New York: Pantheon, ca. 1952.

Houssaye, Arsène. *Man about Paris: The Confessions of Arsène Houssaye.* Trans. and ed. Henry Knepler. London: Victor Gollancz, 1972.

Huret, Jules. *Enquête sur l'évolution littéraire.* Paris: Charpentier, 1891.

Jack, Ian. *Keats and the Mirror of Art.* Oxford: Clarendon Press, 1967.

Jaloux, Edmond. "Elémir Bourges et 'La Nef.'" *Revue Hebdomadaire* (Paris) 31, no. 2 (1922): 5–16.

Juden, Brian. *Traditions orphiques et tendances mystiques dans le romantisme français 1800–1855.* Paris: Editions Klincksieck, 1971.

Kaufman, Walter. *Nietzsche.* New York: Random House, 1968.

———, ed. *Twenty-five German Poets: A Bilingual Collection.* New York: W. W. Norton, 1962.

Kerman, Joseph. "Wagner and Wagnerism." *The New York Review of Books.* (22 December 1983): 27–37.

Klapper, M. Roxana. *The German Literary Influence in Byron.* Salzburg: Institut für Englische Spräche und Literatur, University of Salzburg, 1974.

Kracauer, Siegfried. *Jacques Offenbach; ou le secret du Second Empire.* Trans. Lucienne Astruc. Paris: B. Grasset, 1937.

———. *Orpheus in Paris: Offenbach and the Paris of His Time.* Trans. Gwenda Davis and Eric Mosbacher. New York: Knopf, 1938.

Lagarde, André and Laurent Michard. *XIXe siècle les grands auteurs français.* Paris: Bordas, 1969.

Langlois, Walter, ed. *The Persistent Voice: Hellenism in French Literature since the Eighteenth Century.* New York: New York University Press, 1971.

Larbaud, Valéry. "E. Bourges." *Revue européenne* (Paris) 5 (March 1925): 1–13.

Launay, Louis de. "Orphic," poème, avec préface par Sully Prudhomme. Paris: Lemène, 1951.

Lebois, André. *La Genèse du crépuscule des dieux.* Paris: L'Amitié par le Livre (critical edition), 1954.

———. *Les Tendances du symbolisme à travers de l'oeuvre d'Elémir Bourges.* Paris: L'Amitié par le Livre, 1952.

Lefèbvre, Louis. *Une Grande Figure du symbolisme, Charles Morice, le poète et l'homme. D'après des documents et des manuscrits inédits.* Paris: Perrin, 1926.

Lehmann, Andrew George. *The Symbolist Aesthetic in France.* Oxford: Basil & Blackwell, 1950.

Lorrain, Jean. "La Destinée, Pour Gustave Moreau." La Revue Indépendante 3 (November 1884–April 1885).
———. Le Sang des dieux. Paris: A. Lemerre, 1882.
Maillou, P. Rioux de. Souvenirs des autres. Paris, 1917.
Mallarmé, Stéphane. Oeuvres complètes. Paris: Pléïade, Gallimard, 1945.
———. Selected Prose, Poems, Essays and Letters. Trans. and intro. Bradford Coole. Baltimore: Johns Hopkins, 1956.
———. "Théodore de Banville." Mercure de France 7 (1893).
Manley, Seon and Gogo Lewis, comps. Ladies of Fantasy: Two Centuries of Sinister Stories by the Gentle Sex. New York: Lothrop, Lee & Shepard, 1975.
Marie, Gisèle, ed. Elémir Bourges: ou l'éloge de la grandeur—correspondance inéditée avec Armand Point. Paris: Edition Mercure de France, 1962.
Marshall, L. E. "Greek Myths in Modern English Poetry—"Orpheus and Eurydice." Studi di filologia moderna 5 (1912): 203–32; 6 (1912): 1–32.
Martino, Pierre. Parnasse et Symbolisme. Paris: Librairie Armand Collin, 1970.
Mathews, Andrew Jackson. La Wallonie 1886–1892: The Symbolist Movement in Belgium. New York: King's Crown Press, 1947.
Mauclair, Camille (Faust, Camille). Le Miracle d'Orphée: Lettres détenues, recueillies et publiées par l'Equipe musicale des prisons. Pref. C. Mauclair. Paris: Stock, 1928.
Meantis, George. "Une Resurgence orphique au XIXe siècle." Mélanges d'archéolgie, d'épigraphie et d'histoire offerts à Jérôme Carcopino. Paris: Hachette, 1966.
Michaud, Guy. Mallarmé. Trans. Marie Collins and Bertha Hornez. New York: New York University Press, 1965.
———. Message poétique du Symbolisme. Paris: Librairie Nizet, 1947.
Morice, Charles. Chérubin: trois actes et un prologue. Paris: L. Vanier, 1891.
———. Demain questions d'esthétique. Paris: Perrin, 1888.
———. Discours prononcé au banquet des amis de Paul Verlaine pour le 15eme anniversaire de la mort du poète. Paris: L. Vanier, 1911.
———. Du sens religieux de la poésie: sur le mot poésie le principe sociale de la beauté. Geneva: Eggiman, 1893.
———. L'Esprit belge. Pref. Camille Lemonnier. Brussels: G. Balat, 1899.
———. Il est ressuscité. 2nd editions. Paris: A. Messein, 1911.
———. La Littérature de tout à l'heure. Paris: Perrin, 1889.
———. La Mission. Paris: J. Langlois, 1929.
———. Pages choisies, vers et proses. Paris: A. Messein, 1912.
———. Paul Verlaine. Paris: Vanier, 1888.
———. Tristan Corbière, Conférence faite le 28 mai 1912. Paris: A. Messein, 1912.
Nietzsche, Frederich. The Birth of Tragedy, The Case of Wagner. Trans. and commentary W. Kaufmann. New York: Vintage, 1967.
"Nietzsche's Return." Semiotexte (New York) 3, no. 1 (1978).
Novalis (Friedrich von Hardenberg). Werke. Ed. Hans-Joachim Mähl and Rizhard Samuel. Munich-Vienna: Carl Hanser Verlag, 1978.
Offenbach, Jacques. Orphée aux enfers (English libretto). New York: Program Club, 1956.

O'Malley, Glenn. "Literary Synesthesia." *Journal of Aesthetics and Art Criticism* 15, no. 4 (June 1957): 391–411.
Paris. *Le Cinquantenaire du symbolisme*. Bibliothèque Nationale, 1936.
Paul, Jean. *Ein Stundenbuch für seine Verehrer*. Munich, 1900.
Peyre, Henri. *Qu'est-ce que le symbolisme?* Paris: Presses Universitaires de France, 1974.
———. *What Is Romanticism?* Alabama: Alabama University Press, 1977.
Pouillart, Raymond. *Le Romantisme III, 1809–1896*. Paris: E. Vitte, 1904.
Praz, Mario. *The Romantic Agony*. Trans. from the Italian by Angus Davidson. 2nd edition with a new foreword by Frank Kermode. London and New York: Oxford University Press, 1970.
Raitt, A. W. *Villiers de l'Isle Adam et le Mouvement Symboliste*. Paris: Librairie Jose Conti, 1965.
Raymond, Marcel. *From Baudelaire to Surrealism*. New York: Wittenborn, Schultz, 1950.
Raynaud, Ernest. *La Mêlée symboliste (1870–1910). Portraits et Souvenirs*. Paris: A. G. Nizet, 1971.
Reneville, Roland, de. "Correspondance inédite échangée entre Huysmans et Mallarmé." *Comoedia* (September 1943): 6ff.
Richard, Noël. *A l'aube du symbolisme, hydropaths, fumistes et décadents*. Paris: Nizet, 1961.
Richer, Jean. *Gérard de Nerval et les doctrines ésotériques*. Paris, 1947.
Riffaterre, Hermine B. *L'Orphisme dans la poésie romantique*. Paris: Editions A. G. Nizet, 1970.
Sans, Edouard. *R. Wagner et la pensée Schopenhaurienne*. Paris: Klincksieck, 1969.
Schroder, Maurice. *Icarus: The Image of the Artist in French Romanticism*. Cambridge, Mass.: Harvard University Press, 1961.
Schwab, Raymond. *La Vie d'Elémir Bourges*. Textes et documents médits. Paris: Stock, 1948.
Sewell, Elizabeth. *The Orphic Voice Poetry and Natural History*. New Haven: Yale University Press, 1960.
Shelley, P. B. *Poetical Works*. Ed. Thomas Hutchinson. London and New York: Oxford University Press, 1970.
———. *Selected Poetry and Prose*. Intro. Kenneth Neill Cameron. New York: Holt, Rhinehart and Winston, 1966.
Silvestre, Armand. "La Mort d'Orphée." *L'Artiste* No. 5 (February 1867): 114.
Stedman, Edmund Clarence, ed. *A Victorian Anthology, 1837–1895*. Boston and New York: Houghton, Mifflin, 1895.
Symons, Arthur. *The Symbolist Movement in Literature*. Intro. Richard Ellmann. New York: E. P. Dutton and Co., Inc., 1958.
Thorel, Jean. "Les Romantiques allemands et les symbolistes français." *Entretiens politiques et littéraires* (September 1891).
Ulbach, Louis. "L'Art au théâtre: l'Orphée de Gluck, Madame Viardot." *Gazette des beaux-arts* (1860): 99–105.
Vega Carpio, Lupe Felix de. "Orfeo en lengua castellana." *Biblioteca de antiques libros hispanicos*, sér. A, 14 (1948).

Viatte, Auguste. *Le Catholicisme chez les romantiques.* Paris: E. de Boccard, 1922.
_____. *Victor Hugo et les illuminés de son temps.* Montreal: Editions de l'Arbre, 1942.
Wagner, Richard. *Prose Works.* Trans. William Ashton Ellis. London: K. Paul Trench, Trübner, 1829–1899.
_____. *Art, Life and Theories of Richard Wagner.* Ed. Edward L. Burlingame. New York: H. Holt, 1904 [1909].
Weisberg, G. P. "George de Feure's Mysterious Women: A Study of Symbolist Sources in the Writings of Charles Baudelaire and George Rodenbach." *Gazette des beaux-arts,* sér. 6, 82 [84] (October 1974): 223–32.

The Image of Orpheus in the Visual Arts of the Nineteenth Century

About, E. *Paul Baudry, peintures décoratives exécutées pour le foyer public de l'Opéra.* Paris: Association des Artistes, 1874.
_____. *Peintures décoratives du grand foyer de l'Opéra par Paul Baudry.* Paris: Association des Artistes, 1876.
Adams, Brooks. "The Poetics of Odilon Redon's 'Closed Eyes.'" *Arts Magazine* (January 1980): 130–34.
Adams, Philip Rhys. *A. Bourdelle, 1861–1929.* New York: Slatkin Galleries, 1961.
Andrews, Keith. *The Nazarenes: A Brotherhood of German Painters in Rome.* Oxford: Clarendon Press, 1964.
Angrand, Pierre. "L'Etat micène. Période autoritaire du Second Empire (1851–1860)." *Gazette des beaux-arts* (May–June 1968): 303–48.
Anselm Feuerbach: 1829–1880, Gemälde und Zeichnungen. Munich-Berlin: Deutscher Kunstverlag, 1976.
Ash, Russell. "English Paintings of 1874." *Connoisseur* (January 1974): 32–40.
L'Atelier Nadar et l'art lyrique. Paris: Direction des Musées de France, 1975–76.
Bacou, Rosaline. *Odilon Redon.* Geneva: Pierre Cailler, 1956.
Barazzetti-Demoulin, Suzanne. *Maurice Denis. 25 November 1870–31 November 1943.* Paris: Grasset, 1945.
Bataille, Georges. "Gustave Moreau, l'attitude précurseur du Surréalisme." *Arts* (7 June 1961).
Bénédite, Leonce. "Deux idéalistes: G. Moreau et Edward Burne-Jones." *La Revue de l'art ancien et moderne* (10 April): 265–90; (10 May): 357–78; (10 July): 57–70.
_____. *Notre art, nos maîtres: Puvis de Chavannes, Moreau, Burne-Jones.* Paris, ca. 1922.
_____. *Théodore Chassériau, sa vie et son oeuvre.* 2 vols. Paris, 1931.
Berger, Klaus. *Odilon Redon.* London: Weidenfeld & Nicolson, 1964; New York: McGraw Hill.
Bierbaum, Otto Julius. *Franz von Stuck.* Bielefeld and Leipzig: Velhagen & Klasing, 1899.
Bierhler, Paul. "Gustave Moreau ou l'éternelle jeunesse du mythe." *Atlantis* 226 (1964): 59–84.
Bittler, Paul and Pierre-Louis Mathieu. *Catalogue des dessins de Gustave Moreau.* Paris: Editions de la Réunion des Musées Nationaux, 1983.

Bloy, Léon. *Correspondence de Léon Bloy et Henry de Groux.* Paris: Grasset, 1947.
Boime, A. *The Academy and French Painting in the 19th Century.* London: Oxford, 1971.
Boisseau, Simone. "Le Mythe de Gustave Moreau." Ph.D. thesis, Université de Paris-Sorbonne, 1972.
Boschot, Adolphe. "Un Grand Sculpteur, Injalbert." *Revue politique et littéraire* (Paris) 71 (4 February 1933): 74–75.
Boucher, Marie-Christine. "La Décoration de Puvis de Chavannes pour l'Hôtel Vignon." *Revue du Louvre* 28, no. 2 (1978): 98–106.
Bourdelle, Antoine. *La Sculpture et Rodin.* Paris: Editions Emile-Paul Frères, 1937.
Bouyer, Raymond. "Foreau." *L'Artiste* 2 (1897): 21.
———. "Les Artistes aux salons de 1897." *L'Artiste* 2 (1897): 280, 349.
Breton, André. "Gustave Moreau." In *Le Surréalisme et la Peinture.* Paris: Gallimard, 1965.
Brown, Aimée. "L'Allégoire réelle chez Pierre Puvis de Chavannes." *Gazette des beaux-arts,* Sér. 6, 119 (January 1977): 27–40.
Brussels. *Horta.* Musée Horta, 1973.
Burleigh, Marion. "George Russell (AE), The Painter of the Irish Renaissance." Ph.D. thesis, New York University, Institute of Fine Arts, 1978.
Butler, Ruth. *Rodin in Perspective.* Englewood Cliffs, N. J.: Prentice Hall, 1980.
Cachin, Françoise. *Gauguin.* Paris: Librairie Générale Française, 1965.
———. "Monsieur Venus et l'Ange de Sodome. L'Androgyne au temps de Gustave Moreau." *Nouvelle Revue de Psychanalyse* (Spring 1973): 63–69.
Calloway, Stephen. *Charles Ricketts: Subtle and Fantastic Decorator.* London: Thames and Hudson, 1979.
Cames, G. "Or, éméraudes et griffons." *Gazette des beaux-arts.* sér. 6, 90 (October 1977): 105–8.
Casteras, Susan P. *The Substance or the Shadow: Images of Victorian Womanhood.* New Haven, Conn.: Yale Center for British Art, 1982.
Cham. *Salon de 1866 photographié par Cham.* Paris, 1866.
Chassé, Charles. *Gauguin et le groupe de Pont-Aven. Documents inédits.* Paris: H. Floury, 1921.
———. *Gauguin et son temps.* Paris: Bibliothèque des Arts, 1955.
Chastel, André. "Le Goût des Préraphaelites en France." In *De Giotto à Bellini.* Paris, 1956.
Chesneau, Ernest. "L'Exposition Universelle." *Le Constitutionnel* (10 September 1867).
Chesteron, G. K. *G. F. Watts.* London: Duckworth; New York: E. P. Dutton, 1913.
Chicago. *Corot, 1796–1875.* Art Institute of Chicago, 1960.
Chiollier, Felix. *Dessinateurs lyonnais et foréziens du XIXe siècle.* Saint-Etienne: Musée d'Art et d'Industrie, October–November 1980.
Choix de medailles en vente à la Monnaie. Paris: Musée de La Monnaie, 1926.
Cladel, Judith. *A. Rodin, l'oeuvre et l'homme.* Brussels, 1908.
———. *A. Rodin, pris sur la vie.* Paris: Editions de la Plume, 1903.
———. *Rodin.* Trans. James Whitall. New York: Harcourt Brace & Co., 1937.
———. *Rodin: The Man and His Art.* Trans. S. K. Star; intro. James Honeker. New York: Century, 1917.

———. *Rodin: Sa Vie glorieuse, sa vie inconnue.* Paris: Bernard Grasset, 1936.
Clattenburg, Ellen Fritz. *The Photographic Work of F. Holland Day.* Wellesley, Mass.: Wellesley College Museum, 1975.
Cooper, Jeremy. *Nineteenth-Century Bronzes.* Boston: New York Graphic Society, 1975.
Coquiot, Gustave. *Rodin à l'Hôtel de Biron et à Meudon.* Paris: Ollendorf Editions, 1917.
De Caso, Jacques and Patricia B. Sanders. *Rodin Sculpture. A Critical Study of the Spreckels Collection, California Palace Legion of Honor.* San Francisco: Fine Arts Museums, 1977.
Delevoy, Robert L. *Victor Horta.* Brussels: Editions Meddens, n.d.
Delville, Jean. *The New Mission of Art: A Study of Idealism in Art.* Trans. Francis Colmer; introductory notes Clifford Bax and Edward Schuré. London: Francis Griffiths, 1910.
Denis, Maurice. *ABC de la peinture.* Paris: Floury, 1942.
———. *Du symbolisme au classicisme.* Paris: Hermann, 1964.
———. *Histoire de l'art religieux.* Paris: Flammarion, 1939.
———. *Journal.* 3 vols. Paris: La Colombe, 1957–1959.
———. *Nouvelles Théories sur l'art moderne et sur l'art sacré 1914–1921.* Paris: Rouart and J. Watelin, 1921.
Descarques, Pierre. *Bourdelle.* Paris: Musée Bourdelle, 1954.
Descharmes, Robert. *Auguste Rodin.* Paris: La Bibliothèque des Arts (Edita Lausanne), 1967.
Destrée, Jules. *L'Oeuvre lithographique de Odilon Redon.* Brussels: Edmond Deman, 1891.
Driskl, Michael-Paul. "Eclecticism and Ideology in the July Monarchy: Jules Claude Ziegler's Vision of Christianity at the Madeleine." *Arts* (May 1982): 119–29.
Einem, Herbert von. "Anselm Feuerbach's *Orpheus und Eurydike.*" *Wallraf-Richartz Jahrbuch* 36 (1974): 295–310.
Elsen, Albert E. *In Rodin's Studio: A Photographic Record of Sculpture in the Making.* Ithaca, N.Y.: Cornell University Press, 1980.
———. *Rodin and Balzac: Bronzes from the Cantor, Fitzgerald Collection, Stanford University.* Beverly Hills, Calif.: Cantor, Fitzgerald, 1973.
———. *Rodin's Gates of Hell.* Minneapolis: University of Minnesota Press, 1960.
Ephrussi, Charles. *Paul Baudry, sa vie et son oeuvre.* Paris: Ludovic Baschet, 1887.
Faquet, Emile. *Politiques et moralistes du 19ème siècle.* 2 vols. Paris: Société Française d'Imprimerie et de Libraire, 1890–98.
Finke, Ulrich, ed. *French 19th-Century Painting and Literature with Special Reference to the Relevance of Literary Subject-Matter to French Painting.* New York, Evanston, San Francisco, London: Harper & Row, 1972.
Frongia, Maria-Louisa. "'Finito' et 'non-finito' nell'opera di Gustave Moreau." *Commentari* 23, nos. 1–2 (January–June 1972): 139–51.
———. "I miti classici nelle opere della maturità di Gustave Moreau." *Storia dell'arte* (Florence) No. 13 (1972): 83–96.
———. *Il simbolismo di Jean Delville.* Bologne: Patron, 1978.
Fuchs, George. "Melchior Lechter." *Deutsche Kunst und Dekoration* (Darmstadt) 1 (1897–98): 161–92.
Fusty, G. de. *Alexandre Séon-Silhouettes Foreziennes.* St. Etienne: Bibliothèque de "La Loire Republicaine," 1950.

Gantner, Joseph. *Rodin und Michelangelo*. Vienna: Verlag Anton Schroll, 1953.
Gaunt, William. *The Aesthetic Adventure*. New York: Schocken Books, 1967.
Gauss, Charles E. *The Aesthetic Theories of French Artists: 1855 to the Present*. Baltimore: Md.: Johns Hopkins Press, 1949.
Gautier, Théophile. "Le Panthéon—peintures murales." *L'Art moderne* (Paris) (1856).
———. "Le Salon de 1866." *Le Moniteur universel* (15 May 1866).
Geffroy, Gustave. "L'Oeuvre de Gustave Moreau." *L'Oeuvre d'art* (5 July 1900): 32, illus.
Geissbuhler, Elizabeth Chase. *Rodin's Later Drawings*. With interpretations by Antoine Bourdelle. Boston: Beacon Press, 1963.
Geneva. *Gustave Moreau et le symbolisme*. Musée du Petit Palais, 1977.
Germain, Alphonse. "Un peintre idéaliste-idéiste-symbolisme des Teintes: Alexandre Séon." *L'Art et l'idée*, No. 2 (February 1892): 109–10.
Goldscheider, Cécile. *Rodin*. Paris: Les Productions de Paris, 1962.
———. "Rodin et le mouvement de Victor Hugo." *Revue des Arts* 6 (October 1956).
Goldscheider, Ludwig. *Rodin Sculptures*. Intro. Sommerville Story. Oxford: Phaidon, 1979.
Grantoff, D. *Rodin*. Bielefeld and Leipzig: Verlag von Belhagen and Klafing, 1911.
Greenwood, M. "Gentle Olympian: Pierre Puvis de Chavannes." *Arts Canada* 34 (October–November 1977): 21–34.
Guicheteau, Marcel. *Paul Serusier*. Paris: Editions Side, 1976.
Hahlbrock, Paul. *Gustave Moreau oder das Unbehagen in der Natur*. Berlin: Rembrandt Verlag, 1976.
Harding, James. *Les Peintres pompiers, la peinture académique en France de 1830 à 1880*. Paris: Flammarion, 1980.
Harrison, Martin and Bill Walters. *Burne-Jones*. London: Barsie and Jenkins, 1973.
Hersey, George L. "Delacroix's Imagery in the Palais Bourbon Library." *Journal of the Warburg and Courtauld Institutes* 31 (1968): 383–403.
Hobbs, Richard. *Odilon Redon*. Boston: New York Graphic Society, 1977.
Hofmann, Helga D. "The Villa Stuck: A Masterpiece of the Bavarian Attic Style." *Apollo* (November 1971): 384–95.
Hofstätter, Hans H. *Gustave Moreau, Leben und Werk*. Cologne: Dumont Buchverlag, 1978.
Holten, Ragnar von. "Gustave Moreau, Sculpteur." *La Revue des Arts*, Nos. 4–5 (1959): 208–16.
———. *Gustave Moreau, Symbolist*. Stockholm: Natur och Kultur, 1965.
———. "Le Personnage de Salomé à travers les dessins de Gustave Moreau." *L'Oeil*, Nos. 79–80 (July–August 1968): 44–51, 72.
Houyoux, R. and S. Sulzberger. "Fernand Khnopff and Eugène Delacroix." *Gazette des beaux-arts*, sér. 6, 64 (September 1964): 183–85.
Howe, Jeffery W. *The Symbolist Art of Ferdinand Khnopff*. Ann Arbor: UMI Research Press, 1979.
Iribert, Hughes. *Profils d'artistes contemporaires*. Paris: Fischbacher, 1897.
Ironside, Robin. "Gustave Moreau and Burne-Jones." *Horizon* 1 (June 1940): 406–24.
Jacoby, Karl. "Melchior Lechter und der Kreis der 'Blätter der Kunst.'" *Philobiblion* (Brünn) 11 (1939): 201–12.

Janot, Paul. *Maurice Denis*. Paris: Plon, 1945.
Jean, René. *Puvis de Chavannes*. Paris: F. Alcan, 1925.
Jianou, Ionel and Michel Dufet. *Bourdelle*. Trans. Kathleen Muston, Bryan Richardson. Paris: Arted, 1965.
Jirat-Wasiutynski, Vojtech. *Paul Gauguin in the Context of Symbolism*. New York and London: Garland, 1978.
Johnson, Ron. "Whistler's Musical Modes: Numinous Nocturnes." *Arts Magazine* (April 1981): 169–76.
Jones, Owen. *The Grammar of Ornament*. London: Quaritch, 1868.
Judrin, Claudie. *Rodin et les écrivains de son temps*. Paris: Musée Rodin, 1976.
Judrin, Claudie, Monique Laureat and Dominique Vieville. *August Rodin, Le Monument des Bourgeois de Calais*. Paris: Musée Rodin; Calais: Musée des Beaux-Arts, 1977.
Jugendstil Illustration in München. Munich and Vienna: Albebt es." *Gazette des beaux-arts*, sér. 6, 20 [24] (November 1938): 237–50.
Julia, Emile François. *Bourdelle*. Paris: Librairie de France, 1930.
Jullian, René. "L'Oeuvre de jeunesse de Puvis de Chavannes." *Gazette des beaux-arts*, sér. 6, 20 [24] (November 1938): 237–50.
Kahn, Gustave. "L'Art français à l'Exposition." *La Vogue* (August 1889): 127–30.
Kaplan, Julius. *Gustave Moreau*. Los Angeles: Los Angeles County Museum of Art, 1974.
Koenigsberg, Valdina de. "Gustave Moreau's 'Young Man and Death,' Image of Woman as the Femme Fatale." Qualifying paper for the Masters, New York University, Institute of Fine Arts, 1981.
Kosinski, Dorothy. "Gustave Moreau's *La Vie de l'humanité*: Orpheus in the Context of Relgious Syncretism, Universal Histories and Occultism." *Art Journal* (Spring 1987): 9–13.
Kotzin, M. "Pre-Raphaelitism, Ruskinism and French Symbolism." *The Art Journal* 25 (Summer 1966): 4.
Lafargue, Jacqueline. "The Revival of Decorative Painting in the First Half of the 19th Century." *Apollo* 106 (December 1977): 473–77.
Laforgue, Jules. "A propos de toiles, ça et là." *Le Symboliste*, No. 4 (30 October–6 November 1886).
Lami, Stanislas. *Dictionnaire des Sculpteurs de L'Ecole Française au Dix-Neuvième Siècle*. [Paris, 1914] Nendeln: Neudruck, 1970.
Lamy, M. "Le Préraphaelitisme français de 1850 à 1860." *Notes d'Art et d'Archéologie* (January 1926): 1–7.
Lange, Pauline. "Melchior Lechter." *Westermanns Monatshefte Braunschweig* 97 (1904): 23–39, 194–212.
Larau, J. and André Michel. *Puvis de Chavannes*. Philadelphia: J. B. Lippincott; London: William Heinemann, 1912.
Larroumet, Gustave. "Le Symbolisme de Gustave Moreau." *La Revue de Paris* (15 September 1895): 408–39.
Leprieur, Paul. "Burne-Jones, décorateur et humaniste." *Gazette des beaux-arts* (November 1892): 381.

———. "Gustave Moreau et son oeuvre." *L'Artiste* 59, no. 1 (1889): 161–80; 338–59; 443–55.

Lethève, Jacques. "La Connaissance des peintres préraphaélites en France 1855–1900." *Gazette des beaux-arts* (May–June 1959): 316–28.

———. *Impressionnistes et symbolistes devant la presse*. Paris, 1959.

———. "Les Salons de la Rose + Croix." *Gazette des beaux-arts* (December 1960): 363–74.

———. "Les Thèmes de la décadence dans les lettres françaises à la fin du XIXe siècle." *Revue d'Histoire Littéraire de la France* (January–March 1963): 44–61.

———. *La Vie quotidienne des artistes français au XIXe siecle*. Paris, 1968.

Leymarie, Jean. *Corot*. Geneva, New York: Skira/Rizzoli, 1979.

Lichtenstein, Sara. "Cézanne's Copies and Variants after Delacroix." *Apollo* 101 (February 1975): 116–27.

———. *Delacroix and Raphael*. New York and London: Garland, 1979.

Liebenwein, Renate. *Säkularisierung-Sakralisierung, Studien zur Metamorphose christlicher Bildformen im 19. Jahrhundert*. Frankfurt, 1974.

Le Livre du centenaire: Cent ans de vie française à la "Revue des deux mondes." Paris: Librairie Hachette/Revue des deux mondes, 1929.

Loisel, Abbé. *L'Inspiration Chrétienne du Peintre Gustave Moreau*. Paris: Bloud, 1912.

London. *Burne-Jones: Paintings, Graphics and Decorative Work, 1833–1898*. Great Britain: Arts Council, 1975.

London. *Cézanne, The Early Years, 1859–1872*. Royal Academy, 1988.

London. *Corot*. Great Britain: Arts Council, 1965.

London. *Highly Important 19th-Century European Paintings and Drawings*. Sotheby Parke Bernet, 23 June 1981.

London. *Lord Leverhulme: A Great Edwardian Collector and Builder*. Royal Academy of Arts, 1980.

London. *Odilon Redon, 1840–1916. A Loan Exhibition of Paintings, Pastels and Drawings in Aid of Corneal Graft and Eye Bank Research*. The Mathiesen Gallery.

London. *Odilon Redon: Lithographs*. Sotheby's, 26 March 1968.

Los Angeles. *Homage to Rodin, The B. G. Cantor Collection*. Los Angeles County Museum of Art, 1907.

Los Angeles. *The Romantics to Rodin, French 19th-Century Sculpture from North American Collections*. Organized and ed. by Peter Fusco and H.W. Janson. Los Angeles County Museum of Art, 1980.

Lyon. *Les Peintres de l'âme: Art lyonnais du XIXeme siècle*. Musée des Beaux-Arts, 1981.

Lyon. *Puvis de Chavannes et la peinture lyonnaise du XIXeme siècle*. Palace of Arts, Musée de Lyon, 1937.

Maisels, Ziva. "Gauguin's Philosophical Eve." *Burlington Magazine* 115 (1973): 373–82.

———. "Gauguin's Religious Themes." 2 vols. Ph.D. thesis, Hebrew University, Jerusalem, 1972.

Malle, T. "Alexandre Séon, Galerie Georges Petit." *Le Progrès andelysien* (9 June 1901).

Mamelsdorf, Alice. "Huysmans et Gustave Moreau." *Bulletin de la Société J.-K. Huysmans*, no. hors sér. (1960): 61–71.

Mantz, Paul. "Henri Regnault." *Gazette des beaux-arts* (1872): 66–83.
———. "Salon de 1863." *Gazette des beaux-arts* 4 (June–July 1863): 40.
Marcel, Henry. *La Peinture française aux XIXe siècle.* Paris: A. Picard & Kahn, 1906.
Marseille. *Valère Bernard "Symboliste" 1860–1936.* Musée des Beaux-Arts (July–December 1981).
Marx, Roger. *Les Artistes célèbres, Henri Regnault.* Paris, 1890.
Masson, André. "Mystic with a Method, Odilon Redon." *ARTnews* 55 (January 1957): 40–43, 60–62.
Masson, Frédéric. "Ombres et figures—Ch. Fr. Jalabert." *Le Figaro illustré* 12, no. 133: 2–4.
Mathieu, Pierre-Louis. *Documents inédits sur la jeunesse de Gustave Moreau (1826–1837).* Paris: F. de Nobèle, 1972.
———. *Gustave Moreau.* Trans. James Emmons. Boston: New York Graphic Society, 1976.
———. "Gustave Moreau Amoureux." *L'Oeil* (March 1974).
———. *Gustave Moreau en Italie (1857–1859) d'après sa correspondance inéditée.* Paris: Libr. F. de Nobèle, 1975.
———, ed. *L'Assembleur de rêves: Ecrits complets de Gustave Moreau.* Pref. Jean Paladilhe. Fontfroide: Bibliothèque Artistique & Littéraire, 1984.
Mauclair, Camille. *August Rodin.* London: Duckworth, 1905.
———. *Corot—Peintre-Poète de la France.* Paris: Albin Michel, 1962.
———. *Puvis de Chavannes.* Paris: Librairie Plon, 1928.
———. "Puvis de Chavannes et Gustave Moreau." *International Quarterly* 12 (1905): 240–54.
———. *August Rodin.* London: Duckworth & Co., 1905.
Mauner, George L. *The Nabis: Their History and Their Art, 1888–1896.* New York and London: Garland, 1978.
Maus, Octave. "The Salon of the Libre esthétique." *The Magazine of Art* 24 (1900): 416–20.
———. *Trente années de lutte pour l'art, 1884–1914.* Brussels: Librairie l'Oiseau Bleu, 1926.
McNamara, Mary Jo and Albert Elsen. *Rodin's Burghers of Calais.* The Cantor, Fitzgerald Collection, 1977.
Mellerio, André. *Odilon Redon.* Paris: Société pour l'Etude de la Gravure Française, 1913.
———. *Odilon Redon.* Paris: H. Floury ed., 1923.
Metamorphoses in 19th Century Sculpture. Ed. Jeanne L. Wasserman. Harvard: Fogg Art Museum, 1975.
Milan. *Maurice Denis.* Galleria del Levante (June–July 1966).
Minneapolis. *Victorian High Renaissance.* Minneapolis Institute of Arts (19 November 1978–7 January 1979).
Montifaud, Marc de. "Salon de 1866. I et II." *L'Artiste* (15 May 1866):169–78; (15 June 1866): 196–205.
Moreau, Gustave. *Cahier rouge* (Handwritten notes by the artist). Paris: Gustave Moreau Museum (See published presentation of his writings: *L'Assembleur de rêves*).

Morel, Louis. "L'Influence germanique chez Benjamin Constant—Benjamin Constant à la cour de Benewick." *Revue d'histoire littéraire de la France* (Paris) 22 (1915): 86–112.
Morice, Charles. *Eugène Carrière: L'Homme et sa pensée, l'artiste et son ouevre.* Paris: Société du Mercure de France, 1906.
———. *Paul Gauguin.* Paris: Floury, 1919.
———. *Rodin.* Paris: Floury, 1900.
———. *Quelques maîtres modernes—Whistler, Pissarro, Fantin-Latour, Constantin Meunier, Paul Cézanne.* Paris: Société des Trente, M. Messein, 1914.
Mourey, Gabriel. *D. G. Rossetti et les préraphaélites anglais.* Paris, 1929.
Mras, George P. *Eugène Delacroix's Theory of Art.* Princeton: Princeton University Press, 1966.
———. "Ut Pictura Musica: A Study of Delacroix's *Paragone*." *Art Bulletin* 45 (September 1963): 266–71.
Munich. *Franz von Stuck.* Museum Villa Stuck, 1977.
New York. *The Arts of the American Renaissance.* Hirschl & Adler Galleries, 12 April–31 May 1985.
New York. *Bourdelle.* Grand Central Art Galleries, 1925.
New York. *Carved and Modeled: American Sculpture of 1810–1940.* Hirschl & Adler Gallery, 1982.
New York. *Charles Gleyre.* New York University, Grey Art Gallery and Study Center, 1980.
New York. *Christian Imagery in French Nineteenth Century Art 1789–1906.* Shepherd Gallery, Spring 1980.
New York. *Corot.* Wildenstein, 1969.
New York. *Important 19th and 20th Century Drawings and Watercolors.* Sotheby, Parke, Bernet, 17 May 1979.
New York. *Odilon Redon, Gustave Moreau, Rodolphe Bresdin.* Museum of Modern Art, 1962.
New York. *The Paintings of Bryson Burroughs (1869–1934).* Hirschl & Adler Galleries, 18 February–17 March 1984.
New York. *Symbolism, Art Nouveau and Art Deco: Paintings, Drawings.* Sotheby Parke Bernet, June 1980.
Nice. *Alexis et Gustave Adolf Mossa.* Musée Jules Chevet, 15 March–28 April 1974.
Nice. *Gustave Adolf Mossa et les symboles.* Galerie des Ponchettes (Summer 1978). (Jean Robert Soubiran, catalogue.)
Nîmes. *Charles-François Jalabert 1819–1901.* Musée des Beaux-Arts, Editions Notre-Dame, 1981.
Nordau, Max. *Dégénérescence.* Trans. A. Dietrich. 2 vols. Paris: Alcan, 1894.
Novotny, Fritz. *Painting and Sculpture in Europe, 1780–1880.* Harmondsworth, Middlesex: Penguin, 1960.
Olander, William R. "Fernand Khnopff's Art or the Caresses." *Arts Magazine* (June 1977): 116–21.
Ollendorf, G. *Salon de 1887* (Société des Artistes Français). Paris: L. Baschet, 1887.
Ormond, Léonée and Richard Ormond. *Lord Leighton.* New Haven and London: Yale University Press, 1975.

Ostini, Fritz. *Villa Franz von Stuck.* Darmstadt: A. Koch, 1909.
Ottawa. *Antoine Bourdelle.* National Gallery of Canada, 1961.
Pach, Walter. *Queerthing, Painting.* New York and London: Harper & Bros., 1938.
Paladilhe, Jean. *Gustave Moreau.* Paris: Hazan, 1971.
Paris. *Alphonse Osbert, 1857–1939.* Galerie Coligny, 1980.
Paris. *Artistes de l'âme.* Théâtre de la Bodinière. 1896.
Paris. *Autour de Lévy-Dhurmer: Visionnaires et intimistes en 1900.* Grand Palais, 3 March–30 April 1973.
Paris. *Burne-Jones et l'influence des préraphaëlites.* 1972.
Paris. *Exposition Bourdelle.* Musée de l'Orangerie (14 February–6 April 1931).
Paris: *Exposition de Gustave-Adolf Mossa.* Galerie Georges Petit, 1–15 April 1911.
Paris. *Fernand Khnopff, 1858–1921.* Musée des Arts Décoratifs, 1979. (See also Brussels: Musées Royaux des Beaux-Arts de Belgique; Hamburg, Kunsthalle.)
Paris. *Gustave Moreau.* Musée du Louvre, 1961.
Paris. *Hommage à Alphonse Osbert, 1857–1939.* L'Association, Les Amis du Peintre Alphonse Osbert, 1974.
Paris. *Hommage à Corot.* Musée de l'Orangerie, Editions Musées Nationaux, 1975.
Paris. *Marcel-Beronneau, 1869–1937, Peintre symboliste.* Galerie Alain Blondel, 1981.
Paris. *Maurice Denis.* Musée de l'Orangerie des Tuileries, 8 June–31 August 1970.
Paris. *Mucha, 1860–1930.* Grand Palais, 5 February–28 April 1980.
Paris. *Le Musée du Luxembourg en 1874.* Grand Palais, 31 May–18 November 1974.
Paris. *Musée Gustave Moreau, Catalogue des peintures, dessins, cartons, aquarelles, exposés dans les Galeries.* Editions des Musées Nationaux, 1974.
Paris. *Musée Rodin, Catalogue des oeuvres.* Editions des Musées Nationaux, 1931.
Paris. *Musiciennes du silence, Hébert: un peintre ami de la musique.* Musée Hébert, 1982.
Paris. *Odilon Redon.* Musée de l'Orangerie, October 1956–January 1957.
Paris. *La Peinture lyonnaise du XVIe au XIXe siècle.* L'Orangerie des Tuileries, 1948. (See also Lyon: Musée de la Ville de Lyon.)
Paris. *Puvis de Chavannes.* Grand Palais, 1976. (See also Ottawa, National Gallery of Canada, 1977.)
Paris. *Rodin Collectionneur.* Musée Rodin, 1967–68.
Paris. *Rodin et l'extrême-orient.* Musée Rodin, 1979.
Paris. *Rodin inconnu.* Musée Nationale du Louvre, December 1962–January 1963.
Paris. *Trois générations d'artistes: Maurice Denis, Marcel Poncet, Antoine Poncet.* Musée Bourdelle, June–September 1979.
Pascal, Félicien. "Un prophète de l'avenir." *Correspondant* (Paris) 306 [n.s. 270].
Péladan, Joséphin. "Gustave Moreau." *L'Ermitage* (January 1895): 29–34.
———. "Paul Chenavard," *L'Artiste,* No. 9, n.s. (1895): 356–62.
Philadelphia. *The Second Empire, 1832–1870, Art in France under Napoleon III.* Philadelphia Museum of Art, 1978.
Ponsonailhe, Charles. "Jean Antonin Injalbert." *Revue illustré* 10, no. 19 (1 May 1984): 1–10.
Price, Aimée Brown. "L'Allégorie réelle chez Pierre Puvis de Chavannes." *Gazette des beaux-arts,* sér. 6, 89, 119 (January 1977): 27–40.

Proust, Marcel. "Notes sur le monde mystérieux de Gustave Moreau." In *Contre Sainte-Beuve*. Paris: Pléïade, 1971.
Providence. *Fantastic Illustration and Design in Britain, 1850–1930*. Cat. Diana L. Johnson. Rhode Island School of Design and New York: Cooper-Hewitt Museum, 1979.
Rapsilber, Maxmilian. *Melchior Lechter*. Berlin: E. Wasmuth, 1904.
Raub, Wolfhad. *Melchior Lechter als Buchkünstler Darstellung.* Cologne: Greven, 1969.
Rayssac, Saint-Cyr, de. "La Correspondance de Henri Regnault." *Gazette des beaux-arts* (1873): 119–27.
Redon, Ari. *Lettres de Gauguin, Gide, Huysmans, Jammes, Mallarmé, Verhaeren . . . à Odilon Redon*. Paris: José Corti, 1960.
Redon, Odilon. *A soi-même* (Journal 1867–1915). Paris: H. Fleury, 1922.
———. *Lettres 1878–1916*. Published by his family with a preface by Marius-Ary Leblond. Paris and Brussels: Librairie Nationale d'Art et d'Histoire, G. Van Oest & Cie, 1923.
Renan, Ary. "Gustave Moreau." *Gazette des beaux-arts* 33 (1886): 35–51, 377–94.
———. "Gustave Moreau." *Gazette des beaux-arts* 21 (1899): 5–20, 189–204, 299–312; 22 (1899): 57–70, 414–32, 478–97.
———. *Gustave Moreau (1826–1898)*. Paris: Gazette des beaux-arts, 1900.
Revel, Jean-François. "Delacroix entre les anciens et les modernes." *L'Oeil*, No. 101 (May 1963): 10–19, 67.
Reverseau, Jean-Pierre. "Poètes parnassiens—Peintres symbolistes, l'Inspiration et les Thèmes." Thesis, Ecole du Louvre, 1971.
———. "Pour une Etude du Thème de la Tête Coupée dans la littérature et la peinture dans la seconde partie du XIXe siècle." *Gazette des beaux-arts* (September 1972): 173–84.
La Revue française. "Numéro special consacré à G. Moreau, articles de H. Duvernois, G. Desvallières, etc." No. 11 (15 March 1925).
Rewald, John. *Post-Impressionism: From Van Gogh to Gauguin*. New York: The Museum of Modern Art, 1962.
Rheims, Maurice. *Nineteenth Century Sculpture*. Trans. Robert E. Wolf. New York: Harry N. Abrams, 1977.
Rilke, Rainer Maria. *Rodin*. Leipzig: Insel-Verlag, 1917.
Ringbom, Sixten. "Guérin, Delacroix, and 'The Liberty.'" *Burlington Magazine* 110 (May 1968): 270ff.
Rivier, Georges. "L'Atelier Gustave Moreau et ses élèves." *Apollo* 15 (March 1946): 2.
Robaut, Alfred. *L'Oeuvre complète d'Eugène Delacroix*. [Paris: Charavay, 1885] New York: Da Capo Press, 1969.
———. *L'Oeuvre complète de Corot, catalogue raisonné et illustré*. Paris: Léonce Laget, 1965.
Robert-Jones, Philippe. *La Peinture irréaliste au XIXe siècle*. Paris: La Bibliothèque de Arts, n.d.
Rodin, Auguste. *Art*. Trans. from Paul Gsell by Romilly Fedden. London, NewYork, Toronto: Hodder & Stoughton, 1912.

Rookmaaker, H.R. *Gauguin and Nineteeth Century Art Theory*. Amsterdam: Swets and Zeitlinger, 1972.
_____. *Synthetist Art Theories*. Amsterdam: Swets and Zeitliner, 1959.
Rosenblum, Robert. *Modern Painting and the Northern Romantic Tradition*. New York: Harper & Row, 1975.
Roskill, Mark. *Van Gogh, Gauguin and the Impressionist Circle*. Greenwich, Conn.: New York Graphic Society, 1970.
Saint-Antoine. "Qu'est-ce que le symbolisme?" *L'Ermitage* (June 1894).
Saint-Etienne. *Autour de Félix Chiollier, Dessinateurs lyonnais et foréziens du XIXe siècle*. Musée d'Art et d'Industrie, 1980.
Saint-Etienne. *Peintres Foréziens*. Musée d'Art et d'Industrie, 21 April–21 May 1945.
Saint-Victor, Paul de. "Le Salon de 1869." *La Presse*.
Sanders, Patricia B. and Jacques De Caso. *Rodin's Sculpture: A Critical Study of the Spreckels Collection*. San Francisco: The Fine Arts Museum, 1977.
Sandstrom, Sven. *Le Monde imaginaire d'Odilon Redon*. Lund and New York: Wittenborn, 1955.
Saunier, Charles. "Alexander Séon in 'Gazette d'Art.'" *La Revue blanche* (1951).
_____. "Gazette d'art." *La Revue blanche* 205 (1901): 304.
Scheider, Mechthild. "Künstlerdenkmäler in Frankreich—Ein Thema der Auftragsplastik im 19 Jahrhundert." Ph.D. thesis, Johann-Wolfgang-Goethe Universität, Frankfurt-am-Main, 1977.
Schiff, Gert. *Die seltsame Welt des Malers Gustave Moreau*. Zurich: Du Atlantis, 1965.
Schmutzler, Robert. *Art Nouveau*. New York: Harry N. Abrams, 1978.
Schneider, Pierre. "Fantin-Latour." *ARTnews Annual* 24 (1955): 64–65.
Schnoll, J. A. gen Eisenwerth. *Das Phänomen Franz von Stuck Kritiken Essays: Interviews 1968–1972*. München: Villa Stuck, Stuck Jugendstil-Verein e. V., 1972.
Schuré, Edouard. *Précurseurs et révoltés*. Paris: Perrin, 1920. (Chapter on Gustave Moreau first published in *La Revue de Paris* [1 December 1900]: 587–622.)
Scribe, Léon. *Catalogue officiel de l'Exposition Universelle*. Paris, 1867.
Sebastiana-Picard. "L'influence de Michelangelo sur Odilon Redon." *Revue du Louvre* 3 (1977): 140–52.
Ségalen, Victor. *Gustave Moreau. Maître-Imagier de l'Orphisme*. v. 1908. Unedited typescript, presented by Mme. Joly-Segalen.
Selz, Jean. *Odilon Redon*. New York: Crown Publishers, 1971.
Serullaz, Maurice. *Les Peintures murales de Delacroix*. Paris: Les Editions du Temps, 1963.
Sheffield. *John William Waterhouse, 1849–1917*. Mappin Art Gallery, 1978.
Sheon, Aaron. "French Art and Science in the Mid-19th Century. Some Points of Contact." *Art Quarterly* 34, no. 4 (Winter 1971): 434–55.
Sloane, Joseph C. *French Painting between the Past and the Present Artists, Critics and Traditions from 1848 to 1870*. Princeton, N.J.: Princeton University Press, 1973.
_____. "Paul Chenavard." *Art Bulletin* 33 (December 1951): 240–58.
_____. *Paul Marc Joseph Chenavard, Artist of 1848*. Chapel Hill: University of North Carolina Press, 1962.
Spalding, Frances. *Magnificent Dreamers: Burne-Jones and the Late Victorians*. Oxford: Phaidon, 1978.

Spear, Athena Tacha. *Rodin Sculpture in the Cleveland Museum of Art*. Cleveland: Cleveland Museum of Art, 1967.

———. *A Supplement to Rodin Sculpture in the Cleveland Museum of Art*. Cleveland: Cleveland Museum of Art, 1974.

Stafford, Barbara Maria. *Symbol and Myth. Humbert de Superville's Essay on Absolute Signs in Art*. London: University of Delaware Press, Assoc. University Presses, 1979.

Starzynski, Juilusz. "La Pensée orphique du plafond d'Homère de Delacroix." *Revue du Louvre*, 13: 73–82.

Story, Sommerville. *Rodin*. New York: Oxford University Press, Phaidon, 1939.

Sutton, Denys. "An Aristocrat of Idealism: Puvis." *Apollo* 95 (June 1972): 432–39.

Tancock, John L. *The Sculpture of Auguste Rodin*. The Collection of the Rodin Museum. Philadelphia: Philadelphia Museum of Art, 1976.

———. "Unfamiliar Aspects of Rodin." *Apollo* (July 1974): 46–51.

Thevenin, Leon. *L'Esthétique de Gustave Moreau*. Paris, 1897.

Trapp, Frank Anderson. "The Atelier Gustave Moreau." *The Art Journal* (Winter 1962–63): 92–95.

———. *The Attainment of Delacroix*. Baltimore and London: The Johns Hopkins Press, 1971.

Traz, Georges de. *Bourdelle*. Paris: Gallimard, 1924.

Vachon, Marius. *Puvis de Chavannes*. Paris: Société des Editions Artistique, 1895.

Valbert, G. "Les Monuments de Henri Regnault." *Revue des deux mondes*, sér. 3, 46, no. 17 (1876).

Vanor, Georges. *L'Art symboliste*. Pref. Paul Adam. Paris: Chez le Bibliophile, 1889.

Vanzype, Gustave. "L'Exposition retrospective de l'art belge au XIXe siècle." *L'Art et les artistes* 1, supplément illustré no. 6 (1905): 3–6.

Varnedoe, Kirk. "Rodin and Balzac." *Portfolio* 4, no. 4 (May–June 1982): 94–99.

Venice. *Le Arti a Vienna dalla Secessione alla caduta dell'impero asburgizo*. Palazzo Grassi (ed. La Biennale) 20 March–16 September 1984.

Vial, Eugène. "Les Souvenirs de P. Chenavard." *La Revue du lyonnais* 4 (1921): 547–648.

Viola, Jerome. "Redon, Darwin and the Ascent of Man." *Marsyas* (New York) 11 (1964): 42–57.

Voss, Heinrich. "Franz von Stuck as a Painter." *Apollo* (November 1971): 378–83.

———. *Franz von Stuck, 1863–1928*. Munich: Prestel-Verlag, 1973.

Washington, D.C. *An American Perspective*. National Gallery of Art, 1982.

Washington, D.C. *Leon Spilliaert, Symbol and Expression in 20th Century Belgian Art*. The Phillips Collection, 1980. (See also, New York: The Metropolitan Museum of Art.)

Washington, D.C. *Rodin Rediscovered*. National Gallery of Art, 1981.

Wattenmaker, Richard J. *Puvis de Chavannes and the Modern Tradition*. Toronto: Art Gallery of Ontario, ca. 1976.

Wennberg, Bo. *French and Scandinavian Sculpture in the 19th Century*. Stockholm and Atlantic Highlands, N.J.: Almguist and Wiksell, Int., and Humanities Press, 1978.

Werner, Alfred. *The Graphic Works of Odilon Redon*. New York: Dover, 1969.

Wissman, Jürgen. *Melchior Lechter*. Recklinghausen: A. Bongers, 1966.

Wright, B. and P. Moisy. *Gustave Moreau et Eugène Fromenton, Documents inédits*. La Rochelle, 1972.

Wright, Barbara. "A propos d'une page de Baudelaire: Gustave Moreau et Hector Berlioz." *Studi francesi*, No. 51 (1973): 465–70.
Wytenhove, H. "Don de deux oeuvres de P.-A. Marcel Beronneau." *Revue du Louvre* 5/6 (1980): 357–58.
Wyzewa, Téodor de. "Notes de la musique Wagnérienne Suite." *La Revue wagnérienne* 8 (8 September 1886): 264–65. Geneva: Slatkine reprints, 1968.
———. "Notes sur la peinture Wagnérienne et le Salon de 1886." *La Revue wagnérienne* 2 (8 May 1885): 106. Geneva: Slatkine reprints, 1968.
———. *Peintres de jadis et d'aujourd'hui*. Paris: Perrin, 1903.
Zurich. *Gustave Moreau, Symboliste*. Kunsthaus, 1986.

Nineteenth-Century Symbolism: General

Bailly, J. C. "La Fin d'un siècle: Le Symbolisme en Europe: Grand Palais, Paris." XXe *siècle*, No. 47 (December 1976): 139–41.
Borsi, Franco and Hans Wieser. *Bruxelles—Capitale de l'Art Nouveau*. Trans. Jean-Marie van der Meerschen. Rome: Casa ed. Carlo Colombo, 1971.
Brooklyn. *Belgian Art, 1880–1914*. Brooklyn Museum, 23 April–29 June 1980.
Brussels. *Jugendstil*. Palais des Beaux-Arts, 1 October-27 November 1977.
Budapest 1890–1919 l'anima e le forme. Milano: Gruppo Editoriale Electa, 1981.
Chassé, Charles. *Le Mouvement symboliste dans l'art du XIXe siecle*. Paris: Floury, 1947.
———. *The Nabis and Their Period*. New York: Praeger, 1969.
Dalemans, R. "El Simbolismo en Belgica (1880–1900)." *Goya*, No. 131 (March 1976): 300–304.
Darmstadt. *Plakate um 1900*. Hessisches Landesmuseum, 26 January-1 April 1962.
Delevoy, Robert L. *Symbolists and Symbolism*. New York: Skira (Rizzoli), 1978.
Dorra, Henri. *Visionaries and Dreamers*. Washington: Corcoran Gallery of Art, 1956.
Eldredge, Charles C. *American Imagination and Symbolist Painting*. New York: Grey Art Gallery and Study Center, 1979.
Frongia, Masia-Louisa. "Il mito di Orfeo nella pittura simbolista francese." *Annali della Facoltà di lettere, Filosofia, Magistero* (Università di Cagliari) 36 (1973): 352–94.
Gerhardus, Maly and Dietfried. *Symbolism and Art Noveau, Sense of Impending Crisis, Refinement of Sensibility and Life Reborn in Beauty*. Trans. Alan Bailey. Oxford: Phaidon, 1978.
Goldwater, Robert. *Symbolism*. New York: Harper & Row, 1979.
Hamburg. *Experiment Weltuntergang Wien um 1900*. Kunsthalle, 10 April–3 May 1981.
Hirsh, Sharon. *From Imagination to Evocation: Symbolist Drawings and Sketches*. Carlisle: Dickinson College, 1984.
Hofstätter, Hans H. *Symbolismus und die Kunst der Jahrhundertwende*. Cologne, 1965.
Jullian, Philippe. *Dreamers of Decadence: Symbolist Painters of the 1890s*. New York and Washington: Praeger, 1971.
———. *The Symbolists*. London: Phaidon, 1973.
Kahn, Gustave. *Symbolistes et décadents*. Paris: L. Vanier, 1902.
Legrand, Francine-Claire. *Le Symbolisme en Belgique*. Brussels: Imprimerie Laconti, 1971.

Loevgren, Sven. *The Genesis of Modernism: Seurat, Gauguin, van Gogh and French Symbolism in the 1880s*. Bloomington and London: Indiana University Press, 1971.
London. *French Symbolist Painters: Moreau, Puvis, Redon and Their Followers*. Hayward Gallery, 1972.
London. *Post-Impressionism, Cross-Currents in European Painting*. Royal Academy of Arts, 1979.
Lucie-Smith, Edward. *Symbolist Art*. New York and Washington: Praeger, 1972.
Madrid. *El Simbolismo en la pintura francesa*. Museo Español de Arte Contemporaneo, 1972.
Marie, Gisèle, ed. *Le Théâtre symboliste*. Paris: Nizet, 1973.
Milan. *Maestri del Simbolismo*. Galleria del Levante.
Milner, John. *Symbolists and Decadents*. London: 1971.
Munich. *Symbolismus*. Michael Hasenclever Gallery, 26 October–24 November 1973.
New York. *Painters of the Mind's Eye: Belgian Symbolists and Surrealists*. The New York Cultural Center in association with Farleigh Dickinson University, 1974.
New York. *La Revue Blanche: Paris in the Days of Post-Impressionism and Symbolism*. Wildenstein, 17 November–31 December 1983.
New York. *The Symbolist Aesthetic*. The Museum of Modern Art, 23 December 1980–10 March 1981.
New York. *The Symbolists*. Spencer Samuels Gallery, 1970.
Paris. *L'Art 1900 en Hongrie*. Petit Palais, 1976.
Paris. *Dessins Symbolistes*. Pref. André Breton. Le Bateau Lavoir, 1958.
Paris. *Esthètes et magiciens symbolistes des collections parisiennes*. 1970.
Paris. *Idéalistes et symbolistes: Gustave Moreau*. Galerie J.C. Gaubert, 1973.
Paris. *Peintres de l'imaginaire symbolistes et surréalistes belges*. Galeries Nationales du Grand Palais, 1972.
Reff, Theodore, ed. *Exhibitions of the Rosicrucian Salon*. Modern Art in Paris Series. New York and London: Garland, 1981.
Rotterdam. *Le Symbolisme en Europe*. Museum Boymans-van Beuningen, 1975–76 (also Brussels: Musées Royaux des Beaux-Arts de Belgique; Baden-Baden: Staatliche Kunsthalle; Paris: Grand Palais, 1976).
Saint-Germain-en-Laye, Yvelines. *Symbolistes et Nabis, Maurice Denis et son temps*. Musée Départemental du Prieuré, 1980.
San Bernadino, California. *Symbolism: Europe and America around the end of the 19th Century*. State College, 27 April–10 June 1980.
Spaanstra-Pollak, Bettina. *Het 'Fin-de-siècle' in de Nederlandse Schilderkunst. De Symbolistische Bewegung 1890–1900*. The Hague, 1955.
———. *Symbolism: Art and Architecture in the Netherlands*. Amsterdam: J. M. Meulenhoff, 1967.
Symbolism. A Bibliography of Symbolism, an International Multi-disciplinary Movement. Comp. and ed. David L. Anderson with George S. Maas and Diane-Marie Savoye. New York: New York University Press, 1975.
Turin. *Del Simbolismo*. Galeria Galatea. 20 October–18 November 1970.
Turin. *Il sacro e il profano nell'arte dei Simbolisti*. Galleria Civica d'arte moderna. June–August 1969. (See also Toronto: Art Gallery of Ontario, 1–26 November 1969.)

Ulrich, Christoffel. *Malerei und Poesie: die symbolistische Kunst des 19. Jahrhunderts.* Vienna: Gallus-Verlag, 1948.
Varnedoe, Kirk. *Northern Light Realism and Symbolism in Scandinavian Painting 1880–1910.* New York: The Brooklyn Museum, 10 November 1982–6 January 1983.
Washington, D.C. *Visionaries and Dreamers.* Corcoran Gallery of Art, 1956.

Orpheus in the Twentieth Century: Art, Literature, Criticism, Music

Acéphale: Religion, Sociologie, Philosophie. Paris: Jean-Michael Place, [1936] 1980.
Adema, Marcel. *Apollinaire.* Trans. Denise Folliot. New York: Grove Press, 1955.
Albouy, Pierre. *Mythe et mythologies dans la littérature française.* Paris: Librairie Armand Colin, 1969.
Amyx, Clifford. "Max Beckmann: The Iconography of the Triptypch." *The Kenyon Review* 13 (1951): 610–23.
Anderson, Jack. "A Hard-Headed Miracle: The New York City Ballet Concludes Season with Stravinsky Festival." *Dance Magazine* (September 1972): 26–32.
André Masson. Paris: Editions Filipacchi, 1979.
André Masson. Texts by Jean Louis Barrault, Georges Bataille, André Breton. Rouen: Imprimerie Wolf, 1940.
Anouilh, Jean. *Eurydice suivi de Romeo et Jeannette.* Paris: La Table Ronde, 1971.
Apollinaire, Guillaume. *Le Bestiaire ou cortège d'Orphée.* Trans. Lauren Shakely. New York: The Metropolitan Museum of Art, 1977.
_____. *Lettres à Lou.* Ed. Michel Decaudin. Paris: Gallimard, 1969.
_____. *Poèmes.* Présenté par André Billy. Paris: Gallimard, 1956.
_____. *Le Poète assassiné.* Paris: Gallimard, 1979.
_____. *Selected Writings.* Trans. with critical intro. by Roger Shattuck. New York: A New Directions Book, 1971.
Apollonio, Umbro. *Mondrian P. l'Astrattismo.* Milan: Fabbri, 1970.
L'Art face à la crise, L'Art en Occident 1929–1939. Saint Etienne: Université de Saint-Etienne, Centre Interdisciplinaire d'Etudes et de Recherches sur l'Expression Contemporaine, No. 26.
Avenarius, Ferdinand. *Max Klinger als Poet.* Munich: Im Kunstwartverlag George D. W. Callwey, 1918.
Barzun, Henri-Martin. *Orpheus: Choric Education, A Record of Labors and Achievements.* La Rochelle: French Forum Publications, 1945.
Bataille, Georges. *Histoire de l'oeil.* Paris: René Bonnel, 1928.
_____. *Sacrifices.* [Paris: Guy Lévy Mano, 1936]. In *Oeuvres complètes.* Vol. 1. Paris: Gallimard, 1970.
Bataille 2 André Masson. Billom, Saint-Loup: Les Monts d'Auvergne, 1980.
Bates, Scott. *Guillaume Apollinaire.* New York: Thayne Publishers, 1967.
Batterby, Kenneth A. J. *Rilke and France: A Study in Poetic Development.* London: Oxford, 1966.
Bauer, Arnold. *Rainer Maria Rilke.* Trans. Ursula Lamm. New York: Frederick Ungar, 1972.

Beatty, Frances L. "André Masson and The Imagery of Surrealism." Ph.D. thesis, Columbia University, 1981.
Berckelaers, F. L. (pseud. Michel Seuphor). *Piet Mondrian: Life and Work*. New York: Abrams, 1956.
Bernier, Georges. "Le Surréalisme et après: Un entretien au magnétophone avec André Masson." *L'Oeil* (Paris) (15 May 1955)): 14.
Besançon. *Michel Seuphor, poésie, plastique*. Palais Granuelle, n.d.
Billy, André. *Avec Apollinaire, souvenirs inédits*. Paris: La Palatine, n.d.
Bishop, John Graham. *Jung and Christianity*. London: SPCK, 1966.
Blanchot, Maurice. *The Gaze of Orpheus and Other Literary Essays*. Pref. Geoffrey Hartman, trans. Lydia Davis, ed. with an afterword by P. Adams Sitney. Barrytown, N.Y.: Station Hill Press, 1981.
Blok, C. *Piet Mondrian*. Amsterdam: Meulenhoff, 1974.
Boghosian, V. *Orpheus*. Boston: Swetyoff Gallery, 1951.
Bonfantini, M., ed. *Apollinaire*. Turin and Paris: Giappichelli and Nizet, 1970.
Bouillier, Henry. *Victor Ségalen*. Paris, 1961.
Bowra, Cecil Maurice. *The Heritage of Symbolism*. London: MacMillan, 1962.
Breunig, Leroy C. *Guillaume Apollinaire*. New York/London: Columbia Press, 1969.
———, ed. *Apollinaire on Art: Essays and Reviews*. New York: Viking Press, 1960.
Brosse, Jacques. *Cocteau*. Paris: Gallimard, 1970.
Brown, Fred. *An Impersonation of Angels: A Biography of Jean Cocteau*. New York: Viking, 1968.
Buckberrough, Sherry A. *Robert Delaunay: The Discovery of Simultaneity*. Ann Arbor: UMI Research Press, 1982.
Buenger, Barbara C. "Beckmann's Beginnings: Junge Männer am Meer." *Pantheon* 2, 41 (April, May, June, 1983).
Bultman, Bernhard. *Oskar Kokoschka*. Trans. Michael Bullock. New York: Abrams, 1961.
Cahiers Jean Cocteau I. Paris: Gallimard, 1969.
Cahiers Jean Cocteau II. Paris: Gallimard, 1971.
Cahiers Jean Cocteau V. Jean Cocteau et son théâtre. Paris: Gallimard, 1975.
Campana, Dino. *Orphic Songs*. Trans. Charles Wright. Oberlin: Oberlin College, 1984.
Chadwick, Whitney. "Eros or Thanatos: The Surrealist Cult of Love Reexamined." *Art Forum* 14 (November 1975): 46–56.
———. *Myth in Surrealist Painting 1929–1939*. Ann Arbor: UMI Research Press, 1979.
Chanel, Pierre. *Album Cocteau*. Paris: Tchou, 1970.
Clarke, Mary and Clement Crisp. *Design for Ballet*. New York: Hawthorne Books, 1978.
Claudel, Paul. *Correspondance 1897–1938*. Paris: Gallimard, 1952.
Clébert, Jean-Paul. *Georges Bataille et André Masson*. Paris: Les Lettres Nouvelles, 1971.
———, ed. *Mythologie d'André Masson*. Geneva: P. Cailler, 1971.
Clerx, C. *Le Génie du paganisme: Essais sur l'inspiration artistique dans la littérature française contemporaine*. Paris, 1926.
Cocteau, Jean. *Cocteau on the Film*. Conversations recorded with André Fraigneau. Trans. Vera Traill. New York: Dover, 1972.

———. *Entre Picasso and Radiguet: Textes réunis et présentés par André Fermigier*. Paris: Hermann, 1967.
———. *Entretiens autour du cinématographe*. Recueillis par André Fraigneau. Paris: A. Bonne, 1951.
———. "Entretiens avec André Fraigneau." *Bibliothèque* 10, no. 18 (1955): 53.
———. *Five Plays*. Trans. Carl Wilman et al. New York: Hill and Wang, 1961.
———. *La Machine infernale*. Paris: Le Livre de Poche, 1962.
———. *Orpheus, The Play and The Film*. Ed. E. Freeman. Oxford: Basil Blackwell, 1976.
———. "Paul Valéry." *Partisan Review* 13, no. 1 (Winter 1946): 124–25.
———. *Professional Secrets: An Autobiography of Jean Cocteau*. Trans. Richard Howard. New York: Farrar, Straus, Giroux, 1970.
———. *Two Screenplays: The Blood of a Poet, The Testament of Orpheus*. Trans. Carol Martin Sperry. London: Calder & Boyais, 1970.
Couffignal, Robert. *L'Inspiration biblique dans l'oeuvre de G. Apollinaire*. Paris: Minard-Lettres Modernes, 1966.
Dahl, Ingolf. "The New Orpheus." *Dance Index* 6 (1947): 286.
Davies, Ivor. "Western European Art Forms Influenced by Nietzsche and Bergson before 1914, Particularly Italian Futurism and French Orphism." *Art International* 19, no. 3 (March 1975): 49–55.
Davies, Margaret. *Apollinaire*. Edinburgh and London: Oliver & Boyd, 1964.
Delevèze, J. "Robert Delaunay et le Mouvement." *L'Oeil*, Nos. 252–53 (July–August 1976): 40–45.
Demisch, Heinz. *Vision und Mythos in der Modernen Kunst*. Stuttgart, 1959.
Documents. Paris, 1929–30.
Douglas, Charlotte, C. "Swans of Other Worlds. Kasimir Malevich and the Origins of Suprematism, 1908–1915." Ph.D. thesis, University of Texas, Austin, 1975.
Evans, Arthur B. *Jean Cocteau and His Films on Orphic Identity*. Philadelphia: The Art Alliance Press (Assoc. Univ. Press), 1977.
Fabre, Antonin. "Le Rôle de la musique dans l'oeuvre poétique de Paul Valéry." *Académie de Vaucluse, Mémoires* (Avignon) sér. 3, 3 (1938).
Fingenstein, Peter. "Sprituality, Mysticism and Non-objective Art." *Art Journal* 21 (Fall 1961): 26.
Fischer, Friedheim Wilhelm. *Max Beckmann: Symbol und Weltbild, Grundriss zu einer Deutung des Gesamtwerkes*. Munich: W. Fink, 1972.
Fosca, François. *De Diderot à Valéry les écrivains et les arts visuels*. Paris, 1960.
Fowlie, Wallace. *Jean Cocteau: The History of a Poet's Age*. Bloomington: University of Indiana Press, 1966.
Fraigneau, André. *Cocteau par lui-même*. Paris: Ecrivains de Toujours, Editions du Seuil, 1957.
Franck, Claudine. "Orpheus and Prometheus: A Study in Apollinaire, Mayakovsky and the Visual Arts." Senior thesis, Fine Arts, Princeton University, 1978.
Frommel, Wolfgang. "Max Beckmann, Die Argonauten Aus einem Brief." *Castrum Peregrini* 33 (1957–58).

Gauss, Charles. "Theoretical Backgrounds of Surrealism." *Journal of Aesthetics and Art Criticism* (Fall 1943): 37–44.
Gay, Peter. *Art and Act: Causes in History—Manet/Gropius/Mondrian.* New York: Harper and Row, 1976.
Geelhaar, Christian. *Paul Klee and the Bauhaus.* Greenwich, Conn.: New York Graphic Society, 1973.
Gheorghe, Ian. *Les Images du poète et de la poésie dans l'oeuvre de Valéry.* Paris: Lettres Modernes Minard, 1977.
Golding, John. "Guillaume Apollinaire and the Art of the 20th Century." *The Baltimore Museum of Art News* 26, no. 4; 27, no. 1 (Summer–Fall 1963).
Goldner, Nancy. *The Stravinsky Festival of the New York City Ballet.* New York: Eakins Press, 1974.
Göpel, Erhard. *Max Beckmann: Die Argonauten. Ein Tryptychon.* Stuttgart: Reclam, 1957.
Göpel, Erhard and Barbara Göpel. *Max Beckmann, Katalog der Gemälde.* Vols. 1 and 2. Bern: Verlag Kornfeld, 1976.
Graedener-Hattingberg, Magda von. *Rilke and Benevenuta.* Trans. Cyrus Brooks. New York: W. W. Norton, 1949.
Grohmann, Will. *Paul Klee.* New York: Harry N. Abrams, n.d.
Guillaume Apollinaire. Etudes et informations réunies par Michel Décaudin. *La Revue des lettres modernes,* Nos. 69–70 (Spring 1962)
Hahn, Otto. *Masson.* New York: Abrams, 1965.
Harker, Margaret Florence. *The Linked Ring: The Secession Movement in Photography in Britain, 1892–1910.* London: Heinemann, 1979.
Hartman, Geoffry M. *The Unmediated Vision: An Interpretation of Wordsworth, Hopkins, Rilke and Valery.* New Haven: Yale University Press, 1954; New York: Harcourt Brace World, 1966.
Hassan, Ihab. *The Dismemberment of Orpheus: Toward a Postmodern Literature.* Wisconsin: University of Wisconsin, 1982.
Heilbrun, Carolyn G. *Toward a Recognition of Androgyny.* New York, Evanston, San Francisco, London: Harper & Row, Harper Colophon Books, 1973.
Heller, Erich. *The Disinherited Mind.* Cambridge: Bowes and Bowes, 1952.
Henning, Edward B. *The Spirit of Surrealism.* Cleveland: The Cleveland Museum of Art (Indiana University Press), 1979.
Hess, Thomas. *Barnett Newman.* New York: Walker, 1969.
Hodin, Josef Paul. *Oskar Kokoschka: The Artist and His Time.* Greenwich, Conn.: New York Graphic Society, 1966.
Hofmann, Werner. *Hommage à Schönberg.* Berlin: Nationalgalerie, 1974.
Holthusen, Haus Egon. *Portrait of Rilke.* Trans. W. H. Hargreaves. New York: Herder & Herder, 1971.
Hostie, R. *Du mythe à la religion: la psychologie analytique de C. G. Jung.* Bruges: Desclée De Brouwer, 1955.
Hunter, Sam. *Isamu Noguchi.* New York: Abbeville, 1978.
Jaffe, Hans Ludwig, ed. *De Stijl.* London: Thames & Hudson, 1970.
———. *Piet Mondrian.* New York: Abrams, 1970.

James, Martin S. "Mondrian and the Dutch Symbolists." *Art Journal* 23 (1963–64): 103–11.
Jianou, Ionel. *Zadkine*. Paris: Arted, 1979.
Johnson, Ron. "The 'Demoiselles d'Avignon' and Dionysian Destruction." *Arts Magazine* (October 1980).
Joly-Ségalen, Annie and André Schaeffner. *Ségalen et Debussy*. Monaco, 1961.
Jürgen-Fischer, K. "Kunstkritisches Tagebuch XLVIII Oder Symbolismus in Europa." *Kunstwerk* 29 (May 1976): 17–19.
Jussim, Estelle. *Slave to Beauty: The Eccentric Life and Controversial Career of F. Holland Day*. Boston: David R. Godine, 1981.
Kandinsky, Vasily. *Complete Writings on Art*. Ed. Peter Vergo, Kenneth Lindsay. Boston: G. K. Hall, ca. 1982.
———. *Über das Geistige in der Kunst*. English trans. New York: Wittenborn, Schultz, 1947.
Kandinsky, Vasily and Franz Marc, eds. *The Blaue Reiter Almanac*. New York: Viking, 1974.
Kesser, Armin. *Blick auf Beckmann*. Munich: R. Piper, 1965.
Kessler, Charles S. *Max Beckmann's Triptychs*. Cambridge, Mass.: Belknap Press, Harvard University Press, 1970.
Kihm, J. J., ed. "Jean Cocteau." *La Revue des lettres modernes*, Nos. 298–303 (1972).
Kirby, E. T., ed. *Total Theatre: A Critical Anthology*. New York: Dutton, 1969.
Kloomok, Isaac. *Marc Chagall: His Life and Work*. New York: Philosophical Library, 1951.
Knott, Robert. "The Myth of the Androgyne." *Artforum* 14 (November 1975): 38–45.
Kokoschka, Oskar. *My Life*. Trans. German. London: Thames & Hudson, 1974.
———. "Orpheus und Eurydice." In *Theater der Jahrhunderte*. Pref. Karl Kerenyi. Munich: Albert Langen-Georg Müller Verlag, 1963.
———. "Orpheus und Eurydice." 1915/18. *Vier Dramen*. Berlin: Paul Cassirer Verlag, 1919.
Kosinski, Dorothy. "Nineteenth-Century Sources of Futurism." Master's degree qualifying paper, New York University, 1978.
Kubin, Alfred. *Die andere Seite, phantastischer Roman*. Munich: G. Müller, 1923.
Kühn, Paul. *Max Klinger*. Leipzig: Breitkopf & Härtel, 1907.
Kushner, Eva. *Le Mythe d'Orphée dans la littérature française contemporaine*. Paris: A. G. Nizet, 1961.
Lackner, Stephan. *Max Beckmann*. New York: Abrams, 1977.
———. *Max Beckmann*. Cologne: DuMont Buchverlag, 1978.
———. "Memories of a Friendship." *Arts Yearbook* 4 (New York) (1961): 41.
Lankheit, Klaus. *Franz Marc—Katalog der Werke*. Cologne: DuMont, 1970.
Lathe, Carla. "Edvard Munch and the Concept of 'Psychic Naturalism.'" *Gazette des beaux-arts*, sér. 6, vol. 121, no. 93 (March 1979): 141, fig. 8.
Lawler, J. R. "The Technique of Valéry's Orphée." *A.U.M.L.A., Journal of Australia University Language and Literature Association* (Christchurch, New Zealand), No. 5 (October 1956).

Lederman, Minna. "Stravinsky in the Theatre." *Dance Index* 6, nos. 10, 11, 12 (1947): 250–56.
Leshko, Jaroslaw. "Oskar Kokoschka's 'Still Life with Cat, Rabbit and Child.'" *Arts Magazine* (January 1980): 84–88.
Leslie, Charles. *Wilhelm von Gloeden: Photographer.* New York: Soho Photographic Publishers, 1977.
Levine, Frederick S. *The Apocalyptic Vision: The Art of Franz Marc as German Expressionism.* New York, 1979.
———. "The Iconography of Franz Marc's *Fate of the Animals.*" *Art Bulletin* 58 (1976): 269–97.
Levinson, André. "Stravinsky and the Dance." *Theatre Arts Monthly* (New York) 8 (1924).
Lewis, Michel. *André Masson and His Universe.* Geneva: Editions Trois Collines, 1947.
Lifar, Serge. "Igor Stravinsky, Législateur du ballet." *La Revue musicale* (Paris) (May–June 1939).
Lindsay, Kenneth C. E. "The Genesis and Meaning of the Cover Design for the First *Blaue Reiter* Exhibition Catalogue." *Art Bulletin* 35 (March 1953): 47–50.
Lockspeiser, Edward. *Debussy: His Life and Mind.* London: J. M. Dent, 1962.
London. *Oskar Kokoschka: A Retrospective Exhibition.* Tate Gallery, 14 September-11 November 1962. Great Britain: London Arts Council.
London. *Zadkine.* Great Britain, Arts Council, 1961.
Mackworth, Cecily. *Guillaume Apollinaire and the Cubist Life.* London: John Murray, 1961.
Magny, Jean-Claude Le. *Photographs of the Classical Male Nude: Baron Wilhelm von Gloeden.* New York: Camera/Graphic Press, 1977.
Mahar, William John. "Neo-Classicism in the Twentieth Century: A Study of the Idea and its Relationship to Selected Works of Stravinsky and Picasso." Ph.D. thesis, Syracuse University, 1972.
Malevich, Kasimir. *The Artist, Infinity, Suprematism.* Copenhagen, 1978.
———. *Essays on Art.* Ed. Troels Andersen. Copenhagen: Burgen, 1968.
———. *The Non-Objective World.* Trans. from German by Howard Dearstyne. Chicago: P. Theobald, 1959.
Marc, Franz. "Geistige Güter." *Blaue Reiter Alamanach.* New York, 1974.
Meschonnic, Henri. "Apollinaire illuminé au milieu des ombres." *Europe.* No. spécial sur Apollinaire. Paris: Editions de Minuit, 1966.
Meunier, Micheline. *Jean Cocteau et Nietzsche ou la philosophie du matin.* Paris: Grasset, 1971.
Meyer, Franz. *Marc Chagall: His Graphic Work.* New York: Abrams, 1957.
Meyer, Leonard B. *Music, the Arts and Ideas: Patterns and Predictions in Twentieth-Century Culture.* Chicago and London: The University of Chicago Press, 1967.
Miesel, Victor H., ed. *Voices of German Expressionism.* Englewood Cliffs, N.J.: Prentice Hall, 1970.
Milan. *Michel Seuphor.* Galleria Borgonuovo, 1972.
Milorad. "La Clé des mythes dans l'oeuvre de Cocteau." *Cahiers de Jean Cocteau* (Paris), No. 2 (1971): 12.

———. "Jean Cocteau, Cocteau et les mythes." Ed. J. J. Kihm. In *La Revue des lettres modernes*, Nos. 298–303 (1972): 3.
Mondrian, Piet. *Plastic Art and Pure Plastic Art*. New York: Wittenborn, 1947.
Mondrian. Intro. Harry Holtzman. New York: Pace Editions, 1970.
Mondrian, l'Opera completa. Milano: Rizzoli, 1974.
Munich. *Franz Marc 1880–1916*. Städtische Galerie im Lenbachhaus (Prestel-Verlag), 27 August–26 October 1980.
Munro, Thomas. "The Afternoon of a Faun and the Interrelation of the Arts." *The Journal of Aesthetics and Art Criticism* 10, no. 2 (December 1951): 95–111.
———. *Evolution in the Arts*. New York: Abrams, 1963.
———. "Suggestion and Symbolism in the Arts." *Journal of Aesthetics and Art Criticism* 15, no. 2 (December 1956): 152–80.
Myers, Rollo H. "The Ballet of Igor Stravinsky." *Ballet Annual* (London) 17 (1963): 33–42, 104–11.
Nantes. *Michel Seuphor*. Musée des Beaux Arts, 1966.
New York. *Alfred Kubin: Visions from the Other Side*. Galerie St. Etienne, 22 March–7 May 1983.
New York. *André Masson*. Museum of Modern Art, 1976.
New York. *Exhibition of Works by André Masson*. Wildenstein, 1936.
New York. *Frantisek Kupka 1871–1957: A Retrospective*. The Solomon R. Guggenheim Museum, 1975.
New York. *Kandinsky in Europe, 1896–1914*. The Solomon R. Guggenheim Museum, 1982.
New York. *Mondrian: Centennial Exhibition*. The Solomon R. Guggenheim Museum, 1971.
New York. *Mondrian, De Stijl and Their Impact*. Intro. A. M. Hammacher. Marlborough-Gerson Gallery, April 1964.
New York. *Noguchi: Steel Sculptures*. The Pace Gallery, 10 May–20 June 1975.
New York. *Sculpture of Ossip Zadkine*. Hirschl & Adler Gallery, 7–31 December 1971.
Noguchi, Isamu. *A Sculptor's World*. New York, 1968.
Olivero, Federico. *Rainer Maria Rilke: A Study in Poetry and Mysticism*. Cambridge: W. Heffer & Sons, 1931.
Oppler, Ellen. *Fauvism Re-examined*. New York: Garland, 1976.
"Orpheus di Igor Stravinsky." *Domus* 6, no. 231 (1948): 27–29.
Paris. *André Masson*. Musée Nationale d'Art Moderne, March–May 1965.
Paris. *André Masson Dessins, 1922–1960*. Galerie Louise Leiris, 1960.
Paris. *Apollinaire*. Bibliothèque Nationale, 1969.
Paris. *Hommage à Zadkine*. Musée Rodin, 1972.
Paris. *Kasimir Malevich*. Musée National d'Art Moderne, 1978.
Paris. *Marc Chagall*. Musée des Arts Decoratif, June–October 1959.
Paris. *Michel Seuphor*. Musée National d'Art Moderne, 1977.
Paris. *Michel Seuphor, Oeuvres de 1974*. Attali Galerie, 1975.
Passeron, René. *André Masson et les puissances du signe*. Paris: Denoël, 1975.
Petrie, Brian. "Boccioni and Bergson." *Burlington Magazine* 116 (January–April 1974): 140–47.

Peyre, Henri. "The Significance of Surrealism." *Yale French Studies* (Fall/Winter 1948).
Philipson, Morris. *Jung's Theory of Symbolism as a Contribution to Aesthetics*. New York: Columbia University Press, 1960.
_____. *Outline of a Jungian Aesthetic*. Evanston, Ill.: Northwestern University Press, 1963.
Pia, Pascal. *Apollinaire par lui-même*. Paris: Ecrivains de Toujours aux Editions du Seuïl, 1962.
Proust, Marcel. *Du côté de chez Swann*. Paris: Grasset, 1913.
Rathenau, Ernest, ed. *Oskar Kokoschka Drawings*. Intro. Paul Westheim. London: Thames & Hudson, 1962.
_____, ed. *Oskar Kokoschka Drawings, 1906–1965*. Trans. Henry Norden. Coral Gables, Fla.: University of Miami Press, 1970.
Rehm, Walter. *Orpheus: Der Dichter und die Toten Selbstdeutung und Totenkult bei Novalis, Hölderlin, Rilke*. Düsseldorf: L. Schwann Pädagogischer Verlag und Druckerei, 1950.
Renaud, Philippe. *Lecture d'Apollinaire*. Lausanne: Editions l'Age d'Homme, 1969.
Richardson, Brenda. *Barnett Newman: The Complete Drawings, 1944–1949*. Baltimore: Baltimore Museum of Art, 1979.
Rilke, Rainer Maria. *Duino Elegies and the Sonnets to Orpheus*. Trans. A. Poulin, Jr. Boston: Houghton, Mifflin, 1977.
_____. *Letters to a Young Poet*. Trans. Stephen Mitchell. New York: Random House, 1984.
_____. *The Notebooks of Malte Laurids Brigge*. Trans. M. D. Herter Norton. New York: W. W. Norton, 1949.
_____. *Requiem and Other Poems*. Trans. J. B. Leishman. London: Hogarth Press, 1957.
_____. *Selected Poems of Rainer Maria Rilke*. Trans., sel. and comm. Robert Bly. New York: Harper & Row, 1981.
_____. *The Selected Poetry of Rainer Maria Rilke*. Ed. and trans. Stephen Mitchell with intro. Robert Hass. New York: Random House, 1982.
_____. *Sonnets to Orpheus*. Trans. M. D. Herter Norton. New York: W. W. Norton, Inc. 1942.
_____. *Werke. Erster Band—Gedichte*. Frankfurt: Insel Verlag, 1959.
Ringbom, Sixten. "Art in the Epoch of the Great Spiritual Occult Elements in the Early Theory of Abstract Painting." *Journal of the Warburg and Courtauld Institutes* 29 (1966): 386–418.
_____. *The Sounding Cosmos: A Study in the Spiritualism of Kandinsky and the Genesis of Abstract Painting*. Abo: Akademi, 1970.
Robbins, Daniel. "From Symbolism to Cubism: The Abbaye of Créteil." *Art Journal* 23, no. 2 (Winter 1963–64): 111–16.
Rolleston, James. *Rilke in Transition: An Exploration of His Earliest Poetry*. New Haven and London: Yale University Press, 1970.
Rosenthal, Deborah. "Interview with A. Masson." *Arts Magazine* (November 1980): 88–94.
Rosenthal, Mark. *Franz Marc*. Berkeley: Berkeley University, 1979.
Rotermund, H.M. "Der Gekreuzigte im Werk Chagalls." *Mouseion* (Cologne) (1960).

Rotterdam. *Zadkine.* Essay by A. M. Hammacher. Museum Boymans-van Beuningen, December 1949.
Roudaut, Jean. "La Fête d'Apollinaire," *Critique* (December 1946–47).
Rowell, Margit. "Frantisek Kupka: Prometheus." *Print Collector's Newsletter* 6, no. 5 (November–December 1975): 129–32.
Rubin, William. *Dada and Surrealism.* New York: Abrams, 1969.
Russell, John. "Lincoln Kirstein, A Life in Art." *The New York Times Magazine* (20 June 1982): 24ff.
Saint-Etienne. *Michel Seuphor.* Musée d'Art et d'Industrie, 1971.
Salis, Jean Rodolphe von. *R.M. Rilke, The Years in Switzerland.* Trans. N. K. Cruickshank. Berkeley and Los Angeles: UCLA Press, 1964.
Scarfe, Français. *The Art of Paul Valéry: A Study in Dramatic Monologue.* London: Heinemann, 1954.
Schiff, Gert. "Max Beckmann: Die Ikonographie der Triptychen Umrisse einer geplanten Arbeit." In *Munuscula discipulorum, Kunsthistorische Studien Hans Kauffmann zum 70. Geburstag. 1966.* Ed. Tilman Buddensieg. Berlin: Bruno Hessling, 1968.
———. "The Sun of Taormina," *Print Collector's Newsletter* 9, no. 6 (January–February 1979): 198–201.
Schmidt-Ihms, M. "Rilke's Conception of Poetry with Special Reference to the Sonnets." *Theoria: A Journal of Studies* (Pietermaritzburg), No. 4 (1952): 61–71.
Schoofield, George C. *Rilke's Last Years.* Kansas: University of Kansas Libraries, 1969.
Schwarz, Egon. *Poetry and Politics in the Works of R. M. Rilke.* Trans. David E. Wellbery. New York: Frederick Ungar, 1981.
Ségalen, Victor. *Orphée Roi.* Paris, 1921.
Selz, Peter. *Ferdinand Hodler.* Berkeley: University Art Museum, 1972.
———. *German Expressionist Painting.* Berkeley and Los Angeles: UCLA Press, 1957.
———. *Max Beckmann.* New York: Museum of Modern Art (Doubleday), 1964.
Serota, N., ed. *Max Beckmann: The Triptychs.* London: Whitechapel Gallery, 1980.
Seuphor, Michel. *Ecrits, oeuvres, documents, témoignages.* Paris: C. Martinez, ca. 1976.
———. "L'Orphisme." *Art d'aujourd'hui,* No. 708 (March 1950): 25–26.
Shattuck, Roger. *The Banquet Years: The Origins of the Avant-Garde in France 1885 to World War I. Alfred Jarry, Henri Rousseau, Erik Satie, Guillaume Apollinaire.* New York: Vintage Books, 1968.
Sihare, Laxmi P. "Oriental Influences on Wassily Kandinsky and Piet Mondrian, 1909–1917." Ph.D. thesis, New York University, Institute of Fine Arts, 1957.
Spagnoletti, Giacinto. "Du Symbolisme au Futurisme." *XXe Siècle* 52, no. 2 (1971).
Spate, Virginia. *Orphism, The Evolution of Non-Figurative Painting in Paris, 1910 1974.* Oxford: Clarendon Press, 1979.
Spender, Stephen. *The Creative Element.* London: Hamish Hamilton, 1953.
———. *The Struggle of the Modern.* Berkeley and Los Angeles: UCLA Press, 1963.
Sprigge, Elizabeth and Kihm, Jean-Jacques. *Jean Cocteau: The Man and the Mirror.* New York: Coward-McCann, 1968.
Steegmuller, Francis. *Apollinaire: Poet among the Painters.* New York: Farrar Straus, 1963.
Stewart, William. "Style, Form and Myth: The Orpheus Sonnet of Paul Valéry." In *Stil und Form: Problem der Literatur.* Heidelberg: Carl Winter, 1959.

Strauss, Walter A. *Descent and Return, The Orphic Theme in Modern Literature.* Cambridge: Harvard University Press, 1971.
Stravinsky, Igor. *Orpheus—Ballet in Three Scenes.* Full score. London and New York: Boosey & Hawkes, 1948.
Stravinsky and the Dance, A Survey of Ballet Productions, 1910–1962 in Honor of the 90th Birthday of Igor Stravinsky. New York: New York Public Library, Lincoln Center, Dance Collection, 1962.
Stravinsky and the Theatre, A Catalogue of Decor and Costume. New York: New York Public Library, Lincoln Center, Dance Collection, 1963.
"Stravinsky in the Theatre." Symposium prepared by Minna Lederman. *Dance Index* 6 nos. 10, 11, 12 (1947).
Surrealism. Special issue of *Artforum* (September 1966).
Sweeney, James Johnson. *M. Chagall.* New York: Museum of Modern Art, 1946.
Taper, Bernard. *Balanchine: A Biography.* New York: Macmillan; London: Collier Macmillan Publishers, 1974.
Tobias, Tobi. "Interview with Isamu Noguchi." New York: New York Public Library, Lincoln Center, Dance Collection (January–February 1979).
Towards a New Art: Essays on the Background to Abstract Art 1910–1920. London: The Tate Gallery, 1980.
Troy, Nancy J. *Mondrian and Neo-Plasticism in America.* New Haven: Yale Art Gallery, ca. 1979.
Valéry, Paul. "Amphion, Mélodrame." *Commerce* (Paris) 27 (1931): 5–50.
———. *An Anthology.* Princeton: Bollingen, 1977.
———. *Collected Works.* Vol 4. Trans. William McCausland Stewart. Bollingen Series 45. New York: Pantheon Books, 1956.
———. *Dance and the Soul.* Trans. Dorothy Bussy. London: J. Lehmann, 1951.
———. *Eupalinos.* Paris: Gallimard, 1924.
———. *Eupalinos ou l'architecte.* Montpellier: Musée Fabre, 1971.
———. *Oeuvres complètes.* Paris: Gallimard, 1935.
Vriesen, Gustav and Max Imdahl. *Robert Delaunay: Light and Color.* New York: Abrams, 1967.
Waissenberger, Robert. *Vienna Secession.* New York: Rizzoli, 1977.
Washton-Long, Rose Carol. "Vasily Kandinsky and Abstraction: The Role of the Hidden Image." *Artforum* (June 1982): 42–49.
———. "Vasily Kandinsky's Abstract Style: The Veiling of Apocalyption Folk Imagery." *Art Journal* 34, no. 3 (Spring 1975): 217–28.
Watson-Williams, Helen. *André Gide and the Greek Myth: A Critical Study.* Oxford, 1967.
Webb, Karl Eugene. *Rainer Maria Rilke and Jugendstil Affinities Influences, Adaptations.* Chapel Hill: University of North Carolina Press, 1978.
Weiss, Peg. *Kandinsky in Munich: The Formative Jugendstil Years.* Princeton: Princeton University Press, 1979.
Welsh, Peter P. *P. Mondrian.* Toronto Art Gallery, 1966.
Wiegand, Charmion von. "The Meaning of Mondrian." *Journal of Aesthetics and Art Criticism* 2, no. 8 (Fall 1943): 304–8.

Wijsenbeek, Louis Jacob F. *Piet Mondrian*. Trans. Irene R. Gibbons. Greenwich, Conn.: New York Graphic Society, 1968.
Will-Levaillant, Françoise. *Mythographies Masquées d'André Masson*. Paris: Editions de Minuit, 1977.
Windsor, A. "Apollinaire, Marinetti, Carrà's 'Dipinto Parolibero,'" *Gazette des beaux-arts*, sér. 6, 89 (April 1977): 145–52.
Wingler, Hans Maria. *Oskar Kokoschka*. Salzburg: Verlag Galerie Welz, 1956.
Wingler, Hans M. and Friedrich Welz. *Oskar Kokoschka: Das Druck-graphische Werk*. Salzburg: Verlag Galerie Welz, ca. 1975.
Wise, Stanley C. "Igor Stravinsky as Composer for the Ballet." *Musical America* 23, no. 6 (1915).
Witte, Rose. *Guillaume Apollinaire*. University of London: Athlone Press, 1976.
Wood, Frank. *Rainer Maria Rilke: The Ring of Forms*. Minneapolis: University of Minnesota Press, 1958.
Zabern, Philipp von. *Max Klinger, Wege zum Gesamtkunstwerk*. Hildesheim: Roemer-und Pelizaeus Museum, 1984.

Index

Abstraction, 243, 244, 245, 246, 250
Aeschylus, 3, 5, 16, 190
Alléaume, Ludovic, 197; fig. 5.19
Allegory, 13, 58, 65, 125, 160, 259; vs. symbol, 55, 66
Anouihl, Jean, 243, 267, 270
Antiquity, 1, 2, 5, 7, 14, 15, 18, 50, 58, 72, 85, 88, 190, 193
Apollinaire, Guillaume, 243, 249, 250, 251, 252, 253, 265, 357n.55; orphic Cubism, 249
Argo, 1, 2, 3, 13, 19, 261. See also Orpheus
Art, avant-garde, 249, 254, 265
Art Nouveau, 87
Art, Roman, 6
Art, universal, 50, 260; magic/power, 64, 66, 192; sacred, 64; unity, 68, 155. See also Individual artists; Religion
Aurier, G. Albert, 62, 68

Balanchine, Georges, 266, 269, 270
Ballanche, Pierre Simon, 56, 57, 58, 59, 60, 61, 70, 72, 73, 252; palingenesis, 57, 58, 73
Baroque, 6, 7, 81
Baryshnikov, Mikhail, and Kay Mazzo, fig. 7.18
Bataille, Georges, 262, 263, 365–66n.107
Baudelaire, Charles, 63, 66, 68, 87, 162
Baudry, Paul, 121, 190, 192, 329n.20; figs. 4.20, 6.2
Beckmann, Max, 243, 258, 259, 260, 261, 262, 362n.82; figs. 7.9, 7.10
Bellini, Giovanni, figs. 1.3, 1.6
Bernard, Emile, 62
Bernard, Valère, 69, 199, fig. 6.25

Besant, Annie, 244, 246
Blanchot, Maurice, 125, 126
Blavatsky, Helena Patrovna, 62, 66, 244, 245, 246
Boccaccio, Giovanni, 3, 13, 19
Bouyer, Raymond, 194
Boyé, Abel, 197, fig. 6.17
Brandenburg, Martin, 87, fig. 3.12
Breton, André, 196, 262
Bronzino, Agnolo, figs. 1.7, 1.10
Browning, Robert, 119
Brunetière, F., 54–55
Burne-Jones, Edward, 84, 117; figs. 3.7, 4.10, 4.11, 4.12, 4.13

Canova, Antonio, 15; fig. 1.20a and b
Cézanne, Paul, 258
Chagall, Marc, 243, 253; fig. 7.5
Chenavard, Paul, 56, 57, 58, 59, 60, 61, 70, 72, 73, 311n.44; theory of history, 58–59, 73; fig. 2.1
Christianity, 2, 9, 12, 57, 58–59, 152, 256; biblical, 60, 70, 71, 73, 124, 263; Judeo-Christian, 7, 8, 49, 81; martyrdom, 152, 156, 192; Orpheus/Christ, 8, 9, 71, 156, 193, 202, 251, 256, 264, 265, 268, 270, 297n.45, 298n.51; Orpheus/David/Christ, 7, 8; paganism, 60, 61, 70, 71, 73, 192, 202, 251, 265; symbolism, 124, 152, 192. See also Orpheus; Religion; Symbolism
Clavaud, Armand, 202
Cocteau, Jean, 243, 263, 267, 268, 270, 368n.119; parallel realm of death, 265–66; self-identification, 263–64, 265, 266; figs. 7.15, 7.16
Constant, Benjamin, 53, 307n.12

Corot, Camille, 88, 89, 115, 117, 118, 119, 153; *figs. 3.21, 3.23*
Correspondences, 50, 67, 68, 69, 72, 82, 87, 89, 90, 162, 243, 247, 248, 249, 250, 272; symbolic, 59, 154
Coudray, Marie-Alexandre, 82, 87; *fig. 3.14*
Cox, George W., 51
Creative act, 122, 159, 160, 161, 162, 191, 205
Creuzer, Georg Friedrich, 50, 52, 53, 54, 55, 203

Dahl, Ingolf, 271
Dance, 89, 190, 191, 266, 269–71, 272
Day, F. Holland, 158, 201, 270; *figs. 5.10, 5.11, 6.31*
Death of Orpheus, 1, 11, 15, 19, 61, 121, 124, 125, 189–205, 255, 256, 268, 270; descriptions, 16; and Eurydice, 11, 117, 121; explanations, 15, 16; homosexuality, 18, 189, 196, 266, 303n.93,95; Lyra, 198; severed head, 189, 190, 194, 197, 198, 199, 202; Thracian women, 11, 15, 16, 17, 18, 198, 202, 266. *See also* Eroticism; Eurydice; Mythological characters; Orpheus; Romanticism; Symbolism; Symbols
Debussy, Claude, 243, 267, 268
de Groux, Henry, 82, 83, 322n.5; *figs, 3.4, 3.5*
Delacroix, Eugène, 67, 68, 72, 73; *fig. 2.6*
Delauney, Elie, 118, 250, 254; *fig. 4.15*
Delville, Jean, 66, 83, 115, 116, 193, 198; *figs. 4.7, 6.23*
Denis, Maurice, 62, 66, 68, 89
de Regnier, Henri, 62, 250
de Wyzewa, Téodor, 154, 155, 157
Diel, Paul, 124, 125
di Giorgio, Beccafumi, or Francesco, 6; *fig. 1.7*
d'Olivet, Fabre, 63
Dualities, 2, 261; absolute, 246; death/life, 203, 254, 255, 257, 258, 265–66, 267; death/love, 263, 266; fragmentation/unity, 200, 256, 257, 258, 268; gaze as creation/destruction, 125, 126; good/evil, 13; grieving/creativity, 255; heaven/hell, 13; light/darkness, 13, 251; man/woman, 85; masculine/feminine, 123; morality, 13; spiritual/material, 13, 270. *See also* Individual artists
Duchamp, Marcel, 250
Dufy, Raoul, 243, 251; *fig. 7.4*
Dürer, Albrecht, 17; *fig. 1.24*

Egypt, 4, 9, 52, 57, 59, 62
Encausse, Gérard, 61, 62, 70; cyclical historical process, 61, 73
Enchantment: animals, 5, 6, 7, 19, 71, 81, 82, 83, 85, 86, 89, 200, 245, 251, 255, 261, 269; plantlife, 5, 19, 71, 86, 200, 255. *See also* Music; Mystery; Orpheus
Enckell, Magnus, 204; *fig. 6.37*
Endell, August, 244
Eroticism/sexuality, 161, 189, 191, 192, 202, 262–63, 267, 365n.106, 365–66n.107; castrating female, 191–92, 253, 260, 266, 268, 347n.54. *See also* Death of Orpheus; Psychology
Euripides, 3, 5, 190
Eurydice, 8, 10, 17, 20, 122, 160; creative act/muse, 122, 159, 160, 161; death, 11, 124, 259, 266, 268, 270; evil, 13, 121, 266; humanity, 195; lust/passion, 8, 13; relation with Orpheus, 10, 12, 14, 15, 19, 59, 61, 70, 117, 119, 123, 124; role in tragedy, 119, 120–21, 126, 266–67; snake, 13. *See also* Death of Orpheus; Occult; Orpheus; Symbols

Fabry, Emile, 82, 83, 84, 322nn.6,8; *figs. 3.6, 3.8, 3.9*
Ferrucci, Andrea, 10
Feuerbach, Anselm, 115, 118, 119, 158; *fig. 4.14*
Ficino, Marsilio, 6, 9, 10
Flaubert, Gustave, 202, 252
Français, François Louis, 153, 155; *fig. 5.4*
Francavilla, Pietro, 15; *fig. 1.19*
Franck, César, 268
Freud, Sigmund, 125, 200, 243, 266, 267
Frommel, Wolfgang, 259, 260, 261
Futurism, 69

Gallé, Emile, 121; *fig. 4.21*
Gallen-Kallela, Akseli, 247, 255; *fig. 7.3*
Gauguin, Paul, 49, 62, 63, 68, 73, 154
Gautier, Théophile, 194

George, Stefan, 87, 256, 259
Germain, Alphonse, 157
Giordano, Luca, fig. 1.6
Giorgione, Il, fig. 1.25
Gluck, Christoph, 89, 151, 153, 155, 270
Goblet d'Alviella, Comte Eugène Félicien Albert, 54, 57
Goethe, Johann, 51, 151, 244
Görres, Joseph, 51, 53, 55
Gottlieb, Maurycy, fig. 6.34
Greece, 9, 50, 52, 53, 58, 59, 60, 62, 63, 123, 204, 271, 272; religion, 3, 4, 49, 52, 53
Guigniaut, Joseph Daniel, 53, 55, 57
Gysis, Nikolaus, 82, 87; fig. 3.15

Hades, 1, 8, 10, 11, 12, 14, 15, 17, 19, 115, 117, 122, 123, 126, 161, 191, 255, 258, 266, 269, 270–71; description, 11, 14–15, 116, 269, 301n.78; glance, 119, 120, 124, 125, 126, 160, 302n.80. See also Death of Orpheus; Eurydice; Orpheus; Rodin; Symbols
Helbing, Ferenc, 87; fig. 3.13
Henry, Pierre, 243, 268, 270
Henryson, Robert, 13, 14
Homer, 3, 52, 58
Honneger, Arthur, 249, 268
Horace, 3, 4
Hugo, Victor, 56, 159, 160
Humanism, 10, 50, 72, 81
Huysmans, Joris-Karl, 62

Jacob, Max, 250
Jalabert, Charles François, 89; fig. 3.22
Jouve, Pierre Jean, 267, 268
Kandinsky, Wassily, 243, 244, 245, 246, 250, 255
Klee, Paul, 254; fig. 7.8
Kokoschka, Oskar, 243, 267; fig. 7.17
Kubin, Alfred, 245
Kupka, Frantisek, 243, 246, 247, 250; color symphonist, 246; fig. 7.2

La Forgue, Jules, 194
Landscapes, 6, 7, 81, 82, 87, 122, 153, 154, 155, 156, 162, 194, 296n.38
Laprade, Victor, 56, 59
Leadbetter, Charles W., 244, 246

Lechter, Melchior, 82, 86, 87, 90; fig. 3.11
Léger, Fernand, 250
Leighton, Frederic Lord, 115, 119; fig. 4.17
Lévi, Eliphas, 59, 60, 61, 62, 63, 67, 70, 72, 73, 122, 197; Fourierisme, 59
Lévy, Emile, 190, 192; fig. 6.1
Lévy, Henri Léopold, 197; fig. 6.20
Lorrain, Jean, 194–95, 196
Lydgate, John, figs. 1.13, 1.22

Majer, Friedrich, 51
Mallarmé, Stéphane, 49, 51, 52, 62, 63, 64, 65, 68, 73, 125, 243, 247, 248, 252, 319n.94; architectural ideal, 248
Mannerism, 121
Mantegna, Andrea, 15, 17; figs. 1.4, 1.23
Marc, Franz, 243, 245, 246; fig. 7.1
Marcel-Béronneau, Pierre Amédéé, 116; fig. 4.6
Marcuse, Herbert, 200, 201
Martin, Henri, 82, 87, 88; fig. 3.18
Masson, André, 243, 262, 263, 365n.106; segmentation, 262; figs. 7.11, 7.12, 7.13, 7.14
Maury, Alfred, 53, 59, 204
Mazzo, Kay and Mikhail Baryshnikov, fig. 7.18
Met de Bles, Henry, 14; fig. 1.16
Michelet, Jules, 56, 59, 72
Middle Ages, 10, 12, 121, 266; courtly ideal, 12, 13; mortality, 12, 13, 15, 16, 19; romance, 14, 81
Milhaud, Darius, 243, 268, 270
Millochau, Joseph-Emile, 202; fig. 6.35
Mondrian, Piet, 243, 245, 246, 254, 255; color and sound, 246
Moreau, Gustave, 49, 62, 69, 70, 71, 72, 73, 81, 82, 115, 116, 121, 122, 123, 151–52, 153, 154, 155, 162, 192, 193, 194, 195, 196, 197, 198, 199, 270, 339–40n.15; figs. 2.2, 2.3, 2.4, 2.5, 3.1, 4.22, 4.23, 5.1, 5.2, 5.3, 6.7, 6.8, 6.9, 6.10, 6.12, 6.13, 6.14, 6.15, 6.16, 6.21, 6.33
Morice, Charles, 64–65, 68
Morris, William, 158
Mossa, Gustave Adolf, 191, 192; figs. 6.4, 6.5, 6.6

Müller, F. Max, 51
Müller, K. O., 53
Munch, Edvard, 73, 154
Music, 2, 4, 12, 83, 85, 86, 89, 189, 190, 268, 270, 271, 272; and art, 67, 68, 250; and enchantment, 5, 7, 12, 15, 81, 82, 251; ideal art form, 67, 90, 154, 244, 250, 272; lyre, 2, 7, 19, 71, 84, 115, 251, 254; power, 10, 15, 59, 70, 86, 90, 270; transcending death, 15. *See also* Individual musicians; Mystery; Orpheus
Mysteries/mysticism, 3, 4, 10, 50, 53, 56, 57, 59, 63, 65, 67, 69, 73, 83, 122, 124, 203–4, 243, 245, 246, 248, 256, 258, 259, 261, 267. *See also* Individual artists; Occult; Symbolism
Mythological characters: Apollo, 1, 2, 12, 16, 18, 19, 71, 118, 124, 189, 193, 203, 204, 205, 251, 260, 270, 271; Aristaeus, 13, 14, 17; Athena, 86, 204; Cerberus, 12, 15, 116, 118; Dionysus, 2, 3, 16, 123, 124, 189, 200, 201, 203, 204, 205, 206, 271; Hermes, 11, 85, 116, 118, 121; Maenads, 16, 20, 61, 117, 124, 190, 191, 192, 256; Persephone, 12, 16, 123, 124; Pluto, 12, 115, 116, 269; Prometheus, 71, 200; Zeus, 15, 16, 123, 191, 201. *See also* Death of Orpheus; Orpheus

Nabis, 50, 62, 66, 73
Nadar, Paul, *figs. 4.1, 4.2*
Neo-Impressionism, 89, 157, 250
Neo-Plasticism, 246, 254
Neo-Platonists, 6, 9, 10, 52, 53, 55, 67, 68, 81, 251. *See also* Christiantiy
Nietzsche, Friedrich, 2, 51, 203, 246
Noguchi, Isamu, 243, 269, 270, 271, 272, 369–70n.137

Occult, 6, 10, 50, 56, 57, 59, 60, 63, 65, 67, 69, 70, 72, 73, 122, 158, 203, 245, 250, 252, 258. *See also* Mysteries; Syncretism
Orpheus: androgynous, 81, 116, 157, 195, 196, 197, 201, 268; artist/priest, 49, 81, 85, 159, 160, 161, 195, 205; harbinger of civilization, 3, 4, 10, 20, 50, 52, 81, 88, 204; homosexual, 1, 189, 196, 200, 266, 303n.95; initiate, 1, 3, 12, 13, 49, 58, 59, 60, 61, 62, 69, 72, 73, 81, 90, 195, 196, 203, 205, 255, 258, 261, 272; magician, 6, 20, 73; martyr/saint, 1, 20, 49, 152, 193, 194, 195, 256, 264, 272; musician, 1, 2, 5, 7, 50; poet/musician, 1, 20, 50, 73, 155, 160, 170, 247, 250, 251; poet/priest, 4, 15, 87, 122, 152, 252, 261; poet/teacher, 1, 10; theologian, 3, 4, 11, 255. *See also* Christianity; Death of Orpheus; Enchantment; Eurydice; Middle Ages; Symbols
Orphism, 2, 49, 249, 253, 256; Orphic cults, 1, 3, 8, 20, 50, 52, 123, 124, 189, 203–4, 261, 320n.100; rituals, 3; Zagreus-Dionysus, 1, 8, 16, 123, 189, 200, 201. *See also* Christianity
Osbert, Alphonse, 82, 88, 89, 90, 154; *fig. 3.20*
Ovid, 4, 5, 8, 11, 12, 16, 17, 18, 19, 81, 115, 120, 121, 190, 266

Padovanino, Il, *figs. 1.5, 1.6*
Pausanias, 15, 16
Péladan, Sâr Joséphin, 60, 61, 66, 70, 72, 73, 157, 158, 204, 250; artist/magician, 60; artist/priest, 60; Rosicrucianism, 50, 73, 83; Salons Rose + Croix Catholique, 60, 66, 83, 158, 199
Philology, 49, 50, 51, 52, 54, 56, 57. *See also* Syncretism
Photography, 158, 160; Pictorialist, 158
Picabia, Francis, 250
Picasso, Pablo, 243, 250
Plato, 9, 59, 246
Pre-Raphaelites, 84, 197
Proust, Marcel, 196, 200
Psychology, 2, 15, 82, 89, 155, 243, 253, 259, 260, 266, 268; aspects of myth, 115, 117, 120, 122, 125, 154, 156, 162, 261, 266, 267, 269, 270, 271, 368n.119. *See also* Freud, Sigmund; Landscape; Symbolism; Symbols; Wagner, Richard
Puvis de Chavannes, Pierre, 49, 73, 82, 87, 88, 89, 115, 151, 155, 156, 158, 159, 162, 199; *figs. 3.16, 3.19, 5.5, 5.6*
Pythagoras, 9, 10, 59, 61, 62

Quellinus, Erasmus, 14; *fig. 1.15*
Quinet, Edgar, 53, 56, 59, 72

Redon, Odilon, 49, 73, 115, 154, 193, 199, 200, 201, 262; metamorphosis, 201; unity, 201, 202; *figs. 6.26, 6.27, 6.28, 6.29, 6.30, 6.32*
Regnault, Henri, 115; *figs. 4.3, 4.4, 4.5*
Rehm, Walter, 256
Religion, 4, 50, 56, 60, 253; art, 8, 49, 63, 65, 243, 247; Eastern, 49, 50, 52, 54, 61, 73, 202, 245, 246; historians, 49, 54, 55; language, 54; monotheism, 8, 52; myth, 54; paganism, 8, 9, 49, 60, 72; polytheism, 9, 52; symbol, 54, 55; theater, 203–4, 272; world, 50, 54, 58. *See also* Christianity
Renaissance, 3, 6, 9, 10, 50, 81, 251
Renan, Ary, 152, 195, 196
Renan, Joseph-Ernest, 53, 54, 61
Renard, Camille, 190, 191
Richmond, Sir William Blake, 116, 117; *fig. 4.9*
Ricketts, Charles, 119, 120; *fig. 4.19*
Rilke, Rainer Maria, 243, 254, 255, 256, 257, 258, 261, 265, 360–61nn.70,71
Rodin, Auguste, 73, 118, 119, 151, 258; burden of creativity, 159, 160, 161–62, 191; *figs. 4.16, 5.12, 5.13, 5.14, 5.15, 5.16, 5.17, 5.18, 5.19, 5.20, 5.21, 5.22, 5.23, 5.24, 5.25, 6.3*
Roessler, Arthur, 245
Romano, Giulio, 15; *fig. 1.17*
Romanticism, 64, 67, 69, 73, 89, 247, 256, 268, 309n.30

Sappho, 19, 192, 260
Savery, Roeland, 7; *fig. 1.8*
Schiff, Gert, 259, 260, 261
Schopenhauer, Arthur, 51, 66, 246
Schuler, Alfred, 256
Schuré, Edouard, 62, 66, 73, 123, 153, 154, 155, 195, 204, 244, 246, 252, 331n.34
Sculpture, 5, 6, 15, 59, 118, 272
Secessionism, 86–87
Séon, Alexandre, 82, 87, 88, 115, 156, 158, 162, 167, 193, 198, 199, 270; theory of color, 157; *figs. 3.17, 5.7, 5.8, 5.9, 6.24*

Sérusier, Paul, 62, 63, 66, 154, 204; *fig. 6.36*
Seuphor, Michel, 243, 254; nonfigurative art, 254; *fig. 7.7*
Seurat, Georges, 89
Shelley, Percy Bysshe, 116–17, 151
Solomon, Siméon, 116; *fig. 4.8*
Stravinsky, Igor, 243, 266, 268, 269, 271, 272
Stuck, Franz von, 82, 85–86, 115, 197–98; *figs. 3.10, 6.22*
Styka, Tadeusz, 82; *fig. 3.3*
Surrealism, 262, 264
Swan, John MaCallan, 82; *fig. 3.2*
Symbolism, 1, 18, 20, 49, 52, 63, 64, 69, 73, 82, 89, 115, 121, 151, 157, 158, 191, 192, 193, 194, 197, 202, 203, 205, 245, 247, 248, 250, 252, 256, 260, 262, 267, 268, 270, 272; aesthetic, 54, 90, 154, 162, 243; aesthetic idealism, 51, 67, 68, 157, 193, 205, 247; art/religion, 49, 60, 63, 67, 69, 81; artist/priest, 54, 60, 63, 67, 69, 81, 82, 83, 90, 115, 126; emotion, 154, 155; major tenets, 50, 87; mystery, 54; occult, 60, 62, 63; "piano of colors," 69. *See also* Death of Orpheus; Eurydice; Mysteries, Occult; Orpheus; Psychology; Religion; Wagner, Richard
Symbols, 7, 51, 52, 59, 63, 66, 69, 81, 83, 90, 151, 155, 159, 160, 161, 247, 254, 265, 270, 271; color, 154; color/sound, 154; Eurydice, 8, 12, 13, 121, 122, 124, 151, 159, 162, 195, 266, 271; glance, 15, 125; ladder, 261; *leitmotif*, 68; light, 252; mirror, 6, 19, 265, 266; Orpheus, 7, 10, 50, 58, 72, 151, 162, 189, 203, 253, 254, 263, 272; psychoanalytical, 268; religion, 52, 54, 55, 124; severed head, 11, 15, 18, 19, 20, 195, 205; snakes, 190; universal, 68; Wagnerian, 121, 154; water, 201. *See also* Christianity; Correspondences; Death of Orpheus; Eurydice; Mysteries; Occult; Orpheus; Psychology; Religion; Wagner, Richard
Synaesthesia, 50, 67, 68, 69, 82, 87, 89, 154, 162, 192, 243, 246, 247, 257, 272
Syncretism, 10, 49, 50, 60, 62, 73, 204; histories, 51, 55, 56, 69, 70, 71, 72, 73;

intellectual, 72; language, 50, 51, 53, 56, 69; religion, 53, 54, 55, 56, 58, 59, 61, 69, 72, 192, 193, 202, 251, 265, 305n.1; world mythographies, 50, 51, 52, 56, 57, 59, 63, 69, 72, 73. *See also* Religion
Synthétisme, 154

Tempesta, Antonio, *fig. 1.28*
Theosophy, 62, 65, 66, 73, 83, 195, 204, 243, 245, 246, 247, 250, 255, 258, 265
Thorel, Jean, 55
Tintoretto, Jacopo, *fig. 1.18*
Titian, 14; *fig. 1.14*
Tragedy, 10, 11, 15, 17, 118, 119, 152, 159, 204, 259; art, 160, 161; love, 160
Transformations, 11, 14, 17, 19, 20, 152, 253, 255, 257
Trivet, Nicholas, 10, 13
Truth: universal, 55, 57, 60, 61, 73, 122, 252; divine, 64

Vachon, Marius, 156
Valéry, Paul, 243, 247, 248, 249, 250, 268; architectural ideal, 248
Vanor, Georges, 55
Verlaine, Paul, 63, 89
Vico, Giovanni Battista, 72
Villiers de l'Isle Adam, Philippe Auguste Mathias de, 62, 63
Virgil, 5, 11, 12, 15, 17, 115, 120
von Gloeden, Baron, 158

Wagner, J. J., 51
Wagner, Richard, 51, 65, 66, 68, 154, 155, 202, 204; *leitmotif*, 155; musical revolution, 68, 155; Symbolists, 68, 162, 248
Waterhouse, John William, 197; *fig. 6.18*
Watts, George Frederic, 119, 120; *fig. 4.18*
Whistler, James, 159
Wilde, Oscar, 158
Winckelmann, Johann, 2, 205

Yeats, William Butler, 158, 250

Zadkine, Ossip, 243, 253, 254; *fig. 7.6*